T0214567

Lecture Notes of the Institute for Computer Sciences, Social Informatics and Telecommunications Engineering 254

More information about this series at http://www.springer.com/series/8197

Raheem Beyah · Bing Chang
Yingjiu Li · Sencun Zhu (Eds.)

Security and Privacy in Communication Networks

14th International Conference, SecureComm 2018
Singapore, Singapore, August 8–10, 2018
Proceedings, Part I

 Springer

Editors
Raheem Beyah
Klaus Advanced Computing Building
Georgia Institute of Technology
Atlanta, GA, USA

Bing Chang
Singapore Management University
Singapore, Singapore

Yingjiu Li
School of Information Systems
Singapore Management University
Singapore, Singapore

Sencun Zhu
Pennsylvania State University
University Park, PA, USA

ISSN 1867-8211   ISSN 1867-822X   (electronic)
Lecture Notes of the Institute for Computer Sciences, Social Informatics
and Telecommunications Engineering
ISBN 978-3-030-01700-2   ISBN 978-3-030-01701-9   (eBook)
https://doi.org/10.1007/978-3-030-01701-9

Library of Congress Control Number: 2018940136

This Springer imprint is published by the registered company Springer Nature Switzerland AG
The registered company address is: Gewerbestrasse 11, 6330 Cham, Switzerland

Preface

We are delighted to introduce the proceedings of the 14th European Alliance for Innovation (EAI) International Conference on Security and Privacy in Communication Networks (SecureComm 2018), held in Singapore, in August 2018. SecureComm seeks high-quality research contributions in the form of well-developed papers. Topics of interest encompass research advances in all areas of secure communications and networking.

The technical program of SecureComm 2018 consisted of 33 full papers and 18 short papers in the main conference sessions. The conference sessions were: Session 1, IoT Security; Session 2, User and Data Privacy; Session 3, Mobile Security I; Session 4, Wireless Security; Session 5, Software Security; Session 6, Cloud Security I; Session 7, Mobile Security II; Session 8, Social Network and Enterprise Security; Session 9, Network Security I; Session 10, Applied Cryptography; Session 11, Network Security II; Session 12, Cloud Security II; and Session 13, Web Security.

Aside from the high-quality technical paper presentations, the technical program also featured two keynote speeches and one technical workshop. The two keynote speeches were given by Prof. Robert Deng from Singapore Management University, Singapore, and Prof. Zhiqiang Lin from Ohio State University, USA. The workshop organized was the 6th International Workshop on Applications and Techniques in Cyber Security (ATCS 2018). The ATCS workshop focused on all aspects of techniques and applications in cybersecurity research. The purpose of ATCS 2018 was to provide a forum for the presentation and discussion of innovative ideas, cutting-edge research results, and novel techniques, methods, and applications on all aspects of cyber security and machine learning.

Coordination with the Steering Committee co-chairs, Imrich Chlamtac and Guofei Gu, was essential for the success of the conference. We sincerely appreciate their constant support and guidance. It was also a great pleasure to work with such an excellent Organizing Committee team for their hard work in organizing and supporting the conference. In particular, we thank the Technical Program Committee, led by our co-chairs, Dr. Raheem Beyah and Dr. Sencun Zhu, who completed the peer-review process of technical papers and compiled a high-quality technical program. We are also grateful to the conference coordinator, Dominika Belisova, for her support and all the authors who submitted their papers to the SecureComm 2018 conference and workshops.

We strongly believe that the SecureComm conference provides a good forum for all researchers, developers, and practitioners to exchange ideas in all areas of secure communications and networking. We also expect that future SecureComm conferences will be successful and stimulating, as indicated by the contributions presented in this volume.

September 2018

Raheem Beyah
Bing Chang
Yingjiu Li
Sencun Zhu

Organization

Steering Committee Co-chairs

Imrich Chlamtac   University of Trento, Italy
Guofei Gu   Texas A&M University, USA

Steering Committee Members

Krishna Moorthy   IIT Madras, India
    Sivalingam
Peng Liu   Pennsylvania State University, USA

Organizing Committee

General Chair

Yingjiu Li   Singapore Management University, Singapore

Technical Program Committee Co-chairs

Raheem Beyah   Georgia Tech, USA
Sencun Zhu   Pennsylvania State University, USA

Publications Chair

Bing Chang   Singapore Management University, Singapore

Publicity and Social Media Co-chairs

Yangguang Tian   Singapore Management University, Singapore
Zhao Wang   Peking University, China
Sankardas Roy   Bowling Green State University, USA

Web Chair

Ximing Liu   Singapore Management University, Singapore

Panels Chair

Min Suk Kang   National University of Singapore, Singapore

Local Chair

Li Tieyan   Shield Lab (Singapore), Huawei Technologies Co.,
     Ltd., Singapore

Conference Manager

Dominika Belisova   EAI - European Alliance for Innovation

Technical Program Committee

Elisa Bertino	Purdue University, USA
Alvaro Cardenas	The University of Texas at Dallas, USA
Kai Chen	Institute of Information Engineering, Chinese Academy of Sciences, China
Yu Chen	State University of New York – Binghamton, USA
Sherman S. M. Chow	The Chinese University of Hong Kong, SAR China
Jun Dai	California State University, Sacramento, USA
Mohan Dhawan	IBM Research, India
Birhanu Eshete	University of Illinois at Chicago, USA
Debin Gao	Singapore Management University, Singapore
Le Guan	Pennsylvania State University, USA
Yong Guan	Iowa State University, USA
Yongzhong He	Beijing Jiaotong University, China
Lin Huang	Qihoo 360 Technology Co. Ltd., China
Heqing Huang	IBM Research, USA
Shouling Ji	Zhejiang University, China
Yier Jin	University of Florida, USA
Issa Khalil	Qatar Computing Research Institute (QCRI), Qatar
Lee Lerner	Georgia Institute of Technology, USA
Ming Li	University of Arizona, USA
Qinghua Li	University of Arkansas, USA
Qi Li	Tsinghua University, China
Xiaojing Liao	College of William and Mary, USA
Yue-Hsun Lin	JD.com, USA
Zhiqiang Lin	The Ohio State University, USA
Yao Liu	University of South Florida, USA
Anyi Liu	Oakland University, USA
Giovanni Livraga	Università degli Studi di Milano, Italy
Javier Lopez	University of Malaga, Spain
Rongxing Lu	University of New Brunswick, Canada
Liran Ma	Texas Christian University, USA
Aziz Mohaisen	University of Central Florida, USA
Goutam Paul	Indian Statistical Institute, India
Rui Qiao	LinkedIn, USA
Sankardas Roy	Bowling Green State University, USA
Pierangela Samarati	Università degli Studi di Milano, Italy
Seungwon Shin	KAIST, South Korea
Kapil Singh	IBM Research, USA
Anna Squicciarini	Pennsylvania State University, USA
Martin Strohmeier	University of Oxford, UK

Contents – Part I

Mobile Security

Wireless Security

Contents – Part II

Applied Cryptography

Web Security

ATCS Workshop

IoT Security

A Secure Remote Monitoring Framework Supporting Efficient Fine-Grained Access Control and Data Processing in IoT

Yaxing Chen[1,2]([✉]), Wenhai Sun[2], Ning Zhang[2], Qinghua Zheng[1],
Wenjing Lou[2], and Y. Thomas Hou[2]

[1] School of Electronic and Information Engineering, Xi'an Jiaotong University,
Xi'an 710049, Shaanxi, China
cyx.xjtu@gmail.com, qhzheng@mail.xjtu.edu.cn
[2] Department of Computer Science,
Virginia Polytechnic Institute and State University, Blacksburg, VA 24060, USA
{whsun,ningzh,wjlou,thou}@vt.edu

Abstract. As an important application of the Internet-of-Things, many remote monitoring systems adopt a device-to-cloud network paradigm. In a remote patient monitoring (RPM) case, various resource-constrained devices are used to measure the health conditions of a target patient in a distant non-clinical environment and the collected data are sent to the cloud backend of an authorized health care provider (HCP) for processing and decision making. As the measurements involve private patient information, access control, confidentiality, and trustworthy processing of the data become very important. Software-based solutions that adopt advanced cryptographic tools, such as attribute-based encryption and fully homomorphic encryption, can address the problem, but they also impose substantial computation overhead on both patient and HCP sides. In this work, we deviate from the conventional software-based solutions and propose a secure and efficient remote monitoring framework using latest hardware-based trustworthy computing technology, such as Intel SGX. In addition, we present a robust and lightweight "heartbeat" protocol to handle notoriously difficulty user revocation problem. We implement a prototype of the framework for PRM and show that the proposed framework can protect user data privacy against unauthorized parties, with minimum performance cost compared to existing software-based solutions with such strong privacy protection.

Keywords: Remote patient monitoring · Internet-of-Things (IoT)
Fine-grained access control · Secure hardware · Trusted computing

1 Introduction

Remote patient monitoring is one of the silver applications of the Internet of Things (IoT) system. It allows health care providers to monitor the health conditions of a patient outside the conventional clinical environment, e.g. at the

© ICST Institute for Computer Sciences, Social Informatics and Telecommunications Engineering 2018
R. Beyah et al. (Eds.): SecureComm 2018, LNICST 254, pp. 3–21, 2018.
https://doi.org/10.1007/978-3-030-01701-9_1

patient's home. The measurements are collected in real time from various IoT devices, for example, user activities from audio and video streaming, biometrics such as weight, blood pressure, heart rate via wearable devices on patients' bodies or sensors installed in the room and then sent to the HCP for further functional processing. Instead of maintaining their proprietary infrastructures, nowadays HCPs adopt the public cloud to provide such remote health care services [1].

Due to the private and sensitive nature of the measured information, there is a crucial need for effective and flexible access control and secure data processing to protect user data against unauthorized access while keeping the usability and functionalities of the PRM system. The patient can permit an authorized HCP to access data types based on the offered service. For instance, a cardiovascular HCP may need to access the information of electrocardiogram and heart rate. At the same time, the data processing should be secure against unauthorized parties and adhere to the intended service functions.

Much work has been done in the literature to address this problem. For example, attribute-based encryption (ABE) [2–5] is a well-known technique used in a variety of applications to achieve scalable, secure, fine-grained access control. On the other hand, privacy-preserving date processing can be realized by secure multi-party computation [6], fully homomorphic encryption (FHE) [7]. However, such pure crypto-based solutions typically involve complex crypto operations. RPM at the client side consists of a number of battery-powered and extremely resource-constrained devices, which are likely unable to afford complex computationally-intensive cryptographic operations. Another challenge is the realization of on-demand user revocation and privacy-preserving data protection. The former typically requires a cumbersome large-scale key update as well as storage re-encryption; the latter is usually considered to be prohibitively expensive if we target generic computations, rather than a special class of computation.

In this work, we take the RPM as a case study and propose a secure and efficient remote monitoring framework. In contrast to the software-based solutions that exploit cryptographic primitives as building blocks, we present a novel framework by leveraging the hardware-based trusted computing technology, such as Intel SGX to protect user data privacy and enable secure computations over sensitive data. Specifically, assuming a current smart home IoT platform, e.g. Samsung SmartHome [8], we set up a trusted broker in the home gateway to provide data encryption, remote attestation and key management on behalf of the user (i.e., patient). On the cloud server, access control enforcement and data processing are performed in a trusted execution environment (TEE) protected by secure hardware. Our proposed approach represents a major departure from existing software-based solutions. Due to the use of secure hardware, our scheme is very efficient as we only adopt symmetric encryption, such as AES and carry out the monitoring service (i.e., HCP) functions which could be arbitrary constitution over plaintext data, rather than encrypted ciphertext data.

On the other hand, there is a significant challenge that we need to address before delivering the claimed secure and efficient framework. By our design, the secret keys on the untrusted cloud server never leave the enclave (SGX term for TEE) and the trustworthy executions of the access control enforcement and HCP application are guaranteed by SGX functions. However, strong attackers, such as OS and VM hypervisor, can still launch denial-of-service (DoS) attack [9] to compromise the system. For example, it is expected that the trusted broker can explicitly inform the HCP enclaves to erase the corresponding secret keys to revoke the access permission of the HCP. However, a malicious OS may ignore such request and help the revoked HCP to continue reading the patient's data. Worse still, an HCP may be compromised and fail to invoke corresponding enclave functions in response to the revocation request. In order to solve this problem, we propose a "heartbeat" protocol. In a nutshell, we force the enclave of the revoked HCP to be unavailable if it does not receive a valid heartbeat signal from the trusted broker after the defined time window.

Our contribution can be summarized as follows.

- Building upon recent development of secure processor, we propose a practical secure remote monitoring framework that offers fine-grained access control and privacy-preserving data processing on user information. Compared to existing software-based solutions that rely on cryptographic primitives, the proposed system offers rich functionality while incurring less performance overhead.
- We propose a novel "heartbeat" protocol to address the drawback of Intel SGX architecture, where it is possible for the untrusted cloud server or a monitoring application to selectively drop network traffic to prevent the user from further controlling the enclave upon initial remote attestation. The "heartbeat" protocol allows revocation of previous entrusted key materials in the enclave.
- We implemented a prototype of the framework for remote patient monitoring. Experiments show that the proposed system offers unique protection with little performance overhead. The software has been open-sourced for the community to build upon the existing work.

The rest of this paper is organized as follows. Section 2 introduces the technique of Intel SGX. Section 3 gives a description of the system model, threat model, and design goals. We present the details of our framework and "heartbeat" protocol in Sect. 4, and analyze its security properties in Sect. 5. We describe the implementation of our prototype in Sect. 6 and evaluate it in terms of performance and framework scalability. Section 7 reviews the literature related to our work. Finally, we conclude in Sect. 8.

2 Background

In this section, we provide background knowledge about the used trusted hardware primitive – Intel software guard extensions (SGX).

SGX [10,11] is the latest Intel instruction extensions and allows the host application to reserve a protected memory region as trusted execution environment (TEE), called *enclave*, so that sensitive application operations can run inside securely against privileged system software[1], e.g. OS kernel, VM hypervisor. In addition, SGX provides two other important functions, *storage sealing* and *remote attestation*. Storage sealing allows the enclave to protect its data on the untrusted persistent storage; remote attestation enables a distant entity to check the integrity of the newly generated enclave, including the internal state, code, etc. Should the verification be successful, the entity is able to establish an authenticated secure channel and deliver its secrets into the enclave. Next, we will provide some technical details of these two functions, which are essential building blocks of our framework.

Storage Sealing. Intel SGX platform maintains a seal key to enable cryptographic sealing function, which is derived from a base key called Root Seal Key that is hardcoded when the Intel SGX enabled processor is manufactured. The derivation algorithm supports two policies for data accessibility control. One policy named *sealing to the enclave's identity* bases the seal key on the value of the enclave's MRENCLAVE, which is a SHA-256 digest of an internal log that records all activities done while the enclave is built. It enforces that only the certain enclave can recover sealed data. The other policy is called *sealing to the sealing identity*, which utilizes the value of the enclave's MRSIGNER to generate the seal key. The MRSIGNER is a hash of the public key of the party who signs the enclave prior to distribution. Such a policy facilitates the scenario where an enclave needs to share its sealed data with other enclaves signed by the same party.

Remote Attestation. To enable this functionality, Intel SGX platform provisions a special enclave called quoting enclave. When a challenged enclave remotely attests to an entity, it needs first to locally attest to the quoting enclave as follows. First, the challenged enclave sends a unique signed structure known as REPORT to the quoting enclave, which contains the two enclave's identities, i.e., MRENCLAVE and MRSIGNER, some meta-data and a MAC. The MAC is calculated using a report key derived from the Root Seal Key. After the REPORT is received, the quoting enclave then verifies it by re-computing the MAC over the underlying data of the REPORT with the same report key. If the two MAC values are equal, it shows that the challenged enclave is indeed an enclave running on the same hardware platform with the quoting enclave. In other words, the firmware and hardware of the challenged enclave are trustworthy. Next, the quoting enclave generates a new signed structure called QUOTE by re-signing the underlying data of the report with the Intel Enhanced Privacy ID (EPID), which is an anonymous group signature scheme implemented by Intel. Finally, the QUOTE is delivered to the entity who in turn transfers it to the Intel Attestation Service (IAS) for validation. In principle, any verifiers that possess the group public key can verify the QUOTE.

Intel SGX, however, is known to be vulnerable to various physical and software attacks, for example, side-channel attacks [12,13] including cache-timing

---

[1] The trusted computing base (TCB) of SGX only comprises the CPU and several privileged enclaves.

attack, power analysis attack, branch shadowing attack, etc. Further, the compromised OS can launch DoS attack to disrupt the enclave function as it is still in charge of the underlying resource allocation. Thus, this attack on an intuitive SGX-based RPM system allows the HCP to continue accessing the patient data by dropping off the HCP revocation command from the patient.

3   Problem Formulation

3.1   System Model

A remote patient monitoring system in our design consists of a patient and various health care providers as shown in Fig. 1. At the patient's end, multiple devices, either wearable or physically fixed in the room, are deployed to measure the health conditions of the patient. The health care information collected from the monitoring devices are sent to a patient-controlled gateway, where a trusted broker program executes to manage the access policy for each subscribed HCP, secret keys and data encryption. Then it uploads encrypted data as per device to the cloud storage. HCPs, including hospitals, skilled nursing facilities, disease research centers, etc., have respective specialties in health-related data analysis, assessment and recommendations to the patients. HCPs in our system also outsource their services to the cloud and set up SGX enclaves to perform the computation involving sensitive patient information. To this end, the cloud HCP application first needs to request the corresponding secret keys from the patient gateway after a successful remote attestation. Then the HCP enclave loads the intended ciphertext of patient data from cloud storage and securely process them after decryption. In order to revoke an existing HCP of the patient, a robust "heartbeat" protocol is running between the trusted broker and the HCP enclave. Normally, the enclave will securely erase all the acquired keys when it receives a revocation command along with a heartbeat signal. Any exceptional situations will cause the enclave out of service.

3.2   Threat Model

We assume that the monitoring environment containing IoT devices, the gateway and communication channels between them is trustworthy. In addition, we do not trust the cloud including applications, OS kernels, VM hypervisor, etc., except for CPU and enclave internals, which is consistent with the security of SGX. Thus, we, in general, exclude the relevant physical and software attacks on SGX in this paper. However, we do consider the challenging issue of HCP revocation under the DoS attack by the compromised OS or the malicious host HCP application.

3.3   Design Goals

Our proposed framework aims to achieve the following design goals. With respect to system performance and functionalities,

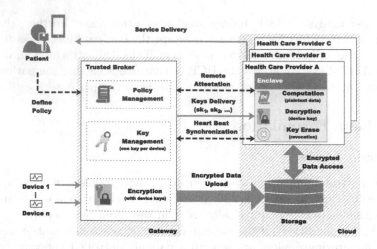

Fig. 1. The proposed framework for remote heath monitoring and protocol flows

- **_Scalability:_** Our scheme should be scalable and allow the patient to subscribe as many HCPs as he/she needs in practice.
- **_Efficiency:_** The overhead of proposed security mechanisms should be minimal.

Pertaining to security, our framework mainly realizes the following goals,

- **_Confidentiality of personal health data and keys:_** It is expected that the measured patient data are well protected when stored and processed in the cloud and the corresponding secret keys will not be disclosed to unintended parties.
- **_Trusted HCP data processing:_** The data processing operations of HCP in the cloud should be verifiable and comply with the prescribed service agreement.
- **_Fine-grained data access control:_** An authorized HCP can only access the data types defined by the patient.
- **_Robust revocation:_** The patient should be able to revoke existing HCPs in the case of service unsubscription.

4   Our Proposed Framework

4.1   Main Idea

In our proposed framework, it is expected that the private patient data should be securely processed and also compliant with the subscribed HCP service. In order to achieve this, we leverage Intel SGX to create an enclave for the patient and put all the sensitive information and computation into the enclave. By remote attestation and computation environment isolation by the enclave, we can ensure that the enclave is faithfully and securely performing the expected HCP functions.

In addition, the patient should be able to enforce access control policy for the subscribed HCPs over his/her outsourced data and revoke the access permission of the unsubscribed HCP. To achieve this, a unique random secret key is assigned to each monitoring device that outputs a specific health-related data type. Data confidentiality can be realized by using the key to encrypt the relevant type of data. Further, the patient can also control which HCP can access what types of patient data by providing the corresponding secret keys. Intuitively, in order to revoke an existing HCP and prevent it from further accessing the patient data, we may re-encrypt the data type that was allowed for the target HCP with updated device keys and redistribute these keys to the remaining affected HCPs. Obviously, this method incurs considerable computation and communication overhead, and cannot revoke the access permission promptly, which is very important for a real-time RPM system. The patient can also choose to explicitly send a revocation command to the enclave to destroy all assigned device keys, but it will fail if the compromised OS or HCP host application intercepts this request. To solve this challenging issue, we present a "heartbeat" protocol in our framework. The core idea is to send a periodical heartbeat signal from the patient side to retain the HCP enclave's vitality and force the enclave to erase all the assigned device keys if it receives an explicit revocation command along with the signal. If the enclave does not receive a valid signal during a predefined time window, it will be no longer available.

Last, we automate the scheme for the patient by executing a trusted broker program in the patient-side gateway device to enable various critical security functions, such as encryption, key management, attestation, etc.

4.2 Framework Description

The proposed scheme comprises five steps: *System Setup, Data Upload, Service Subscription, Secure Data Processing, Service Unsubscription*. Next, we describe them in details. The main notations are summarized in Table 1.

System Setup. In this phase, the patient first bootstraps and configures the trusted broker in the gateway. In particular, an access control list ACL, a device key list DKL and a secret shared key list $SSKL$ are initialized. Then the patient registers all monitoring devices to the trusted broker, who invokes the key management function $\mathbb{F}_{KM}$ to generate a unique secret key sk_i for each registered device i. The key along with the corresponding device ID i is recorded in DKL. On the other side, an HCP sets up its service application in the cloud.

Data Upload. The monitoring devices constantly collect data from the patient and ambient environment, and send them as files to the trusted broker. Each data file j from a particular device is further encrypted into the ciphertext ct_i^j by the encryption function $\mathbb{F}_{Enc}$ using the corresponding device key sk_i. Finally, the ciphertexts are uploaded to the cloud storage and organized as per device, i.e., $CT_i = \{ct_i^j | j \in F_i\}$, where F_i represents the whole file set of device i.

Service Subscription. When the patient subscribes to an HCP p, he/she first defines the access permission rule ζ_p in accordance with the service agreement.

Table 1. Main notations

Notation	Description
$\mathbb{E}_{App}$	The enclave launched by the health care provider
$\mathbb{F}_*$	The function implemented by the trusted broker. $*$ can be KM for key management, Enc for encryption
ssk_p	The shared key generated by the trusted broker for secure communication with the health care provider p
sk_i	The secret key for device i
ct_i^j	The ciphertext of the data file j bound to device i encrypted with sk_i
CT_i	The ciphertexts bound to device i
ζ_p	The access rule defined for the health care provider p
ACL	The access control list maintained by the trusted broker
DKL	The device key list maintained by the trusted broker
$SSKL$	The secret shared key list maintained by the trusted broker

ζ_p explicitly indicates which monitoring devices can be accessed by the HCP. Then, the HCP ID p along with the access rule ζ_p is recorded in the ACL. Meanwhile, the cloud HCP application initializes a dedicated enclave $\mathbb{E}_{App}$ for the target patient. Next, the trusted broker on behalf of the patient begins the remote attestation interaction with the HCP enclave $\mathbb{E}_{App}$ to ensure that all the enclave functions comply with the service agreement. At the end of a successful attestation, a secret key ssk_p is negotiated and shared between the trusted broker and the HCP enclave to generate an authenticated secure channel for subsequent communications. The trusted broker adds (ssk_p, p) to the $SSKL$ and the HCP saves the ssk_p with an internal variable *shared_key*.

Secure Data Processing. Initially, the application enclave $\mathbb{E}_{App}$ of HCP p needs first to request corresponding device secret keys from the trusted broker. After receiving the key request, the trusted broker sends back the device keys according to the defined access rule in ACL. The communication channel is protected using the shared secret key ssk_p. Next, so long as the $\mathbb{E}_{App}$ is not closed by the host application, it can constantly load the intended ciphertexts of patient data from the cloud storage, decrypt them with the obtained device keys and process the plaintext information inside the enclave. In case the enclave is torn down either due to power event or by the application itself, the secret materials can be sealed to the untrusted storage for long-term service delivery. Notably, we limit the enclave to use *sealing to the enclave's identity* policy for storage sealing, so that the obtained secret keys won't be shared with other enclaves not verified by the patient.

Service Unsubscription. The patient is able to unsubscribe a particular HCP service by revoking all the assigned device keys. We propose a lightweight "heartbeat" protocol to enable efficient and robust HCP revocation. In general, the trusted broker adopts an auxiliary function, which will periodically send a heartbeat signal to the HCP enclave $\mathbb{E}_{App}$ after giving out the device keys. The signal carries a state indicating whether or not the HCP has been revoked. Upon receiving a heartbeat signal with revocation state, the $\mathbb{E}_{App}$ will erase all secret keys. Otherwise, it updates an internal variable named *hb_state*, which is critical to sustaining the functionality of enclave. If *hb_state* is not updated after a defined time window, all the functions of the enclave towards secure data processing cannot be executed properly. Thus, it can prevent further data access by the HCP. In what follows, we describe the "heartbeat" protocol in details.

4.3   Heartbeat Protocol

Figure 2 shows the proposed "heartbeat" protocol, which runs between the trusted broker and the HCP.

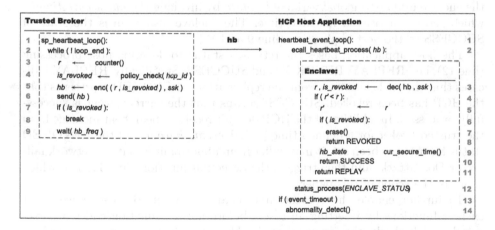

Fig. 2. The "heartbeat" protocol between the trusted broker and HCP enclave

On the Trusted Broker Side. A loop function is implemented to enable periodical heartbeat signal emission and each iteration represents a heartbeat cycle. It also uses a variable *loop_end*, initialized as *false*, to control the on-off switch of emitting heartbeat signal (line 2). During each heartbeat cycle, the trusted broker first calls the *counter()* function to obtain a monotonically increased positive number r (line 3). Then it calls the *policy_access()* function to get the current revocation status of the target HCP, which is stored in a boolean variable *is_revoked* (line 4). It generates a heartbeat signal hb by using authenticated encryption, such as GCM[AES] to encrypt r and *is_revoked* with the shared key ssk of the target HCP and sends it to the HCP host application in the cloud (line 5 and 6). If the HCP has not been revoked, the current process will be suspended for a defined period *hb_freq* before entering the next cycle. Otherwise, it will exit the loop and stops sending the heartbeat signal (line 7–9).

On the HCP Host Application Side. The HCP implements an event response function named *heartbeat_event_loop()* to monitor heartbeat signals (line 1), in which it transfers the received heartbeat message to its enclave by calling the enclave function *ecall_heartbeat_process()* (line 2). Within the enclave, it decrypts the message with the shared key ssk to recover the number r and the revocation status *is_revoked* (line 3). Next, it checks whether r is larger than the number r', which is maintained by the enclave to record the maximum of r that has been received before (line 4). Note that r' is initialized to be -1. If $r \leq r'$, the enclave returns the state of REPLAY (line 11). Otherwise, the enclave stores r as new r' (line 5). Then it checks the revocation status (line 6). Provided that the HCP needs to be revoked, the *erase()* function will be called to free the memory for storing the obtained secret keys from the trusted broker, and return the state of REVOKED to host application (line 7 and 8). Otherwise, the enclave updates a global variable *hb_state* by invoking the *cur_secure_time()*, which returns a trusted machine time. The enclave also returns the state of SUCCESS to the host application (line 9 and 10).

The host application bases the returned status to do some post processing (line 12), i.e., REPLAY, REVOKED and SUCCESS. Specifically, REPLAY indicates that the enclave suffers from the replay attack. REVOKED represents that the HCP has been revoked. SUCCESS means that the current event is successfully processed. In addition, if the HCP doesn't receive a heartbeat message from the trusted broker for a defined time period *event_timeout* and the REVOKED status has not yet been set, it may suffer from abnormalities, either network failure or DoS attack, and thus triggers the detection function (line 12, 13), which is out of the scope of this paper.

To further enable the revocation mechanism, we need to enhance other enclave functions by inserting an assert before normal function codes are executed, which checks the freshness of the *hb_state*. Figure 3 shows the checking algorithm. First, it gets the current trusted machine time *cur_time* by invoking *cur_secure_time()* and computes the difference *diff_time* between *cur_time* and *hb_state* (line 2,3). If *diff_time* is less equal than a defined time window named *threshold*, then it returns true, meaning that the *hb_state* is fresh and that the subsequent codes can be properly executed (line 4,5). Otherwise, it returns false (line 6,7). One non-trivial issue is how to set the value of *threshold*, which is a trade-off between the timeliness of revocation and the robustness of mechanism. Supposed that the *threshold* were very large compared to the heartbeat frequency *hb_freq*, the mechanism can be robust to temporary network failure or compromised OS. However, it will postpone the revocation time of taking effect. For example, when the revocation heartbeat signal is not received by the HCP enclave because of network failure, the HCP can continue processing the patient's data until the time window defined by *threshold* runs out. On the contrary, if the *threshold* is close to the *hb_freq*, it can response revocation event in time but may be vulnerable to the network failure and compromised OS.

```
Enclave:
1 assert():
2     cur_time  ←   cur_secure_time()
3     diff_time  ←   cur_time - hb_state
4     if (diff_time <= threshold):
5         return true
6     else:
7         return false
```

Fig. 3. The freshness check assert

Remark. The proposed "heartbeat" protocol can achieve the desired HCP revocation function. Its correctness can be guaranteed by the follows. In the case of receiving the valid heartbeat signal in the defined time window, if *is_revoked* is false, the HCP can continue to access the patient data. Otherwise, the access permission of the HCP will be revoked by erasing all the assigned secret keys in the enclave. Should the heartbeat signal is not received by the enclave during the defined time window, the abnormality, due to either network delay or the intentional drop off of the revocation signal by the compromised OS or HCP host application, will be detected, which disables the remaining critical HCP enclave functions towards data processing.

5   Security Analysis

In this section, we show that our proposed scheme can achieve the defined security goals.

5.1   Confidentiality of Personal Health Data and Provisioned Key

This property is satisfied by both software-based encryption algorithms, such as AES, and the used secure hardware TEE function, i.e. Intel SGX enclave. When outside the enclave, the patient information collected from various monitoring devices are encrypted using respective device keys and stored in the cloud. After remote attestation, the relevant device keys are provisioned into enclave through an authenticated secure channel. The encrypted patient data can only be decrypted and processed inside the enclave. On the other hand, the shared secret key and assigned device keys by our design never leave the enclave. Thus, the confidentiality of the data and relevant keys are realized in this work.

5.2   Trusted HCP Data Processing

This property is guaranteed by the remote attestation function of Intel SGX. During this process, the patient will verify the integrity and correctness of critical HCP functions that take his/her private data as input. Thus, the patient can be assured of the trustworthy execution of the subsequent data processing and its compliance with the subscribed service agreement.

5.3   Fine-Grained Data Access Control

We use different device-wise keys to encrypt each data type associated with this device. Thus, the patient is able to generate and maintain a straightforward but fine-grained access control policy by explicitly regulating what types of data of the devices can be accessed by the HCP. This is enforced by only giving the HCP the relevant secret device keys.

5.4   Robust HCP Revocation

We leverage the "heartbeat" protocol to efficiently and effectively revoke an existing HCP from the system. The correctness has been stated in Sect. 4.3. Here we focus on the other two security-related aspects.

- *Non-forgeability:* No other parties except for the trusted broker and HCP enclave can access the shared secret key, which is used to encrypt and authenticate the heartbeat messages.
- *Replay attack resistance:* A compromised party, e.g. OS, HCP host application, may replay previously received heartbeat message to the enclave to keep the freshness of hb_state. However, we use a monotonically increased number r to maintain the message order. It is expected that r in newly received heartbeat message should be greater than the stored r' in the enclave. Otherwise, the replay attack can be detected.

6   Implementation and Evaluation

We implemented a prototype[2] in C using the Intel SGX SDK 2.1 for Linux, and enclaves are built as Linux Shared Objects (.so). Our prototype is tested on an Intel NUC7i5BNH, an SGX enabled platform running an Intel Kaby Lake i5-7260U processor at 2.20 GHz (Turbo frequency can reach to 3.40 GHz) with 8 GiB of RAM and Ubuntu 16.01 operating system. Currently, an Intel license is required to build enclaves in release mode, so we compiled the code using g++ in a debug mode.

---

[2] The project is available to access through the GitHub via the following link: https://github.com/yxChen1990/SGXLAB.git.

6.1   Implementation

In our prototype, we implemented the network communication interfaces invoked by the HCP host application with directly stub function calls from the trusted broker. We also implemented a data sample module to imitate the activities of monitoring devices. In particular, it provides a stub function $data\_send()$ for directly invocation by the trusted broker. Besides, we omitted the cloud storage using a stub function $sp\_upload\_data()$ implemented in the trusted broker, which encrypts data sent by the sample module and is further invoked by the HCP host application for loading the ciphertext data. Lastly, the HCP enclave provided abundant ECALL functions for the HCP host application to accomplish designed protocols. Below, we will give the description of each interface in accordance with its functionality.

Remote Attestation. The functions in this module enable the trusted broker to validate the hardware and software TCB of the HCP enclave and agree on the secret shared key between the two entities. Referring to the sample code provided by Intel SDK, we implemented this mechanism by negotiating five core messages between the trusted broker and HCP host application, which are denoted by msg_0, msg_1, msg_2, msg_3, msg_{ret}, respectively. Specifically, the msg_0 carries an Extended GID generated by the HCP host application. It is processed by $sp\_ra\_proc\_msg0\_req()$ in the trusted broker to validate the HCP host application before launching remote attestation. Provided that the validation was passed, the HCP host application will initialize remote attestation by invoking $ecall\_init\_ra()$, which returns an attestation context. Based on the attestation context, the msg_1 including the DHKE public key of the HCP enclave is constructed and sent to the trusted broker. In response, the trusted broker calls $sp\_ra\_proc\_msg1\_req()$ to process msg_1 and returns back msg_2, involving the DHKE public key of the trusted broker. At the moment, a 128-bit asymmetric secret shared key between the trusted broker and HCP enclave can be constructed. Notably, if the final attestation is successful, the shared key will be recorded at both side, i.e., the trusted broker inserts it along with the HCP's ID, denoted by $(hcp\_id,\ ssk)$ to the SSKL and the HCP enclave writes it to the global variable $shared\_key$. In the last round communication, the msg_3, representing the QUOTE generated for the specific HCP enclave, is sent to the trusted broker for verification. Instead of communicating with the IAS, the $sp\_ra\_proc\_msg3\_req()$ locally verifies the MRENCLAVE and MRSIGNER and returns back the final attestation result msg_{ret}. On the HCP's end, it invokes $ecall\_verify\_att\_result\_mac()$ to verify msg_{ret} and further does some post-processing.

Heartbeat. This module includes functions used to synchronize heartbeat messages between the trusted broker and HCP enclave. Following the protocol design in Sect. 4.3, we implemented a $sp\_heartbeat\_loop()$ at the trusted broker's side to constantly emit heartbeat signal msg_{hb} to the HCP enclave and an $ecall\_heartbeat\_process()$ at the HCP enclave's side to handle the captured heartbeat event. In particular, we created a dedicated thread to simulate the protocol execution.

Key Management. This function module facilitates the trusted broker to generate device keys and distribute them to HCP enclaves. The trusted broker maintains two lists, i.e., device key list (DKL) and secret shared key list (SSKL) to support such a functionality. We use two struct arrays to implement them: the first one is defined as *(dev_id, sk)*; the second one is defined as *(hcp_id, ssk)*. It also implements three functions. Specifically, the *key_generate()* function is used to generate keys for registered monitoring devices. The *key_access()* interface enables the access of the two lists by other functions in the trusted broker. To facilitate key distribution, it implements a *sp_km_proc_key_req()* function to deal with key requests from HCP enclaves, which takes the key request message msg_{req} as input and returns back msg_{sk}. More specifically, the msg_{req} includes the HCP ID *hcp_id* and its corresponding ciphertext generated by the HCP enclave using the shared key *shared_key*. The msg_{sk} is a struct encrypted with the same shared key retrieved from SSKL. The underlying struct consists of the key number and target device keys, and can only be recovered to a global variable *device_keys* within the HCP enclave through the invocation of *ecall_put_keys()* by the HCP host application.

Seal Secrets. With regard to the HCP, we offer two ECALL functions in this module to enable that keys received by the HCP enclave can be flushed out to the secondary storage for long-term service provision. The *ecall_create_sealed_policy()* encrypts keys with the platform *seal key* and returns the ciphertext data to the HCP host application, which in turn can be stored in the untrusted storage medium. On the contrary, the *ecall_perform_sealed_policy()* recovers the sealed keys into the HCP enclave. By our design, the exploited policy for deriving the *seal key* is limited to only use *sealing to the enclave's identity*, such that an upgraded enclave need to once again attest to the trusted broker and request keys from it.

Policy Management. For the trusted broker, we also implemented related interfaces to accomplish policy management. The *sp_define_policy()* is provisioned to facilitate a patient to define his/her access policy towards HCPs by inserting access rules to the access control list (ACL). The ACL is implemented by a struct array and the struct is defined as *(hcp_id, dev_id, dev_id,...)*. Correspondingly, we implemented a *policy_access()* function to allow the access of ACL by other functions.

Data Processing. Provided that all above modules were properly functioned, the HCP enclave then could compute over patient's encrypted data. We implemented an *ecall_perform_statistics()* function as an example, which takes two encrypted data as inputs and outputs some statistic measurements like mean and variance of the underlying data.

Last but not the least, to support user revocation, we augment all above defined ECALL functions except those in Heartbeat and Remote Attestation modules by enforcing the freshness assert checking at the point where the function starts. In particular, the freshness time window *threshold* within the assert algorithm is set up as 5 times of the heartbeat frequency *hb_freq*.

6.2 Evaluation

As shown in **Implementation**, our framework involves many function modules. The evaluation of the system aims to answer the following questions:

- How is computation performance when using Intel SGX?
- What is the cost by introducing the heartbeat mechanism?
- How is the scalability of the proposed framework in terms of fine-grained access control?

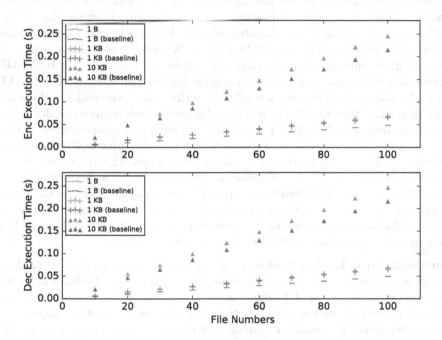

Fig. 4. The computation performance w and w/o Intel SGX

Constant Time Functions. Majority of the aforementioned functions are invoked few times during protocol execution and have constant overhead for each revocation. For example, the functions in key management at both sides either perform an $O(1)$ symmetric *key generation* algorithm or conduct an $O(1)$ *read/write* operation on defined data structure. Similarly, functions in seal secrets module perform a symmetric *encrypt/decrypt* operation and functions in policy management perform a list *read/write* operation. In addition, though the remote attestation between the trusted broker and HCP enclave needs multiple network communications and complex verification computations, it is a one-time protocol finished at the service subscription phase for a given HCP. Therefore, it incurs no performance degradation to the subsequent data processing.

Performance by SGX Enclave. In this experiment, we aim to measure the performance penalty when using Intel SGX. Specifically, we implement a 128 bit AES-GCM scheme and demonstrate the additional cost by SGX through evaluating its performance. In the real world, data collected by different monitoring devices varies greatly. For example, a heart-rate sensor may send a 1-byte data while a footage of an activity monitor with a code rate of 4933 kbps will need about 616 KB frame data per second. To see how the proposed system works under such various conditions, we enable the trusted broker to encrypt files in different sizes. In particular, we chose three file sizes, i.e., 1 B, 1 KB, and 10 KB. In each defined file size, we are also interested in the performance with various number of files since some applications, such as machine learning algorithms, may need to deal with a large number of files. Figure 4 illustrates the performance of the implemented AES-GCM scheme. We use the baseline to represent the same implementation without Intel SGX. It can be observed that Intel SGX is more suitable to process (encryption and decryption) small-sized files, i.e., 1 B and 1 KB, where it only imposes a negligible performance overhead. On the other hand, large-sized files, e.g. 10 KB, will introduce more performance penalty as the file number increases. Note that Intel SGX SDK provides a closed-source trusted cryptographic library named sgx_tcrypto, which includes some well-known cryptographic primitives. In particular, it also provides two AES implementations, i.e., Rijndael 128 bit-GCM and Rijndael 128 bit-CTR. We can choose to use this native 128 bit AES-GCM function to provide the message confidentiality and integrity. It is expected that this optimized AES function will give us a much better performance compared to our own implementation. We will apply this function and evaluate its practical performance in the future.

Heartbeat Cost. The heartbeat mechanism in our framework consists of three critical functions, i.e., the *sp_heartbeat_loop()* at the trusted broker's side, the *ecall_heartbeat_process()* and *freshness_assert()* at the HCP enclave's side. By following numerical analysis, we show that the performance costs of these functions are relatively very small. The main cost of *sp_heartbeat_loop()* is to encrypt the heartbeat message with the shared symmetric key, the complexity of which depends on the underlying message size. By our design, the size of heartbeat message is fixed, including a 4 bytes *counter* and a 1-byte *is_revoked*, so the performance cost can be ignored. Accordingly, in the *ecall_heartbeat_process()*, it mainly performs a reverted decryption operation. Lastly, the *freshness_assert()* obviously comprises no time-consuming operations.

The only potential resource cost introduced by the heartbeat mechanism is that both the trusted broker and HCP host application must maintain a dedicated thread to constantly emit or handle heartbeat messages during the lifetime of the service.

Scalability of the Framework in Terms of Fine-Grained Access Control. On behalf of the patient, a trusted broker is established in the gateway to control the access of his/her monitoring devices by multiple health care providers. In theory, our framework can support the end user to subscribe as many HCPs as he/she needs in practice. On one hand, to accomplish access control, the trusted broker only maintains numbered shared device keys in the DKL for data encryption as per device and two unique tuples for each subscribed HCP, i.e., *(hcp_id, dev_id[])* in the ACL to indicate which device keys can be accessed by the HCP enclave and *(hcp_id, ssk)* in the SSKL to secure the subsequent communication between the two entities, which incurs minimum computation and storage cost. On the other hand, by implementing the heartbeat mechanism, an HCP can be revoked without triggering other time-consuming computations, such as device key re-issuing and data storage re-encryption.

7 Related Work

Attribute-Based Encryption (ABE), first proposed by Sahai and Waters [14], is a promising privacy-preserving data access control technology that achieves fine-grained access control, scalable key management and flexible data distribution. It has been well studied and adopted in many cloud computing applications in the past decade [2–5,15,16]. Recently, Wang et al. [17] give a comprehensive performance evaluation of ABE, focusing on execution time, data and network overhead, energy consumption, and CPU and memory usage, to understand at what cost ABE offers its benefits and under what situations ABE is best suited for use in the IoT. They concluded that the computation cost in encryption and decryption phase may be a heavy burden for those resource-limited devices. Many researchers try to leverage other powerful entities to offload the cumbersome computation. For example, Yang et al. [18] exploit the cloud as an outsourcing entity to encrypt data for publishers and decrypt data for receivers. Huang et al. [19] and Zhang et al. [20] delegate the computation of encryption and decryption to fog nodes, which is a micro data-center adjacent to the end user in fog computing paradigm. Our work, however, avoids such cumbersome cryptography-based methods by utilizing the light-weight hardware, i.e., Intel SGX, to achieve fine-grained access control over user's data while achieving the same security requirements in the challenging IoT scenario.

Intel SGX is a hardware-based trusted computing technology, which has been studied a lot in the literature. Baumann et al. [21] implemented a prototype named Haven to protect unmodified legacy applications against malicious OS by running them in SGX enclaves. Arnautov et al. [22] and Shinde et al. [23] built a secure Linux container with Intel SGX to defend against outside attacks. Fisch et al. [24] propose a system called IRON with Intel SGX to make functional encryption (FE) and multi-input functional encryption (MIFE) practical. Sun et al. [25] exploit Intel SGX to address the challenging searchable encryption (SE) problem. In comparison to existing works, we solve the non-trivial key revocation issue faced by Intel SGX by introducing a "heartbeat" protocol.

8 Conclusion

In this paper, we propose a secure and efficient framework for remote patient monitoring in the context of IoT, which enables two fundamental security functionalities for users (patients), i.e, a user can control which deployed devices can be accessed by which monitoring services (HCPs), and he/she can be further assured that functions over his/her data are securely executed without leaking the privacy information to unauthorized entities. To this end, we leverage the off-the-shelf secure hardware, i.e., Intel SGX to circumvent those cumbersome crypto-based solutions in previous works. Furthermore, we also introduce a "heartbeat" mechanism to efficiently support service unsubscription for users. Lastly, by implementing a prototype, we demonstrate that our framework is feasible in practice and almost raises no performance degradation.

Acknowledgement. This work was sponsored by National Key Research and Development Program of China under Grant No. 2016YFB1000303, Innovative Research Group of the National Natural Science Foundation of China (61721002), Innovation Research Team of Ministry of Education (IRT_17R86), the National Science Foundation of China under Grant Nos. 61502379, 61532015 and 61672420, Project of China Knowledge Center for Engineering Science and Technology, and China Scholarship Council under Grant No. 201606280105. This work was also supported in part by US National Science Foundation under grants CNS-1446478 and CNS-1443889.

References

1. Hassanalieragh, M., Page, A., Soyata, T.: Health monitoring and management using Internet-of-Things (IoT) sensing with cloud-based processing: opportunities and challenges. In: IEEE SCC 2015 (2015)
2. Li, M., Yu, S., Zheng, Y., Ren, K., Lou, W.: Scalable and secure sharing of personal health records in cloud computing using attribute-based encryption. IEEE TPDS **24**(1), 131–143 (2013)
3. Yu, S., Wang, C., Ren, K., Lou, W.: Achieving secure, scalable, and fine-grained data access control in cloud computing. In: IEEE INFOCOM 2010, pp. 1–9 (2010)
4. Sun, W., Yu, S., Lou, W., Hou, Y.T., Li, H.: Protecting your right: attribute-based keyword search with fine-grained owner-enforced search authorization in the cloud. In: IEEE INFOCOM 2014, pp. 226–234 (2014)
5. Wan, A., Liu, J., Deng, R.H.: HASBE: a hierarchical attribute-based solution for flexible and scalable access control in cloud computing. IEEE TIFS **7**(2), 743–754 (2012)
6. Yao, A.C.: Protocols for secure computations. In: IEEE SFCS 1982, pp. 160–164 (1982)
7. Gentry, C.: Fully homomorphic encryption using ideal lattices. In: ACM STOC 2009, pp. 97–105 (2009)
8. Fernandes, E., Jung, J., Prakash, A.: Security analysis of emerging smart home applications. In: IEEE S&P 2016, pp. 636–654 (2016)
9. Costan, V., Devadas, S.: Intel SGX explained. IACR Cryptology ePrint Archive, 86 (2016)
10. McKeen, F., Alexandrovich, L., Berenzon, A., Rozas, C., Shafi, H.: Innovative instructions and software model for isolated execution. In: Hardware and Architectural Support for Security and Privacy (2013)
11. Anati, I., Gueron, S., Johnson, S.P., Scarlata, V.R.: Innovative technology for CPU based attestation and sealing. In: Hardware and Architectural Support for Security and Privacy (2013)

12. Lee, S., Shih, M., Gera, P., Kim, T., Kim, H., Peinado, M.: Inferring fine-grained control flow inside SGX enclaves with branch shadowing. In: USENIX Security Symposium, pp. 557–574 (2017)
13. Wang, W., et al.: Leaky cauldron on the dark land: understanding memory side-channel hazards in SGX. In: ACM CCS 2017, pp. 2421–2434 (2017)
14. Sahai, A., Waters, B.: Fuzzy identity-based encryption. In: Cramer, R. (ed.) EURO-CRYPT 2005. LNCS, vol. 3494, pp. 457–473. Springer, Heidelberg (2005). https://doi.org/10.1007/11426639_27
15. Goyal, V., Pandey, O., Sahai, A., Waters, B.: Attribute-based encryption for fine-grained access control of encrypted data. In: ACM CCS 2006, p. 89 (2006)
16. Bethencourt, J., Sahai, A., Waters, B.: Ciphertext-policy attribute-based encryption. In: IEEE S&P 2007, pp. 321–334 (2007)
17. Wang, X., Zhang, J., Schooler, E.M., Ion, M.: Performance evaluation of attribute-based encryption: toward data privacy in the IoT. In: IEEE ICC 2014, pp. 725–730 (2014)
18. Yang, L., Humayed, A., Li, F.: A multi-cloud based privacy-preserving data publishing scheme for the Internet of Things. In: ACM ACSAC 2016, pp. 30–39 (2016)
19. Huang, Q., Yang, Y., Wang, L.: Secure data access control with ciphertext update and computation outsourcing in fog computing for Internet of Things. IEEE Access 5, 12941–12950 (2017)
20. Zhang, P., Chen, Z., Liu, J.K., Liang, K., Liu, H.: An efficient access control scheme with outsourcing capability and attribute update for fog computing. Future Gener. Comput. Syst. 78(2), 753–762 (2018)
21. Baumann, A., Peinado, M., Hunt, G.: Shielding applications from an untrusted cloud with Haven. ACM TCS 33(3), 1–26 (2015)
22. Abadi, M., Barham, P., Chen, J., et al.: TensorFlow: a system for large-scale machine learning. In: USENIX OSDI 2016, pp. 265–284 (2016)
23. Shinde, S., Tien, D.L., Tople, S., Saxena, P.: PANOPLY: low-TCB Linux applications with SGX enclaves. In: NDSS 2017 (2017)
24. Fisch, B.A., Vinayagamurthy, D., Boneh, D., Gorbunov, S.: Iron: functional encryption using Intel SGX. In: ACM CCS 2017, pp. 765–782 (2017)
25. Sun, W., Zhang, R., Lou, W., Hou, Y.T.: REARGUARD: secure keyword search using trusted hardware. In: IEEE INFORM 2018 (2018)

Securing the Smart Home via a Two-Mode Security Framework

Devkishen Sisodia[1(✉)], Samuel Mergendahl[1], Jun Li[1], and Hasan Cam[2]

[1] University of Oregon, Eugene, OR 97403, USA
{dsisodia,smergend,lijun}@cs.uoregon.edu
[2] United States Army Research Lab, Adelphi, MD 20783, USA
hasan.cam.civ@mail.mil

Abstract. The growth of the Internet of Things (IoT) is contributing to the rise in cyber attacks on the Internet. Unfortunately, the resource-constrained IoT devices and their networks make many traditional security systems less effective or inapplicable. We present TWINKLE, a framework for smart home environments that considers the unique properties of IoT networks. TWINKLE utilizes a two-mode adaptive security model that allows an IoT device to be in regular mode for most of the time which incurs a low resource consumption rate and only when suspicious behavior is detected, switch to vigilant mode which potentially incurs a higher overhead. We show the efficacy of TWINKLE in two case studies that address two types of attacks: distributed denial-of-service (DDoS) and sinkhole attacks. We examine two existing intrusion detection and prevention systems and transform both into new, improved systems using TWINKLE. Our evaluations show that TWINKLE is not only friendly to resource-constrained devices, but can also successfully detect and prevent the two types of attacks, with a significantly lower overhead and detection latency than the existing systems.

Keywords: Internet of Things · Smart home · Security
Resource consumption

1 Introduction

The Internet of Things (IoT) continues to pervade our lives. In 2016, 6.4 billion devices were connected to the Internet [12]. This number is expected to increase to 30 billion by 2020 [15]. However, as IoT devices are connected by the Internet,

This project is in part the result of funding provided by the Science and Technology Directorate of the United States Department of Homeland Security under contract number D15PC00204. The views and conclusions contained herein are those of the authors and should not be interpreted necessarily representing the official policies or endorsements, either expressed or implied, of the Department of Homeland Security or the US Government.

© ICST Institute for Computer Sciences, Social Informatics and Telecommunications Engineering 2018
R. Beyah et al. (Eds.): SecureComm 2018, LNICST 254, pp. 22–42, 2018.
https://doi.org/10.1007/978-3-030-01701-9_2

they also suffer from the same types of attacks that plague traditional Internet-connected machines. In October 2016, for example, the Mirai IoT botnet, which comprised of up to 100,000 infected IoT devices, launched multiple large-scale distributed denial of service (DDoS) attacks [7]. This botnet created a 1.2 terabits per second attack which resulted in the inaccessibility of many popular websites, such as Twitter, Reddit, Netflix, GitHub, and Airbnb.

While IoT devices and traditional machines suffer from the same types of attacks, IoT devices tend to be harder to secure due to some unique properties. IoT devices are often harder to patch and update due to largely non-existent automatic update systems. Also, they tend to have scarce CPU and memory resources, and limited battery capacity, if not plugged into an external power source. IoT devices can have anywhere from a few gigabytes to a few kilobytes of memory. Furthermore, with many different types of IoT devices, IoT networks are far more diverse and heterogeneous than traditional networks. These unique properties, which differentiate IoT devices from traditional machines, hinder the deployment of existing security mechanisms in IoT environments.

Cryptographic protocols and intrusion detection/prevention systems (IDSes/IPSes), developed for the traditional Internet, are designed without the assumption of extremely limited resource and computing power. Even systems that are considered extremely lightweight cannot be installed on memory-constrained devices that have less than 1 MB of available memory [21]. For example, Sehgal et al. [19] show that many IoT devices struggle to run the cryptographic protocol TLS, a traditional Internet security standard. If a security solution needs to probe devices they protect, most devices in an IoT environment may either lack the power or network bandwidth to respond to every probe, or simply wish to stay dormant most of the time. Sometimes a security solution may impose some minor penalties on benign devices while mitigating an attack (e.g., dropping traffic from devices to mitigate a DDoS attack). These minor penalties, when moved to an IoT environment, can become a significant hindrance to those benign devices.

In this paper, we focus on the smart home environment where security and privacy are especially important, and address the ineffectiveness of traditional security mechanisms in the smart home. We introduce a security framework called TWINKLE that supports individual security applications that handle specific attacks in the smart home. By enabling each security application to run in two distinct modes, TWINKLE not only preserves the salient features of classic security solutions, but also addresses the resource limitations that IoT devices face. Every security application, while plugged into TWINKLE, will be running in regular mode for the most time and incur a minimal amount of resource consumption, but when it detects any suspicious behavior that an attack must display, it can readily switch to vigilant mode and engage in sophisticated routines for a short time window during which to cope with the suspicious behavior with strong competence. By only running the heavyweight routines when needed, TWINKLE saves precious resources over methods that run these routines either continuously or periodically.

We further apply the TWINKLE framework to transform two prior attack solutions for the smart home environment. We convert the D-WARD solution [13] that handles DDoS attacks from source networks to D-WARD+; unlike D-WARD, D-WARD+ does not drop packets from benign devices while still effectively keeping the DDoS traffic to an unharmful level. We also convert the SVELTE solution [17] that detects sinkhole attacks to SVELTE+, which does not consume network and power resources unless a suspicious behavior is detected and further adds a routine to remove a sinkhole node once it is detected. Our evaluation further demonstrates that D-WARD+ and SVELTE+ incur much less overhead than D-WARD and SVELTE, respectively, while achieving equal or better efficacy in handling the attacks.

The rest of the paper is organized as follows. In Sect. 2, we describe the TWINKLE framework, including its two modes and its architectural design. In Sect. 3, we describe how D-WARD addresses the DDoS attack from the source and how we design D-WARD+ to address the drawbacks of D-WARD in the smart home environment. In Sect. 4, we describe the sinkhole attack in 6Low-PAN networks and the prior SVELTE solution, and present how we convert SVELTE into the SVELTE+ solution running on TWINKLE. We present the evaluation results of both case studies in Sect. 5, showing that the TWINKLE framework can help reduce the resource consumption in the smart home, compared to D-WARD and SVELTE. In Sect. 6, we discuss the feasibility of deploying TWINKLE, present possible extensions to TWINKLE, and consider open issues that will be addressed in future work. Lastly, we survey related work in Sect. 7 and conclude the paper in Sect. 8.

2   TWINKLE: A Two-Mode Security Framework for the Smart Home

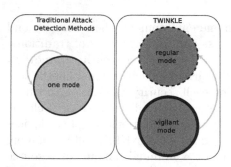
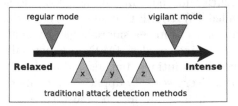

(a) Operational state diagrams   (b) Resource consumption

Fig. 1. Comparison of TWINKLE and traditional defense methods

Many security solutions developed for the traditional Internet, if deployed in an IoT environment such as a smart home, would require more computing power, resources, and energy than what IoT devices can provide. We design a two-mode security framework called **TWINKLE**, **TW**o-mode **IN**-home framewor**K** toward **L**ightweight **SE**curity, that will not only preserve the salient features of classic security solutions, but also address the resource limitations that IoT devices face. We describe our design in this section.

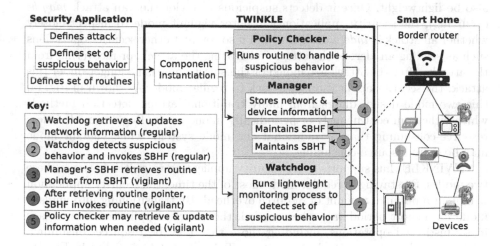

Fig. 2. The basic architecture of TWINKLE

2.1 Basic Design with Two Modes

A smart home requires many types of security applications. It may face various malicious attacks such as an eavesdropping attack that can spy on the traffic between the smart home devices, a sinkhole attack that can misdirect traffic of devices to a sinkhole, a wormhole attack that can reroute data from the smart home to an attacker outside, or an attack that compromises devices at the smart home and turns them into nodes of a botnet. Worse, a smart home may also initiate attacks, such as launching a distributed denial-of-service (DDoS) attack or a phishing campaign through compromised devices at home. The TWINKLE framework thus aims to support various security applications for the smart home, where every security application handles a specific type of attack. For every security application, the user can plug it into the framework when needed, or remove it when it is no longer necessary.

The central dilemma facing these security applications is that they must address the inadequacy of computing power and resources available to smart home devices without compromising their efficacy. If a security application runs directly on a smart home device, it may demand resources from a device that are unavailable; otherwise, a security application may still need devices to respond to its requests, sometimes causing a stretch in the resources at those devices.

We therefore design the TWINKLE framework to address this dilemma. It supports any security application to operate in two distinct modes: *regular mode* for most of the time which has a low resource consumption rate and *vigilant mode* that potentially incurs a high overhead but is infrequent. In regular mode, a security application invokes functions from TWINKLE to detect suspicious behavior that an attack, if occurring, must display, where those functions must also be lightweight. Once it detects suspicious behavior (i.e., an attack *may be* occurring), the security application will enter vigilant mode to inspect closely whether an attack is *indeed* occurring and if so conduct other security operations such as sending an alert of the attack, mitigating the attack, or recovering from the attack. After the attack is handled or the smart home is no longer under this attack, the security application goes back to regular mode. As shown in Fig. 1a, this two-mode design differs from many traditional attack detection methods which either run continuously or periodically in one mode. Regular mode is less resource-consuming than a traditional one mode system, while vigilant mode may be more resource-consuming.

TWINKLE thus supports every security application to switch between these two modes. By staying in regular mode most of the time, the security application will incur a minimal amount of resource overhead. By transitioning into vigilant mode for a short period only when needed, the security application can engage in sophisticated operations, including those that may be resource-consuming, to detect or handle an attack in question. This concept is depicted in Fig. 1b, which represents the resource consumption of the two modes as compared to traditional methods.

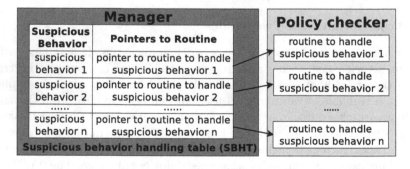

Fig. 3. Diagram of the suspicious behavior handling table (SBHT)

2.2   Architecture of TWINKLE

As shown in Fig. 2, TWINKLE is composed of three main components: *manager*, *policy checker*, and *watchdog*. In general, the manager and policy checker will be running at a central node, such as the border router of a smart home, and the watchdog can be running at every device.

The manager maintains the information of the smart home network, such as the network topology, routing information, or allowed bandwidth of each out bound connection. More importantly, it supports a function to handle suspicious behavior, or the **suspicious behavior handling function (SBHF)**. It maintains a **suspicious behavior handling table (SBHT)**, in which for each suspicious behavior it points to a specific routine for handling that suspicious behavior, as shown in Fig. 3.

The policy checker maintains routines for handling suspicious behavior. Such routines are usually heavyweight and should only be running in vigilant mode when invoked on demand.

The watchdog is a lightweight running process that monitors the smart home for suspicious behavior. Multiple watchdogs can also be running at multiple devices. Whenever a watchdog detects a suspicious behavior, it invokes the function above to process the suspicious behavior. As soon as the function begins its execution, the system will enter vigilant mode. Depending on the security application, a watchdog may perform signature-based detection, behavior-based detection, or a combination of both. In fact, some security applications may not require the watchdog to run on devices in the network. In these cases, off-the-shelf intrusion detection systems (IDSes) can be utilized as the basis for the watchdog that is installed on the border router.

When the TWINKLE framework supports a security application, it will instantiate the manager, the policy checker, and the watchdog according to the security application. The security application must define the attack it targets and the suspicious behavior that its watchdog should monitor. Furthermore, it needs to develop routines to handle each suspicious behavior, plug these routines into the policy checker, and populate the suspicious behavior handling table with every suspicious behavior that the security application is concerned about and the routine that handles the suspicious behavior. Additionally, the security application needs to provide the manager with the necessary information so that the suspicious behavior handling routines can refer to as a basis for their operations.

TWINKLE also provides a dynamic mechanism for a security application to install its watchdog at any device needed. Unlike the manager or policy checker which can run at the central node, depending on the security application in question, the watchdog may need to run on arbitrary devices in the smart home. To cater to this need, TWINKLE deploys a lightweight process called **elf** at each device that may be a candidate for running a watchdog of a security application. When the TWINKLE framework deploys a new security application and needs to run the watchdog code of the application at a device, TWINKLE can communicate with the elf on the device to ship, install, and eventually run the watchdog code on the device. While the watchdog is lightweight, especially compared to traditional methods, installing it on extremely resource-constrained devices may not be possible. This situation is discussed in more detail in Sect. 6.

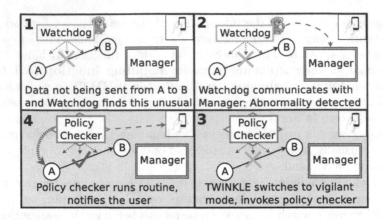

Fig. 4. Jamming attack

2.3 Jamming Attack Scenario

As stated previously, the TWINKLE framework can support various security applications which can be used to handle different types of attacks. In Fig. 4, TWINKLE is being used to handle a jamming attack where the link between devices A and B is being jammed by an unknown attacker. In the first two steps (box 1 and box 2), TWINKLE is running in regular mode. In the first step, the watchdog detects suspicious behavior defined by the security application. In this case, device B is not receiving traffic from device A, which is abnormal. Therefore, the watchdog notifies the manager of the suspicious behavior by invoking the manager's SBHF. As the function begins its execution, the manager switches the security application to vigilant mode (box 3). The manager's SBHT will match the suspicious behavior detected with the routine to handle that suspicious behavior, and the manager will then invoke the policy checker to run that routine. By running the routine, the policy checker will first command A to change its frequency to possibly alleviate the jammed link. The policy checker will also notify the user of the jamming attack (box 4). After mitigating the attack, the policy checker would notify the manager, which returns the security application to regular mode.

3 DDoS Attack Detection by Transforming D-WARD

In this case study, we transform D-WARD, a classic security system for detecting and mitigating DDoS attacks at the source-end of the DDoS traffic, into D-WARD+, a new DDoS defense solution as a security application on TWINKLE.

3.1 DDoS Attacks with IoT Devices

In a DDoS attack, an attacker sends a victim, such as a web server, an overwhelming amount of traffic to make it unavailable. The attacker usually employs a botnet, or a network of compromised devices, to send the traffic. Due to their abundance and the ease to be compromised, IoT devices are easy targets to be recruited by a botnet. As shown in the Mirai attack [7], recent DDoS attacks have been launched from compromised IoT devices and networks.

3.2 Prior Art: D-WARD Against DDoS Attacks

A DDoS defense system placed near the victim may struggle with high volume attacks, but because links closer to the attack sources are less likely to be overwhelmed, filtering attack traffic becomes more feasible for source-end defense systems. One source-end solution example is D-WARD [13]. Deployed at the border router of a policed network, D-WARD consists of an observation module, a rate-limiting module, and a traffic-policing module. The observation module classifies each aggregated flow, or **agflow**, from all devices in the policed network to an entity outside, **receiver**, as good, suspicious, or attack, based on the ratio of sent packets to received packets of each agflow. Also, each agflow consists of multiple connections where each connection is the traffic from a specific device to the receiver, and for each attack agflow, D-WARD classifies each individual connection as good, transient, or bad, also based on the ratio of sent packets to received packets of the connection. The rate-limiting module applies to each bad and transient connection in an agflow, and it cuts the allowed sending rate of each of these connections to a fraction, f_{dec}, of its current amount. If the device complies with the rate-limit, the rate-limit is increased linearly and eventually removed. The traffic-policing module drops all traffic that surpasses the rate-limit.

While D-WARD is primarily designed for DDoS attacks launched from traditional end-hosts on the Internet, when deployed in a smart home environment, it could hurt benign devices if their connections are labeled as transient connections since their traffic, if over the rate limit, will then be dropped. While a traditional benign end-host can recover from the accidental loss of their packets, in a IoT environment such as a smart home, a benign device could instead suffer significantly from such a loss, due to unnecessary retransmissions of lost packets and increased latency, as shown in Subsect. 5.1.

3.3 D-WARD+: A Two-Mode Approach Against DDoS Attacks

We therefore transform D-WARD to D-WARD+ that runs on TWINKLE. To overcome the aforementioned drawback of D-WARD, when detecting a DDoS attack from a policed network, D-WARD+ leverages the *fast retransmit* mechanism in TCP congestion control to reduce the sending rate of transient connections, rather than literally dropping their packets as done in D-WARD. Since these connections could be from benign devices, doing so will not cause their packets to be dropped, while still lowering the amount of DDoS traffic departing from the network.

The manager, watchdog, and policy checker of D-WARD+, all running at the border router, are designed as follows. The manager keeps track of the rate-limit of every connection in every attack agflow. The policy checker consists of an agflow monitoring routine. The watchdog monitors the suspicious behavior of each agflow and has the agflow monitoring routine invoked if it detects an attack agflow.

As a security application of TWINKLE, D-WARD+ handles DDoS attacks by switching between the two modes. Beginning with regular mode, if the watchdog of D-WARD+ detects an attack agflow, it will invoke the manager's function for handling suspicious behavior, including passing the handler a suspicious behavior description block (SDB). The SDB will include the identifier of the attack agflow and other meta-data of the agflow. D-WARD+ then executes this function and enters vigilant mode. In doing so, based on the SDB, the function will determine to invoke the agflow monitoring routine to handle the agflow in question. The routine will then monitor each transient connection of the attack agflow; it will send three duplicate TCP acknowledgments to the device of the connection, which, by following the TCP congestion control design, will reduce its congestion window by half, thus halving its sending rate and mitigating the ongoing DDoS attack. Here, we call the three duplicate TCP acknowledgments a *signal*. In case the device ignores the signal and continues to send its traffic at the original rate, the routine will detect it and label the connection as a bad connection. (Note that if a DDoS device follows the signal in the same way as a benign device, it lowers its sending rate and effectively mitigates the DDoS attack.) Furthermore, if the traffic volume of the connection is still above certain threshold after sending a signal, the routine can send another signal and observe the volume change of the connection, and it can repeat this procedure until the connection is no longer overwhelming its receiver.

Based on the two-mode design above, D-WARD+ is more suitable to a smart home environment than D-WARD. By not literally dropping packets as in D-WARD, D-WARD+ instead informs devices to transmit more slowly. Doing so avoids retransmissions of packets from benign devices, thus lowering network overhead and power consumption.

4   Sinkhole Attack Detection by Transforming SVELTE

In this case study, we transform SVELTE, an IDS for detecting sinkhole attacks in 6LoWPAN networks, into a more resource-efficient security application on TWINKLE.

4.1   Sinkhole Attack in 6LoWPAN Networks

6LoWPAN (IPv6 over Low power Wireless Personal Area Networks) is a wireless technology that combines IPv6 and Low-power Wireless Personal Area Networks (LoWPAN) to enable low-powered devices to communicate using an Internet protocol. A 6LoWPAN network uses RPL (Routing Protocol over Low Powered and

Lossy Networks) as its routing protocol [8]. For each destination in a 6LoWPAN network to reach, RPL creates a graph called *Destination Oriented Directed Acyclic Graph* (DODAG) where every node is a device in the network and the destination is the root. Each node in a DODAG has a set of parents, including a preferred parent, where every parent is a potential next hop to reach the root. Moreover, every node in a DODAG has a *rank* to represent the distance between the device and the root (the distance can be calculated in a number of ways, the simplest being hop-count).

Each device periodically sends out a *DODAG Information Object* (DIO) message to advertise its rank. An entering device, upon the receipt of DIO messages from its neighboring devices, will create its set of parents, choose the preferred parent, and calculate its own rank (which is greater than the rank of each of its parents).

The 6LoWPAN network is subject to the sinkhole attack. In such an attack, a compromised device announces a short path toward a destination node to attract traffic from other nodes to the destination, therefore intercepting or dropping the traffic and creating a sinkhole. A sinkhole attack via RPL can happen when a device sends to its neighbors a DIO message to lie that the device has a low rank. It has been shown that RPL's self-healing and repair mechanisms are not resilient against the sinkhole attack [22].

4.2   Prior Art: SVELTE Against the Sinkhole Attack in 6LoWPAN

SVELTE detects sinkhole attacks in 6LoWPAN networks that occur through RPL rank manipulation. It has three main modules running on the border router (6BR) of a 6LoWPAN network: 6LoWPAN Mapper (6Mapper) that gathers information about the network and determine the DODAG rooted at 6BR, an intrusion detection module that checks the rank inconsistency in data obtained by 6Mapper to detect sinkhole attacks, and a distributed mini-firewall that filters unwanted traffic before it enters the network. 6Mapper sends *probing* messages to nodes in the entire network at regular intervals (e.g., 2 min). Each node then sends a *response* message to 6Mapper, which includes its node ID, node rank, parent ID, and all of its neighbors' IDs and ranks.

Unfortunately, SVELTE's probing mechanism can increase the network overhead, device power consumption, and the latency of detecting sinkhole attacks. Every probe from the 6BR will increase the network overhead. Every response from a device will consume more power. Worst of all, SVELTE has a dilemma in choosing the probing interval: a short interval will lead to a low latency in detecting sinkhole attacks, but a large overhead due to frequent probing and responding; a long interval will result in a low overhead, but a high latency in detecting sinkhole attacks.

4.3   SVELTE+: A Two-Mode Approach Against Sinkhole Attacks

To be more resource-efficient, we transform SVELTE to SVELTE+ that runs on TWINKLE. The essential difference between SVELTE+ and SVELTE is that the 6Mapper in SVELTE+ will not probe the entire network periodically and correspondingly, the intrusion detection component will not run periodically, either.

When SVELTE+ is plugged into TWINKLE, its manager, watchdog, and policy checker are as follows. The manager will consist of the 6Mapper module from SVELTE which runs on the central node and the distributed mini-firewall which may run on devices. The policy checker, which also runs on the central node, will include two suspicious behavior handling routines: (1) a sink-hole detection routine (i.e., the intrusion detection module from SVELTE) that inspects the ranks of nodes in the DODAG graph to determine if a sinkhole attack is occurring; and (2) a sinkhole mitigation routine that SVELTE+ newly introduced to mitigate a detected sinkhole attack. Finally, for each device that originally runs a 6Mapper client, we instead equip it with a SVELTE+ watchdog through TWINKLE; it monitors the RPL ranks of its neighbors and alerts the manager of a suspicious behavior when it receives a new rank advertisement; the manager in turn determines how to handle the suspicious behavior, such as invoking the sinkhole detection routine.

SVELTE+ detects sinkhole attacks by switching between the two modes. It begins in regular mode. Each time a node advertises a new rank, the watchdogs that are within the range of the advertisement will treat the node as a suspect and detect a suspicious behavior. Each watchdog then invokes the manager's function for handling suspicious behavior, including passing to the function a suspicious behavior description block (SDB). The SDB will include the rank of the suspect and the rank of the watchdog itself. More importantly, as soon as the function begins its execution, SVELTE+ enters vigilant mode, allowing it to invoke the corresponding routine to handle the suspicious behavior. Based on the SDB, the function will inspect the behavior and further decides to invoke the sinkhole detection routine inside the policy checker to handle the behavior. The sinkhole detection routine first queries the 6Mapper in the manager for an up-to-date DODAG; then, if the watchdog is a parent (child) of the suspect and its rank is lower (greater) than the rank of the suspect as expected, the routine then has verified the consistency between this watchdog and the suspect. If it has verified the rank consistency with all of the parents and children (or a threshold number of each) of the suspect, it will treat the suspect as a benign node and invoke the 6Mapper to add the node to the DODAG, or simply update its rank if it is already in the DODAG. In case the sinkhole detection routine cannot establish the rank consistency between the suspect and its parents and children, it will detect a sinkhole attack, label the suspect as a sinkhole attacker, and further invoke the sinkhole mitigation routine as described below. The sinkhole detection routine then finishes its execution, followed by the function for handling suspicious behavior, and SVELTE+ returns to regular mode.

The sinkhole mitigation routine's main purpose is to remove a sinkhole node from not only the DODAG, but also the records of any device. Specifically, every parent of the attacker will remove it as their child. Every child of the attacker will remove it as its parent; it may also add a new parent as well as choose a new preferred parent. As a result, the attacker is isolated and can no longer successfully reach any other node.

SVELTE+ outperforms SVELTE in multiple ways. SVELTE+ can reduce the latency in detecting sinkhole attacks to a negligible amount because the watchdog immediately invokes the suspicious behavior handler whenever a new rank is advertised, without having to wait for the next probing interval, as in SVELTE. SVELTE+ also decreases the network overhead and device power consumption as compared to SVELTE; SVELTE+ may incur more overhead in the beginning as nodes join the network, but as the network stabilizes, the amount of times SVELTE+ switches to vigilant mode will be low. An exception here is that a malicious node may frequently advertise a new, legitimate rank, causing SVELTE+ to repeatedly process the suspicious behavior; SVELTE+ sets up an upper bound at which a benign node would advertise a new rank and labels a node as malicious if it advertises a new rank too frequently (it can further remove the node using the sinkhole mitigation routine).

5   Evaluation

We evaluated TWINKLE's two-mode design by showing how D-WARD+ outperformed D-WARD in source-end DDoS defense and how SVELTE+ outperformed SVELTE in sinkhole attack detection. The metrics we focused on were retransmissions and connection duration for the DDoS case study and network overhead and detection latency for the sinkhole case study. For the DDoS case study, we additionally compared the effects of D-WARD+ and D-WARD on a simple TCP flooding attack versus a smart TCP flooding attack. Note that we did not compare D-WARD+ to D-WARD, and SVELTE+ to SVELTE, in terms of detection accuracy because D-WARD+ and SVELTE+ use the same detection modules as D-WARD and SVELTE, respectively.

We implemented D-WARD+, D-WARD, SVELTE+, and SVELTE in Java on a 2015 Dell XPS with a 2.2 GHz Intel Core i5 processor and 8 GB of RAM. Specifically, for the evaluation of D-WARD+ and D-WARD, we constructed a Bluetooth Personal Area Network (PAN) in which a client device transfers 2.5 MB of data to the server through a router on which D-WARD+ and D-WARD are implemented. For the router, we used a 2015 Dell XPS with the same specifications as mentioned previously. In addition to behaving normally, the client device was able to perform simple and smart TCP flooding attacks. Both the client and server utilized TCP New Reno for congestion control. Additionally, for the evaluation of SVELTE+ and SVELTE, we randomly generated mesh IoT network topologies of varying size, which is explained in more detail in Subsect. 5.2.

5.1   D-WARD+ Vs. D-WARD

The main difference between D-WARD+ and D-WARD is that D-WARD+ utilizes the fast retransmit mechanism instead of dropping packets from transient connections. The fast retransmit mechanism allows D-WARD+ to throttle DDoS traffic that leaves the source network it polices and avoid resource penalties on benign traffic. In this section, we analyzed the attainability of these goals in a smart-home network that utilizes D-WARD+. Specifically, we analyzed the following:

1. the ratio of retransmissions D-WARD requires of a benign transient connection over the amount required by D-WARD+;
2. the difference in connection duration of a benign transient connection under D-WARD compared to that of D-WARD+;
3. the maximum length of time that D-WARD+ allows a malicious transient connection to perform a TCP flooding attack; and
4. the maximum length of time that D-WARD+ allows a malicious transient connection to perform a "smart" TCP flooding attack by following TCP congestion control.

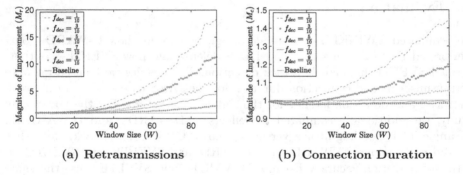

(a) Retransmissions   (b) Connection Duration

Fig. 5. Comparison of retransmissions and connection duration under D-WARD and D-WARD+

Retransmissions. In order to calculate the ratio of retransmissions D-WARD requires of a benign transient connection over the amount required by D-WARD+, we examined the number of retransmissions required of a benign transient connection that attempts to send 2.5 MB of data outside of the policed network under both D-WARD and D-WARD+.

Figure 5a presents the average number of retransmissions that D-WARD+ and D-WARD requires of benign transient connection over two main parameters: the sender's congestion window size, W, at the time D-WARD or D-WARD+ detects an attack agflow, and the pre-set fraction of traffic, f_{dec}, that D-WARD or D-WARD+ allows to leave the source network during a suspected DDoS attack. An f_{dec} of $1/2$ is set as default by Mirkovic et al. [13]. Upon detection of an attack agflow, D-WARD only allows $W * f_{dec}$ segments to the sender each RTT to mitigate any DDoS attacks. Therefore, when the benign transient devices follow TCP congestion control, D-WARD drops $W - W * f_{dec}$ segments every two RTTs. Thus, as W increases or f_{dec} decreases, D-WARD drops more segments which causes more retransmissions. With a large window size and a strict pre-set fraction of allowed traffic, D-WARD may require more than 15 times the number of retransmissions than D-WARD+. Even when the window size is less than 40 and the pre-set fraction of allowed traffic is greater than 0.5, D-WARD still requires more retransmissions than D-WARD+, but to a lesser degree.

Connection Duration. We further compared how long a benign transient connection may last under D-WARD and D-WARD+. Clearly, when transmitting the same amount of data, a shorter duration is desired. We examined the duration of a benign transient connection that attempts to send 2.5 MB of data outside of the policed network at a maximum bandwidth of 250 Kb/s under both D-WARD and D-WARD+.

Figure 5b shows the average difference in connection duration between D-WARD and D-WARD+ over the two main parameters W and f_{dec}. When f_{dec} is set low, D-WARD may punish a transient connection too heavily which leads to long connection durations. However, in cases where f_{dec} is set high and W is large, a transient connection's duration under D-WARD can be slightly faster (at most 3 s) than if it were under D-WARD+.

Simple TCP Flooding Attack. A "simple" TCP flooding attack is one in which the attacker ignores TCP congestion and flow control. We formulate the maximum length of time that D-WARD+ allows a malicious transient device to perform a simple TCP flooding attack as follows. Upon detection of an attack agflow, D-WARD+ provides all transient connections belonging to the attack agflow a window of D seconds to prove the benevolence of their traffic. If a transient device performs a simple TCP flooding attack, it will not follow TCP congestion control which D-WARD+ notices within two RTTs. At this point, D-WARD+ now has high confidence the transient connection is malicious, and begins to drop this connection's traffic, thus ending the DDoS attack.

Smart TCP Flooding Attack. A "smart" TCP flooding attack is one in which the attacker follows TCP congestion control. We formulate the maximum length of time that D-WARD+ allows a malicious device to perform a "smart" TCP flooding attack by following TCP congestion control. Upon detection of an attack agflow, D-WARD+ sends s signals every RTT for the next D seconds to each transient connection belonging to the attack agflow so that after D seconds, each transient connection's congestion window will be below $RECW$.

Figure 6 compares how D-WARD and D-WARD+ handle a smart attacker in TCP Reno. This figure shows two transient connections that belong to an attack agflow, which was detected at 0 RTT. For simplicity, the victim has a constant $RECW$ of 10. Any traffic that surpasses the $RECW$ of 10 is considered DDoS

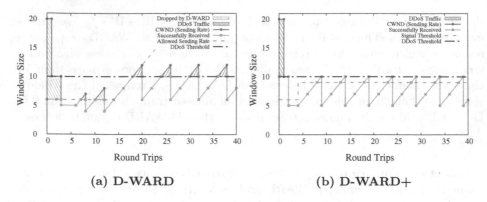

(a) D-WARD   (b) D-WARD+

Fig. 6. Behavior of a smart attacker under D-WARD and D-WARD+ (Color figure online)

traffic. Lastly, the circle-dotted (blue) line represents the amount of traffic sent by the attacker and the square-dotted (green) line represents the amount of traffic that is successfully received by the victim.

In Fig. 6a, D-WARD drops all traffic that surpasses the allowed window size of 6, which in this case means D-WARD set f_{dec} to 0.3. D-WARD initially throttles the smart attacker which forces the attacker to send at the allowed rate (from 0 RTT to 14 RTT), but once the congestion window settles below this initial allowed rate, and because the smart attacker follows TCP congestion control, D-WARD continues to linearly increase the allowed amount even past an amount the receiver can manage (which can be seen at 20 RTT, 25 RTT, 32 RTT, and 37 RTT). This provides the smart attacker an opportunity to successfully send DDoS traffic in the future.

In Fig. 6b, D-WARD+ allows all traffic to be sent to the victim, but sends signals to the smart attacker to force it to send less than or equal to the allowed rate. After 4 RTTs, D-WARD+ will have gained enough information about the victim's *RECW* and increase the signal threshold (the threshold at which 3 duplicate ACK packets will be sent to the attacker) to just below *RECW*. While D-WARD+ allows DDoS traffic for a short period initially (0 RTT to 1 RTT), because the smart attacker follows TCP congestion control, D-WARD+ can continue to preemptively restrict the smart attacker's congestion window preventing any further DDoS attacks.

5.2   SVELTE+ vs. SVELTE

The main difference between SVELTE+ and SVELTE is that SVELTE+ utilizes on-demand probing while SVELTE utilizes periodic probing. In this section, we explored how this difference affected network overhead and detection latency for both security applications.

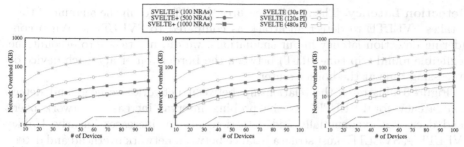

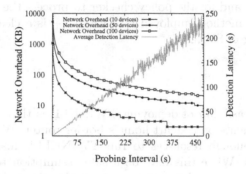

(a) **Average degree of 2** (b) **Average degree of 3** (c) **Average degree of 4**

Fig. 7. Difference in network overhead between SVELTE and SVELTE+ based on probing intervals (PI) and number of new rank advertisements per device (NRA/D)

Fig. 8. The effect of probing interval on network overhead and detection latency for SVELTE

Network Overhead. This metric measures the number of extra bytes that are sent using SVELTE as compared to SVELTE+. Sending traffic requires power consumption and therefore, a security system that sends less extra traffic by power-constrained devices is highly desired.

Figure 7 depicts the difference between SVELTE and SVELTE+ in network overhead. We compare SVELTE with three different probing intervals (30, 120, and 480 s) to SVELTE+ with three different new rank advertisement frequencies (1, 5, and 10 new rank advertisements per device). SVELTE+ incurs less network overhead than SVELTE with probing intervals of 120 s and 30 s. At an average degree of 3 and 4, SVELTE+ with 5 and 10 new rank advertisements per device incur more network overhead than SVELTE with a probing interval of 480 s. However, if a network contains 10 devices and each device advertises a new rank 10 times in a one-hour period, there would be more than 1 new rank advertised each minute. This would be highly unlikely in a stable and stationary environment, such as a smart home. Also, note that while a 480s probing interval for SVELTE incurs a relatively small amount of overhead, the detection latency will be relatively high.

Detection Latency. The metric measures the difference in the amount of time it takes SVELTE to detect an attack as compared to SVELTE+. When considering detection latency in our simulations, we did not take into account the negligible round-trip time (RTT) between the border router and each device or processing time at the border router.

Figure 8 illustrates the relationship between network overhead and detection latency for SVELTE. As the probing interval increases, network overhead decreases exponentially and detection latency increases linearly. Unlike SVELTE+, SVELTE must strike a balance between network overhead and detection latency.

The detection latency with SVELTE+ instead is negligible since it immediately responds to a sinkhole attack on demand. It incurs only some communication delay and processing time for the watchdog to report the manipulation of rank by an attacker and for the policy checker to process the report. Here, the on-demand probing method employed by SVELTE+ is a clear advantage over the periodic probing of SVELTE.

6   Discussion

One factor in the feasibility of deploying TWINKLE is the potential difficulty of installing components on a smart home's border router. We assume that the border router has enough resources to run TWINKLE's manager and policy checker components. While this may be a safe assumption to make for many commercial home routers, we have yet to evaluate this claim. Also, the feasibility of running TWINKLE on routers is highly dependent on the security application. We can estimate the memory consumption of D-WARD+ and SVELTE+ from evaluation done on D-WARD and SVELTE. For example, D-WARD consumes at most 37.581 KB of RAM at the router in a smart home with 100 outbound connections, while SVELTE consumes at most 4.724 KB of RAM (49.924 KB of ROM) at the router in a smart home containing 16 devices.

Another issue is the feasibility of running watchdog code on devices in the smart home. We assume that a watchdog device can run an elf process which can be used to transfer watchdog code onto the device. However, some devices, such as legacy and extremely resource-constrained devices, may not have the ability to install even lightweight processes like elf. Therefore, in some cases, additional devices need to be added to the network to act as watchdogs. Furthermore, watchdogs are required to have enough resources to run the lightweight algorithms of regular mode. Again, the feasibility of running these algorithms is dependent on the security application. SVELTE consumes at most 0.350 KB of RAM (1.414 KB of ROM) at each device while D-WARD does not run any code on the devices.

TWINKLE is a security framework that addresses the resource limitations of IoT devices by giving security applications the ability to run in two modes. However, TWINKLE can be extended to include more than two modes of operation. Certain security applications need to invoke a wide range of functions in order to mitigate an attack. Allowing for multiple levels of granularity in which applications can invoke functions of varying resource-consumption intensity may further reduce resource consumption.

In future work, we plan on studying, and eventually addressing, the aforementioned issues. Specifically, we will evaluate multiple different security applications on TWINKLE and implement TWINKLE on a real IoT testbed to present a more comprehensive study on the feasibility of deploying components on border routers and devices.

7   Background and Related Work

We organize the related work into three sections. The first is on work that provides analysis on smart home security and goals for securing smart home environments. The second is on work that introduces security frameworks and systems targeted towards IoT environments. The last section is on work that motivates different components of our two-mode framework.

7.1   Smart Home Security Analysis

Recent work, [5,6], and [16], explores the current state of smart home security and provide suggestions on improvements in this environment. Denning et al. [5] group security and privacy goals into three categories: device goals (device privacy, device availability, command authenticity, and execution integrity), data goals (data privacy, data integrity, and data availability), and environment goals (environment integrity, activity pattern privacy, sensed data privacy, sensor validity, and sensor availability). Notra et al. [16] report vulnerabilities in various household devices, such as the Phillips Hue light-bulb, the Belkin WeMo power switch, and the Nest smoke-alarm. The main contribution of [6] is the discovery of security-critical design flaws in the SmartThings capability model and event subsystem. These papers give insight into the vulnerabilities and open issues that need to be addressed by smart home security frameworks and systems. Of the three papers, only [16] provides a security solution. However, this solution only provides protection via access control rules deployed at the gateway router to prevent unauthorized in-bound and out-bound traffic. Our framework, not only monitors traffic leaving and entering the network, but also monitors device to device communication from within the network. This allows our framework to potentially detect and prevent attacks that cannot be detected or prevented solely at the gateway router.

7.2   Frameworks and Systems

In this section, we survey select papers which introduce security frameworks for IoT environments [2,3,10], and [20]. In [3], the authors present a security framework based on the Architecture Reference Model (ARM) of the IoT-A EU project. The work in [2], uses game theory and context-aware techniques to create a risk-based adaptive security framework for IoT in an eHealth environment. Both [3] and [2] are proof-of-concept papers that do not provide evidence that the presented frameworks are viable in resource constrained environments. Similar to our framework, the frameworks presented in [20] and [10] are both targeted towards smart home environments. Also, the authors of [20] present a modular security manager which is similar to the Manager component in our framework. However, like [3] and [2], the authors of both papers do not address the limitations of IoT devices nor provide evaluation results for the resource costs of deploying their solutions. In contrast, our framework's primary focus is to reduce resource consumption while maintaining a secure environment. Furthermore, we show that our framework can reduce resource consumption through the evaluation of two concrete case studies.

7.3   Motivation for Certain Components and Policies

Papers [4,9,11], and [14] motivate the need of certain components in a security framework for the smart home environment. Instead of introducing new security countermeasures, the authors of [9] attempt to strengthen security for smart home networks by making it easier for non-expert home owners to set up secure networks and intuitively manage trust and access to their devices. The research in [14] attempts to provide adequate mechanisms to control the flow of data and enforce policies based on users' preferences. In [4], the authors utilize special nodes that monitor traffic within the network to detect certain routing attacks. The work in [9,14], and [4] show the need of user interaction, adjustable policies set by users, and dedicated watchdog nodes for inspection of in-network communication, respectively. Also, the work in [11] provides motivation for allowing security policies, such as using efficient authentication and key agreement methods. The substantial research in the area of security in wireless sensor networks (WSNs), such as the work presented in [1] and [18], can be leveraged to improve TWINKLE. In summary, work presented in this section can supplement and extend our framework.

8   Conclusion

The staggering growth of the Internet of Things (IoT) brings serious security concerns. However, due to the constrained resources of IoT devices and their networks, many traditional attack detection methods become less effective or inapplicable in an IoT environment. Using the smart home as the battleground, this paper proposes a security framework called TWINKLE that endeavors to address a fundamental dilemma facing any security solution for IoT: the solution has to consume as little resources as possible while still aspiring to achieve the same level of performance as if the resources needed are abundant. It introduces a two-mode design to enable security applications plugged into the framework to handle their targeted attacks in an on-demand fashion. Every security application can simply run lightweight operations in regular mode most of the time, and only invoke heavyweight security routines when it needs to cope with suspicious behavior. By applying TWINKLE to distributed denial-of-service (DDoS) and sinkhole attacks, we can successfully convert prior solutions to more resource-efficient versions, as demonstrated by our evaluations.

References

1. Abduvaliyev, A., Pathan, A.S.K., Zhou, J., Roman, R., Wong, W.C.: On the vital areas of intrusion detection systems in wireless sensor networks. IEEE Commun. Surv. Tutor. **15**(3), 1223–1237 (2013)
2. Abie, H., Balasingham, I.: Risk-based adaptive security for smart IoT in eHealth. In: Proceedings of the 7th International Conference on Body Area Networks, pp. 269–275. ICST (Institute for Computer Sciences, Social-Informatics and Telecommunications Engineering) (2012)
3. Bernal Bernabe, J., Hernández, J.L., Moreno, M.V., Skarmeta Gomez, A.F.: Privacy-preserving security framework for a social-aware Internet of Things. In: Hervás, R., Lee, S., Nugent, C., Bravo, J. (eds.) UCAmI 2014. LNCS, vol. 8867, pp. 408–415. Springer, Cham (2014). https://doi.org/10.1007/978-3-319-13102-3_67
4. Cervantes, C., Poplade, D., Nogueira, M., Santos, A.: Detection of sinkhole attacks for supporting secure routing on 6LoWPAN for Internet of Things. In: IFIP/IEEE International Symposium on Integrated Network Management, pp. 606–611. IEEE (2015)
5. Denning, T., Kohno, T., Levy, H.M.: Computer security and the modern home. ACM Commun. **56**(1), 94–103 (2013)
6. Fernandes, E., Jung, J., Prakash, A.: Security analysis of emerging smart home applications. In: IEEE Symposium on Security and Privacy, pp. 636–654. IEEE (2016)
7. Hilton, S.: Dyn analysis summary of Friday October 21 attack (2016). https://dyn.com/blog/dyn-analysis-summary-of-friday-october-21-attack/
8. IETF: Routing over low power and lossy networks (2012)
9. Kalofonos, D.N., Shakhshir, S.: Intuisec: a framework for intuitive user interaction with smart home security using mobile devices. In: IEEE 18th International Symposium on Personal, Indoor and Mobile Radio Communications, pp. 1–5. IEEE (2007)
10. Kang, W.M., Moon, S.Y., Park, J.H.: An enhanced security framework for home appliances in smart home. Human-cent. Comput. Inf. Sci. **7**(1), 6 (2017)
11. Kumar, P., Braeken, A., Gurtov, A., Iinatti, J., Ha, P.: Anonymous secure framework in connected smart home environments. IEEE Trans. Inf. Forensics Secur. **12**, 968–979 (2017)
12. van der Meulen, R.: Gartner says 6.4 billion connected "things" will be in use in 2016, up 30 percent from 2015 (2015). http://www.gartner.com/newsroom/id/3165317
13. Mirkovic, J., Reiher, P.: D-ward: a source-end defense against flooding denial-of-service attacks. IEEE Trans. Dependable Secure Comput. **2**(3), 216–232 (2005)
14. Neisse, R., Steri, G., Baldini, G.: Enforcement of security policy rules for the internet of things. In: IEEE 10th International Conference on Wireless and Mobile Computing, pp. 165–172. IEEE (2014)
15. Nordrum, A.: Popular internet of things forecast of 50 billion devices by 2020 is outdated (2016). http://spectrum.ieee.org/tech-talk/telecom/internet/popular-internet-of-things-forecast-of-50-billion-devices-by-2020-is-outdated

16. Notra, S., Siddiqi, M., Gharakheili, H.H., Sivaraman, V., Boreli, R.: An experimental study of security and privacy risks with emerging household appliances. In: IEEE Conference on Communications and Network Security, pp. 79–84. IEEE (2014)

17. Raza, S., Wallgren, L., Voigt, T.: SVELTE: real-time intrusion detection in the internet of things. Ad hoc Netw. **11**(8), 2661–2674 (2013)

18. Roman, R., Zhou, J., Lopez, J.: Applying intrusion detection systems to wireless sensor networks. In: IEEE Consumer Communications & Networking Conference (CCNC 2006) (2006)

19. Sehgal, A., Perelman, V., Kuryla, S., Schonwalder, J.: Management of resource constrained devices in the internet of things. IEEE Commun. Mag. **50**(12), 144–149 (2012)

20. Simpson, A.K., Roesner, F., Kohno, T.: Securing vulnerable home IoT devices with an in-hub security manager. In: IEEE International Conference on Pervasive Computing and Communications Workshops, pp. 551–556. IEEE (2017)

21. Team, O.P.: Ossec: open source hids security (2010–2017). https://ossec.github.io/index.html

22. Wallgren, L., Raza, S., Voigt, T.: Routing attacks and countermeasures in the RPL-based internet of things. Int. J. Distrib. Sens. Netw. **9**(8), 794326 (2013)

Out of Kilter: Holistic Exploitation of Denial of Service in Internet of Things

Suhas Setikere$^{(\boxtimes)}$, Vinay Sachidananda, and Yuval Elovici

iTrust, Singapore University of Technology and Design, Singapore, Singapore
{suhas_setikere,sachidananda,yuval_elovici}@sutd.edu.sg

Abstract. Internet of Things (IoT) expose various vulnerabilities at different levels. One such exploitable vulnerability is Denial of Service (DoS). In this paper, we showcase our preliminary efforts towards study of various forms of DoS and how it can be exploited in different protocols of IoT. We propose our initial attack and defense framework for IoT and that can perform various forms of DoS on IP and Bluetooth. We show the initial results of DoS vulnerabilities such as Resource Exhaustion and Bluetooth Low Energy (BLE) Packet Injection. In order to understand how resilient is IoT for DoS, we propose a new metric to measure the Resilience against DoS in IoT. We have conducted a real time experimentation with IoT devices in our security IoT testbed. The experiments conducted are for DoS, Distributed Denial of Service (DDoS) by setting up Mirai and Permanent Denial of Service (PDoS) using BrickerBot on various IoT devices.

Keywords: Internet of Things · Denial of Service · Security analysis

1 Introduction

The Internet of Things (IoT) is increasingly becoming an integral part of everyone's lives. IoT devices like smart lights at home [1], motion sensors to detect movements [2] and many more, are continuing to occupy almost every household. Though IoT devices are experiencing an exponential pace of adoption, they have various security loopholes making them vulnerable to numerous attacks. As a case in point, IoT devices have been recently used to launch various attacks such as Denial of Service (DoS) and steal end-user information [3,4]. Recently, Mirai malware had compromised a huge number of Deutsche Telekom routers [3] by performing DDoS attack. There have been instances where it even resulted in Permanent Denial of Service (PDoS) by bricking the IoT devices [5].

Apart from exposing various vulnerabilities IoT devices have less computing power compared to desktop computers and other computing devices and thus, are susceptible and less resilient to such attacks. The IoT devices handle a limited amount of traffic for performing basic applications. In other words, DoS, DDoS and PDoS attacks are a threat to the IoT devices. Current state of the art lacks

© ICST Institute for Computer Sciences, Social Informatics and Telecommunications Engineering 2018
R. Beyah et al. (Eds.): SecureComm 2018, LNICST 254, pp. 43–52, 2018.
https://doi.org/10.1007/978-3-030-01701-9_3

in detailed experimentation and study of various forms of DoS and the resilience of IoT against DoS. In this work, we perform initial study in a logical fashion.

First, in our work, we propose our initial attack and defense framework called OWL (*Optimized Weighted Legitimates and Illegitimates*). OWL is tailored for IoT which can successfuly perform DoS against IP and Bluetooth IoT devices. OWL produces legitimate and illegitimate packets in order to perform the DoS. However, OWL stands out in performing DoS attacks through few mutated packets by exploiting various DoS vulnerabilities of IoT devices. Next, we introduce a DoS and DDoS defense framework for IoT. The framework is capable of analyzing the network traffic to determine if there is a DoS or a DDoS attack on a specific IoT device.

Second, we have introduced *IoT Resilience* (R_{IoT}) metric to evaluate the resilience of an IoT device against DoS, DDoS and PDoS. IoT Resilience will be calculated based on the services running on an IoT device and the security vulnerabilities exposed by the IoT device. Furthermore, we also adopt legacy metrics such as throughput, allocation of resources and normal packet survival ratio.

Finally, we have carried out initial experiments and evaluation of DoS, DDoS and PDoS against IoT. We have performed DoS attacks through TCP connections [6,7], SYN flooding, etc. We have performed Bluetooth Low Energy (BLE) Packet Injection attacks on Bluetooth devices. We carry out DoS attacks through legitimate and illegitimate packets and evaluate the resilience of the IoT devices. We consider legitimate packets (normal) and illegitimate packets (mutated). Furthermore, we have used Mirai (Mirai malware forms a Botnet of IoT devices and tries to compromise various other devices connected to the network) to perform DDoS attacks within a controlled environment. Furthermore, we perform and evaluate PDoS attack using BrickerBot on IoT devices. The experiments are carried out in a controlled environment in our IoT security testbed [8].

In this paper, our contributions are threefold:

- We introduce our preliminary work on new attack and defense framework called OWL for IoT.
- We introduce a new metric to evaluate the IoT Resilience.
- To understand the impact of DoS, DDoS and PDoS on IoT, we have performed real world experiments using our framework in our IoT security testbed.

The structure of the paper is as follows: Sect. 2 introduces our preliminary efforts of attack and defense framework. In Sect. 3, we introduce a new metric and also discuss the adapted legacy metrics. In Sect. 4, we discuss our experimental methodology. Section 5 provides experimental results and in Sect. 6, we discuss the related work. Finally, we conclude in Sect. 7 with the future work.

2   IoT Attack and Defense Framework

In this section, we propose our initial attack and defense framework OWL (*Optimized Weighted Legitimates and Illegitimates*). OWL framework is tailored for IoT and takes into consideration the IP and Bluetooth devices for performing various DoS attacks using legitimate and illegitimate packets. OWL consists of three modules namely Orchestration, Attack and Defense. OWL framework is evaluated on real IoT security testbed which we will explain in Sect. 4.

OWL Orchestration facilitates the scanning, analysis and monitoring for all the IoT devices. **OWL Attack** is responsible for performing DoS attacks on IoT devices. The attack varies on the IoT device. If the IoT device is IP based, then resource exhaustion attack is performed. The resource exhaustion attack is carried out via legitimate packets from the repository. With regard to Bluetooth devices, packet injection attack is carried out. **OWL Defense** caters to the DoS and DDoS defense mechanism functionality. The defense framework performs real time monitoring to identify anomalies in the traffic. For BLE devices, an alert is shown that the corresponding device is under a DoS attack.

3   Denial of Service Metrics

We propose a new metric called *IoT Resilience* and also adapt legacy metrics such as *Throughput, Allocation of Resources and Normal Packet Survival Ratio* [10] to understand how resilient is an IoT against DoS, DDoS and PDoS.

3.1   IoT Resilience

Before we define the *Resilience* of an IoT device, we need to understand its *Permeance* [9]. We define *Permeance* of an IoT device against a DoS, DDoS or a PDoS attack as:

Definition 1 (a): *The total number of packets an IoT device can service over a period of time when it is bombarded with attack packets before the IoT device fails to provide service.*

$$P_{IoT} = S * \frac{(P_n * P_a)}{T_{RRT}}$$

P_n represents the total number of normal packets. P_a represents the total number of attack packets. T_{RRT} represents the *Request Response Time* of the IoT device. S represents the *Resilience constant* specific to an IoT device vulnerability. In [8], the authors have done penetration testing for IoT devices and have identified a metric system for port scanning to rate the vulnerable ports of the IoT device. We make use of the same metric system to measure our constant S. The *Resilience constant* S varies as a function of the risk level of the scanned ports. The total number of open ports running specific services on each one of them indicates a possibility of those services being affected when the device is under a DoS, DDoS or PDoS attack. Higher the number of open ports, higher are the chances of the device being attacked. Keeping this in mind, the authors in [8] calculate the *Exploitability Score* for an IoT device. We use the same methodology to calculate the score of the IoT devices used in our experiments.

The unit of Permeance is p^2/s. From the definition of *Permeance*, we can define *Resilience* of an IoT device against a DoS attack as:

Definition 1 (b): *The resilience of an IoT device is defined as the reciprocal of its permeance.*

$$R_{IoT} = \frac{1}{P_{IoT}}$$

R_{IoT} is the resilience of an IoT device whose unit is s/p^2.

3.2 Legacy Metrics

We identify and discuss an array of DoS metrics known as *Legacy metrics* [10] and utilize them to quantify the impact of such attacks on IoT devices. We have chosen some of the widely used metrics from the state-of-the-art and are as follows:

Throughput. For an IoT device, the throughput continues to increase for requests from users. According to Bhandari et al. [10] the throughput is defined as, *the total number of bytes transferred per unit time from source to the destination.*

$$Throughput = \frac{\Sigma_{i=0}^{n} \ packet \ delivered}{\Sigma_{i=0}^{n} \ (packet \ arrival \ time) - (packet \ start \ time)}$$

Allocation of Resources. According to Bhandari et al. [10], Allocation of resources is defined as *the ratio of bandwidth of legitimate traffic to the bandwidth of attack traffic.*

$$Allocation \ of \ resources = \frac{bandwidth \ of \ legitimate \ traffic}{bandwidth \ of \ attack \ traffic}$$

Normal Packet Survival Ratio. According to Bhandari et al. [10] Normal Packet Survival Ratio (NPSR) is defined as *the ratio of legitimate packets delivered to the user to the total number of packets delivered.*

$$NPSR = \frac{PL}{PL + PA}$$

where, PL represents the number of legitimate packets and PA represents the number of attack packets.

4   Experimental Methodology

Our experiments are conducted in a real-world network topological setup to evaluate our proposed framework and also to calculate the Resilience of IoT devices against various DoS attacks.

Fig. 1. Smart home setup and IoT security testbed

4.1 Denial of Service

For conducting DoS attacks we have used our initial OWL framework. We have performed our experiments in IoT security testbed as shown in Fig. 1. For *IP devices*, we have conducted *Resource Exhaustion* where OWL framework performs resource exhaustion by sending spoofed legitimate packets to the IoT devices. For e.g., The communication between the Android App on the mobile phone and an IP Camera are monitored and the legitimate packets are injected into the communication network channel of the IP camera. This kind of resource exhaustion is done for various IP based IoT devices in our testbed in a Man in the Middle attack fashion.

On **Bluetooth Low Energy (BLE) devices**, we were able to carry out DoS attacks on devices such as Fitbit, Blood Pressure Monitor, etc. *BLE Packet Injection Attack* involves *OWL* bombarding the BLE devices with a large number of illegitimate BLE packets resulting in the devices being overwhelmed.

4.2 Distributed Denial of Service

Compromised IoT devices are capable of carrying out distributed denial of service (DDoS) attacks on other IoT devices, computers or services. One such way of facilitating a DDoS is via malware, such as Mirai [11] that is used in our experimentation.

Mirai. Mirai turns networked devices into remotely controlled Bots and was first detected in August 2016 by the Whitehat malware research group MalwareMustDie [11]. Initial version of Mirai targets IoT devices running on open Telnet/SSH ports and those devices that have default usernames and passwords. Once the devices are infected, Mirai begins targeting other IoT devices by sending a large number of packets. This results in overwhelming the resources of the victim IoT devices.

When we launched a DDoS attack using ten (10) IP cameras on the victim IP camera, we observed that the VSE attack was the one with the highest throughput. This was followed by UDP and GREETH. The worst performing attack were DNS and ACK attack which generated a throughput of 4.2 Mbps and 5.9 Mbps respectively. In our Botnet experimentation, we used a total of eleven (11) D-Link DCS-942L [12] IP cameras, two laptops and a dedicated access point. We monitored the network traffic on a desktop computer through a mirror port.

4.3 Permanent Denial of Service

Permanent Denial of Service (PDoS) involves sabotaging an IoT hardware by exploiting its security flaws. The security flaws allow accessing IoT devices remotely and provides the ability to execute commands that perform various actions including system level operations. The attack involves execution of potentially harmful commands that modify or corrupt an IoT device's firmware, thus rendering it useless, as the IoT device loses its ability to boot or function. BrickerBot is a malware having the ability to carry out a PDoS attack [13].

BrickerBot is a malware that attacks IoT devices that run a specific version of the DropBear SSH server and target Linux devices running *Busybox* (usually IP cameras). The malware removes the default gateway, limits the kernel threads to one and disables timestamps of TCP. It deletes the boot loader and file system consisting of the Linux kernel. Once the file system has been deleted, the IoT device is unable to reboot [15]. When BrickerBot malware ran on an IoT device, the entire file system was wiped out. The IoT resilience would be immaterial because the value is zero for a PDoS attack. In our experimentation, we used two D-Link DCS-942L [12] IP cameras to test BrickerBot.

5 Experimental Results

In this section, we evaluate our initial OWL framework with our proposed metric and provide detailed analysis of all the results induced. Table 1 provides the comprehensive results of all the IoT devices. We have not discussed the results of PDoS as the calculation of metrics such as IoT Resilience would be immaterial and also the entire file system was wiped out when BrickerBot malware was executed.

Table 1. Initial experimental results

Device	Throughput	Allocation	Resilience	NPSR
Amazon echo	5.83E+04	3.96E-04	9.70E-09	9.11E-04
Nestcam	5.59E+05	1.99	1.86E-12	0.48
HP printer	7.34E+04	9.94E-04	2.98E-10	0.02
Samsung TV	2.09E+04	0.13	8.96E-08	0.64
Wink hub	2.6E+04	0.03	1.04E-11	5.14E-02
OmniGuard cam	632.7	0.0018	2.56E-07	0.04
D-Link	772.9	3.9E-04	1.24F-09	0.9
Smart things	1.8E+04	0.012	4.99E-11	0.81
Belkin smart switch	479.1	1.5E-03	1.98E-08	0.52
Fitbit-1	96.28	4.4E-04	2.5E-04	4.1E-03
BP monitor	119.74	0.001	8.18E-05	8.4E-03
BLE watch	72.54	0.001	8.18E-05	1.14E-02

5.1 Denial of Service

From Table 1, we can infer that when OWL was used to perform DoS attacks, the throughput of the attack was low for all the devices. We noticed that OWL was able to completely bring down all the devices at a much faster rate. For e.g., to cause DoS on a Belkin Smart Switch, a throughput of 479.1 Mbps was required by OWL. We can infer that the allocation of resources for OWL took far less attack traffic bandwidth and more legitimate traffic to cause DoS in IoT devices. For e.g., for Smart Things Hub to go down due to DoS, OWL had an allocation of resources value of 0.012. The resilience of IoT devices when OWL was used are, for example, Amazon Echo had a resilience of 9.7E-09 s/p^2. OWL had a higher NPSR rate and required far less number of legitimate and attack packets. For example, NPSR value for Samsung Smart TV under OWL was 0.64.

With regard to Bluetooth devices, OWL framework was able to successfully carry out DoS attacks. For e.g., Fitbit-1 failed to send updates to the Android app when the throughput of the DoS attack reached 96.28 Mbps during a packet injection attack.

5.2 Distributed Denial of Service

When we launched a DDoS attack using ten (10) IP cameras on the victim IP camera, we observed that the VSE attack was the one with the highest throughput. This was followed by UDP and GREETH. The worst performing attack were DNS and ACK attack which generated a throughput of 4.2 Mbps and 5.9 Mbps respectively. We found that ACK and DNS attacks have the highest allocation of resources value followed by SYN attack.

The NPSR was high during a SYN attack while it is the lowest for GREIP and GREETH attacks. This implies that during a SYN attack, the device under attack receives and responds to packets at a higher rate when compared to the other attack types. GREIP attack has the least NPSR value of 0.00023. The IP camera had the least resilience to VSE and UDP attacks. The IoT resilience value for VSE is $2.6E - 10\ s/p^2$ and UDP is $3.8E - 10\ s/p^2$. The IP camera shows a higher resilience compared to the other attacks for DNS attack type with a value of $1.6E - 05\ s/p^2$.

5.3   Defense Framework Analysis

When we conducted successful DoS and DDoS attacks in our experiments, we were able to detect those attacks from our defense framework. The threshold value (maximum number of packets a device can process when it is not under a DoS attack) for each of the IP based devices had been calculated using OWL. When the threshold values were exceeded, necessary steps were taken by defense framework. First, the IoT device's IP was changed as per the defense framework functionality. Second, we observed that during a DDoS attack (in case of Mirai), the attacker devices were immediately removed from the network. Also, the victim camera's IP was changed.

6   Related Work

As DoS is a well-known concept, we have classified the current state-of-the-art according to Mobile Ad-hoc Networks (MANETs), Wired Networks and Internet of Things.

Mobile Ad-hoc Networks (MANETs). Jhaveri et al. [23] carry out a survey of DoS attacks on MANETs and propose methodologies to detect and prevent such attacks. The attacks also include Gray hole, Black hole and Wormhole attacks. Kannhavong et al. [24] provide various details of flooding attacks along with wormhole attacks, replay attacks and link spoofing attacks on MANETs. They also discuss the implementation of various counter measures. Jawandhiya et al. [25] categorize attacks against MANETs into *Passive*, *Active*, and *Miscellaneous*. Passive attacks include Eavesdropping attacks and Traffic monitoring. The authors provide a comprehensive overview of Active attacks such as Jamming attack, Byzantine attack and Transport Layer attacks (SYN flooding). DoS attacks are classified as Miscellaneous where resource exhaustion is carried out in MANETs. In addition, sleep deprivation attacks and routing table overflow attacks are analyzed.

Wired Networks. Zargar et al. [16] classify DDoS flooding attacks as well as their countermeasures. However, networks are limited to wired systems. DDoS attacks arising from Botnets such as IRC-based, P2P-based and Web-based are also discussed. Mirkovic et al. [9,17–21] provides a comprehensive analysis of DDoS on a network including the metrics to measure the impact of DDoS attacks. Bhandari et al. [10] elaborate on the various metrics that could be used to evaluate the performance of DDoS attacks.

Internet of Things. Perakovic et al. [22] analyze protocols like UDP, SYN, NTP, ACK and their impact on connected IoT devices. However, authors in [22] do not involve analysis of varying types of devices present and their resilience against DoS attacks. Mirai's functionalities and operations on IoT devices are discussed by Kolias et al. [14]. The communication sessions between the compromised IoT devices and the Bot servers are analyzed but the effects of several attack types are not discussed.

Nevertheless, none of the aforementioned research evaluated various DoS attacks, Mirai Botnet and BrickerBot Malware through DoS metrics capable of quantifying the impact on IoT devices. Furthermore, the above mentioned work lacks measurement of resilience of IoT against DoS attacks.

7 Conclusion and Future Work

In this paper, we demonstrated and evaluated various forms of DoS attacks on IoT devices. We have done a preliminary study of IP and Bluetooth IoT devices against various DoS attacks. We implemented and demonstrated our initial attack and defense framework called OWL. We proposed a new metric to calculate the Resilience of IoT devices against DoS. We carried out DDoS using IP cameras within a sophisticated environment and discussed the results. In addition, we also carried out PDoS attacks on real IP cameras. We conducted initial experimentation on our IoT security testbed and discuss the preliminary results. We intend to perform a large scale study and extend OWL with complete functionality. We also intend to involve Zigbee devices and perform large scale experiments with more IoT devices.

References

1. Ur, B., Jung, J., Schechter, S.: The current state of access control for smart devices in homes. In: Workshop on Home Usable Privacy and Security (HUPS), HUPS 2014, July 2013
2. Tozlu, S., Senel, M., Mao, W., Keshavarzian, A.: Wi-Fi enabled sensors for internet of things: a practical approach. IEEE Commun. Mag. **50**(6) (2012)
3. Distributed Denial of Service using Mirai. https://www.bankinfosecurity.com
4. Mirai Malware for IoT. https://www.symantec.com
5. Bricker Bot. https://security.radware.com
6. Kuzmanovic, A., Knightly, E.W.: Low-rate TCP-targeted denial of service attacks: the shrew vs. the mice and elephants. In: Proceedings of the 2003 Conference on Applications, Technologies, Architectures, and Protocols for Computer Communications, pp. 75–86. ACM, August 2003
7. Schuba, C.L., Krsul, I.V., Kuhn, M.G., Spafford, E.H., Sundaram, A., Zamboni, D.: Analysis of a denial of service attack on TCP. In: Proceedings of the 1997 IEEE Symposium on Security and Privacy, pp. 208–223. IEEE, May 1997
8. Sachidananda, V., Siboni, S., Shabtai, A., Toh, J., Bhairav, S., Elovici, Y.: Let the cat out of the bag: a holistic approach towards security analysis of the internet of things. In: Proceedings of the 3rd ACM International Workshop on IoT Privacy, Trust, and Security, pp. 3–10. ACM, April 2017

9. Mirkovic, J., Reiher, P.: A taxonomy of DDoS attack and DDoS defense mechanisms. ACM SIGCOMM Comput. Commun. Rev. **34**(2), 39–53 (2004)
10. Bhandari, A., Sangal, A.L., Kumar, K.: Performance metrics for defense framework against distributed denial of service attacks. Int. J. Netw. Secur. **5**(2), 38 (2014)
11. Malware Must Die - Mirai Malware. http://blog.malwaremustdie.org
12. Dlink IP Camera. http://www.dlink.com.sg/
13. Phlashing-PDoS. http://hackersonlineclub.com
14. Kolias, C., Kambourakis, G., Stavrou, A., Voas, J.: DDoS in the IoT: Mirai and other botnets. Computer **50**(7), 80–84 (2017)
15. BrickerBot-Permanent Denial of Service. https://arstechnica.com
16. Zargar, S.T., Joshi, J., Tipper, D.: A survey of defense mechanisms against distributed denial of service (DDoS) flooding attacks. IEEE Commun. Surv. Tutor. **15**(4), 2046–2069 (2013)
17. Mirkovic, J., Prier, G., Reiher, P.: Attacking DDoS at the source. In: Proceedings of the 10th IEEE International Conference on Network Protocols, pp. 312–321. IEEE, November 2002
18. Mirkovic, J., Dietrich, S., Dittrich, D., Reiher, P.: Internet denial of service: attack and defense mechanisms (Radia Perlman computer networking and security) (2004)
19. Mirkovic, J., Arikan, E., Wei, S., Thomas, R., Fahmy, S., Reiher, P.: Benchmarks for DDoS defense evaluation. In: Military Communications Conference, MILCOM 2006, pp. 1–10. IEEE, October 2006
20. Mirkovic, J., et al.: Measuring denial of service. In: Proceedings of the 2nd ACM workshop on Quality of protection, pp. 53–58. ACM, October 2006
21. Mirkovic, J., et al.: Towards user-centric metrics for denial-of-service measurement. In: Proceedings of the 2007 Workshop on Experimental Computer Science, p. 8. ACM, June 2007
22. Peraković, D., Periša, M., Cvitić, I.: Analysis of the IoT impact on volume of DDoS attacks. In: 33rd Symposium on New Technologies in Postal and Telecommunication Traffic (PosTel 2015), pp. 295–304, January 2015
23. Jhaveri, R.H., Patel, S.J., Jinwala, D.C.: DoS attacks in mobile ad hoc networks: a survey. In: 2012 Second International Conference on Advanced Computing and Communication Technologies (ACCT), pp. 535–541. IEEE, January 2012
24. Kannhavong, B., Nakayama, H., Nemoto, Y., Kato, N., Jamalipour, A.: A survey of routing attacks in mobile ad hoc networks. IEEE Wirel. Commun., **14**(5) (2007)
25. Jawandhiya, P.M., Ghonge, M.M., Ali, M.S., Deshpande, J.S.: A survey of mobile ad hoc network attacks. Int. J. Eng. Sci. Technol. **2**(9), 4063–4071 (2010)

Augmented Chain of Ownership: Configuring IoT Devices with the Help of the Blockchain

Sophie Dramé-Maigné[1,2](✉), Maryline Laurent[2], Laurent Castillo[1], and Hervé Ganem[3]

[1] Gemalto SA, 6 rue de la Verrerie, 92190 Meudon, France
sophie.dramemaigne@gmail.com
[2] SAMOVAR, Télécom SudParis, CNRS, Université Paris-Saclay, 9 rue Charles Fourier, 91011 Evry, France
[3] Paris, France

Abstract. Recording the ownership of assets has historically constituted a cumbersome procedure requiring the intervention of third parties that cannot be freely chosen and take a hefty fee. Its high cost had this process reserved for valuable assets such as real estate, cars, jewelry or artwork. The system itself is also vulnerable to corruption as records can be manipulated by malicious actors. The blockchain presents a solution to both these issues.

The blockchain, as a distributed and persistent ledger, removes the need for third parties and lowers the cost of ownership record operations. Consequently, more modest assets such as IoT devices can benefit from this process as well. By registering IoT devices to the blockchain and documenting their transfers, we aim to create a chain of ownership that can be used to keep track and prove the ownership of IoT devices. In this system, a pseudonymous Proof of Ownership (PoO) must be produced and verified before a sale can occur. A PoO can also replace the product's registration process that currently depends on the original product vendor and requires the user to volunteer personal information to a private company.

An extension is proposed to facilitate remote configuration of IoT devices and to improve the management of device-related secrets for owners that must configure a great number of devices.

1 Introduction

In 2008, Nakamoto [15] introduced the concept of the blockchain, a public shared unforgeable ledger that lets participants register transactions in a persistent and decentralized manner. If it was intimately linked with cryptocurrencies at first, the blockchain has since been used in other applications. Amongst them voting [4], online games [3], ride sharing [1], and many others[1]. With properties

---

[1] https://gomedici.com/30-non-financial-use-cases-of-blockchain-technology-infographic/, Last checked Feb, 16th 2018.

© ICST Institute for Computer Sciences, Social Informatics and Telecommunications Engineering 2018
R. Beyah et al. (Eds.): SecureComm 2018, LNICST 254, pp. 53–68, 2018.
https://doi.org/10.1007/978-3-030-01701-9_4

like desintermediation, unforgeability, and decentralization, the blockchain is also very attractive to the Internet of Things (IoT). Its usability in such setting has been studied with mixed results [8,9,12,13].

A common blockchain use case is the tracking of assets' ownership such as houses, cars or artwork [20]. In some countries, because of corrupt officials, the state cannot be trusted to keep accurate records of land ownership. Sweden[2], Georgia[3], and Ukraine[4] are each at different stages of implementing a land entitlement project using the blockchain. Such initiatives have the power to combat that corruption and give power back to farmers and small property owners.

In this paper, we propose to use the blockchain to track IoT devices' ownership. The blockchain is a cheaper alternative to record ownership. Traditional methods involve an outside authority such as notaries that implies trust and drives up cost. Ours is also a simpler and faster process. Thanks to the decreased cost and added usability, ownership records are made available for more low-cost assets such as IoT devices.

This mechanism can also be used to exchange device-related secrets, enabling remote configuration and efficient secret management. IoT use cases can involve many devices deployed in various physical locations. This makes manual configuration inefficient. Smart grids are a good example of hundreds of devices that need to be deployed to cover the entirety of electricity grids. The deployment speed is highly impacted by the configuration method, as many devices need to be configured at once. By leveraging the chain of ownership published in the blockchain, we propose to facilitate remote configuration. Additionally, owners can use the same mechanism to efficiently manage the multiple secrets used to remotely manage their devices.

Related Work. Ownership tracking via a blockchain has already been implemented. On the Bitcoin blockchain, Colored Coins [20] is designed to track asset exchanges. On the Ethereum blockchain [7,22], smart contracts [21] can be programmed to do similar things. Other blockchains such as NXT [6] provide a native asset exchange. There are also front-end applications [2,5] that bridge several blockchains together to facilitate interoperation. These implementations are not IoT-specific but their general-purpose tokens are IoT-compatible. They are however only focused on ownership record and cannot be used for key management.

In the academic literature, the transfer of ownership is addressed at the device level [16,18]. Ownership transfer is defined [19] as "the capability to pass ownership of a tag to a third party without compromising backward untraceability for the said party or forward untraceability for the previous owner." The focus

---

[2] https://www.reuters.com/article/us-sweden-blockchain/sweden-tests-blockchain-te chnology-for-land-registry-idUSKCN0Z22KV, Last checked Feb, 16th 2018.

[3] https://cointelegraph.com/news/georgia-becomes-first-country-to-register-property -on-blockchain, Last checked Feb, 16th 2018.

[4] https://www.bloomberg.com/news/articles/2017-10-03/ukraine-turns-to-blockcha in-to-boost-land-ownership-transparency, Last checked Feb, 16th 2018.

is on key management and domain boundaries. The devices that are concerned by these protocols are RFID tags. No record is kept of past owners. This article precisely focuses on these ownership records.

Table 1. Our notations

Symbol	Description
D	Device
$\{D_i\}_{0 \leq i < n}$	Family of n devices
id_i	Identifier of device D_i
M	Device manufacturer
C	A Company
$addr_A$	Blockchain address of A. $addr_A = Hash(pub_A)$
$(pub_A, priv_A)$	Public/private blockchain key pair linked to $addr_A$
s_i	Secret linked to device D_i
K_A	Master key of A
$k_{A,B}$	Symmetric key derived from K_A and shared with B
$k_{A,i}$	Symmetric key derived from K_A and id_i
tx_k	k^{th} blockchain transaction
out_j^k	j^{th} output of tx_k

Organization. Security assumptions and threat models are presented in Sect. 2. Based on the notations of Table 1, Sect. 3 introduces our tracking of ownership using the blockchain. Section 4 proposes an extension of the approach to configure IoT devices and manage keys for the sake of the owner.

2 Security Considerations

2.1 Security Assumptions

We operate under the following assumptions:

A1 *Secured blockchain keys*: Blockchain keys cannot be stolen, lost or otherwise compromised. This implies good key management.
A2 *Solid cryptographic primitives*: Our proposal uses cryptographic primitives such as signatures, hashes, or encryption. We assume these primitives cannot be broken.
A3 *Blockchain consistency*: Fundamental blockchain properties include consistency amongst nodes and consistency over time [17]. This implies that all nodes in the network will agree on blockchain history, the last few blocks excluded, and that accepted transactions cannot be modified. We assume these properties are verified and the blockchain history cannot be altered.

A4 *Blockchain capability*: Actors (M and C) own a blockchain address, the corresponding public and private key pair, and the means of submitting or retrieving a transaction to or from the blockchain.

A5 *Reputation System*: The actors take part in a reputation system where bad behaviors can be reported. We assume this system cannot be tampered with.

A6 *Unicity of device's serial number*: A device can be uniquely identified by its serial number. We assume this serial number is physically located on the device and cannot be tampered with.

A1 is a very strong assumption that does not really hold. When a private blockchain key is lost, it cannot be changed or retrieved. The assets associated with this key and the corresponding address can no longer be transferred. When a private key is stolen, the victim must race the thief to emit a transaction that will transfer all assets stored on the corresponding blockchain address to another one. Blockchain transactions cannot be reversed. Multisignature addresses can be used to mitigate the risk of theft. However, as this is a core issue for all blockchain applications, there exist a number of methods to safeguard one's key. It can be locked in a safe, stored in a hardware token, put to paper, etc. These considerations are out of the scope of this paper as they have been addressed elsewhere[5].

For the same reasons, we do not address the security of reputation systems (Assumption A5).

2.2   Threat Model

Across our two proposals, we consider three types of attackers: a malicious new owner, a malicious previous owner, and a malicious uninvolved third party. We detail nine possible threats involving these actors. These threats are summarized in Table 2.

Malicious Previous Owners. This attacker's goal is to either fool a potential buyer, by not providing the device after the sale has been concluded, or to retain access to said device and thus gain access to sensitive data belonging to the new owner. As the previous owner, the attacker is in possession of the credentials that, at the time of the handover, enable device access. She can also provision anything unto the device prior to the handover and is able to produce a valid proof of ownership.

When a device is sold and exchanged, the previous owner can use her knowledge to gain access to sensitive information. She can also use the device as an entry point into the new owner's network. This defines Threat $T1$.

A prospective owner can be fooled by the previous owner and buy a device that will not be delivered. This defines Threat $T2$.

When a secret must be provided in order to gain access to the device (see Sect. 4), the attacker may refuse to provide it or falsify it, thus preventing the new owner from accessing his device. This defines Threat $T3$.

---

[5] https://blockgeeks.com/guides/paper-wallet-guide/, Last checked April, 19th 2018
   https://en.bitcoin.it/wiki/Storing_bitcoins, Last checked April, 19th 2018.

Malicious New Owners. The goal of this attacker is to gain access to sensitive information without authorization. As its new owner, the attacker has full access and full control over the device.

After the sale, if the device has not been properly wiped, the new owner can extract potentially sensitive information related to the former owner from the device itself. This defines Threat $T4$.

The new owner can also use the device's identity to gain access to previous owner's data. This can be achieved by interacting with users or devices that still recognize the device as being owned by the previous owner. This defines Threat $T5$.

Malicious Third Party. This attacker's goal is to appear as a legitimate device owner to fool a potential buyer, steal and re-sale a device, disturb the sale transaction or gain information about the parties involved in the ownership transfer. When a public blockchain is used, the attacker has access to all information that transits through the blockchain. She can also produce and submit valid blockchain transactions.

First, the attacker can try to clog the blockchain network. In this event, the network would not be able to process the transaction signaling the ownership transfer. This defines Threat $T6$.

Second, when the transfer occurs, the attacker may try to gain knowledge about the involved parties. This defines Threat $T7$.

Third, the attacker may pretend to be the owner of a device she does not possess or acquired illegally (through theft for instance). This is Threat $T8$.

Fourth, the attacker may fabricate a blockchain trace for a device that does not actually exist. This is Threat $T9$.

Table 2. Threats

Nbr	Attacker type	Description
$T1$	Prev. Owner	Previous owner retains access to the device
$T2$	Prev. Owner	Proof of Ownership is produced but device is not provided
$T3$	Prev. Owner	Secret is not valid. Provided device cannot be accessed
$T4$	New Owner	New owner extracts sensitive data from the device
$T5$	New Owner	New owner uses device to gain access to sensitive data
$T6$	Third Party	Ownership transfer cannot be completed
$T7$	Third Party	Attacker accesses sensitive information by eavesdropping
$T8$	Third Party	Attacker successfully masquerades as the device owner
$T9$	Third Party	Ownership chain with no corresponding device

3   Asset Ownership

3.1   Motivation

As previously mentioned, asset tracking is one of the most straightforward blockchain application. Assets that have been considered for this use case tend to be expensive (i.e. land, cars, houses, paintings, etc.). These objects' ownership will most likely already be tracked using third parties such as notaries, insurance companies, or other government-sanctioned entities. The corresponding administrative procedures can be long and costly. By using the blockchain instead, trust in these third parties and their infrastructure is no longer required. The cost of a transaction is also highly reduced. The transfer of ownership is a simple blockchain operation. For these reasons, ownership records do not have to be confined to expensive items. We propose to apply this principle to IoT devices.

Triggers for ownership transfer in the IoT might be: a user re-selling an old device after it has been replaced by a newer one, an individual looking for cheaper options and turning to the second-hand market, a company re-assigning resources as a project closes, long-term renting of IoT devices, etc.

Benefits of the Proposal. Keeping ownership records on the blockchain offers the following benefits:

- *Desintermediation*: Traditionally, changes in ownership must be attested, assisted, and recorded by third parties. As the blockchain keeps a public proof of the transaction, they are no longer necessary.
- *Shared architecture*: When using existing public or private blockchains, one can take advantage of the infrastructure already deployed by others. This use case does not require the deployment of a dedicated infrastructure nor the federation of a large number of systems to enable interoperability.
- *Decentralized storage*: This pertains to one of the fundamental blockchain property, persistence. Blockchain transactions will be stored in a decentralized fashion, protecting ownership record from loss and alterations.
- *Simplicity*: The process by which the ownership is transferred requires a single transaction. Its simplicity makes it highly usable, even to private individuals.
- *Lower costs*: Ownership transfer usually involves a third party. This third party will take a commission on the sale. The desintermediation therefore has the added benefit of lowering costs.
- *Traceability*: Ownership of an object can be traced back to its original owner. It can also be traced the other way around, from its original owner to the latest one. One interesting consequence is the possibility of issuing security alerts. When an incident affecting a large number of devices occurs, it is currently hard to track owners and warn them of the issue. Owners can be private individuals. They are not likely to follow best security practices. For that reason, in the event of a large scale IoT attack, being able to track and warn device owners could prevent further damage.

- *Proof of ownership (PoO)*: Before a sale or before providing services only the legitimate owner of the device should be able to access, actors can require a proof of ownership. Concerned services would be maintenance operations or customer support for instance. In current systems, this proof takes the form of a certified document. The owner can also be required to prove its identity by answering a number of personal question following a company-dependent registration process. We propose a PoO that is pseudonymous and that can be independently verified, without certification authorities or personal information.
- *Availability*: By its distributed nature, the blockchain offers availability guarantees that the deployment of a private fact recording infrastructure cannot match.
- *Pseudonymity*: Traditionally, ownership records are nominative. This is natural as the PoO is linked to one's identity. When using the blockchain, device ownership is tied to the ownership of the corresponding blockchain private key. This enables the use of pseudonyms.
- *Ownership Transfer notification*: One issue with ownership transfer is the timely revocation of permissions granted to the device. Some access rights can linger, thus weakening a system's security. Recording ownership transfers in the blockchain in a public fashion can enable the automatic revocation of permissions upon ownership transfer. This would enhance the protection of former owners private information.

3.2 Proposal

We take our example at the very beginning of the ownership chain with the sale of a device D. We consider the following actors: the device's manufacturer M, and a company C that wishes to acquire D. Following Assumption $A4$, both M and C possess a blockchain address, the corresponding public and private key pair, and the means of submitting or retrieving a transaction to or from the blockchain.

Table 3. Transaction format

Field	Description	Status
Tx type	Possible values are *genesis* and *transfer*	*Mand*
Nounce	Can be made mandatory for *genesis* tx (see Sect. 3.3)	*Opt*
Inputs	Lists all the inputs of the tx (see Table 4)	*Opt*
Outputs	Lists all the outputs of the tx (see Table 5)	*Mand*

The general idea is to link the asset's exchange to a series of blockchain transactions, thus creating a chain of ownership. There are two types of transaction available. The transaction that creates the link between the asset and its digital

Table 4. Input format

Field	Description	Status
Previous tx	Identifier of previous tx (usually the hash of the tx)	*Mand*
Index	Index of output to be used in previous tx, must be unspent	*Mand*
Public key	Pub key that matches the address in the selected output	*Mand*
Signature	Signed with the priv. key that matches the given pub. key	*Mand*

Table 5. Output format

Field	Description	Status
Destination	Blockchain address of the output owner	*Mand*
Id	Device serial number, mandatory for *genesis* tx	*Opt*
Secret	See Sect. 4	*Opt*

counterpart is the *asset genesis transaction*. Transactions that mark a change in ownership are *transfer* transactions. Transactions follow the Bitcoin [15] model of input/output, meaning that each transaction uses previous transaction outputs as inputs. Transactions are detailed in Table 3. Tables 4 and 5 breakdown the construction of individual inputs and outputs respectively.

For an input to be valid, it must be signed with the private key corresponding to the output's destination address: We take the example of a transaction tx_0 with 2 outputs, out_0^0 sent to $addr_A$ and out_1^0 sent to $addr_B$. Transaction tx_1 uses out_0^0 as input. To be valid, the input must carry the public key corresponding to $addr_A$ along with a valid signature produced using $priv_A$, private key corresponding to $addr_A$. Because outputs only carry blockchain addresses, and because hashes are irreversible, the public key pub_A is needed for the signature validation (reminder: $addr_A = Hash(pub_A)$). Each output in a transaction corresponds to a different asset.

A *genesis*-type transaction has no input. Its outputs however must include an *id* field. According to *A6*, device identifiers are unique and cannot be tampered with. This field, shown in Table 5, therefore strongly affiliates a physical IoT device and its digital counterpart.

Going back to our example, illustrated by Fig. 1, M issues a *genesis* transaction, tx_0, with a single output sent to $addr_M$, her own blockchain address, and carrying D's serial number. This transaction creates device D's digital representation and registers M as the original owner. Before a sale can take place, M must produce a valid proof of ownership to C. To this effect, C sends a challenge message, m, to M. Because the challenge is chosen by C, M cannot reproduce an intercepted message. M signs m with $priv_M$ and sends $(Hash(tx_0), 0, Sign_{priv_M}(m), pub_M)$ back to C. Using the transaction identifier, $Hash(tx_0)$, company C can check for itself the corresponding transaction in the blockchain and the designated output, here the 0th. She validates that out_0^0 is

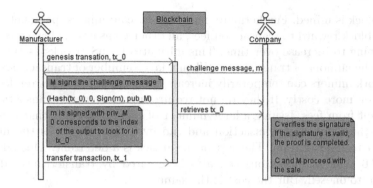

Fig. 1. Proof of ownership and ownership transfer

not spent and was addressed to M. C then verifies the provided signature. If the signature is valid, the PoO is accepted. It is interesting to note that providing such a proof does not compromise the owner's pseudonymity.

Following Assumption $A1$, blockchain keys cannot be stolen. Assumption $A2$ states that the blockchain's cryptographic primitives cannot be broken. This means that the only person capable of producing a valid PoO is the owner of both the blockchain key and the device. Furthermore, since the blockchain history cannot be altered according to Assumption $A3$, once an ownership record has been published or updated, it cannot be modified. This neutralizes Threat $T8$.

A PoO can be useful outside of the scope of a sale. Currently, when buying a device, customers can be required to register themselves with the corresponding brand. This involves personal data that will later be used to identify and authenticate them. A PoO can be used instead, enhancing customer privacy.

Now that M has proven he is the rightful owner of D, the sale can proceed. When C purchases the device, M issues a second transaction of type *transfer*, tx_1. Transaction tx_1 has one input, out_0^0, signed with $priv_M$, and one output, out_0^1 sent to $addr_C$. This second transaction transfers the ownership of D to C.

3.3 Limitations

Blockchain-Related Limitations. The security of the scheme depends on the security of the underlying blockchain [14]. Amongst other issues we can cite 51% attacks, propagation delays [11], withholding attacks [10], the untested scalability of blockchains, their complex governance system, etc. Assumption $A2$ does not cover these issues as they are not crypto-related but rather network-related. However, despite all these theoretical shortcomings, blockchains like Bitcoin and Ethereum have demonstrated their resilience to attacks and only grown stronger as a result.

Another issue that needs addressing is the resistance to DDoS attacks. In the Bitcoin blockchain, the only transactions without inputs are *coinbase* transactions. First transaction of a block, a *coinbase* transaction can only be issued when a block is mined. Furthermore, now that Bitcoin miners' payment is moving from block reward to transaction fees, all other transactions have a cost that is only going to increase over time. This mitigates DDoS attacks as the cost is linear in the number of transactions. When a large number of transactions floods the network, miners can temporarily increase transaction fees, thus rendering an attack even more costly. If they do not require inputs, *genesis* transactions are not exempt from fees. Issuing a large number of them has a cost that is at least linear in the number of transaction and can even grow faster as the miners's fees adapt to the situation. The cost of the attack is a deterrent. This addresses Threat $T6$. Valid transactions can also be created by transferring a device's ownership to oneself. But the cost is the same.

We propose two additional means of mitigation. The first solution is to use a private blockchain where the right to issue *genesis* transactions is limited to pre-approved actors. Manufacturers would need to be registered in a manufacturer consortium, granting them the exclusive right of issuing *genesis* transaction, thus creating new devices. A manufacturer that behaves incorrectly, by advertizing non existing devices or issuing too many *genesis* transactions, would lose its publication privileges. This has the added advantage of addressing Threat $T9$. Private blockchains unfortunately do not offer the same openness and decentralization as public ones.

A second solution consists in increasing the cost of *genesis* transactions. They would require a *nounce* as an input (see Table 4). Similarly to Proof of Work, the *nounce* would be chosen so that the hash of the transaction is lower than a pre-defined threshold. The difficulty does not need to be as high as Bitcoin proof of work's and can be adapted to counter DDoS attacks. The downside is that this increased computational cost will mostly impact manufacturers as they are the most likely to issue *genesis* transactions. This is therefore likely to impact the device's cost in return.

Use-Case-Related Limitations. In the above proposal, a *genesis* transaction creates the digital representation of an IoT device. If the transaction is linked to the device via its serial number, no proof of the existence of this device is required. The production of a valid PoO does not translate to the possession of a real-life IoT device. In case of theft for instance, the original owner can still produce a valid proof but will not be able to produce the device itself. This situation is not different from online shopping where the buyer has to rely on pictures, listings, reputation, or other criteria to decide whether to trust the vendor. Following Assumption $A5$, vendors that do not provide devices after the transaction is complete can be reported. Their reputation score will be lowered and they are less likely to fool someone else in the future. This addresses Threat $T9$.

Similarly, the issuance of a *transfer* transaction does not force the shipping of the device to the new owner. It means however that the previous owner can no longer prove that she owns the device. This is a deterrent as future prospective buyers are unlikely to commit to the sale if the ownership cannot be proven. Blockchain transactions are irreversible. To protect himself, the vendor can be tempted to require payment before the *transfer* transaction is issued. The buyer then runs the risk of that transaction never being issued. Bitcoin multisignature presents a solution to this problem. Multisignature refers to transactions that need more than one signature to be valid. The desired number here is 2 out of 3. The buyer and vendor freely choose a party that they trust to be impartial. The buyer then sends the funds to the multisignature address. If everything goes smoothly, upon reception of the purchased item, the buyer and seller both sign the transaction and funds are sent to the vendor. When a conflict occurs, the third party decides who should receive the funds and signs the transaction together with the interested party. The same can be done with ownership trans-action. This addresses Threat $T2$.

An owner could also try to sell the same device to two different people. This is a problem that is similar to the cryptocurrency double spending. In a similar fashion, both transactions cannot co-exist. New owners should therefore be sure to wait for the blockchain transaction to be confirmed. For Bitcoin, the generic rule is to wait for the transaction to be burried under 5 to 6 blocks, which takes around an hour. For such a use case, this delay is not an inconvenience.

In all of the above cases, bad behavior from any of the involved actors will negatively affect that actor's reputation score (Assumption $A5$). All reporting should include the incriminating transaction(s) when applicable. For a double sale for instance, two transactions spending the same output with valid signatures should be provided as proof of bad behavior.

Finally, malicious previous owners might want to retain control of their former device after it has been shipped to its new owner. To protect against this risk, the device should be wiped clean upon reception and all the credentials should be changed. This addresses Threat $T1$. The same applies to a former device owner who wants to prevent her sensitive data from being accessed by the new owner. Before the device can be shipped, it should be restored to factory default. This addresses Threat $T4$. The necessary steps should also be taken to revoke the device's access to all sensitive services such as a smart home private network. This addresses Threat $T5$. Threats $T4$ and $T5$ are better addressed by Sect. 4.

4   Managing Secrets

4.1   Motivation

Security rests on the sharing of secrets. These secrets are used to secure communications or encrypt data. When a device is manufactured, initial secrets are provisioned to start the security chain. When acquiring a device, its secrets need to be retrieved from the manufacturer or previous owner. The means currently at our disposal to do so lead to slow and cumbersome deployment processes. What is needed therefore is a mean of efficiently retrieving that information to be able to remotely and efficiently configure devices in an industrial context.

Currently, physical access to the device is often necessary. When buying a device, the new owner will have it shipped to her location and configure it. The pin or the password may be written down on the device's box, in the configuration manual or otherwise physically attached to the device and its packaging. Buyer and seller might also choose to call on a trusted third party to take care of the configuration and installation of devices.

The need for an initial physical access is a hindrance on the deployment process. Because many devices need to be configured at once, this method that is slow, costly and may require to trust confidential information to a third party is ill-fitted.

Another issue is the management of these secrets. In IoT scenarios, multiple devices may be owned by the same entity. Furthermore, symmetric cryptography is often preferred due to the constrained nature of IoT devices. This is another multiplying factor for the number of keys involved. This multiplicity implies the need for an efficient management of secrets over the life a device. Based on the blockchain ownership records, we propose a solution that both delivers a device's secret to its newest owner and enable their management over the life of the device.

Benefits of the Proposal. The benefits brought by the proposed scheme are as follows:

- *Simplified deployment process*
- *Cost reduction*
- *Reduction of the number of secret keys*
- *Distributed storage of keys*

As an extension of the proposal from Sect. 3, to the benefits described above we add the advantages described in Sect. 3.1 that are inherent to the use of a blockchain as the underlying mechanism.

4.2   Proposal

For the sake of this proposal, we consider IoT devices as black boxes exposing a number of functions that can be activated either by physical interactions or via a communication channel. In both cases, a secret is required to successfully invoke any function. When the device is manufactured, an initial secret is provided. As for any function, the generation of a new secret requires the previous secret and can be invoked either by physical interaction or through the communication channel.

Once again, we start at the beginning of the ownership chain. The manufacturer M sells a batch of n devices $\{D_i\}_{0 \leq i < n}$ to a company C. Each device has a unique identifier id_i. Additionally, C owns a master key K_C. Used as an input for key derivation, K_C should not be shared and only be known by C. The symmetric key $k_{C,M}$ is derived from K_C and M. This means that a symmetric key is associated with every vendor. Key $k_{C,M}$ will be used to encrypt $\{s_i\}_{0 \leq i < n}$, secrets linked to devices $\{D_i\}_{0 \leq i < n}$ respectively. The blockchain still supports two types of transaction, *genesis* and *transfer*.

Figure 2 illustrates the process by which ownership is transferred and secrets are exchanged:

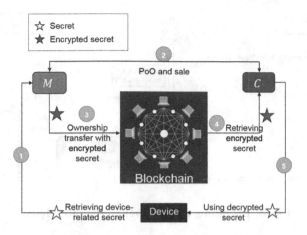

Fig. 2. Transferring ownership and delivering device secret

Step 1 M interacts with each D_i and generates a secret s_i. This secret s_i can be an administrative password, a private key, a pin, etc.

Step 2 M retrieves $k_{C,M}$ from C or from its own record. That information can be provided along with payment information for instance. We assumed $k_{C,M}$ to be a symmetric key that needs to be provided by the buyer. If C prefers using asymmetric cryptography, the key used to encrypt s_i can also be retrieved from a registry storing public key records. These keys are used for applicative purposes and should differ from the keys used for the blockchain protocol. Using $k_{C,M}$, M encrypts each s_i.

Step 3 M issues a *genesis* transaction, tx_0, with n outputs where out_i^0 is linked to D_i through its serial number id_i and is sent to $addr_M$, her own blockchain address. M issues a second transaction of type *transfer*, tx_1, with $\{out_i^0\}$ as inputs, signed with $priv_M$. This transaction yields n outputs, one for each D_i, sent to $addr_C$. In addition to $addr_C$, each output carries $Enc_{k_{C,M}}(s_i)$ (see Table 5).

Step 4 C retrieves $\{Enc_{k_{C,M}}(s_i)\}$ from the blockchain and deciphers them, recovering $\{s_i\}$.

Step 5 Using $\{s_i\}$, C gains access to each D_i. When necessary, s_i is also used for configuration.

Outputs can be separated, enabling devices to be sold separately. This factors the transaction costs.

This scheme involves several keys and secrets, especially when considering devices bought from multiple vendors but only K_C and $priv_C$ need to be safeguarded by C. Each s_i can be recovered from K_C. This greatly simplifies the management of secrets where many devices are involved.

Furthermore, updates can be made to a device's secret, as illustrated by Fig. 3. After buying a device D_i, the new owner should change the corresponding s_i as this secret is known to the previous owner (Threat $T1$). Using s_i, she can

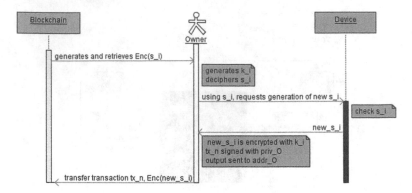

Fig. 3. Publishing a new secret to the blockchain

invoke any function of D_i and generates a new secret, s_i^{new}. This secret can now be stored in the blockchain. The owner simply furthers the ownership chain by sending a *transfer* transaction to herself, replacing $Enc_{k_{C,i}}(s_i)$ by $Enc_{k_{C,i}}(s_i^{new})$, where Enc is the encryption algorithm, and $k_{C,i}$ is a symmetric key derived from K_C and id_i. A single actor can have several blockchain addresses and transfer device ownership between them. Such transactions are made to hide the link between the owner's identity and her blockchain addresses, thus hiding the number of device belonging to a single owner. This also hides how long an actor holds on to a device (Threat $T7$). Note that the new secret should of course be encrypted with a key that is not known to M.

4.3   Limitations

The first delicate point of this scheme is the transmission of the encryption key, $k_{C,M}$, from C to M. If symmetric keys are used, then a secure communication channel should be put in place to enable the exchange. The security of a key during its transmission falls outside of the scope of this document. When a large number of sales involve the same actors, here M and C, the same key is used to encrypt all secrets. The symmetric key must be exchanged only once.

If asymmetric cryptography is used, the public key can simply be transferred or even made available in a registry chosen by the actors. The choice of registry does not affect the scheme. This mitigates Threat $T7$.

Before selling a device, the owner should invoke the secret generation function to bind the device to a new secret. If the secret that is communicated to the new owner via the *transfer* transaction was already in use, it can be used to retrieve private information from the previous owner (Threat $T4$). Similarly, if $k_{C,M}$ is a symmetric key, it should not be reused when a new secret is uploaded to the blockchain. Otherwise, all s_i^{new} are exposed to M (Threat $T1$). To achieve this, $k_{C,i}$ can be derived from elements linked to the blockchain transactions. Let tx_n be the latest transaction that proves M owns D_i. Such a transaction must exist with unspent output otherwise M is not the rightful owner of D_i. In that case,

$Hash(tx_n)$ could be used as an input for key derivation. The *transfer* transaction from M to C, transaction tx_m, will use one of tx_n output as input. Similarly, when updating s_i, an output from tx_m will be used. The hash of the previous transaction is therefore an easy element to recover. It varies with transactions, leading to different $k_{C,i}$.

As stated in Threat $T3$, the new owner runs the risk of receiving the correct device but being given the wrong secret. In such a case, the device is unusable. The motivation behind this can be for the previous owner to retain control of the device (Threat $T1$) while accessing the new owner's network. Devices should not be connected to sensitive infrastructure before the secret has been verified and changed, and the device has been wiped clean. As these are basic precautions, the attack has really low chances of success. Meanwhile the attacker is no longer in possession of the device. Furthermore, such bad behavior can be reported through the reputation system (Assumption $A5$). There are few incentives to engage in this kind of behavior.

One should be careful about publishing encrypted secrets to the blockchain as attackers may try to decipher them (Threat $T7$). The secret should therefore be updated in accordance with the security of the used encryption scheme. Recovery of old secrets is not a threat as they are only used to activate functions and cease to be useful once they have been updated. This, of course, holds if no information about the new secret can be inferred from the old ones.

5   Conclusion

The blockchain has made the tracking of asset's ownership relatively inexpensive. It does not have to be reserved for houses and boats any longer. We therefore propose to use it to track the ownership of IoT devices. The chain of ownership can be augmented by adding additional information to *transfer* transactions. We focused on encrypted device-related secrets that can help owners manage their devices.

We have argued the benefits of these applications. Amongst them, the pseudonymity of the PoO that can be produced to give guarantees to a prospective buyer and replace the registration systems in place, currently run by private companies. Others benefits include the desintermediation and decentralization of classic solutions. Limitations of our proposals have been argued.

A threat model has been detailed and three potential attackers considered: a malicious previous owner, a malicious future owner, and a malicious third party. We have defined six security assumptions and nine security threats involving these attackers. One could argue that blockchain keys should not be considered safe and can easily be lost or compromised. However, the issue of safekeeping a key has been studied extensively and many solutions can be provided. In the current state of affairs, the requirement that every potential owner possesses a blockchain address seems the most unlikely. We believe this is likely to evolve in a near future.

References

1. Arcade City. https://arcade.city/. Accessed 16 Feb 2018
2. Exodus. https://www.exodus.io/. Accessed 23 Feb 2018
3. First blood. https://firstblood.io/. Accessed 16 Feb 2018
4. Follow my vote. https://followmyvote.com/. Accessed 16 Feb 2018
5. Melonport. https://melonport.com/. Accessed 23 Feb 2018
6. Nxt. https://nxtplatform.org/. Accessed 23 Feb 2018
7. Buterin, V., et al.: Ethereum white paper (2013). https://github.com/ethereum/wiki/wiki/White-Paper. Accessed 23 Sept 2016
8. Christidis, K., Devetsikiotis, M.: Blockchains and smart contracts for the internet of things. IEEE Access **4**, 2292–2303 (2016)
9. Conoscenti, M., Vetro, A., De Martin, J.C.: Blockchain for the internet of things: a systematic literature review. In: 2016 IEEE/ACS 13th International Conference of Computer Systems and Applications (AICCSA), pp. 1–6. IEEE (2016)
10. Courtois, N.T., Bahack, L.: On subversive miner strategies and block withholding attack in bitcoin digital currency. arXiv preprint arXiv:1402.1718 (2014)
11. Decker, C., Wattenhofer, R.: Information propagation in the bitcoin network. In: IEEE International Conference on Peer-to-Peer Computing, pp. 1–10 (2013)
12. Huh, S., Cho, S., Kim, S.: Managing IoT devices using blockchain platform. In: 2017 19th International Conference on Advanced Communication Technology (ICACT), pp. 464–467. IEEE (2017)
13. Kshetri, N.: Can blockchain strengthen the internet of things? IT Prof. **19**(4), 68–72 (2017)
14. Lin, I.-C., Liao, T.-C.: A survey of blockchain security issues and challenges. IJ Netw. Secur. **19**(5), 653–659 (2017)
15. Nakamoto, S.: Bitcoin: a peer-to-peer electronic cash system (2008)
16. Osaka, K., Takagi, T., Yamazaki, K., Takahashi, O.: An efficient and secure RFID security method with ownership transfer. In: Kitsos, P., Zhang, Y. (eds.) RFID Security, pp. 147–176. Springer, Boston (2008). https://doi.org/10.1007/978-0-387-76481-8_7
17. Pass, R., Seeman, L., Shelat, A.: Analysis of the blockchain protocol in asynchronous networks. In: Coron, J.-S., Nielsen, J.B. (eds.) EUROCRYPT 2017. LNCS, vol. 10211, pp. 643–673. Springer, Cham (2017). https://doi.org/10.1007/978-3-319-56614-6_22
18. Ray, B.R., Abawajy, J., Chowdhury, M., Alelaiwi, A.: Universal and secure object ownership transfer protocol for the internet of things. Future Gener. Comput. Syst. **78**, 838–849 (2018)
19. Rekleitis, E., Rizomiliotis, P., Gritzalis, S.: How to protect security and privacy in the IoT: a policy-based RFID tag management protocol. Secur. Commun. Netw. **7**(12), 2669–2683 (2014)
20. Rosenfeld, M.: Overview of colored coins. White paper, bitcoil.co.il, p. 41 (2012)
21. Szabo, N.: Formalizing and securing relationships on public networks. First Monday, **2**(9) (1997). https://doi.org/10.5210/fm.v2i9.548
22. Wood, G.: Ethereum: a secure decentralised generalised transaction ledger. Ethereum Project Yellow Paper (2014)

User and Data Privacy

Secure and Efficient Multi-Party Directory Publication for Privacy-Preserving Data Sharing

Katchaguy Areekijseree[1(✉)], Yuzhe Tang[1], Ju Chen[1], Shuang Wang[2],
Arun Iyengar[3], and Balaji Palanisamy[4]

[1] Department of EECS, Syracuse University, Syracuse, NY, USA
{kareekij,ytang100,jchen133}@syr.edu
[2] Department of Biomedical Informatics (DBMI), UCSD, San Diego, CA, USA
shw070@ucsd.edu
[3] IBM T.J. Watson Research Center, Yorktown Heights, NY, USA
aruni@us.ibm.edu
[4] School of Computing and Information, University of Pittsburgh,
Pittsburgh, PA, USA
bpalan@pitt.edu

Abstract. In the era of big-data, personal data is produced, collected and consumed at different sites. A public directory connects data producers and consumers over the Internet and should be constructed securely given the privacy-sensitive nature of personal data.

This work tackles the research problem of distributed, privacy-preserving directory publication, with strong security and practical efficiency. For proven security, we follow the protocols of secure multi-party computations (MPC). For efficiency, we propose a pre-computation framework that minimizes the private computation and conducts aggressive pre-computation on public data. Several pre-computation policies are proposed with varying degrees of aggressiveness. For systems-level efficiency, the pre-computation is implemented with data parallelism on general-purpose graphics processing units (GPGPU). We apply the proposed scheme to real health-care scenarios for constructing patient-locator services in emerging Health Information Exchange (or HIE) networks.

We conduct extensive performance studies on real datasets and with an implementation based on open-source MPC software. With experiments on local and geo-distributed settings, our performance results show that the proposed pre-computation achieves a speedup of more than an order of magnitude without security loss.

1 Introduction

In the era of big-data, personal data is produced, collected and consumed in digital forms, bringing unprecedented convenience to the society. As data production and consumption are decoupled at different sites, sharing person-specific data

© ICST Institute for Computer Sciences, Social Informatics and Telecommunications Engineering 2018
R. Beyah et al. (Eds.): SecureComm 2018, LNICST 254, pp. 71–94, 2018.
https://doi.org/10.1007/978-3-030-01701-9_5

over the Internet becomes a popular application paradigm as widely observed in a variety of domains ranging from electronic healthcare, social networks, Internet of things, malware detection, to many others.

A public directory service is a crucial data-sharing component. In a data-sharing workflow, a data consumer queries the directory service to locate the producer sites that may have the documents of interest. The directory service maintains the private producer-location information, and connects data consumers and producers. For instance, in electronic healthcare, HIE or Healthcare Information Exchange is an emerging data-sharing platform [4,10] where the directory called locator service [1,5,9,11] helps a doctor (data consumer) find the electronic medical records (EMR) of a patient (data producer). The data-location information ("which hospitals a patient has visited") may reveal privacy-sensitive facts; for instance, knowing that a celebrity visited a rehabilitation center, one can infer that s/he may have a drug problem.

A naive way of constructing the directory is for any data producer to directly publish its list of associated people (e.g., the list of patients having visited a hospital). However, this approach discloses the private data-location information to network adversaries performing traffic analysis. This privacy disclosure leaks "identifiable information" and would violate data-protection laws (e.g., HIPAA in USA [6], EC95-46 in European Union [3] and various privacy laws in Asian countries [56]) that govern the data-sharing across borders in regulatory domains.

This work tackles the problem of distributed and privacy-preserving publication of directory, with strong security and high efficiency. In our problem, data producers are operated autonomously and they distrust each other. The publication problem can be modeled as a secure Multi-Party Computation (MPC) problem [25,27,37,52,73] where a joint computation with inputs private to different parties is evaluated in a proven-secure fashion. A naive instantiation of the directory publication is by embedding entire publication logic in an MPC protocol, which however causes high overhead and is impractical, because of the expensive cryptographic primitives used in constructing an MPC. A conventional remedy is to identify the private part of the computation (e.g., by data-flow analysis [17,59]) and to map only this part to the MPC. Unfortunately, this approach is not effective in our problem, as the private and public data flows of the directory-construction logic are inter-tangled and separating them becomes difficult.

In this work, we propose an aggressive pre-computation technique that minimizes (instead of separating) the private computation for multi-party directory publication. Concretely, we conduct the pre-computation by considering all possible values of private data. It then applies expensive MPCs to a simple selection logic, that is, select from the list of pre-computed results by the actual value of private data. At the first glimpse, this optimization technique may seem counter-intuitive as the pre-computation augments the input space exponentially. In practice, particular to our directory construction problem, its effectiveness relies on the application characteristic: The public computation is usually bulky and private identity data is much smaller. For instance, achieving the privacy of t-closeness [51] entails complex computation on the public background knowledge, such as similarity/distance calculation. With a global identity management system, the private identifiable data is minimal. In addition, we propose several policies that vary in the degree of pre-computation aggressiveness. The policies can help the optimization technique adapt to concrete scenarios with different private-data sizes.

To improve the system efficiency, we leverage the data-level parallelism and implement the pre-computation on General-Purpose Graphics Processing Units (GPGPU). We implement our design on real MPC software [25] and conduct performance evaluation in both local and geo distributed settings. Our evaluation verifies the pre-computation speedup by more than an order of magnitude over the conventional approach. Through evaluation on real-world datasets, the assurance of privacy preservation is also verified.

The contributions of this work are listed as following:

- We address the research of constructing privacy-preserving directory in emerging data-sharing applications. We model the general problem as a distributed privacy-preserving data publication problem.
- We propose an application-specific techniques for MPC pre-computation in the directory publication. The insight is based on that the public background knowledge in privacy-preserving publication can be isolated from expensive MPC. We implement this optimization design on real MPC software.
- We propose systems-level optimization by data-parallel pre-computation. We implement the optimization on GPGPU.
- We conduct performance evaluation and demonstrate an order of magnitude performance speedup.

The rest of the paper is organized as following: Sect. 2 formulates the research problem. The proposed technique, pre-computation based MPC for directory publication, is presented in Sect. 3. A case study in healthcare domain is described in Sect. 4. Performance evaluation is presented next in Sect. 5. We discuss the generalizability and extensions of the proposed technique in Sect. 6. Section 7 surveys the related work and Sect. 8 concludes the paper.

2   Research Formulation

This section presents the system and threat model, the security goals, survey of existing techniques, and preliminary on privacy-preserving data publication algorithms.

2.1   System Model

The target eco-system involves three roles: data producers, data consumers, and the host of directory service. Each data producer owns a table of personal records where each record is keyed by the identity of the owner of this record. Given a person of interest, a data consumer would want to find his/her records at all producer sites. The directory service helps the consumer "discover" relevant data producers who maintain the result records.

Formally, sharing personal records in our system works in two steps: First, a data consumer interested in a person's records poses a query to the directory service and looks up the list of producers who have this person's records. Then, the consumer contacts individual producers and locally searches the records there. In this process, the query is based on a personal identity, which we assume is known globally. In practice, this global identity can be maintained physically by an identity-management server or constructed virtually such as by patient record linkage in healthcare [43, 70].

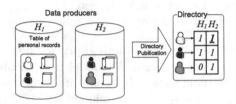

Fig. 1. System model of public directory: Two data producers share three people's records. In the directory, value one means presence and zero means absence (e.g., producer H_1 does not have gray person's records). The underscored one in red is a false positive in the sense that producer H_2 does not have the record of the white person but the directory records the opposite (for the sake of privacy preservation).

We assume each data producer locally has a data-protection mechanism in place (e.g., user authentication and authorization) that prevents an external party from accessing the records without data owner's consent. Figure 1 illustrates the abstract model of our system. The model is applicable to data-sharing applications in regulatory domains; A concrete example is about sharing patient electronic medical records (EMR) in healthcare information exchange networks, where data producers are hospitals, personal data are patients' EMRs and consumers can be physicians diagnosing patient. The details of the scenario will be elaborated in Sect. 4.

The target computation of this work is about building the directory. A baseline is that each data producer sends its local access-control list to the third-party directory which enforces the access control when serving the directory requests. This baseline however becomes problematic when the directory host is untrustworthy (e.g., by third-party clouds): First, enforcing access control with integrity entails user authentication and authorization to be done by a trusted party. Second, the local access-control list reveals the binding between a person and her data producers, which can be privacy-sensitive in many applications. For instance, in Healthcare scenarios, the binding between a patient and a rehabilitation center can reveal that this person may have a drug problem. Even when the directory is protected by the host, an adversary can easily recover the binding by performing network traffic analysis and extracting this information from the side-channel of the consumer access trace.

We consider the privacy-preserving publication of directory. Existing data-privacy definitions, such as k-anonymity, l-diversity, t-closeness, are applicable to our problem. For instance, k-anonymity requires k people have their published lists of producers to be the same. l-diversity requires people placed in the same group have l distinct lists of producers. t-closeness requires each group of people to have similar producer lists to all the producers. In this work, we mainly use the notion of ϵ-privacy [69] to drive further presentation. The main idea of ϵ privacy is to bound the amount of noises or false positives in the published list of producers by a percentage of ϵ. We will discuss the application of our technique to other privacy definitions in Sect. 6.2.

Formally, the notion of ϵ-privacy is adapted to our threat model by being aware of background knowledge—we make the false positive producers indistinguishable from true positives, such that the distribution of true positives is similar to that of false positives. What's noteworthy is that the similarity is measured on the dimension of external, public knowledge. For instance, in HIE, the similarity between hospitals (producers) can be defined by hospital specialties and geographic locations.

Privacy-Preserving Publication Algorithm: Achieving ϵ-privacy can be done by a top-K algorithm. Concretely, given a list of true positive producers, the algorithm finds K negative producers which are closest to the positive ones. The value of K can be simply calculated from ϵ and the number of true producers $|T|$. Listing 2 presents the top-K algorithm which entails the iterative computation of nearest neighbor with similarity/distance defined by public knowledge. The distance computation depends on the metric that represents producers and it can be Euclid distance, Hamming distance, and others.

```
1  TopK(true_producers T, all_producers S){
2    R = T;
3    while (less than K iterations){
4      //find NN in S to T
5      for (any j in S){
6        for (any i in T){
7          min_dist_j = min(dist(T[i],S[j]),min_dist_j);
8          min_j = j;
9        }
10       min_dist = min(min_dist,d);
11     }
12     R.add(S[min_j]);
13     S.remove(S[min_j]);
14   }
15   return R;
16 }
```

Fig. 2. Top-K algorithm to achieve privacy

2.2   Threat Model and Security Goals

This work targets on the *distributed publication of privacy-preserving directory* with untrusting data producers. In our problem, a data producer runs autonomously and distrusts external parties including peer producers. Data producers get engaged in the distributed computation for publishing privacy-preserving directory where they exchange information with each other (Fig. 2).

In the threat model, an adversary can eavesdrop all messages being exchanged during the distributed directory publication. For a producer, the adversary can be a network eavesdropper or a peer producer. Formally, this is the semi-honest model used in formulating a secure multi-party computation problem [21], where the adversary, being a participant in the computation, honestly follows the protocol execution but is curious about any data that flows through her during the execution. Multiple adversaries may collude. Given a network of n producers, we consider the collusion can be up to $n - 1$ peer producers.

The security goal is to assure the data security in the directory-publication process. Our security goal is to ensure perfect privacy (in an information-theoretic sense). Informally, it means an adversary's view only depends on her input and public output. In other words, the messages exchanged in the protocol execution when the input of other parties take one value are "indistinguishable" from those when the input of other parties take another value. More formal treatment of the MPC data security can be found on classic texts [27].

Our threat model and security goal fit in the real-world requirement for policy compliance in data sharing. In many regulatory domains, a data producer has the responsibility of protecting the personal data it maintains and complying data-protection laws. For instance, HIPAA [6] states any identifiable information about a patient cannot be shared to any third-party, without the patient's consent.

Non-goals of this work include directory data authenticity, producer-site data protection, key management, etc. Encrypting data on the directory is orthogonal, as the content of directory is anyway disclosed to the adversary of network eavesdropper performing traffic analysis.

2.3   Preliminary on Multi-Party Computation

In our protocol, we make use of existing multi-party computation (MPC) protocols whose background is presented here. In general, the purpose of MPC is to evaluate a function whose inputs are provided by different parties. Each input is private to its provider party. The protocol of MPC ensures that it does not leak any information about the private inputs even when the computation states are exchanged and shared. Different computational models exist in MPC, including circuit and RAM. After decades of studies, there are a variety of MPC protocols realizing different computation models, specialized for different network scales (for two, three or many parties). In particular, the protocol of GMW [37] is for multi-party, Boolean-circuit based MPC that is constructed based on the primitives of secret-sharing and oblivious transfers. The protocol of multi-server Private-Information Retrieval (ms-PIR) [39,46] is a RAM-based MPC with multiple servers interacting a client on the computation of a simple selection operation (e.g., like a database selection).

MPC causes high overhead, mainly due to the "data -oblivious" representation of the computation and cryptographic primitives being used in the construction. For more-than-three party computation, the use of secret sharing also cause high overhead as the shares need to be broadcast in the entire network. This unscalability (in data and network sizes) makes it challenging to apply MPC for real-world distributed applications.

In practice, the common way MPC is used for many-party distributed applications is based on the "outsourcing" paradigm. That is, given multiple input parties, the GMW protocol distributes the input shares to a small number of computing parties (e.g., three parties as in the Sharemind system [22]). The data security heavily relies on the non-collusion assumption of the computing parties. In our work, we deem this outsourcing model unsuitable for the target application. In HIPAA, a hospital cannot share patient data with *any* third-party entity without patient consent. Therefore, our problem considers each input party as computing party and the MPC protocol needs to run directly on a medium or large network.

3   Secure Directory Publication with Pre-Computation

In this section, we present the secure directory publication and the optimization techniques based on pre-computation. The general idea is to abstract the computation at different levels and precompute the computation at a specific level. This way, we present a series of precomputation techniques (in Sects. 3.2, 3.3) that vary in their aggressiveness. To start with, we present the naive approach based on multi-party computation (MPC) without precomputation.

3.1   MPC-based Publication

Privacy-preserving directory publication is an MPC problem as the input data are spread across multiple producers and are private to them. The naive way to realize directory publication is thus to place the computation as in List 2 into the MPC; this approach is denoted by M_0. Given the circuit representation of MPC program, the algorithm in List 2 can be easily converted to a circuit; the algorithm is a nested loop with pair-wise distance computation, and the data/control flow is essentially oblivious. In particular, we represent each producer by a vector (e.g., specialties of a hospital) and the similarity between producers can be realized by hamming distance. More complex string similarity computation is realized by dynamic-programming based algorithms which are also data oblivious. The security of this approach inherent from that of MPC.

This MPC approach is inefficient especially in big-data sharing scenario where there are a large amount of personal records. This is due to the expensive cryptographic primitives (e.g., oblivious transfers, etc.) used in MPC protocols. To improve the performance, it relies on reducing the use of MPC in the distributed directory publication.

3.2 Full Precomputation Scheme

To reduce the use of MPC, we propose application-level precomputation. Given the $topK(T, S)$ algorithm in List 2 where only input T (the true producers) is private, we pre-compute the algorithm on the public input S and all possible values of private input T. The precomputation result is a table of results under different T values. Then, we use the actual value of T to privately look up this table and to securely retrieve the result entry. This stage can be realized in MPC using protocols such as multi-server private information retrieval (ms-PIR) [39,46]. Formally, the full precomputation is to compute $topK(2^S, S)$ where 2^S is the power set of S which includes all possible values of private T. This scheme is named M_1.

The precomputation is effective in our directory-publication problem, provided the following characteristics. First the $topK$ algorithm invokes some complex computation such as distance computation (i.e. Line 7 in List 2) which involve background knowledge about the producer profiles (e.g., hospital specialties and geographic locations). Precomputation avoids placing these complex computations in MPC which reduces overhead. Second, the precomputation only needs to be done once and its results can be *reused* for publishing different people's entries. Third, given the independence between different values, one can leverage data-parallelism to facilitate the computation. Note that the precomputation needs to be done for all possible value of T, that is, the power set of all producers; although the possibility combination grows exponentially with the number of producers, we only consider the data-producer network is moderately large. For instance, in healthcare, a regional or statewide HIE typically consists of less than hundreds of hospitals in a consortium.

The security of precomputation relies on the fact that no private value is involves in the precomputation. Private data only occurs in the actual MPC computation.

3.3 Selective Precomputation Schemes

The full precomputation scheme considers the directory computation of $topK$ as a whole for precomputation. In this section, we dive into the computation $topK()$ and *selectively* precompute certain computation-intensive parts in $topK()$. Concretely, our selective technique considers $topK$ consists of distance-computation at different granularity. For one, it is to pre-compute the distance between T and $S - T$, considering all possible values of T. This way, we have the selective precomputation, M_2. For the other, it is to pre-compute the distance between all pairwise data producers. This yield the selective precomputation scheme, M_3.

In M_2, the precomputation considers all possible values of true-producer T. Given a value T^*, it precomputes the set-wise distance between T^* and $S - T^*$. This produces a distance table for the subsequent MPC. In the MPC, it first follows the computation in List 2 until Line 6. Then for Line 6 to 9, it is replaced by a secure lookup into the precomputation table. The lookup is realized by the ms-PIR protocol as in M_1.

In M_3, it precomputes the pair-wise distance matrix. That is, for any producer s_1 and $s_2 \in S$, it precomputes their distance and stores it in a table. Then, in the MPC stage, it follows the algorithm in List 2 except that the call to dist(T[i],S[j]) is replaced by a ms-PIR lookup to the precomputation table.

The security of these precomputation schemes are straightforward, as all private-data related computations are placed inside the MPC/ms-PIR protocol whose security is proven. The precomputation only considers the public data.

In summary, the *topK* computation for privacy-preserving directory publication can be modeled as a process that issues a series of call to dist(T[i],S[j]). Our pre-computation schemes partitions this computation process at different "break" points and selectively places a certain partition to precomputation and the rest of computation into MPC/ms-PIR. Table 1 illustrates the three precomputation schemes from this computation-partitioning perspective.

Table 1. Partitioning *topK* algorithm to the precomputation-MPC framework: For notation in this table, T, S are true and all producers as in the *topK*() algorithm in List 2. D_i for $i = 1, 2, 3$ are the table storing precomputation results. *MPC* is secure multi-party computation protocol and *msPIR* is a special MPC protocol for multi-server private information retrieval.

	Pre-compute	MPC+msPIR
M_0	-	$topK(T, S)$
M_1	$D_1 = topK(2^S, S)$	$Lookup_{msPIR}(D_1, T)$
M_2	$D_2 = dist(2^S, S)$	$topK2_{MPC}(T, S)$ invoking $Lookup_{msPIR}(D_2, T)$
M_3	$D_3 = dist(S, S)$	$topK3_{MPC}(T, S)$ invoking $Lookup_{msPIR}(D_3, T[i], S[j])$

3.4   Data-Parallel Pre-Computation

The pre-computation handles multiple independent input values. There is innate data parallelism that can be exploited for better performing pre-computation. In our system, we realize it by data-parallel pre-computation tasks where each task with distinct input value runs in a dedicated thread. Different threads run concurrently and without synchronization. We implement this data-parallel pre-computation framework on both multi-core CPU and general-purpose GPU (GPGPU). Given the large number of possibilities in input values (and the simplicity of each task), GPGPU lends itself to the parallel pre-computation due to its scalable execution model.

In implementation, the CPU implementation is based on pthread library [13]. We pack multiple possible input values in one thread and the number of threads is twice the number of hyper-threads in hardware. The GPGPU implementation is based on CUDA library [2]. In this case, the underlying NVidia-Tesla GPU has global memory of 5 GB and threads run in one grid of 65,635 blocks, each of 1024 GPU threads. This architecture allows to scale the number of threads to 2^{27} and can easily handle the producer networks of more than 27 parties.

4 Case Study: Healthcare Locator

In this section, we present the case study of applying our public locator service in healthcare information exchange networks (HIE). HIE is a health data-sharing network where the data is patient electronic medical records (EMR), data producers are hospitals where each patient visit results in the generation of new entries in an EMR, and data consumers are clinical doctors. A typical application scenario is effective sharing patient's EMR during a clinical visit where the doctor diagnosing a patient needs to view the relevant EMRs of the patient which are produced and stored in remote hospitals.

In this setting, our threat model and security goal apply. Patient EMRs are personal, privacy-sensitive documents, the sharing of which must comply HIPAA [6]. Each hospital has its local information-security infrastructure in place (e.g., access control and user authentication).

A directory service, called HIE locator, can be used to facilitate the EMR sharing between hospitals and to help discovery of a patient's previous hospitals. In the normal case, the list of hospitals is discovered by the doctor asking for it to the patient. However, this is error prone (e.g., the patient forgets about it) and is inapplicable in emergency (e.g., the patient is sent to hospital unconscious). Our privacy-preserving directory can complement the common workflow to improve the quality of healthcare.

Figure 3 illustrates the abstract workflow of sharing EMRs in HIE networks. In a clinic scenario, Alice, the patient, is seeing a physician (data consumer) who interacts with HIE network (directory) to locate the hospitals Alice visited before (data producer). In real HIE applications, the locator service runs healthcare software (e.g., OpenEMPI [11]) and is hosted by Amazon AWS alike public clouds. The public clouds are not trustworthy and it entails the use of our privacy-preserving directory protocol for publishing the HIE locator. Concretely, the life cycle of an EMR, including the data-sharing flow, can be divided into three stages: (1) EMR production where Alice's EMRs are generated or updated to reflect her clinical visit; here we assume Alice has given consent on delegating the EMR to the "producer" hospitals. (2) Locator (periodical) publication where the EMR updates are published to the public directory of HIE locator in a privacy-preserving fashion. This is when our directory publication protocol is being invoked in the overall HIE workflow. (3) Locator service where the locator serves the physician's request to locate Alice's producer hospitals (3.1) and find the EMRs of interest there (3.2). In particular for stage 3.2, after the physician obtains the list of potential hospitals (including both true and false positive ones), he will contact each hospital and find EMRs by going through the local user authentication and access control there.

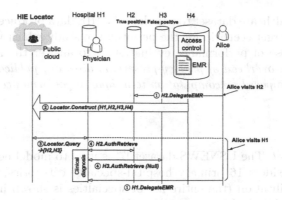

Fig. 3. Data-sharing workflow in the HIE: The figure illustrates how Alice's medical record (EMR) stored on Hospital H_2 is used. It shows the entire life cycle of this EMR: The EMR was produced when Alice paid a clinical visit to H_2 (1). During the current visit in Hospital H_1, Alice's physician requires accessing her EMR in H_2 (3). The physician first contacts the third-party locator service hosted on a public cloud (which is constructed at an earlier time (2)) and obtains the list of candidate hospitals H_2 and H_3. Here, H_3 is a noise for privacy preservation purpose. The physician then contacts both H_2 and H_3, and find EMR on H_2 (4). Note that the physician can do so because she has the credential to access data on both H_2 and H_3. For an adversary obtaining the list of H_2 and H_3, she cannot distinguish which hospitals are noise as she does not have the credential.

Security analysis: In this data-sharing process, the EMR is produced and stored securely (stage 1)) by assuming the producer hospitals' secure and trustworthy local healthcare infrastructure (e.g., faithfully enforcing access control and honest health IT administrator).

The security in publishing the healthcare locator (stage 2)) is based on the security of our privacy-preserving directory protocol, which is further based on the security of MPC protocols [21] and computation-partitioning schemes.

The security in serving the healthcare locator (stage 3.1) is based on the fact that sufficient amount of noise has been injected into the directory, such that an Internet adversary performing traffic analysis and knowing the list of hospitals contacted by the physician can not distinguish between the true positive hospitals and noises. The formal notion of indistinguishability is presented in related work [54,68,69].

The security in searching and retrieving records on individual hospitals (stage 3.2)) is ensured by the security of local healthcare IT (for enforcing access control) and the secure channel on the Internet (e.g., https and underlying PKI [35]).

5 Evaluation

In this section, we study the feasibility of our technique for HIE applications in a holistic manner. Lacking benchmark dataset in existing literature, we first present a real healthcare dataset to populate the HIE data producers and locator. This sets up a target scenario for the performance study which we will present next. The purpose of performance evaluation is to answer the following question: *What is the overhead of privacy-preserving directory publication? and how effective is the proposed precomputation technique in performance optimization?*

5.1   Dataset

USNEWS Dataset. The USNEWS dataset [7] is used to model hospital profiles. The dataset considers 16 primary hospital-specialty categories, such as cardiology and rehabilitation (the entire list of specialties is shown in Table 2). For each category, a hospital is associated with a rating of three grades: "Nationally ranked", "High-performing", and "Null". We map "Nationally ranked" to value 2, "High-performing" to value 1, and "Null" (i.e. the hospital does not have the department for this specialty) to value 0. Each hospital is associated with other profile information, such as the resident city and state. Currently, we select the dataset to include 40 top-ranked hospitals (out of 180) in the New York metropolitan area.

Open-NY Health Dataset ("Sparcs"). To model patient-wise hospital visits, we use an OPEN-NY dataset, called Sparcs [14]. The public dataset includes inpatient discharge records with identifiable information removed. At the finest granularity, it provides per-visit per-patient information (e.g., patient age group, gender, race, ethnicity and other de-identified information), the facility information (e.g., zip-code, name, service areas) and other per-visit information (e.g., admission type, the length of stay). Given the identifiable patient information is removed, we model the per-patient visit history by aggregating the records based on available quasi-identity information (i.e. age group, race, ethnicity, etc.).

5.2   Performance of Directory Publication

We first conduct micro-benchmark to test the performance of data-parallel precomputation. Then, we test the overall performance of secure directory publication, with a machine of multi-core processor and in a geo-distributed setting.

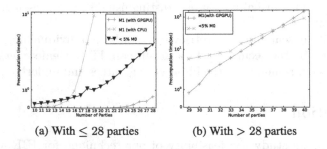

(a) With ≤ 28 parties   (b) With > 28 parties

Fig. 4. Pre-computation performance with GPGPU

Table 2. Specialty catalog in the USNEWS dataset

Index	Name
0	Cancer
1	Cardiology & Heart Surgery
2	Diabetes & Endocrinology
3	Ear, Nose & Throat
4	Gastroenterology & GI Surgery
5	Geriatrics
6	Gynecology
7	Nephrology
8	Neurology & Neurosurgery
9	Ophthalmology
10	Orthopedic
11	Psychiatry
12	Pulmonology
13	Rehabilitation
14	Rheumatology
15	Urology

Table 3. Experiment platform

New York Server	
CPU	Xeon(R) E5-2640 v3 @ 2.60GHz
	2 processors/16 cores/32 hyper-threads
Memory	245 GB

California Server	
CPU	Xeon(R) E5-2687W @ 3.10GHz
	2 processors/16 cores/32 hyper-threads
Memory	256 GB
GPGPU	Nvidia Tesla K20c
	1 grid/65535 blocks/2^{27} threads
	Global Memory 5119MB

Micro-Benchmark of Pre-computation. The pre-computation is implemented with data parallelism (as described in Sect. 3.4) and runs on multi-core CPU and GPGPU. We report the time to pre-compute on GPGPU and that on CPU in Fig. 4. This figure also includes a baseline which is the 5% execution time of running M_0 (i.e. without any precomputation).

The performance result in Fig. 4a shows that GPGPU based pre-computation is effective in reducing the execution time, and its overhead is negligible comparing the baseline. Concretely, the CPU based precomputation has its execution time to quickly surpass the baseline when the network grows over 15 parties.

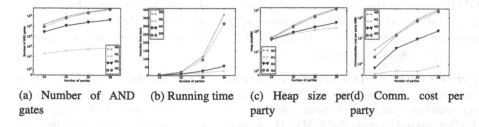

(a) Number of AND gates   (b) Running time   (c) Heap size per party   (d) Comm. cost per party

Fig. 5. Performance of directory publication based on precomputation and MPC

The GPGPU-based precomputation has much lower overhead than the baseline for any network with less than 28 parties.

For more than 28 parties, all GPU threads are occupied and it will need multiple iterations in transferring data from GPU's global memory to host memory. As a result, the GPGPU precomputation time increases exponentially, also reported in the Fig. 4b (note that the y axis is of log scale). With a single GPGPU card, the precomputation time surpasses the baseline when the network is larger than about 40 parties. Here, we stress that the typical scale of a healthcare consortium is usually medium-sized (e.g., tens of hospitals and clinical centers). For nation-wide healthcare systems, there may be thousands of hospitals. In this case, one can use more GPGPU cards to do the precomputation in parallel, while retaining the efficiency.

Overall Performance with MPC The MPC-based implementation of directory publication is realized on the GMW software [25], an open-source MPC software and Percy++ [12], an open-source multi-server PIR software. We note that our precomputation protocol only relies on the general MPC and PIR interface and other MPC "backend" software can be used in our protocol. The GMW protocol exposes a circuit-based programming interface that requires MPC programmers to write a generator for Boolean circuit encapsulating the intended computation logic. At runtime, the GMW protocol runs on multiple parties where each party generates and executes the circuit by iterating through all gates in the circuit (following a topologically sorted order); for each gate, the evaluation is synchronized across all parties. The GMW protocol makes bit-wise use of two cryptographic primitives which provides the security of the protocol, that is, secret sharing [65] and oblivious transfer [62]. In particular, the per-gate evaluation in GMW is to broadcast the shares of input-wire bit to all the parties in the entire network. In our application, we manually express the logic of *topK* algorithm in the GMW Boolean circuit, and tightly estimate the number of gates to pre-allocate so that the unused GMW circuit can be optimized out. Our GMW-based implementation consists of about 1500 lines of C++ code.

Multi-processing execution platform: We first run our protocol on a single node with multi-processing. The machine specs are in Table 3 (the New York server). In this setting, each process represents a data producer and runs a GMW party. In the execution, each process holds a dedicated copy of the entire circuit allocated in its virtual-memory space and without shared memory. The machine has memory large enough (245 GB in total) to hold all circuit copies of the 39 parties without paging.

Results on multi-processing: To measure the performance of MPC, we used four metrics, the number of AND gates (1), end-to-end execution time (2), memory consumption (3) and communication costs (4). (1) We report the number of AND gates in the compiled GMW Boolean circuit. This metric helps evaluate the performance in a hardware-independent fashion. We only consider AND gates in a circuit and ignore other gates (i.e., XOR gates) because evaluating XOR is free

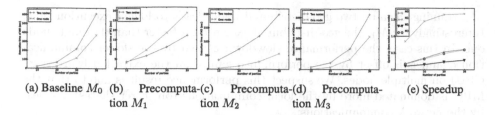

(a) Baseline M_0 (b) Precomputa-(c) Precomputa-(d) Precomputa- (e) Speedup
    tion M_1 tion M_2 tion M_3

Fig. 6. Geo-distributed performance on the Internet

(i.e. free-XOR technique [26]) and evaluating AND gates dominates the cost. (2) We report the wall-clock time from launching the first process to the completion of the last process. (3) We report the size of the heap memory in GMW that stores all circuit gates. It is measured by the Valgrind framework (particularly the Massif memory profiler [64]). (4) We report the party-to-party communication overhead, by monitoring all outbound messages through the socket port of each process using IPTraf[1].

In the experiment, we vary the number of parties (or data producers) and present the result in Fig. 5. Figure 5a reports the result of AND gate number and Fig. 5b reports wall-clock running time. They both show that the pre-computation based schemes (i.e. M_1, M_2, M_3) outperform the baseline without pre-computation. Notably, the M_1 scheme causes the best performance with a speedup of 13 times (comparing the baseline M_0) in the setting of 39 parties. This result demonstrates the effectiveness of pre-computation techniques that off-loads computation from the expensive MPC. In terms of memory consumption in Fig. 5c, M_1 and M_2 are close, reducing up to memory consumption roughly by an order of magnitude comparing M_0 and M_3. It shows that while M_1 produces pre-computation results as additional data, its much smaller circuit (for simple lookup operation in ms-PIR) makes the overall saving of memory footprint as compared to the baseline M_0. In Fig. 5d, the communication overhead of M_1 stays to be the smallest among the four schemes, with a saving of more than 2 orders of magnitudes comparing M_0. This is consistent with the result in the number of AND gates.

Geo-distributed execution platform: We conduct the experiment with two servers set apart more than 3000 miles (one server in the State of New York, and the other in the State of California). The bandwidth is 100 Mbps. The specification of the two servers is illustrated in Table 3. Each server runs half of the parties with multiprocessing. Different parties communicate through sockets. The precomputation runs only in one server.

Results with geo-distributed execution report the execution time of the four schemes in the geo-distributed setting. The results are in Fig. 6. For comparison, we include the results in the single-node setting. The execution time grows super-linearly with the number of parties in a network. For M_0, M_2 and

---

[1] http://iptraf.seul.org/.

M_3, running them on two geo-distributed nodes leads to longer execution time. Interestingly for M_1, the geo-distributed execution is faster than the single-node one. In this case, the performance slowdown caused by the slower communication channels is offset by the performance gain from the extra hardware (e.g., CPU) on multiple nodes. We suspect this performance result is due to that the MPC is dominated more by the local computations (on secret shares) and less by the network communications.

6   Discussion

In this section, we consider the generalizability and extensions of the proposed technique beyond Healthcare Locators. We present the extension to new computation beyond exact-match lookup as in HIE locator and new privacy definitions beyond ϵ privacy.

6.1   Similarity-Based Directory

In this application scenario, a data consumer may want to find data about a group of "similar" people. Comparing the HIE locator that performs exact-match lookup (by a person's ID), the directory here performs similarity search. Take the healthcare domain as an example. The similarity-based directory (e.g., PatientLikeMe.com) entails publishing the binding between a patient, say Alice, and the hospitals that store the EMRs of patients who are similar to Alice, where the similarity can be defined on their syndrome, genome and other bio-medical features.

This directory can be constructed by extending the *topK* algorithm in List 2. In particular, the list of true producers is interpreted as the producers storing the data of people who are similar to the person being queried. The person-person similarity is defined on the external background knowledge as mentioned above. In Line 7 of List 2 the producer-producer distance is defined on the external domain knowledge (e.g., hospital profiles in specialty, locations, etc.).

6.2   Achieving Other Privacy Definitions

Our proposed technique can also be naturally extended to achieving other privacy definitions including k-anonymity, l-diversity, and t-closeness. A general framework for these privacy definitions is that the original data is a table of sensitive data key, quasi-identifier and public attributes. Achieving a specific privacy definition entails finding a "partitioning" solution that partitions the data-table rows based on quasi-identifiers into groups such that each group in the result will meet the privacy definition. There are different algorithms such as generalization, suppression, perturbation, etc. In this section, we consider the Mondrian algorithm [50] that represents the data records as a point in a multi-dimensional space (assuming multi-dimensional quasi-identifiers) and partitions the space by following kd-tree schemes and greedily refining the partition to the smallest units.

One can express the Mondrian algorithm naturally in MPC and the pre-computation stays effective because of extensive complex computation (e.g., computing distances) are based on public knowledge.

In details, adapting the Mondrian algorithm to directory publication can be done by following: For each person the producer vector is her multi-dimensional quasi-identifier and her identity is the data attribute that needs to be searched publicly. In the Mondrian algorithm, it entails determining whether it allows to split the current partition (1) and if it does, finding the dimension and split value (2). In (1) and (2) it involves complex distance computation; for instance, l-diversity requires counting the number of distinct producer vectors in a partition and t-closeness requires computing the group-wise similarity (among all records in a group). The number of distinct producer-vectors and group-wise similarity can both be realized by a nested loop where each iteration computes the pair-wise similarity between two records.

6.3 Data Updates

In many applications, data is being continuously generated. In this case, directory is constructed and updated in batches. In each batch, the latest updates are reflected in the directory incrementally. The $topK$ algorithm can be evaluated for every batch by interpreting the list of `all_producers` to all negative producers before the updates and the list of `true_producers` to be the new producers in the current batch. The content stored in the directory can be time-series data that each update batch is materialized independently.

7 Related Work

7.1 Privacy-Preserving Data Federation

Multi-party Noise Generation. Distributed differential privacy [32,61,72] is proposed to support privacy-preserving aggregations. The randomized response [72] provides differential privacy yet with uncontrollable noises and loss of utility. PrivaDA [34] is proposed to achieve the optimal utility and performance optimization by adopting arithmetic circuit based MPC for the noise generation. Existing multi-party noise generation takes a randomized approach and mainly targets for statistical aggregation (e.g., distributed differential privacy). This is inapplicable to our problem which features deterministic noise generation for the rigorous privacy guarantee, and needs to serve non-aggregation queries.

PPI. Privacy-Preserving Index or PPI is proposed to federate and index distributed access-controlled documents [18,19] and databases (e.g., patient medical records in the HIE locator service) [69] among autonomous providers. Being stored on an untrusted server, PPI entails preserving the content privacy of all participant providers or hospitals. Inspired by the privacy definition of K-anonymity [67], existing PPI work [18,19,69] follows the *grouping-based* approach; it organizes providers into disjoint privacy groups of size K, such that providers from the same group are indistinguishable. However, K-anonymity, while easy to construct, does not guarantee high-quality privacy preservation. In addition, early approaches of PPI construction [54,68] are based on randomized responses [72], an iterative protocol that takes indefinite number of rounds to converge and may produce incorrect result (with certain probability). To avoid those drawbacks, ϵ-PPI combines randomized responses with a minimal use of multi-party computation to construct PPI correctly and efficiently.

Multi-party Join. DJoin [60] is a federated database system built on top of multi-party joins, which are realized by privacy-preserving set intersections and general-purpose MPC for re-distributing noises. Its performance practicality has been demonstrated in small network with 3 to 5 parties. Multi-party joining has the potential to be applied in private record linkage problem (PRL) which is to match and link remote records of the same principle (e.g., patient in the health-care domain) across multiple sites. While PRL has been studied for decades in the health-care domain, the recent advances include improved linking precision [44], providing privacy guarantee [24] and building a practical system [8,11,70]. Particularly in [24] the authors identify the performance problem of using MPC for PRL and propose to publish differential private synopsis of tables to avoid MPC and improve performance. Our work, focused on noising locator service, is orthogonal and complementary to the record linkage and joining, and can be integrated to an overall federated system of HIE.

7.2 Distributed Privacy-Preserving Mining

Distributed privacy-preserving data mining [45,71] relies on algorithm/query-specific approaches to secure data-mining computations. For instance, association rule mining over vertically-partitioned databases [45,71] reduces to scalar product which is secured by the impossibility of solving n equations in more than n unknowns. In addition, by assuming no collusion at all [22,31], the secure data mining can be realized by efficient operations such as secret sharing and random number generation without using expensive protocols (e.g., oblivious transfers [62]). Our work is distinguished from privacy-preserving data mining in that we consider strong provable security against the worst-case collusion (e.g., all other parties may collude) which entails an extensive use of cryptographic protocols at fine granularity, rendering performance a critical issue.

7.3 MPC Frameworks and Optimization

In the last decade, practical MPC has attracted a large body of research work with a focus on programming language support and optimization [16,20–22,25,40,48,57,63]. Practical MPCs are built on top of cryptographic protocols, such as Yao's garbled circuits [73] or GMW protocol [37], with protocol-level optimization, such as Oblivious Transfer (OT) extensions [41], or for stronger security, such as resilience with dishonest majority [28]. The MPC protocols assume a circuit interface to express the computation, and practical programming support focuses on compiling a program written in a high-level language into the circuit. Existing MPC protocols and systems mainly focus on a small-scale computing that involves 2 or 3 parties. To the general MPC problem, a fundamental trade-off exists between performance and computation generality; for instance, randomized responses [72] and other techniques for privacy-preserving data mining take an ad-hoc and domain-specific approach, which can be efficient at scale. By contrast, the general-purpose MPC is rather expensive.

MPC Optimization. High performance overhead stays to be one of the major hurdles to applying MPC in practice, which is partly caused by MPC's fine-grained use (e.g., per single bit) of expensive cryptographic primitives, and the need to transfer all *possible* computation results for the "obliviousness" of computation flow. Various optimization techniques are proposed to utilize the programming semantics to reduce the circuit size and depth (e.g., by using the hardware synthesis tools [29,66]) and optimize the resource utilization (e.g., just-in-time compilation and pipelined execution [40,48]). Program analysis [47] is used to automatically infer privacy-sensitive data and constraints MPC only to the sensitive data. [49] conducts pre-processing on verification of MPC and results in general transformation from a passively secure protocol to an actively secure one. Our MPC optimization is currently specific to the directory construction problem, while holding the potential to apply to more generic computations.

Some programming frameworks support high-level programming languages with compilers (e.g., Fairplay(MP) for SFDL [21,57], Sharemind for SecreC [42], CBMC-GC for ANSI C [36], PCF for C [48], Wysteria for a high-level typed specification language [63], PICCO for C with extension [75]), while others expose a quite low-level circuit based interface (e.g., GMW [25], JustGarble [20], OTExtension [16]); particularly both boolean circuit (e.g., GMW) and arithmetic circuit (e.g., SEPIA [23]) are considered. In addition, some advanced technique designs based on hybrid model that combines both boolean or arithmetic circuits (e.g., ABY [30], TASTY [38], Wysteria [63]).

7.4   Anonymization Definitions

Publishing public-use data about individuals without revealing sensitive information has received a lot of research attentions in the last decade. Various anonymization definitions have been proposed and gained popularity, including K-anonymity [67], l-diversity [55], t-closeness [51], and differential privacy [33]. In addition, prior work [58] formally studied the information leakage under background knowledge attacks by formulating the problem using a proposed declarative language. These anonymity notions however are generally inapplicable to the PPI problem – they are mainly designed for statistic analysis or aggregation style computation where the result is global per-table data, while PPI needs to serve queries specific to individual records.

r-confidentiality [74] is a privacy notion specific to the PPI problem. It assumes a probabilistic attacker on PPI and considers the increase of attack success-rate with/without using the background knowledge. By contrast, our proposed ϵ-privacy considers to bound the attack success-rate (instead of the increase) which we believe provides better privacy control.

8   Conclusion

This work presents an MPC-precomputation framework tailored for privacy-preserving data publication for data-sharing applications. The pre-computation framework improves the performance by minimizing the private-data computation and realizing the public-data only pre-computation in a data-parallel fashion. Several pre-computation policies are proposed with varying degrees on the aggressiveness. It is demonstrated that the proposed pre-computation scheme is applicable in real health-care scenarios. Based on real datasets and implementation on open-source MPC software, the performance study shows that the proposed pre-computation achieves a speedup of more than an order of magnitude without security loss.

Acknowledgement. The authors would thank anonymous reviewers for their constructive suggestions. The first three authors were supported by the Cyber Research Institute in Rome, NY, under Grant Number #28254. Shuang Wang was supported by NIH R00HG008175.

References

1. CommonWell. http://www.commonwellalliance.org/
2. Cuda. https://en.wikipedia.org/wiki/cuda
3. Directive 95/46/EC of the European parliament and of the council
4. GaHIN. http://www.gahin.org/
5. HealthEConnections. http://www.healtheconnections.org/rhio
6. HiPAA. http://www.cms.hhs.gov/hipaageninfo/
7. http://health.usnews.com/best-hospitals/area/new-york-ny/specialty
8. Nextgate. http://www.nextgate.com/our-products/empi/
9. NHIN Connect. http://www.connectopensource.org/
10. NHIN. https://www.healthit.gov
11. OpenEMPI. http://www.openempi.org/
12. Percy++/PIR in C++. http://percy.sourceforge.net/
13. pthread. https://en.wikipedia.org/wiki/posix_threads
14. SPARCS. http://www.health.ny.gov/statistics/sparcs/
15. 2015 IEEE Symposium on Security and Privacy, SP 2015, San Jose, CA, USA, 17–21 May 2015. IEEE Computer Society (2015)
16. Asharov, G., Lindell, Y., Schneider, T., Zohner, M.: More efficient oblivious transfer and extensions for faster secure computation. In: 2013 ACM SIGSAC Conference on Computer and Communications Security, CCS 2013, 4–8 November 2013, Berlin, Germany, pp. 535–548 (2013)

17. Bater, J., Elliott, G., Eggen, C., Goel, S., Kho, A.N., Duggan, J.: SMCQL: secure query processing for private data networks. CoRR, abs/1606.06808 (2016)
18. Bawa, M., Bayardo Jr., R.J., Agrawal, R., Vaidya, J.: Privacy-preserving indexing of documents on the network. VLDB J. **18**(4), 837–856 (2009)
19. Bawa, M., Bayardo Jr, R.J., Agrawal, R.: Privacy-preserving indexing of documents on the network. In: VLDB, pp. 922–933 (2003)
20. Bellare, M., Hoang, V.T., Keelveedhi, S., Rogaway, P.: Efficient garbling from a fixed-key blockcipher. In: 2013 IEEE Symposium on Security and Privacy, SP 2013, 19–22 May 2013, Berkeley, CA, USA, pp. 478–492. IEEE Computer Society (2013)
21. Ben-David, A., Nisan, N., Pinkas, B.: Fairplaymp: a system for secure multi-party computation. In: Ning, P., Syverson, P.F., Jha, S. (eds.) ACM Conference on Computer and Communications Security, pp. 257–266. ACM (2008)
22. Bogdanov, D., Laur, S., Willemson, J.: Sharemind: a framework for fast privacy-preserving computations. In: Jajodia, S., Lopez, J. (eds.) ESORICS 2008. LNCS, vol. 5283, pp. 192–206. Springer, Heidelberg (2008). https://doi.org/10.1007/978-3-540-88313-5_13
23. Burkhart, M., Strasser, M., Many, D., Dimitropoulos, X.: SEPIA: privacy-preserving aggregation of multi-domain network events and statistics. In: Proceedings of 19th USENIX Security Symposium, 11–13 August 2010, Washington, DC, USA, pp. 223–240. USENIX Association (2010)
24. Cao, J., Rao, F., Bertino, E., Kantarcioglu, M.: A hybrid private record linkage scheme: Separating differentially private synopses from matching records. In: 31st IEEE International Conference on Data Engineering, ICDE 2015, 13–17 April 2015, Seoul, South Korea, pp. 1011–1022 (2015)
25. Choi, S.G., Hwang, K.W., Katz, J., Malkin, T., Rubenstein, D.: Secure multi-party computation of boolean circuits with applications to privacy in on-line marketplaces. In: Dunkelman, O. (ed.) CT-RSA 2012. LNCS, vol. 7178, pp. 416–432. Springer, Heidelberg (2012). https://doi.org/10.1007/978-3-642-27954-6_26
26. Choi, S.G., Katz, J., Kumaresan, R., Zhou, H.-S.: On the security of the "Free-XOR" technique. In: Cramer, R. (ed.) TCC 2012. LNCS, vol. 7194, pp. 39–53. Springer, Heidelberg (2012). https://doi.org/10.1007/978-3-642-28914-9_3
27. Cramer, R., Damgård, I., Nielsen, J.B.: Secure Multiparty Computation and Secret Sharing. Cambridge University Press, Cambridge (2015)
28. Damgård, I., Keller, M., Larraia, E., Pastro, V., Scholl, P., Smart, N.P.: Practical covertly secure MPC for dishonest majority – or: breaking the SPDZ limits. In: Crampton, J., Jajodia, S., Mayes, K. (eds.) ESORICS 2013. LNCS, vol. 8134, pp. 1–18. Springer, Heidelberg (2013). https://doi.org/10.1007/978-3-642-40203-6_1
29. Demmler, D., Dessouky, G., Koushanfar, F., Sadeghi, A.R., Schneider, T., Zeitouni, S.: Automated synthesis of optimized circuits for secure computation. In: Ray, I. Li, N., Kruegel, C. (eds.) Proceedings of the 22nd ACM SIGSAC Conference on Computer and Communications Security, 12–6 October 2015, Denver, CO, USA, pp. 1504–1517. ACM (2015)
30. Demmler, D., Schneider, T., Zohner, M.: Aby - a framework for efficient mixed-protocol secure two-party computation. In: Network and Distributed System Security Symposium, NDSS 2015, February 2015
31. Du, W., Atallah, M.J.: Protocols for secure remote database access with approximate matching. In: Ghosh, A.K. (ed.) E-Commerce Security and Privacy. ADIS, vol. 2, pp. 87–111. Springer, Boston (2001). https://doi.org/10.1007/978-1-4615-1467-1_6

32. Dwork, C., Kenthapadi, K., McSherry, F., Mironov, I., Naor, M.: Our data, ourselves: privacy via distributed noise generation. In: Vaudenay, S. (ed.) EUROCRYPT 2006. LNCS, vol. 4004, pp. 486–503. Springer, Heidelberg (2006). https://doi.org/10.1007/11761679_29

33. Dwork, C., McSherry, F., Nissim, K., Smith, A.: Calibrating noise to sensitivity in private data analysis. In: Halevi, S., Rabin, T. (eds.) TCC 2006. LNCS, vol. 3876, pp. 265–284. Springer, Heidelberg (2006). https://doi.org/10.1007/11681878_14

34. Eigner, F., Maffei, M., Pampaloni, F., Pryvalov, I., Kate, A.: Differentially private data aggregation with optimal utility. In: Proceedings of the 30th Annual Computer Security Applications Conference, ACSAC 2014, 8–12 December 2014, New Orleans, LA, USA, pp. 316–325 (2014)

35. Ferguson, N., Schneier, B., Kohno, T.: Cryptography Engineering - Design Principles and Practical Applications. Wiley, Hoboken (2010)

36. Franz, M., Holzer, A., Katzenbeisser, S., Schallhart, C., Veith, H.: CBMC-GC: an ANSI C compiler for secure two-party computations. In: Cohen, A. (ed.) CC 2014. LNCS, vol. 8409, pp. 244–249. Springer, Heidelberg (2014). https://doi.org/10.1007/978-3-642-54807-9_15

37. Goldreich, O., Micali, S., Wigderson, A.: How to play any mental game or a completeness theorem for protocols with honest majority. In: Aho, A.V. (ed.) Proceedings of the 19th Annual ACM Symposium on Theory of Computing, New York, New York, USA, pp. 218–229. ACM (1987)

38. Henecka, W., Kögl, S. K., Sadeghi, A.-R., Schneider, T., Wehrenberg, I.: Tasty: tool for automating secure two-party computations. In: ACM CCS, pp. 451–462 (2010)

39. Henry, R., Olumofin, F.G., Goldberg, I.: Practical PIR for electronic commerce. In: Proceedings of the 18th ACM Conference on Computer and Communications Security, CCS 2011, 17–21 October 2011, Chicago, Illinois, USA, pp. 677–690 (2011)

40. Huang, Y., Evans, D., Katz, J., Malka, L.: Faster secure two-party computation using garbled circuits. In: USENIX Security Symposium. USENIX Association (2011)

41. Ishai, Y., Kilian, J., Nissim, K., Petrank, E.: Extending oblivious transfers efficiently. In: Boneh, D. (ed.) CRYPTO 2003. LNCS, vol. 2729, pp. 145–161. Springer, Heidelberg (2003). https://doi.org/10.1007/978-3-540-45146-4_9

42. Jagomägis, R.: Secrec: a privacy-aware programming language with applications in data mining

43. Jurczyk, P., Lu, J.J., Xiong, L., Cragan, J.D., Correa, A.: FRIL: a tool for comparative record linkage. In: American Medical Informatics Association Annual Symposium, AMIA 2008, 8–12 November 2008, Washington, DC, USA (2008)

44. Jurczyk, P., Lu, J.J., Xiong, L., Cragan, J.D., Correa, A.: FRIL: a tool for comparative record linkage. AMIA Annu. Symp. Proc. **2008**, 440 (2008)

45. Kantarcioglu, M., Clifton, C.: Privacy-preserving distributed mining of association rules on horizontally partitioned data. IEEE Trans. Knowl. Data Eng. **16**(9), 1026–1037 (2004)

46. Keller, M., Scholl, P.: Efficient, oblivious data structures for MPC. In: Sarkar, P., Iwata, T. (eds.) ASIACRYPT 2014. LNCS, vol. 8874, pp. 506–525. Springer, Heidelberg (2014). https://doi.org/10.1007/978-3-662-45608-8_27

47. Kerschbaum, F.: Automatically optimizing secure computation. In: Proceedings of the 18th ACM Conference on Computer and Communications Security, CCS 2011, 17–21 October 2011, Chicago, Illinois, USA, pp. 703–714 (2011)

48. Kreuter, B., Shelat, A., Mood, B., Butler, K.R.: PCF: a portable circuit format for scalable two-party secure computation. In: Proceedings of the 22th USENIX Security Symposium, 14–16 August 2013, Washington, DC, USA, pp. 321–336 (2013)
49. Laud, P., Pankova, A.: Preprocessing-based verification of multiparty protocols with honest majority. IACR Cryptology ePrint Archive 2015:674 (2015)
50. LeFevre, K., DeWitt, D.J., Ramakrishnan, R.: Mondrian multidimensional k-anonymity. In: Liu et al. [53], p. 25 (2006)
51. Li, N., Li, T., Venkatasubramanian, S.: t-closeness: Privacy beyond k-anonymity and l-diversity. In: Proceedings of the 23rd International Conference on Data Engineering, ICDE 2007, 15–20 April 2007, The Marmara Hotel, Istanbul, Turkey, pp. 106–115 (2007)
52. Liu, C., Wang, X.S., Nayak, K., Huang, Y., Shi, E.: Oblivm: a programming framework for secure computation. In: 2015 IEEE Symposium on Security and Privacy, SP 2015, 17–21 May 2015, San Jose, CA, USA [15], pp. 359–376 (2015)
53. Liu, L., Reuter, A. Whang, K., Zhang, J. (eds.): In: Proceedings of the 22nd International Conference on Data Engineering, ICDE 2006, 3–8 April 2006, Atlanta, GA, USA. IEEE Computer Society (2006)
54. Liu, Y.T.L.: Privacy-preserving multi-keyword search in information networks. IEEE Trans. Knowl. Data Eng. 27(9), 2424–2437 (2015)
55. Machanavajjhala, A., Gehrke, J., Kifer, D., Venkitasubramaniam, M.: l-diversity: privacy beyond k-anonymity. In: Liu et al. [53], p. 24 (2006)
56. Makulilo, A.B.: Asian Data Privacy Laws, Trade and Human Rights Perspective, By Graham Greenleaf, vol. 23, no. 3, pp. 322–324. I. J. Law and Information Technology (2015)
57. Malkhi, D., Nisan, N., Pinkas, B., Sella, Y.: Fairplay - secure two-party computation system. In: Blaze, M. (ed.) USENIX Security Symposium, pp. 287–302. USENIX (2004)
58. Martin, D.J., Kifer, D., Machanavajjhala, A., Gehrke, J., Halpern, J.Y.: Worst-case background knowledge for privacy-preserving data publishing. In: Proceedings of the 23rd International Conference on Data Engineering, ICDE 2007, 15–20 April 2007, The Marmara Hotel, Istanbul, Turkey, pp. 126–135 (2007)
59. McCamant, S., Ernst, M. D.: Quantitative information flow as network flow capacity. In: Proceedings of the ACM SIGPLAN 2008 Conference on Programming Language Design and Implementation, 7–13 June 2008, Tucson, AZ, USA, pp. 193–205 (2008)
60. Narayan, A., Haeberlen, A.: DJoin: differentially private join queries over distributed databases. In: OSDI, October 2012
61. Pettai, M., Laud, P.: Combining differential privacy and secure multiparty computation. In: Proceedings of the 31st Annual Computer Security Applications Conference, 7–11 December 2015, Los Angeles, CA, USA, pp. 421–430 (2015)
62. Rabin, M.O.: How to exchange secrets with oblivious transfer. IACR Cryptology ePrint Archive 2005:187 (2005)
63. Rastogi, A., Hammer, M.A., Hicks, M.: Wysteria: a programming language for generic, mixed-mode multiparty computations. In: 2014 IEEE Symposium on Security and Privacy, SP 2014, 18–21 May 2014, Berkeley, CA, USA, pp. 655–670. IEEE Computer Society (2014)
64. Seward, J., Nethercote, N., Weidendorfer, J.: Valgrind 3.3-Advanced Debugging and Profiling for GNU/Linux Applications. Network Theory Ltd., UK (2008)
65. Shamir, A.: How to share a secret. Commun. ACM 22(11), 612–613 (1979)

66. Songhori, E.M., Hussain, S.U., Sadeghi, A.R., Schneider, T., Koushanfar, F.: Tiny-garble: highly compressed and scalable sequential garbled circuits. In: 2015 IEEE Symposium on Security and Privacy, SP 2015, 17–21 May 2015, San Jose, CA, USA [15], pp. 411–428 (2015)
67. Sweeney, L.: K-anonymity: a model for protecting privacy. Int. J. Uncertain. Fuzziness Knowl.-Based Syst. **10**(5), 557–570 (2002)
68. Tang, Y., Liu, L., Iyengar, A., Lee, K., Zhang, Q.: e-PPI: locator service in information networks with personalized privacy preservation. In: IEEE 34th International Conference on Distributed Computing Systems, ICDCS 2014, 30 June–3 July 2014, Madrid, Spain, pp. 186–197 (2014)
69. Tang, Y., Wang, T., Liu, L.: Privacy preserving indexing for ehealth information networks. In: CIKM, pp. 905–914 (2011)
70. Toth, C., Durham, E., Kantarcioglu, M., Xue, Y., Malin, B.: Soempi: A secure open enterprise master patient index software toolkit for private record linkage. In: AMIA Annual Symposium Proceedings, vol. 2014, p. 1105. American Medical Informatics Association (2014)
71. Vaidya, J., Clifton, C.: Privacy preserving association rule mining in vertically partitioned data. In: Proceedings of the Eighth ACM SIGKDD International Conference on Knowledge Discovery and Data Mining, 23–26 July 2002, Edmonton, Alberta, Canada, pp. 639–644 (2002)
72. Warner, S.L.: Randomized response: a survey technique for eliminating evasive answer bias. J. Am. Stat. Assoc. **60**(309), 63–69 (1965)
73. Yao, A.C.: How to generate and exchange secrets (extended abstract). In: 27th Annual Symposium on Foundations of Computer Science, 27–29 October 1986, Toronto, Canada, pp. 162–167. IEEE Computer Society (1986)
74. Zerr, S., Demidova, E., Olmedilla, D., Nejdl, W., Winslett, M., Mitra, S.: Zerber: r-confidential indexing for distributed documents. In: EDBT, pp. 287–298 (2008)
75. Zhang, Y., Steele, A., Blanton, M.: PICCO: a general-purpose compiler for private distributed computation. In: 2013 ACM SIGSAC Conference on Computer and Communications Security, CCS 2013, 4–8 November 2013, Berlin, Germany, pp. 813–826 (2013)

A Formal Logic Framework for the Automation of the Right to Be Forgotten

Abhishek Tiwari[1]([✉]), Fabian Bendun[2], and Christian Hammer[1]

[1] University of Potsdam, Potsdam, Germany
{tiwari,chrhammer}@uni-potsdam.de
[2] Saarland University, Saarland, Germany
bendun@cs.uni-saarland.de

Abstract. The right to be forgotten results from a ruling of the European Court of Justice. It empowers individuals to control the display of their personal data indexed by a search engine. Specifically, it requires Internet search engine operators to deploy a process for individuals to file requests concerning the removal of their personal data from search indices.

To support the right to be forgotten, search engine operators such as Google, Microsoft and Yahoo currently provide a web form where users submit all relevant information. A subsequent manual process by the search engine operators assesses whether the author of the request is eligible to exercise the right to be forgotten and if the request itself is lawful. However, manual verification is inefficient, unscalable, and prone to subjective judgment. A framework for automated reasoning about case law ("PriCL") could in principle tell whether some precedents lead to the conclusion that some action is legal or illegal. However, PriCL leverages first order logic, and hence, is insufficient to determine *similarity* of cases. In this paper, we design a framework that extends PriCL's logic with similarity measures in order to automate the enforcement of the right to be forgotten. Our implementation of this logic leverages the Z3 theorem prover. We evaluate the framework by performing 10 case studies on the right to be forgotten. Each case was decided correctly in less than 1 s.

Keywords: Formal language definitions · Verification and validation
Privacy protections

1 Introduction

In 2010, a Spanish citizen filed a complaint against La Vanguardia Ediciones SL as well as Google Spain and Google Inc. He argued that the indexed information concerning himself had been fully resolved for a number of years and that reference to it was now entirely irrelevant. In May 2014, the Luxembourg-based EU court of justice agreed and ruled that all online search engines must provide

© ICST Institute for Computer Sciences, Social Informatics and Telecommunications Engineering 2018
R. Beyah et al. (Eds.): SecureComm 2018, LNICST 254, pp. 95–111, 2018.
https://doi.org/10.1007/978-3-030-01701-9_6

an interface for EU citizens to request the removal of their personal information from search results, referred to as the "right to be forgotten".

At present, search engine operators such as Google, Microsoft and Yahoo provide a simple web form that requires users to provide all relevant information relating to their case [7]. This is followed by a manual evaluation by the search engine operators to assess whether the author of the request is eligible and the request itself is lawful. "According to Google's transparency report, the number of removal requests that have been submitted to Google since the court decision in May 2014 has already exceeded 1/5 of a million and the number of URLs that Google has evaluated for removal are approximately 3/4 of a million" [6].

However, the manual verification has the following drawbacks:

1. *Time/cost.* A person working for a search engine operator needs to manually understand the query, reason about it and then provide the response. Taking into account the number of increasing queries over last years [6], it will be a time consuming and inefficient process, which requires more and more resources and thus, more money.
2. *Scalability.* The system needs to keep growing in capacity to accommodate all the user queries with a timely response.
3. *Subjective judgment.* Decisions are human made, thus possibly biased by subjective judgment, and prone to the risk of human error.

Our Contributions. In this paper, we provide a framework for the automation of the right to be forgotten, i.e., we propose an automated scenario in which search engine operators no longer need to verify all requests manually. An employee working for the indexing system manually evaluates the user query and acknowledges the user with a success or failure message. Our aim is to automate this manual procedure at the indexing system such that the user query is processed automatically for the verification of the right to be forgotten. We need to reason automatically with the user query based on the legal requirement. We leverage the PriCL framework [15] to evaluate the user query according to the right to be forgotten.

Technically, we make the following contributions:

1. *Logic for similarity measure.* PriCL provides automatic reasoning on privacy case law by means of precedents. However, PriCL currently supports first order logic for all reasoning algorithms and we have only one legal case for the right to be forgotten to compare against. To be useful PriCL would need to consider similarities regarding the justification, i.e., it should abstract away some details of the original case. Therefore, we extended PriCL's logic with similarity measures, which account for similarities between new cases and the existing one. With similarity measures PriCL can identify precedents that may replace the originals in the line of arguments.
2. *Formalization of the original case.* In order to deduce the facts from the 2014 ruling, we first analyse the case document. The case document consists of 23 pages and 100 paragraphs involving arguments (reference, axioms) and

decisions. Each argument and judgment from the case is converted into logical (predicate) form.

3. *Implementation.* We implemented the similarity measures for PriCL's logic and designed a framework that takes as input the user queries. These queries are then evaluated for the right to be forgotten using PriCL with similarity measures.

4. *Verification in the Z3 theorem prover and evaluation.* We modeled the logic with similarity measures using the Z3 theorem prover and provide several test cases to evaluate the similarity measures. Finally, we performed the validation for the right to be forgotten for several user queries using our framework. Our evaluation shows an accuracy of 100% while only requiring less than a second for processing each case.

2 Motivation and Background

In this section we will start with a simple example. We will elucidate the inadequacy of the first order logic employed by the current approach (PriCL framework). We will further explain our approach towards solving the aforementioned shortcoming. Let us assume, we have a case with the following court ruling:

Case A: Tom killed Adam and Tom goes to prison. The ruling implies that killing a person is a crime. Following is another case for which we want to deduce the ruling:

Case B: Amy killed a fly. Deciding the fate of *Amy*, given rulings from *case A*, appears trivial. However, automation of this decision is a non-trivial task. PriCL [15] is a framework for expressing and automatically reasoning about the case law by means of *precedents*. *Precedents* are cases that have been concluded in the past and already have a decision.

PriCL converts each precedent into a specific case format and stores them in a (case law) database. A case consists of a decision formula, a case description, a court and a proof tree. Defining the proof tree is more involved since it needs to capture the judge's justification. There are two main types of nodes in the proof tree: inner nodes (which may have other children) and leaf nodes. Inner nodes are deduced from their children. Inner nodes can be of type *AND*, when all of the arguments are necessary to reach their conclusion. They can be of type *OR*, when any one of the provided arguments are sufficient to reach the conclusion. There are a few argumentations that are neither explicitly covered by a decision nor by a case reference. These argumentations are provided in a knowledge base denoted KB_w.

Leaf nodes of the proof tree can be of three types: Axiom (sentences which are axiomatic statements), Assess (sentences assessing the truth value of a particular statement) and Reference (sentences in the legal case referring to another case). Leaf nodes, denoted as *facts*, are additionally associated with a prerequisite condition. The prerequisite condition is denoted as *pre*. These nodes are represented as $(pre \rightarrow fact)$ in the proof tree.

In our example, *Case A* is the precedent. It can be converted into the logical format as, *killed(Tom, Adam)* ∧ *prisoned(Tom)*. In this scenario, the *fact* is *prisoned(Tom)* and the *pre* is *killed(Tom, Adam)*. Thus, the proof tree node can be visualized as, (*killed(Tom, Adam)* → *prisoned(Tom)*). The *Case B* can be converted to logical format as, *killed(Amy, fly)*. In order to check the deducibility of formula *prisoned(Amy)*, PriCL checks the following (explaining the exact algorithm is out of scope for this paper):

$$killed(Amy, fly) \vDash killed(Tom, Adam) \text{ (A } \vDash \text{ B means, B holds given A)}$$
$$killed(Amy, fly) \wedge prisoned(Tom) \vDash prisoned(Amy)$$
$$killed(Amy, fly) \wedge prisoned(Tom) \nvDash \bot \text{ (}\bot \text{ denotes the value } false)$$

PriCL assumes first order logic, which is not sufficient for similar situations, e.g., *killed(Tom, Adam)* and *killed(Tom, Bob)* are not similar as per first order logic. However, for court rulings they could be similar since killing a person is a crime. To overcome this limitation, we extend the entailment (⊨) in PriCL with similarity measures. We define a *similarity measure function*, to evaluate the similarity between predicates, considering following points:

1. *Similarity between names of predicates.* Predicates with the same name or predicates that are synonyms should only be considered for the similarity check. For example, *killed(Amy, fly)* should be compared with *killed(Tom, Adam)* (and its synonyms, e.g., *murdered(Tom, Adam)*).
2. *Similarity between arguments of the predicate.* We need to consider the similarity between all possible pairs of arguments.
3. *Order of arguments.* Considering the order of arguments is important, e.g., between predicates *killed(Tom, Adam)* and *killed(Amy, fly)*, *Tom* should be compared with *Amy*, and *Adam* should be compared with *fly*.
4. *Weighting of arguments.* Deciding the weight of similarity between pair of arguments is important, e.g., between predicates *killed(Tom, Adam)* and *killed(Amy, fly)*, similarity between Adam and fly makes a deciding role.

Example 1. Define the similarity between predicates *killed(Tom, Adam)* and *killed(Amy, fly)*.

1. Both predicates have the same name, i.e., *killed*. Thus, they should be compared for similarity.
2. *Tom, Adam, Amy* are human being and *fly* is an insect. The similarity between the human and the insect should be low, i.e., *similarity(Tom, fly)* = *low* = *similarity(Adam, fly)*.
3. In this example, the correct pair of arguments to be compared are: *(Tom, Amy)* and *(Adam, fly)*.
4. In this example, the similarity between *(Adam, fly)* plays a deciding role. Since *similarity(Adam, fly)* ≡ *similarity(human, insect)* = *low*, the similarity between predicates *killed(Tom, Adam)* and *killed(Amy, fly)* is low.

Next, we define the similarity between formulas. A formula is created from conjunction, disjunction or implication between different predicates, e.g., *killed(Tom, Adam)* ∧ *prisoned(Tom)* is a formula. Intuitively, two formulas are similar if they have the same operators and the respective predicates are similar to each other, e.g., *killed(Tom, Adam)* ∧ *prisoned(Tom)* and *killed(Amy, fly)* ∧ *prisoned(Amy)* are not similar since predicates *killed(Tom, Adam)* and *killed(Amy, fly)* are not similar predicates (Example 1). Finally, we define the extended entailment (⊨) for two formulas ϕ and φ. Intuitively, if a formula ϕ holds under a given condition I ($I \vDash \phi$), and formula φ is similar to ϕ, then φ also hold under I.

Using above constructs, we can see that in the *Case B, killed(Amy, fly)* ⊭ *killed(Tom, Adam)* and hence *prisoned(Amy)* does not hold. In the next section, we provide formal definitions and proofs required for above constraints.

3   Similarity Measures

The goal of this work is to decide a novel judicial case with respect to a case that has already been conclusively ruled by some court. In this section, we will start by comparing cases of law. We will elaborate on the role of similarity measures to approximate the correspondences between two cases. Since we convert cases into a logical format, we use the small-step syntax and semantics of the PrivacyLFP [3] logic and extend it to include similarity measures. We define a structure ζ as an abstraction of legal cases. For a formula ϕ, we write $\zeta \vDash \phi$ to mean that "ϕ is true in the structure ζ". We say a formula ϕ is false in the structure ζ if $\zeta \vDash \bar{\phi}$.

3.1   Case Law

We are interested in the evaluation if a novel judicial case can be decided in analogy to an already decided case, a *precedent*. To that end, we leverage an already existing tool, called PriCL [15], that builds an argument tree (*proof tree*) based on the precedent's court decision argument structure and compares whether another case can also be structured in the same tree with the same facts. However, in practice, the new case is not exactly identical to the precedent but somewhat similar. In particular, we expect it to be similar to the same line of arguments as the precedent, i.e. we expect the *structure* of the decision tree to be identical. At the same time, the instances of the circumstances are not identical but should be similar such that the line of reasoning is not invalidated. We call these leaf nodes in the proof tree that are case-dependent *decision nodes*. If we can assert that all decision nodes from the precedent have an equivalent instance in the current case, then we can assume that the judgment is also valid for the new case.

Therefore, the general scheme to decide analogies for case law as the "right to be forgotten" is:

– analyze the precedent and structure it in a proof tree in a logical format where children are either conjunctively (all sub-arguments must hold) or disjunctively (at least one sub-argument holds) combined.

– match the case-specific arguments in the decision nodes with equivalent facts from the new case.

If we can assert that all decision nodes have similar pendants then we will conclude that these cases should come to the same judgement. However, there are two issues to be solved here: First, matching the case-specific arguments is in general an NP-hard problem and, second, we need to define what we assume to be similar enough in order to consider it equivalent.

Decision nodes have a format of $(pre \rightarrow fact)$, i.e., *facts* are based on preconditions, e.g., in *case A* from Sect. 2, "Tom goes to prison" ($prisoned(Tom)$) is a *fact* and precondition for this *fact* is "Tom killed Adam" ($killed(Tom, Adam)$). Considering all such facts from decision nodes, the final judgement is made.

The case description from new cases is short and does not contain well-organized argument structure. It contains few preconditions and facts that are not sufficient to derive a proof tree. However, we need to derive a proof tree to compare it with the precedent's proof tree. To achieve this, We need to create a new proof tree based on precedent's argument structure. Intuitively, for every decision node, $(pre \rightarrow fact)$ in precedent, if the *pre* condition holds in the new case description, then we add this decision node in the new proof tree. To check the former, we need to find a similar condition in the case description. We do the following to achieve it:

– Find all possible formulas pre', by replacing predicates in pre by predicates of case description.
– Check if any one of the formulas is similar to pre.

Finding all possible formulas pre' is exponential in order. However, we can reduce all possible formulas to one in the case of *Synonyms*[1]. Let us explain this using a simple example as follows:

Example 2. Let's assume we have a decision node $(pre \rightarrow fact)$ in the precedent case as: $killed(Tom, Adam) \land category(Adam, human) \rightarrow prisoned(Tom)$. Following is a case description, which we want to decide: $killed(Amy, fly) \land bitten(fly, Amy) \land dangerous(insect) \land category(fly, insect)$.

To create a proof tree for this case description, we need to check if the precondition from decision node holds in the case description, i.e., $killed(Tom, Adam) \land category(Adam, human)$ is *true* in case description. The total number of formulas pre' are:

$$pre'_1 = killed(Amy, fly) \land category(fly, insect)$$
$$pre'_2 = killed(Amy, fly) \land bitten(fly, Amy)$$
$$pre'_3 = killed(Amy, fly) \land dangerous(insect)$$
$$pre'_4 = bitten(fly, Amy) \land category(fly, insect)$$
$$pre'_5 = bitten(fly, Amy) \land dangerous(insect)$$
$$pre'_6 = dangerous(insect) \land category(fly, insect)$$

---

[1] Synonyms express the word property.

The next step is to check if any of the above formulas is similar to *pre*. In order to check the similarity between formulas, it is sufficient to check for similarity between predicates that are replaced, e.g., formula pre'_1 is created by replacing *killed(Tom, Adam)* by *killed(Amy, fly)* and *category(Adam, human)* by *category(fly, insect)*, so if we can verify that predicates *killed(Tom, Adam)* is similar with *killed(Amy, fly)* and *category(Tom, human)* is similar with *category(fly, insect)* then the formula *pre* and pre'_1 will be similar formulas.

To evaluate the similarity between predicates, we define a similarity measure function. It returns a value in the range from 0 (dissimilar) to 1 (equal). The definition of the similarity measure function is as follows:

Definition 1 (Similarity Measure Function). *For all predicates $P^n(X)$, $Q^m(Y)$, where X and Y as the argument vectors of predicates P and Q of arity n and m, respectively, we assume:*

- $\mathcal{P}$ *be the set of all predicates.*
- *similarity : $U \times U \to [0, 1]$ is a symmetric function, where U is a universe of words. The function similarity intends to define the similarity between arguments of predicate, e.g., for predicates killed(Tom, Adam) and killed(Amy, fly), similarity(Tom, Amy) $\equiv$ similarity(Person, Person) $\approx$ 1 and similarity(Adam, fly) $\equiv$ similarity(Person, Insect) $\approx$ 0. We use Named-Entity-Relationship [11] to categorize the entities, i.e., Tom is a person.*
- $\eta_{P,Q} : [0, 1]^{n \times m} \to [0, 1]$ *is a weighing function where for any matrix $A \in [0, 1]^{n \times m} : \eta_{P,Q}(A) = \eta_{Q,P}(A^T)$*

Then, we define a function $K : P(X) \times Q(Y) \to [0, 1]$ as:

$$K(P(X), Q(Y)) = \eta_{P,Q} \left(\left[similarity(x_i, y_j) \right]_{i=1\ldots n \times j=1\ldots m} \right)$$

and call it a similarity measure function for $\mathcal{P}$.

Intuitively, the weighing function $\eta_{P,Q}$ takes as a input a matrix created by similarity of arguments and returns a similarity value based on the weighing of arguments. In our case, $\eta_{P,Q}$ returns the lowest similarity value, e.g., for predicates killed(Tom, Adam) and killed(Amy, fly), the similarity matrix is:

$$A = \begin{bmatrix} similarity(Tom, Amy) & similarity(Tom, fly) \\ similarity(Adam, Amy) & similarity(Adam, fly) \end{bmatrix}$$

$\eta_{killed,killed}(A) = $ similarity(Adam, fly) ≈ 0 (lowest of all similarities). Hence $K(killed(Tom, Adam), killed(Amy, fly)) = \eta_{killed,killed}(A) \approx 0$.

It is trivial to see that the similarity measure function is symmetric, i.e., $K(P(X), Q(Y)) = K(Q(Y), P(X))$. This property ensures that the similarity measure function will always produce the same results for two predicates $P(X), Q(Y)$ irrespective of their argument order.

It is important to note that the similarity is not absolute, so we define a similarity threshold, λ, which quantifies the similarity between predicates or formulas. The value of λ ranges from 0 to 1. The higher the value of λ the more similar are the predicates or formulas to each other. In simple words, if two predicates/formulas have λ value one then they are identical and if they have λ value 0, then they are distinct. Any value in between 0 to 1 quantifies the similarity between two predicates/formulas. The value of λ can be decided manually or automatically based on the criticality of situation, e.g., for the legal cases, high precision is required and hence it should have a high value. With enough number of sample cases, we can also use machine learning approaches to decide the λ value. Due to lack of real time use cases, we approximated λ value in our implementation as 0.8. This approximation is based on the evaluation with 10 sample use cases designed by us. Given the similarity threshold, we define the λ-similarity as follows:

Formally, lets assume a set $\mathcal{U}(\mathcal{P}) = \{P(\boldsymbol{X}) | \boldsymbol{X} \subseteq U^n, P \in \mathcal{P}, P \subseteq U^n\}$ and a similarity threshold $\lambda \in [0, 1]$, then we define:

Definition 2 (λ-similar predicates). *Let $\mathcal{L}$ be a mapping function $\mathcal{L}: \mathcal{U}(\mathcal{P})$ $\rightarrow \mathcal{U}(\mathcal{P})$ such that for all $P(\boldsymbol{X}) \in \mathcal{U}(\mathcal{P})$ we have:*
$K(P(\boldsymbol{X}), \mathcal{L}(P(\boldsymbol{X}))) \geq \lambda$
Then predicates $P(\boldsymbol{X})$ and $\mathcal{L}(P(\boldsymbol{X}))$ are λ-similar predicate.

Definition 3 (λ-similar Formula). *Let φ be a formula. Fixing the mapping function $\mathcal{L}$ such that, if the formula ϕ is generated by replacing all predicates $P(\boldsymbol{X}) \in \varphi$ by $\mathcal{L}(P(\boldsymbol{X}))$ then ϕ and φ are called λ-similar formula.*

Definition 4 (Extended $\vDash$). *Let ϕ, φ be formulas. We define ζ, $\lambda \vDash \phi$ if and only if ϕ is a λ-similar formula to φ and $\zeta \vDash \varphi$.*

3.2   Modelling the Similarity Measures ($\zeta, \lambda \vDash \phi$)

In this section, we model the similarity measures Definition 4, i.e., for a formula ϕ we implement $\zeta, \lambda \vDash \phi$. We identify two major tasks:

Task 1. Find a formula φ which is a λ-similar formula to ϕ.
Task 2. Check if $\zeta \vDash \varphi$.

To solve the first task, we leverage the definition of λ-similar formula 3. We define a mapping set $\mathcal{L}$ which maps all predicates of formula ϕ to some or all predicates in the structure ζ. If predicates of each pair in $\mathcal{L}$ are λ-similar to each other then we call this mapping as λ-similar mapping. Finally, we define a formula φ which is generated by replacement of predicates in ϕ by corresponding λ-similar mapping. In accordance with Definitions 2 and 3, φ is a λ-similar formula to ϕ. There can be several λ-similar mappings; we aggregate them along with their corresponding λ-similar formulas in a set $\mathcal{S}$.

To solve the second task, we define a formula $\mathcal{V}$ such that it contains logical OR between all λ-similar formulas from the set $\mathcal{S}$. Intuitively, $\mathcal{V}$ is true if any of the λ-similar formula (φ) is true in ζ.

For all predicates $P^n(X), Q^m(Y)$, where $\boldsymbol{X}$ and $\boldsymbol{Y}$ as the argument vectors of predicates P and Q of arity n and m, respectively, let ϕ be a formula such that it contains $\{P_1(\boldsymbol{X_1}), .., P_k(\boldsymbol{X_k})\}$ and $\zeta \vDash Q_1(\boldsymbol{Y_1}), .., Q_j(\boldsymbol{Y_j})$. We define:

– A function *lambda-similar* such that it takes two predicates as input and returns boolean. Internally, it implements the *Similarity Measure Function 1*. Formally, for two predicates $P(\boldsymbol{X})$, $Q(\boldsymbol{Y})$:

$$lambda\text{-}similar(P, Q) = \begin{cases} true, & \text{if P and Q are } \lambda\text{-}similar \\ false, & \text{otherwise} \end{cases} \qquad (1)$$

– A mapping set $\mathcal{L} = \{l_1, l_2, .., l_n\}$, such that $l_i = (P_i, Q_j)$ where $j = \{1$ to $m\}$. In simple words, it maps all predicates of the formula ϕ to some or all predicates in ζ. The total number of possible mappings are finite and equal to j^k. If predicates of each pair in the mapping are λ-similar to each other then we call this mapping a λ-similar mapping.
– A function $\mathcal{H}$ such that it takes mapping $\mathcal{L}$ as input and returns boolean. Formally for any mapping $\mathcal{L}$:

$$\mathcal{H}(\mathcal{L}) = \begin{cases} true, & \text{if } \mathcal{L} \text{ is a } \lambda\text{-similar mapping} \\ false, & \text{otherwise} \end{cases} \qquad (2)$$

– A formula φ such that it is generated by replacing each predicate in ϕ by the predicates in ζ corresponding to the mapping $\mathcal{L}$. For example:
if $\phi = P_1 \wedge P_2$ and $\mathcal{L} = \{(P_1, Q_1), (P_2, Q_2)\}$, then $\varphi = Q_1 \wedge Q_2$.
– A set $\mathcal{S}$ such that for the given ϕ, ζ, it contains the formula φ for all possible λ-similar mappings $\mathcal{L}$. Formally:

$$\mathcal{S} = \{\varphi \mid \text{if } \mathcal{H}(\mathcal{L})\} \qquad (3)$$

– A formula $\mathcal{V}$ such that for a given $\mathcal{S}$ it is the logical OR between each element of $\mathcal{S}$. If the set $\mathcal{S}$ is an empty set then it is equivalent to the truth value *false*. Formally $\mathcal{V}$, for a given $\mathcal{S}$, is defined as:

$$\mathcal{V} = \begin{cases} \varphi_1 \vee .. \vee \varphi_n, & \text{if } \mathcal{S} = \{\varphi_1, .., \varphi_n\} \\ false, & \text{if } \mathcal{S} = \emptyset \end{cases} \qquad (4)$$

Thus, if $\mathcal{V}$ is *true* then at least one of the formula φ that is a λ-similar formula to ϕ is true. Hence, from Defintion 4, $\zeta, \lambda \vDash \phi$.

Example 3. Let $\phi = killed(Amy, fly) \wedge prisoned(Amy)$ and $\zeta \vDash \{killed(Tom, Adam), prisoned(Tom)\}$ then:

$\mathcal{L}_1 = \{(killed(Amy, fly), killed(Tom, Adam)), (prisoned(Amy), prisoned(Tom))\}$

$\mathcal{H}_1(\mathcal{L}_1) = lambda\text{-}similar(killed(Amy, fly), killed(Tom, Adam))$

$\wedge\ lambda\text{-}similar(prisoned(Amy), prisoned(Tom))$

$= false(see\ Definition\ 1)$

$\varphi_1 = killed(Tom, Adam) \wedge prisoned(Tom)$

$\mathcal{L}_2 = \{(killed(Amy, fly), killed(Tom, Adam)), (prisoned(Amy), killed(Tom, Adam))\}$

$\mathcal{H}_2(\mathcal{L}_2) = lambda\text{-}similar((killed(Amy, fly), killed(Tom, Adam))$

$\wedge\ lambda\text{-}similar(prisoned(Amy), killed(Tom, Adam))$

$= false(see\ Definition\ 1)$

$\varphi_2 = killed(Tom, Adam) \wedge killed(Tom, Adam)$

$\mathcal{L}_3 = \{(killed(Amy, fly), prisoned(Tom)), (prisoned(Amy), killed(Tom, Adam))\}$

$\mathcal{H}_3 = lambda\text{-}similar((killed(Amy, fly), prisoned(Tom))$

$\wedge\ lambda\text{-}similar(prisoned(Amy), killed(Tom, Adam))$

$= false(see\ Definition\ 1)$

$\varphi_3 = prisoned(Tom) \wedge killed(Tom, Adam)$

$\mathcal{L}_4 = \{(killed(Amy, fly), prisoned(Tom)), (prisoned(Amy), prisoned(Tom))\}$

$\mathcal{H}_4 = lambda\text{-}similar((killed(Amy, fly), prisoned(Tom))$

$\wedge\ lambda\text{-}similar(prisoned(Amy), prisoned(Tom))$

$= false(see\ Definition\ 1)$

$\varphi_4 = prisoned(Tom) \wedge prisoned(Tom)$

The set $\mathcal{S} = \emptyset$ & $\mathcal{V} = false$. Thus $\zeta, \lambda \nvDash \phi$.

Lemma 1. *Given ϕ, ζ and λ, for all possible mappings $\mathcal{L}$ and their corresponding φ, if $\mathcal{H}(\mathcal{L})$ is true then φ is λ-similar formula to ϕ.*

Proof. By Definition 2, $\mathcal{H}(\mathcal{L})$ returns true only if $\mathcal{L}$ is a λ-similar mapping, i.e., predicates of each pair in mapping $\mathcal{L}$ are λ-similar to each other. Given $\mathcal{H}(\mathcal{L})$ is true, φ is generated by replacing all predicates of ϕ with corresponding λ-similar predicates. Therefore, by definition (3) of λ-similar formula, φ is a λ-similar formula to ϕ.

Lemma 2. *Given ϕ, ζ and λ, if there exist at least one φ that is λ-similar formula to ϕ and $\mathcal{O}$ is logical OR of all such φ, then $\mathcal{V}$ is equivalent to $\mathcal{O}$.*

Proof. For a non-empty set $\mathcal{S}$, $\mathcal{V}$ is equivalent to the logical OR between each element of $\mathcal{S}$ (Definition 4). For a given mapping $\mathcal{L}$, $\mathcal{S}$ contains the corresponding φ only if $\mathcal{L}$ is a λ-similar similar mapping, i.e., $\mathcal{H}(\mathcal{L})$ returns true. By Lemma 1 we know that if $\mathcal{H}(\mathcal{L})$ returns true then corresponding φ is λ-similar formula to ϕ. Thus, we can say that $\mathcal{V}$ is equivalent to logical OR of all φ that are λ-similar formula to ϕ, which is equivalent to $\mathcal{O}$.

Theorem 1. *For all ϕ, ζ and λ, Given ζ, $\mathcal{V}$ is true iff ζ, $\lambda \vDash \phi$.*

Proof (by contradiction). Let us assume that the above statement is false, then their are two possible cases:

(1) $\mathcal{V}$ is true in the structure ζ ($\zeta \vDash \mathcal{V}$) and $\zeta, \lambda \nvDash \phi$.

As $\mathcal{V}$ is true, $\mathcal{S}$ contains at least one formula φ (Definition 4). By Defintion 3, $\mathcal{L}$ corresponding to this φ is a λ-similar similar mapping, i.e., $\mathcal{H}(\mathcal{L})$ returns true. By Lemma 1 we know that if $\mathcal{H}(\mathcal{L})$ returns true then the corresponding φ is a λ-similar formula to ϕ. As $\zeta \vDash \mathcal{V}$ is equivalent to $\zeta \vDash \varphi$ and φ is a λ-similar formula to ϕ, we have $\zeta, \lambda \vDash \phi$ (Defintion 4). However, this contradicts our assumption.

(2) $\zeta, \lambda \vDash \phi$ and $\mathcal{V}$ is false in the structure ζ ($\zeta \nvDash \mathcal{V}$).

By Defintion 4 (Extended $\vDash$), if $\zeta, \lambda \vDash \phi$, then there exists at least one φ that is a λ-similar formula to ϕ and $\zeta \vDash \varphi$. By Defintion 3, $\mathcal{S}$ will at least contain this φ. As $\mathcal{V}$ is the logical OR between all φ from $\mathcal{S}$ and $\zeta \vDash \varphi$, $\zeta \vDash \mathcal{V}$ (as logical OR of *true* with any formula is *true*). However, this contradicts our assumption.

3.3 λ-Similarity ($\zeta, \lambda \vDash \phi$) for Synonyms

In this subsection, we model the λ-similarity for the predicates that are synonyms to each other. Synonyms express word properties, i.e., search and explore are synonyms to each other. This gives us the advantage of eliminating all other mappings that have at least one pair of predicates that are not synonyms. We show that by using the transitive property of synonyms, we can reduce the total number of mappings to exactly one.

For all predicates $P^n(X), Q^n(Y)$, where X and Y as the argument vectors of predicates P and Q of arity n, let ϕ be a formula such that it contains $\{P_1(X_1), .., P_k(X_k)\}$ and $\zeta \vDash Q_1(Y_1), .., Q_j(Y_j)$. If the predicate P_1 is synonym to the predicates $Q_1, Q_2, .., Q_i$, then by the transitive property of synonyms[2], $Q_1, Q_2, .., Q_i$ are also synonyms to each other. If $Q_1, Q_2, .., Q_i$ are true given a structure ζ, then they are equivalent instances of each other. Thus, the mapping (P_1, Q_1) is equivalent to taking all mappings $\{(P_1, Q_1), ..(P_1, Q_i)\}$.

Example 4. Let(($killed(Tom, Adam) \wedge category(Tom, human)$) $\rightarrow$ $prisoned$ (Tom) ($pre \rightarrow fact$) be a node in precedent. We have the following case description for the new case:
$killed(Amy, fly) \wedge category(fly, insect)$
Then the total number of mappings from pre to case description are:

1. $killed \rightarrow killed, category \rightarrow category$
2. $killed \rightarrow category, category \rightarrow killed$
3. $killed \rightarrow category, category \rightarrow category$
4. $killed \rightarrow killed, category \rightarrow killed$

However, we are only interested in mappings that contain synonyms predicate pairs. Thus, the total number of mappings can be reduced from 4 to 1, i.e., $killed \rightarrow killed, category \rightarrow category$.

Z3 [16] theorem prover is used to model the implementation of the λ-similarity for synonyms. It is developed by Microsoft Research and based on SMT-LIB 2.0 standard.

---

[2] If A is synonym to B and C, then B and C are also synonyms to each other.

3.4   Formalization of the Mr. Mario Costeja Gonzalez's Case

In this section, we describe the formalization of Mr. Gonzalez's case. To convert it into the PriCL case format, we divide the formalization into two phases:

1. Understanding and analyzing the legal case document. As the case document involves arguments and judgments in the natural language, we need to convert it into the logical format.
2. The next task is to identify the type of arguments, e.g., arguments referring of other cases. After determining the type of arguments, we identified their structure and converted them into the proof tree format as required by PriCL.

Analysis of the Case of Mr. Gonzalez: To deduce facts from the Mr. Mario Costeja Gonzalez's case, we analyze the case document which consists of 23 pages and 100 paragraphs involving arguments (reference, axioms) and decisions. Arguments and judgments are converted into the logical form. Below is one of the examples of the conversion from natural language to the logical form:
Textual Sentence from the Case:

"*Mr Costeja Gonzalez, a Spanish national resident in Spain, lodged with the AEPD a complaint against La Vanguardia Ediciones SL, which publishes a daily newspaper with a large circulation, in particular in Catalonia (Spain) ('La Vanguardia'), and against Google Spain and Google Inc.*"
Logical Form:

```
national(costeja_gonzalez, Spanish) /\
resident_of(costeja_gonzalez,Spain) /\
logged_complaint_with(costeja_gonzalez,AEPD) /\
logged_complaint_against(costeja_gonzalez ,La_Vanguardia_Ediciones_SL) /\
logged_complaint_against(costeja_gonzalez ,Google_Spain,Google_Inc) /\
publishes(La_Vanguardia_Ediciones_SL,a_daily_newspaper) /\
publishes_at(La_Vanguardia_Ediciones_SL,Catalonia).
```

In this example, we have used a predicate *national(person_name, Spanish)* to indicate that Mr. Costeja Gonzalez is a Spanish national. A variant of this predicate can also be *citizen(person, country)*. We have covered all such predicates, i.e., similar predicates or synonyms of the predicates. It is important to see that Mr. Costeja lodged the same complaint against both *La Vanguardia Ediciones SL* and *Google Spain*. Thus, we use a generic predicate *logged_complaint_against(person, entity)*, which covers all such cases. As *La Vanguardia Ediciones SL* is a daily newspaper, we use a predicate *publishes* to show the same.

After converting the entire document, we identified a total of 205 unique predicates. As we saw above (*national(person, country)* and *citizen(person, country)*), we can have various variations of the same predicate. We have included all such variations.

Automatic conversion of text to logical form is out of the scope of this paper. We have done the conversion manually, but NLP (natural language processing) could be used in practice to automate this process.

Structuring the Arguments (ProofTree): To convert the entire case into the PriCL case format [15], we need to identify the argumentation structure. We have identified arguments based on their types, i.e., whether they are decision nodes providing the rulings of the court or they are axiom nodes providing the universally true statements. We have generated one pictorial form of the tree using word tree [8]. Figure 1 is one snapshot of the entire tree. Reference nodes are black, Assess nodes are red, Axioms are green, and the Root node is of blue color.

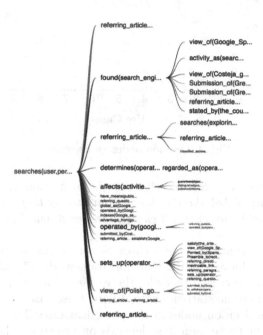

Fig. 1. Proof tree (Color figure online)

4 Evaluation

We empirically evaluated our framework with ten different use cases. We had to create use cases manually as real use cases (submitted to search engines) are not available publicly. Each case is differentiated based on following criteria (extracted from the rulings of the Mr. Costeja's case):

1. Whether the information is indexed by the search engine,
2. Whether the citizen lives in European Union,
3. Whether the information indexed is indeed affecting to the user,
4. Whether the indexed information is invalid at present.

All experiments mentioned were performed on a MacBook Air with Mac OS X 10.11.1 installed, a 1.6 GHz Intel core i5 processor and 4 GB RAM. Below is one of the use case taken for evaluation:

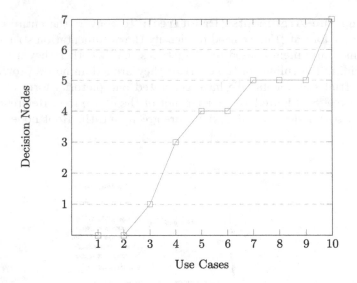

Fig. 2. Decision nodes vs use case

Alice lives in Germany. She searched Google for her name. She found a link to a newspaper stating that she was found convicted of theft. This information was published in 1990. However, all charges on her dropped by the court in the year 1992.

Checking the authenticity of use cases is not in the scope of this paper. This can be easily achieved by the Oblivion framework [17], which verifies the connection between the citizen that files the request and the data the request is about. Following are some statistics with different use cases:

There are seven decision nodes in the precedent case. The total time taken to evaluate the right to be forgotten depends on the time taken to create the proof tree from use cases. Graph in Fig. 2 shows the number of decision nodes (for which the pre condition is entailed by the use case) entailed by each use case. Use cases are arranged from the lowest number of entailed decision nodes to the highest, on X-coordinate (numbered from one to ten). The Y-coordinate contains values from zero to seven. Case ten contains most similarities with the precedent case and entails all of the decision nodes. As a result, case ten creates the exact decision tree of the precedent and thus requires maximum amount of time Fig. 3 (0.25 s by Z3 and 0.851 s in total). On the contrary, case one and two take minimum amount of time Fig. 3 (0.098 s by Z3 and 0.26 s in total) and do not entail any pre condition from the precedent, i.e., they are completely dissimilar to the precedent.

4.1   Discussion

At the time of writing this paper, we have only one case (Mr. Costeja's) with a legal ruling from the court. We use this case as the precedent. However, if in the future more cases concerning the right to be forgotten appear in the court,

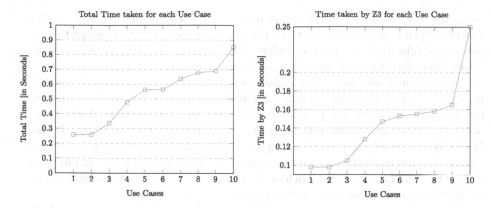

Fig. 3. Time vs use case

we can easily integrate them in our framework. It is important to note that the right to be forgotten only removes the indexing of information. The original publication itself is not removed from the web, i.e., the information will no longer be searched by a search engine but at the same time it can be accessed directly.

5 Related Work

Measuring semantic similarity between two texts or defining a logic for textual entailment has always been a topic of research in the field of artificial intelligence. Various approaches have been taken towards solving this problem [4,13,14]. Thanh Ngoc Dao and Troy Simpson [20] used tokenization, word stemming, part of speech tagging, word sense disambiguation, and then building a semantic similarity relative matrix of each pair of the word. They emphasized on formulating the problem of capturing semantic similarity between sentences as the problem of computing a maximum total matching weight of a bipartite graph.

Takale and Nandgaonkar [19] discussed several approaches to measure the similarity between words using web documents. Their work mainly emphasized on snippet extraction and snippet preprocessing. They used five different strategies for similarity measure including *Jaccard similarity coefficient*, which is used for comparing the similarity and diversity of sample sets. Rest of the strategies include *Dice's coefficient, Overlap coefficient, Cosine similarity measures* and *Simple matching index. Dice's coefficient* and *Overlap coefficient* are related to the *Jaccard similarity coefficient*, while the *cosine similarity* is a measure of similarity between two vectors of n dimensions by measuring the angle between them.

These methods evaluated the similarity between two sentences either by calculating the distance vector or counting the recurrence of words and then performing some computations. These estimates may not be precise. However, in this paper, we need accurate results as it involves legal judgment. We calculate the similarity between predicates and formulas and define the extended entailment to achieve the desired results. We calculate the similarity in more complex scenarios, e.g, similarity between predicates *kills(Ben, Human)* and *kills(Ben, Insect)* depends on the similarity of the second argument. To achieve this, we define a similarity function to calculate the similarity of arguments and finally a weighing matrix to evaluate the similarity between predicates.

Some approaches have been considered in the past to express the privacy policies [1,2,5,9]. Considering only first order logic does not suffice to express privacy policies as privacy policies need to consider several other factors such as partial structure, time, and similarity. A technical report of Garg, Jia and Datta [3] expressed the privacy policy using first-order temporal logic including propositional temporal logics and first-order metric temporal logic. In our work, we use the small step syntax provided by PrivacyLFP [3], i.e., a smaller sublogic without temporal connectives and negation.

It is essential to check the satisfiability and validity of a formula to verify the logical entailment. A lot of theorem provers are providing the logical theorem proving [10,12,16,18,21]. E [18] is, a high-performance theorem prover, based on equational superposition calculus. It is implemented in C; thus, portable to most of the UNIX dialects. Vampire and Spass [10,21] are automatic theorem provers for the first-order classical logic. Z3 [16] is a high performance and efficient theorem prover based on SMT-LIB 2.0 standard. It supports propositional logic, arithmetic, fixed-size bit-vectors, extensional arrays, data types, uninterpreted functions, and quantifiers. We are using Z3 prover in our approach because it provides high performance, efficient theorem proving, and support for propositional logic.

6   Conclusions

In this work we propose a novel logic for the automation of the right to be forgotten. We formalize the legal case of Mario Costeja Gonzalez's, which is the only legal case for the right to be forgotten. We analyze the case document of 23 pages and converted 100 paragraphs from the natural language to the logical format. We implement the essential reasoning tasks (*similarity measures*) that are needed for the automation. Finally, we evaluate our implementation on ten different use cases. The average run time for the evaluation of a use case is approximately one second, which is in turns much better than the manual verification.

References

1. Basin, D., Klaedtke, F., Samuel, M.: Monitoring security policies with metric first-order temporal logic. In: Proceedings of the 15th ACM Symposium on Access Control Models and Technologies, pp. 23–34. No. 12 in SACMAT 2010. ACM, New York (2010)
2. Giblin, C., Liu, A.Y, Müller, S., Pfitzmann, B., Zhou, X.: Regulations expressed as logical models (REALM). In: 18th Annual Conference on Legal Knowledge and Information Systems (JURIX), pp. 37–48. IOS Press, Amsterdam (2005)

3. Garg, D., Jia, L., Datta, A.: A logical method for policy enforcement over evolving audit logs*. Technical report, CMU-CyLab-11-002 (2011)
4. Agirre, E., Cer, D., Diab, M., Gonzalez Agirre, A., Guo, W.: Semantic textual similarity, including a pilot on typed similarity. In: The Second Joint Conference on Lexical and Computational Semantics (2013)
5. Baader, F., Bauer, A., Lippmann, M.: Runtime verification using a temporal description logic. In: Ghilardi, S., Sebastiani, R. (eds.) FroCoS 2009. LNCS (LNAI), vol. 5749, pp. 149–164. Springer, Heidelberg (2009). https://doi.org/10.1007/978-3-642-04222-5_9
6. Google: European privacy requests for search removals, January 2015. https://www.google.com/transparencyreport/removals/europeprivacy/?hl=en
7. Google: September 2015. https://support.google.com/legal/contact/lr_eudpa?product=websearch
8. Google: Word tree, July 2016. https://developers.google.com/chart/interactive/docs/gallery/wordtree?hl=en
9. DeYoung, H., Garg, D., Jia, L., Kaynar, D., Datta, A.: Experiences in the logical specification of the HIPAA and GLBA privacy laws. In: Proceedings of the 9th Annual ACM Workshop on Privacy in the Electronic Society (WPES), Chicago, Illinois, USA, pp. 12–20. ACM (2010)
10. Max-Planck Institute: SPASS. http://www.mpi-inf.mpg.de/departments/automation-of-logic/software/spass-workbench/, July 2017
11. Finkel, J.R., Grenager, T., Manning, C.: Incorporating non-local information into information extraction systems by Gibbs sampling. In: Proceedings of the 43rd Annual Meeting of the Association for Computational Linguistics (ACL 2005), pp. 363–370. Association for Computational Linguistics, Stroudsburg (2005)
12. Argonne National Laboratory: Otter, August 2004. http://www.mcs.anl.gov/research/projects/AR/otter/
13. Han, L., Kashyap, A., Finin, T., Mayfield, J., Weese, J.: UMBC EBIQUITY-CORE: semantic textual similarity systems. Technical report. University of Maryland (12)
14. Metzler, D., Dumais, S., Meek, C.: Similarity measures for short segments of text. In: Amati, G., Carpineto, C., Romano, G. (eds.) ECIR 2007. LNCS, vol. 4425, pp. 16–27. Springer, Heidelberg (2007). https://doi.org/10.1007/978-3-540-71496-5_5
15. Backes, M., Bendun, F., Hoffmann, J., Marnau, N.: PriCL: creating a precedent, a framework for reasoning about privacy case law. In: Focardi, R., Myers, A. (eds.) POST 2015. LNCS, vol. 9036, pp. 344–363. Springer, Heidelberg (2015). https://doi.org/10.1007/978-3-662-46666-7_18
16. Microsoft: Z3 prover, January 2017. http://rise4fun.com/z3/tutorial
17. Simeonovski, M., Bendun, F., Asghar, M.R., Backes, M., Marnau, N., Druschel, P.: Oblivion: mitigating privacy leaks by controlling the discoverability of online information. CoRR abs/1506.06033, 01 July 2015
18. Schulz, S.: E theorem prover, July 2017. http://wwwlehre.dhbw-stuttgart.de/~sschulz/E/E.html
19. Takale, S.A., Nandgaonkar, S.S.: Measuring semantic similarity between words using web search engines. In: Proceedings of the 16th International Conference on World Wide Web, pp. 757–766. ACM, New York (2007)
20. Dao, T.N, Simpson, T.: Wordnet-based semantic similarity measurement (2005). www.codeproject.com. (1 Oct 2011)
21. Voronkov, A.: Vampire, July 2017. http://www.vprover.org/

Privacy-Preserving Biometric-Based Remote User Authentication with Leakage Resilience

Yangguang Tian[1(✉)], Yingjiu Li[1], Rongmao Chen[2], Nan Li[3], Ximeng Liu[1], Bing Chang[1], and Xingjie Yu[1]

[1] School of Information Systems, Singapore Management University, Singapore, Singapore
{ygtian,yjli,xmliu,bingchang}@smu.edu.sg, stefanie.yxj@hotmail.com
[2] College of Computer, National University of Defense Technology, Changsha, China
chromao@nudt.edu.cn
[3] School of Electrical Engineering and Computing, University of Newcastle, Callaghan, Australia
nan.li@newcastle.edu.au

Abstract. Biometric-based remote user authentication is a useful primitive that allows an authorized user to authenticate to a remote server using his biometrics. Leakage attacks, such as side-channel attacks, allow an attacker to learn partial knowledge of secrets (e.g., biometrics) stored on any physical medium. Leakage attacks can be potentially launched to any existing biometric-based remote user authentication systems. Furthermore, applying plain biometrics is an efficient and straightforward approach when designing remote user authentication schemes. However, this approach jeopardises user's biometrics privacy. To address these issues, we propose a novel leakage-resilient and privacy-preserving biometric-based remote user authentication framework, such that registered users securely and privately authenticate to an honest-but-curious remote server in the cloud. In particular, the proposed generic framework provides optimal efficiency using lightweight symmetric-key cryptography, and it remains secure under leakage attacks. We formalize several new security models, including leakage-resilient user authenticity and leakage-resilient biometrics privacy, for biometric-based remote user authentication, and prove the security of proposed framework under standard assumptions.

Keywords: Remote user authentication · Leakage-resilient Biometrics privacy · Generic framework

1 Introduction

User authentication is the first line of defense in most information systems. While password-based user authentication is still pervasive, it triggers increasing

© ICST Institute for Computer Sciences, Social Informatics and Telecommunications Engineering 2018
R. Beyah et al. (Eds.): SecureComm 2018, LNICST 254, pp. 112–132, 2018.
https://doi.org/10.1007/978-3-030-01701-9_7

concerns over security (e.g., password leakage and correlated passwords) and usability (e.g., many passwords for each user to remember and frequent update of passwords). To address these concerns, biometrics based user authentication has become increasingly popular in practice in recent years. We focus on biometric-based remote user authentication in this work.

Biometrics (such as face, fingerprint, iris and voice) based remote user authentication may be vulnerable to some leakage attacks in the real world, such as "side channel attacks" on computation time, power consumption, radiation/noise/heat emission. An attacker is able to obtain some imperfect information of the secrets (e.g., biometrics) stored at either user or remote server's side. Specifically, if an impersonator is able to obtain imperfect/partial knowledge of one user's biometrics stored in cloud, then user's authenticity may be compromised. To capture such leakage attacks in biometrics-based remote user authentication setting is the main motivation of this work.

Furthermore, we consider user's biometrics as a secret value in this work. One may argue that biometrics is public information [2,7,28] such as face or fingerprint, but certain liveness detection systems in the literature [24,32] confirmed that biometrics acts as a secret key for (remote) user authentication. In particular, we consider biometrics privacy against an honest-but-curious remote cloud server.

The proposed leakage-resilient and privacy-preserving biometric-based remote user authentication framework has the following properties: (1) user's secret biometrics is hidden to the public; (2) user relies on encryption technique to protect biometrics, the encryption key is permanently stored locally and user's encrypted biometrics is stored in remote cloud; (3) user's encryption key and encrypted biometrics remain secure under certain leakage attacks.

The proposed biometrics-based and privacy-preserving remote user authentication framework is significantly useful in many real-world applications. We take mobile device users enrolling/logging in a service provider in cloud as an example, where they have their respective roles (i.e., client and server). The user authenticity of proposed framework assists in ensuring that a registered user and the remote service provider are performing authentication successfully using encrypted biometrics that are stored in cloud. In other words, user authenticity aims to capture impersonation attacks performed by outsider attackers. The biometrics privacy prevents the honest-but-curious remote service provider from revealing the registered user's secret biometrics. Furthermore, these aforementioned attacks will not be successful under the leakage of secret values.

1.1   This Work

In this work, we introduce the notion of leakage-resilient and privacy-preserving biometric-based remote user authentication (LR-BUA), allowing registered users authenticate to an honest-but-curious remote server using biometrics, and at the same time ensuring leakage resilience to any secrets stored on physical medium and privacy protection on biometrics. Our contributions can be summarized as follows.

- We present the formal security definitions for biometrics-based and privacy-preserving remote user authentication schemes. In particular, we propose a user authenticity model to capture impersonation attacks, and a biometrics privacy model to address an honest-but-curious remote server.
- We present the *first* leakage-resilient user authenticity security model and biometrics privacy model to capture the computationally hard-to-invert leakage attacks on all secret values in the auxiliary inputs model.
- We present the *first* generic construction on leakage-resilient and privacy-preserving biometric-based remote user authentication, and prove that the proposed LR-BUA generic construction can achieve leakage-resilient user authenticity and biometrics privacy under standard assumptions.
- We show the instantiations of all the building blocks. In particular, we present a lightweight biometrics-based remote user authentication scheme and its overall performance analysis.

Table 1. A comparative summary of biometrics-based user authentication.

Function/scheme	[2]	[29]	[18]	[28]	[15]	[23]	Ours
Biometrics privacy	✓	✓	✓	×	✓	✓	✓
†-Factor authentication[a]	Two	One	One	One	Three	One	Two
Lightweight cryptography[b]	✓	✓	×	×	×	✓	✓
Remote user authentication	✓	×	×	✓	✓	×	✓
Leakage-resilient w.r.t user	×	×	×	×	×	×	✓
Leakage-resilient w.r.t server	×	×	×	×	×	×	✓

[a]† denotes number of factors for authentication/identification.
[b]Lightweight Cryptography means symmetric key cryptography (e.g., symmetric key encryption [29]) rather than public key cryptography (e.g., homomorphic encryption [18,27]).

1.2   Related Work

Biometric-based Authentication. Atallah et al. [2] proposed the first lightweight biometrics-based authentication using cryptographic hash functions, and formally defined security requirements for biometrics-based authentication including confidentiality, integrity and availability. Notice that some research work in the literature [2,7,28] assume that the biometrics is a public value (such as fingerprint and face), and their *privacy* concern is the relationship between a biometric information and user's real identity.

However, three-factor [15,17] and multi-factor [16] authentication (such as smart card, password and biometrics) in the literature formed an opposite research direction, such that biometrics acts as a secret key for (remote) user authentication, and the proposed three/multi-factor solutions are able to provide enhanced security on user authentication. Meanwhile, another research line [24,32] also confirmed this assumption. One well-known three-factor authentication was done by Fan and Lin [15], in which an efficient three-factor authentication with privacy protection on biometrics was proposed, and formally proven in Bellare and Rogaway's [4] model. Specifically, they require user's biometrics is not sharing with remote server, and the biometrics matching is performed by remote server.

Moreover, some research work focused on privacy-preserving (remote) user biometrics authentication/identification, and a few novel solutions [18,23,27,29] are mainly for biometrics *identification* in the cloud. For instance, Schoenmakers and Tuyls [27] proposed to use a homomorphic encryption scheme for efficient biometric authentication by employing multi-party computation techniques. Wang et al. [29] used invertible matrices as symmetric-key secrets to encrypt biometrics and the exact biometrics matching are executed in the transformed (i.e., encrypted) domain, namely, transformation-based cancellable biometrics [22]. In Table 1, we compare our proposed solution with typical works on biometric-based authentication/identification to highlights our distinctions: it shows that our proposed solution is the first lightweight biometrics based remote user authentication with leakage-resilient and biometrics privacy.

"Fast Identity Online" (FIDO) alliance [1] is an industry consortium to address the lack of interoperability between authentication devices and user authentication experiences. Specifically, FIDO is used to enhance user authentication security (e.g., using biometrics) on local devices, while we focus on remote biometric-based user authentication in this work.

Modelling Leakage Attacks. Biometrics and secret values used in biometrics-based user authentication may be subject to leakage attacks. Micali and Reyzin [25] firstly introduced a leakage-resilient cryptography model to capture various side-channel attacks. Specifically, an adversary is allowed to access a leakage oracle: Adversary can query a polynomial time computable function f, and receive the output of $f(x)$, where x is user's secret key. They also put some restrictions on $f(x)$ such that the adversary is not able to recover the secret key x completely through the chosen function f, and the amount of leakage $f(x)$ must be less than $|x|$. Later on, Naor and Segev [26] relaxed the restriction on $f(x)$, and stated that the lower bound of leaked bits is confined to the minimal entropy of secret key x, namely, "noisy leakage" model.

Dodis et al. [12] proposed a more general model: "auxiliary inputs". Instead of min-entropy requirement on secret key x, they only require the chosen leakage functions to be computationally hard to compute x given $f(x)$. The adversary is allowed to obtain the leakage bits larger than any upper bound that defined in the bounded/noisy leakage models, and the chosen functions f must "hard-to-invert". Notice that leakage-resilient cryptography (e.g., [10,30,31]) has been extensively studied in the auxiliary inputs model. However, all the previous leakage-resilient works didn't address the leakages on secret biometrics in the (remote) user authentication systems, such as the secret (encrypted) biometrics stored in the remote server. Furthermore, the leakage attacks on secret biometrics become more challenging as those encrypted biometrics is a key to the authentication success, and the adversarial capability has not been formally captured by the existing leakage models.

Fuzzy Extractor. Fuzzy extractor is one of the building blocks for constructing biometric-based remote user authentication in this work. Juels and Wattenberg [21] introduced a new type of cryptography primitive "fuzzy commitment scheme". It is particularly useful for biometric authentication systems because error-correcting property within a suitable metric. Juels and Sudan [20] proposed another novel construction "fuzzy vault scheme". It is based on set distance rather than hamming distance used in [21]. Specifically, the fuzzy vault scheme randomly creates a secret k degree polynomial $p(x)$ during the sketch generation procedure. Given valid biometric information, a user can reproduce the polynomial and recover x. Dodis et al. [14] formally introduced the notion of secure sketches and fuzzy extractors, and use biometrics to derive a cryptographic key for various cryptographic applications, such as password-based authentication.

Recently, Li et al. [23] proposed the first fuzzy extractor based biometric identification protocol using a newly built fuzzy extractor, which is focusing on real number strings with Chebyshev distance. In particular, the proposed fuzzy extractor is suitable for efficient user identification, but its drawback is less error-tolerance than hamming distance or edit distance. In order to achieve fast remote user authentication on-line, we implement this succinct fuzzy extractor in our proposed instantiation scheme.

With regard to specific attacks on fuzzy extractor, Boyen et al. [6] introduced a notion called "robust sketches", and provided a generic conversion to prevent an active attack, such that adversary can modify the public helper data so as to compromise the security of secure sketches and fuzzy extractors. Later on, Canetti et al. [8] presented another notion, namely "reusable fuzzy extractor" (the prior work is [5]). It addressed an issue that user has multiple sketches from the same sketch scheme, and his (low-entropy) biometrics information may be leaked.

2   Security Model

In this section, we firstly present the system model for biometric-based remote user authentication, then we present the security models for LR-BUA.

Notation. We define a system with n users. We denote the i-th session established by a user as Π_U^i, and identities of all the users recognised by Π_U^i during the execution of that session by partner identifier pid_U^i. We define sid_U^i as the unique session identifier belonging to the session i established by the user U. Specifically, $\mathsf{sid}_U^i = \{m_j\}_{j=1}^n$, where $m_j \in \{0,1\}^*$ is the message transcript among users.

We say an oracle Π_U^i may be *used* or *unused*. The oracle is considered as unused if it has never been initialized. The oracle is initialized as soon as it becomes part of a group. After the initialisation the oracle is marked as used

Table 2. Summary of notations

Notation	Definition
pk_i/sk_i	User i' public key/private key
$ID_i/ID_{\widehat{S}}$	Identity of user i/server $\widehat{S}$
$dist(x, y)$	Distance between vector x and vector y
$t \in \mathbb{R}^+$	Threshold value (positive real number)
$\mathcal{B}$	Biometrics information
$\mathcal{C}$	Encrypted biometrics information
T_{Enc}	One-way transformation-based encryption scheme
$\mathsf{Ext}(x, r)$	Strong extractor

and turns into the *stand-by* state where it waits for an invocation to execute a protocol operation. Upon receiving such invocation the oracle Π_U^i learns its partner identifier pid_U^i and turns into a *processing* state where it sends, receives and processes messages according to the description of the protocol. During that phase, the internal state information $state_U^i$ is maintained by the oracle. The oracle Π_U^i remains in the processing state until it collects enough information to finalise the user authentication. As soon as the authentication is accomplished Π_U^i *accepts* and *terminates* the protocol execution meaning that it would not send or receive further messages. If the protocol execution fails then Π_U^i terminates without having accepted. In addition, we present the commonly used notations (see Table 2) in this paper.

2.1 System Model

In this work, we present a biometric-based remote user authentication system involving two entities: user and cloud server. We then define a biometric-based remote user authentication framework which consists of the following algorithms:

- Registration. This is an algorithm that executed between a user and a cloud server $\widehat{S}$ in a secure channel. User registers his identity ID along with a reference biometric information $\mathcal{B}^1$ to cloud server $\widehat{S}$.
- Authentication. This is an interactive algorithm between a registered user and a cloud server $\widehat{S}$ in a public channel. User sends his identity ID and specific information associates with a candidate biometric information $\mathcal{B}'$ to cloud server $\widehat{S}$, while $\widehat{S}$ accept it if and only if $t' = dist(\mathcal{B}', \mathcal{B}) \leq t$.

2.2 Security Model

We define a formal user authenticity model to capture the impersonation attacks performed by outsider adversaries, and a formal biometrics privacy

---

[1] Reference biometrics can be interpreted as either encrypted biometrics [9] or plain biometrics.

model to capture an honest-but-curious server for biometric-based authentication/identification protocols. Furthermore, we extend both user authenticity and biometrics privacy models to the leakage-resilient against auxiliary inputs models for tackling leakage attacks, such as side-channel attacks.

Authenticity. Informally, an adversary $\mathcal{A}$ attempts to impersonate a registered user and authenticate to a cloud server. We then define a formal authenticity game between a probabilistic polynomial-time (PPT) adversary $\mathcal{A}$ and a simulator $\mathcal{S}$ (i.e., challenger) as follows.

- Setup. $\mathcal{S}$ first generates identity/static key pair $(ID_i, \mathtt{sk}_i)$ for n users and an identity $ID_{\widehat{S}}$ for cloud server in the system, where $\mathtt{sk}_i$ denotes the secret key of user i. In addition, $\mathcal{S}$ honestly generates user's reference biometric information $\{\mathcal{B}_i\}$. Eventually, $\mathcal{S}$ sends user/cloud server's identities $(\{ID_i\}, ID_{\widehat{S}})$ to $\mathcal{A}$.
- Training. $\mathcal{A}$ can make the following queries in arbitrary sequence to $\mathcal{S}$.
  - Send: If $\mathcal{A}$ issues a send query in the form of (U, i, m) to simulate a network message for the i-th session of user U, then $\mathcal{S}$ would simulate the reaction of instance oracle Π_U^i upon receiving message m, and return to $\mathcal{A}$ the response that Π_U^i would generate; If $\mathcal{A}$ issues a send query in the form of $(U, \text{'}start\text{'})$, then $\mathcal{S}$ creates a new instance oracle $\Pi_{U'}^i$ and returns to $\mathcal{A}$ the first protocol message.
  - Biometric Reveal: If $\mathcal{A}$ issues a biometric reveal query to user i, then $\mathcal{S}$ returns user i's reference biometric information $\mathcal{B}_i$ to $\mathcal{A}$.
  - Static Key Reveal: If $\mathcal{A}$ issues a static key reveal (or corrupt, for short) query to user i, then $\mathcal{S}$ returns user i's static secret key $\mathtt{sk}_i$ (e.g., static key stored in ROM) to $\mathcal{A}$.
  - State Reveal: If $\mathcal{A}$ issues a state reveal query to (possibly unaccepted) instance oracle $\Pi_{U_i}^j$ $(j \neq i)$, then $\mathcal{S}$ will return all internal state values (e.g., ephemeral key stored in RAM) contained in $\Pi_{U_i}^j$ at the moment the query is asked.
- Attack. $\mathcal{A}$ wins the game if all of the following conditions hold.
  - $\mathcal{S}$ accept user i; It implies $\mathsf{sid}_{\widehat{S}}^s$ exists.
  - $\mathcal{A}$ did *not* issue Biometric Reveal query with regard to user i;
  - $m_i \in \mathsf{sid}_{\widehat{S}}^s$, *but* there exists *no* $\Pi_{U_i}^s$ which has sent m_i (m_i denotes the message transcript from user i)[2].

We define the advantage of an adversary $\mathcal{A}$ in the above game as

$$\mathtt{Adv}_{\mathcal{A}}^{BUA}(\lambda) = |\Pr[\mathcal{A}\,wins]|.$$

Definition 1. *We say a biometric-based remote user authentication (BUA) scheme has* authenticity *if for any PPT $\mathcal{A}$, $\mathtt{Adv}_{\mathcal{A}}^{BUA}(\lambda)$ is a negligible function of the security parameter λ.*

---

[2] We do not consider the collude attack between an impersonator and a curious server in this work.

Biometrics Privacy. Informally, an adversary (i.e., server) attempts to learn user's plain biometrics. Below is the biometrics privacy game between an adversary $\mathcal{A}$ and a simulator $\mathcal{S}$.

- Setup: $\mathcal{S}$ first generates the identity/static key pair $(ID_i, \mathbf{sk}_i)$ for n user in the system, where $\mathbf{sk}_i$ denote the secret key of user i. In addition, $\mathcal{S}$ honestly generates user's reference biometric information $\{\mathcal{C}_i\}^3$. Eventually, $\mathcal{S}$ sends user's identities $\{ID_i\}$ to $\mathcal{A}$. We denote the original n users set as $\mathcal{U}$.
- Training: $\mathcal{A}$ is allowed to issue Send, Biometric reveal, State reveal and at most n-1 Static key reveal queries to $\mathcal{S}$. We denote the honest (i.e., uncorrupted) user set as $\mathcal{U}'$.
- Challenge: $\mathcal{S}$ randomly selects a reference biometrics information $\mathcal{C}_i$ ($ID_i \in \mathcal{U}'$) as challenge candidate, and send it to $\mathcal{A}$. $\mathcal{A}$ wins the game if $\mathcal{B}_i \leftarrow \mathcal{A}(\mathcal{C}_i)$. We then define the advantage of an adversary $\mathcal{A}$ in the above game as

$$\mathrm{Adv}_{\mathcal{A}}^{BUA}(\lambda) = |\Pr[\mathcal{A}\ wins]|. \tag{1}$$

Definition 2. *We say a BUA scheme has* biometrics privacy *if for any PPT $\mathcal{A}$, $\mathrm{Adv}_{\mathcal{A}}^{BUA}(\lambda)$ is a negligible function of the security parameter λ.*

Authenticity Against Auxiliary Inputs. To model the leakage on both the biometric information and the static key with respect to auxiliary inputs, we first define a set of admissible functions $\mathcal{H}$. According to the work of Dodis et al. [12], we define two classes of auxiliary input leakage functions below.

- Let $\mathcal{H}_{ow}(\epsilon_{bio})$ be the class of all the polynomial-time computable functions $h : \{0,1\}^{|bio|} \to \{0,1\}^*$, such that given $h(bio)$ (for a randomly generated biometric information bio), no PPT adversary can find bio with probability $\geq \epsilon_{bio}$. The function $h(bio)$ can be viewed as a composition of $q_{bio} \in \mathbb{N}^+$ functions, i.e., $h(bio) = (h_1(bio), \cdots, h_{q_{bio}}(bio))$ where for all $i \in \{1, \cdots, q_{bio}\}, h_i \in \mathcal{H}_{ow}(bio)$.
- Let $\mathcal{H}_{ow}(\epsilon_{sta})$ be the class of all the polynomial-time computable functions $h : \{0,1\}^{|sta|} \to \{0,1\}^*$, such that given $h(sta)$ (for a randomly generated static key sta), no PPT adversary can find sta with probability $\geq \epsilon_{sta}$. The function $h(sta)$ can be viewed as a composition of $q_{sta} \in \mathbb{N}^+$ functions, i.e., $h(sta) = (h_1(sta), \cdots, h_{q_{sta}}(sta))$ where for all $i \in \{1, \cdots, q_{sta}\}, h_i \in \mathcal{H}_{ow}(sta)$.

We then present the new security model, i.e., leakage-resilient biometric-based user authenticity model (LR-BUA), which is an extension of previous authenticity model. Specifically, we provide two leakage queries for $\mathcal{A}$ in the LR-BUA model.

- Biometric Leakage: If $\mathcal{A}$ issues a biometric leakage query to user i (i.e., $\mathcal{O}_{bio}(i)$), then $\mathcal{S}$ returns $f_{Bio}(\mathcal{B}_i)$ to $\mathcal{A}$, where $f_{Bio} \in \mathcal{H}_{ow}(\epsilon_{bio})$, and $\mathcal{B}_i$ denotes the reference biometric information of user i.

---

^{3} The secret key is used to protect biometrics, such as $\mathcal{C}_i \leftarrow F(\mathbf{sk}_i, \mathcal{B}_i)$, where F denotes a one-way function.

- Static Key Leakage: If $\mathcal{A}$ issues a static key leakage query to user i (i.e., $\mathcal{O}_{sta}(i)$), then $\mathcal{S}$ returns $f_{Sta}(Sta_i)$ to $\mathcal{A}$, where $f_{Sta} \in \mathcal{H}_{ow}(\epsilon_{sta})$, and Sta_i denotes the static key of user i.

A General Trivial Attack. Consider an adversary is allowed to reveal user's secret key Sta in the LR-BUA model, she then can launch a trivial attack by encoding the reference derivation function into the leakage function of f_{Sta}, hence obtains biometrics information $\mathcal{B}_i$ and wins the leakage-resilient user authenticity game. Similarly, an adversary can launch another trivial attack by encoding the static key derivation function into the leakage function of f_{Bio} if user's reference biometrics is revealed, which is corresponding to the leakage-resilient biometrics privacy game below.

Our Treatment. In our proposed leakage-resilient biometric-based user authenticity model, we ask the adversary to submit two leakage function sets $\mathcal{F}_{Bio} \subseteq \mathcal{H}_{ow}(\epsilon_{bio}), \mathcal{F}_{Sta} \subseteq \mathcal{H}_{ow}(\epsilon_{sta})$, where both $\mathcal{F}_{Bio}$ and $\mathcal{F}_{Sta}$ are polynomial in the security parameter λ, prior to game Setup which is observed in [10]. During the LR-BUA security game, $\mathcal{A}$ is allowed to adaptively access both biometric leakage oracle f_{Bio} and static key leakage oracle f_{Sta}. We require that $f_{Bio} \in \mathcal{F}_{Bio}, f_{Sta} \in \mathcal{F}_{Sta}$ and $\mathcal{A}$ is not allowed to leak reference biometric information $\mathcal{B}_i$ entirely. We define the advantage of an adversary $\mathcal{A}$ in the LR-BUA game as

$$\mathrm{Adv}_{\mathcal{A}}^{LR-BUA}(\lambda) = |\Pr[\mathcal{A} \ wins]|.$$

Definition 3. *We say a BUA scheme has* leakage-resilient authenticity *if for any PPT* $\mathcal{A}$, $\mathrm{Adv}_{\mathcal{A}}^{LR-BUA}(\lambda)$ *is a negligible function of the security parameter* λ.

Biometrics Privacy Against Auxiliary Inputs. In this extended biometrics privacy against auxiliary inputs model, $\mathcal{A}$ is additionally allowed to access challenge user's Static Key Leakage oracle $\mathcal{O}_{sta}(i)$, and $\mathcal{A}$ is not allowed to leak static secret key sk_i entirely. We follow the same treatment described above and define the advantage of an adversary $\mathcal{A}$ in the biometrics privacy game as

$$\mathrm{Adv}_{\mathcal{A}}^{LR-BUA}(\lambda) = |\Pr[\mathcal{A} \ wins]|. \tag{2}$$

Definition 4. *We say a BUA scheme has* leakage-resilient biometrics privacy *if for any PPT* $\mathcal{A}$, $\mathrm{Adv}_{\mathcal{A}}^{LR-BUA}(\lambda)$ *is a negligible function of the security parameter* λ.

3   Our Construction

In this section, we present the proposed generic fuzzy extractor that will be used in the proposed generic construction, and present our proposed LR-BUA generic framework and security analysis respectively.

3.1   Generic Fuzzy Extractor

We present a generic fuzzy extractor with hard-to-invert auxiliary inputs, which is built on top of a (robust)[4] secure sketch [14] and a (δ, ϵ)-strong extractor with hard-to-invert auxiliary inputs [10,12,31].

Definition 5. *A generic fuzzy extractor with ϵ-hard-to-invert auxiliary inputs consists of two randomised procedures* (Gen, Rep) *with the following properties.*

- Gen: *Let* SS *be a secure sketch and* Ext *be a strong extractor with ϵ-hard-to-invert auxiliary inputs. Given an input x,* $\text{Gen}(x; r_1, r_2) \rightarrow (P, R)$, *such that*
$$P = (\text{SS}(x; r_1), r_2), \quad R = \text{Ext}(x; r_2).$$

- Rep: *Given an noisy input x' and P, recover the original input $x = \text{Rec}(x', \text{SS}(x; r_1))$, then compute $R = \text{Ext}(x; r_2)$.*

Theorem 1. *The proposed generic fuzzy extractor with ϵ-hard-to-invert auxiliary inputs is secure if the (robust) secure sketch is secure and the (δ, ϵ)-strong extractor with hard-to-invert auxiliary inputs is secure.*

The security of proposed generic fuzzy extractor is based on the statistical indistinguishability of two distributions below.

$$| \Pr[\mathcal{A}(r_2, f(x), \text{SS}(x; r_1), \text{Ext}(x; r_2)) = 1]|$$
$$-| \Pr[\mathcal{A}(r_2, f(x), \text{SS}(x; r_1), u) = 1]| < \delta$$

Where $x, r_1 \in_R \{0,1\}^{l_1}, r_2 \in_R \{0,1\}^{l_2}, u \in_R \{0,1\}^m$ and $f \in \mathcal{H}_{ow}(\epsilon)$.

Proof. We use (δ, ϵ)-strong extractor with hard-to-invert auxiliary inputs to derive the strong extractor Ext from the proposed generic fuzzy extractor. The (δ, ϵ)-strong extractor with hard-to-invert auxiliary inputs can guarantee the security of such (leakage-resilient) strong extractor of proposed generic fuzzy extractor. In other words, the output string $\text{Ext}(x; r_2)$ is statistically indistinguishable with a string u which is generated uniformly at random, even if a leakage function f is provided. Furthermore, the secure sketch $\text{SS}(x; r_1)$ is secure due to the fact that adversary can recover x with a negligible advantage [14]. Therefore, the proposed generic fuzzy extractor with ϵ-hard-to-invert auxiliary inputs is secure.

Remark. The proposed fuzzy extractor with ϵ-hard-to-invert auxiliary inputs is a *stronger* assumption than a generic fuzzy extractor defined in [14], which allows adversary to access a leakage function f (adaptively). We stress that

---

[4] It can detect the modification of helper data P_i over public channel (secure in the random oracle model), please refer to [6,13,23] for detailed generic construction of *robust secure sketch*.

the proposed fuzzy extractor with ϵ-hard-to-invert auxiliary inputs is a generic construction (i.e., without concrete construction). To this end, Dodis et al. [12] constructed the first reusable (and robust) extractor with hard-to-invert auxiliary inputs at the non-fuzzy case (i.e., without helper data and Rep algorithm, or when $x = x'$, where x' denotes a noisy input). Meanwhile, as stated by Canetti et al. [8], most constructions of fuzzy extractor are not reusable (except [5,8]), and adding error-correcting codes to a strong extractor with hard-to-invert auxiliary inputs at the fuzzy case (i.e., when $x \neq x'$) is a challenging task.

3.2   Generic Framework

High-level Description. User submits his/her reference biometrics to a remote server during registration phase; Remote server then acknowledges user's authenticity if and only if user's candidate biometrics is statistically "close" to his/her reference biometrics during authentication phase. We define a collision-resistant hash function as $H : \{0,1\}^* \rightarrow \mathbb{Z}_q$, a strong extractor with ϵ_2-hard-to-invert auxiliary inputs $\mathsf{Ext}_2 : \{0,1\}^{l'_1(\lambda)} \times \{0,1\}^{l'_2(\lambda)} \rightarrow \{0,1\}^{m_2(\lambda)}$ and a generic fuzzy extractor with ϵ_1-hard-to-invert auxiliary inputs ($\mathsf{Ext}_1 : \{0,1\}^{l_1(\lambda)} \times \{0,1\}^{l_2(\lambda)} \rightarrow \{0,1\}^{m_1(\lambda)}$) in the system.

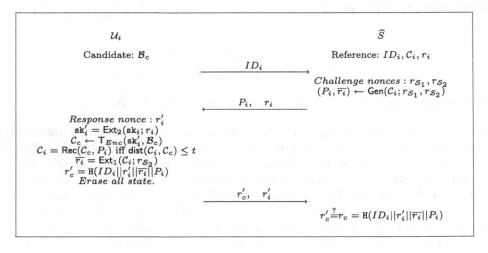

Fig. 1. Authentication. (public channel)

– Registration. A user i performs below.
1. Generate a biometric information $\mathcal{B}_i$, and a secret key sk_i along with a public randomness r_i; Note that user i takes sk_i as a secret key and stores it locally.
2. Compute an encryption key $\mathsf{sk}'_i = \mathsf{Ext}_2(\mathsf{sk}_i; r_i)$ using fuzzy extractor with ϵ_2-hard-to-invert auxiliary inputs Ext_2;

3. Compute the reference biometrics $C_i = \mathsf{T}_{Enc}(\mathsf{sk}'_i, \mathcal{B}_i)$, and sends (ID_i, C_i, r_i) to a cloud server $\widehat{S}$.

Note that cloud server $\widehat{S}$ takes/stores reference biometrics C_i as a shared secret key with user i, and the registered user erases sk'_i after the generation of reference biometrics.

- Authentication. The interaction between a registered user and cloud server performs as follows (see Fig. 1).

  - Upon receiving a request ID_i from user i, cloud server $\widehat{S}$ performs below.
    1. Compute the challenge nonces $r_{\mathcal{S}_1}, r_{\mathcal{S}_2}$;
    2. Run the generic fuzzy extractor with ϵ_1-hard-to-invert auxiliary inputs to obtain $(P_i, \overline{r_i}) \leftarrow \mathsf{Gen}(C_i; r_{\mathcal{S}_1}, r_{\mathcal{S}_2})$, where $P_i = (\mathsf{SS}(C_i; r_{\mathcal{S}_1}), r_{\mathcal{S}_2}), \overline{r_i} = \mathsf{Ext}_1(C_i; r_{\mathcal{S}_2})$;
    3. Send (P_i, r_i) to user i.

  - Then user i performs below.
    1. Generate a candidate biometric information $\mathcal{B}_c$ and compute $C_c = \mathsf{T}_{Enc}(\mathsf{sk}'_i, \mathcal{B}_c)$, where encryption key $\mathsf{sk}'_i = \mathsf{Ext}_2(\mathsf{sk}_i; r_i)$ is computed using locally stored secret key sk_i and public randomness r_i;
    2. Run the generic fuzzy extractor with ϵ_1-hard-to-invert auxiliary inputs to obtain $C_i = \mathsf{Rec}(C_c, P_i)$ ($P_i = (\mathsf{SS}(C_i; r_{\mathcal{S}_1}), r_{\mathcal{S}_2})$ if and only if $\mathsf{dist}(C_i, C_c) \leq t$, and compute $\overline{r_i} = \mathsf{Ext}_1(C_i; r_{\mathcal{S}_2})$;
    3. Choose a response nonce r'_i and compute the token $r'_c = \mathsf{H}(ID_i \| r'_i \| \overline{r_i} \| P_i)$;
    4. Erase all state and send (r'_c, r'_i) to cloud server $\widehat{S}$.

  - Eventually, cloud server $\widehat{S}$ computes the token $r_c = \mathsf{H}(ID_i \| r'_i \| \overline{r_i} \| P_i)$ and checks $r'_c \overset{?}{=} r_c$. If it does hold, accept; Otherwise, reject.

3.3 Security Analysis

Theorem 2. *The proposed LR-BUA achieves leakage-resilient authenticity (Definition 3) in the random oracle model if the generic fuzzy extractor with ϵ_1-hard-to-invert auxiliary inputs is secure, where ϵ_1 is negligible.*

High-Level Discussion. Before we present detailed security proof, we clarify the motivation of each game for leakage-resilient user authenticity security. Game $\mathbb{G}_1$ is used to prevent replay attacks; Game $\mathbb{G}_2$ is used to capture an adversary, who is allowed to reveal the static key of user i, aims to impersonate *corrupted* user i to authenticate to a remote server $\widehat{S}$.

Proof. We define a sequence of games $\{\mathbb{G}_i\}$ and let Adv_i^{LR-BUA} denote the advantage of the adversary in game $\mathbb{G}_i$. Assume that $\mathcal{A}$ activates at most m sessions in each game.

- $\mathbb{G}_0$: This is the original game for leakage-resilient authenticity security.

- $\mathbb{G}_1$: This game is identical to game $\mathbb{G}_0$ except that $\mathcal{S}$ will abort if challenge/response nonce (i.e., $r_{\mathcal{S}_\in}, r_i'$) is used twice by the server/user in two different sessions. Therefore, we have

$$\left|\mathsf{Adv}_0^{LR-BUA} - \mathsf{Adv}_1^{LR-BUA}\right| \le m^2/2^\lambda \tag{3}$$

- $\mathbb{G}_2$: This game is identical to game $\mathbb{G}_1$ except that in the "Attack" session, $\mathcal{S}$ replaces the real value $\overline{r_i}$ by a random value $R \in \{0,1\}^{m_1(\lambda)}$ with regard to instance oracle $\Pi_{U_i}^i$. Below we show the difference between $\mathbb{G}_1$ and $\mathbb{G}_2$ is negligible under the assumption that the generic fuzzy extractor with ϵ_1-hard-to-invert auxiliary inputs is secure.

Let $\mathcal{S}$ denote an adversary, who is given $(r, f_1(\mathcal{C}_i), \cdots, f_{q_{Bio}}(\mathcal{C}_i), \mathsf{SS}(\mathcal{C}_i; r_1), T_b)$, aims to break the generic fuzzy extractor with ϵ_1-hard-to-invert auxiliary inputs. $\mathcal{S}$ simulates the game for $\mathcal{A}$ as follows.

- **Setup.** $\mathcal{S}$ sets up the game for $\mathcal{A}$ by creating n users with the corresponding identity, secret key and public randomness $\{ID_i, \mathsf{sk}_i, r_i\}$. $\mathcal{S}$ randomly selects an index i and guesses that the "Attack" event will happen with regard to user i. In addition, $\mathcal{S}$ honestly generates rest user's biometrics information $\{\mathcal{B}_j\}_{j \ne i}^n$ and their corresponding reference biometrics $\{\mathcal{C}_j\}$. It is obvious that $\mathcal{S}$ can answer all the queries made by $\mathcal{A}$ except user i (w.r.t. reference biometrics $\mathcal{C}_i$). Below we mainly focus on the simulation of user i only.

- **Training.** $\mathcal{S}$ answers $\mathcal{A}$'s queries as follows.
  - If $\mathcal{A}$ issues a send query in the form of ID_i to $\mathcal{S}$ w.s.t instance oracle $\Pi_{U_i}^i$, $\mathcal{S}$ forwards it to his challenger and obtains a helper data P_i (where $P_i = (\mathsf{SS}(\mathcal{C}_i; r_1), r)$, and (r_1, r) are chosen by his challenger), and returns (P_i, r_i) to $\mathcal{A}$ as the query response. Note that r_i is the public randomness chosen by $\mathcal{S}$.

    If $\mathcal{A}$ issues a send query in the form of (P_i, r_i) to $\mathcal{S}$, $\mathcal{S}$ randomly chooses a response nonce r_i' and sets $\overline{r_i} = T_b$; $\mathcal{S}$ then computes the token $r_c' = \mathsf{H}(ID_i||r_i||\overline{r_i}||P_i)$ and returns (r_c', r_i') to $\mathcal{A}$. Note that T_b can be either $T_0 = \mathsf{Ext}_1(\mathcal{C}_i; r)$ or $T_1 \in_R \{0,1\}^{m_1(\lambda)}$.
  - If $\mathcal{A}$ issues a static key leakage query to user i, then $\mathcal{S}$ randomly chooses a leakage function $f_{Sta} \in \mathcal{F}_{Sta} \subseteq \mathcal{H}_{ow}(\epsilon_2)$ and returns $f_{Sta}(\mathsf{sk}_i)$ to $\mathcal{A}$ as the leakage query outputs. Note that $\mathcal{A}$ is allowed to reveal sk_i entirely.
  - If $\mathcal{A}$ issues a biometric leakage query to user i, then $\mathcal{S}$ returns $f_1(\mathcal{C}_i)$, $\cdots, f_{q_{Bio}}(\mathcal{C}_i)$ as the leakage query outputs.
  - If $\mathcal{A}$ issues a state reveal query to an instance oracle $\Pi_{U_i}^i$, then $\mathcal{S}$ returns (r_i', r) to $\mathcal{A}$.

If the challenge of $\mathcal{S}$ is $T_0 = \mathsf{Ext}_1(\mathcal{C}_i; r)$, then the simulation is consistent with $\mathbb{G}_1$; Otherwise, the simulation is consistent with $\mathbb{G}_2$. If the advantage of $\mathcal{A}$ is significantly different in $\mathbb{G}_1$ and $\mathbb{G}_2$, then $\mathcal{S}$ can break the generic fuzzy extractor with ϵ_1-hard-to-invert auxiliary inputs. Therefore we have

$$\left|\mathsf{Adv}_1^{LR-BUA} - \mathsf{Adv}_2^{LR-BUA}\right| \le n \cdot m \cdot \mathsf{Adv}_{\mathcal{S}}^{\mathsf{Ext}_1}(\lambda) \tag{4}$$

- $\mathbb{G}_3$ This game is identical to game $\mathbb{G}_2$ except that in the "Attack" session, we replace the token r'_c by a random value R. Since we model H as a random oracle, if the replay attacks (w.r.t., $\mathbb{G}_1$) and impersonation attacks (w.r.t., $\mathbb{G}_2$) did not happen, then we have

$$\mathsf{Adv}_2^{LR-BUA} = \mathsf{Adv}_3^{LR-BUA}$$

It is easy to see that in game $\mathbb{G}_3$, $\mathcal{A}$ has no advantage, i.e.,

$$\mathsf{Adv}_3^{LR-BUA} = 0 \qquad (5)$$

Combining the above results together, we have

$$\mathsf{Adv}_{\mathcal{A}}^{LR-BUA}(\lambda) \leq m^2/2^\lambda + n \cdot m \cdot \mathsf{Adv}_{\mathcal{S}}^{\mathsf{Ext}_1}(\lambda)$$

Theorem 3. *The proposed LR-BUA achieves leakage-resilient biometrics privacy (Definition 4) if Ext_2 is a strong extractor with ϵ_2-hard-to-invert auxiliary inputs, where ϵ_2 is negligible.*

Proof. Let $\mathcal{S}$ denote an adversary, who is given $(r, f_1(\mathsf{sk}_i), \cdots, f_{q_{Sta}}(\mathsf{sk}_i), T_b)$, aims to break the strong extractor with ϵ_2-hard-to-invert auxiliary inputs. $\mathcal{S}$ simulates the game for $\mathcal{A}$ as follows.

- Setup. $\mathcal{S}$ sets up the game for $\mathcal{A}$ by creating n users with the corresponding identity/biometric $\{ID_i, \mathcal{B}_i\}$. $\mathcal{S}$ randomly selects an index i and guesses that the challenge reference biometrics $\mathcal{C}^*$ will happen with regard to user i. In addition, $\mathcal{S}$ honestly generates rest user's secret key and public randomness pair $\{\mathsf{sk}_j, r_j\}_{j\neq i}^n$ and their corresponding reference biometrics $\{\mathcal{C}_j\}$. Eventually, $\mathcal{S}$ sends all the reference biometrics (include $\mathcal{C}^*$) to $\mathcal{A}$. It is obvious that $\mathcal{S}$ can answer all static secret reveal queries made by $\mathcal{A}$ except user i. Below we mainly focus on the simulation of user i only.
- Training. $\mathcal{S}$ answers $\mathcal{A}$'s queries as follows.
  - If $\mathcal{A}$ issues a send query in the form of (P_i, r) to $\mathcal{S}$, then $\mathcal{S}$ performs the simulation as follows. Firstly, $\mathcal{S}$ chooses the response randomness r'_i, and computes the challenge reference biometrics $\mathcal{C}^* = \mathsf{T}_{Enc}(T_b, \mathcal{B}_i)$; Secondly, $\mathcal{S}$ runs the generation of generic fuzzy extractor to obtain $(P_i, \overline{r_i}) \leftarrow \mathsf{Gen}(\mathcal{C}_i; r_{i1}, r_{i2})$, where P_i denotes a helper date and $\overline{r_i} = \mathsf{Ext}_1(\mathcal{C}_i; r)$, and (r_{i1}, r_{i2}) are randomly chosen by $\mathcal{S}$; Eventually, $\mathcal{S}$ computes the token $r'_c = \mathsf{H}(ID_i || r'_i || \overline{r_i} || P_i)$ and sends (r'_c, r'_i) to $\mathcal{A}$ as the query response. Note that T_b can be either $T_0 = \mathsf{Ext}_2(\mathsf{sk}_i; r)$ or $T_1 \in_R \{0,1\}^{m_2(\lambda)}$.
    We assume user i may use same $\mathsf{sk}_i, \mathcal{B}_i$ with different public randomness $r^* \neq r_i$ at most $n(\lambda)$ times (where n is a polynomial in the security parameter λ) for generating different references during registration. For instance, $\mathcal{C}_i^* = \mathsf{T}_{Enc}(\mathsf{sk}_i^*, \mathcal{B}_i)$, $\mathsf{sk}_i^* = \mathsf{Ext}_2(\mathsf{sk}_i; r^*)$.
  - If $\mathcal{A}$ issues a static key leakage query to user i, then $\mathcal{S}$ returns $f_1(\mathsf{sk}_i), \cdots, f_{q_{Sta}}(\mathsf{sk}_i)$ as the leakage query outputs.

- If $\mathcal{A}$ issues a state reveal query to an instance oracle $\Pi_{U_i}^i$, then $\mathcal{S}$ returns (r_i', r_{i2}) to $\mathcal{A}$.

Finally, $\mathcal{S}$ outputs whatever $\mathcal{A}$ outputs. If $\mathcal{A}$ guesses the random bit correctly, then $\mathcal{S}$ can break the strong extractor with ϵ_2-hard-to-invert auxiliary inputs. Hence, we have

$$\mathsf{Adv}_{\mathcal{A}}^{LR-BUA}(\lambda) \leq n(\lambda) \cdot \mathsf{Adv}_{\mathcal{S}}^{\mathsf{Ext}_2}(\lambda) \tag{6}$$

4   Instantiation

In this section, we first present a lightweight biometric-based remote user authentication scheme using an efficient fuzzy extractor proposed in [23]. We then present the performance analysis and efficiency analysis respectively. Note that the work in [31] showed that a strong extractor with auxiliary inputs can be constructed from the modified Goldreich-Levin theorem (refer to [31] for detailed instantiation).

4.1   The Lightweight Biometric-Based Remote User Authentication Scheme

We present a lightweight and efficient biometric-based remote user authentication scheme below.

- Registration. A user i performs below.
  1. Generate a biometric information vector $\mathcal{B}_i = [b_{i1}, b_{i2}, \cdots, b_{in}]$ ($b_i \in \mathbb{Z}_q$);
  2. Choose an encryption key $\mathsf{sk}_i' \in_R \{0,1\}^{n|q|}$;
  3. Compute the reference biometric information $\mathcal{C}_i = \mathsf{sk}_i' \oplus \mathcal{B}_i$ and send $(ID_i, \mathcal{C}_i)$ to cloud server $\widehat{S}$.
- Authentication. The interaction between a user and the cloud server performs as follows.
  - Upon receiving a request ID_i from user i, cloud server $\widehat{S}$ performs below.
    1. Compute a challenge nonce $r_{\mathcal{S}} \in \mathbb{Z}_p$;
    2. Run the fuzzy extractor in [23] to obtain $(P_i, \overline{r_i}) \leftarrow \mathsf{Gen}(\mathcal{C}_i; r_{\mathcal{S}})$, where $P_i = (\mathsf{SS}(\mathcal{C}_i), r_{\mathcal{S}}), \overline{r_i} = \mathsf{Ext}(\mathcal{C}_i; r_{\mathcal{S}})$;
    3. Send P_i to user i.
  - Then user i performs below.
    1. Generate a candidate biometric information vector $\mathcal{B}_c = [b_{c1}, b_{c2}, \cdots, b_{cn}]$, and computes the candidate biometrics $\mathcal{C}_c = \mathsf{sk}_i' \oplus \mathcal{B}$;
    2. Run the fuzzy extractor in [23] to obtain $\mathcal{C}_i = \mathsf{Rec}(\mathcal{C}_c, P_i)$ ($P_i = (\mathsf{SS}(\mathcal{C}_i), r_{\mathcal{S}})$ if and only if $\mathsf{dist}(\mathcal{C}_i, \mathcal{C}_c) \leq t$, and compute $\overline{r_i} = \mathsf{Ext}_1(\mathcal{C}_i; r_{\mathcal{S}})$;
    3. Choose a random nonce $r_i' \in \mathbb{Z}_p$ and computes the token $r_c' = \mathsf{H}(ID_i \| r_i' \| \overline{r_i} \| P_i)$;

Candidates:	$|q|$	n
Fingerprint [3, 29]	4-8	16-640
Face [33]	4-8	1024 - 16384

Fig. 2. General parameters.

4. Erase all state and send (r'_c, r'_i) to cloud server $\widehat{S}$.

- Eventually, cloud server $\widehat{S}$ computes the token $r_c = \text{H}(ID_i||r'_i||\overline{r_i}||P_i)$ and checks $r'_c \overset{?}{=} r_c$. If it does hold, accept; Otherwise, reject.

A Trivial Attack. We notice that both user authenticity and biometric privacy may suffer to brute force attacks. For instance, an adversary may choose a random candidate biometrics $C^* \in \{0,1\}^{n|q|}$ for remote user authentication. More formally, adversary wins the user authenticity game with probability $(C^0_{n|q|} + C^1_{n|q|} + \cdots C^t_{n|q|})/2^{n|q|}$ (C denote the combinatorial number system in the form of $C^n_m = m!/n!(m-n)!$), which is negligible in terms of security parameters.

4.2 Performance Analysis

This experiment was run on virtual machines (3.6 GHz single-core processor and 6 GB RAM memory). In this experiment, we use Fingerprint and Face as candidates biometrics to initialize biometric-based remote user authentication scheme (BUA) (see Fig. 2). The experiment assumes that user biometric data has been converted into the format needed (we focus on real number strings here because the input requirement of fuzzy extractor [23]), because the representation (depends on the feature extraction algorithms) of biometric data could be vary. Without loss of generality, we use simulated data which is independent from various type of biometrics. We analyze the BUA in terms of computation cost and communication overhead, and we assume an identity has 256-bit size, a hash function SHA-256 has 256-bit output size, and the helper data of fuzzy extractor includes a secure sketch with $n \cdot log(k \cdot a + 1)$-bit output size (Refer to [23] for detailed description of parameters, such as t, k, a).

- Fingerprint 3a: Typically, the bit length of FingerCode (Refer to [19]) is ranging from 64 bits to 5120 bits. Specifically, a proper fingerprint has the following parameters: 2–5 concentric bands, 4–16 sectors, 2–8 Gabor filters, quantised with 4–8 bits and stored with five different orientations [3,19]. Note that there are two main factors that affect the computation cost: (1) Length of b_i (4–8 bits); (2) Dimension of FingerCode n (16–640).
From Fig. 3a, we can see that the running time increases linearly with whole size of bit length because the computational cost of fuzzy extractor and XOR operation are relying on the actual size of biometrics. Furthermore, we take $b_i = 4$ and $n = 640$ as a sample FingerCode, it requires about 6.16 ms for efficient computation (w.r.t. authentication) on-line. If we assume $p = 256$, then server and user has 703-bit and 768-bit communication overhead respectively. Note that the output size of secure sketch is $447 \approx 640 \cdot log(4 + 1)$ bits.

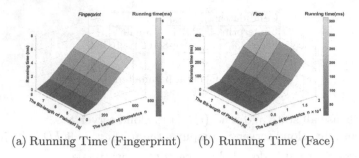

(a) Running Time (Fingerprint)   (b) Running Time (Face)

Fig. 3. Evaluation findings

– Face 3b: An image pixel is usually quantised to store from 4-bit to 8-bit length, and the size of image is ranging from 32×32 to 128×128 with respect to grayscale image. Note that 32×32 is the minimal recognised value of a grayscale image, and 128×128 is a most used image size according to the experimental results (see Table 3 in [33]). From Fig. 3b, the running time also increases linearly with whole size of bit length (the same reason as explained above). We then take $b_i = 4$ and $n = 16384$ as a sample of face recognition, it requires about 277.46 ms for efficient computation (w.r.t. authentication) on-line. Furthermore, server and user has 11707-bit and 768-bit communication overhead respectively, and in particular, the user' communication overhead is a constant value. Note that the output size of secure sketch is $11451 \approx 16384 \cdot log(4 + 1)$ bits.

Remark. Note that some types of biometric data such as iris or an audio recording of a voice, are typically quantised in the binary format [11,32] which can also be processed using above fuzzy extractor. The reason is that, the input of fuzzy extractor [23] is actually a ciphertext, which means any specified format (such as binary, integer, vector and matrix) will be transformed into a real random string using XOR operation (recall that $b_i \in \mathbb{Z}_q$).

4.3   Efficiency Analysis

We then present an efficiency comparison among relevant lightweight biometric-based and fuzzy-extractor based user authentication and identification schemes in terms of storage costs and computational costs. We consider a two-party (namely, user and server) setting only for fair comparison.

– Storage cost: Let $\mathcal{L}_\mathcal{B}$ denote the length of biometrics $\mathcal{B}$ (e.g., $|q|n$); $\mathcal{L}_{\mathbb{Z}_q}$ denote the length of element in $\mathbb{Z}_q$. In Table 3, user's storage cost (such as encryption key or randomness) in our proposed solution is less than [23] since cloud server stores the encrypted biometrics and the corresponding helper data, and user does not need to run Gen algorithm during authentication phase. As for the basic scheme in [29], it requires more storage due to two diagonal matrixes are replying on flexible dimension of biometrics. Thus our proposed generic construction has less storage cost than [23,29] from user's perspective.

Table 3. Storage costs in various schemes.

Schemes	Public/secret key (user)	Stored info (server)
[29]	$(\mathcal{L_B} + 2)^2$	$(\mathcal{L_B} + 2)^2$
[23]	$\mathcal{L_B} + \mathcal{L}_{\mathbb{Z}_q}$	$\mathcal{L_B} + 2\mathcal{L}_{\mathbb{Z}_q}$
LR-BUA	$2\mathcal{L}_{\mathbb{Z}_q}$	$\mathcal{L_B} + 3\mathcal{L}_{\mathbb{Z}_q}$

– Computational cost: Let T_{Mul} denote the multiplication operation; T_{Ext} denote the fuzzy extractor; $T_{\mathsf{Ext}'}$ denote the strong extractor (non-fuzzy case); T_{KG} denote the key generation algorithm; T_{Enc} denote the encryption scheme; T_{Sign} denote the digital signature scheme; T_{H} denote the hash function. In Table 4, user's computational cost of our proposed construction at registration phase is larger than [23] since additional encryption Enc algorithm is required for biometrics privacy and Ext' is required for preventing leakage attacks. However, user has less computational cost than [23] during authentication phase. Specifically, user may perform lightweight Enc algorithm as above instantiation described, when it compared to the Sign algorithm in [23]. Furthermore, the computational cost of our proposed construction and [23] are linear, while [29] requires cubic growth of computational cost which is relying on the dimensional of biometrics. According to the performance analysis, we can infer that the computational cost in [29] is more efficient than [23] and LR-BUA at low-dimensional (of biometrics) case, but it performs worse compared to [23] and LR-BUA at high-dimensional case.

Table 4. Computational costs in various schemes.

Schemes	Registration	Authentication
[29]	$\mathcal{O}(\mathcal{B}^3)[T_{Mul}]$	$\mathcal{O}(\mathcal{B}^3)[T_{Mul}]$
[23]	$\mathcal{O}(\mathcal{B})[T_{\mathsf{Ext}} + T_{\mathsf{KG}}]$	$\mathcal{O}(\mathcal{B})[T_{\mathsf{Ext}} + T_{\mathsf{KG}} + T_{\mathsf{Sign}}]$
LR-BUA	$\mathcal{O}(\mathcal{B})[T_{\mathsf{Ext}'} + T_{\mathsf{Enc}}]$	$\mathcal{O}(\mathcal{B})[T_{\mathsf{Ext}} + T_{\mathsf{Ext}'} + T_{\mathsf{Enc}} + T_{\mathsf{H}}]$

5   Conclusion

In this paper, we proposed a notion of leakage-resilient biometric-based remote user authentication and its generic framework, and a lightweight instantiation with overall efficiency analysis. We also defined the new formal security models for leakage-resilient user authenticity and biometrics privacy, and proved the security of the proposed generic construction under standard assumptions. We leave the construction of leakage-resilient and privacy-preserving biometric-based user authentication against impersonation attacks from multiple remote servers as our future work.

Acknowledgements. This work is supported by the Singapore National Research Foundation under NCR Award Number NRF2014NCR-NCR001-012, the National Natural Science Foundation of China (Grant No. 61702541,61702105), the Young Elite Scientists Sponsorship Program by CAST (Grant No. 2017QNRC001) and the Science Research Plan Program by NUDT (Grant No. ZK17-03-46).

References

1. Fido alliance (2017). https://fidoalliance.org
2. Atallah, M.J., Frikken, K.B., Goodrich, M.T., Tamassia, R.: Secure biometric authentication for weak computational devices. In: Patrick, A.S., Yung, M. (eds.) FC 2005. LNCS, vol. 3570, pp. 357–371. Springer, Heidelberg (2005). https://doi.org/10.1007/11507840_32
3. Barni, M., et al.: Privacy-preserving fingercode authentication. In: Proceedings of the 12th ACM Workshop on Multimedia and Security, pp. 231–240 (2010)
4. Bellare, M., Rogaway, P.: Entity authentication and key distribution. In: Stinson, D.R. (ed.) CRYPTO 1993. LNCS, vol. 773, pp. 232–249. Springer, Heidelberg (1994). https://doi.org/10.1007/3-540-48329-2_21
5. Boyen, X.: Reusable cryptographic fuzzy extractors. In: ACM CCS, pp. 82–91 (2004)
6. Boyen, X., Dodis, Y., Katz, J., Ostrovsky, R., Smith, A.: Secure remote authentication using biometric data. In: Cramer, R. (ed.) EUROCRYPT 2005. LNCS, vol. 3494, pp. 147–163. Springer, Heidelberg (2005). https://doi.org/10.1007/11426639_9
7. Bringer, J., Chabanne, H., Izabachène, M., Pointcheval, D., Tang, Q., Zimmer, S.: An application of the goldwasser-micali cryptosystem to biometric authentication. In: Pieprzyk, J., Ghodosi, H., Dawson, E. (eds.) ACISP 2007. LNCS, vol. 4586, pp. 96–106. Springer, Heidelberg (2007). https://doi.org/10.1007/978-3-540-73458-1_8
8. Canetti, R., Fuller, B., Paneth, O., Reyzin, L., Smith, A.: Reusable fuzzy extractors for low-entropy distributions. In: Fischlin, M., Coron, J.-S. (eds.) EUROCRYPT 2016. LNCS, vol. 9665, pp. 117–146. Springer, Heidelberg (2016). https://doi.org/10.1007/978-3-662-49890-3_5
9. Castiglione, A., Choo, K.-K.R., Nappi, M., Narducci, F.: Biometrics in the cloud: challenges and research opportunities. IEEE Cloud Comput. **4**(4), 12–17 (2017)
10. Chen, R., Mu, Y., Yang, G., Susilo, W., Guo, F.: Strongly leakage-resilient authenticated key exchange. In: Sako, K. (ed.) CT-RSA 2016. LNCS, vol. 9610, pp. 19–36. Springer, Cham (2016). https://doi.org/10.1007/978-3-319-29485-8_2
11. Daugman, J.: How iris recognition works. In: The Essential Guide to Image Processing, pp. 715–739 (2009)
12. Dodis, Y., Kalai, Y.T., Lovett, S.: On cryptography with auxiliary input. In: STOC, pp. 621–630 (2009)
13. Dodis, Y., Kanukurthi, B., Katz, J., Reyzin, L., Smith, A.: Robust fuzzy extractors and authenticated key agreement from close secrets. IEEE Trans. Inf. Theory **58**(9), 6207–6222 (2012)

14. Dodis, Y., Ostrovsky, R., Reyzin, L., Smith, A.D.: Fuzzy extractors: how to generate strong keys from biometrics and other noisy data. SIAM J. Comput. **38**(1), 97–139 (2008)
15. Fan, C., Lin, Y.: Provably secure remote truly three-factor authentication scheme with privacy protection on biometrics. IEEE Trans. Inf. Forensics Secur. **4**(4), 933–945 (2009)
16. Huang, X., Xiang, Y., Bertino, E., Zhou, J., Xu, L.: Robust multi-factor authentication for fragile communications. IEEE Trans. Dependable Secur. Comput. **11**(6), 568–581 (2014)
17. Huang, X., Xiang, Y., Chonka, A., Zhou, J., Deng, R.H.: A generic framework for three-factor authentication: preserving security and privacy in distributed systems. IEEE Trans. Parallel Distrib. Syst. **22**(8), 1390–1397 (2011)
18. Huang, Y., Malka, L., Evans, D., Katz, J.: Efficient privacy-preserving biometric identification. In: NDSS (2011)
19. Jain, A.K., Prabhakar, S., Hong, L., Pankanti, S.: Fingercode: a filterbank for fingerprint representation and matching. In: 1999 IEEE Computer Society Conference on Computer Vision and Pattern Recognition, vol. 2, pp. 187–193 (1999)
20. Juels, A., Sudan, M.: A fuzzy vault scheme. Des. Codes Cryptogr. **38**(2), 237–257 (2006)
21. Juels, A., Wattenberg, M.: A fuzzy commitment scheme. In: ACM CCS, pp. 28–36 (1999)
22. Kanade, S.G., Petrovska-Delacrétaz, D., Dorizzi, B.: Enhancing Information Security and Privacy by Combining Biometrics with Cryptography. Synthesis Lectures on Information Security, Privacy, and Trust. Morgan & Claypool Publishers, San Rafael (2012)
23. Li, N., Guo, F., Mu, Y., Susilo, W., Nepal, S.: Fuzzy extractors for biometric identification. In: ICDCS, pp. 667–677 (2017)
24. Li, Y., Li, Y., Yan, Q., Kong, H., Deng, R.H.: Seeing your face is not enough: an inertial sensor-based vileness detection for face authentication. In: ACM CCS, pp. 1558–1569 (2015)
25. Micali, S., Reyzin, L.: Physically observable cryptography. In: Naor, M. (ed.) TCC 2004. LNCS, vol. 2951, pp. 278–296. Springer, Heidelberg (2004). https://doi.org/10.1007/978-3-540-24638-1_16
26. Naor, M., Segev, G.: Public-key cryptosystems resilient to key leakage. In: Halevi, S. (ed.) CRYPTO 2009. LNCS, vol. 5677, pp. 18–35. Springer, Heidelberg (2009). https://doi.org/10.1007/978-3-642-03356-8_2
27. Schoenmakers, B., Tuyls, P.: Efficient binary conversion for paillier encrypted values. In: Vaudenay, S. (ed.) EUROCRYPT 2006. LNCS, vol. 4004, pp. 522–537. Springer, Heidelberg (2006). https://doi.org/10.1007/11761679_31
28. Tang, Q., Bringer, J., Chabanne, H., Pointcheval, D.: A formal study of the privacy concerns in biometric-based remote authentication schemes. In: Chen, L., Mu, Y., Susilo, W. (eds.) ISPEC 2008. LNCS, vol. 4991, pp. 56–70. Springer, Heidelberg (2008). https://doi.org/10.1007/978-3-540-79104-1_5
29. Wang, Q., Hu, S., Ren, K., He, M., Du, M., Wang, Z.: CloudBI: practical privacy-preserving outsourcing of biometric identification in the cloud. In: Pernul, G., Ryan, P.Y.A., Weippl, E. (eds.) ESORICS 2015. LNCS, vol. 9327, pp. 186–205. Springer, Cham (2015). https://doi.org/10.1007/978-3-319-24177-7_10
30. Yang, G., Mu, Y., Susilo, W., Wong, D.S.: Leakage resilient authenticated key exchange secure in the auxiliary input model. In: Deng, R.H., Feng, T. (eds.) ISPEC 2013. LNCS, vol. 7863, pp. 204–217. Springer, Heidelberg (2013). https://doi.org/10.1007/978-3-642-38033-4_15

31. Yuen, T.H., Zhang, Y., Yiu, S.M., Liu, J.K.: Identity-based encryption with post-challenge auxiliary inputs for secure cloud applications and sensor networks. In: Kutyłowski, M., Vaidya, J. (eds.) ESORICS 2014. LNCS, vol. 8712, pp. 130–147. Springer, Cham (2014). https://doi.org/10.1007/978-3-319-11203-9_8
32. Zhang, L., Tan, S., Yang, J., Chen, Y.: Voicelive: a phoneme localization based liveness detection for voice authentication on smartphones. In: ACM CCS, pp. 1080–1091 (2016)
33. Zhao, W., Chellappa, R., Phillips, P.J., Rosenfeld, A.: Face recognition: a literature survey. ACM Comput. Surv. (CSUR) 35(4), 399–458 (2003)

Differentially Private High-Dimensional Data Publication via Markov Network

Fengqiong Wei, Wei Zhang$^{(\boxtimes)}$, Yunfang Chen, and Jingwen Zhao

School of Computer Science,
Nanjing University of Posts and Telecommunications, Nanjing, China
{1016041011,zhangw,chenyf,1017041019}@njupt.edu.cn

Abstract. Differentially private data publication has recently received considerable attention. However, it faces some challenges in differentially private high-dimensional data publication, such as the complex attribute relationships, the high computational complexity and data sparsity. Therefore, we propose *PrivMN*, a novel method to publish high-dimensional data with differential privacy guarantee. We first use the Markov model to represent the mutual relationships between attributes to solve the problem that the direction of relationship between variables cannot be determined in practical application. We then take advantage of approximate inference to calculate the joint distribution of high-dimensional data under differential privacy to figure out the computational and spatial complexity of accurate reasoning. Extensive experiments on real datasets demonstrate that our solution makes the published high-dimensional synthetic datasets more efficient under the guarantee of differential privacy.

Keywords: Differential privacy · High-dimensional data
Data publication · Markov network

1 Introduction

With the emergence of big data era, a large amount of user data is generated and accumulated, which becomes a new generation of resources to be urgently developed and utilized [1]. For instance, purchase records of online users is helpful for E-businesses to enhance the user experience and induce more consumption; patient information is helpful for doctors to improve the accuracy of diagnosis and level of medical services; population genetic database is helpful for scientists to predict disease and reduce the risk of illness. These data resources have such tremendous potential value. Therefore, how to make reasonable utilization is particularly important.

A vital issue of mining and using big data is privacy protection, which often involves the user's personal privacy leakage. If the data are shared directly or indirectly among the illegal person, it will make serious consequences [2]. Aiming at the problem of sharing and publishing private data, traditional solutions

© ICST Institute for Computer Sciences, Social Informatics and Telecommunications Engineering 2018
R. Beyah et al. (Eds.): SecureComm 2018, LNICST 254, pp. 133–148, 2018.
https://doi.org/10.1007/978-3-030-01701-9_8

widely use anonymization technologies [3]. However, these anonymization technologies exist two obvious defects, cannot be quantified and cannot resist background attacks. In 2006, Dwork proposed the concept of differential privacy [4], which is a model of strict mathematical foundation and good robustness for privacy protection by adding controllable noise. Furthermore, it can resist the type of attacks in case of an attacker with specific background knowledge, and control the privacy leakage risk within acceptable limits. Differential privacy has been widely recognized in the industry and it has become a practical standard for privacy protection.

Differential privacy was originally designed to deal with simple relational data. However, with the development of big data, many high-dimensional and heterogeneous data appeared in practical applications. In the process of dealing with high-dimensional data, the biggest problem is the curse of dimensionality, that is, as the number of dimensions increases, the complexity and cost of analyzing and processing multi-dimensional data increases exponentially. Thus, one of the problems of high-dimensional data publishing is the sparsity of high-dimensional data. In consequence, it cannot guarantee utility by differential privacy since original data were covered by noise. Another problem, which is more prominent in high-dimensional data differential privacy publishing, is that the relationship between high-dimensional data is rather complicated and the change of single record will have a wider range of impact on the entire data, which results in the increase of data sensitivity. Therefore, for releasing high-dimensional data under differential privacy, it is important to reduce the data dimension and simplify the relationship between attributes to make the sensitivity controlled within a certain range.

To deal with the problem of high-dimensional data representation, researchers in the field of the Probabilistic Graphical Model [5] provide a new idea. They take advantage of the graph structure to represent the hidden relationship between various types of data and map all kinds of problems in applications onto the problem of calculating the probabilistic distribution of certain variables in the probabilistic model. The probabilistic graphical model provides the possibility of concise representation, efficient inference and learning various types of probability models. Therefore, it has been widely applied in many fields such as data processing and mining.

In this paper, considering the characteristics of high-dimensional data, we present a probabilistic graphical model for high dimensional data modeling and simplify the complex relationships between data onto the mutual relationship between variables. Specifically, we use Markov network to represent the probabilistic distribution of multiple random variables, consequently reducing the high-dimensional data dimension effectively and improving data utility. In addition, the inference algorithm in the probabilistic graphical model can effectively reduce computational complexity. Our contribution of this paper are as follows:

1. We propose the Markov network model to represent relationships between the variables without specifying directions of dependencies. The design of the potential function in undirected graph model is not constrained by the

probability distribution and more flexible. Meanwhile, it also avoids the constraint of global acyclic in directed graph model.

2. We develop the propagation-based approximate inference algorithm to deal with the NP-hard problem of exact inference algorithm as its computational complexity and spatial complexity grows exponentially. We specifically infer the distribution by the confidence-update propagation algorithm and this method can be applied to any structure network.

The remainder of the paper is organized as follows. The related work is presented in Sect. 2. Then, we describe some preliminaries in Sect. 3. The details of PrivMN are proposed in Sect. 4, followed by an extensive experimental evaluation in Sect. 5. Finally, a conclusion is depicted in Sect. 6.

2 Related Work

At present, the main research of differentially private data publication is how to guarantee the publishing accuracy of query result with the privacy budget. There are two kinds of applications, interactive data publishing and non-interactive data publishing.

The main question of interactive data publishing is how to answer as many data queries as possible with a limited privacy budget. In the early stage, Roth et al. [6] improved the *Laplace mechanism* proposed by Dwork et al. This method provides more inquiries under the same privacy budget. Gupta et al. [7] proposed a universal iterative dataset generation framework, which supports more queries as a whole. In general, the algorithm of interactive publishing method is relatively complicated, and the unknown of subsequent queries makes it have many limitations on query quantity and application mode.

The main problem of the non-interactive data publishing is how to design an efficient publishing algorithm to make it not only satisfy the differential privacy, but also has more utility. There are two main non-interactive data publishing strategies. One is adding noise to the original data and then optimize the data and publish the optimized result. Dwork [8] is an early representative method, which combines with *Laplace mechanism* to publish an equal-width histogram under differential privacy guarantee. However, one of the problems of histogram releasing is the consistency of the range query results. Therefore, many researchers propose some techniques to improve the availability and accuracy of the published equal-width histograms. For example, the post-processing method proposed by Hay et al. [9] makes the result of the publication guarantee the consistency under the condition of differential privacy, which not only satisfies the query accuracy but also reduces the noise addition.

However, the privacy cost of the above releasing strategy is relatively high. Therefore, another strategy is generally adopted, that is, convert or compress the original data first and then add noise to the processed data. For instance, Xiao et al. [10] first propose a multi-dimensional histogram distribution method DPCube that effectively reduces the query error. The wavelet transform method proposed by Xiao et al. [11] performs wavelet transform on the data before adding noise, which improves the accuracy of counting query to a certain extent. Barak et al. [12] propose the method of Fourier transform contingency table, which achieves the non-redundant encoding of marginal frequency. Meanwhile, the addition of the noise in the Fourier domain will not undermine the consistency between the edge frequencies.

When it comes to dealing with the problem of differential privacy protection for high-dimensional data, a basic idea is to propose an effective variable selection method to reduce the dimension to a reasonable degree (dimensionality reduction) on the premise of losing less information and then process the low-dimensional data. For example, Qardaji et al. [13] evenly divide two-dimensional spatial data onto equal-width cells and then add noise to each cell. Chen et al. [14] use a classification tree to generalize the high-dimensional dataset and finally publish noise counts. The *PriView* method proposed by Qardaji et al. [15] uses the cover design method of combination principle to select views, which decomposes the high-dimensional data onto the low-dimensional views, and then adds the noises to form the low-dimensional noisy marginal table, and finally uses the maximum entropy optimization algorithm to reconstruct the k-attribute marginal table for data publishing. Due to the increasing perturbation errors and computation complexity, Xu et al. [16] propose *DPPro* that publishes high-dimensional data via random projection to maximize utility while guaranteeing privacy. Ren et al. [17] identify correlations and joint distributions among multiple attributes to reduce the dimensionality of crowdsourced data, which achieves both efficiency and effectiveness.

Some attempts on differentially private data publishing have been made in the field of the probabilistic graphical model. Since Pearl [18] and Lauritzen [19] first introduced the concept of the graphical model into the field of artificial intelligence and statistical learning in the late 1980s, the graphical model has been rapidly applied to many fields. Zhang et al. [20] propose the *PrivBayes* method that uses the Bayesian network of the digraph model to represent the relationship between data attributes and combine a series of low-dimensional noise conditional probability tables by the chain rule of the Bayesian network to form a joint distribution for data publishing. Based on *PrivBayes*, Su et al. [21] present *DP-SUBN*, which develops a non-overlapping covering design (NOCD) method for generating all 2-way marginals of a given set of attributes to improve the fitness of the Bayesian network and reduce the communication cost. In addition, Xiao et al. [22] propose another scheme, which mainly uses attribute dependence graph to form attribute clusters, then adds noise to form low-dimensional noise marginal table, and finally publishing by sampling.

Different from the above solutions, we focus on the mutual relationship between multiple attributes, as well as the computational complexity and spatial complexity. To solve these problems, *PrivMN* uses the method of high-dimensional contingency table data publication and provides an approximate distribution of the original dataset based on the inference theory of probabilistic graphical model.

3 Preliminaries

3.1 Differential Privacy

Basic Definition. For a finite domain Z, $z \in Z$ is the element in Z. The dataset D is consist of z sampled from Z, its sample size is n and the number of attributes is dimension d.

Let datasets D and D' have the same attribute structure. The difference between them is denoted as $D \Delta D'$ and $\mid D \Delta D' \mid$ indicates the number of records in $D \Delta D'$. If $\mid D \Delta D' \mid = 1$, D and D' are called adjacent datasets.

Definition 1. ϵ-*Differential privacy [23]. A randomized algorithm M satisfies ϵ-Differential privacy, if for any two neighboring databases D and D', and for any $o \subseteq Range(M)$, $Pr[M(D) \in o] \leq \exp(\epsilon) \cdot Pr[M(D') \in o]$. Where the probability $Pr[\cdot]$ is taken over M's randomness and is the risk of privacy leakage. The parameter ϵ is privacy protection budget.*

From Definition 1, we can see that the privacy budget ϵ is used to control algorithm M to obtain same output probability ratio of two neighboring datasets, which reflects the level of privacy protection in fact. The smaller the value of ϵ, the higher the level of privacy protection. When ϵ equals 0, the protection level reaches the highest. At this time, the algorithm will output two identical probability distribution results for any neighboring dataset, but these results will not have any available information for a user.

Global Sensitivity. Differentially private protection can be achieved by adding an appropriate amount of interference noise to the return values of query function. Too much noise will affect the availability of the output, while too little will not provide enough security. The size of the noise is generally controlled by global sensitivity.

Definition 2. *Sensitivity [4]. Let f be a function that maps a dataset into a fixed-size vector of real numbers (i.e. $D \rightarrow R^d$). For two any neighboring databases D and D', the sensitivity of f is defined as $GS_f = \max_{D,D'} \parallel f(D) - f(D') \parallel_p$. Where p denotes L_p norm used to measure Δf, and we usually use L_1 norm.*

Noisy Mechanism. In practice, we usually add noise to algorithms to achieve differential privacy. In this paper, we rely on two best known and widely used, namely *Laplace mechanism* [8] and *exponential mechanism* [24]. The *Laplace mechanism* is suitable for numerical datasets, while the *exponential mechanism* is suitable for non-numerical datasets.

Laplace Mechanism. Laplace mechanism realizes the differential privacy by adding random noises that obey Laplace distribution to perturb the exact query result.

Theorem 1. *For any function $f : D \rightarrow R^d$, the mechanism M, $M(D) = f(D) +$ Y, satisfies ϵ-Differential privacy, where $Y \sim Lap(\frac{\Delta f}{\epsilon})$ is i.i.d. Laplace variable with scale parameter $\frac{\Delta f}{\epsilon}$. The greater the sensitivity of algorithm M, the more amount of noise added.*

Exponential Mechanism. If the output is not numeric, we need to use availability function to evaluate the output. Let the output domain of query function is *Range*, and each value $r \in Range$ in the domain is an entity object. Under the *exponential mechanism*, the function $q(D, r) \rightarrow R$ is the availability function of the output value r, which is used to evaluate the quality of r.

Theorem 2. *Let the input of random M is dataset D, and output is an entity object $r \in Range$. $q(D, r)$ is availability function with its sensitivity, Δq. The mechanism M, $M(D, q) = \{r :| Pr[r \in Range] \propto \exp(\frac{\epsilon q(D,r)}{2\Delta q})\}$, satisfies ϵ-Differential privacy.*

3.2 Markov Network

Basic Conception. Markov Random Field (MRF) is also known as Markov Network. In general, the Markov Network is a complete joint probability distribution model for a group of random variables X which have Markov property [27], and *ISing Mode* is one of the earliest Markov Networks.

Definition 3. *Let $G = (V, E)$ be an undirected connection graph, where node $V_j \in V$ represents a random variable. If the node V_i and V_j in edge $(V_i, V_j) \in E$ satisfy the local Markov property:*

1. The probability of each possible distribution is greater than 0.
2. The conditional probability distribution of an arbitrary node is only related to the value of its adjacent node (Locality).

Then the network structure is called Markov Network, denoted as $\mathcal{H}$.

Conditional Independence. In the Markov network, there is a conclusion on the property of independence that if X_B 'splits' X_A and X_C, X_A and X_C are independent when X_B is given, and this property is also called Markov property.

Definition 4. *If a set of observed variables Z is given, there is no path between any two nodes $x \in X$ and $y \in Y$, then we call node set Z separates x and y in Markov network $\mathcal{H}$ and denoted as $sep_{\mathcal{H}}(X; Y \mid Z)$. The global independence associated with $\mathcal{H}$ is defined as: $I(\mathcal{H}) = \{X \perp Y \mid Z\} : sep_{\mathcal{H}}(X; Y \mid Z)$.*

Joint Probability Distribution

Definition 5. *According to Hammersley-Clifford Theorem [25, 26] and Local Markov Property, the joint probability distribution of Markov network is defined as: $p(x) = \frac{1}{z} \prod_i \psi_i(x_i)$. $\psi_i(x_i)$ is a non-negative real-valued function of x_i, which is usually called the potential function of a clique, and the variable x_i belongs to set X. Z is the normalization constant of partition function and its value is $Z = \sum_x \prod_i \psi_i(x_i)$.*

4   PrivMN Algorithm

4.1   PrivMN Overview

In this paper, we consider the following problem: Given a dataset D with d attributes, we want to generate a synthetic dataset that has approximate the joint distribution of original dataset D while satisfying differential privacy.

The method proposed in this paper includes the following four steps and the process of *PrivMN* is showed in Fig. 1:

1. Represent attributes relationship: we use a graphical model to represent the relationship between attributes and establish the Markov model.
2. Approximate inference: we infer approximately on the model based on the method of cluster graph confidence-propagation and obtain a series of low-dimensional marginal tables.
3. Generate noisy marginal: we add noise to the low-dimensional marginal table by *exponential mechanism* to form noisy marginal table.
4. Publishing synthetic datasets: we combine the noisy marginal tables and the Markov model to generate a synthetic dataset.

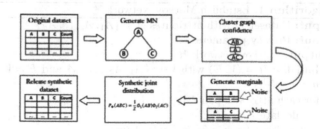

Fig. 1. The detail steps of *PrivMN*

4.2   Represent Attributes Relationship

As mentioned before, we use Markov network to represent the relationship between attributes. Firstly, we need to measure the relationship between attributes, there are many kinds of measures, such as chi-square test, mean-square contingency, Cramer's V coefficient, mutual Information and so on. In this paper, we choose mutual information to measure the correlation between two attributes. One reason is that mutual information is different from other correlation coefficients, that it is not limited to real-valued random variables and can express the degree of similarity generally. The other is not only for its small sensitivity but also for its capability of seizing the linear and non-linear correlations.

Given two attributes A_k and A_l, the mutual information $I(A_k, A_l)$ is defined as:

$$I(A_k, A_l) = \sum_{i=1}^{|\Omega_k|} \sum_{j=1}^{|\Omega_l|} p_{ij} \log \frac{p_{ij}}{p_i.p._j} \tag{1}$$

where p_{ij} is the joint distribution of A_k and A_l. $p._j = \sum_j p_{ij}$ and $p._j = \sum_i p_{ij}$ is marginal distribution.

In this paper, we consider that A_k and A_l are independent if $I(A_k, A_l) \leq \theta_{kl}$ for some small threshold $\theta_{kl} > 0$. We choose Cramer's V coefficient as the threshold and Cramer's V coefficient is a method to calculate the correlation degree of between attributes in contingency table which attribute is greater than 2×2.

Cramer's V coefficient is calculated as follows:

$$\theta_{kl} = \sqrt{\frac{\chi^2}{n \min[(| \Omega_k | -1)(| \Omega_l | -1)]}} \tag{2}$$

where n is the size of a sample formed by two attributes, the domain of an attribute A_i is represented by Ω_i and its size is $| \Omega_i |$. χ^2 is the value of chi-square.

We present the process of establishing Markov network in Algorithm 1:

Algorithm 1. Establish Markov Network

Input: Dataset D with attributes $A = \{A_1, A_2, \ldots A_d\}$
Input: Privacy parameter ϵ_1
Output: Markov network $\mathcal{H}$
1: Initialize $H = (V, E)$ with $V = \{A_1, A_2, \ldots A_d\}$ and $E = \emptyset$;
2: $\eta = Lap(\frac{1}{\epsilon_1})$;
3: for each attribute pair (A_k, A_l) do
4:    calculate $I(A_k, A_l)$;
5:    if $I(A_k, A_l) + \eta \geq \theta_{kl} + Lap(\frac{1}{\epsilon_1})$ then
6:       Add edge (A_k, A_l) into $\mathcal{H}$;
7: return $\mathcal{H}$;

4.3 Approximate Inference

We have obtained the Markov network by Algorithm 1 which reveals attribute relations obviously. Then, we need to infer the model and the purpose of the inference is to achieve the marginal distribution and the conditional distribution of the given model. However, it is still complicated to obtain the required marginal distribution by inferring directly on the Markov network. Therefore, we need further clustering on the Markov network to reduce the computational complexity.

The cluster graph that we constructed in this step is a data structure, which provides a flowchart of the factor processing. Each node in the cluster graph is a cluster associated with a subset of the variables. The graph also contains undirected edges that connect non-empty intersection sets in the domain. Each edge between a pair of clusters C_i and C_j is relevant to a cut set $S_{i,j}$ that $S_{i,j} \subseteq C_i \cap C_j$. In addition, we make use of a simple structure called Bethe clustering graph, which can transform a general clustering graph into a clustering graph satisfying the confidence-propagation algorithm.

We obtain a series of clusters C_i and cut sets $S_{i,j}$ after clustering Markov network that satisfy the family-preserving of cluster graph: Each factor $\phi \in \Phi$ is related to a cluster graph C_i, expressed as $\alpha(\phi)$, and satisfy $Scope[\phi] \subseteq C_i$.

After obtaining the clustering graph, we ratiocinate in the clustering graph by the confidence-propagation algorithm in Algorithm 2. Confidence-propagation Algorithm of clustering Graph is an approximate calculation and iterative algorithm based on the undirected graph model. It updates the current probability distribution of the entire clustering graph by exchanging information between the nodes in the clustering graph. Moreover, it can solve probabilistic inference problems of the probabilistic graphical model and spread all information on parallel.

After several iterations, the confidence of all nodes is no longer changed. At this time, the clustering graph reaches the convergence state. Moreover, the marginal distribution of each cluster is the optimal solution. This cluster graph is called a cluster graph calibrated, that is, for each edge $(i - j)$ between connected clusters C_i and C_j in the cluster graph, there is

$$\mu_{i,j}(S_{i,j}) = \sum_{C_i - S_{i,j}} \beta_i(C_i) = \sum_{C_j - S_{i,j}} \beta_j(C_j) \tag{3}$$

Therefore, the confidence set $Q = \{\beta_i : i \in vertex\ set\} \cup \{\mu_{i,j} : i - j \in edge\ set\}$ is a distribution similar to datasets. Where β_i denotes the confidence on C_i and $\mu_{i,j}$ represents the confidence on $S_{i,j}$.

We present the process of approximate inference in Algorithm 2:

Algorithm 2. Approximate Inference

Input: Markov network $\mathcal{H}$

Input: Factor set Φ

Output: Confidence set Q

1: Bethe cluster graph $\mathcal{U} \longleftarrow$ BehteGraphCreateAlgorithm($\mathcal{H}$);

2: confidence set $Q \longleftarrow$ CGraph-SP-Calibrate($\mathcal{U}, \Phi$);

3: return Q;

4.4 Generate Noisy Marginal

In this section, we use the *Laplace mechanism* to add noise to the marginal tables of each cluster to generate the noisy marginal tables and consequently realize the differential privacy protection for the attributes in the cluster.

Let the number of clusters be m. For each clusters marginal table, we add Laplace noise $Lap(\frac{m}{\epsilon_2})$ to each entry's count. Therefore, the privacy budget of a single cluster for privacy protection is $\frac{\epsilon_2}{m}$. According to the combinatorial property of the differential privacy protection algorithm, the differential privacy protection for different clusters in the same dataset provides the sum of all budgets. Therefore, the noisy marginal tables satisfy ϵ_2-differential privacy.

In order to reduce the error caused by adding noise and ensure the availability of noise-added data, we will post-process the noisy marginal tables. We cite the post-processing technique in [22] to ensure consistency even if the noisy marginal tables are of different sizes and attributes are not binary.

Let $A = C_1 \cap C_2 \cap \cdots C_m \neq \emptyset$, the public attribute of cluster group. We use T_{c_i} to denote C_i's noisy marginal table, $T_{c_i}[A]$ to denote A's marginal constructed from C_i and $T_{c_i}[A] \equiv T_{c_j}[A]$ to denote that two marginal tables are identical. We want to ensure $T_{c_i}[A] \equiv \cdots \equiv T_{c_m}[A]$, that is, all noisy marginal tables of an attribute are coincident.

We achieve this goal in two steps. Where a is a possible value in As domain and $T_A(a)$ is the count of a in As noisy marginal table.

1. Generate the approximate value of $T_A(a)$. The best estimate of $T_A(a)$ is the minimum noise variance. Therefore, we use inverse-variance weighting to obtain the variance of the weighted average as follows:

$$T_A(a) = \frac{\sum_{i=1}^{m} \frac{T_{c_i}(a)}{\sigma_i^2}}{\sum_i \frac{1}{\sigma_i^2}} \tag{4}$$

where $\sigma_i^2 = \prod_{A_j \in (c_i \setminus A)} |\Omega_j|$ is proportional to the variance of $T_{c_i}[A](a)$.

2. Update all T_{c_i}s to be consistent with T_A:

$$T_{c_i}(e) \leftarrow T_{c_i}(e) + \frac{T_A(a) - T_{c_i}(a)}{\prod_{A_j \in (c_i \setminus A)} |\Omega_j|} \tag{5}$$

where e is the a after the update.

To make all marginal tables consistent, we need to perform a series of mutual consistency steps.

In addition, in order to reduce the bias caused by rounding the negative noisy to 0 and assuring the accuracy, we turn negative counts into 0 while decreasing the counts for its neighbors to maintain overall count unchanged. Specifically, we choose a threshold θ that close to 0. The sum above the threshold is n and the sum below the threshold is k. For each count c above the threshold, we subtract $|k| * \frac{c}{n}$ as the last value of it, and the value below the threshold becomes 0.

4.5   Publishing Synthetic Datasets

Combining with the previously obtained clustering graph and the noisy marginal tables, we can calculate the joint distribution of attributes. Based on the joint probability calculation formula in Markov networks, the confidence set, and the noisy marginal tables, we can get the non-normalized distribution as follows:

$$\mathcal{P}_\Phi(\mathcal{H}) = \frac{\prod \beta_i(C_i)}{\prod \mu_{i,j}(S_{i,j})} \tag{6}$$

The normalization constant is usually obtained by the sum of all states, that is, $Z = \frac{\sum_{C_i} \prod \beta_i(C_i)}{\sum_{S_{i,j}} \prod \mu_{i,j}(S_{i,j})}$. Therefore, the joint distribution is calculated as follows:

$$P_\Phi(\mathcal{H}) = \frac{1}{Z} \mathcal{P}_\Phi(\mathcal{H}) = \frac{1}{Z} \frac{\prod \beta_i(C_i)}{\prod \mu_{i,j}(S_{i,j})} \tag{7}$$

However, directly sampling a synthetic dataset from the joint distribution is computationally prohibitive. Therefore, we use the clustering graph and the noisy marginal tables to generate a synthetic dataset. Specifically, the steps are as follows: 1. Randomly select a cluster in the cluster graph and sample its attributes from its noisy marginal distribution. 2. Continuously sample other attributes in the cliques adjacent to the cliques, that is, they share a common separator, and repeat the above operation. 3. Terminate this process until all the attributes have been sampled.

After the sampling, we calculate the joint distribution by using the joint probability calculation formula given earlier. Thus, we obtain the required joint distribution, which satisfies the differential privacy protection of the complete dataset.

In the four steps of *PrivMN*, only the first and third steps require access to the original dataset, so we divide the total privacy budget ϵ into two portions with ϵ_1 being used for the first step and ϵ_2 for the third step by the composition property [8,28]. Therefore, the first and third steps are ϵ_1- and ϵ_2-differential privacy respectively, and *PrivMN* satisfies -differential privacy as a whole, where $\epsilon = \epsilon_1 + \epsilon_2$.

5   Evaluation

We make use of three standard real datasets (both binary and non-binary) in our experiments. For binary datasets, we choose **Retail** referred from [22]. **Retail** is a retail market basket dataset, where each record consists of the distinct items purchased in a shopping visit. We preprocess **Retail** to include 50 binary attributes and its domain size is 2^{50}. For non-binary datasets, we use the same datasets used in [20]. **Adult** contains census data from 1994 US census. There are 15 non-binary attributes in it and its domain size is about 2^{52}. **TPC-E** contains information of 'Trade', 'Security', 'Security status' and 'Trade type' tables in the **TPC-E** benchmark. It consists of 24 non-binary attributes and its domain size is about 2^{77}.

We evaluate the *PrivMN* in two aspects: One is the construction of marginal table, which used to measure the accuracy of methods. The other is to train multiple SVM classifiers on the same dataset to predict attributes. We first generate synthetic datasets and then use these datasets to build SVM classifiers. The correct rate or error rate is the judgment of all data, which is the overall evaluation of the classifier and suitable for the evaluation of the experiment. Therefore, we use the error rate to measure the performance of the classifier and the property of the algorithm.

Since *PriView* [15] only works for binary datasets and cannot generate synthetic datasets for SVM classification, for binary datasets we only report the results on marginal tables. Due to L_2 error and Jensen-Shannon divergence are similar, we use the same evaluation scheme used in *PriView*, that is, we plot the average L_2 error where privacy budget $\epsilon \in \{0.1, 1.0\}$ and generate 200 random k-way marginal tables for each $k \in \{4, 6, 8\}$.

For non-binary datasets, when k is relatively large, a k-way marginal table is normally very sparse and the evaluation scheme used in binary datasets may be significantly biased. Therefore, we choose to follow the same methodology used in *PrivBayes* [20]. We generate all 2-way and 3-way marginal tables and perform the average total variation distance between the original datasets and the noisy datasets. In addition, we use the same method used in *PrivBayes* to test the classification results with SVM classifiers. We report the results on Adult, which is the most widely used benchmark dataset for SVM classification analysis. We train SVM classifiers on Adult to predict where an individual (1) is a male, (2) holds a post-secondary degree, (3) has salary $> 50k$ per year, and (4) has never married. We evaluate each classification task with privacy budget $\epsilon \in \{0.2, 0.5, 0.8, 1.0\}$. Each task uses 80% of the datasets as the training set and the remaining 20% for prediction. We employ the misclassification rate as the performance metric.

5.1   Contrast on Binary Datasets

In the first part of experiments, we compare the accuracy of four algorithms on the binary dataset by assigning different privacy budgets. The results are presented in Fig. 2.

It can be seen that our method, *PrivMN*, is far superior to *PrivBayes* in most cases and has some advantages over *PriView*. In Fig. 2(a), *PriViews* L_2 error is higher than *PrivBayes* when $k = 8$. It means that *PriView* is not stable and there is a substantial decrease in the performance of the property with the amount of attributes increase. Although *PrivMN* is similar to *JTree*, the error of *PrivMN* is smaller than *JTree*. Our method still maintains certain advantages as attributes increase. In general, the advantage of *PrivMN* is more observable when $\epsilon = 0.1$, that is, when ϵ is small, it is still the overall optimal without excessive volatility. Therefore, we consider the synthetic dataset generated by

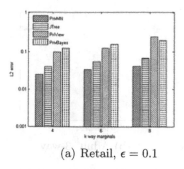
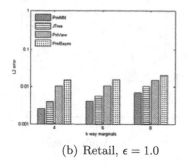

(a) Retail, $\epsilon = 0.1$ (b) Retail, $\epsilon = 1.0$

Fig. 2. L_2 error of k-way marginals on binary datasets

PrivMN can meet different analysis needs. In addition, *PrivMN* can be applied to non-binary datasets, which is of great significance for practical applications.

5.2   Contrast on Non-binary Datasets

k-**Way Marginal Tables.** In the second part of the experiment, we compare the average total variation distance of three algorithms for varying privacy budgets on non-binary datasets and present the results in Fig. 3.

Since *PriView* cannot apply to non-binary datasets, we only compare the remaining three methods. It can be seen from the figure that the experimental results of *PrivMN* are far superior to *PrivBayes*. Under the condition of different datasets and different k-way marginal tables, the error of *JTree* is large when $\epsilon = 0.2$, and the overall change range is wide, especially in Fig. 3(c), (d). Although *PrivMN* makes more errors than *JTree* when $\epsilon = 0.5$ in Fig. 3(a), (b), it is relatively flat as a whole. With the gradual increase of the privacy budget, the added noise is less, and the average total variation distance is gradually reducing. Therefore, *PrivMN* is suitable for extensive datasets and is utility for many real-world applications.

SVM Classification. In the last part of experiments, we compare the misclassification rate to measure the performance of *PrivMN*, *JTree*, and *PrivBayes* on non-binary datasets. We report the results on Adult with different ϵ values in Fig. 4.

Non-Private is the misclassification rate of the original dataset, which is also the best experimental result we can achieve. In Fig. 4, *PrivMN* is far superior to *PrivBayes* in all cases. Compared with *JTree*, *PrivMN* decreases more slowly with different privacy budget, and the overall performance is better. In particular, *PrivMN* performs even better in Fig. 4(a), (b), (c). When $\epsilon = 0.2$ in Fig. 4(d), *PrivMN* has a slight fluctuation, but still within the acceptable range while *JTree* gets an obvious error. Although the property of the dataset generated by *PrivMN* is lower than that of the original dataset, it can satisfy the requirement of differential privacy and is superior to general methods. Therefore,

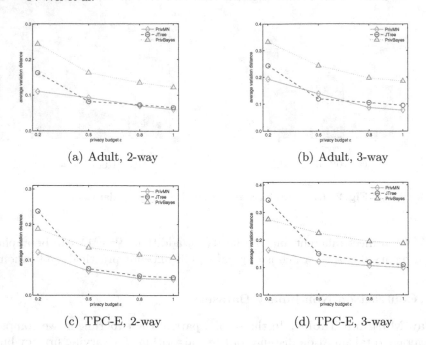

Fig. 3. Total variation distance of k-way marginal tables on non-binary datasets

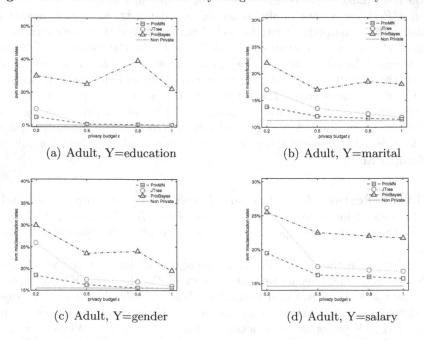

Fig. 4. SVM misclassification rates on non-binary datasets

PrivMN provides a generic data publishing solutions and it has certain practical significance.

6 Conclusion

Differentially private high-dimensional data publication is one of most challenging research issues and an important problem to be solved urgently. In this paper, we propose to use the Markov network model to represent the mutual relationships between attributes to solve the problem that the direction of relationship between variables cannot be determined in practical application. Morcover, we take advantage of approximate inference to calculate the joint distribution of high-dimensional data under differential privacy to figure out the computational and spatial complexity of accurate reasoning. Experiments on several real standard datasets demonstrate that *PrivMN* is significant in practice.

Acknowledgments. The authors would like to express their thanks to the anonymous reviewers for their constructive comments and suggestions. This work was supported by the National Natural Science Foundation of China under grants 61272422, 61672297.

References

1. The Economist: The worlds most valuable resource is no longer oil, but data, May 2017
2. Yu, S.: Big privacy: challenges and opportunities of privacy study in the age of big data. IEEE Access **2017**(4), 2751–2763 (2017)
3. Sweeney, L.: k-anonymity: a model for protecting privacy. Int. J. Uncertain. Fuzziness Knowl.-Based Syst. **10**(5), 557–570 (2002)
4. Dwork, C.: Differential privacy. In: Bugliesi, M., Preneel, B., Sassone, V., Wegener, I. (eds.) ICALP 2006. LNCS, vol. 4052, pp. 1–12. Springer, Heidelberg (2006). https://doi.org/10.1007/11787006_1
5. Koller, D., Friedman, N.: Probabilistic Graphical Models: Principles and Techniques - Adaptive Computation and Machine Learning. MIT Press, Cambridge (2009)
6. Roth, A., Roughgarden, T.: Interactive privacy via the median mechanism. In: Proceedings of the 42nd ACM Symposium on Theory of Computing, Cambridge, USA, pp. 765–774 (2010)
7. Gupta, A., Ligett, K., McSherry, F., et al.: Differentially private approximation algorithms (2009)
8. Dwork, C., McSherry, F., Nissim, K., Smith, A.: Calibrating noise to sensitivity in private data analysis. In: Halevi, S., Rabin, T. (eds.) TCC 2006. LNCS, vol. 3876, pp. 265–284. Springer, Heidelberg (2006). https://doi.org/10.1007/11681878_14
9. Hay, M., Rastogi, V., Miklau, G., et al.: Boosting the accuracy of differentially private histograms through consistency. Proc. VLDB Endow. **3**(1–2), 1021–1032 (2010)
10. Xiao, Y., Gardner, J., Xiong, L.: DPCube: releasing differentially private data cubes for health information. In: IEEE International Conference on Data Engineering, pp. 1305–1308. IEEE Computer Society (2012)

11. Xiao, X., Wang, G., Gehrke, J.: Differential privacy via wavelet transforms. IEEE Trans. Knowl. Data Eng. **23**(8), 1200–1214 (2011)
12. Barak, B., Chaudhuri, K., Dwork, C., et al.: Privacy, accuracy, and consistency too: a holistic solution to contingency table release. In: Proceedings of the 26th ACM SIGMOD-SIGACT-SIGART Symposium on Principles of Database Systems, Beijing, China, pp. 273–282 (2007)
13. Qardaji, W., Yang, W., Li, N.: Differentially private grids for geospatial data. In: IEEE International Conference on Data Engineering, pp. 757–768. IEEE Computer Society (2013)
14. Chen, R., Mohammed, N., Fung, B.C.M., Desai, B.C., Xiong, L.: Publishing set-valued data via differential privacy. PVLDB **4**(11), 1087–1098 (2011)
15. Qardaji, W., Yang, W., Li, N.: Priview: practical differentially private release of marginal contingency tables. In: SIGMOD (2014)
16. Xu, C., Ren, J., Zhang, Y., et al.: DPPro: differentially private high-dimensional data release via random projection. IEEE Trans. Inf. Forensics & Secur. **12**(12), 3081–3093 (2017)
17. Ren, X., Yu, C.M., Yu, W., et al.: LoPub: high-dimensional crowdsourced data publication with local differential privacy. IEEE Trans. Inf. Forensics & Secur. **13**(9), 2151–2166 (2016)
18. Pearl, J.: Probabilistic Reasoning in Intelligent Systems: Networks of Plausble Inference. Morgan Kaufmann Publishers, Burlington (1988)
19. Lauritzen, S.L., Spiegelhalter, D.J.: Local computations with probabilities on graphical structures and their application to expert systems. J. R. Stat. Soc. Ser. B (Methodol.) **50**(2), 157–224 (1988)
20. Zhang, J., Cormode, G., Procopiuc, C.M., Srivastava, D., Xiao, X.: Privbayes: private data release via Bayesian networks. In: SIGMOD (2014)
21. Su, S., Tang, P., Cheng, X., et al.: Differentially private multi-party high-dimensional data publishing. In: IEEE International Conference on Data Engineering, pp. 205–216. IEEE (2016)
22. Chen, R., Xiao, Q., Zhang, Y., et al.: Differentially private high-dimensional data publication via sampling-based inference. In: ACM SIGKDD International Conference on Knowledge Discovery and Data Mining. ACM (2015)
23. Dwork, C.: A firm foundation for private data analysis. Commun. ACM **54**(1), 86–95 (2011)
24. Mcsherry, F., Talwar, K.: Mechanism design via differential privacy. In: Proceedings of the 48th Annual IEEE Symposium on Foundations of Computer Science, Providence, Rhode Island, USA, pp. 94–103 (2007)
25. Hammersley, J.M., Clifford, P.: Markov fields on finite graphs and lattices (1971)
26. Cliord, P.: Markov random fields in statistics. Disord. Phys. Syst. A **14**(1), 128–135 (1990)
27. Zhang, J., Xiao, X., Xie, X.: PrivTree: a differentially private algorithm for hierarchical decompositions. In: International Conference on Management of Data, pp. 155–170. ACM (2016)
28. Li, D., Zhang, W., Chen, Y.: Differentially private network data release via stochastic kronecker graph. In: Cellary, W., Mokbel, M.F., Wang, J., Wang, H., Zhou, R., Zhang, Y. (eds.) WISE 2016. LNCS, vol. 10042, pp. 290–297. Springer, Cham (2016). https://doi.org/10.1007/978-3-319-48743-4_23

Mobile Security

Automated Identification of Sensitive Data via Flexible User Requirements

Ziqi Yang[✉] and Zhenkai Liang

National University of Singapore, Singapore, Singapore
{yangziqi,liangzk}@comp.nus.edu.sg

Abstract. Protecting sensitive data in web and mobile applications requires identifying sensitive data, which typically needs intensive manual efforts. In addition, deciding sensitive data subjects to users' requirements and the application context. Existing research efforts on identifying sensitive data from its descriptive texts focus on keyword/phrase searching. These approaches can have high false positives/negatives as they do not consider the semantics of the descriptions. In this paper, we propose S3, an automated approach to identify sensitive data based on user requirements. It considers semantic, syntactic and lexical information comprehensively, aiming to identify sensitive data by the semantics of its descriptive texts. We introduce the notion *concept space* to represent the user's notion of privacy, by which our approach can support flexible user requirements in defining sensitive data. Our approach is able to learn users' preferences from readable concepts initially provided by users, and automatically identify related sensitive data. We evaluate our approach on over 18,000 top popular applications from Google Play Store. S3 achieves an average precision of 89.2%, and average recall 95.8% in identifying sensitive data.

1 Introduction

Web and mobile applications are becoming an essential part of our daily life, including online banking, social network service, health care, etc. These online services handle users' sensitive data, such as passwords, health records, and financial information. Protecting users' sensitive data on web and mobile platforms is getting more and more important. Recent incidents [5,33] have leaked information of hundreds of millions of users.

Separating and protecting user data is a basic principle of computer security. User data protection requires to distinguish sensitive data and insensitive data, and provide stronger but more expensive mechanisms to ensure sensitive data security against a powerful adversary. There are many existing research efforts [3,7,17,18,27,36,37] on protecting sensitive data both on web and mobile applications. Researchers develop solutions that utilize other secure devices (including mobile phones) [4,23,28,29] to protect the security of sensitive data in the web platform from affected. Other solutions [7,15,17,27] perform taint analysis based on user-specified sensitive data sources in the mobile platforms.

© ICST Institute for Computer Sciences, Social Informatics and Telecommunications Engineering 2018
R. Beyah et al. (Eds.): SecureComm 2018, LNICST 254, pp. 151–171, 2018.
https://doi.org/10.1007/978-3-030-01701-9_9

The solutions to protect sensitive data often need developers/users to identify sensitive data, which is a challenging task. Deciding whether a piece of data is sensitive subjects to users' preference and the application context. User's privacy preference may change with the application scenario. Identifying sensitive data typically needs intensive manual efforts [21], which prevents large-scale analysis of sensitive data. Therefore, we need a way that can automatically identify sensitive data based on users' requirements.

Sensitive data is hardly distinguishable from insensitive data in the programming representations of web and mobile applications. For example, the `<span>` element displaying a user's bank balance is same as the `<span>` element displaying the website title in terms of a machine. However, it's easy for the user to know that her bank balance is more sensitive than the website title, because she understands the meaning of the data or its surrounding descriptive text. Therefore, instead of analyzing source code of applications, it is more accurate and efficient to identify sensitive data from the user interface (UI), and understand the semantic meaning of data or its surrounding descriptive text.

Several solutions have been proposed to identify sensitive data using the descriptive text in mobile applications. Supor [10] identifies sensitive input data of Android applications by keyword based searching on descriptive texts. UIPicker [21] utilizes SVM (Support Vector Machine) to learn sensitive descriptive texts with sensitive keywords as features. AutoCog [26] identifies the real permissions an Android application requires from its descriptions on Google Play, by analyzing the semantic meaning of noun phrases, verb phrases and possessives. Whyper [24] considers both actions and noun phrases to further increase the accuracy. However, all the existing approaches are based on only key word/phrase/counterpart searching, with no complete semantic information considered. For instance, all of them incorrectly classify the sentence *"Facebook will not save your password"* as sensitive because of the detection of a sensitive phrase "save your password", though it is only a normal claim message. Moreover, none of the prior work takes into account the flexible user requirements.

In this paper, we propose a more advanced technique, S3[1], to identify sensitive data. S3 aims to understand users' preferences by extracting the semantic concepts from a set of user-provided texts, and identifies unseen sensitive data with a learning-based approach. Instead of outputting a Boolean result in prior work, S3 produces a probability of a text being sensitive to make the measurement controllable by setting a threshold in different strictness levels. Besides, S3 classifies sensitive data as multiple categories such as credential data, profile data and financial data, in a more fine-grained way, so that users and developers are able to choose different categories of sensitive data on demand for further protection.

Contributions.

– To the best of our knowledge, S3 is the first automated approach to precisely identify sensitive data by analyzing its semantic meaning on a large scale. S3

---

[1] S3 stands for *semantics*, *syntax*, and *sentiment*.

reduces much manual effort of identifying sensitive data for further protection and research on it.

- S3 supports flexible user requirements in defining sensitive data. It enables users to define sensitive data on demand by providing initial concepts. Then S3 is able to automatically identify unseen sensitive data by learning from the concepts.
- We conduct a series of evaluation, and compare S3 with existing approaches. Evaluation results show that S3 is able to identify sensitive data with high precision and recall, and can correctly identify instances which are not handled in existing approaches.

2   Overview

In this section, we introduce our motivation, and analyze the challenges faced by sensitive data identification. We then introduce techniques used in natural language processing (NLP) as a background. At last, we give an overview of our solution.

2.1   Motivation

Sensitive data (e.g., login input box, shopping history, and profile data) in a UI widget is usually surrounded or embedded with a descriptive text [10,21], indicating its functionality. Our approach leverages such descriptive texts to measure its sensitiveness, following the same setting in [21]. The descriptive texts in mobile applications are usually short, and well-spelled, which makes S3 quite effective in identifying sensitive data. Users can define sensitive data categories on demand, by providing concept texts for S3 to learn from. For example, one may use "password", "pin code", etc., to define credential data.

2.2   Challenges in Sensitive Data Identification.

Importance of Semantics. The data sensitiveness is highly dependent on its semantic meaning. For instance, the sentence *"Facebook will not save your password."* does not indicate sensitive data, because it is just a declaration text showing Facebook will not violate users' privacy. Prior work [10,21,24,26] incorrectly identifies this text as sensitive because of the detection of a key phrase "save your password". Consider two sentences, *"Register account"* and *"Account registered"*. The former one describes a sensitive operation *requesting* information, and the latter one is a hint text *confirming* that the account has already been registered. Existing work cannot distinguish the sensitiveness of the two sentences, because they are composed of same sensitive keywords "register" and "account". Another representative example is *"Log in"* and *"Logged in"*. The first one describes a sensitive operation but the second one is a normal message indicating the user has already logged in. Both of them have the same words, regardless of their forms, but their sensitiveness are significantly different, because of the different part of speech of "log". Therefore, to give a more accurate measurement of the sensitiveness, we have to learn its semantic meaning.

Flexible User Requirements. Sensitive data are subjective to users' preference and application context. For instance, a banking application is most likely to handle users' sensitive financial data, while a social network application contains mostly sensitive profile data instead. However, existing work treats all of them equally, which is not reasonable to users. It is preferable to identify sensitive data in a more flexible way, by allowing users to customize the classification of sensitive data they are really cared about.

2.3 NLP Background

The semantic meaning of texts is critical for correctly identifying sensitive data. To understand the semantics of a text, we need NLP techniques to process it. With advance of existing NLP techniques, the grammatical structure of a natural language sentence can be parsed accurately. We next briefly introduce the key NLP techniques used in our work.

Parts Of Speech (POS) Tagging [12,32]. It is also called *"word tagging"*, *"grammatical tagging"* and *"word-category disambiguation"*. POS tagging is able to identify the part of speech (such as nouns and verbs) a particular word in a sentence belongs to. Current state-of-the-art approaches have been shown to achieve 97% [19] accuracy in classifying POS tags for well-written news articles.

Named Entity Recognition [8]. It is also known as *"entity identification"* and *"entity extraction"*, and works as a subtask of information extraction. These techniques are able to classify words in a sentence into predefined categories such as names, quantities, and expressions of time.

Phrase and Clause Parsing. It is also known as *"chunking"*. This technique divides a sentence into a constituent set of words (or phrases) that logically belong together (such as a Noun Phrase and Verb Phrase) to analyze the syntax of the sentence. Current state-of-the-art approaches can achieve around 90% [19] accuracy in classifying phrases and clauses over well-written news articles.

Syntactic Parsing [11]. It generates a parse tree of a sentence showing the hierarchical view of the syntax structure for the sentence. By traversing the parse tree, we are able to identify target phrases (such as noun phrases and verb phrases) and POS tags.

2.4 Approach Overview

The overall architecture of S3 is illustrated in Fig. 1. S3 takes a raw text as input. *Preprocessor* processes this text to generate an intermediate structure.

Table 1. Members of the intermediate structure.

Item	Description
Noun phrase list	Reflect the content of the data it describes
Verb phrase list	Reflect the operation it guides users to perform
Modifiers	Adjectives of nouns in noun phrases
Lemma list	Mapping of original word to its lemma form
POS tag list	Mapping of a word to its pos tag
Parse tree	Hierarchical view of the syntax structure for the sentence

The intermediate structure is a data structure holding all the required information for further analysis. It contains the syntax information and other information such as noun phrases, verb phrases, POS tags, etc. Then S3 analyzes its topic by extracting its semantic meaning, and produces a candidate sensitive category. Finally, S3 decides its sensitiveness by analyzing its syntax, POS, and sentiment information.

Each sensitive category is represented as a set of vectors, called *concept space* in the following, constructed from concept words/phrases provided by users. The knowledge base is a large corpus of texts, from which S3 is able to identify the semantic relation of unseen texts and the concept space, and thus determines its topic.

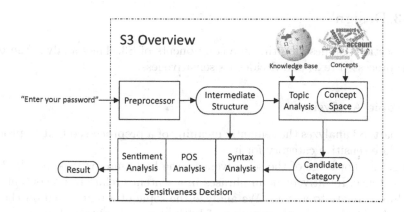

Fig. 1. Overall architecture of S3.

Preprocessing Inputs. The NLP techniques we have discussed above are used as a preprocessor in S3 to accept the raw natural-language sentences as input and produces an intermediate structure for further analysis. It uses standard NLP techniques to perform text splitting, stopword removal, phrase collection, modifier extraction, lemma recovery, part of speech tagging, and syntactic parsing. Figure 2 gives an illustrating example of partial preprocessing result. The sentence node is labeled as S. It is the child of the root node. The interior nodes of the tree are labeled by non-terminal tags (e.g., verb phrases VP and noun phrases NP). The leaf nodes are labeled by terminal tags (e.g., pronouns $PRP\$$ and nouns NN). In summary, Table 1 lists the members of the intermediate structure of a text after preprocessing.

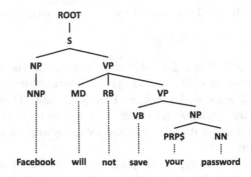

Fig. 2. Preprocessing of a sample sentence.

3   S3 Design

In this section, we describe the core components of S3. They analyze the topic of a preprocessed text, and decides its sensitiveness.

3.1   Topic Analysis

In this part, S3 analyzes the semantic meaning of a preprocessed text to produce a candidate sensitive category for it.

To get a knowledge of the sensitiveness, the first thing is to know the topic of the sentence. Intuitively, noun phrases in a sentence relate to its content, and verb phrases relate to actions. We analyze the topic of a text based on the two phrases. In S3, the semantic meaning of both phrases is obtained by measuring the semantic distance of the target phrase and each sensitive category in a vector space, where each category has its own cluster, referred to as *concept space*. The closest sensitive category is chosen to classify its sensitiveness.

Concept Space. We use vector representations of words [20] to create a domain of sensitive category to represent *concept space* in our approach. The intuition is to cluster closely related sensitive words/phrases in the vector space, so that we are able to classify unseen texts based on the clusters. Such words and phrases in the clusters are called *concepts*, provided by users or developers. For example, one may create a category "Credentials" by feeding concepts of "username", "password" and "pin code". S3 then constructs a concept space based on them for this category.

An unseen word/phrase is classified to a sensitive category based on K-Nearest Neighbors (KNN) algorithm [6]. It first transforms the word/phrase to its vector representation, and then calculates K nearest vectors under a predefined threshold of similarity distance in the concept space of each category. A word/phrase is classified to the i-th sensitive category if K_i is maximum, and assigned with the maximum similarity score in the concept space as its probability. If no neighbors are found, this word/phrase is classified as insensitive. The similarity distance between two vectors is measured using cosine similarity [9], which is a standard way of quantifying the similarity between two documents in the vector space in document retrieval [31]. In order to improve the result of classification, S3 uses the lemma form of each word in noun phrases and verb phrases. The lemma forms can be obtained in the intermediate structure.

Modifier Analysis. The semantic meaning of concepts are affected by the words modifying it. Specifically, a noun phrase often contains adjectives that can affect its sensitiveness. For instance, the sentence "*Email address*" describes sensitive profile information but the sentence "*Invalid email address*" is a normal hint message. Therefore it is necessary to analyze the sentiment of the adjectives to improve the accuracy. In our approach, we use SentiWordNet [2] to give a sentiment score of an adjective. A negative adjective is assigned a negative value. The more negative the word is, the larger the absolute value of its sentiment score is. S3 first collects adjectives in a noun phrase using POS information in the intermediate structure. Then it adds the sentiment score to its probability of being sensitive if the sentiment score is negative and thus reduces its probability.

3.2 Sensitiveness Decision

Topic analysis, giving only candidate sensitive category, is not sufficient to determine the sensitiveness. For instance, the sentence "*Register account*" describes a sensitive action but the sentence "*Account registered*" is an insensitive message showing that the account has already been registered. However they are both classified as the same sensitive category because they consist of same words in lemma form. Therefore, despite topic analysis, S3 also performs syntax, lexical and sentiment analysis to finally determine the sensitiveness.

Syntax Analysis. Empirically, we observe noun phrases and verb phrases in sensitive descriptive texts usually have fixed syntactic patterns, and we note such nodes a *Candidate Block* (CB) in the parsing tree. We summarize three syntactic patterns with CB notations of a descriptive text as follows:

- **Noun phrase only** (CB_{NP}). The noun phrase directly indicates the content of the surrounding data. For instance, "*Your password*" indicates a password input box.

- **Verb only** (CB_A). The action (verb) indicates some operation. For instance, *"Log in"* and *"Register"* describe sensitive account operations. *"Pay with Paypal"* is also a CB_A, as shown in Fig. 3c, where "Paypal" is removed as a name of entity.
- **Verb phrase (verb+noun phrase)** (CB_{ANP}). In the parsing tree of a sentence, if a noun phrase node has an ancestor verb phrase node (VP), we say the noun phrase is dominated by the action in the VP. For instance, in *"Register account"*, the noun phrase node "account" has a father VP node of action "Register" as shown in Fig. 3a, then the noun phrase is dominated by the action.

In the case of CB_A and CB_{NP} co-existing in a text without forming a CB_{ANP}, we empirically defines the priority of CB_{NP} is higher than that of CB_A. For example, in the case of *"Account registered"* as shown in Fig. 3b, the noun phrase "account" is the emphasis of the sentence, and the action "registered" modifies it.

After S3 collects all the CBs, it checks if their ancestor nodes or sibling nodes contain verb phrases. If verb phrases are found, the sentence is identified as insensitive. This is because the surrounding verb phrases can reduce the sensitiveness of a CB significantly. In Fig. 3b, the CB_{NP} "Account" has a sibling verb phrase "registered". Therefore the meaning of this sentence is to state the noun phrase is operated by the action and thus the sensitiveness of the noun phrase is reduced to insensitive by the action. In Fig. 3a, the CB_{ANP} has no surrounding nodes containing verb phrases, so the whole sentence is sensitive.

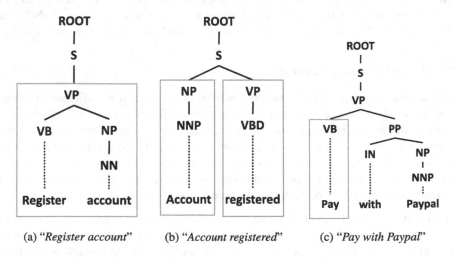

(a) *"Register account"*   (b) *"Account registered"*   (c) *"Pay with Paypal"*

Fig. 3. Syntax analysis illustration. The red rectangles indicate CBs. (Color figure online)

POS Analysis. For sentences containing only a CB_A, e.g., *"Log in"* and *"Logged in"*, POS affects the sensitiveness of the CB_A significantly. In our approach, we assume only the base form (noted as *VB* in the parse tree) and non-3rd person singular present (noted as *VBP* in parse tree) of a verb remain the sensitiveness. Other forms of a verb will reduce the sensitiveness of the CB_A to insensitive. For example, the word "Logged" is tagged as *VBN* (past participle) in the sentence *"Logged in"*. The sensitiveness of this sentences is reduced to insensitive. S3 checks POS of the action in a CB_A of a sentence to revise its sensitiveness.

Sentiment Analysis. We observe that negative sentiment of descriptive texts makes it insensitive (e.g., *"Login failed"*). We have tried Stanford Sentiment Analysis [30] but it does not produce satisfactory results of identifying the sentiment of texts in our problem domain. We have observed that most of the negative descriptive texts include some common keywords like "fail", "no", "error", etc. In our approach, we make a list of such negative words. S3 performs a keyword-based searching in a sentence to analyze its sentiment. A sentence is negative if it contains any of the negative keywords.

4   Evaluation

In this section, we present the evaluation of S3. Given a piece of text, S3 classifies it to some sensitive category with a probability. We first introduce the experiment setup of evaluation. Then we analyze the results of evaluation, and compare S3 with related work. Finally we analyze the causes of producing false positives and false negatives.

We implemented the preprocessor based on Stanford CoreNLP [19] to generate the intermediate structure, which is a state-of-the-art suit of core NLP tools including Stanford Parser from Stanford. To map words to the concept space, we implemented Stanford GloVe [25] for vector representation of words. We use English Wikipedia 2014 and Gigaword version 5 [14] as the base corpus. Each word is represented as a vector of 300 dimensions.

4.1   Evaluation Setup

We evaluate S3 on Android applications. We get all the text resources of an Android application using *decompiling* technique. In this paper, we use texts from a snapshot of popular Android applications. The app data set was generated from the official Google Play Store in November 2016. It contains the top 500 free applications in each category (34 categories totally). Except some connection errors occurred in the downloading process, we collected 18,681 applications totally. For each application, we extract texts from */res/values/strings.xml* file after decompiling it. We remove non-English texts from all the 18,681 applications and finally get 1,741,143 distinct English texts. We sort them based on the frequency of each text appearing in all the applications. In our evaluation, we manually define 7 sensitive categories. For each category, we define concepts for noun phrases, actions and single actions respectively. Information of the 7 categories is illustrated in Table 2.

Table 2. Categories of sensitive data.

Category	# CoNP	# CoA	# CoSA
Account	5	16	6
Calendar	4	5	0
Credential	16	18	0
Finance	30	10	4
Profile	45	21	0
Search & history	6	6	2
Setting	8	9	1

#CoNP: Number of noun phrases; #CoA: Number of actions; #CoSA: Number of single actions.

We first manually annotate the top 5,152 frequent texts using the listed categories. In our evaluation, we invite five volunteers to annotate these texts independently. A text is annotated as one category only if at least three volunteers label the text as the same category. Then S3 is applied on these texts to output results under different thresholds of similarity distance from 0.5 to 1.0 with 0.05 as interval. For each threshold, we measure the number of *true positives (TP), false positives (FP), true negatives (TN)* and *false negatives (FN)*, which are illustrated as follows:

- **TP**: A text which S3 correctly identifies as sensitive (category).
- **FP**: A text which S3 incorrectly identifies as sensitive (category).
- **TN**: A text which S3 correctly identifies as not sensitive (category).
- **FN**: A text which S3 incorrectly identifies as not sensitive (category).

In statistical classification [22], *Precision* is defined as the ratio of the number of true positives to the total number of items reported to be true, and *Recall* is defined as the ratio of the number of true positives to the total number of items that are true. *F-score* is defined as the weighted harmonic mean of Precision and Recall. *Accuracy* is defined as the ratio of sum of true positives and true negatives to the total number of items. Higher values of precision, recall, F-Score, and accuracy indicate higher quality of S3 to identify sensitive data. Based on the total number of TPs, FPs, TNs, and FNs, we compute the precision, recall, F-score, and accuracy of S3 in identifying sensitive texts as follows:

$$Precision = \frac{TP}{TP + FP} \tag{1}$$

$$Recall = \frac{TP}{TP + FN} \tag{2}$$

$$F\text{-}score = \frac{2 \cdot Precision \cdot Recall}{Precision + Recall} \tag{3}$$

$$Accuracy = \frac{TP + TN}{TP + FP + TN + FN} \tag{4}$$

4.2   Results

In this section, we describe the evaluation results and compare S3 with related work. We first measure the effectiveness of S3 under different thresholds in identifying sensitive texts to find the optimal threshold. Then we analyze in detail the effectiveness under the optimal threshold. Finally, we compare S3 with other approaches.

Threshold Setting. Errors of S3 come from false positives and false negatives. S3 seeks to achieve higher performance than prior work by reducing false positives and false negatives. However, to choose the optimal threshold in the trade-off of false positives and false negatives, we seek less false negatives than false positives. This is because false positives identify normal data as sensitive, and thus cause over protection, while false negatives leave sensitive data unprotected, and cause more serious consequences, e.g., data exposed to attackers. In statistics, *Recall* can reflect the measure of false negatives and *Precision* reflects false positives. Therefore we seek higher recall value than precision value in this paper.

The threshold controls the relatedness measure between a target noun phrase and action with concept spaces. A higher threshold indicates that the target is classified into a concept space only with closer relation with the concept space. Evaluation results differ under different thresholds as illustrated in Fig. 4. We compute average precision, recall, F-score and accuracy of the 7 categories for each threshold. The threshold ranges from 0.5 to 1.0 with 0.05 as interval. The results show that as threshold increases, precision first increases sharply before threshold 0.7 and then increases smoothly. Recall first increases smoothly before threshold 0.7 and then decreases sharply. The reason of such trend is that a higher threshold means S3 identifies a text as sensitive more strictly which causes less false positives but more false negatives. The accuracy differs more smoothly than precision, recall and F-score. This is because the number of negative samples (4588 identified by human) is much larger than the number of positive samples (564 identified by human) in 5152 texts. Therefore the fluctuation between true positives and true negatives is small and thus affects accuracy little. We can conclude from the results that under threshold 0.70, recall (95.8%) gets its maximum value and both F-score (92.2%) and accuracy (99.7%) get the maximum value as well.

Effectiveness Analysis. In this section, we evaluate the effectiveness of S3 in identifying sensitive texts. We take the optimal threshold 0.7 as an example to describe the evaluation results. Table 3 shows the evaluation results under threshold 0.7. Column "Category" lists names of the 7 predefined categories of sensitive data. Column "H_I" lists the number of texts identified as corresponding category of sensitive data by human users. Column "M_I" lists the number of texts identified as corresponding category of sensitive data by S3. Columns "TP", "FP", "TN" and "FN" list the number of *true positives, false positives, true negatives* and *false negatives* respectively. Columns "$P(\%)$", "$R(\%)$",

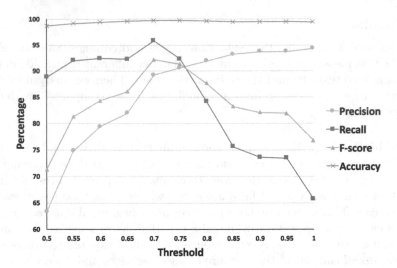

Fig. 4. Evaluation results under different thresholds.

Table 3. Evaluation results under threshold 0.7.

Category	H_I	M_I	TP	FP	TN	FN	$P(\%)$	$R(\%)$	$F_S(\%)$	$Acc(\%)$
Account	66	66	63	3	5083	3	95.5	95.5	95.5	99.9
Calendar	18	19	17	2	5132	1	89.5	94.4	91.9	99.9
Credential	77	87	75	12	5063	2	86.2	97.4	91.5	99.7
Finance	83	103	81	22	5047	2	78.6	97.6	87.1	99.5
Profile	200	232	193	39	4913	7	83.2	96.5	89.4	99.1
Search & history	42	41	39	2	5108	3	95.1	92.9	94.0	99.9
Setting	78	78	75	3	5071	3	96.2	96.2	96.2	99.9
Average	–	–	–	–	–	–	89.2	95.8	92.2	99.7
*OneCategory**	564	626	545	81	4507	19	87.1	96.6	91.6	98.1

H_I: Number of texts identified by human as sensitive (category); M_I: Number of texts identified by S3 as sensitive (category); TP: Number of true positives; FP: Number of false positives; TN: Number of true negatives; FN: Number of false negatives; P: Precision; R: Recall; F_S: F-score; Acc: Accuracy; *: The last row is computed by treating all sensitive texts as one category.

"$F_S(\%)$" and "$Acc(\%)$" list the percentage of *Precision, Recall, F-score* and *Accuracy* respectively. The evaluation results show that S3 effectively identifies and classifies sensitive texts out of top 5152 frequent texts with average precision, recall, F-score, and accuracy of 89.2%, 95.8%, 92.2% and 99.7% respectively. If we treat sensitive data as one category, S3 achieves precision, recall, F-score, and accuracy of 87.1%, 96.6%, 91.6%, and 98.1% respectively. Evaluation results show that S3 produces less false negatives than false positives in most categories which is in line with our expectations. We will discuss the reasons of producing false positives and false negatives in Sect. 4.3.

Comparison with Related Work. In this section, we compare S3 with related approaches in identifying sensitive texts. Table 4 shows the comparison results among different approaches in identifying sensitive texts. We select eight typical instances to present the comparison process.

Table 4. Comparison of S3 and related work.

Sentence	Supor	UIPicker	Whyper	AutoCog	S3
Enter your password	✓	✓	✓	✓	✓
Facebook will not save your password	✗	✗	✗	✗	✓
Register account	✓	✓	✓	✓	✓
Account registered	✗	✗	✓	✗	✓
Log in	✓	✓	✗	✗	✓
Logged in	✗	✗	✗	✗	✓
Your password	✓	✓	✓	✓	✓
Invalid password	✗	✗	✗	✗	✓

✓: The sentence is correctly identified. ✗: The sentence is incorrectly identified.

For the sentence *"Enter your password"*, it describes an input box receiving user's password. It contains sensitive keywords "Enter" (an action) and "password" (a noun phrase). All the approaches are able to correctly identify this sentence as sensitive. Moreover, S3 can classify it as category "Credential". The second sentence *"Facebook will not save your password"* also contains sensitive keywords "save" (an action) and "password" (a noun phrase). However it is only a normal hint sentence and describes no sensitive data. Both Supor and UIPicker incorrectly identify it as sensitive because it contains sensitive keywords. Whyper also fails because the sentence contains a sensitive noun phrase "your password" with dominant action "save". AutoCog fails as well because the sentence has a sensitive verb phrase "save your password", a sensitive noun phrase "your password". However even though the sentence has a sensitive noun phrase with dominant action (make up a CB_{ANP}), it does not guarantee that it is the point of the sentence. S3 correctly identifies it because it finds that the CB_{ANP} is dominated by "Facebook will" (has an ancestor node of verb phrase) so that the CB_{ANP} is not the point of the sentence and thus the whole sentence is not sensitive.

Another comparison example is sentences *"Register Account"* and *"Account registered"*. Both of the two sentences have sensitive keywords "Register" and "Account", but the meanings of them are significantly different. The former one describes an account registration manner but the latter one is a hint message saying that the account is already registered. All the related approaches can correctly identify the former sentence but fail for the latter sentence. As we are not sure if an action check is compulsory or not in Whyper, we here assume it is not compulsory so that Whyper correctly identifies the sentence. S3 first identifies the sensitive noun phrase "Account" which makes up a CB_{NP}. It then analyses that the CB_{NP} has a sibling action (verb phrase) "registered" which does not dominate the noun phrase. As a result, S3 correctly identifies it as insensitive.

The part of speech of a word is able to affect the sensitiveness of a text. Take two sentences "*Log in*" and "*Logged in*" as an example. Both contain sensitive keyword "log" (assuming all the approaches can transform the original token to its lemma form correctly). Supor and UIPicker can correctly identify "Log in". Whyper and AutoCog fail because they are not able to identify single actions. However all the related approaches fail in identifying "Logged in". Even though it contains sensitive keyword, it is a hint text showing the user has already logged in. They fail because the part of speech of tokens is not considered in the related approaches. S3 can correctly identify such texts.

Sentiment also affects the sensitiveness of a text. For instance, the sentence "*Your Password*" describes an input box receiving user's password but "*Invalid password*" is a hint text showing the user has typed a wrong password even though it contains the sensitive keyword "password". Such negative text reduces its sensitiveness. All the related approaches do not consider the sentiment of a text, so all fail. S3 correctly identify such text.

4.3   FP/FN Analysis

In this section, we analyze the causes of false positives and false negatives under threshold 0.7. Here we select representative examples to discuss the causes.

First we present why S3 incorrectly identifies a text as some category of sensitive data, which produces false positives.

– **Inaccurate underlying NLP infrastructure.** One major source of false positives is the incorrect syntactic parsing of texts by the underlying NLP infrastructure. Take the text "Send Email" as an instance. It is not labeled as sensitive data by our volunteers. However, the underlying Stanford Parser is not able to correctly parse its syntax in original form. It annotates the whole text as a noun phrase. S3 then analyzes its topic and finally classifies it as category "Profile" with maximum probability 85.3% as it has three neighbors "email", "e-mail" and "email address" while zero neighbors in other categories. However, it correctly parses the syntax in lowercase form: an action "send" followed by a noun phrase "email". The noun phrase "email" is classified as category "Profile" but the dominant action "send" has no neighbors within threshold in category "Profile". Therefore, S3 classifies the text as insensitive in the lowercase form. Due to the classification priority, S3 chooses the category with the higher probability among original and lowercase form, such text is eventually identified as category "Profile". We observe that a majority of false positives result from incorrect syntactic parsing. Such cases can be addressed with the advancement in underlying NLP infrastructure.
– **Inaccurate threshold control.** Take the text "*Product ID:*" as an example, S3 successfully identifies it as a noun phrase "Product ID"/"product id" (in original and lowercase form respectively) with a following colon. This text

matches the pattern that only contains a noun phrase. In topic analysis, S3 classifies the text using 7 concept spaces. It finds 2 neighbors "id" and "user id" within the threshold with maximum probability 80.1% in category "Profile" while zero neighbors in other categories. Then the text is incorrectly identified as category "Profile", but actually it is a normal text describing a product. Such false positives result from inaccurate threshold control and can be addressed by increasing the threshold.

Next we present why S3 incorrectly identifies a text as insensitive, which produces false negatives.

- **Inaccurate underlying NLP infrastructure.** Consider the text *"Zip Code"*. It is labeled as category "Profile" by volunteers, but S3 identifies it as insensitive. S3 correctly parses the text as a noun phrase in the original form. However, both the token "Zip" and "Code" are identified as names of entities and then removed. In the lowercase form, the text is incorrectly parsed as an action "zip" followed by a noun phrase "code". Although the noun phrase "code" has neighbors in category "Profile", the dominant action "zip" has zero neighbors in any categories so the text is identified as insensitive. In this instance, the syntax is parsed correctly in the original form but the underlying named entity analysis is incorrect. Such instances can be addressed with the improvement of underlying named entity parser. In *"Change Passcode"* of the original form, S3 incorrectly parses its syntax as a noun phrase and in the lowercase form it parses its syntax as an action "change" followed by an adjective "passcode". It is easy to know the correct syntax should be an action "change" followed by a noun phrase "passcode". Such instances can be addressed with the advancement of the underlying NLP infrastructure.
- **Incomplete knowledge base.** For instance, the word "logout" is not found in the top frequent words of our base corpus English Wikipedia 2014 and Gigaword version 5. It causes S3 to incorrectly identify the text *"logout"* as insensitive. Such issues can be addressed by collecting more words from the knowledge base corpus.
- **Incomplete concept space.** There are a few false negatives caused by the incomplete concept space. For example, the text *"Use street address"* is parsed correctly as an action "use" followed by a noun phrase "street address". However, the dominant action "use" has zero neighbors of the concept spaces of actions in any categories. Therefore S3 incorrectly identifies it as insensitive. This case can be addressed by extending concept spaces or decreasing the threshold.
- CB **priority.** A small source of false negatives results from the priority issue in processing CB. For instance, the sentence *"Allow Ad to create a calendar event?"* describes a "Setting" manner, but S3 identifies it as insensitive. S3 correctly parses its syntax as an action "Allow" followed by a noun phrase "Ad" and an action "create" followed by a noun phrase "a calendar event". S3 first identifies the sensitive candidate noun phrase "a calendar event" because it has three neighbors in category "Calendar" while noun phrase "Ad" has no

neighbors in any categories. Then S3 identifies the noun phrase "a calendar event" is dominated by an action "create". This action also has neighbors in concept space of actions in category "Calendar". Then the noun phrase "a calendar event" and its dominant action "create" make up a CB_{ANP}. Since the noun phrase "Ad" is insensitive but its dominant action "Allow" has neighbors in category "Setting", the action "Allow" makes up a CB_A. Because the CB_{ANP} has higher priority than CB_A, S3 identifies the sensitiveness of the text based on the CB_{ANP} "create a calendar event". However the syntax check fails because the CB_{ANP} is dominated by another action "Allow" (the ancestor node is a verb phrase). Such issue can be addressed by processing the CB sequentially until it reaches a sensitive category rather than only processing the top priority CB.

- CB **definition**. Rare false negatives result from the issue in defining CB in cases that the noun phrase and its dominant action belonging to different categories. Take the text *"Search by location"* as an instance. It describes a "Search" manner, but S3 identifies it as insensitive. S3 correctly parses its syntax as an action "Search" followed by a noun phrase "location". The noun phrase "location" has neighbors in category "Profile", but its dominant action "Search" has no neighbors in category "Profile". Therefore the noun phrase and its dominant action cannot form a CB_{ANP}, and is thus classified as insensitive. Such issue can be addressed by forming two separate CBs for the noun phrase and its dominant action.

4.4   Performance

We evaluate the performance of S3 by measuring the average time of identifying a text and its memory usage. We use S3 to identify top 20,000 out of 1,741,143 texts and measure the average time for each text. The experiment is performed on a Dell PowerEdge R730 server with 20 cores (40 threads) of Intel(R) Xeon(R) CPU E5-2660 v3 @ 2.60 GHz and 64 GB memory. The operating system is 64 bit Ubuntu 14.04.1 with Linux 3.19.0 kernel. The total time of processing 20,000 texts is 8682.4 s. The average time for each text is 0.43 s. Memory usage is 1,502 MB including the base corpus.

5   Related Work

To the best of our knowledge, S3 is the first systematical tool to automatically identify sensitive data including input data and output data from descriptive texts in mobile applications. Our approach utilizes NLP and learning based methods to analyze descriptive texts. Related research efforts using NLP and/or learning based methods to analyze texts/documents mainly are: (1) Sensitive input data identification in Android applications [10,21]; (2) Detecting mismatches between Android UIs and program behaviors [1]; (3) Description/Review-to-Behavior fidelity analysis in Android applications [13,24, 26,35]; and (4) Automatic discovery of Indicators of Compromise (IOC) [16].

Sensitive Input Data Identification in Android Applications. Supor [10] analyzes the descriptive texts of input boxes to analyze their sensitiveness. It first locates all the input boxes of a UI and then searches for their descriptive text. It uses keyword based searching to analyze such texts, and thus could cause many FP and FN because no semantic and syntactic information are considered. Moreover, the process of generating keywords needs much manual effort and also lacks flexibility of involving new sensitive data categories. UIPicker [21] utilizes SVM (Support Vector Machine) to learn the descriptive texts. The features are a set of sensitive keywords. The accuracy tends to increase as the size of training set increases. However it is also the limitation of this approach, because it causes much manual effort to prepare a well-labeled training set. The features are also limited by the size of sensitive keywords, so that it cannot handle unknown words. Compared with such approaches, S3 considers complete semantic and syntactic information to give accurate sensitiveness of a descriptive text. Besides, S3 does not require much manual effort to prepare massive keywords or training set.

Detecting Mismatches Between Android UIs and Program Behaviors. BackStage [1] checks the advertised functionality of Android UI elements (e.g., buttons) against their implemented functionality to detect such mismatches. To get the advised functionality, it analyzes the descriptive texts of these elements. It collects all the verbs and nouns from their application dataset and then clusters them into 250 classes. It gets the advertised functionality by testing the membership of a target UI element among the 250 clusters. The approach of BackStage is similar to the topic analysis of S3, but it does not consider syntactic information. Therefore, BackStage is able to get only the approximate meaning of a descriptive text, and is thus not applicable to identifying sensitiveness.

Description/Review-to-Behavior Fidelity Analysis in Android Applications. Approaches are proposed to identify the real permissions an Android application needs from its descriptions (Description-to-Behavior fidelity) or users' reviews (Review-to-Behavior fidelity). AutoCog [26], Whyper [24], and TAPVerifier [35] analyze Description-to-Behavior fidelity. AutoCog uses a learning based method to generate a dataset of noun phrases with corresponding verb phrases and possessives (called *np-counterpart* in the paper) if any. It performs an np-counterpart based searching on descriptions to identify the real permissions. Actually it is an extension of keyword based searching, and does not consider complete syntactic information as well. Whyper first extracts related noun phrases and actions from API documents. Then it checks if the noun phrase is dominated by the action in a description. It considers syntactic information, but it is not complete, and no other semantic information (e.g., POS, sentiment) is considered. TAPVerifier first collects verbs in different actions and then defines semantic patterns of descriptions. However, only verbs are not sufficient to analyze the sensitiveness of a text in our problem domain. AUTOREB [13] analyses Review-to-Behavior fidelity. The approach of AUTOREG is similar to UIPicker. It also uses a machine learning method and the features of the classifier are keywords as well. The difference is that AUTOREB utilizes the "relevance feedback" technique [34] to add relevant words to the keyword list. Syntactic information is not considered in AUTOREG either.

Automatic Discovery of Indicators of Compromise (IOC). IOC is an artifact observed on a network or in an operating system that with high confidence indicates a computer intrusion. It can be converted into a machine-readable OpenIOC format for automatically analysis. iACE [16] is proposed to discover IOC data in online pages (e.g., blogs, forums) and creates IOC in OpenIOC format. It first identifies IOC sentences in a document by searching IOC tokens and context terms. It identifies IOC tokens with regrexes and uses keyword based searching to identify context terms. Then it checks the relation between IOC tokens and context terms by graph mining. Finally, it creates IOC if the relation passes the check. Though iACE considers relatively complete syntactic information, regrex matching of identifying IOC tokens and keyword based searching of identifying context terms could cause many FPs and FNs.

In our problem domain, it is impossible to standardize sensitive data because different users may care about different sensitive data. Therefore it requires an approach that allows users to define sensitive data on demand. This is a key aspect of S3. It proposes the notion of *concept space* to represent a category of sensitive data. None of the related approaches have such flexibility to define a category on demand. S3 performs a careful revision of sensitiveness with complete syntax, POS and sentiment information taken into account. None of the related approaches are applicable in our problem domain.

6   Conclusion

In this paper, we propose S3, an automated approach to identify sensitive data from flexible user requirements. S3 takes semantic, syntactic and lexical analysis into account to understand the semantic meaning of sensitive data and then decides its sensitiveness. To enable S3 to support flexible user requirements in defining sensitive data, we propose the notion *concept space* which is constructed by initial readable concepts provided by users. S3 is able to learn users' preferences from the concept space, and automatically identify related sensitive data. We evaluate S3 on 18,681 application from top 500 free applications in 34 categories of Google Play. We classify sensitive data into 7 categories. S3 achieves an average precision of 89.2%, and average recall 95.8% (within threshold 0.7) in classifying sensitive data.

Acknowledgment. This research is supported by the National Research Foundation, Prime Ministers Office, Singapore under its National Cybersecurity R&D Programme (Grant No. NRF2015NCR-NCR002-001).

References

1. Avdiienko, V., Kuznetsov, K., Rommelfanger, I., Rau, A., Gorla, A., Zeller, A.: Detecting behavior anomalies in graphical user interfaces. In: Proceedings of the 39th International Conference on Software Engineering Companion (ICSE-C). IEEE (2017)
2. Baccianella, S., Esuli, A., Sebastiani, F.: SentiWordNet 3.0: an enhanced lexical resource for sentiment analysis and opinion mining. In: Proceedings of the 7th International Conference on Language Resources and Evaluation. European Language Resources Association (2010)
3. Budianto, E., Jia, Y., Dong, X., Saxena, P., Liang, Z.: You can't be me: enabling trusted paths and user sub-origins in web browsers. In: Stavrou, A., Bos, H., Portokalidis, G. (eds.) RAID 2014. LNCS, vol. 8688, pp. 150–171. Springer, Cham (2014). https://doi.org/10.1007/978-3-319-11379-1_8
4. Bursztein, E., Soman, C., Boneh, D., Mitchell, J.C.: SessionJuggler: secure web login from an untrusted terminal using session hijacking. In: Proceedings of the 21st International Conference on World Wide Web (WWW). ACM (2012)
5. CNBC: Driver's license, credit card numbers: The equifax hack is way worse than consumers knew. https://www.cnbc.com/2018/02/12/the-equifax-hack-is-way-worse-than-consumers-knew.html
6. Cunningham, P., Delany, S.J.: K-nearest neighbour classifiers. Multiple Classif. Syst. **34**, 1–17 (2007)
7. Enck, W., et al.: TaintDroid: an information-flow tracking system for realtime privacy monitoring on smartphones. In: Proceedings of the 9th USENIX Conference on Operating Systems Design and Implementation (USENIX OSDI). USENIX Association (2010)
8. Finkel, J.R., Grenager, T., Manning, C.: Incorporating non-local information into information extraction systems by gibbs sampling. In: Proceedings of the 43rd Annual Meeting of the Association for Computational Linguistics (ACL). Association for Computational Linguistics (2005)
9. Gabrilovich, E., Markovitch, S.: Computing semantic relatedness using Wikipedia-based explicit semantic analysis. In: Proceedings of the 20th International Joint Conference on Artifical Intelligence (IJCAI). Morgan Kaufmann Publishers Inc. (2007)
10. Huang, J., et al.: SUPOR: precise and scalable sensitive user input detection for android apps. In: 24th USENIX Security Symposium (USENIX Security). USENIX Association (2015)
11. Jurafsky, D., Martin, J.H.: Speech and Language Processing, vol. 3. Pearson, London (2014)
12. Klein, D., Manning, C.D.: Fast exact inference with a factored model for natural language parsing. In: Proceedings of the 15th International Conference on Neural Information Processing Systems (NIPS). MIT Press (2002)
13. Kong, D., Cen, L., Jin, H.: AUTOREB: automatically understanding the review-to-behavior fidelity in android applications. In: Proceedings of the 22nd Conference on Computer and Communications Security (CCS). ACM (2015)
14. LDC: English gigaword fifth edition. https://catalog.ldc.upenn.edu/LDC2011T07
15. Li, X., Hu, H., Bai, G., Jia, Y., Liang, Z., Saxena, P.: DroidVault: a trusted data vault for android devices. In: Proceedings of the 19th International Conference on Engineering of Complex Computer Systems (ICECCS). IEEE (2014)

16. Liao, X., Yuan, K., Wang, X., Li, Z., Xing, L., Beyah, R.: Acing the IOC game: toward automatic discovery and analysis of open-source cyber threat intelligence. In: Proceedings of Conference on Computer and Communications Security (CCS). ACM (2016)

17. Lu, K., et al.: Checking more and alerting less: detecting privacy leakages via enhanced data-flow analysis and peer voting. In: Proceedings of the Network and Distributed System Security Symposium (NDSS) (2015)

18. Mannan, M., van Oorschot, P.C.: Using a personal device to strengthen password authentication from an untrusted computer. In: Dietrich, S., Dhamija, R. (eds.) FC 2007. LNCS, vol. 4886, pp. 88–103. Springer, Heidelberg (2007). https://doi.org/10.1007/978-3-540-77366-5_11

19. Manning, C.D., Surdeanu, M., Bauer, J., Finkel, J., Bethard, S.J., McClosky, D.: The Stanford CoreNLP natural language processing toolkit. In: Association for Computational Linguistics (ACL) System Demonstrations, pp. 55–60 (2014). http://www.aclweb.org/anthology/P/P14/P14-5010

20. Mikolov, T., Sutskever, I., Chen, K., Corrado, G., Dean, J.: Distributed representations of words and phrases and their compositionality. In: Proceedings of the 26th International Conference on Neural Information Processing Systems (NIPS). Curran Associates Inc. (2013)

21. Nan, Y., Yang, M., Yang, Z., Zhou, S., Gu, G., Wang, X.: UIPicker: user-input privacy identification in mobile applications. In: Proceedings of the 24th USENIX Security Symposium (USENIX Security). USENIX Association (2015)

22. Olson, D.L., Delen, D.: Advanced Data Mining Techniques. Springer, Heidelberg (2008). https://doi.org/10.1007/978-3-540-76917-0

23. Oprea, A., Balfanz, D., Durfee, G., Smetters, D.K.: Securing a remote terminal application with a mobile trusted device. In: Proceedings of the 20th Annual Computer Security Applications Conference (ACSAC). IEEE (2004)

24. Pandita, R., Xiao, X., Yang, W., Enck, W., Xie, T.: WHYPER: towards automating risk assessment of mobile applications. In: Proceedings of the 22nd USENIX Security Symposium (USENIX Security). USENIX Association (2013)

25. Pennington, J., Socher, R., Manning, C.D.: GloVe: global vectors for word representation. In: Empirical Methods in Natural Language Processing (EMNLP) (2014)

26. Qu, Z., Rastogi, V., Zhang, X., Chen, Y., Zhu, T., Chen, Z.: AutoCog: measuring the description-to-permission fidelity in android applications. In: Proceedings of the 2014 ACM SIGSAC Conference on Computer and Communications Security (CCS). ACM (2014)

27. Rastogi, V., Chen, Y., Enck, W.: AppsPlayground: automatic security analysis of smartphone applications. In: Proceedings of the 3rd ACM Conference on Data and Application Security and Privacy. ACM (2013)

28. Roalter, L., Kranz, M., Diewald, S., Möller, A., Synnes, K.: The smartphone as mobile authorization proxy. In: Proceedings of the 14th International Conference on Computer Aided Systems Theory (EUROCAST), pp. 306–307 (2013)

29. Sharp, R., Madhavapeddy, A., Want, R., Pering, T.: Enhancing web browsing security on public terminals using mobile composition. In: Proceedings of the 6th International Conference on Mobile Systems, Applications, and Services (MobiSys). ACM (2008)

30. Socher, R., et al.: Recursive deep models for semantic compositionality over a sentiment treebank. In: Proceedings of the Conference on Empirical Methods in Natural Language Processing (EMNLP) (2013)

31. Steinbach, M., Karypis, G., Kumar, V., et al.: A comparison of document clustering techniques. In: KDD Workshop on Text Mining, Boston, vol. 400, pp. 525–526 (2000)
32. Toutanova, K., Klein, D., Manning, C.D., Singer, Y.: Feature-rich part-of-speech tagging with a cyclic dependency network. In: Proceedings of the 2003 Conference of the North American Chapter of the Association for Computational Linguistics on Human Language Technology (NAACL). Association for Computational Linguistics (2003)
33. Wikipedia: Yahoo! data breaches. https://en.wikipedia.org/wiki/Yahoo!_data_breaches
34. Xu, J., Croft, W.B.: Query expansion using local and global document analysis. In: Proceedings of the 19th Annual International ACM SIGIR Conference on Research and Development in Information Retrieval (SIGIR). ACM (1996)
35. Yu, L., Luo, X., Qian, C., Wang, S.: Revisiting the description-to-behavior fidelity in android applications. In: Proceedings of the 23rd International Conference on Software Analysis, Evolution, and Reengineering (SANER). IEEE (2016)
36. Zhou, Y., Jiang, X.: Detecting passive content leaks and pollution in android applications. In: Proceedings of the 20th Network and Distributed System Security Symposium (NDSS) (2013)
37. Zhou, Y., Evans, D.: Protecting private web content from embedded scripts. In: Atluri, V., Diaz, C. (eds.) ESORICS 2011. LNCS, vol. 6879, pp. 60–79. Springer, Heidelberg (2011). https://doi.org/10.1007/978-3-642-23822-2_4

Understanding Android Obfuscation Techniques: A Large-Scale Investigation in the Wild

Shuaike Dong[1], Menghao Li[2], Wenrui Diao[3], Xiangyu Liu[4], Jian Liu[2(✉)],
Zhou Li[5], Fenghao Xu[1], Kai Chen[2], XiaoFeng Wang[6], and Kehuan Zhang[1(✉)]

[1] The Chinese University of Hong Kong, Sha Tin, Hong Kong
{ds016,xf016,khzhang}@ie.cuhk.edu.hk
[2] Institute of Information Engineering, Chinese Academy of Sciences, Beijing, China
{limenghao,liujian6,chenkai}@iie.ac.cn
[3] Jinan University, Guangzhou, China
diaowenrui@link.cuhk.edu.hk
[4] Alibaba Inc., Hangzhou, China
eason.lxy@alibaba-inc.com
[5] ACM Member, Boston, MA, USA
lzcarl@gmail.com
[6] Indiana University Bloomington, Bloomington, IN, USA
xw7@indiana.edu

Abstract. Program code is a valuable asset to its owner. Due to the easy-to-reverse nature of Java, code protection for Android apps is of particular importance. To this end, code obfuscation is widely utilized by both legitimate app developers and malware authors, which complicates the representation of source code or machine code in order to hinder the manual investigation and code analysis. Despite many previous studies focusing on the obfuscation techniques, however, our knowledge of how obfuscation is applied by real-world developers is still limited.

In this paper, we seek to better understand Android obfuscation and depict a holistic view of the usage of obfuscation through a large-scale investigation in the wild. In particular, we focus on three popular obfuscation approaches: identifier renaming, string encryption and Java reflection. To obtain the meaningful statistical results, we designed efficient and lightweight detection models for each obfuscation technique and applied them to our massive APK datasets (collected from Google Play, multiple third-party markets, and malware databases). We have learned several interesting facts from the result. For example, more apps on third-party markets than malware use identifier renaming, and malware authors use string encryption more frequently. We are also interested in the explanation of each finding. Therefore we carry out in-depth code analysis on some Android apps after sampling. We believe our study will help developers select the most suitable obfuscation approach, and in the meantime help researchers improve code analysis systems in the right direction.

Keywords: Android · Obfuscation · Static analysis · Code protection

© ICST Institute for Computer Sciences, Social Informatics and Telecommunications Engineering 2018
R. Beyah et al. (Eds.): SecureComm 2018, LNICST 254, pp. 172–192, 2018.
https://doi.org/10.1007/978-3-030-01701-9_10

1   Introduction

Code is a very important intellectual property to its developers, no matter if they work as individuals or for a large corporation. To protect this property, *obfuscation* is frequently used by developers, which is also considered as a double-edged sword by the security community. To a legitimate software company, obfuscation keeps its competitors away from copying the code and quickly building their own products in an unfair way. To a malware author, obfuscation raises the bar for automated code analysis and manual investigation, two approaches adopted by nearly every security company. For a mobile app, especially the one targeting Android platform, obfuscation is particularly useful, given that the task of disassembling or decompiling Android app is substantially easier than doing so for other sorts of binary code, like X86 executables.

Android obfuscation is pervasive. On the one hand, there are already more than 3.5 million apps available for downloading just in one app market, Google Play, up to December 2017 [13]. On the other hand, many off-the-shelf obfuscators are developed, like ProGuard [14], DashO [7], DexGuard [8], DexProtector [9], etc. Consequently, the issues around app obfuscation attract many researchers. So far, most of the studies focus on the topics like what obfuscation techniques can be used [20], how they can be improved [38], how well they can be handled by state-of-art code analysis tools [37], and how to deobfuscate the code automatically [22]. While these studies provide solid ground for understanding the obfuscation *techniques* and its *implications*, there is still an unfilled gap in this domain: how is obfuscation *actually used* by the vast amount of developers?

We believe this topic needs to be studied, and the answer could enlighten new research opportunities. To name a few, for developers, learning which obfuscation techniques should be used is quite important. Not all obfuscation techniques are equally effective, and some might even have bad influence on the performance of a program. Plenty of code analysis approaches were proposed, but their effects are usually hampered by obfuscation and the impact greatly differs based on the specific obfuscation technique in use, e.g., identifier renaming is much less of an issue comparing to string encryption. Knowing the preferences of obfuscation techniques can better assist the design of code analysis tools and prioritize the challenges need to be tackled. All roads paving to the correct conclusions call for measurement on real-world apps, and only the result coming from a comprehensive study covering a diverse portfolio of apps (published in different markets, in different countries, from both malware authors and legitimate companies) is meaningful.

Our Work. As the first step, in this paper, we systematically study the obfuscation techniques used in Android apps and carry out a large-scale investigation for apps in the wild. We focus on three most popular Android obfuscation techniques (identifier renaming, string encryption, and Java reflection) and measure the base and popular implementation of each technique. To notice, the existing tools, like deobfuscators, cannot solve our problem here, since they either work well against a specific technique or a specific off-the-shelf obfuscator (e.g.,

ProGuard). As such, they cannot be used to provide a holistic view. Our key insight into this end is that instead of mapping the obfuscated code to its original version, a challenge not yet fully addressed, we only need to *cluster* them based on their code patterns or statistical features. Therefore, we built a set of lightweight detectors for all studied techniques, based on machine learning and signature matching. Our tools are quite effective and efficient, suggested by the validation result on ground-truth datasets. We then applied them on a real-world APK dataset with 114,560 apps coming from three different sources, including Google Play set, third-party markets set, and malware set, for the large-scale study.

Discoveries. Our study reveals several interesting facts, with some confirming people's intuition but some contradicting to common beliefs: for example, as an obfuscation approach, identifier renaming is more widely-used in third-party apps than in malware. Also, though basic obfuscation is prevalently applied in benign apps, the utilization rate of other advanced obfuscation techniques is much lower than that of malware. The detailed statistical results are provided in Sect. 4. We believe these insights coming from *"big code"* are valuable in guiding developers and researchers in building, counteracting or using obfuscation techniques.

Contributions. We summarize this paper's contributions as below:

- **Systematic Study.** We systematically study the current mainstream Android obfuscation techniques used by app developers.
- **New Techniques.** We propose several techniques for detecting different obfuscation techniques accurately, such as n-gram -based renaming detection model and backward slicing-based reflection detection algorithm.
- **Large-scale Evaluation.** We carried out large-scale experiments and applied our detection techniques on over 100K APK files collected from three different sources. We listed our findings and provided explanations based on in-depth analysis of obfuscated code.

Roadmap. The rest of this paper is organized as follows: We systematically summarize popular Android obfuscation techniques in Sect. 2.2. Section 3 overviews the high-level architecture of our detection framework. The detailed detection strategies and statistical results on large-scale datasets are provided in Sect. 4. Also, we discuss some limitations and future plans in Sect. 5. Section 6 reviews the previous research on Android obfuscation, and Sect. 7 concludes this paper.

2   Background

In this section, we briefly introduce the structure of APK file and overview some common Android obfuscation techniques.

2.1   APK File Structure

An APK (Android application package) file is a zip compressed file containing all the content of an Android app, in general, including four directories (res, assets, lib, and META-INF) and three files (AndroidManifest.xml, classes.dex, and resources.arsc). The purposes of these directories and files are listed as below.

res This directory stores Android resource files which will be mapped to the .R file in Android and allocated the corresponding ID.

assets This directory is similar to the res directory and used to store static files in the APK. However, unlike res directory, developers can create subdirectories in any depth with the arbitrary file structure.

lib The code compiled for specific platforms (usually library files, like .so) are stored in this directory. Subdirectories can be created according to the type of processors, like armeabi, armeabi-v7a, x86, x86_64, mips.

META-INF This directory is responsible for saving the signature information of a specific app, which is used to validate the integrity of an APK file.

AndroidManifest.xml This XML file is the configuration of an APK, declaring its basic information, like name, version, required permissions and components. Each APK has an AndroidManifest file, and the only one.

classes.dex The dex file contains all the information of the classes in an app. The data is organized in a way the Dalvik virtual machine can understand and execute.

resources.arsc This file is used to record the relationship between the resource files and related resource ID and can be leveraged to locate specific resources.

2.2   Android Obfuscation Characterization

In general, obfuscation attempts to garble a program and makes the source or machine code more difficult for humans to understand. Programmers can deliberately obfuscate code to conceal its purpose or logic, in order to prevent tampering, deter reverse engineering, or behave like a puzzle for someone reading the code. Specifically, there are several common obfuscation techniques used by Android apps, including identifier renaming, string encryption, excessive overloading, and so forth.

Identifier Renaming. In software development, for good readability, code identifiers' names are usually meaningful, though developers may follow different naming rules (like CamelCase, Hungarian Notation). However, these meaningful names also accommodate reverse-engineers to understand the code logic and locate the target functions rapidly. Therefore, to reduce the potential information leakage, identifier's names could be replaced by meaningless strings. In the following example, all identifiers in class Account are renamed.

```
1  public class a{
2      private Integer a;
```

```
3      private Float = b;
4      public void a(Integer a, Float b){
5          this.a = a + Integer.valueOf(b)
6      }
7 }
```

String Encryption. Strings are very common-used data structures in software development. In an obfuscated app, strings could be encrypted to prevent information leakage. Based on cryptographic functions, the original plaintexts are replaced by random strings and restore at runtime. As a result, string encryption could effectively hinder *hard-coded* static scanning. The following code block shows an example.

```
1 String option = "@^@#\x '1 m*7 %**9_!v";
2 this.execute(decrypt(option));
```

Java Reflection. Reflection is an advanced feature of Java, which provides developers with a flexible approach to interact with the program, e.g., creating new object instances and invoking methods dynamically. One common usage is to invoke nonpublic APIs in the SDK (with the annotation @hide). The following code gives an example of reflection that invokes a hidden API batteryinfo.

```
1 Object object = new Object();
2 Method getService = Class.forName("android.os.
     ServiceManager").getMethod("getService", String.class);
3 Object obj = getService.invoke(object, new Object[]{new
     String("batteryinfo")});
```

As an obfuscation technique, reflection is a good choice of hiding program behaviors because it can transfer the control to a certain function implicitly, which can not be well handled by state-of-the-art static analysis tools. Therefore, malware developers usually heavily employ reflection to hide malicious actions.

3   System Design

Our target is to systematically study the Android obfuscation techniques and carry out a large-scale investigation. As the first step, we design an efficient Android code analysis framework to identify the obfuscation techniques used by developers. Here we overview the high-level design of this framework and introduce the datasets prepared for the subsequent large-scale investigations.

3.1   System Overview

To detect the usage of obfuscation techniques, we propose an architecture to analyze APK files automatically, as illustrated in Fig. 1. After the APK files collected from several channels (details are provided in Sect. 3.2) are stored on our server, this detection framework will try to unpack them for the primary testing. Some damaged APK files failing to pass this step will be discarded and manually checked to make sure the samples used in the following phases are valid. Then this framework applies three targeted detection methods to identify obfuscated Smali code blocks. These detection methods could be classified into two categories: signature-based and machine learning-based.

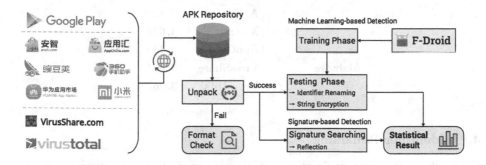

Fig. 1. Android app obfuscation detection framework

3.2 APK Dataset

We are interested in the obfuscation usage status of apps in different types, so three representative APK datasets were used in our experiment: Google Play set (26,614 samples), third-party market set (65,666 samples), and malware set (22,280 samples). These samples were collected during 2016 and 2017. In total, our experiment dataset contains 114,560 sample with the size of around 1.521TB. More details are given in Table 1.

As the official app store for Android, Google Play is the main Android app distribution channel. Thus, its sample set could reflect the deployment status of obfuscation used by mainstream developers. Also, due to the policy restriction, in some countries (such as China), Google Play is not available, and users have to install apps from third-party markets. Therefore, in the second dataset, we select six popular app markets from China (say Anzhi [4], Xiaomi [19], Wandou-jia [18], 360 [1], Huawei [10], and AppChina [5]) and developed the corresponding crawlers to collect their apps. Note that the replicated samples from different markets have been excluded. Lastly, except for legitimate app samples, we are also curious about whether malware authors heavily use obfuscation skills to hide their malicious intentions. So, the last dataset contains the malware samples coming from VirusShare [16] and VirusTotal [17,30].

4 Obfuscation Detection and Large-Scale Investigation

In this section, we introduce the detection approaches for each obfuscation technique and summarize our findings based on large-scale experiments.

Table 1. APK dataset for investigation

Type	Source	Number
Official Market	Google Play	26,614
3rd-party Market	Wandoujia	8,979
	360	18,724
	Huawei	22,048
	Anzhi	7,121
	Xiaomi	4,649
	AppChina	4,145
Malware	VirusShare	19,004
	VirusTotal	3,267

4.1 Identifier Renaming

Generally, in the software development, the names of identifiers (variable names, function names, and so forth) are usually meaningful, which could provide good code readability and maintainability. However, such *clear* names may leak much information due to the easy-to-reverse feature of Java. As a solution, identifier renaming is proposed and widely used in practice.

The renaming operation can be appended at different stages of APK file packaging. For example, ProGuard [14] and Allatori [2] work at the source-code level, mapping the original names to mangled ones based on the user's configuration. The other obfuscators, like DashO [7], DexProtector [9], and Shield4J [15], can work directly on APK files, modifying `.class` and `.dex` files.

Given an identifier, we can easily tell whether some obfuscator has renamed it based on the information it contains. In other words, if an identifier name is obscure and meaningless, it can be regarded as obfuscated because it tries to hide the actual intention. A typical renaming operation is changing the original name to a single character (like "a", "b") or some kind of puzzling string (like "IIIIIIII", "oO0OO0oo") [20]. However, the manual check is obviously not qualified for our large-scale scanning goal. Moreover, we focus on the whole APK contents rather than a single identifier. Therefore, we need to design a representation which can measure the overall extent of identifier renaming given an app.

Beyond that, as a special case of identifier renaming, the *excessive overloading* technique utilizes the overloading feature of Java and could map irrelevant identifier names to the same one, making the code more confusing to analysts [21]. For example, in the sample idfhn[1], more than 46 functions are named as idfhn (the same as the package name). Though the compiler could distinguish these variables with the same name, security analysts have to face more troubles. In our research, we also paid attention to the application of overloading feature and its impact on code analysis.

---

[1] MD5: `7d9eb791c09b9998336ef00bf6d43387`.

Identifier Renaming Detection. To the above challenges and targets, we combine the computational linguistics and machine learning techniques for accurate renaming detection. The high-level idea is based on the probabilistic language model. The insight is that identifier renaming will lead to the abnormal distribution of characters and character combinations, which distinguishes from normal ones (non-obfuscated). The model outputs 1 or 0 according to whether the app is judged as using identifier renaming. Here we give our three-step approach:

1. *Data Pre-processing.* All the identifier names of the target APK sample are extracted as the training candidates. Note that, software developers often introduce third-party libraries into their apps. However, those third-party libraries may contain obfuscated code, which does not reflect the protection deployed by developers. Therefore we also pre-removed over 12,000 common third-party libraries to avoid the inference using the approach of Li et al. [32].
2. *Feature Generation.* The amount of identifiers varies among different apps. To build a uniform expression, we apply the n-gram algorithm [12] to generate a fixed-length [2] feature vector for each app. An n-gram is a contiguous sequence of n items from a given sequence of text or speech. Through our small-scale tests, we found 3-gram [3] can well depict the distribution of character combinations while restricting the length of the vector. Then we applied it to traverse each name string in extracted raw name set to form the feature vector. Each element of the vector records the frequency of a certain character combination and will be normalized. Note that, the vector also involves the frequencies of fewer-than-three character combinations (a, ab, etc.) due to the length of an identifier may be smaller than three.
3. *Classification.* We collected apps from F-Droid and applied different obfuscators on them to generate the training set. Due to our model is a two-class classifier, we decided to use Supported Vector Machine (SVM) as the classification algorithm for its powerful learning ability. After the training phase, we applied it to our large-scale dataset.

Experiment Settings. We implemented a prototype of our detection model based on Androguard [3] with more than 1,500 Python lines of code. For training, we downloaded 3,147 apps with their corresponding source code from F-Droid. Two obfuscators, ProGuard and DashO, were used to generate variant obfuscated samples because they have different renaming policies. Note that, due to the diversity of apps' project configurations, not all of them can be processed by both ProGuard (2,107 successful samples) and DashO (654 successful samples). Among them, we randomly chose 500 original apps and 500 successful obfuscated apps (250 from Proguard and 250 from DashO) as the training set. We

---

[2] The length is restricted by the legal characters sets used for contracting a name in Java: ["a-z", " A-Z", "0-9", "_", "$", "\"].
[3] For example, if there is a string "abcdefgh", all of the 3-gram sequences it contains are {abc, bcd, cde, def, efg, fgh}.

then randomly selected 500 original, 250 Proguard-obfuscated and 250 DashO-obfuscated apps from the remaining set to do the validation. Our model reached 0.6% FN rate and 0.0% FP rate, which is quite satisfactory. We then collected another testing set consisting of 200 samples obfuscated by another obfuscator called Allatori. The completely successful classification results showed the strong generalization ability of our model.

Large-Scale Investigation and Findings. We carried out a large-scale detection on the three typical datasets (Google Play, third-party markets, and malware) mentioned in Sect. 3.2. The obfuscation detection result by dataset is given in Fig. 2. According to such statistics, we have two immediate findings:

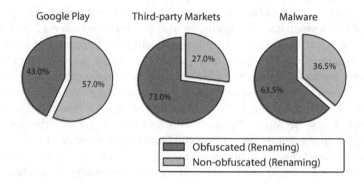

Fig. 2. Ratio of identifier renaming in three datasets

⇒ 1. Compared with the apps on Google Play, the ones from third-party markets apply more renaming operations.
⇒ 2. Over one third of malware don't apply identifier renaming.

To the first finding, we ascribe it to the discrepancy between app market environments. The piracy issue in Chinese app markets are quite severe, say nearly 20% apps are repacked or cloned [24]. Such situation urges developers to put more effort into protecting their apps. On the other hand, Google Play provides more strict and timely supervision, which mitigates the severity of software piracy largely. The better application ecosystem makes many developers believe obfuscation is just an optional protection approach.

To the second finding, the percentage of malware utilizing identifier renaming is only 63.5%, slightly less than third-party apps, which is opposite our traditional opinion. After manually checking the code of malware without renaming-obfuscation, we conclude that two aspects contribute to such phenomenon.

– *Script Kiddies.* Many entry-level malware authors only could develop simple malicious apps and lack the knowledge of how to disguise malicious behaviors through obfuscation. A few codes and clumsy class structures are two main features of those entry-level apps. The vicious behaviors of the malware are usually exposed to analysts due to the rough implementation.

- *False Alarmed "Malware"*. For some apps, their main bodies are benign and non-obfuscated, while the imported third-party libraries contain some kinds of sensitive and suspicious behaviors which are recognized as malicious by some anti-virus software. A common example is the advertising library.

In addition, we explored the difference in renaming implementation between malware and benign apps. The result reflects:

⇒ 1. Malware authors prefer to use more complex renaming policies.
⇒ 2. Malware may use irrelevant names to hide the true intention.

We find that, in benign apps (the samples on Google Play and third-party markets), most identifier names are mapped to {a, b, aa, ab, aaa, ... } and so on, in lexicographic order. In fact, such renaming rules accord with the default configurations of many obfuscators (such as ProGuard). That is to say, app developers do not intend to change the renaming rules to more ingenious ones. However, malware authors usually put more effort into configuring the renaming policies. For example, some malware samples utilize special characters (encoded in Unicode) as obfuscated names (e.g., É, ô), which seems very odd but still be regarded as legal by Java compilers. Also, some dazzling weird names (like {llllllll, oO0O0O0oo, ... }) could be found. Such renaming policy can actually make manual analysis more strenuous.

Apart from that, we find that overloading, as a grammar feature provided by Java, is also applied by malware to confuse analysts. In sample `tw.org.ncsist. mdm`[4], the name of overloaded function `attachBaseContext` (A `protected` method in class `android.app.Application`) will mislead security analysts because the logic of this function is actually implemented for encryption.

4.2 String Encryption

The strings in a `.dex` (Dalvik executable) file may leak a lot of private information about the program. As security protection, those hard-coded texts can be stored in an encrypted form to prevent reverse analysis. In this section, we take a deep insight into the string encryption and focus on two aspects:

1. Detect whether an app uses the string encryption.
2. Analyze the cryptographic functions invoked by apps.

String Encryption Detection. Similar to the approach for identifier renaming detection (Sect. 4.1), we trained a machine-learning based model to classify encrypted strings and plain-text strings. We reused the 3-gram algorithm, SVM algorithm, and the open-source apps from F-Droid. Here we only describe the different steps. At first, all strings appeared in an app are extracted. Next, a

---

[4] MD5: `01a93f7e94531e067310c1ee0f083c07`.

vector was generated for each app. Distinct from the setting for identifier renaming detection, there is no restriction on the content of a string. Therefore, we extended the acceptable character set to all ASCII codes[5].

In the implementation, we reused most code of identifier renaming detection model. Since string encryption is not a common function provided by off-the-shelf obfuscators, we chose DashO and DexProtector to generate the ground truth and finally obtained 737 string-encrypted samples for training. To avoid the overfitting caused by unbalanced data, we randomly selected 500 original apps and 500 string-encrypted apps to train our model. To verify the effectiveness, we randomly selected another 100 original apps and 100 string-encrypted apps for testing. The result shows our model could achieve 98.5% success rate with FP 1% and FN 2%.

Cryptographic Function Detection. Previous work has proposed various approaches to identify cryptographic functions in a program, like [23,28,34]. Those methods were specifically designed for the identification of the standard, modern cryptographic algorithms in binary code, like AES, DES, and RC4. The features used by the previous commonly include entropy analysis, searchable constant patterns, excessive use of bitwise arithmetic operations, memory fetch patterns and so on, besides, the dynamic binary instrument is also widely-used by analysts to better locate and identify the cryptographic primitives. However, previous approaches do not fit android platform very well due to three reasons: (1) Smali instructions have different representations from the x86 assembly language, especially for memory access. (2) Java provides the complete implementations of standard cryptographic algorithms through Java Cryptography Extension [11]. Therefore, in most cases, developers do not need to implement cryptographic related functions again. (3) Java provides a series of string & character operations, like `concat()`, `substring()`, `getChars()`, `strim()` and so on, which can be used to build an encrypted string.

To better handle the identification in Android apps, we extended the previous approaches with more empirical features, shown as below.

- The ratio of bit and loop operations.
- The usage of Java Cryptography Extension API invoking.
- The amount of operations on string & character variables.
- The frequency of encrypted strings as function parameters (for decryption).

Large-Scale Investigation and Findings. We applied our string encryption detection model on the testing datasets. The results are presented in Fig. 3. The direct findings are that:

> ⇒ 1. Nearly all benign apps don't use string encryption.
> ⇒ 2. String encryption is more popular in malware.

---

[5] Unicode codes can be represented in the form of $\backslash uxxxx$, where $xxxx$ is a 4-digit hexadecimal number.

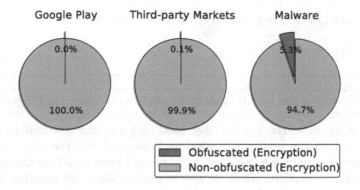

Fig. 3. Ratio of string encryption in three datasets

These statistical results comply with our perception, and we could understand it from three perspectives. (1) String encryption is not a common feature provided by off-the-shelf obfuscators (Proguard). The obfuscators offering the string encryption feature are expensive (DexGuard, DexProtector). (2) Many developers may lack the knowledge or awareness of deploying more advanced obfuscation techniques. They may believe the default identifier renaming is enough for code protection and it is not necessary to consider other techniques. (3) String encryption can help malware evade the signature scanning of some anti-virus software and hidden the intention effectively, leading to a higher rate of utilization than benign apps.

We then manually analyzed the implementations of cryptographic functions extracted from malware set and got the following findings.

⇒ The cryptographic functions usually disguise its true intention by changing to an irrelevant name.

For instance, in sample `com.solodroid.materialwallpaper`[6], the decryption function is disguised as a common legitimate API `NavigationItem;->getDrawable()` which should be used for retrieving a drawable object.

⇒ About 17.6% of string-encrypted malware implement multiple cryptographic functions and take turns to use them in a single app.

In sample `com.yandex.metrica`[7], four different cryptographic functions were implemented. All of them first initialize the key, then doing the encryption/decryption. However, the key initialization procedures are quite different from each other. As a result, the workload of restoring rises significantly for analysts.

```
1  // In class com.yandex.metrica.impl.ad;
2  static final String a(String str){
3  if (c == null){
```

---

[6] MD5: `fab2711b0b55eb980f44bfebc2c17f1f`.
[7] MD5: `95f7d37a60ef6d83ae7443a3893bb246`.

```
4      a13840(); // key initialization function
5 }
6      Continue ...
7 }
```

⇒ The secret keys can be either statically defined or dynamically generated.

In the static case, the key is either hard-coded or directly imported as the parameter, which can be easily located and obtained. On the other hand, the dynamic key is usually generated at runtime and even could be fluctuating in different runtime context, which is nearly impossible to be handled by static analysis. The following code snippet shows an example of dynamic key genera-tion, in which elements[3] is not a fixed value because of the uncertain stack trace at runtime.

```
1 StackTraceElement[] elements = Thread.currentThread().
      getStackTrace();
2 int hashCode = elements[3].getClassName()+elements[3].
      getMethodName().hashCode();
```

4.3 Reflection

Reflection allows programs to create, modify and access an object at runtime, which brings many flexibilities. However, such dynamic feature also impedes static analysis due to those reflective invocations, especially those invoking other functions. Such uncertain behaviors could result in that the static analysis cannot capture the real intention.

In this section, we explore two questions on reflection:

1. How widespread is the reflection used in the wild?
2. Among all the usage, how many of them are for the obfuscation purpose?

Reflection provides diverse APIs targeting at different objects like Class, Method and Field. In practice, particular APIs are often executed in sequence to achieve specific functionalities. In our study, we focus on the sequence pattern [Class.forName() → getMethod() → invoke()] which is the most frequent pattern for reflective calls mentioned by Li et al. [31]. Also, in this sequence, the execution of the program is implicitly transferred to another function (the function targeted by getMethod()), which has an obvious influence on program status, especially the control flow.

Reflection Detection. First, we located the reflective invocations by searching for the certain APIs, Class.forName(), etc. Then we managed to recover the real target of the reflective calls, actually the parameters of Class.forName() and getMethod(). In theory, dynamic analysis is the best way to find the input parameter. However, its low path coverage and efficiency issues are not suitable for large-scale scanning. To balance the efficiency and coverage, we developed a light-weight tool to trace the input parameters. The high-level idea is to find the real content of the parameters through backward slicing.

More details, first our tool scans the function body and locates two reflection calls – Class.forName() and getMethod(). The parameter registers will be set as *slicing criterion*. Then it traces back from the locations, analyzing each instruction to find the corresponding *slices*. After that, this tool parses and simulates each instruction in *slices*, and calculates the final value of the *slicing criterion*.

Here, we use a real-world example (see the below code block) to illustrate such work flow. In this case, our tool will mark the positions of *blue-highlighted* reflective calls and trace the data flow of *red highlighted* registers. The final output would be {"android.os.SystemProperties", "get"}.

```
1 const/4 v1, 0
2 const-string v0,'android.os.SystemProperties'
3 invoke-static v0,Ljava/lang/Class;->forName(Ljava/lang/String
      ;)Ljava/lang/Class;
4 const-string v2, 'get'
5 ...
6 invoke-virtual v0, v2, v3, Ljava/lang/Class;->getMethod(Ljava/
      lang/String; [Ljava/lang/Class;)Ljava/lang/reflect/
      Method;
```

Note that, to reduce the maintenance complexity, we do not carry out recursive function invoking resolution. If the content of the target register is the return value of another function, the metadata of that function will be recorded (name, parameters, etc.). Besides, due to our tool works at the static level, predicates (if and switch, etc.) may lead to the failure of recovering the real target. Whenever the target can not be definitely obtained by our tool, a null will be recorded instead. We then measured the successful recovery rate of our static-level tool. Among all 121,262 occurrences of reflective calls, 116,595 (96.2%) non-null targets were recorded, which means our tool can work effectively.

Large-Scale Investigation and Findings. The implementation of our detection model (reflection usage and invoked functions in reflection) is still based on Androguard with around 1600 Python lines of code. After experiments on our APK dataset, the reflection statistics are shown in Fig. 4. We could find:

⇒ The proportions of reflection deployment in benign apps and malware are similar.

To the successfully recovered functions, we further explore why these reflection implementations are necessary. According to different APK dataset, the most frequently invoked functions are listed in Tables 2, 3, and 4 respectively. These lists reflect:

⇒ Most of the reflection cases are used to invoke hidden functions or to support backward compatibility.

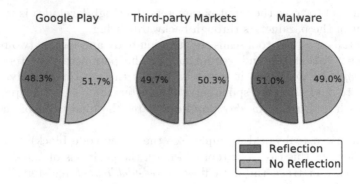

Fig. 4. Ratio of reflection in three datasets

Table 2. Functions invoked via reflection (Google Play)

Frequency	Recovered Function
2,275	android.support.v4.content.LocalBroadcastManager.getInstance
1,297	android.webkit.WebView.onPause
1,250	android.os.SystemProperties.get
821	org.apache.harmony.xnet.provider.jsse.NativeCrypto.RAND_seed
523	com.google.android.gms.common.GooglePlayServicesUtil. isGooglePlayServicesAvailable

Table 3. Functions invoked via reflection (3rd-p Market)

Frequency	Recovered Function
3,859	android.os.SystemProperties.get
1,800	android.support.v4.content.LocalBroadcastManager.getInstance
1,158	org.apache.harmony.xnet.provider.jsse.NativeCrypto.RAND_seed
721	android.os.ServiceManager.getService
613	android.os.Build.hasSmartBar

Table 4. Functions invoked via reflection (malware)

Frequency	Recovered Function
2,977	java.lang.String.valueOf
2,142	android.telephony.gsm.SmsManager.getDefault
687	android.os.SystemProperties.get
518	java.lang.String.charAt
352	java.lang.String.equals

In Android system, the functions related to the Android framework and OS itself are usually annotated with the label "@hide", which can only be called through reflection. In above three tables, all functions starting with `android.os.*` and `android.webkit.*` are hidden-annotated.

We also manually checked the use case of `android.support.v4.content.` `LocalBroadcastManager.getInstance`. We found that the corresponding reflective calls are usually enclosed in a *try-catch* block, aiming to handle the not-found exception caused by discrepancy among systems with different versions. Such pattern is a programming standard recommended by the official Android documents [6].

To malware samples, we find:

⇒ Compared with benign apps, malware prefers to use more complex reflection invoking patterns to hide its intentions.
⇒ String operations are usually combined with reflection to enhance the complexity of the code.

For example, the following code block is extracted from an obfuscated malware[8]. After analysis, the function invoked by reflection could be restored as:

```
if (!ò.trim().toLowerCase().contains(Ô("G))OCH")))
```

As a comparison, the original code is shown below. In this case, all string operations can be written in non-reflection forms. We could find such reflection usage makes the code structure more complicated and confusing, which enhances the effect of code obfuscation.

```
if (!((Boolean) Class.forName("java.lang.String").
    getMethod("contains", new Class({CharSequence.class}).
    invoke(Class.forName("java.lang.String").getMethod("
    toLowerCase", null).invoke(Class.forName("java.lang.
    String").getMethod("trim", null).invoke(ò, null), null)
    , new Object[]{Ô("G))OCH")}))).booleanValue())
```

5   Discussion

In this section, we discuss some limitations of our study and then describe the future plan. Though we have conducted a large-scale investigation of mainstream obfuscation techniques used in Android apps, we should point out there are still some existing techniques not involved in our research, say control flow obfuscation and native code obfuscation.

According to our investigation, the control flow obfuscation is non-universal and only provided by two available Android obfuscators, DashO and Allatori. Moreover, we believe both tools cannot provide a strong control flow obfuscation implementation as they claimed. In our experiments, less than 5% methods

---

[8] MD5: `7ff1b8afd22c1ed77ed70bfc04635315`.

contained in our sample APKs were obfuscated in the control flow, and the obfuscation implementations were trivial (such as only adding some simple "try-catch" combinations). Therefore, at this moment, we cannot capture enough meaningful (real-world) control-flow obfuscated samples for study.

Another topic not involved in this paper is native code obfuscation. As an advanced programming skill, developers can implement components in native code with the help of Android NDK. However, the implementation of native code is quite different from Java-level techniques, which makes the native code obfuscation could be treated as an independent research topic. Therefore, we leave it as our future study.

6   Related Work

Obfuscation is always a hot research topic in Android ecosystem, and there are several studies performed on how to obfuscate Android apps effectively and how to measure the obfuscation effectiveness.

6.1   Obfuscation Measurement and Assessment

Obfuscation techniques have been widely used in the Android app development. Naturally, in academia, researchers are interested in whether these techniques do work. An early attempt is [27] which empirically evaluates a set of 7 obfuscation methods on 240 APKs. Also, Park et al. [35] empirically analyzed the effects of code obfuscation on Android app similarity analysis. Recently, Faruki et al. [26] conducted a survey to review the mainstream Android code obfuscation and protection techniques. However, they concentrated on the technical analysis to evaluate different techniques, not like our work based on a large-scale dataset. They show that many obfuscation methods are idempotent or monotonous. Wang et al. [41] defined the obfuscator identification problem for Android and proposed a solution based on machine learning techniques. The experiments indicated that their approach could achieve about 97% accuracy to identify ProGuard, Allatori, DashO, Legu, and Bangcle. Duan et al. [25] conducted a comprehensive study on 6 major commercial packers and a large set of samples to understand Android (un)packers. On the aspect of deobfuscation research, Bichsel et al. [22] proposed a structured prediction approach for performing probabilistic layout deobfuscation of Android APKs and implemented a scalable probabilistic system called DeGuard.

Different from above research, our work is based on large Android app datasets which cover official Google play store, third-party Android markets, and update-to-date malware families. We attempt to understand the distribution of Android obfuscation techniques and provide the up-to-date knowledge about app protection.

6.2   Security Impact of Android Obfuscation

As discussed earlier, the obfuscation will create barriers for Android program analysis. Works on clone/repackage detection [40,42] find that obfuscations can impair detection results.

Studies of malware detection also showed that obfuscation is an obstacle to malware analysis. Rastogi et al. [37] evaluated several commercial mobile anti-malware products for Android and tested how resistant they are against various common obfuscation techniques. Their experiment result showed anti-malware tools make little effort to provide transformation-resilient detection (in the year 2013). After that, Maiorca et al. [33] conducted a large-scale experiment in which the detection performance of anti-malware solutions are tested against malware samples under different obfuscation strategies. Their results showed the improvement of anti-malware engines in recent years. Recently, Hoffmann et al. [29] developed a framework for automated obfuscation, which implemented fine-grained obfuscation strategies and could be used as test benches for evaluating analysis tools. Similar works are also completed by Preda et al. [36]. To handle obfuscated samples, Suarez-Tangil et al. [39] propose DroidSieve, an Android malware classifier based on static analysis and deep inspection that is resilient to obfuscation.

For malware detection, researchers mainly discussed arms race between obfuscation and malware detection. Although some malware detection tools claim to still work well in the presence of obfuscation, none could eliminate the obfuscation effects in their experimental evaluation. Our study focuses on the empirical study of security impacts of obfuscation in the wild from different views, which are complementary to existing works. That is, we statistically evaluate the distribution of obfuscation methods from views of different markets, hardening capability of obfuscations and temporal evolution, with a light-weight and scalable obfuscation detection framework. We believe some of our findings would be useful for developers and researchers to better understand the usage of obfuscation, for example, keeping pace with the development of obfuscation technique.

7   Conclusion

In this paper, we concentrate on exploring the current deployment status of Android code obfuscation in the wild. For this target, we developed specific detection tools for three common obfuscation techniques and performed a large-scale scanning on three representative APK datasets. The results show that, to different techniques and app categories, the status of code obfuscation differs in many aspects. For example, the basic renaming obfuscation has become widely-used among Chinese third-party market developers, while still not pervasive in Google Play market. Besides, malware authors put great efforts on more advanced code protection skills, like string encryption and reflections. Also, we provide the corresponding illustrations to enlighten developers to select the most suitable code protection methodologies and help researchers improve code analysis systems in the right direction.

Acknowledgement. We thank anonymous reviewers for their insightful comments. This work was partially supported by National Natural Science Foundation of China (NSFC) under Grant No. 61572415 and 61572481, Hong Kong S.A.R. Research Grants Council (RGC) Early Career Scheme/General Research Fund No. 24207815 and 14217816.

References

1. smartphone assistant. http://zhushou.360.cn/
2. Allatori. http://www.allatori.com/
3. Androguard. https://github.com/androguard/androguard
4. Anzhi. http://www.anzhi.com/
5. Appchina. http://www.appchina.com/
6. Backward compatibility for android applications. https://android-developers. googleblog.com/2009/04/backward-compatibility-for-android.html
7. DashO. https://www.preemptive.com/products/dasho/overview
8. Dexguard. https://www.guardsquare.com/en/dexguard
9. DexProtector. https://dexprotector.com/
10. Huawei appstore. http://appstore.huawei.com/
11. Java Cryptography Extension. http://www.oracle.com/technetwork/java/javase/ downloads/jce8-download-2133166.html
12. n-gram. https://en.wikipedia.org/wiki/N-gram
13. Number of available applications in the Google Play Store from December 2009 to December 2017. http://www.statista.com/statistics/266210/number-of-available-applications-in-the-google-play-store/
14. ProGuard. http://proguard.sourceforge.net/
15. Shield4J. http://shield4j.com/
16. Virusshare. https://virusshare.com/
17. Virustotal. https://www.virustotal.com/
18. Wandoujia. https://www.wandoujia.com/
19. Xiaomi application store. http://app.mi.com/
20. Apvrille, A., Nigam, R.: Obfuscation in android malware, and how to fight back. Virus Bull. 1–10 (2014)
21. Balachandran, V., Tan, D.J., Thing, V.L.: Control flow obfuscation for android applications. Comput. Secur. **61**, 72–93 (2016)
22. Bichsel, B., Raychev, V., Tsankov, P., Vechev, M.T.: Statistical deobfuscation of android applications. In: Proceedings of the 2016 ACM SIGSAC Conference on Computer and Communications Security (CCS) (2016)
23. Calvet, J., Fernandez, J.M., Marion, J.: Aligot: cryptographic function identification in obfuscated binary programs. In: Proceedings of the 19th ACM Conference on Computer and Communications Security (CCS) (2012)
24. Chen, K., Liu, P., Zhang, Y.: Achieving accuracy and scalability simultaneously in detecting application clones on Android markets. In: Proceeding of the 36th International Conference on Software Engineering (ICSE) (2014)
25. Duan, Y., et al.: Things you may not know about android (un)packers: a systematic study based on whole-system emulation. In: Proceedings of 25th Annual Network and Distributed System Security Symposium (NDSS) (2018)
26. Faruki, P., Fereidooni, H., Laxmi, V., Conti, M., Gaur, M.S.: Android Code Protection via Obfuscation Techniques: Past, Present and Future Directions. CoRR abs/1611.10231 (2016)

27. Freiling, F.C., Protsenko, M., Zhuang, Y.: An empirical evaluation of software obfuscation techniques applied to Android APKs. In: Tian, J., Jing, J., Srivatsa, M. (eds.) SecureComm 2014. LNICST, vol. 153, pp. 315–328. Springer, Cham (2015). https://doi.org/10.1007/978-3-319-23802-9_24

28. Gröbert, F., Willems, C., Holz, T.: Automated identification of cryptographic primitives in binary programs. In: Sommer, R., Balzarotti, D., Maier, G. (eds.) RAID 2011. LNCS, vol. 6961, pp. 41–60. Springer, Heidelberg (2011). https://doi.org/10.1007/978-3-642-23644-0_3

29. Hoffmann, J., Rytilahti, T., Maiorca, D., Winandy, M., Giacinto, G., Holz, T.: Evaluating analysis tools for android apps: status quo and robustness against obfuscation. In: Proceedings of the Sixth ACM on Conference on Data and Application Security and Privacy (CODASPY) (2016)

30. Huang, H., et al.: Android malware development on public malware scanning platforms: a large-scale date-driven study. In: Proceeding of the 2016 IEEE International Conference on Big Data (BigData) (2016)

31. Li, L., Bissyandé, T.F., Octeau, D., Klein, J.: DroidRA: taming reflection to support whole-program analysis of android apps. In: Proceedings of the 25th International Symposium on Software Testing and Analysis (ISSTA) (2016)

32. Li, M., et al.: LibD: scalable and precise third-party library detection in Android markets. In: Proceedings of the 39th International Conference on Software Engineering (ICSE) (2017)

33. Maiorca, D., Ariu, D., Corona, I., Aresu, M., Giacinto, G.: Stealth attacks: an extended insight into the obfuscation effects on Android malware. Comput. Secur. **51**, 16–31 (2015)

34. Matenaar, F., Wichmann, A., Leder, F., Gerhards-Padilla, E.: CIS: the crypto intelligence system for automatic detection and localization of cryptographic functions in current malware. In: Proceeding of the 7th International Conference on Malicious and Unwanted Software (MALWARE), 16–18 October 2012, Fajardo, PR, USA (2012)

35. Park, J., Kim, H., Jeong, Y., Cho, S., Han, S., Park, M.: Effects of code obfuscation on Android app similarity analysis. J. Wirel. Mob. Netw. Ubiquitous Comput. Dependable Appl. **6**(4), 86–98 (2015)

36. Preda, M.D., Maggi, F.: Testing Android malware detectors against code obfuscation: a systematization of knowledge and unified methodology. J. Comput. Virol. Hacking Tech. **13**(3), 209–232 (2017)

37. Rastogi, V., Chen, Y., Jiang, X.: DroidChameleon: evaluating Android antimalware against transformation attacks. In: Proceedings of the 8th ACM Symposium on Information, Computer and Communications Security (ASIACCS) (2013)

38. Shu, J., Li, J., Zhang, Y., Gu, D.: Android app protection via interpretation obfuscation. In: Proceeding of the 12th IEEE International Conference on Dependable, Autonomic and Secure Computing (DASC) (2014)

39. Suarez-Tangil, G., Dash, S.K., Ahmadi, M., Kinder, J., Giacinto, G., Cavallaro, L.: DroidSieve: fast and accurate classification of obfuscated Android malware. In: Proceedings of the Seventh ACM on Conference on Data and Application Security and Privacy (CODASPY) (2017)

40. Wang, H., Guo, Y., Ma, Z., Chen, X.: WuKong: a scalable and accurate two-phase approach to Android app clone detection. In: Proceedings of the 2015 International Symposium on Software Testing and Analysis (ISSTA), Baltimore, MD, USA, 12–17 July 2015 (2015)

41. Wang, Y., Rountev, A.: Who changed you? Obfuscator identification for Android. In: Proceedings of the 4th IEEE/ACM International Conference on Mobile Software Engineering and Systems (MOBILESoft) (2017)
42. Zhang, F., Huang, H., Zhu, S., Wu, D., Liu, P.: ViewDroid: towards obfuscation-resilient mobile application repackaging detection. In: Proceedings of 7th ACM Conference on Security & Privacy in Wireless and Mobile Networks (WiSec) (2014)

Transparent Low-Latency Network Anonymisation for Mobile Devices

Martin Byrenheid[✉], Stefan Köpsell, Alexander Naumenko,
and Thorsten Strufe

Chair of Privacy and Data Security, Technische Universität Dresden,
Dresden, Germany
{martin.byrenheid,stefan.koepsell,thorsten.strufe}@tu-dresden.de,
alexnau@posteo.de

Abstract. Mobile devices such as smartphones and tablets have become increasingly popular tools for Internet-based communication such as web browsing and text messaging. At the same time however, mobile devices fail to provide important privacy guarantees for their users. In particular, mobile devices per default neither conceal which services they are contacting nor hide their source IP addresses. Solutions to these problems exist, but either do not provide sufficient protection or have not gained widespread use due to a lack of usability. In this paper, we therefore present an architecture that combines the transparent tunneling of traffic with the strong protection of low-latency anonymisation networks. We furthermore present and discuss trade-offs that can be made to reduce the latency and overhead caused by the transparent tunneling of traffic. Based on measurements taken from a testbed setup, we show that our solution provides anonymity at the IP layer with acceptable energy consumption and goodput penalties.

1 Introduction

Wireless and mobile communication technologies such as Wi-Fi, UMTS and LTE allow mobile connectivity to the Internet at speeds sufficient for email, instant messaging, web browsing, and even video streaming. As a consequence, mobile devices such as smartphones and tablets became widely used for Internet-based communication.

Similar to desktop devices, smartphones and tablets per default do not provide sufficient concealment of the users communication activities. On the one hand, mobile devices do not hide the IP addresses of the services they are contacting, consequently leaking this information to the Internet service provider (ISP) and to local Wi-Fi access point providers. On the other hand, mobile devices do not hide their own IP addresses from the services they are contacting. Thus if the service colludes with the ISP of the user, both entities are able to link the service with the real-world identity of the user.

© ICST Institute for Computer Sciences, Social Informatics and Telecommunications Engineering 2018
R. Beyah et al. (Eds.): SecureComm 2018, LNICST 254, pp. 193–209, 2018.
https://doi.org/10.1007/978-3-030-01701-9_11

Virtual Private Network (VPN) services like Mullvad[1] and Private Internet Access[2] allow users to mitigate these problems by installing an application on their devices that tunnels all traffic through the VPN provider's servers. While VPN services typically act transparently and can be set up easily, they require the user to trust the VPN provider, since the latter can easily observe which services the user is contacting [1,2]. Applications like Orbot[3] and ANONDroid[4] in contrast utilise low-latency anonymisation networks and thus provide anonymisation without the user having to trust a single entity. At the same time however, these applications do not yet provide the same level of transparency as VPN services do. The ANONdroid application only provides a local SOCKS-interface, so that only applications that support SOCKS can profit from anonymization. Orbot already provides a VPN mode that achieves a similar level of transparency as applications from VPN providers do. However, Orbot only supports anonymisation of TCP traffic[5] and we are not aware of any documentation or evaluation of Orbot's architecture and performance.

Motivated by the need for easy-to-use and strong IP layer anonymisation, we present the following contributions in this paper:

- Inspired by virtual private network technology, we propose an architecture for transparent tunneling of arbitrary IP traffic through low-latency anonymisation. We furthermore discuss protocol-specific optimisations for UDP, TCP and DNS traffic.
- We present results from experiments on a testbed, where we measured the average goodput and energy consumption during the download of data under different settings. In particular, we compare the performance of different devices with different versions of Android for the cases that OpenVPN for Android, Orbot or our solution is used for anonymisation.

The paper is structured as follows: In the next section, we first give a short introduction to mix networks and highlight how low-latency mix networks differ from traditional mix networks. In Sects. 3 and 4, we state the goals that guided the design of our solution and discuss to which extend these goals have been addressed in the literature. In Sects. 5 and 6, we subsequently present our solution in detail and discuss protocol-specific optimisations. Section 7 discusses to which extend the optimisations we proposed weaken the privacy guarantees of the low-latency anonymisation service that is used. In Sect. 8, we present and discuss our experimental results. Section 9 then provides summary of our results.

---

[1] Mullvad. https://www.mullvad.net/en/, 2018-01-05.

[2] Private Internet Access. https://www.privateinternetaccess.com/. 2018-01-05.

[3] "Orbot: Tor for Android". Guardian Project. https://guardianproject.info/apps/orbot/. 2018-01-05.

[4] "ANONdroid". JAP-Team. https://play.google.com/. 2018-01-23.

[5] "Tor Project: FAQ". Tor Project. https://www.torproject.org/docs/faq.html.en. 2018-01-05.

2   Background

Our work addresses privacy issues of mobile devices such as smartphones and tablets that are connected to the Internet via Wi-Fi or mobile communications. We consider a user, who runs one or more applications on his device. Each application in turn contacts a number of Internet services to exchange data. Depending on the service, the respective application might need to provide login credentials in order to gain access.

To protect his privacy, the user wants to set up his mobile device in such a way that the installed applications never contact Internet services directly, but instead utilise an anonymisation service like Tor [3] or AN.ON [4] to contact services privately. In particular, the user expects the service to provide *sender anonymity*, meaning packets sent by the user's device cannot be linked to it anymore after being processed by the network.

Low-latency mix networks are based on the mix concept introduced by Chaum [5]. To conceal its communication using a sequence of mix nodes, a client pads each packet to a fixed length and performs layered encryption, where each layer is encrypted with the key of the corresponding mix node. Low-latency mix networks designed for use cases where a high latency results in unacceptable slowdown, such as web browsing or multimedia streaming. Instead of encrypting each mix packet separately using public key cryptography, low-latency mix networks therefore only make use of public key cryptography once to exchange symmetric keys between senders and mixes. A set of symmetric keys is then called an *anonymous channel* or *circuit* and is used for multiple packets. The low-latency mix networks considered in our work furthermore provide reliable communication, automatically performing retransmission of lost packets.

Due to the absence of any artificial delay during the processing of mix packets by mixes, low-latency mix networks are vulnerable to traffic analysis attacks based on timing. Thus, low-latency mix networks can only protect against a *local adversary* that can observe or compromise a fraction of the mixes by generating, modifying or dropping packets. Furthermore, low-latency mix networks do not provide anonymity for a particular channel if the first and last mix of the channel are under control of the adversary.

3   Goals

In our opinion, a useful and effective mechanism for mobile devices that provides anonymisation of traffic at the network and transport layer should achieve the following goals:

1. **Strong anonymisation of traffic:** The mechanism must support obfuscation of arbitrary traffic at the network and transport layer in a manner that does not open up new attacks for the local adversary described in Sect. 2.
2. **Low setup complexity:** The mechanism needs to be easy to setup on current operating systems for mobile devices. In particular, it shall be implementable without requiring modifications of the operating system kernel or

unlocking of administrative privileges (e.g. rooting on Android or jailbreaking on iOS). Furthermore, the solution should provide protection for all installed applications per default without the need to make changes to any application.
3. **Low overhead:** The anonymisation should not result in a significant loss of network throughput nor increase the latency significantly. Furthermore, the solution should consume a low amount of energy.

We consider anonymisation at the application layer out of scope, since latter cannot be done in general without changing the code of the applications themselves. For example, web browsers typically protect the confidentiality and integrity of their traffic by means of Transport Layer Security (TLS). Consequently, a transparent proxy application cannot erase identifying information from the web traffic without being able to compromise TLS encryption, which is clearly undesirable.

4   Related Work

According to our knowledge, the integration of low-latency anonymisation services into mobile devices so far received only few attention by the research community. Wiangsripanawan et al. [6] proposed game-based definitions for location privacy as well as for sender anonymity, receiver anonymity and unlinkability together with three different mechanisms that allow mobile Tor clients to avoid loss of existing circuits after their IP address have changed. Andersson and Panchenko [7] investigate the differences regarding anonymity and performance for the cases that the Tor client is running directly on the mobile device, the Tor client is running on a computer at the home of the user and the case that the mobile device connects to a third party Tor client. More recently, the work of Doswell [8] presents a field study along with network simulation and mathematical modelling, showing the impact of congestion and circuit build time on the achievable data transfer speed. Furthermore, Doswell proposes a design called *mBridge*, which employs a trusted bridge relay as first hop and Mobile IP [9] to handle changes of the mobile devices' IP address.

Fundamentally, all previous work on low-latency anonymisation that we are aware of focuses on efficient maintenance of connectivity to the anonymisation service. Thus, there still is a need for investigation regarding how an anonymisation client can be integrated into the mobile device in an effective and resource-efficient manner.

5   Design

Existing low-latency anonymisation networks like Tor [3] or AN.ON [4] typically provide a client software that is run as a background service on the user's system. In order to make the anonymous communication service accessible to other applications, the client software implements a proxy interface and can therefore be used like a regular proxy (usually SOCKS or HTTP proxy). While this approach has the advantage that it only requires processing of application layer data and is thus easy to implement, it currently fails in practice, as Android and iOS do not support a corresponding permanent global setting. Instead, Android and iOS only allow manual proxy settings per network [10,11], which would have to be done manually by the user and thus is error-prone.

To overcome the aforementioned problem, we instead utilise a virtual network interface (VNI), which is already provided by Android and iOS [12,13]. Latter is handled by the operating system like a real network interface. The interfaces provided by Android and iOS furthermore automatically set up their forwarding table so that whenever an application sends a packet to an arbitrary destination, this packet will be enqueued in the VNI until it is processed by a dedicated process that we call *mediator service* in the following.

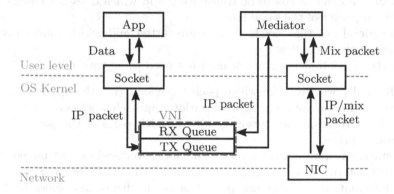

Fig. 1. The architecture of the software running on the user's smartphone.

Figure 1 illustrates the architecture of the software running on the user's device in detail. Except for the mediator service, all packets sent by user-level applications are appended to the VNIs *transmission queue* (TX queue) by the operating system. We assign an IP address from a private address space (10.0.0.0/8 or 172.16.0.0/12) to the VNI in order to avoid overlap with IP addresses of the Internet.

The only process that is able to exchange IP-packets with the external network is the mediator service. Latter is aware of the VNI and is able to read and remove IP-packets from the transmission queue. Additionally, the mediator service is able to append IP-packets to the *reception queue* (RX queue) of the VNI. The operating system subsequently delivers all IP-packets added to the reception queue to the corresponding applications.

For each IP-packet read from the transmission queue, the mediator service extracts the relevant header data and payload, sets up a new channel through the anonymisation service if necessary and submits the extracted data over the channel. Whenever the mediator service receives data from the anonymisation service, it assembles a corresponding IP-packet and appends it to the reception queue. If necessary, the mediator service then closes the channel through the anonymisation service.

5.1 Improving Efficiency and Anonymity Considering Transport Layer Packet Streams

Since we focus on current mobile devices based on Android and iOS, the primary consideration that influenced our design is that latter devices mainly communicate in the form of TCP and UDP flows, where each flow consists of multiple packets destined to the same recipient.

From the perspective of the mediator service introduced above, we assign each field of a packet header to one of the following three categories:

- **Static:** Data that needs to be transmitted and which does not change from packet to packet of the same flow.
- **Dynamic:** Data that needs to be transmitted and which differs between packets of the same flow.
- **Private:** Data that must not or does not need to be transmitted.

Additionally we treat the whole packet payload (i.e. the application layer data) as dynamic because our anonymisation approach works on the transport layer and has therefore no knowledge about which parts of the payload are in fact static or private.

For static data, we can trade off transmission overhead against memory consumption (in terms of keeping state). To do so, the mediator *only once* sends control information that contains the set of header fields and values that shall be used for all packets of the corresponding flow. The last relay then keeps this information in memory until the flow has been terminated.

Dynamic data in turn allows a trade-off between overhead and latency. Since the encapsulation process of the low-latency anonymisation protocol enforces a fixed length for the resulting mix packets, the dynamic data contained in one packet might only use a fraction of the space reserved for anonymous payload data, thus resulting in significant padding overhead. To reduce the needed amount of padding, the mediator can wait a certain amount of time for further packets and if successful, encapsulate the dynamic data of multiple packets within one mix packet.

In the following we describe how we adapted the general approach described above to the important transport layer protocols UDP and TCP and how we deal with the remaining IP traffic.

UDP: The UDP header contains four fields, namely the destination port, the source port, the payload length and a checksum. The destination port is considered to be static data and thus will be transmitted (together with the destination IP address) only once per UDP packet flow. Additionally we treat the source port as static data. The checksum is handled as private data and therefore not transmitted. As the anonymous channel offers reliable transport, the checksum will be recreated by the last relay before sending the UDP packet to the final destination. The UDP payload length is considered to be dynamic. We assume that many application layer protocols on top of UDP expect to receive non-fragmented data units (e.g. RTP packets) and thus we must preserve the UDP packet size while sending the UDP packet from the last relay to the final destination.

TCP: For TCP, the situation is more complex, since a naive transmission of TCP header data and payload would neglect the fact that low-latency anonymisation services already provide reliable transmission of data, thus resulting in an undesirable transport of TCP over TCP. Additionally it turned out that most of the TCP header fields could or should be treated as private. The former for efficiency reasons, the latter due to anonymity reasons, e.g. to avoid leakage of details about the sender's TCP implementation (which in turn could be related to revealing the operating system used etc.). Therefore our general approach is to basically only transport the TCP payload but not the TCP header. The only exception is that we treat the destination port number (and destination address) as static data.

To achieve this, we employ a minimal user-level TCP stack that allows the mediator service to transparently interact with the TCP streams of local applications. Since the mediator service and the application that uses TCP are running on the same device, the user-level stack does not need any sophisticated mechanisms for detection of packet loss and congestion control, allowing us to avoid high computational overhead. Figure 2 illustrates the interaction between the local application, the mediator service, the anonymisation service and the recipient upon initiation of a new TCP connection by the local application. Whenever the mediator service takes a TCP SYN packet from the transmission queue, it opens a new anonymous channel and sends a signalling packet with the corresponding IP address and port number to the last relay of the anonymisation service. Latter then initiates a TCP connection using the given address and port number and responds with a signalling message that indicates whether the connection has been set up successfully. If the connection succeeded, the mediator service generates a TCP packet for the local application with the SYN and ACK flag set. Otherwise, the mediator service generates a TCP packet with RST bit set and appends it to the reception queue.

During transmission of data by the local application, the mediator will transparently extract the payload from the packets and send it over the established anonymous channel. When the application terminates the connection by sending a packet with the FIN flag set, the mediator will signal the anonymisation service to close the associated connection. If the recipient terminates the connection, the anonymisation service will notify the mediator, which in turn will shut down the TCP connection of the corresponding application.

IP. Although the official APIs of Android and iOS currently only support UDP and TCP, we also discuss anonymisation solely at the IP layer in the following.

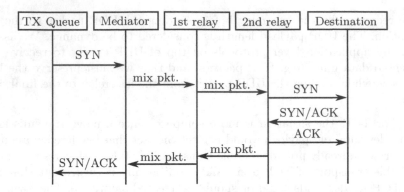

Fig. 2. Interaction between the local application, the mediator service and the anonymisation service for TCP transmissions (pessimistic mode of operation).

This allows us to provide at least a minimal protection in the case that other transport layer protocols are supported by Android or iOS in the future.

We treat all IP-traffic which is neither TCP nor UDP in the same way. First of all each IP-packet flow is transmitted over an individual channel to reduce linkability. For each IP-packet we send certain header information (as explained below) and the IP-packet payload. The last relay will create IP-packets out of this information and sends them to the final recipient.

Considering IP version 4 and IP version 6, the *Version* field, and the *Destination Address* clearly belong to the static data. The *Total Length/Payload Length* field belong to the dynamic data. The *Source Address* and the *Header Checksum* belong to private data.

Additionally, we categorise the *Differentiated Services Code Point (DSCP)* and *Explicit Congestion Notification (ECN)* as well as *Traffic Class* as private data. The reason is, that we are not aware of any low-latency anonymisation service which supports different service/traffic classes, thus limiting their effectiveness to only the path between the last relay and the recipient.

For IPv4 packets, we think that data related to fragmentation (*Identification, Flags, Fragment Offset*) can be treated as private data, if anonymity has priority. Fragmentation is rarely used in practice – and IPv6 does not even support it. In this case all fragmented IPv4 packets will be dropped. The *Time to Live (TTL)/Hop Limit* field can also be treated as private in case of prioritising anonymity. Therefore the last relay will set this field to a predefined fixed value. Nevertheless there might be cases where this field is used in protocols (traceroute would be one example). Therefore we consider it as dynamic data if compatibility needs to be prioritised.

The IP header supports optional headers by the *Options* and *IHL* fields in case of IPv4 and by the *Next Header* field in case of IPv6. Again, if anonymity should be prioritised, we consider these fields as private. More specific, we drop all IP-packets which have optional headers. If compatibility has priority, we do not change the fields and therefore consider them as dynamic data.

6   Optimistic DNS

In this section we will describe some efficiency improvements related to DNS, which we treat in a special way due to its importance.

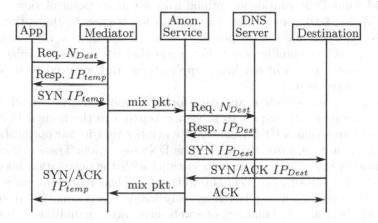

Fig. 3. Interaction between the local application, the mediator service and the anonymisation service for DNS requests.

One fundamental advantage of VNI-based anonymisation over SOCKS-based solutions is that the operating system can be configured to use the VNI for DNS name resolution. All DNS requests, including those triggered by applications, will then be appended to the transmission queue of the VNI, thus allowing the mediator service to perform name resolution over the anonymisation service. However, since DNS resolution needs to be completed before any packets can be sent to the intended recipient, we face the problem that the anonymisation of the DNS request by means of rerouting over multiple mixes introduces significant latency. We therefore propose an optimistic DNS resolution, which is illustrated in Fig. 3. Upon arrival of a DNS request, the mediator service immediately chooses a local, temporary IP address and generates a corresponding DNS response. The mapping from the temporary IP address to the DNS name is kept in memory by the mediator service, so that subsequent packets can be correctly associated with their destination. As soon as the mediator starts submission of data to the anonymisation service, it prepends signalling data containing the DNS hostname, leaving the task of DNS name resolution to the last relay.

In order to avoid that the DNS lookup table grows infinitely, we set the time-to-live (TTL) field in our DNS responses to 60 s and remove outdated DNS entries after 70 s. These timeout values reflect the default lifetime of application level DNS caches as used by Mozilla Firefox and Google Chrome.

7 Discussion

Considering TCP, we only transmit the minimal necessary data, namely the destination IP and port number and the payload itself. Since we do not see how to further reduce this information without breaking application layer compatibility we consider our TCP solution as optimal from a privacy point of view.

Considering UDP, our current implementation is close to the optimal case. The only field which we could possibly avoid to transmit is the source port number. In fact some preliminary tests suggest that letting the last relay choose a random source port will not break applications. But we need to do a more profound analysis here.

Considering our optimistic approach for DNS resolution, we see advantages and disadvantages with respect to privacy compared to the normal DNS resolution using anonymous UDP channels. Remember that in our optimistic DNS approach, the last relay eventually does the DNS resolution. Thereby it can link the payload of the related anonymous channel with the destination host name contained in the signalling packet. This in fact could leak more information compared to the case, where the last relay only learns the destination IP address (but not the host name). Think e.g. of a web server hosting multiple web sites. A common approach to distinguish the different web sites is based on the requested host name. Therefore the last relay will learn which of the multiple web sites was in fact requested (in case of optimistic DNS) while in case of normal DNS it will not learn this (assuming that in both cases the HTTP protocol itself is encrypted by TLS).

On the other hand, the optimistic DNS approach could also offer some privacy benefits compared to the normal anonymous DNS lookup. Assuming that there is a web-site https://gugle.com operated by Numbers Inc., the DNS servers of Numbers Inc. could respond with a new unique IP address for each DNS request for gugle.com. Usually DNS responses are cached on the client side, meaning that subsequent HTTP requests sent from the same client to gugle.com will all use the same destination IP address while HTTP requests originated from different clients will use different destination IP addresses. Therefore the web servers of Numbers Inc. can distinguish different users even if all of them use an anonymisation service for their communication (including DNS requests). In case of our optimistic DNS resolution, all DNS requests will be made by the same client, namely the last relay of the anonymisation service. Thus it will prevent the attack described above.

8 Evaluation

Network layer anonymisation on mobile devices is particularly challenging due to their constrained resources. A high computational overhead will result in low throughput and high battery drain, thus severely limiting the usefulness of the device. To evaluate the practical value of the design presented in Sect. 5, we implemented our solution (named *ANONguard*[6]) for the Android operating system and performed experiments on a local testbed[7]. We chose to evaluate our solution in a local testbed to obtain upper bounds on the performance of our solution in an idealized setting in which there is almost no network latency and congestion.

As depicted by Fig. 4, we set up a 802.11ac-capable wireless access point (AP) that allows a mobile device to connect with a dedicated measurement host. For our measurement, we used a Motorola Moto X Style running Android 7.0 and an ASUS Nexus 7 (2nd generation) running Android 6.0.1. Both devices were running the latest official version of Android that was provided by the manufacturer. To generate arbitrary traffic workloads, we implemented a measurement client for Android along with a measurement server application for Linux. The instrumentation host was used to perform repeated measurements in an automated fashion, as it controls the setup of the anonymisation software on the mobile device, starts the measurement client and extracts the measurement results from the device.

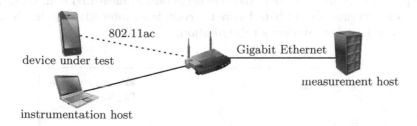

Fig. 4. The setup of the testbed used for experimental evaluation.

8.1   Goodput

In our first experiment, we investigated the loss of goodput due to network layer anonymisation. Clearly, we expect a certain loss of goodput due to the encapsulation of traffic into fixed-size packets that are smaller than the Maximum Transmission Unit (MTU) of the network card, which in itself does not necessitate measurements. However, even though many current smartphones have sufficient computational power, frequent multi-layer encryption and decryption might lead to high temperatures that force the device to slow down and thus limit the actually achievable bandwidth. Furthermore, the utilisation of a virtual network interface incurs additional computational overhead whose impact is hard to estimate analytically.

---

[6] A test version of ANONguard can be installed from Google Play (https://play.google.com/store/apps/details?id=anonvpn.anon_next.android).

[7] The source code for our evaluation tools as well as the used anonymisation tools can be found on https://dud-scm.inf.tu-dresden.de/ANON-Public.

Methodology: To obtain measurements, we first deployed a set of mixes on the measurement host and start the anonymisation software on the mobile device. Afterwards, we set up our measurement client to constantly download data from the measurement server as fast as possible and record the total number of bytes received within 10 min. To avoid errors due to instrumentation, the recording was started one minute after the download had began.

We performed measurements with one, two and three mixes to evaluate the impact of encryption and decryption on the achievable goodput, since each mix requires one decryption operation per incoming packet. In the case of one mix anonymisation, we used version 0.7.3 of OpenVPN for Android. For the two and three mix scenario, we used our solution as well as Orbot version 15.5.1-RC-2 (Tor version 0.3.1, compiled with Android NDK Rev. 15c). As reference, we also performed measurements without any anonymisation. Furthermore, we performed measurements where the client directly connects to our mixes and thus avoids any overhead associated with the usage of a virtual network interface.

Results: Figure 5 shows our results for different configurations and devices. Each dot represents the mean value of the average goodput, measured in megabit per second, over 10 runs and the bars denote the confidence intervals for a significance level of 95% based on Student's t-distribution.

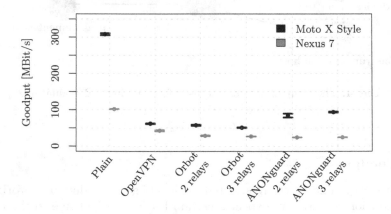

Fig. 5. Mean values for the average goodput during a continuous download for different devices and anonymisation solutions.

Clearly, the employment of current implementations of transparent tunneling leads to a significant drop in network performance. In the case of OpenVPN, the average goodput dropped from 308.2 ± 2.5 Mbit/s to 61.9 ± 0.9 Mbit/s on the Moto X Style and from 102.0 ± 0.5 Mbit/s to 42.8 ± 1.9 Mbit/s on the Nexus 7. Orbot achieved similar results, allowing 57.5 ± 1.5 Mbit/s on the Moto X and 28.8 ± 1.1 on the Nexus 7 if two relays are used and 51.0 ± 0.7 Mbit/s as well as 27.1 ± 0.1 Mbit/s if three relays are used. On the Moto X Style, the ANONguard application achieved a notably higher goodput than OpenVPN and Orbot, allowing 84.5 ± 5.2 Mbit/s if two relays are used. This is surprising, since the whole tunneling and anonymisation functionality of OpenVPN and Orbot is running as native code while ANONguard is purely written in Java. We experimented with different settings for OpenVPN and Orbot but were not able to substantially improve their performance. Another surprising observation is that the average goodput of ANONguard slightly improved to 93.5 ± 1.4 Mbit/s when three relays were used. Unfortunately, we did not find a definitive answer for this result in the time available for the measurement study.

While the Nexus 7 showed a rather continuous performance during each measurement run, performance on the Moto X dropped during each run where anonymisation was enabled. In all our results, we only included runs where the initial temperature of the Moto X was between 35 and 40° Celsius. During each run, the temperature of the device increased to a value close to 60° Celsius and then stabilised at a value around 53° Celsius after the CPU frequency has been automatically reduced. However, the drop in performance was not dramatic compared to the drop from goodput without anonymisation: in the first two minutes of the measurement, the average goodput of ANONguard with two relays reached 103.4 ± 2.5 Mbit/s whereas in the remaining 8 min, the average goodput reduced to 79.7 ± 6.8 Mbit/s. Similarly, Orbot's goodput dropped from 68.1 ± 1.4 Mbit/s to 54.9 ± 1.7 Mbit/s.

While the results shown on Fig. 5 have been obtained by a single TCP-connection, we performed the same measurements with 3 simultaneous TCP transmissions. In this setting, the average goodput without any anonymisation increased to 335.2 ± 16.3 Mbit/s, whereas the goodput using ANONguard increased to 98.9 ± 2.4 Mbit/s. We observed similarly low increases in goodput for OpenVPN and no difference for Orbot. Consequently, the number of simultaneous transmissions does not have a strong impact on our results.

Analysis of Goodput Degradation: To evaluate possible causes for the strong degradation of goodput, we performed additional measurements to asses the particular impact of encryption and decryption as well as interaction with the virtual network interface. The results presented by Fig. 5 indicate that encryption and decryption do not have a major impact on goodput, since the number of relays did not have a notable impact on the results of Orbot and ANONguard. To verify this claim, we ran the goodput measurement with a modified version of ANONguard where encryption and decryption has been disabled. Afterwards, we furthermore integrated the AN.ON client implementation that is used in the ANONguard application directly into the measurement client application, thus avoiding the overhead associated with the virtual network interface and conducted measurements without the ANONguard application. Even if cryptography as well as transparent tunneling is disabled, the AN.ON client just achieves 115.59 ± 10.50 Mbit/s of average goodput on the Moto X and 47.3 ± 0.6 Mbit/s on the Nexus 7. An initial runtime profiling indicates that internal synchronisation is a primary cause for the loss of performance of ANONguard. After we re-enabled encryption, the goodput slightly dropped to 108.1 ± 3.2 Mbit/s on the Moto X and 43.5 ± 4.5 Mbit/s on the Nexus 7. Using just transparent tunneling without encryption yielded a goodput of 83.6 ± 1.2 Mbit/s on the Moto X and 25.3 ± 0.9 Mbit/s on the Nexus 7. Besides internal synchronisation, profiling in latter case suggests that the frequent computation of TCP checksums contributes to the loss of performance.

Discussion: Our measurements suggest that current solutions for network layer anonymisation significantly reduce the achievable goodput on mobile devices. However, the observed loss of performance mostly seems to stem from networking-related performance issues such as synchronisation of concurrent threads as well as computation of checksums. We did not observe a strong additional loss of goodput after enabling the virtual network interface together with encryption and decryption, which indicates that our current results underestimate the actual goodput that is achievable if there are no networking-related performance bottlenecks.

8.2   Energy Consumption

Complementary to our measurements regarding goodput, our second experiment focuses on the energy consumption of the transparent anonymisation.

Methodology: To obtain samples, we performed the same steps as described in the previous section but before launching the measurement client, we disabled the power supply of the mobile device and used the Trepn Power Profiler[8] to record the battery power of the device every 100 ms (which is the highest frequency Trepn supports). If available, the Trepn Power Profiler reads battery power from the fuel gauge of the battery pack [14]. After 12 min have passed, we stop the recording of the battery power and use the mean value of all data points between the second and 12th minute as sample value. Before the next measurement run was started, we charged the battery of the device to 95%. Since the Motorola Moto X Style does not have an integrated fuel gauge, we only performed measurements with the Nexus 7, which comes with a BQ2751 fuel gauge from Texas Instruments (according to the kernel log messages of the device).

Our measurement procedure provides a worst case perspective on the increase in battery drain, since it seems unlikely that smartphones constantly have to cope with one or more running TCP transfers. However, we are not aware of any published models or datasets that allow us to emulate the variety of dynamic workloads that mobile devices typically have to deal with.

As a reference, we performed measurements without anonymisation on minimal screen brightness and also on maximum screen brightness. All measurements involving anonymisation were recorded with minimal screen brightness. The wakelock acquired by the Trepn profiler ensured that the device did not change its screen brightness or went to sleep mode during the transfer. We also recorded the average goodput of each run and observed a decrease of around 5 Mbit/s for the setting without anonymisation and the setting with OpenVPN.

---

[8] https://developer.qualcomm.com/software/trepn-power-profiler, 2018-02-16.

In all other settings, the observed decrease in average goodput was less than 2 Mbit/s, rendering the impact of the power profiling on average goodput negligible.

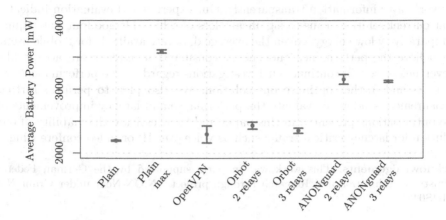

Fig. 6. Mean values for the average energy consumption during a continuous download for different devices and anonymisation solutions.

Results: The results of our measurements are depicted by Fig. 6, where each dot represents the mean value of the average battery power, measured in milliwatt, over 10 runs and the bars denote the confidence intervals for a significance level of 95% based on Student's t-distribution. On maximum screen brightness, we measured an average battery power of 3590.3 ± 24.8 mW during the download if no anonymisation is enabled. On minimal screen brightness, we observed an average battery power of 2197.1 ± 8.6 mW. While OpenVPN and Orbot with 2 relay channels additionally require 98.1 ± 132.4 mW and 234.0 ± 54.8 mW of power on average, our solution currently requires 957.6 ± 75.9 mW of additional power if 2 relays are used. Similar to the results from the previous section, we identified networking-related implementation issues to be the main source of energy consumption. Without cryptography, the ANONguard application still demanded 867.2 ± 47.5 mW of power. If the measurement client contacted the AN.ON mixes directly, 468.7 ± 11.9 mW of power were additionally required without use of cryptography.

Discussion: Ultimately, our measurements indicate that current state of the art solutions like OpenVPN and Orbot only require few additional battery power, suggesting that transparent anonymisation can be implemented without causing prohibitive energy consumption. Our Java-based solution currently consumes significantly more energy than OpenVPN and Orbot, whose anonymisation and VNI handling is implemented natively. However, it remains open if the high energy consumption is inherent in the use of Java or if they can be solved by an improved control and data flow.

9 Conclusion

In this paper we described the design of a low-latency network layer anonymisation solution for mobile devices that uses a virtual network interface to obfuscate network layer information transparently. Our experimental evaluation indicates that current solutions cause a significant loss of achievable goodput but require comparatively low energy. Given the average data rate available for mobile users, we believe the performance and energy consumption impacts are acceptable. Nevertheless we will continue our investigations regarding the performance bottlenecks and further optimise our solution. We also plan to perform further measurement studies to evaluate the performance and latency improvements of the optimisations presented in this paper and to investigate the viability of our solution for latency-critical traffic such as voice over IP or video conferencing.

Acknowledgements. This work was in parts supported by the German Federal Ministry of Education and Research through project AN.ON-Next under Grant No. 16KIS0421.

References

1. Hide My Ass! Blog: Lulzsec fiasco. https://blog.hidemyass.com/lulzsec-fiasco. Accessed 02 Mar 2018
2. Khandelwal, S.: FBI Arrests A Cyberstalker After Shady "No-Logs" VPN Provider Shared User Logs. https://thehackernews.com. Accessed 02 Mar 2018
3. Dingledine, R., Mathewson, N., Syverson, P.: Tor: the second-generation onion router. Technical report, Naval Research Lab, Washington, D.C. (2004)
4. Berthold, O., Federrath, H., Köpsell, S.: Web MIXes: a system for anonymous and unobservable internet access. In: Federrath, H. (ed.) Designing Privacy Enhancing Technologies. LNCS, vol. 2009, pp. 115–129. Springer, Heidelberg (2001). https://doi.org/10.1007/3-540-44702-4_7
5. Chaum, D.L.: Untraceable electronic mail, return addresses, and digital pseudonyms. Commun. ACM **24**(2), 84–90 (1981)
6. Wiangsripanawan, R., Susilo, W., Safavi-Naini, R.: Achieving mobility and anonymity in IP-based networks. In: Bao, F., Ling, S., Okamoto, T., Wang, H., Xing, C. (eds.) CANS 2007. LNCS, vol. 4856, pp. 60–79. Springer, Heidelberg (2007). https://doi.org/10.1007/978-3-540-76969-9_5
7. Andersson, C., Panchenko, A.: Practical anonymous communication on the mobile internet using Tor. In: SecureComm, pp. 39–48. IEEE (2007)
8. Doswell, S.: Measurement and management of the impact of mobility on low-latency anonymity networks. Ph.D. thesis, Northumbria University (2016)
9. Perkins, C.: IP Mobility Support for IPv4, Revised. RFC 5944, November 2010
10. Google: Connect to Wi-Fi networks - Nexus Help. https://support.google.com/ See "Advanced Network Settings". Accessed 01 Mar 2018
11. Apple Inc.: Connect to the Internet - iPhone User Guide. https://help.apple.com/. Accessed 01 Mar 2018

12. Android Open Source Project: VpnService—Android Developers. https://developer.android.com. Accessed 02 Mar 2018
13. Apple Inc.: NetworkExtension—Apple Developer Documentation. https://developer.apple.com. Accessed 02 Mar 2018
14. Qualcomm Developer Network: How does Trepn Power measure battery power? https://developer.qualcomm.com. Accessed 02 Mar 2018

Inferring UI States of Mobile Applications Through Power Side Channel Exploitation

Yao Guo[✉], Junming Ma, Wenjun Wu, and Xiangqun Chen

Key Laboratory of High-Confidence Software Technologies (Ministry of Education),
School of EECS, Peking University, Beijing, China
{yaoguo,majunming,wuwenjun,cherry}@pku.edu.cn

Abstract. The UI (user interface) state of a mobile application is important for attackers since it exposes what is happening inside an application. Attackers could initiate attacks timely according to this information, for example inserting fake GUIs or taking screenshots of GUIs involving user's sensitive data. This paper proposes PoWatt, a method to infer the timing of sensitive UI occurrences by exploiting power side channels on mobile devices such as smartphones. Based on power traces collected and power patterns learned in advance, PoWatt applies a pattern matching algorithm to detect target UI occurrences within a series of continuous power traces. Experiment results on popular Android apps show that PoWatt can detect sensitive UI loading with an average precision of 71% (up to 98%) and an average recall rate of 70% (up to 88%) during offline detection. In real-time experiments for online detection, PoWatt can still detect sensitive UIs with a reasonable precision and recall, which can be successfully exploited by real-world attacks such as screenshot-based password stealing. Finally, we discuss the limitations of PoWatt and possible mitigation techniques.

Keywords: Side channels · Power traces · Power side channels
UI inference · Smartphones

1   Introduction

Side channel attacks have been studied extensively. The goal of side channel attacks is gaining confidential information from the targeted computing system, while leveraging *side channels* that are not directly revealing sensitive information. Previously discovered side channels include timing information [4,18,21], sound [22], shared memory/registers/files between processes [16] and power consumption [8,15], etc.

Power side channels (or power analysis attacks) have become an important type of covert side channels. One well-known example of power side channels is the recovery of an encryption key from a cryptosystem [7,8]. Messerges *et al.* examined both *simple power analysis (SPA)* and *differential power analysis*

© ICST Institute for Computer Sciences, Social Informatics and Telecommunications Engineering 2018
R. Beyah et al. (Eds.): SecureComm 2018, LNICST 254, pp. 210–226, 2018.
https://doi.org/10.1007/978-3-030-01701-9_12

(DPA) attacks [14] against the data encryption standard algorithm and managed to breach the security of smart-cards using signal-to-noise ratio (SNR) based multi-bit attack. For mobile systems such as smartphones, researchers have shown that power information can also be used to infer users' locations [15].

Goal Overview. This paper introduces *a new power side channel*, which can be exploited to initiate side channel attacks by inferring UI (user interface) states on mobile devices such as smartphones. We investigate the feasibility of using unprivileged power traces to infer sensitive UI states of mobile applications (*apps* for short), such that the attacker would learn the exact timing to initiate the corresponding attacks.

For example, in order to initiate activity hijacking attacks on Android, attackers need to know when the user login UI will be prompted so that they can intercept the UI state transition and insert fake user login UIs that could steal user credentials. In our work, *we regard the UI states of a mobile app as the confidential information that the attacker wants to gain through side channel attacks; while the power traces, as an unprivileged resource, can be used as a side channel to achieve this goal.*

Our Proposal. This paper proposes PoWatt (*PoWer Attack*), a method to infer sensitive UI states based on power traces collected on Android smartphones, in order to demonstrate the feasibility of power side channel exploitation. Specifically, we investigate the effectiveness of capturing sensitive UI loading events from power traces collected during app execution.

The key idea of PoWatt is based on the fact that *power patterns of each UI loading even in Android apps has unique features that distinguish it from other UI loading events.* We can study the power patterns of a sensitive UI in advance and detect its occurrences on another phone based on the learned pattern. PoWatt is thus designed as a typical pattern matching approach, which involves *training data collection, model training* and *target UI detection.*

During training data collection, we design a method to identify the starting point of a UI loading event and use automated scripts to collect the power trace of a target UI. The power traces are collected with a software-based approach that can read power values from the smartphone profile.

In the model training phase, we generate a prediction model by splitting the training data into different groups and finding the most accurate parameters to generate the most matches between these groups. The result of model training includes fitting curves and accompanying parameters for each sensitive UI.

The detection phase can be conducted either offline or online. In offline detection, we use the trained model to detect the target UI from continuous power traces collected separately from training data collection. The algorithm detects matching target UIs with a time window sliding along the time-indexed power trace. In online detection, the algorithm is the same, while we add the detecting algorithm running in background in the training phase to reduce its impact on the power patterns. We carry out real-time experiments by inviting several volunteers to use the above-mentioned apps with our exploitation tool running in the background.

Results Overview. We perform experiments on four popular Android apps, include Alipay, Amazon, WeChat, and Word. Most experiments are conducted on a Nexus 5 smartphone. We collect power traces with automated scripts manipulating these apps traversing different UIs including the target sensitive UIs, and detect the occurrences of these sensitive UIs with PoWatt using the trained models for each app.

In experiments with offline detection, we split the collected data into five groups and performed five-cross evaluation. Results show that we can achieve an average precision of about 71% (up to 98%) and an average recall rate of about 70% (up to 88%) to detect given sensitive UIs For online detection, PoWatt detects 45–85% of the target UI occurrences in real-time cases, with an average precision of 66%.

The results demonstrate that we are able to infer a target UI state from the power trace of a running app with a reasonable precision and recall rate, thus it is practical for attackers to exploit power traces to infer UI states.

Although our approach is not perfect in terms of detection accuracy, it presents a real threat to user privacy as an attacker is able to detect the presence of a particular UI with a reasonable successful rate, revealing that attacking based on power side channel is becoming a practical concern.

2   Background and Motivation

2.1   Power Measurements

The power consumption of a smartphone can be measured with both hardware-based and software-based methods. Although power measurements based on hardware meters are very accurate, it is not applicable to real-world scenarios, thus we use a software-based measurement method to record power traces on a smartphone.

Power related readings are publicly accessible on most smartphone OSes such as Android. In general, instant power numbers can be calculated based on voltage and current readings of BMU (Battery Monitoring Unit) [20]. The battery status information is accessible by most apps without system-level privilege, as many mobile apps need to know the battery status to carry out responses such as saving user context before the battery dies.

The power numbers can be calculated by polling battery status files. Battery device drivers are required to updating these files in order to provide instant power numbers of Android system. Within these files, power consumption is specified in microamps (μA) of current and in microvolts (μV) of voltage. The update frequency varies with different devices, ranging from 10 to 100 times per second.

2.2   Distinguishability in Power Patterns

Our study is based on the following hypothesis: *different UIs within an app are distinguishable based on their power patterns* since different UIs have different usage of network communication, calculation tasks and UI rendering.

We use software-based method to measure the user login UI from the Amazon app running on a Nexus 5 smartphone with Android 6.0. Figure 1 shows the power traces of the user login UI in three different test runs. We can see that the power patterns exhibit obvious similarity for the same UI on different test runs, which makes it distinguishable in a continuous power trace.

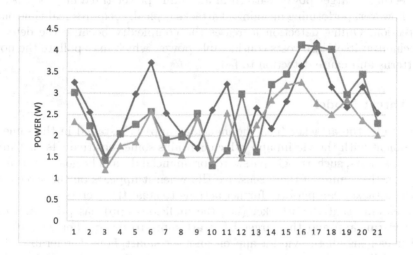

Fig. 1. Power traces collected for the log-in UI for the Amazon app through software-based measurement, in three different runs.

Based on the measurement results, we observed the existence of power side channels that can be used to distinguish between different UI States, which is potentially exploitable for attackers to infer sensitive UI loading phases such as user login (password input) UIs. This motivates us to conduct further studies on the feasibility of exploiting power side channels to infer sensitive UI states. More details on the measurement study can be found in our earlier work [19].

3   PoWatt Overview

The goal of our study is to demonstrate the feasibility of inferring sensitive UI states of mobile apps through power side channels on mobile devices. In order to achieve this goal, we face the following challenges:

- *How do we capture the power pattern for a target UI?* A user may visit dozens (or even hundreds) of different UIs when using a mobile app, thus we need to find a way to specify the particular UI that might be interested to the attacker. We also need to specify the starting and ending points of a UI loading phase before we learn its pattern.

- *How do we detect the occurrence of a target UI based on its power pattern?* Even we have obtained a unique power pattern for a target UI, we need to find a way to detect the power pattern in a continuous power trace, as the user will use the app in a continuous manner. Furthermore, the exact power readings and loading time might vary in different occurrences of the same UI, even it runs on the same smartphone.
- *How do we conduct real-time online detection of the target UI?* Detecting a target power pattern in an offline power trace may be easier to do, however, performing meaningful attacks typically requires real-time online detection. Online detection increases the complexity because the detection mechanism itself also costs considerable power, which may pollute the power patterns and cause detection to fail.

3.1 Threat Model

In our study, the attacker (i.e., the malicious app) is installed in the same OS environment with the victim app, which contains some sensitive UIs that might reveal its secrets, such as login passwords or financial data. The goal of the attack is to learn the timing of these sensitive UIs when it appears on the screen such that the attacker can perform further actions to steal the secrets.

We assume that the attacker (i.e., the malicious app) has prior knowledge on the victim app and the target UI it attempts to detect. For example, the attacker can install the victim app on another smartphone (preferably of the same model) and collect the power traces to study the power patterns of the target UI state, such as a login screen.

When the malicious app is conducting real-time power side channel exploitation, it runs in the background recording the power data while the victim app runs in the foreground. The malicious app attempts to infer sensitive UI states of the victim app based on the power trace it collects, initiating further attacks once it detects the correct timing.

3.2 Overview of PoWatt

The purpose of PoWatt is to find an effective method to capture the occurrences of the target UI from a continuous power trace collected from an app. Figure 2 presents an overview of PoWatt, which involves the following main steps.

Training Data Collection. The first step is collecting training data. We first specify a sensitive UI (i.e. the target UI) within the target app, for instance, the user login UI. Then we run the target app in the foreground and the data collecting program in the background to collect multiple power traces continuously.

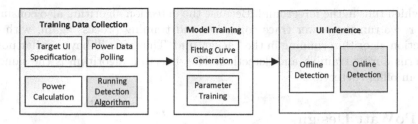

Fig. 2. Overview of PoWatt. (Note that the shaded components are used for real-time online detection only.)

In our experiments, we use an automated script to visit different UIs in this app, with the target UI (e.g., the login UI) visited multiple times during the process. The result is a continuous power trace that includes the power patterns of the target UI and other UIs as well.

During *online detection*, running a real-time pattern matching algorithm in the background will increase power consumption and affect the pattern matching accuracy. In order to simulate the same environment as in the detection phase, we also let the same pattern matching algorithm running in the background while collecting power data for the training dataset on the target UI for online detection.

Model Training. Based on a subset of the collected power traces (the rest will be used in testing), we then train a model to identify the target UI. These power traces are basically time-indexed power numbers recording the occurrence of the target UI. In order to obtain the fitting curve, we first apply several pre-processing steps including calculating an average curve and smooth the data with moving average to eliminate noises.

After pre-processing, we split the training data into two separate sets. We first calculate a fitting curve with one part of the training data and use it to detect the target UI in the rest of the data. We use a simple genetic algorithm to find the parameters that yield the best overall accuracy (considering both precision and recall). These fitting curves and accompanying parameters will be used to conduct the detection in the next phase.

UI Inference. We perform both offline and online detection to demonstrate the possibility of detect the target UI while exploiting the power side channel.

For *offline detection*, we use the model trained with training data to detect the target UI in the testing data. We apply a time-window based pattern matching algorithm with the trained model. Offline detection is used to demonstrate the feasibility of power trace exploitation, thus we do not run the detection algorithm in real-time to prevent it from polluting the power trace.

We also perform *online detection* in a more realistic environment, where the detection algorithm runs in the background on a smartphone to detect the target

UI, which runs in the foreground. Because the detection algorithm also consumes power, we run the power trace collection and training process again, with the detection algorithm running in the background. Thus we will have similar power patterns during training and detection. The detection algorithm is the same as used in offline detection.

4   PoWatt Design

4.1   Data Collection

Target UI Specification. Mobile apps are composed of different UI components (*i.e., Activities* in Android). In a single app, the user typically navigates through multiple UIs to use some specific app functionality. In Android, current and past UIs are saved and maintained in a stack data structure called a *Back Stack*. When a new UI is loaded, it is pushed on the top of the stack. If the current UI has a "parent" UI (e.g., the UI has a "back" button), it gets popped out the stack when the user returns to its "parent" UI. As a result, when the loading process of some specific UI happens, there are two possibilities of the trigger source: (1) the user creates a new instance of the UI; (2) the user navigates back from one of its "children" UIs.

A typical UI loading process in the Android framework works as follows: (1) The `ActivityManager` component calls `performLaunchActivity()` API; (2) the `onCreate()` or `onPause()` function (both of them are implemented by the app) gets called depending on the source of trigger; (3) After that, the `performTraversal()` API is called, in which the loaded UI will be put into the framebuffer and the screen gets repainted; (4) Finally, if the UI is newly created, it will be pushed into the *Back Stack*, and the current one will be destroyed; if the UI is the parent of the current one and it gets resumed, the current one will be popped out and destroyed.

Each UI loading process is unique because it involves loading different resources in different sequences, and showing different color schemes on the screen.

We modify the Android framework to record power traces of the target UI. When we record the power trace of each UI loading, we use the `performLaunchActivity()` API calling point as the starting point a UI process, and monitor it until the completion of the `performTraversal()` API.

Power Data Polling and Calculation. We collect the power numbers of the target UI to form a power trace, which is used to reflect its power characteristics. To collect the power numbers, we use the built-in software-based measuring method. Instant current and voltage numbers can be acquired by polling system battery status files.

Adaptation for Online Detection. The above procedure works well for offline detection of the target UI in a continuous power trace. However, when we try to conduct online detection, the detection algorithm itself consumes significant power, which affects the power consumption patterns of the target app.

In order to minimize the influences of the online detection algorithm, we run the algorithm in the background when we collect the training power data. In this way, we simulate the same environment as in the detection phase while collecting power data for the training dataset on the target UI.

4.2 Model Training

During model training, our goal is to generate a representing power pattern (i.e., fitting curves) and accompanying parameters (thresholds), which is used to identify the target UI in a power trace during the detection phase. In our study, we generate the fitting curve based on the power consumption time series $TS_1, TS_2, ..., TS_n$ extracted from the power traces, which contains n runs of the loading phase of the target UI.

After collecting the training dataset, we first calculate an average power pattern based on the set of different power patterns $(TS_1, TS_2, ..., TS_n)$ for the same UI, and then apply a Gaussian filter to smooth the power curve by calculating their moving average. The result is the main fitting curve (FC).

As a supplement to the power traces, we also calculate a *power differential series* (DS) that considers the difference of the power numbers in each adjacent pairs in the trace. For each $TS_i = p_1, p_2, ..., p_n$, its corresponding DS_i is calculated as $p_2 - p_1, p_3 - p_2, ..., p_n - p_{n-1}$. We calculate the average DS and apply the same Gaussian filter to smooth the curve. The resulting differential curve (FC') is used to represent the power trend for the target UI, which we consider as an important supplement to the main fitting curve.

For the generated fitting curve FC, we then calculate the distance of each power pattern to the fitting curve, and use the average distance as the threshold (Th). For the differential curve FC', we calculate a threshold (Th') using the same method.

We can use either fitting curve and the corresponding threshold to detect the target UI in a continuous power trace. However, we want to train a model that involves both fitting curves to achieve better accuracy. For each time series TS_i, we add two parameters P_1 and P_2, and use the following criteria to determine whether is a match:

$$Sigmoid(\frac{Dist(TS_i, FC)}{Th} + P_1 \times \frac{Dist(DS_i, FC')}{Th'}) > P_2$$

where P_1 and P_2 will be trained using a simple genetic algorithm to maximize the F-Measure value:

$$F\_Measure = 2 \times \frac{precision \times recall}{precision + recall}$$

When calculating distances between two time series, we use the square of the actual distance, since the Euclidean norm is better than Manhattan norm in terms of preventing overfitting.

We use a sliding window approach as shown in Fig. 3 to detect whether there is positive match in a power trace based on the above criteria. Once we detect the match, the sliding window will jump to the end of the match and continue. The matching algorithm is the same as used later in the UI inference step. The parameters P_1 and P_2 will be initially set as a number from (0.2, 0.5) and (0.5, 0.7), respectively. For the genetic algorithm, we generate 200 instances for each generation and train them over 10 generations, in order to find the best possible parameters (P_1 and P_2).

Please note that the model training process for online detection is the same as for offline detection. The only difference is that the power traces used when training for online detection include the power consumption of the detection algorithms running in the background.

4.3   UI Inference

In the UI Inference phase, PoWatt applies the same detection algorithm as used in training based on the fitting curves (FC and FC'), the thresholds (Th and Th'), and the trained parameters (P_1 and P_2), to detect whether there is a match to the target UI in the testing power trace.

Offline Detection. For offline detection, the goal is to identify the occurrence of the target UI in a continuous power trace in an offline manner, after we record the power trace.

The detection process is depicted in Fig. 3. We create a time window along the time series with window size equaling the longest power pattern for the target UI during training. Then we apply the detection algorithm mentioned earlier to repeatedly calculate the distance between the fitting curves and the times series in the current window. We find a match when the distances satisfy the given criteria for the trained parameters and thresholds.

Without real-time background noises, offline detection can demonstrate the capability of PoWatt to detect the target UI in ideal situations.

Online Detection. The method we adopt in online detection is the same as in offline detection. However, because we apply pattern matching in real-time, it adds extra power consumption to the power trace, such that we need to re-train the model with the power traces collected with the detection algorithm running in the background. Fortunately, the detection algorithm itself is not power hungry and its power consumption patterns is regular. Thus we are still able to find a power pattern to match the target UI even with detection in the background.

Online detection will be performed by volunteers, such that we can demonstrate the capability of PoWatt to detect sensitive UIs in real scenarios.

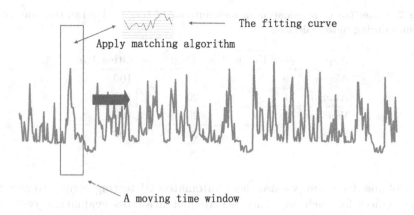

Fig. 3. The workflow of the UI detection algorithm.

5 Experiments and Results

5.1 Experimental Setup

In our experiments, we choose four popular Android apps from including Alipay, Amazon, WeChat and Word. Details of these apps are shown in Table 1. We consider the user login or payment password input UI of each app as the target UI, as attackers may try to steal user passwords from these apps. We use a Nexus 5 smartphone with Android 6.0 for most of our experiments.

Table 1. Details of the mobile apps used in our experiments.

App	Version	Category	Target UI
Alipay	9.5.3	Payment	Password input
Amazon	6.4.0.100	Shopping	Log in
WeChat	6.3.15	Communication	Password input
Word	1.0.1	Productivity	Log in

For each app, we write an automated UI testing script based on a technique for building test cases for Android apps [10]. We do not use the popular MonkeyRunner here since it requires adb connection, which will result in big influence on the power patterns. Within each automated UI testing script, we try to reach multiple UIs while achieving the desired number of occurrences (20 in each trace) of the target UIs.

Table 2 shows the power trace statistics. For each app, we include 20 occurrences of the target UI, as well as 100 occurrences of other UIs (including different unique UIs as list in the table). We use the automated scripts to collect five traces for each app.

Table 2. Power trace specification in each automated script. (We ran the same script five times during data collection.)

App	# of Unique UIs	Target UIs	Other UIs
Alipay	9	20	100
Amazon	11	20	100
WeChat	10	20	100
Word	9	20	100

For offline detection, we use these automated UI testing scripts to generate 5 power traces for each app, then we conduct five-cross evaluation, each time using four power traces as training data and the remaining power trace as the testing data. We train a model with the four training power traces and use the model to predict target UIs in the testing trace. Offline detection is performed on a desktop PC with the power traces.

In order to evaluate the effectiveness of real-time online detection, we invite volunteers from our lab to use the apps listed in Table 1 on the Nexus 5 smartphone.

With the online detection program running in the background, all the participants are trained to perform two different tests: one using a given UI sequence which is the same as the in the automated test script; the other asking the volunteer to visit different UIs inside each app with randomized order and number of visits. In both tests, they are asked to visit the target UIs (login UIs) for exactly 20 times. Each participant has 10 min to finish the experiments. If a positive matching of the target UI is detected, a notification will be pushed on top of the screen in the notification area to remind the user. We ask all participants to count the number of total positive detection notifications, and whether it is a true positives (or false positive).

5.2 Results and Analysis

Offline Detection. Table 3 shows the results of UI inference during offline detection. We perform five-cross evaluation with the five power traces collected for each app. The results include the precision and recall numbers in each test, as well as their average value.

We can see that the Word app has the best overall result in both precision and recall of 98% and 88%, respectively. The reason is because the long in UI of the Word app is implemented as a webpage in WebView, thus its loading time is relatively long. A long loading time will expose more features of the target UI, thus increasing the detection accuracy. For the other three apps, their detection precision are all at about 60%, which is acceptable. In all four apps, Amazon fares the worst with an average recall of only 49%.

Although the results still have space for improvement, they are good enough to be used in meaningful attacks as attacks do not have to be successful every time. We have accomplished our goal to demonstrate the effectiveness of inferring UI states exploiting a power side channel.

Table 3. UI Inference results for offline detection on collected power traces. We show five-cross examination results, and their average.

App	Run #1		Run #2		Run #3		Run #4		Run #5		**Overall**	
	prec.	recall	prec.	recall	prec.	recall	prec.	recall	prec.	recall	**prec.**	**recall**
Alipay	64%	80%	68%	85%	65%	85%	67%	80%	55%	85%	**64%**	**83%**
Amazon	43%	50%	55%	55%	68%	65%	79%	55%	57%	20%	**60%**	**49%**
WeChat	56%	70%	67%	50%	67%	60%	58%	90%	62%	40%	**62%**	**62%**
Word	91%	100%	100%	90%	100%	100%	100%	55%	100%	95%	**98%**	**88%**

Online Detection. Table 4 shows online detection results following the same UI sequences as in the automated scripts. Because there are no new UIs introduced during the test, the detection accuracy remains comparable to what we have as for offline detection. On average, we are able to detect the target UI in real-time with an average precision of around 66% and an average recall rate of 59%. The highest detecting precision and recall is on the Word app with 94% and 85%, respectively.

We then show online detection results with random UI sequences in Table 5. The average precision now drops to 43% while the average recall drops to 54%.

Although both the precision and recall rates are lower than those from the previous power trace study, this is expected because real-time pattern matching brings instability to the power patterns. However, even with the Amazon app, we are still able to detect the timing of user login with a one in three chance. Even there is a 72% chance that we might mispredict, we are still able to perform meaningful attacks with a reasonable success rate.

Table 4. Results of online detection (on a Nexus 5 smartphone with Android 6.0). The volunteers followed the UI sequence in the automated script.

App	Unique UIs	Target	P	FP	Prec.	Recall
Alipay	9	20	16	6	63%	50%
Amazon	11	20	18	7	61%	55%
WeChat	10	20	20	11	45%	45%
Word	9	20	18	1	94%	85%

Table 5. Results of online detection (on a Nexus 5 smartphone with Android 6.0). The volunteers were free to click as many different UIs as possible.

App	Unique UIs	Target	P	FP	Prec.	Recall
Alipay	45	20	29	20	31%	45%
Amazon	25	20	25	18	28%	35%
WeChat	23	20	26	17	35%	45%
Word	12	20	23	5	78%	90%

6   Case Study

To show that our methodology in PoWatt can pose real-world threats on smartphones, we present a case study of a real-world attack exploiting power side channels. The attack we demonstrate here is a screenshot-based UI attack, which is introduced in ScreenMilker [11]. The attackers could steal user passwords through this attack on smartphones.

We assume that the attack happens in an environment of common configurations where the Android OS does not have be compromised and the malicious app is a totally legit non-system app with no extra permissions needed (we may need the "network" permission to broadcast the attacking results, but it is in fact unnecessary). The malicious app and the victim app are co-installed on the same Android OS, and our case study show that the malicious app could successfully steal confidential information from the victim app with the hints provided by PoWatt.

We assume that the attacker has prior knowledge of the victim app and has already generated a detection engine using the online detection model training techniques described in PoWatt. The malicious app then runs in the background and collects the power trace continuously in real-time. While collecting the power data, it continuously applies real-time detection to check whether the user has attempted to load the target UI (login UI in this example). Once it detects that the login UI has been loaded, the malicious app starts to take screenshots of the victim app in order to steal sensitive information (i.e., username or passwords) from it.

We implemented our attack on a Nexus 5 smartphone and choose the Alipay app as our victim app. Alipay is a popular mobile payment app with multiple functions including payment, money transfer and investment. We consider the user passwords of Alipay app to be highly sensitive.

Figure 4 shows the screenshots taken in our case study. Once the malicious app detects the loading of the user login UI, it will continuously take screenshots of the victim app. With the default prompt of the keyboard animation on tapped keys, the attacker is able to steal the user's Alipay password ("**mypw**"). Attacker could achieve this either programmatically with some graphical recognition algorithms or manually with full images acquired.

Although the attack is pretty straightforward to apply, the most important thing in the attack procedure is that the attacker has to know when to start taking screenshots. Although the login UI for the Alipay app is not guaranteed to be detected each time it loads, with several more attempts, the attacker will eventually get the chance to detect the occurrence of the target UI and capture the desired passwords successfully.

Please note that in this attacking example, the malicious app requires extra permissions to take screenshots, which is not considered a very sensitive permission in Android as many apps are allowed to perform the action. However, when the seemingly innocuous privilege is exploited together with power side channels, the attacker can successfully steal sensitive information from the apps.

Fig. 4. The attacker steals user credentials by continuously taking screenshots of the Alipay login UI after detecting the timing of its loading.

7   Discussions

Threats to Validity. We have demonstrated that we are able to infer sensitive UI states with power side channels and perform real-time attacks to steal user information. There are a few limitation of this work that might affect its validity.

Power side channels might only be distinguished for a limited set of UI operations whose power patterns are consistent each time it is loaded. Some other UIs might exhibit different power patterns each time it is loaded. For example, an image display app may consume different power while loading image thumbnails if the number of images it processes are different. Fortunately, we observe that sensitive UIs involving login passwords or financial data are typically stable and exhibit unique power patterns.

Possible Mitigations. In order to protect users from power side channel attacks, we could make modifications to mobile apps or the OS itself.

- **Energy obfuscation through code injection.** One straightforward mitigation approach is that we can inject meaningless code into mobile apps while
  performing sensitive user interactions, in order to insert power bursts into its
  power pattern to make it unpredictable. This can be achieved at the source
  code level during the app development process, or through instrumentation
  to the bytecode for app binaries.
- **Randomly changing display/color parameters.** One interesting feature
  for the OLED or AMOLED displays used for smartphones is that it consumes
  different power when different color schemes are used [5]. Thus we can vary the
  displaying color and other parameters each time the sensitive UI is displayed
  on the screen. This could be achieved during app development or through
  bytecode instrumentation [9].
- **Raising the privilege needed to access power files.** Of course, we can
  always make the power information privileged, such that not all apps could
  access these data directly. As a matter of fact, mobile apps probably do not
  need to read low-level power related files containing raw voltage or current
  readings. The only thing that most apps need to know is how much battery
  is still remaining, which should not pose serious threats as a side channel.

8   Related Work

8.1   Power Side Channels

Power analysis attacks (or power side channels) [1] have become an important
type of side channel attacks in recent years. One well-known example of power
analysis is the recovery of an encryption key from a cryptosystem [7,8]. Messerges
et al. [13,14] examined both simple power analysis(SPA) and differential power
analysis (DPA) attacks against the data encryption standard (DES) algorithm
and managed to breach the security of smart-cards using the proposed signal-
to-noise ratio (SNR) based multi-bit attack [12].

On mobile platforms, Michalevsky *et al.* proposed PowerSpy [15], which inves-
tigates the relation between signal strength and the power pattern of the smartphone and showed that they can infer smartphone users' whereabouts based on
the power traces.

Our work also focuses on the mobile platform, but we have presented a different and more general attack in UI state inference based on power traces.

8.2   UI-Based Attacks

The UI security of an application has been studied extensively [3,6,17]. On
traditional desktop platforms, UI-based attacks are basically categorized as UI
spoofing attacks [3,6]. Recently, UI-based attacks start to emerge on mobile
platforms. For example, ScreenMilker [11] can take screenshots of the foreground
app covertly and steal user credentials.

Chen *et al.* propose an attack on the Android platform called UI inference
attack [2]. They use the share-memory side channel to infer UI states, in order

to detect the correct timing for attacks. Our work targets at a similar attack in UI inference, but we have achieved it through power side channel exploitation.

9   Conclusions

In this paper, we present PoWatt, a method that demonstrates the existence of a new side channel to infer UI states of mobile apps: the *power side channel*. Attackers can infer the UI states of a mobile app in the foreground with an un-privileged app running in the background, which helps to identify the timing of attacking on sensitive user inputs or screen outputs based on power traces.

The results demonstrate that we are able to infer a target UI state from the power trace of a running app with a reasonable precision and recall rate, thus it is practical for attackers to exploit power traces to infer UI states. Although this study on power side channels is only a small step towards understanding the power side channel issues on mobile devices, it shows that there are new ways to perform attacks based on unprotected power information. More studies are needed to investigate its potential damages and possible mitigation techniques.

Acknowledgments. This work was partly supported by the National Natural Science Foundation of China (No. 61772042).

References

1. Brier, E., Clavier, C., Olivier, F.: Correlation power analysis with a leakage model. In: Joye, M., Quisquater, J.-J. (eds.) CHES 2004. LNCS, vol. 3156, pp. 16–29. Springer, Heidelberg (2004). https://doi.org/10.1007/978-3-540-28632-5_2
2. Chen, Q.A., Qian, Z., Mao, Z.M.: Peeking into your app without actually seeing it: UI state inference and novel android attacks. In: Proceedings of the 23rd USENIX Conference on Security Symposium, pp. 1037–1052 (2014)
3. Chen, S., Meseguer, J., Sasse, R., Wang, H.J., Wang, Y.-M.: A systematic approach to uncover security flaws in GUI logic. In: IEEE Symposium on Security and Privacy, S&P 2007, pp. 71–85. IEEE (2007)
4. Chen, S., Wang, R., Wang, X., Zhang, K.: Side-channel leaks in web applications: a reality today, a challenge tomorrow. In: Proceedings of the 2010 IEEE Symposium on Security and Privacy, pp. 191–206 (2010)
5. Dong, M., Zhong, L.: Power modeling and optimization for OLED displays. IEEE Trans. Mob. Comput. **11**(9), 1587–1599 (2012)
6. Fischer, T., Sadeghi, A., Winandy, M.: A pattern for secure graphical user interface systems. In: The 20th International Workshop on Database and Expert Systems Application, DEXA 2009, pp. 186–190, August 2009
7. Kocher, P., Jaffe, J., Jun, B.: Introduction to differential power analysis and related attacks (1998). http://www.cryptography.com/resources/whitepapers/DPATechInfo.pdf
8. Kocher, P., Jaffe, J., Jun, B.: Differential power analysis. In: Wiener, M. (ed.) CRYPTO 1999. LNCS, vol. 1666, pp. 388–397. Springer, Heidelberg (1999). https://doi.org/10.1007/3-540-48405-1_25

9. Li, D., Tran, A.H., Halfond, W.G.J.: Making web applications more energy efficient for OLED smartphones. In: Proceedings of the 36th International Conference on Software Engineering, ICSE 2014, pp. 527–538. ACM (2014)

10. Li, Y., Yang, Z., Guo, Y., Chen, X.: Droidbot: a lightweight UI-guided test input generator for android. In: Proceedings of the 39th International Conference on Software Engineering Companion, ICSE-C 2017, pp. 23–26 (2017)

11. Lin, C.-C., Li, H., Zhou, X., Wang, X.: Screenmilker: how to milk your android screen for secrets. In: Proceedings of The 21th Annual Network and Distributed System Security Symposium (NDSS) (2014)

12. Mangard, S., Oswald, E., Popp, T.: Power Analysis Attacks: Revealing the Secrets of Smart Cards, vol. 31. Springer, Heidelberg (2008)

13. Messerges, T.S., Dabbish, E.A., Sloan, R.H.: Power analysis attacks of modular exponentiation in smartcards. In: Koç, Ç.K., Paar, C. (eds.) CHES 1999. LNCS, vol. 1717, pp. 144–157. Springer, Heidelberg (1999). https://doi.org/10.1007/3-540-48059-5_14

14. Messerges, T.S., Dabbish, E.A., Sloan, R.H.: Examining smart-card security under the threat of power analysis attacks. IEEE Trans. Comput. 51(5), 541–552 (2002)

15. Michalevsky, Y., Nakibly, G., Schulman, A., Boneh, D.: PowerSpy: location tracking using mobile device power analysis. In: 24th USENIX Security Symposium (USENIX Security 15), Washington, D.C., August 2015

16. Qian, Z., Mao, Z.M., Xie, Y.: Collaborative TCP sequence number inference attack: how to crack sequence number under a second. In: ACM Conference on Computer and Communications Security, CCS 2012, pp. 593–604 (2012)

17. Shapiro, J.S., Vanderburgh, J., Northup, E., Chizmadia, D.: Design of the EROS trusted window system. In: Proceedings of the 13th Conference on USENIX Security Symposium, vol. 13, p. 12 (2004)

18. Wray, J.C.: An analysis of covert timing channels. In: Proceedings of 1991 IEEE Computer Society Symposium on Research in Security and Privacy, pp. 2–7 (1991)

19. Yan, L., Guo, Y., Chen, X., Mei, H.: A study on power side channels on mobile devices. In: Proceedings of the Seventh Asia-Pacific Symposium on Internetware (Internetware 2015) (2015)

20. Yoon, C., Kim, D., Jung, W., Kang, C., Cha, H.: AppScope: application energy metering framework for Android smartphone using kernel activity monitoring. In: USENIX Annual Technical Conference, pp. 387–400 (2012)

21. Zhang, D., Askarov, A., Myers, A.C.: Predictive mitigation of timing channels in interactive systems. In: Proceedings of the 18th ACM Conference on Computer and Communications Security, pp. 563–574. ACM (2011)

22. Zhuang, L., Zhou, F., Tygar, J.D.: Keyboard acoustic emanations revisited. ACM Trans. Inf. Syst. Secur. 13(1), 3:1–3:26 (2009)

PoliteCamera: Respecting Strangers' Privacy in Mobile Photographing

Ang Li[1(✉)], Wei Du[2], and Qinghua Li[1]

[1] Department of Computer Science and Computer Engineering,
University of Arkansas, Fayetteville, USA
{angli,qinghual}@uark.edu
[2] Department of Electrical and Computer Engineering,
Michigan State University, East Lansing, USA
duwei1@msu.edu

Abstract. Camera is a standard on-board sensor of modern mobile phones. It makes photo taking popular due to its convenience and high resolution. However, when users take a photo of a scenery, a building or a target person, a stranger may also be unintentionally captured in the photo. Such photos expose the location and activity of strangers, and hence may breach their privacy. In this paper, we propose a cooperative mobile photographing scheme called PoliteCamera to protect strangers' privacy. Through the cooperation between a photographer and a stranger, the stranger's face in a photo can be automatically blurred upon his request when the photo is taken. Since multiple strangers nearby the photographer might send out blurring requests but not all of them are in the photo, an adapted balanced convolutional neural network (ABCNN) is proposed to determine whether the requesting stranger is in the photo based on facial attributes. Evaluations demonstrate that the ABCNN can accurately predict facial attributes and PoliteCamera can provide accurate privacy protection for strangers.

Keywords: Mobile phone · Photo · Privacy

1 Introduction

Nowadays mobile phones usually have built-in cameras that facilitate capturing photos. For instance, iPhone 7 is embedded with a 12-megapixel camera [23]. However, an increasing privacy concern has arisen as more and more pictures are taken in people's daily lives. When a user takes a photo of a scenery or a friend with a mobile phone, it is likely that a stranger can also be accidentally included in the photo, with the face clearly recognizable. Figure 1 illustrates two examples. In Fig. 1(a), the building is the target but a stranger is captured; in Fig. 1(b), the photographer intends to picture the target person but two strangers

---

W. Du—This work was done when Wei Du was at the University of Arkansas.

are accidentally included. In these examples, the photo can breach the stranger's privacy by revealing the stranger's location and activity. Thus strangers' privacy should be protected.

(a) A stranger is included when the photographer pictures a building.

(b) Two strangers are included when the photographer pictures a target person.

Fig. 1. Privacy issues with photos taken by mobile phones.

Based on advanced techniques in computer vision, there exist several applications which can blur faces in a photo, such as ObscuraCam [2], Point Blur [6] and [8]. However, none of these commercial applications can inform the inclusion of a stranger in a photo and allow him to decide whether to blur his face or not. Only the photographer is allowed to determine the necessity of blurring the stranger's face.

Several recent works have been done to protect strangers' privacy in photos through blurring their faces. They differ in the way of determining whether a stranger is in the photo or not. Our previous work [14] checks whether a stranger is in a photo or not based on GPS locations of the photographer and the stranger. Due to the dependence on GPS location, it does not work well indoor due to the unavailability or inaccuracy of GPS. Wang et al. [27] design a system for protecting photo privacy that identifies a stranger in a photo by recognizing his motion patterns and visual appearance (e.g., clothes color) profiled into the system in advance. However, users' visual fingerprints need to be updated whenever they change (e.g., changing clothes), which is not convenient. Zhang et al. [28] propose a server-based system to protect privacy of photographed users that compares the portrait of a user uploaded to the server and the portrait of the persons included in photos. Their scheme considers full portrait captured in the photo (i.e., the whole body), which is quite different from this paper that only considers face. Also, their scheme assumes a trusted server from the privacy perspective, which is not always available.

In this paper, we use facial attributes that do not change frequently (e.g., black hair or blond hair) to determine whether a stranger is in a photo or not. Since such facial attributes are relatively stable, if a person is in a photo, by comparing the faces in the photo with his recent profile photo in facial attributes, the person can be correctly matched to his face in the photo. Also, in photographing scenarios, it is not very likely that the facial attributes of two nearby strangers are exactly same, since the number of persons in a limited geographic area around the photographer is usually not large. That means if facial attributes can be accurately identified from photos, mismatch between faces and strangers will be of a low chance. Thus intuitively facial attribute-based face-stranger matching is a promising method to explore.

Based on facial attributes, we design a cooperative scheme *PoliteCamera* to protect the privacy of strangers who are unintentionally included in photos taken by mobile phones. PoliteCamera works as an application on the mobile phones for both the photographer and the stranger. When a photographer takes a photo, he (via the mobile phone) will notify nearby strangers of the potential risk of being included in the photo via peer-to-peer short-range wireless communications (e.g., WiFi Direct [4]). If a stranger prefers not to be included in the photo, he can send a blurring request to the photographer together with his facial attributes included in the request. The photographer will check whether the requesting stranger's face appears in the photo or not based on the facial attributes sent from the stranger and the facial attributes of faces captured in the photo. If the attributes of a face in the photo match those of the requesting stranger, that face is considered to be the stranger's and it will be blurred in the photo.

The set of facial attributes will be carefully selected so that a combination of attribute values is specific enough to differentiate different strangers nearby the photographer but is not specific enough to uniquely identify who the requesting stranger is in the real world. The number of possible attribute value combinations should be reasonably large (e.g., tens of thousand). Then the probability for two different strangers to have the same combination is low, since the number of strangers around a photographer is usually small. The number of possible combinations should also not be too large. In this way, each combination could be owned by many people in the real world, and thus cannot be used to infer who the stranger is. As described later, approximate match instead of exact match will be used in PoliteCamera, which makes linking multiple appearances of the same person difficult. Thus, the privacy risk of re-identification will be low. Moreover, privacy-preserving computing technologies can also be applied to complete the matching of facial attributes without sending the stranger's facial attributes to the photographer in cleartext, and in this way further protect the stranger's facial attributes from the photographer (see Sect. 2.4 for a discussion).

The privacy protection offered by PoliteCamera is based on the cooperation between photographers and strangers. Although these two roles are separately discussed, real-world users can take either role in different scenarios. Since every user can be a stranger in many scenarios, users have a motivation to use this system, and participation in this system means mutually protecting each other's privacy and benefiting everyone including self. This inter-user cooperation design is also motivated by many real-world systems such as collaborative filtering recommender systems [19] and peer-to-peer video streaming systems [15]. Users' privacy can be better protected when more people use this system. Although it is not a perfect solution for the problem, it still significantly advances the state of the art in this domain.

The contribution of this paper is summarized as follows:

- We propose a facial attribute-based system PoliteCamera for protecting strangers' privacy in mobile photographing. To the best of our knowledge, PoliteCamera is the first scheme that makes nearby strangers aware of possible inclusion in a photo when the photo is being taken, allowing them to determine whether to blur their face in the photo or not, and protects strangers' privacy under both indoor and outdoor scenarios, without using any trusted server, human gesture, or special wearables.
- We design a novel adapted balanced convolutional neural network (ABCNN) that can simultaneously predict multiple facial attributes from a photo, and use it to determine the existence of requesting strangers in a photo.
- To avoid identifying the real target persons of a photo as a stranger, a heuristic approach is employed to effectively filter targets to prevent incorrect blurring.
- The proposed system is implemented, and extensively evaluated on real datasets and in the field. Experimental results show the excellent performance of the system.

The rest of the paper is organized as follows. Section 2 introduces the design of PoliteCamera. Section 3 presents implementation. Section 4 shows evaluation results. Section 5 reviews related work. Section 6 concludes the paper.

2   System Design

This section describes the design of PoliteCamera.

2.1   System Overview

Three types of entities are involved in the system: the *photographer* who takes a photo, the *target* who is intentionally captured by the photographer, and the *stranger* who is near the target and might be accidentally included in the photo.

The system is designed to protect the stranger's privacy by giving an option to the stranger to opt out from the photo. The general idea is that the system notifies nearby strangers the possible inclusion in a photo, and blurs a stranger's face if the stranger sends a blurring request. A naive approach is to blur every stranger's face in the photo. However, this is not an ideal solution, since blurring will inevitably affect the quality of the photo. To minimize the effect on photo quality, our design only blurs a stranger's face if he requests to do so. We assume PoliteCamera is installed on both the photographer's and the stranger's mobile phone. Each user of PoliteCamera provides one of his photos to the PoliteCamera app upon the installation of the system. Each user's facial attributes are learned from this base photo and stored in the system for future use. (The base photo can be updated by the user but this does not need to be done frequently since facial attributes do not change frequently.) When a stranger requests a photographer to blur his face, he can send these attributes to the photographer and the photographer will determine whether his face is in the photo based on these facial attributes and blur his face if so.

There are two challenges with the approach. Firstly, there might be multiple nearby strangers who receive the notification of potential privacy leakage by the photo. Some of them may request to blur their faces but others may not request so. Hence, we need to determine if the requesting stranger's face is in the photo or not, which is not trivial. Secondly, when the target is a single person or multiple persons, we need to keep the target unblurred even if the target's phone mistakenly sends out a blurring request. Telling the target from the stranger is necessary but difficult.

2.2 The Architecture and Workflow of PoliteCamera

As Fig. 2 shows, the system consists of six major modules: *face detection and preprocessing, blurring request and collection, facial attributes classifier, target filter, stranger determination* and *face blurring*. When a photographer takes a photo, the face detection module will run on the captured image. If any face is detected, the notification of possible inclusion in the photo will be sent to nearby strangers via peer-to-peer short-range wireless communications. If a stranger would like to blur his face in the photo, he sends a blurring request to the photographer. To help the photographer determine if the requesting stranger is in the photo, this stranger also sends his pre-computed facial attributes (e.g., gender, obtained from his face image when initializing the PoliteCamera app). Upon receiving blurring requests, the photographer crops all the faces in the picture, and then feed them into the pre-trained facial attributes classifier. By comparing the facial attributes of requesting strangers and the attributes of detected faces in the photo, the stranger determination module of photographer can identify those requesting strangers captured in the photo. If a requesting stranger is in the photo, the face blurring module of the photographer smoothly blurs the corresponding face; otherwise, the request is ignored. In case the target mistakenly sends a blurring request, the target filter module distinguishes the target from the stranger based on specific defined rules, and keeps the target unblurred in the photo.

The design of PoliteCamera depends on several available technologies in mobile phones. In particular, face detection and preprocessing can be implemented using APIs provided by the operating system on mobile phones, such as the *FaceDetector* APIs in Android SDK. Similarly, peer-to-peer short-range wireless communications can be set up by available technologies on most modern mobile phones, such as WiFi Direct [4] and Bluetooth. We will introduce the implementation of these two modules in Sect. 3. Next, we will illustrate more details about the rest four modules.

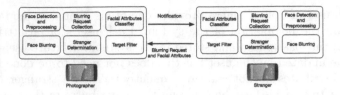

Fig. 2. The architecture of PoliteCamera.

2.3   Facial Attribute Classifier

Given an input face image in pre-defined dimensions, this module aims to simultaneously output a set of facial attributes associated with this input image. In particular, each facial attribute is a binary label, where $+1$ indicates the presence of the corresponding attribute, and -1 means its absence. In this paper, we propose to train a facial attribute classifier through the ABCNN model where a weighted objective function is constructed to maximize the prediction accuracy.

Formally, let $\mathbb{I}$ be the set of input images, and N be the number of facial attributes. For a given image $x \in \mathbb{I}$, let $y_i \in \{-1, +1\}$ be the binary label of the ith attribute, where $i \in \{1, 2, \dots, N\}$ is the index of facial attributes. Let $\mathbb{H}$ be the hypothesis space of possible decision functions, and $f_i(\theta^T x)$ be the decision function, where $\theta = \{\theta_1, \theta_2, \dots, \theta_N\}$ is the network weights. Hence, the loss function of the ith facial attribute can be defined as $L_i(f_i(\theta^T x), y_i)$. Let $\mathbb{E}(L_i)$ be the expected loss over the range of inputs $\mathbb{I}$. Then the optimization task is to minimize the expected squared error for each attribute.

$$\forall i : f_i = \arg\min_{f_i \in \mathbb{H}} \mathbb{E}(L_i) \tag{1}$$

For each input x and attribute i, the corresponding classification result $c_i(x)$ and the according accuracy $acc_i(x)$ can be obtained from the output of $f_i(x)$ described as:

$$c_i(x) = \begin{cases} +1 & f_i(x) > 0 \\ -1 & \text{otherwise,} \end{cases}$$

and

$$acc_i(x, y) = \begin{cases} +1 & y_i(x)c_i(x) > 0 \\ 0 & \text{otherwise} \end{cases} \tag{2}$$

As discussed above, the traditional approach treats facial attributes as N independent tasks, and each classifier is trained independently. The typical loss function for the ith facial attribute is constructed by choosing the hinge-loss function, which is shown as:

$$\arg\min_{\theta_i} L_i(f_i(\theta^T x), y_i) = \arg\min_{\theta_i}(\max(0, 1 - y_i(x)f_i(\theta^T x))) \tag{3}$$

However, a problem with the traditional approach is that training independent classifiers cannot learn the latent correlations between attributes. To exploit such correlations, the classifier should be constructed to learn all of these facial attributes simultaneously. In addition, the attribute label distribution in the training set should match with the corresponding distribution in the testing set. Therefore, it is necessary to balance the dataset to train a better classifier. One way to obtain a balanced dataset is to perfectly collect evenly distributed dataset of images for each attribute. However, it will cause extra efforts since most of data in real application is not evenly distributed, and finding such dataset may be very challenging especially at a large scale. An alternative solution is to modify the loss function in order to simulate a balanced dataset. In our proposed ABCNN, some changes are made to the objective function to address the imbalance between the training dataset and the test dataset. Specifically, a mixed objective function is proposed by considering the distribution difference between training data and testing data as adapted weights. Firstly, the training distribution S_i for each attribute i is computed by calculating the fraction of positive samples $Train_i^+$ ($0 < Train_i^+ < 1$) and fraction of negative samples $Train_i^-$ ($0 < Train_i^- < 1$) in the training set. Given the binary testing target distribution $Target_i^+$ and $Target_i^-$ (where $Target_i^+ + Target_i^- = 1$), an adapted weight is assigned for each class of attribute i, as shown in Eqs. (4) and (5):

$$p(i| + 1) = 1 + \frac{\Delta T^+}{Target_i^+ + Train_i^+} \tag{4}$$

$$p(i| - 1) = 1 + \frac{\Delta T^-}{Target_i^- + Train_i^-} \tag{5}$$

where $\Delta T^+ = Target_i^+ - Train_i^+$ and $\Delta T^- = Target_i^- - Train_i^-$. It can be seen from the above equations that we will increase the weight of the ith facial attribute if the fraction of positive or negative labels in the training data is less than the testing data. The intuition is that the increment of those weights will help balance the distribution difference between training data and testing data. Correspondingly, we will decrease the fraction weights of positive or negative labels in the training data if it is higher than that in the testing data. Then, these adapted weights are incorporated into the mixed objective function. Instead of using the hinge-loss function, a weighted mixed task square error is adopted as the loss function, and the optimization problem of ABCNN can be expressed as:

$$\forall i : \underset{f_i \in \mathbb{H}}{\arg\min}\ \mathbb{E}(L(x,y)) = \underset{f_i \in \mathbb{H}}{\arg\min}\ \mathbb{E}(\textstyle\sum_{i=1}^{N} p(i|y_i(x))\|f_i(x) - y_i(x)\|^2) \tag{6}$$

The optimization problem aims to find the optimal decision function f that has the smallest error between predictions and target labels. Over an M-element training set X with labels Y, from Eq. (6) we can get:

$$\forall i : \underset{f_i \in \mathbb{H}}{\arg\min}\ \mathbb{E}(L(X,Y)) = \underset{f_i \in \mathbb{H}}{\arg\min}\ \mathbb{E}(\textstyle\sum_{j=1}^{M} \sum_{i=1}^{N} p(i|Y_j i(x))\|f_i(X_j) - Y_j i\|^2) \tag{7}$$

The ABCNN architecture can be built by replacing the standard loss layer of a deep convolution neural network (DCNN) with a layer implementing Eq. (7). After the above classifier is trained, we can predict facial attributes by inputting a face image with fixed dimensions (which are consistent with that of training images) to the classifier.

2.4 Stranger Determination

This module aims to determine if a requesting stranger is included in the photo or not and which face matches the stranger. This is done though thresholding the difference between the facial attributes of the detected faces and those of the requesting stranger. In fact, facial attributes predicted by the classifier is a vector of binary values, where $+1$ indicates the presence of the corresponding attribute, while -1 represents its absence. The difference is defined as the number of different attributes between two faces under the same set of attributes. Formally, let N be the number of attributes associated with a face. For a given face, its corresponding attributes vector $V = [a_1, \ldots, a_N]$, where $a_i \in \{-1, +1\}$ represents the ith facial attribute. We use V_r and V_s to represent the facial attributes of the requesting stranger and a specific detected face respectively. The inner product of V_r and V_s is $V_r \cdot V_s = \sum_{i=1}^{N} V_r[i]V_s[i]$. If all the attributes are identical that inner product should be N. The $V_r[i]V_s[i]$ is -1 only when the ith attribute in V_r and the ith attribute in V_s are different. Hence, the difference can be obtained as:

$$diff = \frac{N - V_r \cdot V_s}{2} \tag{8}$$

As discussed before the facial attributes cannot be used to uniquely identify a stranger. In order to further protect the stranger's facial attributes from the photographer, inner product computation can be done with a two-party privacy-preserving scheme [5]. Usually the predication results from two images from the same person cannot match exactly due to angle difference or some other reasons. Thus a threshold is set to tolerate such minor deviations. The rule is that only the difference between facial attributes of the requesting stranger and any specific detected face is less than or equal to the threshold, we consider the detected face belongs to the requesting stranger. Our evaluations show that it is a good choice to set 1 as the threshold.

2.5 Target Filter

This module is designed to distinguish the target from the stranger in a photo, so that the target's face will not be blurred even if the target mistakenly sends a blurring request. Specifically, if the target of a photo is one or multiple persons, the task is filtering out the targeted faces; if the target is a building or something else, we would like to avoid the stranger being mistakenly identified as the target. Therefore, a heuristic approach is proposed to achieve this goal. Based on our observations from real-world experience, the target is usually associated with the following properties in the photo:

- One common goal of taking photos is recording beautiful moments. The target is likely to be smiling when he is being pictured, since smiles make a person more attractive and confident.
- The photographer usually intentionally makes the target's face significantly larger than others who are accidentally included in the photo. For instance, if a stranger is too close to the camera and hence his face is larger than the target's, the photographer will usually stop picturing or move a little bit so that the target is better captured into the photo. Moreover, considering that there might be multiple targets appearing in the photo but with slightly different face sizes (e.g., a group of people taking a picture), we expect to filter all targets in the photo by comparing a detected face with the largest face in the photo, which is considered as one of the targets' faces by default. If the size difference is less than a pre-defined threshold, we consider the detected face as one of the target faces.
- Similarly, the photographer usually puts the target in a dominant position of the photo. The central region is one of the most popular options, which can highlight the target in the photo.

Consequently, **smiling**, **face size** and **face position** can facilitate determining if a face belongs to the target or not. Based on these observations, we propose three rules to determine whether a person in the photo is a target or not.

1. The person is smiling.
2. The person's face is the largest one in the photo or slightly smaller than the largest one by a pre-defined threshold. Based on our test, we find that the average size difference between two targets' faces in a photo is around 10%. Hence, if more than one face is detected, we compare the largest one with the others. If the size difference between the largest one and a certain face is less than or equal to 10%, we consider that face as one target face. Otherwise, the detected face will not be treated as a target.
3. The person's face appears at the central region of the photo. The central region is defined as the middle section of horizontal trisections of a photo.

However, it is too strict if we determine a detected face is the target only when all those three rules are satisfied, since sometimes not all of them are satisfied. For instance, the target is not always smiling when the photo is taken. Considering this, we determine that the face is the target if at least two of the three rules are satisfied.

2.6 Face Blurring

The purpose of face blurring is to mask the features of a face in order to make the face not recognizable, without degrading the quality of photo much. Similar to our previous work [14], we adopt an approach based on the Gaussian Blur algorithm [21] to smoothly blur faces. To conduct face blurring, we need to determine a blurring area in the face enclosing the main identifiable features of the face. In particular, we draw a square whose side length is 2.4 times of the distance between eyes, and whose center is the middle point between eyes. Then the Gaussian Blur operation can be performed in the square blurring area.

3 Implementation

The facial attribute classifier was implemented using Python 2.7 and MxNet [3], which is an open-source deep learning framework. WiFi Direct was used to conduct peer-to-peer communications between the stranger and the photographer. The face blurring module was implemented as same as our previous work [14], so some details are omitted here.

3.1 Face Detection and Preprocessing

Face detection is based on the *FaceDetector* class provided in Android SDK. Faces in an image can be detected by calling the *findFaces* method of *FaceDetector*. This method detects faces by finding pupils in the image, and returns a number of detected faces into an array of FaceDetector.Faces class. For each instance of *Face* class, the distance between two eyes of a face and the coordinate of the middle point between two eyes can be obtained. Then we crop each detected face with a square area, which is the same as the blurring square described in Sect. 2.6. Also, the size of the cropped square is used to represent the size of the corresponding face in the target filter module. To prepare for target filtering, we need to detect the position of each face in the photo. To do so, we evenly divide the picture into three regions (left, middle, right) along the horizontal direction. Then for each detected face, we calculate the middle point between its eyes. If the middle point is located in the middle region, we say this face is in the central region.

3.2 Facial Attribute Classifier

This module aims to predict a set of facial attributes from a given face image. As described in Sect. 2.3, we use ABCNN to predict the facial attributes and ABCNN is implemented by the Python interface of MxNet [3]. In particular, we build the ABCNN network by replacing the final loss layer of a 16-layer VGG network from [22] by the loss function in Eq. (7), and the architecture shown in Fig. 3. The architecture consists of 16 weight layers, including 13 convolution layers and 3 fully connected layers, which are associated with over one million weights. Since the network only accepts RGB image input with dimensions of 128 * 128 pixels, each cropped face obtained from the face detection and preprocessing module should be scaled to that size before being sent into this classifier.

In this paper, the ABCNN network is trained on the CelebA dataset [16], which is a large-scale facial attributes dataset. It contains 20 images for each of over 10K celebrities, hence with a total of more than 200K images. The first 160K images are used for training, and the remaining 40K images are used for

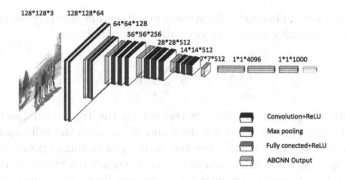

128*128*3   128*128*64
64*64*128
56*56*256
28*28*512
14*14*512
7*7*512   1*1*4096   1*1*1000

■ Convolution+ReLU
■ Max pooling
■ Fully conected+ReLU
■ ABCNN Output

Fig. 3. Architecture of the ABCNN network.

validation and testing, specifically, 20K for validation and 20K for testing. For our implementation, we use a set of pre-cropped and aligned face images provided by the CelebA dataset, and scale the dimensions of training RGB images from 178 * 218 pixels to 128 * 128 pixels. Each image in the CelebA dataset is annotated with binary labels of 40 facial attributes (e.g., 'Young' and 'Male'). However, in this work, we choose 16 out of the 40 attributes that do not change frequently for the same person as our considered attributes. The 16 chosen facial attributes include {*Arched Eyebrows, Bushy Eyebrows, Big Lips, Big Nose, Point Nose, Black Hair, Blond Hair, Brown Hair, Gray Hair, Eyeglasses, Bald, High Cheekbones, Narrow Eyes, Oval Face, Male, Young* }. In addition, since the 'smiling' attribute is required for target filtering, we also add it into the classifier (note that it is not used for stranger determination but only for target filtering).

4 Evaluations

To train the classifier, we set the batch size to 384 images per training iteration, and hence the training process requires approximately 420 iterations to finish a full epoch on the training set. The learning rate is initialized as 0.05, and reduced by a factor of 0.8 every four epochs until it decays to 0.000001. We train the ABCNN for 110 epochs with all images from training set on two NVidia K80 GPUs.

4.1 Model Selection

Classification accuracy is defined as the number of correctly predicted cases divided by the number of testing images. From Eq. (2), we can derive the classification accuracy of each attribute i:

$$e_i(X, Y) = \frac{1}{N_{test}} \sum_{j=1}^{N_{test}} acc_i(X_j, Y_j) \qquad (9)$$

Consequently, we can evaluate the average classification accuracy by calculating the average classification accuracy over all the N attributes:

$$E(X,Y) = \frac{1}{N} \sum_{i=1}^{N} e_i(X,Y) \tag{10}$$

The ABCNN prediction model is trained on the training dataset, but the number of training epochs needed is determined based on the validation dataset. Specifically, the accuracy trend when the number of training epochs increases is shown in Fig. 4. As the training continues, the accuracy over the training dataset keeps increasing. However, training for more epochs means higher cost. Thus, based on the maximum accuracy over the validation dataset, we stop training the ABCNN network after 80 epochs (with 89.84% validation accuracy) and use the resulted model for performance evaluations in order to guarantee the coverage of the model without too high cost.

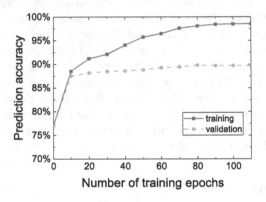

Fig. 4. Average classification accuracy vs training epochs.

Then based on Eq. (9) we evaluate the classification accuracy of each facial attribute on the test dataset, including 16 attributes used for stranger determination and the 'Smiling' attribute for target filtering. The average accuracy over those 16 attributes is also tested according to Eq. (10). As Fig. 5 shows, the average accuracy is 88.53% (see the horizontal dashed line) which is pretty high. Out of the first 16 facial attributes, 6 attributes outperform the average performance, including *Bushy Eyebrows*, *Black Hair*, *Blond Hair*, *Gray Hair*, *Eyeglasses*, *Bald* and *Male*. For example, the classification accuracies of *Eyeglasses* and *Bald* achieves 98.31% and 98.34%, respectively.

To measure the performance of our proposed ABCNN in predicting the facial attributes, we compared it with the state-of-art algorithm proposed in [17]. They also construct a multi-task training classifier and the corresponding facial attribute prediction and average accuracy are represented with the blue dashed line and the horizontal blue solid line in Fig. 5, respectively. In addition, we also compared the proposed ABCNN with [16] which uses the basic CNN model to select features and inputs them to the SVM classifier for training. Its performance is displayed by green line and green dashed line for facial attributes prediction accuracy and average accuracy, respectively. ABCNN outperforms both the multi-task training classifier in [17] and the CNN-SVM model [13].

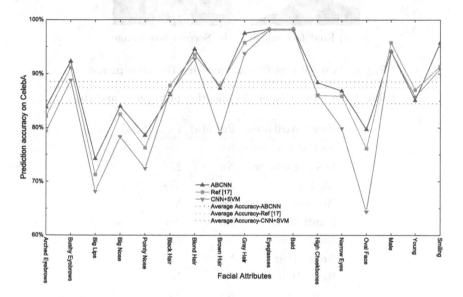

Fig. 5. Classification accuracy of each attribute and average accuracy in testing. (Color figure online)

4.2   Classification Consistency

Since the facial attributes are used for stranger determination, the trained classifier is expected to make consistent predictions given a specific person. That is, given two different face images of the same person, ideally all the 16 facial attributes obtained from the two images are identical. To evaluate classification consistency, we use the LFW image database [7] that has been widely used in the literature. Since images in the LFW database are organized by person, it is more efficient to sample images for experiment. In this experiment, we randomly pick 50 persons, and a pair of different face images of each person (see Fig. 6 as an example). The classification results over the two images in Fig. 6 are presented in Table 1. It can be seen that the classified facial attributes of these two images are exactly the same except 'Big Lips', 'Brown Hair' and 'High Cheekbones'. Out of the 50 persons, the classification results for 32 persons are fully consistent. For the rest 18 persons, 7 persons have 15 identical attributes, 8 persons have 14 identical attributes, and the remaining 3 persons have 13 identical attributes.

Besides, we examine the classification consistency on persons with more than 4 face images in the LFW dataset. In particular, we pick 2 pairs of different face

(a) First face image   (b) Second face image

Fig. 6. Two different face images from the same person.

Table 1. Facial attributes classification of Fig. 6(a) and (b).

Facial attributes	Fig. 6(a)	Fig. 6(b)
Arched Eyebrows	No	No
Bushy Eyebrows	No	No
Big Lips	No	Yes
Big Nose	Yes	Yes
Pointy Nose	No	No
Black Hair	No	No
Brown Hair	Yes	No
Blond Hair	No	No
Gray Hair	No	No
Eyeglasses	No	No
Bald	No	No
High Cheekbones	No	Yes
Narrow Eyes	No	No
Oval Face	No	No
Male	Yes	Yes
Young	No	No

images for each of those 10 persons. Then we compare the predicted attributes pair by pair, and hence perform 20-pair comparisons. As Table 2 shows, 8 pairs of face images are labeled with the exactly the same attributes, and only 6 pairs are labeled with 3 or more different attributes.

Furthermore, we examine the possibility of two different persons being predicted with identical attributes. We randomly pick 100 persons from the LFW dataset, and perform facial attribute classification on a face image of each person. Then, we compare facial attributes of every person with those of the other 99 persons and hence 4950 pairs are compared in total. Only 144 pairs have exactly the same attributes. All these results show that the classification consistency is high.

Table 2. Classification consistency of 10 persons with 2 pairs of face images each.

Number of identical attributes	16	15	14	13	12	11	10
Number of pairs	8	4	2	2	2	1	1

4.3 Optimal Thresholding

The above consistency experiments show that facial attributes of two face images from the same person may not be perfectly identical. Hence, a scheme that depends on exactly matching of facial attributes between two faces will not work for stranger determination. The stranger determination is implemented by thresholding the difference of facial attributes between two compared face images to allow a reasonable difference between these two faces. Hence, it is needed to find a proper threshold. The goal is that we can obtain more true positives without causing too many false positives under the threshold. Here, true positive means two different face images of the same person being determined as the same person. False positive means images of two different persons being determined are from the same person. In this experiment, we pick 50 persons from the LFW database, and two different face images with each person. In order to evaluate false positive, 50 tests are conducted. In each test, we pick one face image from the above 50 persons as the target, and choose another face image from a different person to compare with the target. From the above classification consistency evaluations, we consider 0, 1 and 2 as reasonable threshold candidates and show the results in Table 3. Based on these results, we choose 1 as the threshold in stranger determination which has good performance in both true positive and false positive.

Table 3. Effectiveness of stranger determination under different threshold with 50 tests.

	Threshold = 0	Threshold = 1	Threshold = 2
# True positives	36	45	48
# False positives	1	3	12

4.4 Effectiveness of Target Filter

This test aims to examine how well the target filter module can detect the target from a photo. In this experiment, we perform target filter on field photos from two different sources where multiple targets might be in one photo. We use *false filtering rate* to measure the performance, which is defined as the percentage of times when not all targets in the photo are successfully detected or any stranger appearing in the photo is mistakenly detected as the target.

First, we evaluate the effectiveness of target filter on 100 photos, which we have pictured by mobile phone in the past, and at least one target person is included in each photo. The result shows that the false filtering rate is only 8%, which means the target filter only fails to detect the target in 8 photos. Figure 7 illustrates two example photos of our test. Figure 7(a) is a successful example, but Fig. 7(b) is a failed example. The reason for unsuccessful target detection is that the face is not at the central region of the photo, and 'Smiling' attribute is falsely predicted as 'No'. Based on our proposed three rules, only the rule based on face size can be satisfied, and hence the target is not successfully detected.

(a) A test photo where the target is successfully detected. (b) A test photo where the target filter failed.

Fig. 7. Target filter test on photos taken by the authors.

Then we pick 100 photos shared by our friends in Facebook from 10/01/2016 to 12/26/2016. At least one target person is included in each photo. Figure 8 shows some example photos, where faces are blurred upon the friends' request. Similar to the above test, we run target filtering on these 100 photos. The false filtering rate is 12%, which means the target filtering operation fails in 12 photos. We look into each of those 12 photos, and find the same reason causing false target filtering. When multiple targets are shown in the photo, the target at the rightmost or leftmost is detected as out of the central region of the photo. Also, this target was not smiling when the photo was taken or the 'Smiling' attribute is falsely predicted as 'No'. As a result, in those cases, the rules based on face position and smiling cannot be satisfied, and hence the target filter cannot successfully detect all the targets in the photo. However, the overall target filtering accuracy is still high.

Fig. 8. Target filter test on photos shared by friends on Facebook.

4.5   Accuracy of Protection

This part evaluates the effectiveness of our system in protecting the stranger's privacy. The experiments are conducted on our campus. Figure 9 shows two example experiment scenes.

Fig. 9. Example experiment scenes

True Protection Rate: This group of tests considers the scenario where one target person and two strangers appear in the photo. We assume either one of the two strangers or both of them request face blurring. The *true protection rate* is defined as ratio of times when the faces of the requesting strangers are blurred in the photo. For each requesting stranger, we conduct 10 tests separately. Figure 10 shows an example where the right stranger's face is successfully blurred. Table 4 shows the true protection rate which is high.

Fig. 10. Example of a successful protection.

False Protection Rate: Again we consider the scenario where one target person and two strangers appear in the photo. Suppose the two strangers in the photo do not request to blur their faces but other nearby strangers who are not in the photo submit blurring requests. In this case, we define *false protection rate*

Table 4. True protection rate

# Requesting strangers	True protection rate
1	90%
2	80%

as the percentage of times when any of two strangers in the photo is mistakenly detected as a requesting stranger and hence falsely blurred. To evaluate the false protection rate in a noisy environment, we conduct simulations with 1, 3, 5 and 10 nearby requesting strangers separately. Specifically, in each test, we randomly pick a certain number of entities from the LFW database, who act as nearby requesting strangers, and one face image for each selected person. For each specific number of requesting strangers, 50 tests are conducted separately. Table 5 shows results with different number of requesting strangers. We can see that false protection rate increases with the increasing number of nearby requesting strangers. This is because the more nearby requesting strangers, the higher possibility of their facial attributes being overlapped with that of strangers in the photo. Note that the false protection rate is as low as 3% with only one nearby requesting stranger. Even under noisy environment with 3 nearby strangers who request face blurring, the false protection is only 8%. The false protection rate increases to 24% with 10 nearby requesting strangers, but this case does not occur often in the real world.

Table 5. False protection rate

	# Nearby requesting strangers			
	1	3	5	10
False protection rate	3%	8%	14%	24%

5   Related Work

Photo and Video Privacy. Jung and Philipose [11] propose a system to protect video privacy. If it detects the person being recorded is making certain gestures like waving hands, the wearable camera will stop recording that person. Raval et al. [18] design a system called *MarkIt* to protect video privacy. It detects sensitive objects predefined by users in video, and those sensitive objects will be covered with markers before releasing the video to third-party applications. Jana et al. [9] design an OS abstraction *Recognizer* to enforce fine-grained access control in augmented reality system by reducing the quality of raw sensor data. *Darkly* [10] restricts untrusted applications from accessing raw data from perceptual sensors.

Schiff et al. [20] implement a system to protect photo privacy by detecting persons that wear special tracking markers and blurring their faces in photos. However, people who want to protect their privacy must wear special markers beforehand which is not suitable for our considered daily scenarios. Bo et al. [1] propose a protocol to protect the privacy of people being pictured based on a physical tag, which contains their privacy preferences. However, people have to wear clothes with QR-code as privacy tags. Visual fingerprints have also been used to detect whether a user is in a photo [27], but their scheme requires update of visual fingerprints whenever there is any change (e.g., clothes change), requiring too much intervention from people. Templeman et al. [25] propose an approach to prevent photos from being shared with others by checking the attributes extracted from the photo, such as location and content. *PlaceAvoider* [26] is a context-aware system which can notify the photographer when an application is going to capture photos in sensitive places. Zhang et al. [28] design a photo capturing and sharing system to protect people's privacy based on graph representations of people's portraits. *Notisense* [17] is implemented to notify bystanders of nearby mobile sensing activities. Tan et al. [24] implement a system to protect photo privacy based on the recognition of persons who are known to the phone owner, and deny third-party applications to access these photos.

Facial Attributes Classification. Kumar et al. [13] propose an approach to train facial attribute classifiers. Features from manually-picked facial regions for each facial attribute are separately optimized using AdaBoost algorithms. In addition, independent SVM classifiers are trained by feeding optimized features. In this approach, various features are learnt for each facial attribute, and an independent SVM classifier is separately trained. Even though it is a valid approach, it is not efficient for feature extraction and classification. Recently, with the increasing popularity of convolution neural network (CNN), it has been leveraged to extract more sophisticated features of facial attributes. For instance, Kang et al. [12] propose gated CNNs, which aim to determine which regions of a face are most correlated to corresponding attributes. Then, the output of such CNNs is encoded into a global feature vector for training independent binary SVM classifiers. Zhang et al. [29] apply CNNs to learn facial attributes, which are used to infer social relations between pairs of identities with an image. Liu et al. [16] design three CNNs, including two localization networks (LNets) and an attribute recognition network (ANet). LNet is designed for localizing features in face images, while ANet is trained on face identities and attributes to extract features. Then, independent SVM classifiers are trained on those extracted features. However, none of them can be directly used for imbalanced distributed datasets.

6   Conclusion

We proposed a system PoliteCamera to protect strangers' privacy who are accidentally captured in a photo taken by mobile phones. The system can inform nearby strangers that they are possibly included in a photo and give them an option to blur their faces in the photo. A novel ABCNN structure is designed to predict facial attributes, where the facial attributes are used to determine whether a requesting stranger is in the photo and which face in the photo belongs to him. We implemented a prototype system, and evaluated its performance through experiments. The accuracy of the facial attributes prediction is better than the state of the art, and experimental evaluations demonstrate that the system can effectively protect strangers' privacy.

References

1. Bo, C., Shen, G., Liu, J., Li, X.Y., Zhang, Y., Zhao, F.: Privacy.tag: privacy concern expressed and respected. In: Proceedings of the 12th ACM Conference on Embedded Network Sensor Systems, pp. 163–176. ACM (2014)
2. Camera OTP (2013). https://play.google.com/store/apps/details?id=org.witness.sscphase1&hl=en
3. Chen, T., et al.: MXnet: a flexible and efficient machine learning library for heterogeneous distributed systems. arXiv preprint arXiv:1512.01274 (2015)
4. Wi-Fi Direct (2015). http://www.wi-fi.org/discover-wi-fi/wi-fi-direct
5. Dong, W., Dave, V., Qiu, L., Zhang, Y.: Secure friend discovery in mobile social networks. In: 2011 Proceedings of IEEE, INFOCOM, pp. 1647–1655. IEEE (2011)
6. Blur DSLR PBP (2016). https://play.google.com/store/apps/details?id=jp.co.pointblur.android.app.quick&hl=en
7. Huang, G.B., Ramesh, M., Berg, T., Learned-Miller, E.: Labeled faces in the wild: a database for studying face recognition in unconstrained environments. Technical report 07–49. University of Massachusetts, Amherst (2007)
8. Blur Image (2016). https://play.google.com/store/apps/details?id=com.inglesdivino.blurimage&hl=en
9. Jana, S., et al.: Enabling fine-grained permissions for augmented reality applications with recognizers. In: USENIX Security, pp. 415–430 (2013)
10. Jana, S., Narayanan, A., Shmatikov, V.: A scanner darkly: protecting user privacy from perceptual applications. In: 2013 IEEE Symposium on Security and Privacy, SP, pp. 349–363. IEEE (2013)
11. Jung, J., Philipose, M.: Courteous glass. In: Proceedings of the 2014 ACM International Joint Conference on Pervasive and Ubiquitous Computing: Adjunct Publication, pp. 1307–1312. ACM (2014)
12. Kang, S., Lee, D., Yoo, C.D.: Face attribute classification using attribute-aware correlation map and gated convolutional neural networks. In: 2015 IEEE International Conference on Image Processing, ICIP, pp. 4922–4926. IEEE (2015)
13. Kumar, N., Belhumeur, P., Nayar, S.: FaceTracer: a search engine for large collections of images with faces. In: Forsyth, D., Torr, P., Zisserman, A. (eds.) ECCV 2008. LNCS, vol. 5305, pp. 340–353. Springer, Heidelberg (2008). https://doi.org/10.1007/978-3-540-88693-8_25
14. Li, A., Li, Q., Gao, W.: PrivacyCamera: cooperative privacy-aware photographing with mobile phones. In: 2016 13th Annual IEEE International Conference on Sensing, Communication, and Networking, SECON, pp. 1–9. IEEE (2016)
15. Liu, Y., Guo, Y., Liang, C.: A survey on peer-to-peer video streaming systems. Peer-to-Peer Netw. Appl. 1(1), 18–28 (2008)

16. Liu, Z., Luo, P., Wang, X., Tang, X.: Deep learning face attributes in the wild. In: Proceedings of the IEEE International Conference on Computer Vision, pp. 3730–3738 (2015)
17. Pidcock, S., Smits, R., Hengartner, U., Goldberg, I.: NotiSense: an urban sensing notification system to improve bystander privacy. In: PhoneSense (2011)
18. Raval, N., Cox, L., Srivastava, A., Machanavajjhala, A., Lebeck, K.: MarkIt: privacy markers for protecting visual secrets. In: Proceedings of the 2014 ACM International Joint Conference on Pervasive and Ubiquitous Computing: Adjunct Publication, pp. 1289–1295. ACM (2014)
19. Schafer, J.B., Frankowski, D., Herlocker, J., Sen, S.: Collaborative filtering recommender systems. In: Brusilovsky, P., Kobsa, A., Nejdl, W. (eds.) The Adaptive Web. LNCS, vol. 4321, pp. 291–324. Springer, Heidelberg (2007). https://doi.org/10.1007/978-3-540-72079-9_9
20. Schiff, J., Meingast, M., Mulligan, D.K., Sastry, S., Goldberg, K.: Respectful cameras: detecting visual markers in real-time to address privacy concerns. In: Senior, A. (ed.) Protecting Privacy in Video Surveillance, pp. 65–89. Springer, London (2009)
21. Shapiro, L., Stockman, G.: Computer Vision, Chap. 12, pp. 137–150. Prentice Hall, New Jersey (2001)
22. Simonyan, K., Zisserman, A.: Very deep convolutional networks for large-scale image recognition. arXiv preprint arXiv:1409.1556 (2014)
23. iPhone 7 technical specifications (2016). http://www.apple.com/iphone-7/specs/
24. Tan, J., Drolia, U., Martins, R., Gandhi, R., Narasimhan, P.: Short paper: chips: content-based heuristics for improving photo privacy for smartphones. In: Proceedings of the 2014 ACM Conference on Security and Privacy in Wireless & Mobile Networks, pp. 213–218. ACM (2014)
25. Templeman, R., Kapadia, A., Hoyle, R., Crandall, D.: Reactive security: responding to visual stimuli from wearable cameras. In: Proceedings of the 2014 ACM International Joint Conference on Pervasive and Ubiquitous Computing: Adjunct Publication, pp. 1297–1306. ACM (2014)
26. Templeman, R., Korayem, M., Crandall, D., Kapadia, A.: PlaceAvoider: steering first-person cameras away from sensitive spaces. In: Network and Distributed System Security Symposium (NDSS) (2014)
27. Wang, H., Bao, X., Roy Choudhury, R., Nelakuditi, S.: Visually fingerprinting humans without face recognition. In: Proceedings of the 13th Annual International Conference on Mobile Systems, Applications, and Services, pp. 345–358. ACM (2015)
28. Zhang, L., Liu, K., Li, X.Y., Liu, C., Ding, X., Liu, Y.: Privacy-friendly photo capturing and sharing system. In: Proceedings of the 2016 ACM International Joint Conference on Pervasive and Ubiquitous Computing, pp. 524–534. ACM (2016)
29. Zhang, Z., Luo, P., Loy, C.C., Tang, X.: Learning social relation traits from face images. In: Proceedings of the IEEE International Conference on Computer Vision, pp. 3631–3639 (2015)

Lexical Mining of Malicious URLs
for Classifying Android Malware

Shanshan Wang[1], Qiben Yan[2], Zhenxiang Chen[1(✉)], Lin Wang[1],
Riccardo Spolaor[3], Bo Yang[1], and Mauro Conti[3]

[1] Shandong Provincial Key Laboratory of Network Based Intelligent Computing,
University of Jinan, Jinan, China
czx@ujn.edu.cn
[2] Department of Computer Science and Engineering, University of Nebraska-Lincoln,
Lincoln, NE, USA
[3] Department of Mathematics, University of Padova, Padua, Italy

Abstract. The prevalence of mobile malware has become a growing issue given the tight integration of mobile systems with our daily life. Most malware programs use URLs inside network traffic to forward commands to launch malicious activities. Therefore, the detection of malicious URLs can be essential in deterring such malicious activities. Traditional methods construct blacklists with verified URLs to identify malicious URLs, but their effectiveness is impaired by unknown malicious URLs. Recently, machine learning-based methods have been proposed for malware detection with improved performance. In this paper, we propose a novel URL detection method based on Floating Centroids Method (FCM), which integrates supervised classification and unsupervised clustering in a coherent manner. The proposed method uses the lexical features of a URL to effectively identify malicious URLs while grouping similar URLs into the same cluster. Our experimental results show that a URL cluster exhibits unique behavioral patterns that can be used for malware detection with high accuracy. Moreover, the proposed behavioral clustering method facilitates the identification of malicious URL categories and unseen malware variants.

1 Introduction

Malicious software, or malware, has become a major threat to the growing mobile ecosystem. Recently, the number and sophistication of mobile malware, particularly those target Android platforms, have increased dramatically [1]. The Android platform and mobile anti-virus scanners provide security protection mechanisms to protect Android devices, yet an increasing number of advanced mobile malware can still penetrate the mobile system by evading these mechanisms. As mobile devices are increasingly associated with personal information, an effective mobile malware detection system is urgently needed.

Malware authors have adopted repackaging and code obfuscation techniques to generate a large number of malware variants. These malware variants exhibit

© ICST Institute for Computer Sciences, Social Informatics and Telecommunications Engineering 2018
R. Beyah et al. (Eds.): SecureComm 2018, LNICST 254, pp. 248–263, 2018.
https://doi.org/10.1007/978-3-030-01701-9_14

similar malicious behaviors at runtime, which can be clustered together to identify their common behaviors. The vast majority of malware programs launch their malicious activities through network (e.g., sending spam, exfiltrating private data, and downloading malware updates). Thus, we can use the malware's network behaviors to conduct classification.

Clustering algorithm is an unsupervised learning method, which groups the samples into different families based on their similarities with each other. However, the challenge of the clustering algorithms is to accurately cluster the same family of malware together, while avoiding the inclusion of benign apps. Some clustering algorithms can effectively discover the differences and commonalities between malicious samples, and with these features they can divide malicious samples into multiple categories. However, this approach does not have the ability to efficiently distinguish between benign and malicious samples, i.e., it is highly likely that a benign sample will be included into a malicious cluster when it has some similar characteristics with a certain type of malware.

In this paper, we introduce a novel machine learning technique, Floating Centroid Method (FCM) [2] for mobile malware detection and malware family clustering. FCM can cluster similar samples with the same label, while separating samples with different labels as much as possible that effectively avoids the inclusion of benign samples into a malicious cluster. Note that most malware programs use URLs to execute or transfer commands to support their malicious behaviors [3]. So the method that extracts URLs in HTTP traffic to detect malware can be effective in most cases. Using FCM, malicious URLs can be clustered and identified. By analyzing clustering results, we can find more valuable information about malware's network behaviors. The contribution can be summarized as follows:

- Through the analysis on URLs, we discover the many-to-many relationship between URLs and malware family labels. Based on this observation, we propose a novel network-level behavioral clustering method.
- We use Canopy algorithm [4] to improve the selection of cluster number in FCM. The improved FCM can quickly determine the optimal cluster number. With the improved FCM algorithm, we create a novel model that can cluster and detect malicious URLs based on similar lexical features which has a higher accuracy than traditional clustering algorithms.
- We mine the rich information within each URL cluster and perform statistical and manual analysis to reveal different behavioral patterns in different clusters which helps in finding malicious variants.

The rest of the paper is organized as follows: related works are introduced in Sect. 2. We give a detailed description on the method implementation in Sect. 3. The experimental results and comparative analysis are discussed in Sect. 4. The limitation of this method is introduced in Sect. 5. The conclusions are provided in Sect. 6.

2 Related Work

Malware detection has traditionally been implemented based on static and dynamic analysis methods. Static analysis can identify malicious behaviors of suspicious apps without code execution. DroidMat [5], Drebin [6], and Droid-Miner [7] are static analysis methods that utilize the machine-learning algorithm to detect anomalies by analyzing permissions, called APIs or bytecode instructions. However, static analysis is challenged by the code polymorphism and obfuscation of malware. In dynamic analysis methods, the app is executed in a sandbox environment. Dynamic analysis systems [8,9] have been proposed to analyze system calls to detect malicious behaviors. However, these dynamic analysis methods are difficult to deploy due to their complexity.

In addition, suspicious apps can be analyzed by observing their network traffic. We briefly review the mechanisms that use network traffic for malware detection. Some malware detection methods focus on a specific network protocol [10], which considers some basic information about the TCP header. Other studies have focused on the HTTP application-layer traffic between the attackers and victims, such as works [11–13]. The flower system [11] is an automatic app signature system that only considers the key value pair and hostname in HTTP header. TrafficAV [12] uses four fields (request method, request host, request URL, and user-agent) in HTTP header and combines the decision-tree algorithm to create an effective malware detection model. Recon [13] reveals privacy leaks in mobile network traffic by observing the keys that appear in the URLs. Work [14] also focus on the URLs. The authors design and implement AURA, a framework for identifying the hosts that an app talks to and evaluating the risks communication entails. Many studies focus on the clustering of malware samples to perform malware detection or explore malicious behavior of a certain type of malware. Shabtai et al. [15] analyzed a large amount of Android network traffic to identify malicious attacks by repackaging. They pointed out that the apps should be grouped into different categories based on the statistical characteristics of network data. They also summarized the deviation between benign and malicious network behaviors. Gorla et al. [16] focused on the market descriptive information of the app to extract keywords for clustering different apps. They identified the most unusual apps in each cluster as suspicious apps because apps in the same cluster would have similar attributes or behaviors, while the suspicious apps are drastically different from other apps. However, this method has a high false-positive rate.

Our proposed method differs from the above classification and clustering methods, as we integrate classification and clustering into a holistic model. The benign URLs are for the convenience of people's memory, while malicious URLs do not want to attract people's attention. Malicious URLs are often filled with a lot of junk characters and change encoding methods, use IP addresses instead of domain names, and randomly generate domain names. From this point of view, lexical mining of malicious URLs is a viable way. So our work clusters and identifies malicious URLs based on their lexical features. FCM algorithm is used to effectively cluster similar URLs into a group while identifying malicious URLs within the clustered URLs, attaining a better clustering performance.

3   Methodology

Our goal is to cluster similar samples together while keeping benign and malicious samples separated. Figure 1 presents an overview of our method, including URL extraction, feature representation as well as clustering and detection.

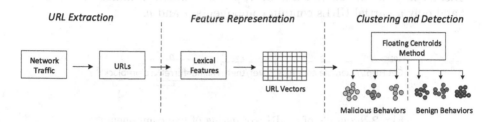

Fig. 1. The overview of URL clustering and detection method

3.1   URL Extraction

We design a traffic collection platform to collect network data generated by Android apps during network interaction. Then, we extract URL samples from the network traffic. A large number of network traffic data generated by both benign and malicious apps is collected. This module consists of two components: app execution and network traffic collection.

We run the apps on multiple Android emulators. Every app is driven by the Android tool Monkey [17], which can randomly send some events to the device during the execution of each app. In the process of traffic collection, additional operations of simulator restart and random event generation are used to trigger the malware's malicious activities as much as possible. To avoid the network traffic mixing by different apps, we only execute one app every time. Before running the next app, the emulator will be destroyed and a new emulator is re-established, which ensures that no app is running in the background when each app is executed. We then extract URLs from traffic data using the tshark tool [18].

3.2   Feature Representation

(1) **Component Description:** We divide each URL into five components and process them separately. The five components are shown in Fig. 2. The component m represents the request method, such as "GET","POST" and "HEAD". The component h represents the hostname. This field is specific

for the Internet host and port number of the requested resource. The component p stands for page, which includes the path and page name. We use the "/" character to segment this string and regard each word as a candidate feature after page segmentation. The component n represents the set of parameter names (i.e., n = {name, color}). The parameter names are always followed by the page and start with the character of "?". The component v is the set of parameter values (i.e., v = {ferret, black}). The parameter values are usually followed by the parameter names and connected to the parameter name with "=". Not all of the URLs contain these five components. In general, components m, h, p are common in almost every URL, and only a partial URLs contain components n and v.

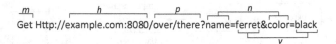

Fig. 2. Example of a URL consisting of five components

(2) **Feature Selection:** We process each component separately. For m component, we save all the request methods appearing in our dataset into a dictionary. For h component, we use another dictionary to save all the different hostnames that appear in our dataset. For the word in components p, n and v, we consider using an automatic feature selection algorithm (chi-square test [19]) to automatically identify meaningful features. This approach accounts for the relevance of a single word to the final category label and ignores the frequency of each feature appears. The formula of the chi-square test is as follows:

$$\chi^2(t, c) = \sum_{e_t \in 0,1} \sum_{e_c \in 0,1} \frac{(N_{e_t e_c} - E_{e_t e_c})^2}{E_{e_t e_c}} \tag{1}$$

where $N_{e_t e_c}$ refers to the occurrence number of feature t and class c, and $E_{e_t e_c}$ is the expected occurrence number of feature t and class c when they are independent of each other. The e_t and e_c are boolean, and value "0" indicates that the feature t is not in the word set from class c, whereas e_t with a value of "1" indicates that word set of class c contains feature t. We use all the lexical features in the components of m, h and select 100 features with high chi-square test score from components p, n and v respectively.

(3) **Vectorization:** We vectorize the selected features since the adopted machine-learning algorithm can only accept numerical data as input. We use one-hot encoding method to encode selected features obtained in feature selection section. In one-hot encoding, each word will be converted into m bits, among which only one bit is set to 1 and the others are set to 0. Notably, we make a distinction between the words belonging to components

m, h, p, n and v. This is done by having a separate dictionary for each component. After encoding words from different components, we also need to vectorize each URL. Given a URL, the resulting vector can be stitched together with multipart vectors. In this vector, the value of 1 indicates that the word appears in the URL, and 0 otherwise.

3.3   Clustering and Detection Model

The original FCM algorithm comprises of two parts. The first part is a three-layer feedforward neural network and the second part is a K-Means clustering algorithm. The K-Means algorithm needs to set the K value in advance. However, the K selection is a difficult but critical issue. Thus, we propose to enhance the FCM by adding the Canopy algorithm [4] for data coarse clustering. The modified FCM uses Particle Swarm Optimization (PSO) [20] algorithm to adjust the parameters of the neural network in accordance with the clustering accuracy of K-Means. The schematic of the modified FCM is shown in Fig. 3 and we elaborate on the details of each part in the following.

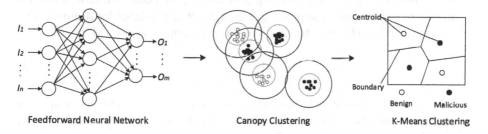

Fig. 3. The schematic diagram of improved FCM algorithm

(1) **Neural Network Mapping:** A mapping relationship refers to the transfer of training data samples from the original data space to the partition space. For this mapping, the input dimension is N and the output dimension is M, so the mapping is from a vector of N-dimensional elements to a vector of M elements. Specifically, the N-dimensional URL vector is fed into the neural network and then is mapped as a vector with M-dimensions. Given that the feedforward neural network can fit any nonlinear function, it is suitable to use feedforward neural network for mapping completion.

(2) **Canopy Clustering:** To determine the optimum K value quickly and accurately, we use Canopy algorithm to cluster data roughly, and then obtain K according to Canopy-clustering results. Specifically, the Canopy algorithm is used to cluster data mapped by the neural network roughly and then calculate the best cluster number for the dataset. Although the Canopy clustering algorithm has low accuracy, it has a great advantage in speed and thus is often used with K-Means.

Algorithm 1. PSO algorithm optimizes the feedforward neural network

---

Input: Dataset S and the structure of feedforward neural networks
Output: Best neural network and its corresponding clustering model
1: Initializing 20 different neural networks as individuals
2: **while** maximum generation has not been reached **do**
3:     **for** id:=1 to the number of individuals **do**
4:         Map dataset S to the partition space
5:         Canopy algorithm clusters the mapped dataset to obtain the K
6:         K-Means algorithm clusters the mapped dataset
7:         According to clustering result to calculate E value as this individual's fitness
8:     Update individuals by their fitness
9: **return** Best neural network and its corresponding clustering model

---

(3) **K-Means Clustering:** The optimum K is determined by Canopy clustering, and then K-Means algorithm is used to divide the mapped data into K disjoint clusters. The center of each cluster is called centroids. After calculating K centroids, each cluster is marked as malicious or benign in a process called coloring. To prevent coloring bias toward the class with more samples, in practice we balance the problem through setting weights for samples. The sample weight belonging to class i with $|S_i|$ samples is defined as follows:

$$W_i = \frac{1}{|S_i|} \tag{2}$$

The principle of coloring is that if the sum of weights of malicious samples in a cluster takes the majority, the cluster is colored as malicious. Otherwise, the cluster is marked as benign.

(4) **Learning Process:** We first define a variable z to evaluate a mapped point in the partition space whose formula is shown in Formula 3. For a point in the partition space, d_{min}^{self} represents the euclidean distance between the point and the closest centroid with the same label. Similarly, d_{min}^{noself} is the distance between the point and the nearest centroid having different labels with it. When no cluster has the same label or has different labels for this point, z is assigned as the *maximum* that is a number. Under a limited condition, if a sample happens to be mapped to a cluster center whose label is consistent with the sample, then z equals 0; if not, then z equals 1.

$$z = \begin{cases} \frac{d_{min}^{self}}{d_{min}^{self}+d_{min}^{noself}} & \exists \ell_{self\,class} \wedge \ell_{noself\,class} \\ maximum & Else \end{cases} \tag{3}$$

Finally, the optimization target function is defined as follows:

$$E = \sum_{l=0}^{s} \frac{1}{1 + e^{a(1-2Z_l)}}, \tag{4}$$

where Z_l is the z value of the lth sample, s is the total number of samples in the training set, and a is a real constant determining *tortuosity*, and E is the target of neural network optimization. A smaller E indicates a better neural network and partition space.

Based on the optimization target function, the PSO algorithm is used to optimize the neural network and simultaneously obtain the final partition space. The detail of how the PSO algorithm utilizes the clustering result of K-Means to optimize the feedforward neural network is shown in Algorithm 1. With the optimized neural network, unseen URL vector can be mapped as a new vector. The data space where the vector is located has a clear boundary between benign and malicious samples, and then the vector is clustered by K-Means to a specific cluster. The prediction label of the URL vector is the same as the nearest cluster centroid, and the URL vector shares some attributes with other samples in this cluster.

4   Evaluation

For evaluating the proposed method, we first introduce the dataset used in our method, and then analyze some parameters that affect the model's performance. Next, we compare our performance with other state of the art methods. Some interesting findings are presented. Lastly, we apply the model on the wild apps, and compare the detection results with different anti-virus scanners.

4.1   Data Set

Malicious apps originate from VirusShare website [21]. This library, which is constantly updated, is one dedicated to providing a large number of malware datasets for security researchers. We downloaded 27127 samples from this website dated between July 2014 and September 2016. We collected the network traffic generated by these malicious apps and finally obtained 18.9 GB traffic. We extracted URL samples from the network traffic. Notably, not all URLs requested by malware are malicious, and malicious URLs may only account for a small part. So to let our training set have correct labels, we screened all URLs using the detection report from VirusTotal [22]. Only explicitly malicious URLs were added to the collection of malicious URLs. Eventually, only 11251 explicitly malicious URLs are added to our dataset.

As for the benign data set, we downloaded a total of 6072 apps from multiple third-party application markets (hiapk, wandoujia, and yinyongbao). Similarly, the apps we downloaded from the app markets were not always benign. So we also used VirusTotal to screen these apps. Only apps that VirusTotal confirms benign are added to our benign app collection. And then the traffic-collection platform was used to obtain their traffic data. Ultimately, we obtains 25276 benign URLs from the 14.2 GB collected traffic. Although benign URLs are more than twice of malicious URLs, the FCM algorithm sets different weights (see Formula 2) for samples from different class which helps balance the problem.

4.2   Evaluation of Clustering and Detection Model

The parameters of FCM algorithm are related to the structure of the feedforward neural network, which is determined by the number of neurons that are included in the input, hidden, and output layers. According to the empirical analysis of FCM [2], we set the number of hidden-layer neurons in the neural network to 15 and the neurons number in the output layer to 9. Given that the neuron number of the input layer is determined by the data set, we set the neuron number in the input layer to 475 according to the length of URL vector.

(1) **The Effect of Neural Network Mapping:** We use a feedforward neural network to map training data from the initial data space to the partition space. The 475-dimensional data are mapped to 9 dimensional. In theory, a clear division exists among the different categories of mapped data. To verify that our optimal neural network can be helpful for clustering, we display the training data before and after neural-network mapping. We use Principal Component Analysis (PCA) to process and subsequently visualize the data. Figure 4(a) shows the initial data, where different shapes represent different categories (solid points represent benign samples, and hollow points represent malicious samples). We find that a large part of different category data are mixed together. If directly clustering these data, we will end with a false inclusion of benign samples in malicious clusters. A clear boundary is observed between benign and malicious samples after mapping in Fig. 4(b), and only a few samples fall into other categories. Thus, from the figures, we can clearly conclude that the data after mapping are more helpful in improving clustering accuracy than data before mapping.

(2) **The Impact of URL's Different Components on Model:** We divide a URL into five components and deal with each component separately. By intuition, each of the five components plays a different role on malicious URL clustering and detection model. In this section, we assess the impact of different components of a URL on final results. In the experiment, we vectorize the components m, h, p, n, and v, respectively. Each component after vectorization is then fed to the improved FCM algorithm to train the corresponding clustering and detection model. Training set and test set are separated randomly and the test set occupy 30% of total samples. According to the accuracy of different models on test set, we plot the line chart (Fig. 5).

The horizontal axis represents the optimization generation of PSO optimizing target function (see Formula 4), and the vertical axis represents the Accuracy of the model at different optimization generations. Each type of line represents a different model trained by different components of the URL. We can see that the components p and h have greater contributions to the model than components of m, n and v. Component m of the URL has the poorest recognition because the request method is not diverse enough and almost all of request methods are "GET" and "POST". Each component plays a role in malicious URL detection, so we can derive a better model by combining all URL components.

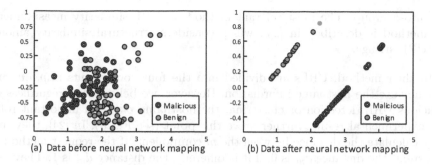

Fig. 4. Training data distribution before and after neural network mapping

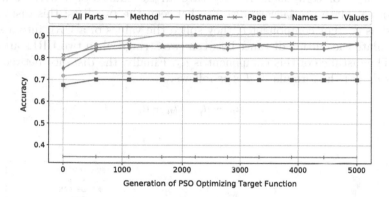

Fig. 5. Different components of URL affect on the accuracy with the optimization generation increasing

4.3   Comparison with State of the Art

(1) **Comparison with Other Clustering Algorithms:** FCM can cluster similar samples into the same group. Here, we compare the clustering performance of FCM with other popular clustering algorithms. We have selected several popular clustering algorithms, i.e., K-Means, DBSCAN, Brich, and Hierarchical Clustering. For each algorithm, we attempt to use multiple sets of parameters to maximize the performance of each algorithm. The final results of different algorithms are shown in Fig. 6. Regarding malware identification performance, FCM performs best in terms of Accuracy, Precision, F-Measure, and FPR. Only DBSCAN algorithm has higher TPR than FCM, but DBSCAN algorithm has a very high false-positive rate. Regarding clustering performance, we compare the Silhouette Coefficient (SC) [23] of each algorithm. A higher SC score means a model with better-defined clusters. Figure 6 shows that the SC score of FCM is 0.4, which is much higher than that of other algorithms.

(2) **Comparison with Other URL-similarity Measurement Methods:** We claim that we can use the lexical features of URL to cluster similar URLs

into a group. The most relevant method on URL-similarity measurement method is described in [24], which considers structural similarity among URL strings.

In their method, URLs are divided into the four components m,p,n,v and does not use the hostname information. However, we believe that regardless of malicious URL detection or clustering, the hostname plays an important role. Our experimental results further prove this point (see Fig. 5). In [24], they initially calculate the distance between the m component. If the request method is consistent, the distance d_m is 0; if it is different, the distance d_m is 1. They use the edit distance to count the distance between the p component of two URLs, named as d_p. For component n, they save all the names of a URL to an list and then calculate the jaccard distance between the two lists; this distance is recorded as d_n. For component v, they splice the values of a URL into a string and calculate the editing distance between two strings when two URLs are compared. The distance of this component is d_v. Finally, the distance between two URLs is d, and the formula of d is as follows:

$$d = d_m + d_p + d_n + d_v \tag{5}$$

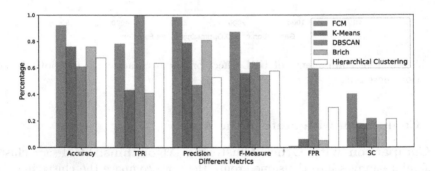

Fig. 6. The model evaluation of FCM with the traditional clustering algorithms

To compare two URL-similarity measurement methods, we use K-Means algorithm to cluster the data sets obtained by the two methods. Figure 7 shows the clustering results of both methods. We can see that our methods have obvious advantages over structural similarity method [24] in all metrics.

4.4   Interesting Findings

FCM algorithm divides our data into 26 small clusters and each cluster is labeled benign or malicious. The URLs in a cluster are grouped together based on similar lexical features. We analyze each cluster and discover that each one has some

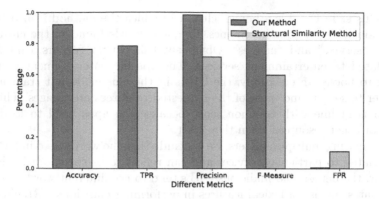

Fig. 7. The clustering results comparison of our method and structured similarity method [24]

interesting characteristics. We use DOM Tree technology to visualize each cluster. Here, we show two examples. One cluster is marked as malicious (see Fig. 8), and the other is benign (see Fig. 9).

Figure 8 shows a total of 114 URLs in the cluster. The request methods in the cluster are all "GET", and contain six unique hostnames. The different paths are followed by the hostnames. Words ending with the symbol "=" are keys in query strings. The corresponding values of the keys are not shown because the values are usually alphanumeric strings that are unique for the app itself or for third-party providers. The hostname "stat.appsgeyser.com" is malicious as validated with VirusTotal. However, no detailed information on malicious behavior about the hostname is found in VirusTotal. We can see that the keys in query strings are "action", "name", "id", "p", "age", "stall" and "system". The values of "name", "id" and "age" are related to the private data of users and devices. The word "ad" appearing in multiple URLs shows that the URLs may be related to the advertising service.

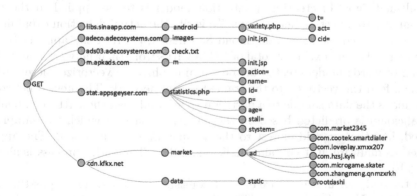

Fig. 8. An example of malicious cluster

The cluster in Fig. 9 is a benign cluster in which the method is also "GET" and contains three unique hostnames. Frequent words found in the cluster are "tingsh", "service" and "images". Obviously, this cluster gathers a number of flows related to entertainment services. The specific entertainment service is listening to books. Interestingly, the URLs in the cluster do not transmit any parameter to server, and most of the requested resources are images. This phenomenon is in line with common sense because the apps need to load some pictures or other resources when they start.

By comparing multiple clusters, we conclude that the words used in URLs are always related to particular services and can reflect some specific behaviors. In particular, the benign and malicious URLs tend to use different words, so it further validates the use of lexical features in performing malicious URL clustering and detection. The analysis on the cluster will help us gain more understanding of malware's network behaviors.

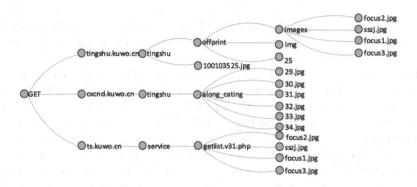

Fig. 9. An example of benign cluster

4.5   URL Detection in the Wild

The ultimate goal of creating a detection model is to be applied to the real environment to detect malicious apps. To verify the actual detection capabilities of the established model, we download 833 new apps from the app market in December 2017, and extract a total of 10473 URLs from their network traffic. We use bag of words model created in the training phase to vectorize these URLs, and then feed the vectors into the trained neural network. The neural network, which maps the data sample to a partition space, and then the URL (i.e., benign or malicious) is predicted based on the partition space in which the sample is located, i.e., the centroid closest to the sample after the mapping. The app is marked as malware, if it contains malicious URLs. The entire process is shown in Fig. 10.

In the end, our new malware dataset consists of 305 malicious apps that are confirmed by VirusTotal reports. The 305 malware are filtered by 59 anti-virus scanners in VirusTotal; however, each scanner in VirusTotal can only detect

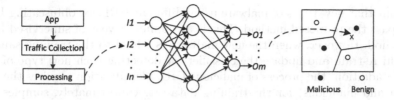

Fig. 10. The detection process for unseen app

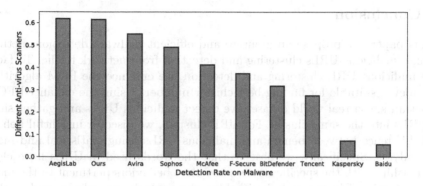

Fig. 11. Detection rate comparison with novel malware in the wild using our method and other anti-virus scanners

part of these malware samples. We select nine popular anti-virus scanners which are AegisLab, Avira, Sophos, McAfee, F-Secure, BitDefender, Tencent, Kaspersky and Baidu respectively. The detection results of scanners are derived from the VirusTotal service, which vary considerably. The best anti-virus scanner is AegisLab which can detect 189 out of 305 malware and the detection rate is 61.9%, whereas the Baidu scanner only discovers 17 malware in the wild app set whose detection rate is only 5.6%. Figure 11 shows the detailed statistics. In contrast, our detection model can identify 188 out of 305 apps and the detection rate is 61.6% that is on par with the best performing scanner, and outperforms eight other anti-virus scanners. Note that detecting novel malicious apps is a notoriously difficult task, and all existing methods are not able to achieve high detection rate due to the malware's high adaptability. Thus, the comparison result validates the capability of our model in scanning wild apps.

5   Limitations

Our method only focuses on the URLs in HTTP traffic which brings its limitation on identifying traffic using non-HTTP protocols or HTTP encryptions (i.e., HTTPs). We have conducted a statistical analysis on the collected traffic, and the proportion of malware samples using unencrypted HTTP protocol for communication is 83.67% [25]. From the statistics, we can conclude that our method will be effective in detecting most of the real-world malware samples.

We admit that new types of malware using different URLs or obfuscating URLs can bypass the proposed method. This is a common caveat of supervised learning method. However, when the new malware is added to the training samples, we could re-train and update the classifier for detecting such new type of malware. In addition, the process of malicious URL identification requires the label (benign and malicious) for the training data set. Unfortunately, samples with specific labels across the entire network are relatively hard to find.

6 Conclusion

In this paper, we propose an accurate and efficient malware detection method through malicious URLs clustering and detection from network traffic. To facilitate malicious URL clustering and detection, we enhance the FCM algorithm to render it suitable for finding best cluster number. Using the enhanced FCM algorithm and a real-world dataset, we detect malicious URLs and gather similar URLs into the same cluster. For URL clusters, we discover insightful behavioral difference between benign and malicious URLs using statistical and manual analyses. Specifically, we observe that the words used in URLs have close relationships with the specific services or reflect behaviors pertinent to the malicious activities. Cluster analysis simplifies the analysis on malware and further improves malware detection at the network-level.

Acknowledgement. This work was supported by the National Natural Science Foundation of China under Grants No. 61672262, No. 61573166 and No. 61572230, the Shandong Provincial Key R&D Program under Grant No. 2016GGX101001 and No. 2018CXGC0706, CERNET Next Generation Internet Technology Innovation Project under Grant No. NGII20160404. This work is also supported in part by NSF grant CNS-1566388.

References

1. Security threat report 2014. http://www.sophos.com/en-us/medialibrary/PDFs/other/sophossecurity-threat-report-2014.pdf
2. Wang, L., et al.: Improvement of neural network classifier using floating centroids. Knowl. Inf. Syst. **31**(3), 433–454 (2012)
3. Specification of malicious url 2013. http://www.antiy.net/p/specification-of-malicious-url
4. Canopy clustering algorithm. https://en.wikipedia.org/wiki/Canopy_clustering_algorithm
5. Wu, D.J., Mao, C.H., Lee, H.M., Wu, K.P.: Droidmat: android malware detection through manifest and api calls tracing. In: Information Security, pp. 62–69 (2012)
6. Arp, D., Spreitzenbarth, M., Hubner, M., Gascon, H., Rieck, K.: DREBIN: effective and explainable detection of android malware in your pocket. In: Proceedings of the Network and Distributed System Security Symposium (NDSS) (2014)
7. Yang, C., Xu, Z., Gu, G., Yegneswaran, V., Porras, P.: DroidMiner: automated mining and characterization of fine-grained malicious behaviors in android applications. In: Kutyłowski, M., Vaidya, J. (eds.) ESORICS 2014. LNCS, vol. 8712, pp. 163–182. Springer, Cham (2014). https://doi.org/10.1007/978-3-319-11203-9_10

8. Yan, L.K., Yin, H.: DroidScope: seamlessly reconstructing the OS and Dalvik semantic views for dynamic android malware analysis. In: Proceedings of the 21st USENIX Conference on Security Symposium, p. 29 (2013)

9. Rastogi, V., Chen, Y., Enck, W.: AppsPlayground: automatic security analysis of smartphone applications. In: ACM Conference on Data and Application Security and Privacy, pp. 209–220 (2013)

10. Narudin, F.A., Feizollah, A., Anuar, N.B., Gani, A.: Evaluation of machine learning classifiers for mobile malware detection. Soft Comput. **20**(1), 1–15 (2016)

11. Xu, Q., et al.: Automatic generation of mobile app signatures from traffic observations. In: Computer Communications, pp. 1481–1489 (2015)

12. Wang, S., Chen, Z., Zhang, L., Yan, Q., Yang, B.: Trafficav: an effective and explainable detection of mobile malware behavior using network traffic. In: Proceedings of IEEE/ACM International Symposium on Quality of Service (IWQOS), pp. 1–6 (2016)

13. Pizzato, L., Rej, T., Chung, T., Koprinska, I., Kay, J.: RECON: a reciprocal recommender for online dating. In: ACM Conference on Recommender Systems, pp. 207–214 (2010)

14. Wei, X., Neamtiu, I., Faloutsos, M.: Whom does your android app talk to? In: Global Communications Conference (GLOBECOM), pp. 1–6. IEEE (2015)

15. Shabtai, A., Tenenboim-Chekina, L., Mimran, D., Rokach, L., Shapira, B., Elovici, Y.: Mobile malware detection through analysis of deviations in application network behavior. Comput. Secur. **43**(6), 1–18 (2014)

16. Gorla, A., Tavecchia, I., Gross, F., Zeller, A.: Checking app behavior against app descriptions. In: Proceedings of the 36th International Conference on Software Engineering, pp. 1025–1035. ACM (2014)

17. Android monkey tool. http://developer.android.com/tools/help/monkey.html

18. Tshark - dump and analyze network traffic. https://www.wireshark.org/docs/man-pages/tshark.html

19. Yang, Y., Pedersen, J.O.: A comparative study on feature selection in text categorization. In: Fourteenth International Conference on Machine Learning, pp. 412–420 (1997)

20. PSO tutorial. http://www.swarmintelligence.org/tutorials.php

21. Virusshare.com - because sharing is caring. https://virusshare.com/

22. Virustotal. https://www.virustotal.com/

23. Aranganayagi, S., Thangavel, K.: Clustering categorical data using silhouette coefficient as a relocating measure. In: Conference on Computational Intelligence and Multimedia Applications. International Conference on, vol. 2, pp. 13–17. IEEE (2007)

24. Perdisci, R., Lee, W., Feamster, N.: Behavioral clustering of HTTP-based malware and signature generation using malicious network traces. In: Usenix Conference on Networked Systems Design and Implementation, p. 26 (2010)

25. Wang, S., Yan, Q., Chen, Z., Yang, B., Zhao, C., Conti, M.: Detecting android malware leveraging text semantics of network flows. IEEE Trans. Inf. Forensics Secur. **PP**(99), 1 (2017)

GranDroid: Graph-Based Detection of Malicious Network Behaviors in Android Applications

Zhiqiang Li(✉), Jun Sun, Qiben Yan, Witawas Srisa-an, and Shakthi Bachala

Department of Computer Science and Engineering, University of Nebraska–Lincoln,
Lincoln, NE 68588, USA
{zli,jsun,qyan,witty,sbachala}@cse.unl.edu

Abstract. As Android malware increasingly relies on network interfaces to perform malicious behaviors, detecting such malicious network behaviors becomes a critical challenge. Traditionally, static analysis provides soundness for Android malware detection, but it also leads to high false positives. It is also challenging to guarantee the completion of static analysis within a given time constraint, which is an important requirement for real-world security analysis. Dynamic analysis is often used to precisely detect malware within a specific time budget. However, dynamic analysis is inherently unsound as it only reports analysis results of the executed paths. In this paper, we introduce GRANDROID, a graph-based hybrid malware detection system that combines dynamic analysis, incremental and partial static analysis, and machine learning to provide time-sensitive malicious network behavior detection with high accuracy. Our evaluation using 1,500 malware samples and 1,500 benign apps shows that our approach achieves 93% accuracy while spending only eight minutes to dynamically execute each app and determine its maliciousness. GRANDROID can be used to provide rich and precise detection results while incurring similar analysis time as a typical malware detector based on pure dynamic analysis.

1 Introduction

As Android devices become the most popular end-hosts for accessing the Internet, cybercriminals have increasingly exploited Android's network connectivity to glean sensitive information or launch devastating network-level attacks [11,14,20]. Significant research efforts have been spent on studying the network usage of Android devices for detecting malicious Android apps using both static and dynamic analyses approaches.

Static analysis approaches [7,12,19,27] perform sound analysis in an offline manner and thus incur no runtime overhead. However, static analysis can result in excessive false positives. Dynamic analysis approaches, on the other hand, are more precise but incur additional runtime overhead [10,15,28]. However, recent reports indicate that dynamic analysis can be easily defeated if an app being

© ICST Institute for Computer Sciences, Social Informatics and Telecommunications Engineering 2018
R. Beyah et al. (Eds.): SecureComm 2018, LNICST 254, pp. 264–280, 2018.
https://doi.org/10.1007/978-3-030-01701-9_15

analyzed can discover that it is being observed (e.g., running in an emulator), and as a result, it behaves as a benign app [16,18].

Due to the aforementioned limitations, it is not a surprise that recently introduced malware detection approaches perform hybrid analysis, leveraging both static and dynamic information. In general, hybrid analysis approaches statically analyze various application components of an app, execute the app, and then record runtime information. Both static and dynamic information is then used to detect malicious apps, which can lead to more in-depth and precise results. However, most of the existing Android malware analysis approaches detect Android malware by matching manually selected characteristics (e.g., permissions) [12,19,23] or predefined programming patterns [27]. *The existing approaches do not capture the programming logic that leads to malicious network behaviors.*

Our key observation about a typical hybrid analysis approach is that a significant amount of efforts are spent on constructing various static analysis contexts (e.g., API calls, control-flow and data-flow graphs). Yet, the malicious network behaviors are only induced by specific programming logic, i.e., *the network-related paths or events* that have been dynamically executed. This can lead to wasteful static analysis efforts. Furthermore, running an instrumented app or modified runtime systems (e.g., Dalvik or ART) to log events can incur significant runtime overhead (e.g., memory to store runtime information, and network or USB bandwidth to transport logged information for processing). Consequently, it is challenging for hybrid analysis to be able to complete its analysis within a given time budget (e.g., five minutes). *Adhering to a time budget, however, is an important criterion for real-world malware analysis and vetting systems.*

In this paper, our research goal is to enhance the capability of hybrid analysis and evaluate if the analysis result is sufficiently rich to detect malicious network behaviors in malware running on real devices (to avoid evasion attacks) given a specific time budget. In this work, we introduce GRANDROID, a graph-based malicious network behavior detection system. We extract four network-related features from the network-related paths and subpaths that incorporate network methods, statistic features of each subpath, and statistic features on the sizes of newly-generated files during the dynamic analysis. These features uniquely capture the programming logic that leads to malicious network behaviors. We then apply different types of machine learning algorithms to build models for detecting malicious network behaviors. We evaluate GRANDROID using 1,500 benign and 1,500 malicious apps collected recently, and run these apps on real devices (i.e., Asus Nexus 7 tablets) using event sequences generated by UIAUTOMATOR[1]. Our evaluation results indicate that GRANDROID can achieve high detection performance with 93.2% F-measure.

The contribution of our paper includes the following:

1. We develop GRANDROID based on system-level dynamic graphs to detect malicious network behaviors. Unlike prior work that rely on network traffic

---

[1] Available from: https://developer.android.com/training/testing/ui-automator.html.

information to detect network-related malware, GRANDROID utilizes detailed network-related programming logic to automatically and precisely detect the sources of malicious network behaviors.

2. GRANDROID enables partial static analysis to expand the analysis scope at runtime, and uncover malicious programming logic related to dynamically executed network paths. This can make our analysis approach more sound than a traditional dynamic analysis approach.

3. We perform an in-depth evaluation of GRANDROID to evaluate the runtime performance and the efficacy of malicious network behavior detection. We show that GRANDROID can run on real devices efficiently, achieving a high accuracy in detecting malicious network behaviors.

2 Motivation

BOUNCER, the vetting system used by Google, can be bypassed by either delaying enacting the malicious behaviors or not enacting the malicious behaviors when the app is running on an emulator instead of a real device. Figure 1 illustrates a code snippet from Android.Feiwo adware [5], a malicious advertisement library that leaks user's private information including device information (e.g., IMEI) and device location. The Malcode method checks fake device ID or fake model to determine whether the app is running on an emulator.

```
1:  public static Malcode(android.content.Context c) {
2:     ...
3:     v0 = c.getSystemService("phone").getDeviceId();
4.     if (v0 == 0 || v0.equals("000000000000000") == 0) {
5.         if ((android.os.Build.MODEL.equals("sdk") == 0) &&
        (android.os.Build.MODEL.equals("google_sdk") == 0))  {
6:             server = http.connect (server A);}
7:         else{
8:             server = http.connect (server B); }}
9:     else{
10:      server = http.connect (server B);}
11:    // Send message to server through network interface
12:    ...}
```

Fig. 1. Android.Feiwo Adware example

In this example, if the app is being vetted through a system like BOUNCER, it would be running on an emulator that matches the conditions in Lines 4 and 5. As a result, it will then connect to a benign server, i.e., *server A*, which serves benign downloadable advertisement objects (i.e., Line 6). However, if the app is running on a real device, it will make a connection to a malicious server, i.e., *server B*, which serves malicious components disguised as advertisements (i.e.,

Lines 8 and 10). An emulator-based vetting system then classifies this app as benign since the application never exhibits any malicious network behaviors.

For static analysis approaches, the amount of time to analyze this app can vary based on the complexity of code. Furthermore, there are cases when static analysis cannot provide conclusive results as some of the input values may not be known at the analysis time (e.g., the location of *server B* can be read in from an external file). This would require additional dynamic analysis to verify the analysis results. Therefore, using static analysis can be quite challenging for security analysts if each app must be vetted within a small time budget (e.g., a few minutes).

Our proposed approach attempts to achieve the best of both static and dynamic approaches. As an example, when we use our approach to analyze Malcode, it would first run the app for a fixed amount of time. While the app is running, our hybrid analysis engine pulls all the loaded classes (including any of its methods that have been executed and any classes loaded through the Java reflection mechanism) and incrementally analyzes all methods in each class to identify if there are paths in an app's call graph that contain targeted or suspicious network activities. Despite the malware's effort in hiding the malicious paths, our system would be able to identify the executed path that includes the network related API calls on Lines 6, 8 and 10. These paths are then decomposed into subpaths and submitted to our classifier for malicious pattern identification.

There are two notable points in this example. First, our approach can analyze more information within a given time budget than using dynamic analysis alone. This would allow vetting techniques including BOUNCER to achieve a higher precision without extending the analysis budget. Second, unlike existing approaches such as DROIDSIFT, which only considers APIs invoked in the application code [29], our approach also retrieves low level platform and system APIs that are necessary to perform the targeted actions. This allows our approach to build longer and more comprehensive paths, leading to more relevant information that can further improve detection precision. In the following section, we describe the design and implementation of GRANDROID in detail.

3 System Design

We now describe the architectural overview of our proposed system, which operates in three phases: *graph generation, feature extraction*, and *malicious network behavior detection*, as shown in Fig. 2. Next, we describe each phase in turn.

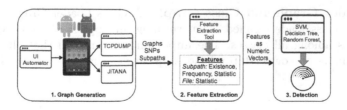

Fig. 2. System architecture

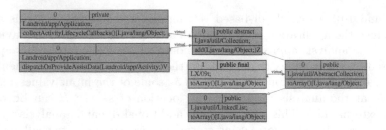

Fig. 3. Method graph

3.1   Graph Generation

GRANDROID detects malicious network behaviors by analyzing program contexts based on system-level graphs. As illustrated in Fig. 2, the process to generate the necessary graphs involves three existing tools and an actual device or an emulator (we used an actual device in this case). First, we install both malicious and benign apps with known networking capability on several Nexus 7 tablets. Next, we select malware samples and benign apps that can be *exercised* via UIAUTOMATOR and can *produce network traffic* (we monitored traffic via TCP-Dump). Incomplete malware samples and the ones that produce no network traffic are discarded, as GRANDROID currently focuses on detecting malicious network behaviors. For future work, we plan to extend GRANDROID to cover other types of malware (e.g., those that leak information via intents).

Next, we use JITANA [21], a high-performance hybrid program analysis tool to perform on-the-fly program analysis. While UIAUTOMATOR exercises these apps installed on a tablet, JITANA *concurrently* analyzes loaded classes to generate three types of graphs: classloader, class, and method call graphs that our technique utilizes. JITANA performs analysis by off-loading its dynamic analysis effort to a workstation to save the runtime overhead. It periodically communicates with the tablet to pull classes that have been loaded as a program runs. Once these classes have been pulled, JITANA analyzes these classes to uncover all methods and then generates the method call graph for the app. As such, we are able to run JITANA and TCPDUMP simultaneously, allowing the data collection process to be completed within one run. For the apps that we cannot observe network traffic, we also discard their generated graphs. Next, we provide the basic description of the three types of graphs used in GRANDROID.

Class Loader Graph and Class Graph. A Class Loader Graph of an app includes all class loaders called when running an app. A Class Graph shows relationships among all classes. The important information that these graphs provide includes the ownership relationship between methods, classes, and the app that these classes belong to (based on the class loader information). Such information is particularly useful for identifying paths and subpaths as it can help resolving ambiguity when multiple methods belonging to different classes share the same name and method's signature.

Method Graph. Our system detects malicious network behaviors by exploring the invoking relationship of methods in the Method Graph. As shown in Fig. 3, blocks represent methods, and edges indicate invoking relationship among methods. Each block contains the name of the method, its modifiers and the class name which this method belongs to. *Sensitive Network Paths (SNPs)* are defined as paths that contain network related APIs. We generate SNPs from the method graph of each app.

Note that these dynamically generated graphs are determined by the event sequences that exercise each app. As such, they actually reflect the runtime behavior of an app. Another useful information contained in these graphs include the specific Android APIs provided by Google and used by each app. We observe that detecting an actual malicious act often boils down to detecting critical Android APIs that enable the malicious behaviors. For example, if a malicious app tries to steal users' private information by sending it through the Internet, network related APIs must be used to commit this malicious act. In addition to network related APIs, there are also other system-level and user-defined methods that can be exploited by malware authors. JITANA is able to capture the invocations of these APIs and any lower level APIs that can help with identifying SNPs and their subpaths formed by these sensitive method invocations. The information can be extracted from the Method Graph of each app. Next, we describe the process of generating SNPs and the corresponding subpaths.

Sensitive Network Path (SNP) Generation. An SNP (a path related to network behavior) can be used to determine if an app exhibits malicious network behaviors. To generate SNPs, we extract all the network related Android APIs provided by Google, and network related APIs from third party HTTP libraries, such as Volley [4] and Okhttp [2]. In the Method Graph, we consider all nodes whose in-degree are zero as sources, and all network related method nodes as destinations. GRANDROID generates SNPs from sources to destinations via depth first search (DFS). Each SNP contains all the methods (nodes) from the program entry points to network related destinations. Figure 4 illustrates the SNP Generation. There are two sources (Node 1 and Node 2, marked as red) and two destinations (Node 7 and Node 11, marked as green) in the graph. SNP preserves the order of methods, and we believe that paths from malware have different patterns compared to those from benign apps. In the following section, we will explain our strategies in extracting features from SNP.

Sensitive Network Subpath (SNS) Generation. In order to extract features, we also need to extract all the subpaths from each SNP. These subpaths

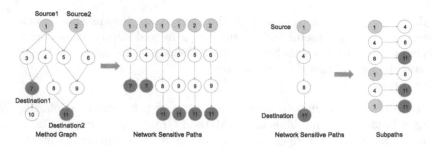

Fig. 4. Path generation (Color figure online)   **Fig. 5.** Subpath generation

are regarded as patterns for machine learning classification. In our system, we only use the starting node and the ending node to indicate subpath, and ignore all the nodes between them. Figure 5 shows the process of generating subpaths. These subpaths are then converted into numeric vectors in the Feature Extraction phase.

3.2   Feature Extraction

We now describe the features that our system extracts from the information generated by the Graph Generation phase. Our features come from the generated graphs, paths, and subpaths. We also consider the amount of the generated features for each malware sample as another feature. To quantify this, we use the size of the file that is used to store each feature for each app. File size provides a good approximation of the volume of each generated feature.

Subpath Existence Feature (F1). We extract all the SNSs for each malicious app in the training set, and build a database to store them. We order these subpaths by their names, and form a Boolean vector from these subpaths. For each sample in the testing set, GRANDROID generates the SNSs for each app and we check whether these subpaths match any paths stored in the database. A matching subpath indicates a malicious pattern, and the corresponding bit in the Boolean vector is set to 1. Otherwise, the corresponding bit remains at 0. Even though our training set contains more than 20,000 subpaths, the vectorization process can be efficient when a database management system (e.g., SQLite) is used. This subpath vector provides an enriched feature for classification. The subpaths reflect the programming logic of malware, and therefore, GRANDROID inherently captures the relationship among methods in the network-related paths.

Subpath Frequency Feature (F2). As mentioned above, Subpath Existence Feature is extracted to form a numeric vector based on network subpaths of malware in the training set. To generate Subpath Existence Feature, we check if the identified subpath exists in the database or not. However, in generating Subpath Frequency Feature, we count how many times the subpath appears for each sample.

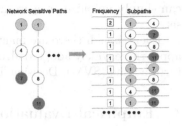

Fig. 6. Subpath frequency feature

To do so, we use both SNP and SNS information. As shown in Fig. 6, instead of marking 1 or 0 to build Subpath Existence Feature, we mark the frequency value in the vector position. Intuitively, the frequency of the subpaths can be useful in representing the usage pattern of malicious programming logic.

Path Statistic Feature (F3). We collect several statistic features for each Android app from its Network Sensitive Path. We use nine statistical features that include the lengths of the longest and short paths, the average path length, the number of paths, the number of classes and methods in all paths, the sum of lengths of all paths, and the average numbers of classes and methods per path. We observe that these statistical features can represent malicious network behaviors.

File Statistic Feature (F4). For each app, we save all of the graphs, paths and feature information into separate files. We hypothesize that the size of these files can be used to form another numeric feature vector for our machine learning based detection system, because the file size accurately reflects the amount of generated information that can provide some insight about the complexity of these network paths (e.g., the numbers of API calls and the number of paths). In the end, the attributes we use to form the File Statistic Feature for each app include the size of each graph (method graph, class graph, and class-loader graph) and each generated feature (SNPs, subpaths, subpath existence, subpath frequency and path statistics).

3.3 Detection

In the Detection phase, we apply three well-recognized machine learning algorithms to automatically determine if an Android app has malicious network behaviors.

Our system utilizes four different features (F1–F4) as previously mentioned. Intuitively, we consider that each of the four feature sets can reflect malicious network behaviors in some specific patterns. In order to get the best detection result, we need to mine the dependencies of features within each feature set and relationship between different feature sets. We discussed approaches to convert feature set F1, F2, F3 and F4 into numeric vector in the previous section. We can simply unionize or aggregate different feature sets into a combined feature set.

Even though there are many supervised learning algorithms to use, we only apply three widely adopted algorithms to build malware detectors: Support Vector Machine (SVM), Decision Tree and Random Forest.

4 Empirical Evaluation

We present the results of our empirical evaluation of GRANDROID. We first explain the process to collect our experimental objects. Next, we report our detection results by using different sets of features. We also compare our methods with other related approaches. Lastly, we report the runtime performance of GRANDROID.

4.1 Data Collection

Initially, our dataset consists of 20,795 apps from APKPure [1] collected from January 2017 to March 2017. We also downloaded 24,317 malware samples from VirusShare [3]. Note that these samples are newer than those from the Android Genome Project [31], a popular malware repository that was also used by DROID-MINER.

To ensure that our experimental environment has not been contaminated after executing a malware sample, we turn off common features that generate network traffic such as auto updates for apps and systems. We also manually checked that there is no background traffic. This is done to ensure that the network traffic seen is generated by our malware sample and not from residual effects from previously exercised malware samples. After running a few samples, we also reflash our devices to ensure that they are free from contaminations.

As previously mentioned, we also run TCPDUMP packet analyzer in each tablet to capture the network traffic information and save it as a PCAP file. Usually, malware which conducts malicious network behaviors regularly sends and receives HTTP packets. As such, we only select apps by mainly focusing on their HTTP traffic in the PCAP files. Initially, we have 11,238 benign apps and 24,317 malicious apps. After removing apps without HTTP traffic, only 1,725 malicious apps and 1,625 benign apps remain. In order to have a balanced dataset, we randomly select 1,500 benign and 1,500 malicious apps to form our dataset.

4.2 Detection Result

For each experiment, we run the 10-fold cross validation on the dataset. We generate different sets of features for these dataset by ways explained in previous sections, and apply three different machine learning methods to build our detection system. In order to compare the performance with other methods, we also implement one popular approach based on our dataset.

Table 1. The performance of GRANDROID using five different features (F1–F4, F3 & F4) and three different Machine Learning algorithms: Support Vector Machine (SVM), Decision Tree (DT) and Random Forest (RF).

	F1			F2			F3			F4			F3 ∪ F4		
	SVM (%)	DT (%)	RF (%)	SVM (%)	DT (%)	RF (%)	SVM (%)	DT (%)	RF (%)	SVM (%)	DT (%)	RF (%)	SVM (%)	DT (%)	RF (%)
I. Accuracy	79.3	84.3	83.3	60.3	82.7	83.0	88.7	86.3	87.7	50.3	91.0	91.7	50.3	89.0	92.3
II. Precision	71.6	95.6	94.6	55.9	74.7	91.6	92.6	85.2	86.5	50.2	7.7	91.9	50.2	88.7	92.1
III. Recall	97.3	72.0	70.7	97.3	98.7	72.7	84.0	88.0	89.3	100	95.3	91.3	100	89.3	92.7
IV. F-Measure	82.5	82.1	80.9	71.0	85.1	81.0	88.1	86.6	87.9	66.8	91.4	91.6	66.8	89.0	92.4

Result Based on F1. We first implement our system based on Subpath Existence Feature (F1). Table 1:F1 shows the result of applying SVM, Decision Tree and Random Forest on F1. We compare four metrics for each classification method in Table 1. The accuracy for F1 when using SVM is 79.3%; however Decision Tree achieves the highest accuracy at 84.3% and Random Forest achieves the accuracy of 83.3%. It is also worth noting that F1 is similar to the modality feature used by DROIDMINER. As such, we can also regard GRANDROID's performance based on F1 as that of a reimplemented DROIDMINER being applied to our dataset, i.e., the reported results for F1 are representative of the results of DROIDMINER.

Result Based on F2. As explained in Sect. 3, Subpath Frequency Feature (F2) is based on F1. It builds feature vector based on the frequency of each subpath. Table 1: F2 shows the detection result. For F2, Decision Tree achieves the highest F-measure of 85.1%. It achieves the accuracy of 82.7% with 74.7% precision and 98.7% recall. It appears that F2 only slightly affects the overall performance of our system.

Result Based on F3. F1 and F2 are created by checking the existence and frequency of subpaths in the training set. In essence, these first two vectors can be classified as signature-based features as they correlate existence of a subpath and its frequency to malware characteristic.

To overcome this shortcoming, we extract statistical information from SNP to construct Path Statistic Feature (F3). As illustrated in Table 1: F3 obviously achieves higher performance than F1 and F2 in terms of all four metrics. This indicates that statistical information related to paths is an important factor that can improve detection performance.

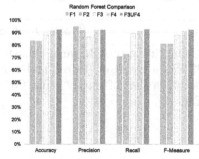

Fig. 7. Performance of random forest

Result Based on F4. Besides the statistical feature from paths, we also convert the size all the graph and feature files into numeric vectors. We refer to this feature as File Statistic Feature (F4). Table 1: F4 shows the result based on F4. F4 surprisingly outperforms F1, F2 and F3. When F4 is used with Random Forest, it can achieve F-measure of 91.6%.

Result Based on F3 $\bigcup$ F4. We have shown that statistical feature sets, F3 and F4, provide higher detection accuracy than F1 and F2. Intuitively, we hypothesize that we may be able to further improve performance by combining F3 and F4. To do so, we concatenate the feature vector of F3 with the feature vector of F4 and refer to the combined vector as $F3 \cup F4$.

Table 1: F3∪F4 validates our hypothesis. In this case, Random Forest achieves 92.3% detection accuracy, which is better than using either feature individually. Figure 7 graphically illustrates the comparison of different feature sets via Random Forest, which also shows that F3 $\cup$ F4 yields the best F-Measure.

4.3   Evaluating Aggregated Features

By concatenating F3 and F4, we can achieve better performance than using those two features individually. However, we hypothesize that the richness of path information contained in F1 and F2 may help us identify additional malicious apps not identified by using $F3 \cup F4$. As such, we first experiment with applying Random Forest on a new feature based on concatenating all features ($F1 \cup F2 \cup F3 \cup F4$). We find that the precision and F-measure are significantly worse than the results generated by just using $F3 \cup F4$ due to an increase of false positives.

Next, we take a two-layer approach to combine the *classified results* and not the features. In the first layer, we simply use Random Forest with features $F1$, $F2$, and $F3\cup F4$, to produce three classification result sets ($\theta_{F1}, \theta_{F2}, \theta_{F3\cup F4}$). As Table 1 shows that the results in θ_{F1} and θ_{F2} contain false positives, we combat this problem by only using results that appear in both result sets (i.e., $\theta_{F1} \cap \theta_{F2}$). We then add the intersected results to $\theta_{F3\cup F4}$ to complete the combined result set ($\theta_{combined}$). $\theta_{combined}$ is then used to compare against the ground truth to determine the performance metrics. In summary, we perform the following operations on the three classification result sets produced by the first layer:

$$\theta_{combined} = \theta_{F3\cup F4} \cup (\theta_{F1} \cap \theta_{F2})$$

Using this approach, we are able to achieve an accuracy of 93.0%, a precision of 92.9%, a recall of 93.5%, and a F-measure of 93.2%. This performance is higher than that of simply using $F3 \cup F4$ as the feature for classification (refer to Table 1).

4.4 Comparison with Related Approaches

Existing dynamic analysis techniques use network traffic behaviors to detect malware and botnets [15,30]. The major difference is that their works observe dynamic network traffic information while our approach focuses on programming logic that can lead to invocations of network-related methods. If a malicious traffic behavior is detected by executing an app, the app is then classified as malware.

Table 2. Utilized HTTP statistic features

Feature description
The number of HTTP requests
The number of HTTP requests per second
The number of GET requests
The number of GET requests per second
The number of POST requests
The number of POST requests per second
The average amount of response data
The average amount of response data per second
The average amount of post data
The average amount of post data per second
The average length of URL

Next, we show how GRANDROID performs against one of these purely dynamic analysis approaches.

HTTP Statistic Feature. Prior research efforts have used network traffic information to conduct the malware or botnet detection [30]. Their work mainly focuses on extracting the statistical information from PCAP files, converting such information into features, and then applying machine learning to construct the detection system.

To facilitate a comparison with GRANDROID, we re-implement their system. Table 2 lists all the extracted features. Table 3 reports the detection results. As shown, Random Forest achieves the best F-measure of 80.6%. This is significantly lower than our approach when F3 and F4 are used with Random Forest. As a reminder, our approach achieves the F-measure of 93.2%.

In summary, GRANDROID outperforms this popular approach in terms of Android malicious network behavior detection. We observe that the overall performance of Random Forest is better than other classifiers. Table 4 summarizes the overall performances of

Table 3. The performance of HTTP statistic approach based on using Support Vector Machine (SVM), Decision Tree (DT) and Random Forest (RF).

	HTTP statistic approach		
	SVM (%)	DT (%)	RF (%)
I. Accuracy	57.0	76.0	79.7
II. Precision	53.8	75.3	77.0
III. Recall	99.3	77.3	84.7
IV. F-Measure	69.8	76.3	80.6

Table 4. Detection result comparison

Method	DROIDMINER (F1) (%)	HTTP statistic approach (%)	GRANDROID (%)
Accuracy	84.3	79.7	93.0
F-Measure	80.9	80.6	93.2

all approaches consisting of DROIDMINER (F1), HTTP Statistic Approach and GRANDROID. For DROIDMINER's results, we use Decision Tree. For GRANDROID's results, we use Random Forest. We see that GRANDROID achieves higher detection accuracy and F-measure than other approaches. Particularly, GRANDROID achieves a 93.0% detection accuracy, much higher than that of DROIDMINER (84.3%) and that of HTTP Statistic Approach (79.7%). Even though DROIDMINER has about 5% FP rate, and GRANDROID has about 8% FP rate, GRANDROID achieves a much higher F-Measure than those of other approaches.

4.5   Average Malware Detection Time

On average, the time to execute an application using UIAutomator was about 5 min, our feature extraction time was 1.76 s, and the model training time using Random Forest, the best performing algorithm, was 1.14 s.

Consider a situation when a security analyst needs to vet an app for malicious components. Prior work by With BOUNCER, each app is also executed for 5 min to observe if there are any malicious behaviors. The time of 5 min is also confirmed by Chen et al. [8] when they reported that most malware would generate malicious traffic in the first 5 min. As such, our approach also executes an app for about 5 min and within that time, it can achieve the average accuracy and F-measure that are comparable to those achieved by approaches that rely on sound static analysis. Based on this preliminary result, GRANDROID has the potential to significantly increase the effectiveness of dynamic vetting processes commonly used by various organizations without incurring additional vetting time.

In addition, the time requires to train a detection model is also very short (i.e., 1.14 s). This means that we can quickly update the model with newly generated features, which indicates that GRANDROID can be practically used by security analysts to perform time-sensitive malware detection.

5   Discussion

We have shown that GRANDROID can be quite effective in detecting network related malware. However, similar to other hybrid analysis or classifier based detectors, GRANDROID also has several limitations. First, as an approach that relies on executing apps, the quality of event sequences used to exercise the apps can have a major impact on code coverage. Currently, automatically generating event sequences for Android apps that can reach any specific code location or provide good coverage is still an open research problem [9]. As such, it is possible that our system can perform better if we have a better way to generate input that can provide higher code coverage. In this regard, static analysis would be able to explore more code but it might not be able to adhere to strict vetting time budget.

Second, our analysis engine, JITANA only works on dex code and cannot analyze native code. As such, implementations of network related APIs that utilize JNI to directly execute native code would not be fully analyzed by our approach. However, there are existing work that attempt to perform native code analysis. For example, Afonso et al. [6] perform an analysis of the native code usage in Android apps, and they report that sandboxing native code can be quite useful in practice. Approaches such as this can be incorporated into our work to extend the analysis capability.

Third, as a learning based detector, evasion is a common problem as cyber-criminals may try to develop attacks that are so much different than those used in the training dataset [24]. However, as mentioned by the authors of DROIDSIFT, semantic- or action-based approaches are more robust and resilient to attack variations than syntax- or signature-based approaches [29]. This is because semantic- or action-based approaches focuses their efforts on actual events. It is difficult to instigate a particular network related event (e.g., downloading a malicious component) without utilizing network related APIs. While it is possible for cyber-criminal to evade our detector, it would require significant more efforts than trying to evade signature-based detectors.

Fourth, our current implementation only supports network related APIs, which are widely used to carry out malicious attacks. However, our approach can be extended to cover other classes of APIs. The key in doing so is to identify relevant APIs that can be exploited to conduct a specific type of attacks. For example, a malicious app that destroys file system would need to use file related APIs. Fortunately, there are some existing approaches that can help identify these relevant APIs [17].

6   Related Work

Network traffic has been used to detect mobile malware [15,22,30]. However, these studies have also shown that such systems can be evaded by simply delay the malicious behaviors so that only benign traffic is generated within observation window. Another important observation is that by simply looking at usage of such APIs is not sufficient to distinguish between benign and malicious apps as both types of apps with network functionalities would need to use those APIs. Our approach tries to overcome this ambiguity by considering execution paths that include framework, system, and the third party library's code that often invokes network related APIs [25].

Past research efforts to address this problem statically analyze various program contexts to help distinguish between benign and malicious apps [7,12,13, 19,25,27]. APPCONTEXT creates contexts by combining events that can trigger the security sensitive behaviors (referred to as *activation events*) with control flow information starting from each entry point to the method call that triggers an activation event (referred to as *context factors*). Machine learning (i.e., SVM) method is then applied on these contexts to detect malware, achieving 92.5% precision and 77.3% recall. DROIDMINER applies static program analysis to generate two-tiered behavior graph to extract modalities (i.e., known logic segments in the graph that correspond to malicious behaviors) and then aggregates these modalities into vectors that can be used to perform classification. It is worth noting that their approach suffers from scalability issues. As the number of methods in an app increases from 5,000 to 19,000, the analysis time also increases from a few seconds to over 250 s [26].

The work that is most closely related to our work is DROIDSIFT [29], which uses API dependency graphs to classify Android malware. The basic idea is to develop program semantics by establishing API dependency graph that is then used to construct a feature set. However, their main feature is weighted graph similarity while our approach considers network path-related features that aim at detecting malicious network behaviors. While GRANDROID takes a hybrid program analysis approach, DROIDSIFT, on the other hand, takes a static analysis approach. It uses SOOT as the program analysis platform. GRANDROID presents several advantages. First, DROIDSIFT only focuses on application code and does not include underlying framework or third party library code, while our analysis can capture these third party and framework codes. Second, as a static analysis approach, DROIDSIFT cannot deal with components that are loaded at runtime through Java reflection or Android Dynamic Code Loading (DCL), but our approach can easily deal with these dynamically loaded components. Third, their analysis time can also vary due to different application size and complexity. They report an average detection time of 3 min but the detection time for some apps can exceed 10 min. Thus, the approach cannot guarantee to complete under tight vetting time budget. We have reached out to the authors of DROIDSIFT to access their implementation to be used as another baseline system. Unfortunately, we have not received the response.

7   Conclusion

In this work, we present GRANDROID, a graph based malware detection system that utilizes dynamic analysis and partial static analysis to deliver high detection performance that is comparable to approaches that rely mainly on static analysis. When we use Random Forest with two of our feature sets, we can achieve over 93.2% F-measure which is about 10% higher than the F-Measure that can be achieved by DROIDMINER when applied to our dataset. We also demonstrate that we can achieve this level of performance by spending on average 8 min per apps on analysis and detection. While we only focus on detecting network-related malware in this work, our approach, by considering sensitive APIs, can be extended to detect other types of malicious apps designed to, for example, drain power or destroy resources. Such extension is possible because GRANDROID focuses its analysis efforts on paths that can lead to specific API invocations. It is thus possible to detect different forms of malware by knowing specific APIs that they use to perform attacks.

Acknowledgement. This work was supported in part by US National Science Foundation under grant CNS-1566388.

References

1. Apkpure.com. https://apkpure.com/. Accessed Dec 2017
2. An http client for android and java applications. http://square.github.io/okhttp/. Accessed Dec 2017
3. Virusshare.com. https://virusshare.com/. Accessed Dec 2017
4. Volley overview. https://developer.android.com/training/volley. Accessed Dec 2017
5. Android feiwo. https://goo.gl/AAY8xp. Accessed Feb 2018
6. Afonso, V., et al.:. Going native: using a large-scale analysis of android apps to create a practical native-code sandboxing policy. In: The Network and Distributed System Security Symposium, pp. 1–15 (2016)
7. Arp, D., Spreitzenbarth, M., Hubner, M., Gascon, H., Rieck, K., Siemens, C.: DREBIN: effective and explainable detection of android malware in your pocket. In: NDSS (2014)
8. Chen, Z., et al.: A first look at android malware traffic in first few minutes. In: Trustcom/BigDataSE/ISPA, vol. 1, pp. 206–213. IEEE (2015)
9. Choudhary, S.R., Gorla, A., Orso, A.: Automated test input generation for android: are we there yet? In: Proceedings of ASE, Lincoln, NE, pp. 429–440 (2015)
10. Enck, W., et al.: Taintdroid: an information-flow tracking system for realtime privacy monitoring on smartphones. ACM TOCS **32**(2), 5 (2014)
11. Enck, W., Octeau, D., McDaniel, P., Chaudhuri, S.: A study of android application security. In: USENIX Security Symposium, vol. 2, p. 2 (2011)
12. Felt, A.P., Chin, E., Hanna, S., Song, D., Wagner, D.: Android permissions demystified. In: Proceedings of CCS, pp. 627–638. ACM (2011)
13. Grace, M., Zhou, Y., Zhang, Q., Zou, S., Jiang, X.: Riskranker: scalable and accurate zero-day android malware detection. In: Proceedings of MobiSys, pp. 281–294 (2012)
14. Kelly, G.: Report: 97% of mobile malware is on android. This is the easy way you stay safe. In: Forbes Tech (2014)
15. Li, Z., Sun, L., Yan, Q., Srisa-an, W., Chen, Z.: DroidClassifier: efficient adaptive mining of application-layer header for classifying android malware. In: Deng, R., Weng, J., Ren, K., Yegneswaran, V. (eds.) SecureComm 2016. LNICST, vol. 198, pp. 597–616. Springer, Cham (2017). https://doi.org/10.1007/978-3-319-59608-2_33
16. Messmer, E.: Black Hat demo: Google Bouncer Can Be Beaten. http://www.networkworld.com/news/2012/072312-black-hat-google-bouncer-261048.html
17. Rasthofer, S., Arzt, S., Bodden, E.: A machine-learning approach for classifying and categorizing android sources and sinks. In: Proceedings of of NDSS (2014)
18. Storey, O.: More malware found on google play store. https://www.eset.com/uk/about/newsroom/blog/more-malware-found-on-google-play-store/. Accessed June 2017
19. Sun, L., Li, Z., Yan, Q., Srisa-an, W., Pan, Y.: SigPID: significant permission identification for android malware detection. In: Proceedings of MALWARE, pp. 1–8. IEEE (2016)
20. Symantec. Latest intelligence for March 2016. In: Symantec Official Blog (2016)
21. Tsutano, Y., Bachala, S., Srisa-An, W., Rothermel, G., Dinh, J.: An efficient, robust, and scalable approach for analyzing interacting android apps. In: Proceedings of ICSE, Buenos Aires, Argentina (2017)

22. Wang, S., et al.: TrafficAV: an effective and explainable detection of mobile malware behavior using network traffic. In: Proceedings of IWQoS, pp. 1–6. IEEE (2016)
23. Wang, W., Wang, X., Feng, D., Liu, J., Han, Z., Zhang, X.: Exploring permission-induced risk in android applications for malicious application detection. IEEE Trans. Inf. Forensics Secur. 9(11), 1869–1882 (2014)
24. Xu, W., Qi, Y., Evans, D.: Automatically evading classifiers. In: Proceedings of NDSS (2016)
25. Yang, C., Xu, Z., Gu, G., Yegneswaran, V., Porras, P.: DroidMiner: automated mining and characterization of fine-grained malicious behaviors in android applications. In: Kutyłowski, M., Vaidya, J. (eds.) ESORICS 2014. LNCS, vol. 8712, pp. 163–182. Springer, Cham (2014). https://doi.org/10.1007/978-3-319-11203-9_10
26. Yang, C., Xu, Z., Gu, G., Yegneswaran, V., Porras, P.: Droidminer: automated mining and characterization of fine-grained malicious behaviors in android applications, Technical report. Texas A&M (2014)
27. Yang, W., Xiao, X., Andow, B., Li, S., Xie, T., Enck, W.: Appcontext: differentiating malicious and benign mobile app behaviors using context. In: Proceedings of ICSE, Florence, Italy, pp. 303–313 (2015)
28. Yang, Y., Wei, Z., Xu, Y., He, H., Wang, W.: Droidward: an effective dynamic analysis method for vetting android applications. Cluster Comput. December 2016
29. Zhang, M., Duan, Y., Yin, H., Zhao, Z.: Semantics-aware android malware classification using weighted contextual API dependency graphs. In: Proceedings of CCS, pp. 1105–1116 (2014)
30. Zhao, D., Traore, I., Sayed, B., Lu, W., Saad, S., Ghorbani, A., Garant, D.: Botnet detection based on traffic behavior analysis and flow intervals. Comput. Secur. 39, 2–16 (2013)
31. Zhou, Y., Jiang, X.: Dissecting android malware: characterization and evolution. In: Proceedings of IEEE S&P, pp. 95–109 (2012)

FGFDect: A Fine-Grained Features Classification Model for Android Malware Detection

Chao Liu[1], Jianan Li[1,2], Min Yu[1,2(✉)], Bo Luo[3], Song Li[1,2],
Kai Chen[1], Weiqing Huang[1], and Bin Lv[1]

[1] Institute of Information Engineering, Chinese Academy of Sciences,
Beijing, China
yumin@iie.ac.cn
[2] School of Cyber Security, University of Chinese Academy of Sciences,
Beijing, China
[3] Department of Electrical Engineering and Computer Science,
University of Kansas, Lawrence, Kansas, USA

Abstract. In Android malware detection, fine-grained features can provide a more accurate description of the application's behavior. Nonetheless fine-grained feature extraction has not been done perfectly, hence, invalid features will not only bring additional overhead but also reduce the detection accuracy. In this paper, we propose FGFDect, a malware classification model by mining Android applications for fine-grained features. Our work aims to handle two types of features that frequently appear in Android malware. One of them refers to the permissions that have been registered, but actually not been used. The other is the API called via the reflection mechanism. This information improves the precision of static analysis, which no longer need to make conservative assumptions about coarse-grained features. These two feature sets are fed into the machine learning algorithms to classify the app into benign or malware. FGFDect is evaluated on a large real-world data set consisting of 6400 malware apps and 4600 popular benign apps. Compared with those traditional approaches with coarse-grained features, extensive evaluation results demonstrate that the proposed approach exhibits an impressive detection accuracy of 96.7% with the false positive rate of 0.7%. In addition, the proposed approach complements existing permission-based approaches and API-based approaches.

Keywords: Permission · API · Reflection · Static analysis · Fine-grained

1 Introduction

Nowadays, Android is the most widely used mobile OS [1] and it plays an important role in our daily life. This development platform allows every mobile device manufacturer who intends to join them to become a member of the Android alliance. However, Android malware attack technology has become increasingly mature. Emerging malware has many characteristics related to the field of wide, difficult to detect, reveal state secrets and cause users economic losses [2]. Although there are a

© ICST Institute for Computer Sciences, Social Informatics and Telecommunications Engineering 2018
R. Beyah et al. (Eds.): SecureComm 2018, LNICST 254, pp. 281–293, 2018.
https://doi.org/10.1007/978-3-030-01701-9_16

large number of detection methods, there is still no ideal detection rate for some malware. A crucial factor is that many applications over-claim permissions in order to facilitate the development and upgrade of the applications. This caused trouble with permission-based malware detection. Another reason is that over 90% of static analysis techniques for Android apps do not account for reflection calling issues [3]. Recent reports [4] also pointed out that the reflection calling is an important factor in the poor performance of many malware detection tools.

Most of the previous work [5–8] only extracted features from Android application behaviors (e.g., permission request and API calls), then note that each feature is binary, indicating when a data feature occurs in an app, its value is 1, otherwise, its value is 0. Ultimately, machine learning algorithms are employed to perform classification of benign and malicious applications. However, the feature extracted by this method is coarse-grained, which will affect the judgment of the application. For permission, there is a problem that developers over-request, but in fact the application does not use. The current research on this issue is still rare and needs to be solved urgently. For API, scanning reflection calls API is still a difficult task. To the best of our knowledge, there is one work presented by Barros et al. [9] who proposed a solution for reflection analysis of Android apps. However, their approach focuses on checking information flows from developer's perspective, but the source code of Android is hard to obtain by for most market applications. Haohua et al. [10] for the first time, covers reflection invocation via array assignment, but the number of such applications is relatively small and the detection rate is not significantly improved.

In order to reduce system overhead and improve the low accuracy caused by the coarse-grained features of traditional methods. This paper proposes a fine-grained feature classification model named FGFDect for Android application detection, which can more truly describe the behavior of the application and eliminate the interference of unrelated information. The most important thing is that experiments show that our method does achieve the expected effect of improving the detection accuracy without causing any additional system overhead. A brief summary of our contributions is given below:

- This model could extract fine-grained API, including scanning smali files one by one for API called directly, in addition, also including variable assignment reflection calls for API (Sect. 3.2).
- After that, this model found out the used permissions according to the API-permission mapping library constructed by ourselves, and removed the applied but unused permissions to determine the final fine-grained permission feature (Sect. 3.3).

The reminder of this paper is organized as follows. Section 2 presents the necessary background about our study. After that in Sect. 3, this paper present the model by mining fine-grained features for Android application, the design of FGFDroid. In Sect. 4, this paper introduce the results of the experiment and compare to the related work. And last, this paper close with conclusion and future work in Sect. 5.

2 Preliminaries

In this section, permission-API mapping and reflection mechanism related background information will be introduced.

2.1 Permission-API Mapping

The main purpose of Android to set up permission mechanism is that it can make detailed distinction and access control to some specific operations performed by the application [6]. Through the API call, the application can access and obtain some sensitive data in the phone, such as contacts, geographies, photos and accounts, or trigger some high-risk behaviors such as sneaking into the network and sending deductions SMS [11]. As with permission information, APIs vary widely in usage due to differences between normal and malware.

Permission information and API information can all reflect the characteristics of a program to a certain extent. However, it has some limitations, the false positive rate of the classification results will have some impact. For example, in the actual development process, programmers will tend to request too much permissions in order to facilitate the development and upgrade of the application, resulting in a lot of permissions in the application has not been used. Therefore, this paper combines permission features and API features by using previous work [12] which is PScout to obtain permissions-API mapping so as to remove useless permissions. This tool has been constantly updated, the fact proved that Android permission system has little redundancy and it remains relatively stable as the Android OS evolves. Fortunately, PScout's analysis found over 32 thousand mappings between API calls and permissions until now. Part of its mapping as shown in Table 1, which can be processed as {permission 1: [API$_1$, API$_2$...], permission 2: [API$_1$, API$_2$, ...], ..., permission N: [API$_1$, API$_2$...]} by ourselves. This will surely provide enough help for our later static analysis.

Table 1. The part of the permission-API mapping provided by PScout.

CallerClass	CallerMethod	Permission
android/server/wifi/WifiServiceImpl	enableNetwork	CHANGE_WIFI_STATE
android/server/wifi/WifiServiceImpl	addOrUpdateNetwork	CHANGE_WIFI_STATE
android/server/wifi/WifiServiceImpl	checkAndStartWifi	CHANGE_WIFI_STATE
android/location/LocationManager	requestLocationUpdates	DUMP
android/location/LocationManager	getLastKnownLocation	DUMP
android/internal/telephony/PhoneSubInfo	getImei	READ_PHONE_STATE
android/internal/telephony/PhoneSubInfo	getDeviceId	READ_PHONE_STATE
android/internal/telephony/PhoneSubInfo	getSubscriberId	READ_PHONE_STATE
android/internal/telephony/UiccSmsController	sendText	SEND_SMS

2.2 The Reflection Mechanism

Android applications are based on Java language development, so it can take full advantage of Java's reflection mechanism. According to previous work [3] has shown

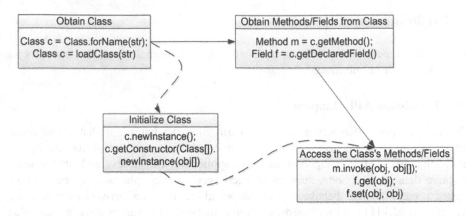

Fig. 1. Abstract pattern of reflection usage.

that reflection is frequently used by Android developers to (1) provide genericity, e.g., using reflection to implement generic functions. (2) Maintain backward compatibility. (3) Reinforce app security. (4) Access inaccessible APIs.

Unfortunately, in recent years, malware makers have used reflection mechanisms as an important way to hide malicious behavior in software [13]. In order to avoid static analysis, malicious applications can propagate malicious code by invoking sensitive methods through reflection at runtime. Lindorfer et al. [14] also pointed out that from 2010 to 2014, the proportion of Android malware using the reflection mechanism increased from 43.87% to 78%. In addition, since 2010 this proportion has never been eased.

In order to tame the reflections of static analysis methods, [15] investigated the sequence invocation of reflection methods and summarized their common usage patterns by randomly selecting 500 applications. Figure 1 could illustrate how reflection is used by developers, which is able to model the most typical usage of reflection calls. Among them, solid arrows indicate if they have been statically declared, you can use the reflection method or field directly. Otherwise, they must be used after the class has been initialized as indicated by the dotted arrow.

Due to the characteristics of the reflection mechanism, the API extraction is not comprehensive enough. Therefore, it poses challenges for many static analysis tools. At present, the detection of reflection method calls is relatively deficient.

3   System Design

We start with getting and parsing the *AndroidManifest.xml* and *classes.dex* file. *Classes.dex* file [16] is converted into *.smali* files (an interpreted language that syntactically approaches pure source codes) with APKTool. As shown in Fig. 2, the system consists of four steps. Firstly, we constructed a permission-API mapping library based on prior knowledge [12]. Secondly, we can get the APIs directly called by scanning the *.smali* files, then get the APIs reflected call by scanning the variable

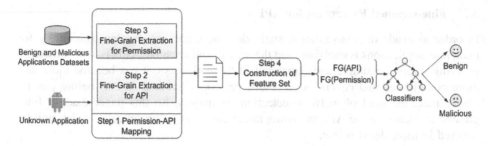

Fig. 2. Overview of FGFDect.

assignments. Thirdly, by scanning the *AndroidManifest.xml* files, the fine-grained permissions can be obtained based on the mapping library. Lastly, the feature vector are constructed and fed into machine learning algorithms to detect whether the app is malicious or benign.

3.1 Building a Permission-API Mapping Library

There are tens of thousands of permission-API mappings provided by PScout, and some of them are useless, which can lead to unnecessary system overhead and affect system efficiency. Therefore, this paper designs a filtering algorithm based on the semantics, and finally selects more than 600 groups of the most helpful mapping for classification.

Part of the data provided by the PScout as shown in Table 1 (Sect. 2.1), we used three columns of its contents, namely the CallerClass, CallerMethod and Permission. Firstly, we need to process these data into a consistent form with the *.smali* file as mentioned in the second paragraph of Sect. 2.1. We are interested in APIs that can get the personal information. For example, function *getDeviceId ()* indicates *"Returns the unique device ID, for example, the IMEI for GSM and the MEID or ESN for CDMA phones"*. After that we chose 652 APIs to get the following crucial information: device ID, IP address, location (include latitude, longitude), email, wifi, postal code, account, phone number, sim serial number, installed application list, audio/video, cookies, visited URLs, and browser bookmarks. Finally, the permission-API mapping library built by us is shown in Fig. 3.

```
{android.permission.READ_PHONE_STATE:
[getVoiceMailNumber, getDeviceSvn, getSubscriberId,
getLine1Number, getDeviceId, getIccSerialNumber,...],
android.permission.MANAGE_ACCOUNTS:
[clearPassword, updateCredentials, removeAccount,...],
android.permission.ACCESS_COARSE_LOCATION:
[requestLocationUpdates, getLastLocation,...] ... }
```

Fig. 3. Part of permission-API mapping.

3.2   Fine-Grained Extraction for API

In order to evade the conventional static detection, hackers develop technology for malicious applications is evolving, and the way to call sensitive APIs is also constantly evolving. From the simple and direct call of the early days, it has become more and more complicated and covert. As a result, get coarse-grained API as before can no longer meet the need of malware detection techniques. So this paper made a fine-grained extraction of the API, including direct calls and reflection calls, which will be covered in more detail below.

(1) Directly call the API: An application that uses this kind of invocation style, if it needs to get some network information, then call the corresponding function that is *getNetworkInfo()*. This method takes an approach that scanning all API's usage in . *smali* file directly to check for the presence of related function calls. The method includes the following steps:

Step 1: Exclude some unrelated files from all *.smali* files, such as *R.smali, R$attr. smali, R$layout.smali, R$id.smali* and so on. Because these documents do not belong to the main function file, there will be no sensitive function calls in them, there is no need for analysis;

Step 2: Scan the remaining smali files one by one, analyze the file contents line by line. Then match with the API library we built in the previous section. If a program contains invoke-virtual and the corresponding sensitive function, it means that the application does indeed call the relevant sensitive API. Figure 4 describes a file named VirusShare_0b2e2250b514297 adb7da45b5d22dae8.apk in VirusShare dataset by calling *getNetworkInfo* function to get a smali code snippet of network information. The first line invoke-virtual shows virtual method call, the method of calling at run time confirms the actual call. General API are used this way to call;

```
1 invoke-virtual {v0, v3},
2 Landroid/net/ConnectivityManager;->getNetworkInfo(I)
3 Landroid/net/NetworkInfo;
```

Fig. 4. Smali code snippet for getting network information.

Step 3: The APIs obtained in this section build a set called *DC (API)*, meaning the collection of APIs that are scanned directly. If all the files are scanned but no sensitive function call can be found, it indicates that there is no direct API call in the application. We need to further analyze whether the sensitive API is invoked in a more subtle way.

(2) Reflection call API: Let us take Fig. 5 as an example to better explain the idea of reflection call API, where the code snippet is extracted from an app of DroidBench named Reflection3.apk [17]. This case is used by many testing tools (such as Flow-Droid [17]) to evaluate performance, but does not work well because it contains reflection calls. In this example, first *forName* method is used to get the class where the method is called, which is *ReflectiveClass* (line 3-4). Then initialize the object (line 5). The *getMethod* method is finally used to retrieve the API of the reflection call and using

the *invoke* method to execute (lines 6-10). Among them, the called *setImei* formed by string splicing, *getImei* is directly assigned. In addition, the string can be assigned to the variable, then the variable as a parameter of *getMethod*. Whatever the method, it is essentially a reflection call to a variable assignment type.

Sensitive API calls made this way cannot be detected by scanning the *.smali* file directly. Therefore, this paper based on the method framework in [3] namely DroidRA to detect such hidden calls. For the method in Fig. 5, DroidRA can detect that lines 6-8 use the reflection call "*setImei*" and lines 9-10 use the reflection call "*getImei*". The method first preprocesses the APK file: converts to Jimple code, determines the analysis entry, and ensures that all application code is covered. Then, the preprocessed code is reflected and analyzed. A context-based, dataflow-based analysis method is used to detect whether the reflection is invoked by the Android application. Finally, given the reflection call parameters (class name, method name and method parameters).

In order to enhance the detection efficiency of our system. On the basis of DroidRA, this paper delete the application's permission, package name, entry page and other initialization work, because such work has been completed in the decompilation phase. Finally, the extracted reflection call API built into a set of *RC (API)*, meaning the collection of APIs that are reflected call.

3.3 Fine-Grained Extraction of Permission

First of all, after reversing the Android application, get all the permissions of the application in the *AndroidManifest.xml* file. Then these permissions be built a set called *CG (Permission)*, which is the coarse-grained collection of permissions. Then according to the API-permission mapping library provided by Sect. 3.1, we find out the permissions that have been used, remove the applied but unused permission, in order to determine the final fine-grained permission set named *FG (Permission)*.

Algorithm 1 Generate FG(Permission)

Input: CG (Permission); FG(API);
    Permission-API Mapping Library
Output: FG(Permission)
for i **to** CG(Permission) **do**
  if i == Permission-API Mapping Library.getkey() **then**
  value[] = Permission-API Mapping Library.get(key)
  for j **to** FG(API) **do**
    if FG[j] == value[] **then**
      continue
    EA(Permission)[] = i
    end if
  end for
  end if
end for
FG(Permission) = CG(Permission) − EA(Permission)
return FG(Permission)

```
1     TelephonyManager telephonyManager = //default;
2     String imei = telephonyManager.getDeviceId();
3     Class c =
4          Class.forName("de.ecspride.ReflectiveClass");
5     Object o = c.newInstance();
6   ⌈ Method m = c.getMethod("setIme" + "i",
7   ⎰    String.class);
8   ⌊ m.invoke(o,imei);
9   ⌈ Method m2 = c.getMethod("getImei");
10  ⌊ String s = (String) m2.invoke(o);
11    SmsManager sms = SmsManager.getDefault();
12    sms.sendTextMessage("+49 1234", null, s, null, null);
```

Fig. 5. Code excerpt of de.ecspride.MainActivity from Reflection3.apk.

Algorithm 1 highlights the step of generating the *FG (Permission)* set with the input of *CG (Permission)*, *FG (API)* of a given app and the Permission-API mapping. We put each permission without the appropriate API into the collection *EA (Permission)*, meaning excessively applied permissions. *FG (Permission)* is finally obtained by removing the permissions of the overly applied from the coarse-grained permission set.

3.4   Construction of Feature Set

The fine-grained feature set of FGFDect is co-constructed with a fine-grained set of APIs and a fine-grained set of permissions. The fine-grained API set contains two parts: API direct call and API reflection call. The fine-grained set of permissions removes the permissions that have been applied but not actually used from coarse-grained permissions. The feature space is represented as follows:

$$
\begin{pmatrix}
FG(API) & \begin{pmatrix} DC(API) \\ RC(API) \end{pmatrix} \\
FG(Permission) & (CG(Permission) - EA(Permission))
\end{pmatrix}
\tag{1}
$$

4   Evaluation and Analysis

To evaluate the effectiveness of our approach, we first introduce the dataset and the metrics (see Sect. 4.1 for details). We then evaluated our approach based on the fine-grained features compare with coarse-grained features of other baseline approaches (see Sect. 4.2 for details). Afterward, we proved that the advantage of the FGFDect design and performance through testing with four machine learning algorithms (see Sect. 4.3 for details).

4.1 Dataset and Metrics

In order to perform experiments, a large number of datasets need to be selected. From the perspective of comprehensiveness and applicability, experiments have been performed on the dataset consists of 11000 applications on a computer with Intel Core i7-6500HQ 2.50 GHz CPU and 16 GB memory. The 6400 malicious samples of this experiment come from the data set in [18] and VirusShare [19], the latter is a very authoritative malicious sample library website and the malicious samples are confirmed by more than 50 security engines. At the same time, this paper also climbed telephone communications, social, life, video, travel, shopping 6 different types of applications from Google Play and Anzhi Market. Using the malware detection tool VirusTotal, Virscan scans for confirmation, collecting a total of 4,600 non-malicious applications.

The metrics used to measure our detection results are shown in Table 2. The goal of any malware detection research is to achieve a high value for ACC and a low value for FPR.

4.2 Analysis of Features

(1) Analysis of reflection call API: The goal of our reflection analysis is to provide analysts (or other methods) with the necessary information to better understand how reflection is used by Android applications. Therefore, in this experiment, we did not consider all reflection-related methods, but chose the ones that are of most interest to the analyst.

At first, we compute the coverage of reflection calls that FGFDect identifies and inspects the results. We randomly selected 800 Android applications (400 benign applications and 400 malicious applications) for testing, of which about 56 (7%) of applications cannot get an API call by scanning directly, but scan again by our reflection call method, which is called sensitive API can be obtained. In addition, 588 (79%) of them also include API reflection calls for applications that can scan directly to the API.

Most importantly, according to our manual analysis, we found that about 263 (75%) of the malicious applications that APIs are called via reflection are related to its major malicious function. This will be helpful to improve the classification accuracy rate. Because this part of the APIs are not available if we still use the traditional method. For example, the aforementioned APK named Reflection3.apk, the traditional method cannot get its API called through the reflection mechanism, and just this API is closely related to its malicious function. Eventually this application is mistakenly identified as a benign application if the traditional method is used.

Finally, we also randomly extracted 50 of our applications containing reflection call APIs to compare our system to other open source tools. The results show that the open source tools such as FlowDroid, Androguard, Androwarn really cannot extract API called by reflection.

(2) Analysis of fine-grained permission: For the fine-grained analysis of permissions, we still randomly selected 800 applications. The number of benign and malicious applications each accounts for half of the total. Performing our experimental methodology, we found that 186 of the 800 applications did indeed excessive apply

permissions. To our surprise, 137 of them are benign applications. Figure 6 shows the average number of coarse-grained and fine-grained permissions in 800 randomly selected applications. We found that transitional application of permission in benign applications is more severe than malicious applications.

Table 2. Descriptions of the used metrics.

Term	Abbr.	Definition
True Positive	TP	Malicious apps classified as malicious apps
True Negative	TN	Benign apps classified as benign apps
False Negative	FN	Malicious apps classified as benign apps
False Positive	FP	Benign apps classified as malicious apps
True Positive Rate	TPR	TP/(TP + FN)
False Positive Rate	FPR	FP/(FP + TN)
Accuracy	ACC	(TP + TN)/(TP + TN + FN + FP)
Precision	PRE	TP/(TP + FP)

This result shows that during the initial stages of program development, the developers of normal applications do apply a lot of permissions that are not necessary in order to facilitate the next development and upgrade. As a result, rely on the traditional coarse-grained extraction methods must lead to the benign applications classified to be malicious. However, using our permission extraction method greatly reduces this false positive rate. Because the permissions we extract are the permissions that the application really uses.

4.3   Performance of FGFDect

Four different classifiers are employed to evaluate our approach. These classifiers are Random Forest, Decision Tree (C4.5), Nearest Neighbor and Logistic Regression. All the 4600 benign apps and 6400 malicious apps are mixed together. After the extraction and analysis of the fine-grained features with our approach, each app is first represented as a feature vector provided by Sect. 3.4. Then, on the training dataset (consisting of 2600 benign apps and 3400 malicious apps), the known malicious application has a classification label of 1 and the known benign application has a label of −1 so that the classifier can understand the difference between the malicious application and the benign application. After the training sample's classification label is generated, four kinds of machine learning algorithms can be used to train the four classifiers. Finally, when a sample without classification label is entered into the classifier, the classifier can also determine whether it is benign or malicious.

The detection performances are shown in Fig. 7. The result indicates that all four classifiers can achieve a high value for TPR and a low value for FPR. In particular, Random Forest performs best among four classifiers. With Random Forest, the detection performance yields a TPR of 0.965 at an FPR of 0.007, and the ACC is 0.967.

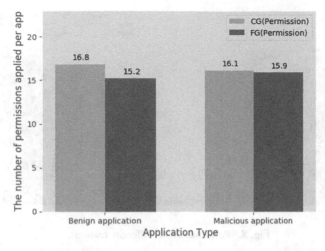

Fig. 6. The average number of coarse and fine grained permissions in random applications.

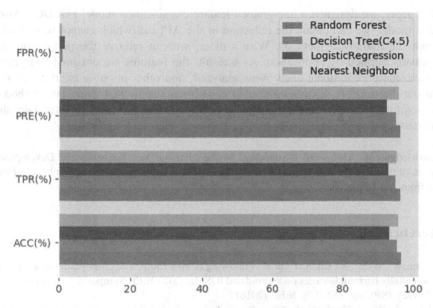

Fig. 7. The performance of FGFDect under different classification algorithms.

Since Random Forest algorithms have the best performance, we use Random Forest algorithms to test the performance of the system when using different feature sets. As shown in Fig. 8, which is almost in line with our expectation, the use of fine-grained feature sets has significantly higher accuracy and lower false positive rate due to remove excessive application of permissions and obtain APIs for reflection calls.

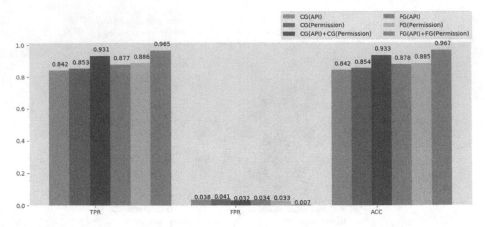

Fig. 8. Performance of different features.

5 Conclusion

In this paper, we designed a fine-grained feature classification model FGFDect, based on this model, we can obtain the reflection of the API call which cannot be extracted through the traditional methods. What's more, we can remove the permission that excessively applied by application. As a result, the features we obtained were more accurate, some exceptional cases were analyzed, and other possible interference was ruled out. Fortunately, a large number of experiments show that using our method is very helpful to improve the classification accuracy, and the false positive rate also decreased.

Acknowledgment. This work is supported by the National Key Research and Development Program of China (2016YFB0801001, 2016YFB0801004), and is supported in part by a research grant from Ant Financial.

References

1. Chen, K., Wang, X., Chen, Y., et al.: Following devil's footprints: cross-platform analysis of potentially harmful libraries on android and iOS. In: 2016 IEEE Symposium on Security and Privacy (SP), pp. 357–376. IEEE (2016)
2. Chen, J., Wang, C., Zhao, Z., Chen, K., et al.: Uncovering the face of android ransomware: characterization and real-time detection. IEEE Trans. Inf. Forensics Secur. **13**, 1286–1300 (2017)
3. Li, L., Bissyandé, T.F., Octeau, D., et al.: DroidRa: taming reflection to support whole-program analysis of android apps. In: Proceedings of the 25th International Symposium on Software Testing and Analysis, pp. 318–329. ACM (2016)
4. Rastogi, V., Chen, Y., Jiang, X.: DroidChameleon: evaluating android anti-malware against transformation attacks. In: Proceedings of the 8th ACM SIGSAC Symposium on Information, Computer and Communications Security, pp. 329–334. ACM (2013)

5. Yuan, Z., Lu, Y., Xue, Y.: DroidDetector: android malware characterization and detection using deep learning. J. Tsinghua Univ. (Sci. Technol.) **21**(1), 114–123 (2016)
6. Ping, X., Xiaofeng, W., Wenjia, N., et al.: Android malware detection with contrasting permission patterns. China Commun. **11**(8), 1–14 (2014)
7. Li, M., Liu, Y., Yu, M., et al.: FEPDF: a robust feature extractor for malicious PDF detection. In: Trustcom/bigdatase/icess. IEEE (2017)
8. Jiang, J., et al.: A deep learning based online malicious URL and DNS detection scheme. In: Lin, X., Ghorbani, A., Ren, K., Zhu, S., Zhang, A. (eds.) SecureComm 2017. LNICST, vol. 238, pp. 438–448. Springer, Cham (2018). https://doi.org/10.1007/978-3-319-78813-5_22
9. Barros, P., Just, R., Millstein, S., Vines, P., Dietl, W., Ernst, M.D.: Static analysis of implicit control flow: resolving Java reflection and android intents. In: Proceedings of the IEEE/ACM International Conference on Automated Software Engineering, ASE, Lincoln, Nebraska (2015)
10. Haohua, H., Zhanqi, C., Minxue, P., et al.: Automatic detection of malicious Android applications based on static and dynamic combination. J. Inf. Secur. **2**(4), 27–40 (2017)
11. Yu, L., Zhang, T., Luo, X., et al.: Toward automatically generating privacy policy for Android apps. IEEE Trans. Inf. Forensics Secur. **12**(4), 865–880 (2017)
12. Au, K.W.Y., Zhou, Y.F., Huang, Z., et al.: PScout: analyzing the android permission specification. In: Proceedings of the 2012 ACM Conference on Computer and Communications Security, pp. 217–228. ACM (2012)
13. Kazdagli, M., Huang, L., Reddi, V., et al.: Morpheus: benchmarking computational diversity in mobile malware. In: Proceedings of the Third Workshop on Hardware and Architectural Support for Security and Privacy, p. 3. ACM (2014)
14. Lindorfer, M., Neugschwandtner, M., Weichselbaum, L., et al.: ANDRUBIS–1,000,000 apps later: a view on current Android malware behaviors. In: 2014 Third International Workshop on Building Analysis Datasets and Gathering Experience Returns for Security (BADGERS), pp. 3–17. IEEE (2014)
15. Li, L., Bissyandé, T.F., Octeau, D., et al.: Reflection-aware static analysis of android apps. In: Proceedings of the 31st IEEE/ACM International Conference on Automated Software Engineering, pp. 756–761. ACM (2016)
16. Zhang, Y., Luo, X., Yin, H.: DexHunter: toward extracting hidden code from packed android applications. In: Pernul, G., Y A Ryan, P., Weippl, E. (eds.) Computer Security–ESORICS 2015. LNCS, vol. 9327, pp. 293–311. Springer, Cham (2015). https://doi.org/10.1007/978-3-319-24177-7_15
17. Arzt, S., Rasthofer, S., Fritz, C., et al.: FlowDroid: precise context, flow, field, object-sensitive and lifecycle-aware taint analysis for Android apps. ACM Sigplan Not. **49**(6), 259–269 (2014)
18. Arp, D., Spreitzenbarth, M., Hubner, M., et al.: DREBIN: effective and explainable detection of Android malware in your pocket. In: Ndss, vol. 14, pp. 23–26 (2014)
19. Virus Share [EB/OL]. https://virusshare.com/. Accessed 12 Nov 2017

Wireless Security

An Adaptive Primary User Emulation Attack Detection Mechanism for Cognitive Radio Networks

Qi Dong[1]([⊠]), Yu Chen[1], Xiaohua Li[1], Kai Zeng[2], and Roger Zimmermann[3]

[1] Department of Electrical and Computer Engineering, Binghamton University,
Binghamton, NY 13902, USA
{qdong3,ychen,xli}@binghamton.edu
[2] Volgenau School of Engineering, George Mason University,
Fairfax, VA 22030, USA
kzeng2@gmu.edu
[3] School of Computing, National University of Singapore,
Singapore 117417, Singapore
rogerz@comp.nus.edu.sg

Abstract. The proliferation of advanced information technologies (IT), especially the wide spread of Internet of Things (IoTs) makes wireless spectrum a precious resource. Cognitive radio network (CRN) has been recognized as the key to achieve efficient utility of communication bands. Because of the great difficulty, high complexity and regulations in dynamic spectrum access (DSA), it is very challenging to protect CRNs from malicious attackers or selfish abusers. Primary user emulation (PUE) attacks is one type of easy-to-launch but hard-to-detect attacks in CRNs that malicious entities mimic PU signals in order to either occupy spectrum resource selfishly or conduct Denial of Service (DoS) attacks. Inspired by the physical features widely used as the fingerprint of variant electronic devices, an adaptive and realistic PUE attack detection technique is proposed in this paper. It leverages the PU transmission features that attackers are not able to mimic. In this work, the transmission power is selected as one of the hard-to-mimic features due to the intrinsic discrepancy between PUs and attackers, while considering constraints in real implementations. Our experimental results verified the effectiveness and correctness of the proposed mechanism.

Keywords: Cognitive radio networks (CRNs)
Primary user emulation (PUE) attacks · Detection
Hard-to-mimic features

1 Introduction

The rigid spectrum allocation scheme regulated by governmental agencies leads to great deficit on spectrum band resources. Static spectrum access technology

© ICST Institute for Computer Sciences, Social Informatics and Telecommunications Engineering 2018
R. Beyah et al. (Eds.): SecureComm 2018, LNICST 254, pp. 297–317, 2018.
https://doi.org/10.1007/978-3-030-01701-9_17

results in lots of waste on wireless spectrum resources. The emergence of new intelligent spectrum allocation/re-allocation schemes, especially cognitive radio network (CRN), are studied elaborately in the last decade, due to the ever-increasing wireless applications. Cognitive radio (CR), or known as secondary user (SU) in CRN, is a technology that allows wireless devices (unlicensed users) access spectrum resources dynamically without introducing major interference to licensed primary users (PUs). Because of the great difficulty and high complexity in dynamic spectrum access (DSA), and many open issues on security deployment, CRN study still under development [25].

Spectrum sensing allows CRs acquire real-time spectrum occupation status such that interleaving communications shared by PUs and SUs become feasible. Basically, a well-designed CRN aims to serve for two purposes [3]: to maximize the usage of spare spectrum resource as well as to protect the incumbent primary system from secondary network interference. Due to the requirement to SUs that they shall not interfere the PU functionalities, SUs should adapt their behaviour in accordance to PU activities. Such requirement can be regarded as two separate parts: (1) monitoring PU activities, and (2) behaving properly.

In general, knowing PU activities is essentially critical for cognitive radios to share the spectrum resource with legitimate users. One of the effortless ways to acquire PU activity information is that PUs are able to notify SUs their spectrum usage status; or there exist a third party as an inquiry center that knows what PUs will do in the near future. An alternative solution is to develop robust and efficient spectrum sensing technique to acquire knowledge on PU activities. Also, the spectrum sharing efficiency greatly depends on a secure CR operating environment. In addition, due to the opportunistic spectrum access (OSA) nature, CR systems encounter several CR-specified security problems.

Regarding spectrum sensing, one major challenge is to detect PU signals with high accuracy while maintain low false alarm rate. The false detection rate may become extraordinarily high when primary user emulation (PUE) attacks happen. A PUE attack is that malicious entities mimic PU signals in order to either occupy spectrum resource selfishly or conduct Denial of Service (DoS) attacks. PUE attacks can be easily implemented in CRNs. It introduces great overhead on cognitive radio communication and causes chaos in dynamic spectrum sensing [9,10]. However, defense against the PUE attacks is nontrivial because traditional authentication and authorization (AA) methods are no longer applicable to CR systems. A more adaptive and practical PUE attack detection technique is highly desired.

Inspired by radiometric used to identify short range transceivers and the interpulse/intrapulse fingerprint in radar identification, we propose to detect PUE attacks in CRN environment leveraging the hard-to-mimic PU transmission features. As one type of hard-to-mimic feature, the PU transmission features are determined by the inherent physical characteristics of the device. Attackers are not able to generate such kind of features. A received signal strength (RSS)-based hypothesis detection mechanism is designed, which can detect attackers who attempt to fool the system by mimicking PUs' patterns.

In general, RSS-based approaches have been studied elaborately in many literatures for PUE attack defense. It is applied either as one direct rudimentary feature of PU [6], or as the premise for PU localization [8,13,17]. These works can be challenged by either smart attackers or the practical constraints such as SUs are unaware of their geographical information. There are two major advantages that make our work more feasible and efficient in real-world applications than exiting solutions: (1) in general, our proposal allows mobility of nodes in the CRN and does not require prior geographical information of either PUs, SUs, or attackers; and (2) compared to machine learning or neural network based methods, our proposal does not need the training process.

The rest of this paper is organized as follows. Section 2 provides background knowledge that motivated this work. Section 3 describes a practical CRN model on which our detection mechanism is built. Section 4 discusses a PUE attack intuition under perfect propagation model assumptions. The proposed RSS-based PUE attack detection method is introduced in Sect. 5. Section 6 presents a tentative trail based on real-world measurements. Section 7 shows our numerical experimental results and comparison to other related schemes, and finally, Sect. 8 concludes this paper.

2 Background Knowledge and Related Work

According to Federal Communications Commission (FCC): *"no modification to the incumbent signal should be required to accommodate opportunistic use of the spectrum by Secondary Users (SUs)"* [1]. Obviously FCC places constraints on PUs such that PUs are not obligated to notify CR users with their activity scheduling and intention, neither to provide AA services. Consequently, CR systems are expected to collect and process sufficient and highly accurate information of the spectrum environment without imposing overhead on incumbent users by adding new features, such as redundant symbolic pads or authentication protocols.

In CR systems, it is necessary to distinguish attacker signals from PU signals in spectrum sensing stage. PUE attacks will cause severe problems on the efficiency of spectrum utility. Since no obligation is imposed on PUs, it is natural to explore the features of different wireless transceivers. In general, there are two categories of transceiver features: the primary/strong radiometric/fingerprint, and the secondary/weak radiometric. The primary radiometric denotes the intrinsic characteristics or imperfections of wireless transceivers, that can be used to identify the uniqueness of the hardware. Transient is one of the most discussed radiometric that can be used to identify short range transceivers. Transient is the part of the signal where the amplitude rises from background noise to full power. In literature, five transient features are used [22]:

1. The length of the transient, along the x-axis;
2. The variance of the normalized amplitude of the transient;
3. The number of peaks (periods) of the carrier signal in the transient;

4. The first part of a discrete wavelet transform of the transient; and
5. Difference between the normalized mean and the normalized maximum value of the transient.

It is proved that transient features are useful fingerprints for wireless transceivers identification. They are not well studied in PU recognition in CRNs, however, due to the difficulties in detecting transient on the scale and scope of CRNs.

Another inspiration comes from radar identification, in which two kinds of fingerprint are usually discussed. One is interpulse fingerprint that considers factors including frequency, amplitude, pulse width, pulse repetition rate, etc. The other one is intrapulse fingerprint that pays attention to pulse waveform characteristics, such as unintentional modulation on pulse (UMOP) feature [15] and time domain waveform feature, including rise slope and fall time, falling angles, angle of pulse, and pulse point [14]. It looks intriguing, but requires accurate measurements on signals that is usually not available for CRs.

There are other ideas based on the imperfections of transceivers such as frequency offset error caused by different transmitter and receiver oscillators, or modulation errors caused by the imperfection of electric circuits [5]. Usually, those fingerprint extraction requires prior knowledge of modulation/mulplexing technology, and it is often very computational intensive.

The secondary/weak radiometric usually does not identify signals from a particular transceiver. Instead, it identifies signal characteristics that are not reproducible to attackers. A smart attacker is able to mimic some PU signal features such as spectrum bandwidth, activity pattern, and adaptively change transmission power. Many studies tried to extract features of communication channel of the wireless environment [6,7,13], which is known as geometrical information of the PU transmitter, because PUs and attackers are unlikely be at the same place.

Two types of channel fingerprint detection approaches are well discussed. The first category is distance-based approaches [6]. A rudimentary approach is to use RSS-based location estimation techniques, which record the received energy level from the PU as the reference radiometric, and compare with the sensed spectrum signal strength for detection. A novel idea was proposed to deploy helper nodes around PUs, which are able to help verify PU signal based on helper node's authentic link signatures [16]. A smart attacker model was presented to prove that the first order feature of RSS is not adequate for PUE attacks detection, and then a RSS detection method using second order feature is proposed to confront the smart attackers [6]. However, the assumption that all SUs and PUs' positions are prefixed and known is not applicable to many situations in CRNs. The second category is location-based approach [13], which requires geographical information from at least part of network participators. In those proposals, peripherals such as GPS, helper nodes and prior knowledge of PU position, are necessary.

PUE attack detection happens in spectrum sensing stage. In 2010, FCC announced that they adopted condition a device's use of TV White Spaces on its consultation of a geolocation database to ensure the availability of the desired spectrum [4]. Several literatures have discussed the feasibility of constructing PU activity database and the details in design of prototypes [11,18,21,24]. The database will record, model and predict PU activities in order to regulate CR access and optimize spectrum use efficiency. These base stations are able to provide many critical PU information, such as geographical location, activity pattern, and modulation/mulplexing technology. Even further, a FCC Commission's Rule proposes that PUs such as Federal Primary Users are going to register in a database before accessing 3.5 GHz band [2].

On one hand, while such kind of database model can eliminate PUE attacks, they do violate the original FCC requirement [1]. Database enabled spectrum sensing provides a new inspirations on against of PUE attack, but still remains problematic. As the general PU information is known to CRs with involvement of regular database, smart attackers can mimic PU signal features. In addition, the geographic information of PU is not available for moving base stations or radars. On the other hand, the PU registry approach has been deployed in very limited scale, which is only in federal PU environments [2].

As discussed above, a more adaptive and practical PUE attack detection technique is highly desired. Considering the limited prior knowledge of PUs and constraints on computing resources of CRs, it is natural to extend our vision on hard-to-mimic PU signal features for PUE attack detection. While the secondary radiometric can be easily reproduced by smart attackers, the actual transmission power is an exception. Although the attacker can smartly adapt their transmission power to disguise their locations, they are usually incapable of mimicking counterpart power as PUs. PUs are usually radars, TV stations, and cellular base stations, which signal strength is normally tens to thousands of times higher comparing to what PUE attackers can produce [19]. For example, the strength of CRs signals is normally in scale of milliwatts [19]. With cooperative spectrum sensing, and involvement of a fusion center (FC), the emitter transmission power based PUE detection is applicable without requiring any prior knowledge of PUs and CRs location information.

3   Detection Model

In CR spectrum sensing study, the cooperative sensing method is preferable due to the well-known "hidden PU problem". This problem happens when a SU cannot sense an active PU either due to the PU signal is out of range or because the signal faded away in concurrent wireless fading channel. In cooperative spectrum sensing, CRs have to share their sensing results to obtain the most comprehensive knowledge of the desired spectrum environment. In centralized CRNs, a fusion center can collect and synthesize sensed spectrum information from all CRs, and make a joint decision on PU appearance. Our detection model is based on such deployment with the following assumptions.

- The PUs are either public infrastructures (i.e. TV stations) or federal facilities (i.e. weather radar system). They have powerful transmission capability to serve their own purposes.
- The PUs are not required to be geographically fixed, such that PUs including moving radars or stations are considered.
- Without loss of generality, assume CRs and the FC are randomly scattered in an circular area with radius of r_{CRN}. CRs are not equipped with localization peripherals, and they are unaware of the location of either themselves or the peers.
- CRs are able to sense the radio environment and report processed spectrum features to the FC.
- The FC can collect spectrum features from CRs and perform deliberate analysis. The FC has knowledge of general information of measured PUs, such as their occupied spectrum bands, their approximate propagation power, etc.

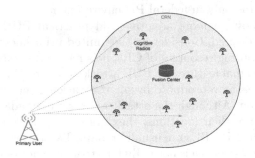

Fig. 1. A centralized CRN sharing the spectrum with a PU.

Figure 1 shows a scenario of centralized CRN jointly share the spectrum resource with a PU. In order to be more consistent to real-world situation, in our detection model, the position of the PU and distances among each parties are unknown, and there is not localization peripherals, such as GPS, time of arrival (TOA) based equipment, is equipped by CRs because these peripherals are unaffordable in many applications. In consequence, this detection model poses a higher challenge on PUE attacks detection.

4   PUE Attacks Detection Under Perfect Propagation Model

As discussed earlier, the attackers can hardly emit the magnitude of signal power as PUs do, so the propagation power becomes a useful hard-to-mimic secondary radiometric of transmitters. The challenge is, however, such a secondary radiometric feature remains unmeasurable in wireless environment. Usually, the receiver can measure the RSS, which is determined by many factors, such as transmission power, propagation environment, and transmission distance.

An ideal propagation model, Free-Space Path Loss (FSPL) model, assumes no obstructions between the transmitter and receiver, and the signal propagate along a line-of-sight (LOS) channel. This ideal propagation model inspires a reasonable intuition on PUE attacks detection. In this section, our new idea on PUE attacks detection is introduced with consideration of some restrictions in real world such as unknown PU and CRs locations, but we assume an ideal wireless propagation environment. The FSPL model is expressed as:

$$\frac{P_r}{P_t} = \frac{G_l \cdot \lambda^2}{(4\pi d)^2} \tag{1}$$

where P_r and P_t are received signal power and transmitted signal power respectively; λ is signal wave length; d is the LOS distance between transmitter and receiver; G_l is the product of the transmit and receive antenna field radiation patterns, and it is a constant if the pattern is known. Thus, the received to transmitted power ratio is proportional to the reciprocal of d^2 as:

$$\frac{P_r}{P_t} \propto \frac{1}{d^2} \tag{2}$$

4.1   A Naive Detection Model

In the ideal propagation model, given the RSS measurement and global information of PU propagation power, the transmitter-receiver distance is deducible, which gives us a hint on the relation between the uncloneable radio feature P_t and the wireless channel feature d. In our PUE attacks detection model, a hypothesis test is adopted to decide the presence of the attacker.

- $\mathcal{H}_0$: the signal is from the PU
- $\mathcal{H}_1$: the signal is from the attacker

The PU propagation power is usually in scale of hundreds or thousands of watts, defined as $P_{t,pu}$. In contrast, the attacker, usually comparable to CRs, has the propagation power of tens to hundreds of milliwatts, defined as $P_{t,attacker}$. Thus, the ratio of PU propagation power to attacker propagation power is computed as $R = P_{t,pu}/P_{t,attacker}$.

In a CRN with N CRs, the transmitter-receiver distance d_i $(i = 1, 0, \cdots, N)$ can be easily computed given the propagation power $P_{t,pu}$ and individual CR received power $P_{r,i}$. If the signal is transmitted by the PU, the distance is computed as:

$$d_i = M \cdot \sqrt{\frac{P_{t,pu}}{P_{r,i}}} = d_{i,pu} \tag{3}$$

Here, M is defined as a constant $M = \sqrt{\frac{G_l \cdot \lambda^2}{(4\pi)^2}}$. Similarly, if the signal is transmitted by the attacker, the distance is computed as:

$$d_i = M \cdot \sqrt{\frac{P_{t,pu}}{P_{r,i}}} = M \cdot \sqrt{\frac{P_{t,attacker}}{P_{r,i}}} \cdot \sqrt{R}$$

$$= d_{i,attacker} \cdot \sqrt{R} \tag{4}$$

Further, if the distance between individual CR and the FC $d_{i,fc}$ is also known, ideally, it is easy to infer to the distance between the PU and the FC in a range $d_{pu,fc} \in [max(|d_i - d_{i,fc}|), min(d_i + d_{i,fc})]$. If the signal is transmitted by the PU, the computed $d_{pu,fc}$ does not belong to an empty set, as demonstrated in Fig. 2. If the signal is transmitted from the attacker, the distance is computed as $d_i = d_{i,attacker} \cdot \sqrt{R}$, according to Eq. 4. Thus, the range set $d_{attacker,fc} \in [max(|d_{i,attacker} \cdot \sqrt{R} - d_{i,fc}|), min(d_{i,attacker} \cdot \sqrt{R} + d_{i,fc})]$ is possibly empty as shown by Fig. 3. The FC can apply the hypothesis test by:

- If $(d_i + d_{i,fc}) \geq |d_j - d_{j,fc}|, \forall i, j = 1, 2, \cdots, N$, the signal is from the PU ($\mathcal{H}_0$); or
- If $(d_i + d_{i,fc}) < |d_j - d_{j,fc}|, \exists i, j = 1, 2, \cdots, N$, the signal is from the attacker ($\mathcal{H}_1$).

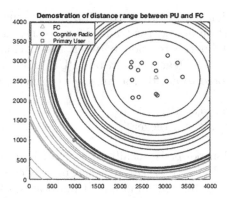

Fig. 2. In the case of PU transmission, compute distance range between the transmitter and the FC. The radius of blue circles are the lower bounds of $d_{pu,fc}$, computed as $|d_i - d_{i,fc}|$; the radius of green circles are the upper bounds of $d_{pu,fc}$, computed as $d_i + d_{i,fc}$. The PU is supposed to locate between the lower and upper bounds. (Color figure online)

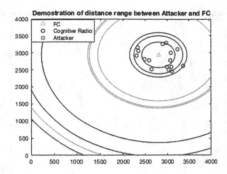

Fig. 3. In the case of PUE attacks, compute distance range between the transmitter and the FC. The radius of blue circles are the lower bounds of $d_{attacker,fc}$, computed as $|d_i - d_{i,fc}|$; the radius of green circles are the upper bounds of $d_{attacker,fc}$, computed as $d_i + d_{i,fc}$. The figure shows no intersection between the lower and upper bounds. (Color figure online)

Following the hypothesis test, the detection rate P_d is calculated as:

$$P_d = 1 - P_{fn}$$
$$\geq 1 - \Pr\{d_{i,attacker} - d_{j,attacker} \leq \frac{d_{i,fc} + d_{j,fc}}{\sqrt{R}},$$
$$\forall i, j = 1, 2, \cdots, N\}$$
$$\geq 1 - (1 - (\frac{r_{CRN} - \frac{max(d_{i,fc}+d_{j,fc})}{\sqrt{R}}}{r_{CRN}})^2)^N, \qquad (5)$$

where $P_{fn} = \Pr(\mathcal{H}_0|\mathcal{H}_1)$ is the false negative probability. In Eq. 5, the first inequality originates from the expansion of the inequality to the absolute value of $|d_i - d_{i,fc}|$. The second inequality can be explained that the greatest false negative probability happens (suppose $\frac{max(d_{i,fc}+d_{j,fc})}{\sqrt{R}} \leq r_{CRN}$) when the attacker is located in the center of CRN, and all CRs are located in the ring-shape area centered at the attacker with inner radius of $r_{CRN} - \frac{max(d_{i,fc}+d_{j,fc})}{\sqrt{R}}$ and outer radius of r_{CRN}. The false positive probability $P_{fp} = \Pr(\mathcal{H}_1|\mathcal{H}_0)$ is zero under such hypothesis test condition.

4.2 Evaluation of Hypothesis Test by Monte Carlo Method

A Monte Carlo method is applied to calculate the detection accuracy in a scenario where CRs and attackers are randomly distributed in an circular area, which is centered at the FC with radius r_{CRN}. Figure 4 shows the result. The detection accuracy P_d increases dramatically as the number of CRs increases. And P_d is approaching one when there are more than four CRs in the testing scenario.

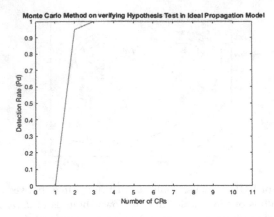

Fig. 4. The detection accuracy of the hypothesis test computed by Monte Carlo method with different number of CRs in the CRN. For each different number of CRs, repeat the hypothesis test for 100000 times.

5   A RSS Based PUE Attack Detection Approach

The above hypothesis test is discussed under ideal propagation model, which provides a reasonable intuition on PUE attack detection, with the given propagation power features of PUs and attackers. But, in reality, the RSS based distance measurement method is not well applicable for several reasons. First of all, the FSPL propagation model cannot faithfully describe the actual propagation environment. Secondly, signal propagation patterns are variant in different environments. Also, RSS can be vary by a large magnitude over short distances.

Therefore, we choose the single transmitter log-normal shadowing fading propagation model to describe the relationship among transmitted power P_t, received signal power P_r, and distance d between transmitter and receiver.

$$P_r(dBm) = P_t(dBm) + K(dB) - 10\gamma log_{10}\frac{d}{d_0} + G \tag{6}$$

where P_t and P_r are measured in dBm. K is the path loss variable at the reference distance d_0, which depends on the antenna characteristics and propagation environment. γ is the empirical path loss exponent, which is learned to have different values in different environment [12]. Table 1 presents some γ values measured by empirical studies. G is a normal random variable with zero mean and standard deviation σ. Most empirical studies for outdoor channels measure the standard deviation $\sigma \in (5, 12)$ in macrocells and $\sigma \in (4, 13)$ in microcells [12].

Over the years of development, a number of propagation models have been developed in different wireless environments, such as Hata model, COST231 model, piecewise linear model, etc. [12]. In some literatures, a statistical model is used to obtain maximum likelihood of the propagation model parameters with great fitness [23]. In our work, we assume the model parameters with some errors,

Table 1. Empirical path loss exponents γ

Environment	γ range
Urban macrocells	3.7–6.5
Urban microcells	2.7–3.5
Factory	1.6–3.3

are accessible either from historically empirical study, or statistical estimation. Thus, the path loss propagation model, inferred from Eq. 6, can be written as Eq. 7, where C is a constant determined by reference propagation path loss, and Γ is the empirical path loss exponent.

$$L = P_t - P_r = C + \Gamma \cdot log_{10}d + G \qquad (7)$$

Because G is a normal random variable, the optimal estimator of $log_{10}d$ is obtained by averaging the propagation loss L. Thus, we smooth the RSS by using a local averaging method from neighboring CR groups. Then, we apply our hypothesis test to detect PUE attacks.

5.1 CRs Grouping

A RSS smoothing method that divides secondary network into circular areas has been studied [6]. One major restriction of this method lies in the requirement that all CR positions are known globally and CRs remain geographically static. In our work, as discussed in Sect. 3, a dynamic CRN is assumed where CRs can be either static or mobile, and the CRs are assumed unaware of their positions. In order to estimate distance to the PU in a small area, a CR grouping technique is applied, which assumes the distances between the PU and CRs in a group can be uniformly treated as $d_{i,pu}$, where i represents the i-th CR as the group leader.

In comparison to clustering patterns in traditional wireless sensor networks (WSNs), CRs grouping does not meant to construct a hierarchical CRN structure. Instead, it is a logical grouping process that is completed by the FC. The grouping process is shown in Fig. 5. Every CR will maintain a dynamic neighbor list by intermittently requesting in a short broadcasting range $r_{neighbor}$. In spectrum sensing stage, CRs will send their neighbor list along with the RSS measurements to the FC, which enables the FC create a $N \times N$ binary CR neighbor matrix $A_{neighbor}$ with each element be denoted as $a_{i,j}$. The FC will group RSS measurements by rows (for every $cr(i)$), shown in Fig. 6. In each group, the averaged propagation loss is computed as $L_i^* = P_{t,pu} - mean(P_{r,k}|\forall a_{i,k} = 1)$. Further, the distance between the PU and each group is estimated as $d_{i,pu}$, when it assumes all CRs in a group have approximately the same distance to the PU, because $d_{i,pu} \gg r_{neighbor}$.

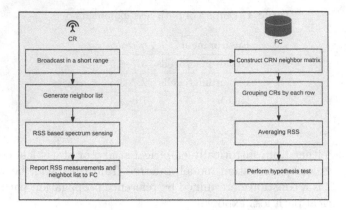

Fig. 5. Process of CR grouping and PUE attack detection.

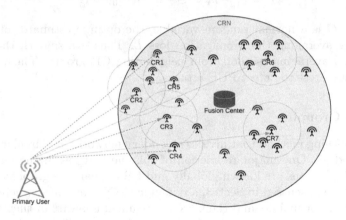

Fig. 6. CRs grouping and RSS smoothing diagram.

5.2 Hypothesis Test of PUE Attack Detection

In practical PUE attack detection, the hypothesis test defined in Sect. 4 is adopted. The propagation powers of the PU and attacker are denoted as $P_{t,pu}(dBm)$ and $P_{t,attacker}(dBm)$, respectively, where the propagation power difference, regarded as radiometric difference, is calculated as $F(dB) = P_{t,pu} - P_{t,attacker}$.

Refer to Eq. 7, the distance between a transmitter and the i-th CR group is estimated as:

$$\hat{d}_i = 10^{(L_i^* - C - \varepsilon)/\Gamma} \tag{8}$$

where ε is the remaining error term. If the signal is transmitted by the PU, the estimated distance is the approximate distance between i-the CR and the PU $\hat{d}_{i,pu}$:

$$\hat{d}_i = \hat{d}_{i,pu} \tag{9}$$

If the signal is transmitted by the attacker, the path loss is computed as:

$$L_i^* = (P_{t,attacker} + F) - mean(P_{r,k}|\forall A_{i,k} = 1) \tag{10}$$

Thus, the estimated distance is a scaled approximate distance between i-the CR and the attacker $\hat{d}_{i,attacker}$:

$$\hat{d}_i = \hat{d}_{i,attacker} \cdot 10^{F/\Gamma} \tag{11}$$

As assumed in Sect. 4, all CRs are randomly distributed in a circular area with radius of r_{CRN}. The transmitter-receiver distances satisfy:

$$d_{i,pu} - d_{j,pu} \leq 2 \cdot r_{CRN}, \forall i,j = 1, 2, \cdots, N \tag{12}$$

$$(d_{i,attacker} - d_{j,attacker}) \cdot 10^{F/\Gamma} \leq 2 \cdot r_{CRN} \cdot 10^{F/\Gamma},$$
$$\forall i,j = 1, 2, \cdots, N \tag{13}$$

Refer to Eqs. 9 and 11, the FC can apply the following hypothesis test:

- If $\hat{d}_i - \hat{d}_j \leq T, \forall i,j = 1, 2, \cdots, N$, the signal is from the PU ($\mathcal{H}_0$), or
- If $\hat{d}_i - \hat{d}_j > T, \exists i,j = 1, 2, \cdots, N$, the signal is from the attacker ($\mathcal{H}_1$)

Here T is the threshold factor that affects the accuracy of the hypothesis test. The probability of false negative can be calculated as:

$$P_{fn} = \Pr\{max(\hat{d}_{i,attacker}) - min(\hat{d}_{j,attacker}) \leq \frac{T}{10^{F/\Gamma}},$$
$$\forall i,j = 1, 2, \cdots, N\}$$
$$\begin{cases} \leq 1, \text{ if } \frac{T}{10^{(F+\varepsilon')/\Gamma}} > r_{CRN} \\ \leq (1 - (\frac{r_{CRN} - \frac{T}{10^{(F+\varepsilon')/\Gamma}}}{r_{CRN}})^2)^N, \\ \text{if } \frac{T}{10^{(F+\varepsilon')/\Gamma}} \leq r_{CRN} \end{cases}$$
$$\tag{14}$$

where ε' is the error term. The interpretation to Eq. 14 is similar to the one to Eq. 5. It is noteworthy that the equality happens only when attacker is located at some particular locations. The probability of false positive can be calculated as:

$$P_{fp} = \Pr\{max(\hat{d}_{i,pu}) - min(\hat{d}_{j,pu}) > T,$$
$$\exists i,j = 1, 2, \cdots, N\}$$
$$\begin{cases} = 0, \text{ if } \frac{T}{10^{\varepsilon'/\Gamma}} \geq 2 \cdot r_{CRN} \\ < 1 - (\frac{\alpha - \frac{T}{10^{\varepsilon'/\Gamma}}}{\pi})^N, \\ if \frac{T}{10^{\varepsilon'/\Gamma}} < 2 \cdot r_{CRN} \end{cases}$$
$$\tag{15}$$

where $\cos\alpha = \frac{r_{CRN}-T/10^{\epsilon'/\Gamma}}{r_{CRN}}$. The Eq. 15 can be explained as the complementary of the probability to the case that all CRs are located in the intersection area between a ring-shape area with width of $\frac{T}{10^{\epsilon'/\Gamma}}$ and the CRN distributed area. According to Eqs. 14 and 15, with larger value of F and lower value false negative rate P_{fn}, better hypothesis threshold factor T can be designed. With the larger number of CRs N, the lower false negative rate P_{fn} can be achieved, but a higher false positive rate P_{fp} may occur.

6   Real-World Emulation Trial

In this section, a deployment trail of our method in real-world PUE attack detection is presented. To perform spectrum sensing in CRN, we used Universal Software Radio Peripheral (USRP) N210 as the sensing nodes, one of which acts as a smart PUE attacker. Due to the practical limitations, we are unbale to emulate PU activities. Thus, we regard one of the local digital television (DTV) station as the primary user. The PUE attacker impose malicious signal on another unused spectrum band. In order to conduct effective attacks, the smart attacker will mimic the DTV behavior: it will record the DTV signal from near spectrum band and broadcast the exact received signal data.

We implemented the experiment in our lab. The attacker (one USRP N210) is allocated to a fixed spot, and the sensing nodes (other USRP N210 Devices) are placed in 6 different places/rooms, shown in Fig. 7. Due to lack of empirical

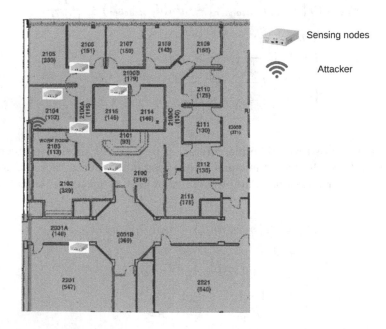

Fig. 7. Experiment deployment.

model parameters, we directly applied Hata propagation model for urban environment [12]. The PU signal information is presented in Table 2, where h_T is the transmitter height. Accordingly, we take of the value of receiver height h_R as 10 m.

Table 2. PU parameters

Frequency	590–596 MHz
Power	345 kW
h_T	278 m

The result is shown in Fig. 8, which indicates an almost perfect detection. It is because the great discrepancy between PU transmission power and attacker transmission power (over 60 dB difference), despite the inaccurate propagation model parameters. The sensing nodes will receive a relatively high power of PUE attack signal if near to the attacker, but receive barely nothing if too far away from the attacker. In next section, we will present more detail discussions on detection performance regarding to model parameter errors and attacker transmission power.

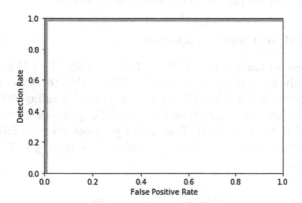

Fig. 8. ROC of emulation.

7   Numerical Evaluation

7.1   Practical Model Evaluation

Further, a numerical experiment with more comprehensive network topology, is designed to evaluate the proposed hypothesis test. The parameters in Eq. 7

is estimated from empirical study, which may not be the best estimation. The empirical model we used for distance estimation is:

$$L = C_{est} + \Gamma_{est} \cdot log_{10}d + G \tag{16}$$

While the best fit propagation model is:

$$\begin{aligned} L &= (C_{est} - \varepsilon\_C) + (\Gamma_{est} - \varepsilon\_\Gamma) \cdot log_{10}d + G \\ &= C_{est} + \Gamma_{est} \cdot (log_{10}d - \frac{\varepsilon\_C}{\Gamma} - \frac{\varepsilon\_\Gamma}{\Gamma}log_{10}d) \end{aligned} \tag{17}$$

where ε_C and ε_Γ are the empirical propagation model estimation errors ($C_{est} - C_{best} = \varepsilon\_C$ and $\Gamma_{est} - \Gamma_{best} = \varepsilon\_\Gamma$). Thus, the estimated distance is, if signal is transmitted by the PU:

$$\hat{d}_i = (\hat{d}_{i,pu})^{(1-\varepsilon\_\Gamma/\Gamma)} \cdot 10^{-\varepsilon\_C/\Gamma} \tag{18}$$

Similarly, the estimated distance calculated based on the attacker transmission signal is:

$$\hat{d}_i = (\hat{d}_{i,attacker})^{(1-\varepsilon\_\Gamma/\Gamma)} \cdot 10^{(-\varepsilon\_C/\Gamma+F/\Gamma)} \tag{19}$$

Compared to Eqs. 14 and 15, the empirical propagation model estimation errors may increase both the false positive and false negative probabilities, due to the increasing uncertainty from the estimated distance.

7.2   Numerical Test and Comparison

The designed test scenario is in a 3000m × 3000m field. The PU and the FC are initially randomly located in the field. The PU is able to move. CRs and the attacker are randomly distributed in a circular area with radius 500 m. The best fitted propagation model parameters, C_{best} and Γ_{best}, are designed by referring to the empirical Hata model [12]. The model parameter errors follow Gaussian distribution, defined as $\varepsilon\_C \sim (0, \sigma^2_{\varepsilon\_C})$ and $\varepsilon\_\Gamma \sim (0, \sigma^2_{\varepsilon\_\Gamma})$. The details are shown in Table 3.

Table 3. Parameter setting

Field	3000m × 3000m
C_{best}	111.76
Γ_{best}	31.8
G	$\sim(0, 8^2)$
ε_C	$\sim(0, \sigma^2_{\varepsilon\_C})$
ε_Γ	$\sim(0, \sigma^2_{\varepsilon\_\Gamma})$
$P_{t,pu}$	50 (dBw) = 100 (W)
PU mobility	Yes

We have compared the performance of our proposal with a back propagation neural network (BPNN) based approach [20]. It is a PUE attack detection scheme that does not need geographical information of the PU, which is similar to our work. However, it does require CRs' geographical information for both training and testing process. Although there are other PUE attacks detection methods, their strong assumptions make it inappropriate to compare them with our approach. In the evaluation test, we apply a three layer BPNN with three input nodes, four hidden nodes and two output nodes, as shown in Fig. 9.

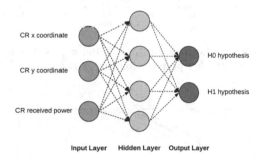

Fig. 9. BPNN structure for PUE attack detection.

Figures 10, 11, 12, and 13 present the comparison between our proposal and the BPNN approach using the receiver operating characteristics (ROC) curves corresponding to different number of CRs (N) and different propagation power differences (F) under several different parameter error propagation models.

The performance evaluation results in the figures show that both our proposed approach and BPNN approach for PUE attack detection have achieved better performance when there are larger number of CRs and larger propagation power difference between the PU and the attacker. When compared all result

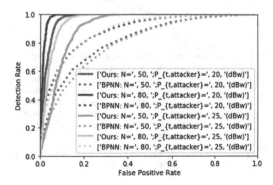

Fig. 10. ROC of two approaches, when $\sigma_{\varepsilon\_C} = 0$ and $\sigma_{\varepsilon\_\Gamma} = 0$, with different number of CRs (N) and different attacker propagation power $P_{t,attacker}$.

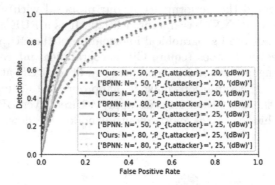

Fig. 11. ROC of two approaches, when $\sigma_{\varepsilon\_C} = 3$ and $\sigma_{\varepsilon\_\Gamma} = 1$, with different number of CRs (N) and different attacker propagation power $P_{t,attacker}$.

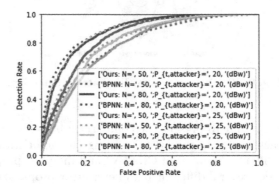

Fig. 12. ROC of two approaches, when $\sigma_{\varepsilon\_C} = 5$ and $\sigma_{\varepsilon\_\Gamma} = 2$, with different number of CRs (N) and different attacker propagation power $P_{t,attacker}$.

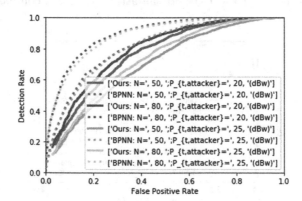

Fig. 13. ROC of two approaches, when $\sigma_{\varepsilon\_C} = 10$ and $\sigma_{\varepsilon\_\Gamma} = 3$, with different number of CRs (N) and different attacker propagation power $P_{t,attacker}$.

figures, however, it is shown that the BNPP approach is not sensitive to model parameter errors σ_{ε_C} and $\sigma_{\varepsilon\_\Gamma}$, while the performance of our approach greatly depends on the accuracy of model estimation. It is because the training data feeding to the neural network in BPNN approach is directly from real propagation environment, thus the testing process does not rely on the propagation model estimation. As shown in Figs. 10 and 11, on the other hand, our approach achieves a superior performance when the propagation model is well estimated.

However, the comparison based only on performance does not provide a comprehensive vision. The BPNN is robust against the inaccuracy in propagation model estimation because it is essentially empirical and learns from historical data. Actually the BPNN detector does not work with the same inputs that are required by our proposed method.

In summary, our proposed detection approach possesses two major advantages over the BPNN detector. Firstly, the BPNN approach requires CRs' geographical information in both training and testing process, which may greatly increase the cost by equipping CRs with extra peripherals, such as GPS, while our approach does not rely on any prior geographical information. Secondly, in our approach, no training process, especially supervised training process, is required. In PUE attack detection, training signal at receiver sides with tag of the PU is not always available in practical. Therefore, our approach, compared to BPNN detector, is more feasible in a wide selection of scenarios.

8   Conclusions

In this work, we proposed a novel PUE attack detection approach leveraging the hard-to-mimic feature of high PU transmission power, compared to the attacker transmission capability. The detection model considered many constraints in real-world situations, such as mobile PUs, unknown geographical information of each party, and the geographical randomness of PUs and attackers as well as the CRN formation. Both theoretical analysis and experimental results have validated our proposal.

Acknowledgement. Q. Dong, Y. Chen and X. Li are supported by the NSF via grant CNS-1443885. K. Zeng is partially supported by the NSF under grant No. CNS-1502584 and CNS-1464487.

References

1. Federal Communications Commission: Facilitating opportunities for flexible, efficient, and reliable spectrum use employing spectrum agile radio technologies. Et et docket (03–108) edn, December 2003
2. Federal Communications Commission: Enabling innovative small cell use in 3.5 GHz band NPRM & order, December 2012
3. Adelantado, F., Verikoukis, C.: Detection of malicious users in cognitive radio ad hoc networks: a non-parametric statistical approach. Ad Hoc Netw. **11**, 2367–2380 (2013)

4. Baker, M.A.: Introductory remarks: panel on the future of radio technology. Technical report, Federal Communications Commission (2010)
5. Brik, V., Banerjee, S., Gruteser, M., Oh, S.: Wireless device identification with radiometric signatures. ACM (2008)
6. Chen, R., Park, J.M., Reed, J.H.: Defense against primary user emulation attacks in cognitive radio networks. IEEE J. Sel. Areas Commun. **26**(1), 25–37 (2008)
7. Chen, Z., Cooklev, T., Chen, C., Pomalaza-Ráez, C.: Modeling primary user emulation attacks and defenses in cognitive radio networks. In: 2009 IEEE 28th International Performance Computing and Communications Conference (IPCCC), pp. 208–215. IEEE (2009)
8. Das, D., Das, S.: Primary user emulation attack in cognitive radio networks: a survey. IRACST-Int. J. Comput. Netw. Wirel. Commun. **3**(3), 312–318 (2013)
9. Dong, Q., Yang, Z., Chen, Y., Li, X., Zeng, K.: Anomaly detection in cognitive radio networks exploiting singular spectrum analysis. In: Rak, J., Bay, J., Kotenko, I., Popyack, L., Skormin, V., Szczypiorski, K. (eds.) MMM-ACNS 2017. LNCS, vol. 10446, pp. 247–259. Springer, Cham (2017). https://doi.org/10.1007/978-3-319-65127-9_20
10. Dong, Q., Yang, Z., Chen, Y., Li, X., Zeng, K.: Exploration of singular spectrum analysis for online anomaly detection in CRNs. EAI Endorsed Trans. Secur. Saf. **4**(12), e3 (2017)
11. Feng, X., Zhang, J., Zhang, Q.: Database-assisted multi-AP network on TV white spaces: architecture, spectrum allocation and AP discovery. In: 2011 IEEE Symposium on New Frontiers in Dynamic Spectrum Access Networks (DySPAN), pp. 265–276. IEEE (2011)
12. Goldsmith, A.: Wireless Communications. Cambridge University Press, Cambridge (2005)
13. Huang, L., Xie, L., Yu, H., Wang, W., Yao, Y.: Anti-PUE attack based on joint position verification in cognitive radio networks, vol. 2. IEEE (2010)
14. Kawalec, A., Owczarek, R.: Specific emitter identification using intrapulse data. In: Radar Conference, 2004. EURAD. First European, pp. 249–252. IEEE (2004)
15. Langley, L.E.: Specific emitter identification (SEI) and classical parameter fusion technology. In: WESCON/1993. Conference Record, pp. 377–381. IEEE (1993). 0780399706
16. Liu, Y., Ning, P., Dai, H.: Authenticating primary users' signals in cognitive radio networks via integrated cryptographic and wireless link signatures, pp. 286–301. IEEE (2010)
17. Marinho, J., Granjal, J., Monteiro, E.: A survey on security attacks and countermeasures with primary user detection in cognitive radio networks. EURASIP J. Inf. Secur. **2015**(1), 4 (2015). ISSN 1687-417X
18. Murty, R., Chandra, R., Moscibroda, T., Bahl, P.V.: Senseless: a database-driven white spaces network. IEEE Trans. Mob. Comput. **11**, 189–203 (2012)
19. Paisana, F., Marchetti, N., DaSilva, L.A.: Radar, TV and cellular bands: which spectrum access techniques for which bands? IEEE Commun. Surv. Tutor. **16**(3), 1193–1220 (2014)
20. Peng, K., Zeng, F., Zeng, Q.: A new method to detect primary user emulation attacks in cognitive radio networks. In: International Conference on Computer Science and Service System (CSSS 2014) (2014)
21. Pesko, M., Javornik, T., Kosir, A., Stular, M., Mohorcic, M.: Radio environment maps: the survey of construction methods. TIIS **8**(11), 3789–3809 (2014)

22. Rasmussen, K.B., Capkun, S.: Implications of radio fingerprinting on the security of sensor networks. In: Third International Conference on Security and Privacy in Communications Networks and the Workshops, SecureComm 2007, pp. 331–340. IEEE (2007)
23. Roos, T., Myllymaki, P., Tirri, H.: A statistical modeling approach to location estimation. IEEE Trans. Mob. Comput. 99(1), 59–69 (2002)
24. Yilmaz, H.B., Tugcu, T., Alagoz, F., Bayhan, S.: Radio environment map as enabler for practical cognitive radio networks. IEEE Commun. Mag. 51(12), 162–169 (2013)
25. Zhang, X., Jia, Q., Guo, L.: Secure and optimized unauthorized secondary user detection in dynamic spectrum access. In: IEEE Conference on Communications and Network Security (CNS), pp. 1–9, October 2017

VeReMi: A Dataset for Comparable Evaluation of Misbehavior Detection in VANETs

Rens W. van der Heijden$^{(\boxtimes)}$, Thomas Lukaseder, and Frank Kargl

Ulm University, Albert-Einstein-Allee 11, 89081 Ulm, Germany
{rens.vanderheijden,thomas.lukaseder,frank.kargl}@uni-ulm.de

Abstract. Vehicular networks are networks of communicating vehicles, a major enabling technology for future cooperative and autonomous driving technologies. The most important messages in these networks are broadcast-authenticated periodic one-hop beacons, used for safety and traffic efficiency applications such as collision avoidance and traffic jam detection. However, broadcast authenticity is not sufficient to guarantee message correctness. The goal of misbehavior detection is to analyze application data and knowledge about physical processes in these cyber-physical systems to detect incorrect messages, enabling local revocation of vehicles transmitting malicious messages. Comparative studies between detection mechanisms are rare due to the lack of a reference dataset. We take the first steps to address this challenge by introducing the Vehicular Reference Misbehavior Dataset (VeReMi) and a discussion of valid metrics for such an assessment. VeReMi is the first public extensible dataset, allowing anyone to reproduce the generation process, as well as contribute attacks and use the data to compare new detection mechanisms against existing ones. The result of our analysis shows that the acceptance range threshold and the simple speed check are complementary mechanisms that detect different attacks. This supports the intuitive notion that fusion can lead to better results with data, and we suggest that future work should focus on effective fusion with VeReMi as an evaluation baseline.

Keywords: Misbehavior detection · Vehicular networks
Intrusion detection

1 Introduction

Vehicular Ad-hoc Networks (VANETs) have received extensive attention in the research community in the past two decades as a potential enabling technology for improved road safety and efficiency. These networks, consisting of vehicles with ad-hoc wireless communication modules, are gaining importance in the context of cooperative autonomous driving applications. The idea is that communication can significantly improve autonomous driving by essentially increasing

© ICST Institute for Computer Sciences, Social Informatics and Telecommunications Engineering 2018
R. Beyah et al. (Eds.): SecureComm 2018, LNICST 254, pp. 318–337, 2018.
https://doi.org/10.1007/978-3-030-01701-9_18

the availability of information within the vehicle. However, for these applications to work correctly, this information needs to be authenticated and verified for correctness [14]. Standardization agencies have already defined cryptographic (IEEE 1609.2), communication (IEEE 802.11p, IEEE 1609), and application (ITS-G5, SAE J2735) standards, but addressing the correctness of the transmitted data has largely been a research issue. Cryptographic solutions (e.g., vehicular PKIs) only provide message integrity, and do not ensure message correctness; detecting the lack of correctness in authentic messages is referred to as *misbehavior detection*. These are typically classified into *data-centric* and *node-centric* [20], depending on the semantics of the decision: in data-centric detection, the data is *reliable*, while in node-centric detection, the sender is *trustworthy* (and thus the messages sent by it should be trusted).

There are many remaining research challenges in the area of misbehavior detection for VANETs. For example, similar to the area of intrusion detection, it is intuitively obvious that it is hard to build a single detection mechanism that detects all possible attacks. Instead, many proposals aim to either detect specific attacks [19] (i.e., particular types of behavior that are malicious), or they try to protect a specific application by structuring the checks such that only correct messages are accepted [18]. Many authors have proposed to apply some type of data fusion as a tool to combine information from multiple sources [5,13,19], but it is not well-studied how individual detection mechanisms compare. In this article, we inform this discussion with data, and argue that it is necessary to have a clear understanding of how mechanisms behave to maximize fusion performance. For this purpose, we also introduce a new metric that can be used to study the weaknesses and strengths of specific mechanisms by looking at how their error rates are distributed over the detecting vehicles. If the errors are concentrated in a certain area, one can either redesign the mechanism or use a situation detection mechanism (as suggested by our previous work). In this entire process, the essential step is a large common dataset that can be shared as input for multiple mechanisms; this dataset is the VeReMi dataset (Vehicular Reference Misbehavior Dataset), one of the two main contribution of this work. To the best of our knowledge, this is the first of such datasets that is publicly available.

To illustrate the need for such a public dataset, it is worth looking at the different approaches taken to evaluate VANET applications, which can be categorized in three groups: real-world field studies, analytical models and simulations. Field studies are effective for some scenarios, but especially for security and for large scale applications, this leads to prohibitive cost, especially for attacks aiming to disrupt traffic and cause accidents. Analytical models typically assume significant simplifications to keep the evaluation manageable. Therefore, simulation studies are often used as the primary evaluation methods for VANETs [14]. Even when using simulation, the computational cost for a representative analysis is significant, suggesting that common datasets could be useful. The state of datasets for intrusion detection evaluation is best illustrated by a recent survey by Mitchell and Chen [12], who analysed intrusion detection techniques for cyber-physical systems, which is closely related to VANETs. Out of 30 ideas discussed in [12], 4 used a public dataset, 22 papers did not release their dataset, and 4 did not use any dataset at all. For VANETs specifically, even releasing source code is uncommon, and sometimes it is not even declared which tools are used for simulation [8]. Although some authors in this field now have started to release material for reproducibility [9,22], this is still highly uncommon [7]. This is also a challenge for the security community within VANET research; this work requires both reliable, representative VANET simulations, and public attacker implementations, to enable comparisons between different detectors. This paper aims to address this need and push the community towards a more rigorous, scientifically valid approach to meet these and future challenges within our field.

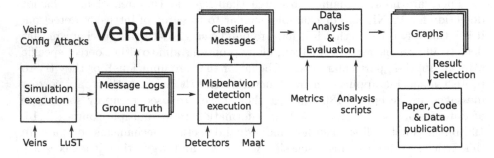

Fig. 1. Evaluation workflow

There are many different methodologies that can be used to evaluate misbehavior detection systems (and indeed, intrusion detection in general). In this paper, we focus on the evaluation workflow shown in Fig. 1, which basically consists of a system simulation step, a detection step, and an analysis step. In the system simulation step, a scenario (with or without attack(s)) is executed, and message reception is logged; in the detection step, a detection system is fed with the corresponding message logs, and the analysis step consists of computing relevant metrics and visualizing the results. Our simulations are performed within the LuST scenario [2], using VEINS [17] for the simulation of vehicles; more details are provided in Sect. 2. The message classification process is done using our evaluation framework Maat, which executes multiple parallel detectors, as discussed in detail in Sect. 4. This workflow is particularly effective for the evaluation of a broad spectrum of scenarios, and can be used to estimate the overall detection performance in a potential system deployment. For some evaluation goals (e.g., intrusion response effectiveness), where detection must be part of the system execution, the simulation and detection steps should be combined. In this paper, we focus on study designs that can be performed independently of the system simulation.

In summary, this paper has two major contributions; in Sect. 2, we introduce a dataset that can serve as a broad baseline for misbehavior detection evaluations, while Sect. 3 describes how to aggregate and present the results. We then show how to apply this dataset in our second major contribution, which is a broad evaluation of plausibility mechanisms proposed by previous authors in Sect. 4. We conclude with a discussion of future work in Sect. 5.

2 Dataset

The first contribution of this paper is a dataset intended to provide a common base line for misbehavior detection evaluation. Previous studies have always relied on individually designed simulation studies: although this has the advantage of customizable attacks and flexibility with respect to the specifics of the scenario, it makes it difficult to compare mechanisms with each other. The purpose of our dataset is to provide an initial baseline with which detection mechanisms can be compared. This reduces the time required for researchers to perform high-quality simulation studies, and it makes it easier for readers to compare the results of different papers. We acknowledge that no dataset can completely replace a detailed analysis of a detection mechanism; however, the current state of the art, where a comparison with any other scheme requires a time-intensive and error-prone re-implementation of every scheme, is unacceptable. Our dataset will provide the first step towards a comprehensive evaluation methodology for this field.

The dataset we introduce essentially consists of message logs for every vehicle in the simulation and a ground truth file that specifies the attacker's behavior. Local information from the vehicle is included through messages of a different type (representing periodic messages from a GPS module in the vehicle). Any detector can thus read the sequence of messages and determine the reliability of every message (or a subset thereof). Our dataset and the source code used to generate it[1] is publicly available, and consists of 225 individual simulations, with 5 different attackers, 3 different attacker densities, 3 different traffic densities, and 5 repetitions for each parameter set (with different random seeds). A detailed discussion of these aspects and the choices made in the generation process is provided below. Note that anyone can reproduce and extend our dataset in a consistent way using the provided source code, enabling anyone to extend the evaluation of any detector that was studied with VeReMi.

2.1 Scenario Selection

The purpose of our dataset is to provide a holistic basis for evaluation of misbehavior detection mechanisms, rather than a specific traffic situation that works well or poorly for a specific mechanism. This is aimed to reduce unintentional selection bias based on properties of the mechanism and the scenario, sacrificing the level of detail with which individual scenarios are studied. The alternative approach that is often taken is to pick a few specific traffic scenarios to be studied (e.g., congested highways, free-flowing traffic in a Manhattan grid setting)

---

[1] https://veremi-dataset.github.io/.

and analyze these in detail. This provides detailed information on mechanism behavior, but relies on a lot of manual decision making, making fair comparisons between mechanisms difficult. We instead focus on how mechanisms behave in a variety of different scenarios. To this end, we provide a much larger dataset that can be used to assess the overall performance, before looking at individual scenarios to provide specific improvements for specific detection mechanisms. In order to achieve this, we selected a representative sample of the entire simulation scenario, based on the included road types and the associated traffic densities.

Our work is based on the Luxembourg traffic scenario (LuST), originally introduced by Codeca et al. [2], who aimed to provide a comprehensive scenario for evaluation of VANET applications. Although this scenario is very suitable for traffic engineering, the simulation cost for the simulation of a city-scale VANET over multiple hours is prohibitive[2]. For this reason, reproduction of an entire study performed by other research groups is quite rare in our community – most papers that reference results from other articles are follow-up work. This is where our dataset comes in: it provides a simple message stream per vehicle, making it much easier to reproduce detection studies. Table 1 describes some core parameters of the simulation – more information can be obtained in the OMNeT++ configuration file in our source code.

Table 1. Simulation parameters

Parameter	Value	Notes
Mobility	SUMO LuST (DUA static)	[2]
Simulation start	(3, 5, 7) h	Controls density
Simulation duration	100 s	
Attacker probability	(0.1, 0.2, 0.3)	Attacker with this probability
Simulation area	2300, 5400–6300, 6300	Various road types
Signal interference model	Two-ray interference	VEINS default
Obstacle shadowing	Simple	VEINS default
Fading	Jakes	VEINS default
Shadowing	Log-normal	VEINS default
MAC implementation	802.11p	VEINS default
Thermal noise	−110 dbm	VEINS default
Transmit power	20 mW	VEINS default
Bit rate	6 Mbps	VEINS default (best reception)
Sensitivity	−89 dBm	VEINS default
Antenna model	Monopole on roof	VEINS default
Beaconing rate	1 Hz	VEINS default

---

[2] For illustration purposes; our 100 s excerpt of the scenario at high densities contains hundreds of vehicles and runs for a few hours – a significant part of this cost is the realistic simulation of signals bouncing off the ground and various buildings.

2.2   Attacks and Implementation

We implemented an initial set of attacks associated with position falsification, the type of attack that is most well-studied in our field (and for which many mechanisms have been designed [20]). Rather than implement a broad set of attacks, we focused on this specific attack to show the efficacy of our approach. We foresee that other researchers can contribute new attack implementations and corresponding datasets to the central VeReMi repository, which we will maintain. By focusing on a specific attack in this paper, we show how VeReMi is useful for other researchers and provide an initial starting point for the community. Since the data is published as a list of message logs, which include speed, claimed transmission time, reception time, position, and RSSI for each receiver, it is easy to take a newer version of VeReMi and run it through detectors that have already been published. This enables researchers to directly compare their detector against existing ones, and any new attack against a variety of detectors (as long as their source code is published).

The attackers we implement are the constant attacker, the constant offset attacker, the random attacker, the random offset attacker, and the eventual stop attacker. The constant attacker transmits a fixed, pre-configured position; the constant offset attacker transmits a fixed, pre-configured offset added to their actual position; the random attacker sends a random position from the simulation area; the random offset attacker sends a random position in a preconfigured rectangle around the vehicle; the eventual stop attacker behaves normally for some time, and then attacks by transmitting the current position repeatedly (i.e., as if it had stopped). The random attacks (4 and 8) take a new random sample for every message. The parameters for our attacks are shown in Table 2; the numbers are based on previous work [19].

Table 2. Attacker parameters

ID	Attack	Parameters
1	Constant	$x = 5560, y = 5820$
2	Constant offset	$\Delta x = 250, \Delta y = -150$
4	Random	Uniformly random in playground
8	Random offset	$\Delta x, \Delta y$ uniformly random from $[-300, 300]$
16	Eventual stop	Stop probability $+ = 0.025$ each position update (10 Hz)

2.3   Characteristics

The dataset consists of a total of 225 simulation executions, split into three density categories. The low density (corresponding to a run starting at 3:00) has 35 to 39 vehicles, while the medium density (a run at 5:00) has between 97 and 108 vehicles, and the high density (7:00) has between 491 and 519 vehicles. Out of these vehicles, a subset is malicious: this decision is made by sampling a uniform distribution ($[0, 1]$) and comparing it to the attacker fraction parameter, essentially assigning each vehicle to be an attacker with that probability. All of the vehicles classified as attacker execute the same attack algorithm (described in the previous section). Each receiver generates a reception log containing all periodic position updates generated by SUMO (10 Hz) and all received messages (i.e., beacons from other vehicles). Each of these log entries contains a reception time stamp, the claimed transmission time, the claimed sender, a simulation-wide unique message ID, a position vector, a speed vector, the RSSI, a position noise vector and a speed noise vector. In addition, a ground truth file is updated whenever a message is sent by any vehicle: this file contains the transmission time, sender, attacker type, message ID, and actual position/speed vectors. The attacker type is set to 0 for legitimate vehicles. The following describes the dimensions of the VeReMi dataset in terms of messages and reception events per density.

The amount of messages transmitted in the simulations varies between the simulations and densities; at low densities, 908 to 1144 messages are sent, at medium densities, there are between 3996 and 4489, and at high densities, there are 20482 to 21878 messages sent. The corresponding reception events are much more scattered; each vehicle at different densities can receive 0 messages (e.g., if they are not close to any other vehicles). For low density, a vehicle receives up to 278 reception events (total over all low density simulations is 277916 events spread over 2820 receivers), while at medium density this number goes up to 911 reception events (total over all 1815215 spread over 7695 receivers). Finally, for a high density, a single vehicle processes up to 5468 reception events in the 100 simulation seconds (total over all simulations over all 37500 vehicles is 37043160), or about 1000 messages per vehicle (10 per second, i.e., roughly 100 nearby vehicles at a beaconing rate of 1 Hz if we ignore lost messages). A graphical view of reception event frequency is given in the histogram in Fig. 2.

The scenario also includes a wide variety of traffic behavior, as illustrated in Fig. 3, which shows aggregate speed statistics over all runs in a specific density. The statistics were computed by taking the current local speed vector for every vehicle for every position update (which happens at 10 Hz) and aggregating all these samples. This results in a mean speed of 24.36 m/s for the low density scenario, with a very large standard deviation of 13.73 m/s; since the median speed is 30 m/s, this suggests that most of the deviation is due to traffic lights. In the medium density configuration, the median (13.33 m/s) and mean (15.06 m/s) drop significantly, although the amount of vehicles in the simulation is fairly low (only about 2.5 times the vehicles compared to a low density); the standard deviation is still very high (12.34 m/s), indicative of the wide variety of driving behavior. Finally, our high density scenario drops down further to a mean speed of 12.81 m/s, with a standard deviation of 10.94 m/s, while the median is 12.81 m/s.

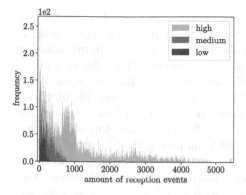

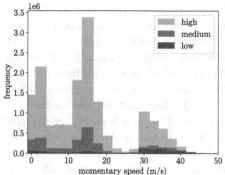

Fig. 2. Histogram showing the raw amount of reception events in the simulations.

Fig. 3. Histogram showing distribution of speed in the simulations.

2.4 Limitations

Our dataset cannot be fully representative of all possible attacks in VANETs, especially because the implemented attacks are representative of a specific type of attack. Investigating the effect of multiple attack types across a single simulation is not possible with this dataset. We argue that our dataset should be used as a starting point for a more rigorous approach to the evaluation of such systems – other researchers can use this process to find weaknesses in our detection approaches and implement new attacks. We believe this process is essential to achieving scientifically meaningful results: existing work nearly always relies on non-published code in some way, and thus it is very difficult to verify others' results. This leads to difficulty in replication of results, especially for complex detection systems that have many moving parts. The purpose of this dataset publication is to alleviate this: authors can make verifiable and reliable comparisons between their schemes and ours.

Another important limitation of our dataset is that the evaluation workflow in Fig. 1 is fundamentally non-interactive: it is designed for *detection*, not for *response*. This means that some specific misbehavior detection schemes that rely on interactivity or application decisions based on the detection of an attack (e.g., increasing safety distance in autonomous driving) cannot be evaluated with our dataset directly. However, for systems that protect specific applications, a comparison with other schemes always requires custom implementation. The core weakness of our approach is that we cannot directly evaluate trust over time without major modifications to our workflow, since trust schemes often do not output decisions for every message.

3 Metrics

Detection performance is a complicated and multi-faceted issue, whose definition also varies across publications, depending mostly on the purpose of the detector.

Even in intrusion detection in general, determining how to evaluate detection mechanisms and how to choose the appropriate mechanism for deployment, is considered a challenging issue, and the trade-off is non-trivial [1]. In misbehavior detection specifically, many authors use false positive/negative rates or equivalent metrics to determine how well attacks are detected, and this is combined with other performance metrics (such as latency, or application-specific metrics). Although these metrics are useful to compare performance of mechanisms, we find that there is a lack of metrics that are useful for the development of new detectors. In this section we propose an additional metric that fills this gap.

Another issue that should be addressed is specific to detection in *distributed* peer-to-peer systems: how should detection metrics be aggregated across participants? For example, given a simulation with two honest vehicles and one attacker, how do we characterize the detection performance of the same detection system (running within two vehicles independently)? We previously touched on this issue in a discussion with the vehicular communication community [21]. In this paper we will quantify the detection quality by classifying every detection event as true/false positive or as true/false negative; a detection event occurs whenever a message is received (i.e., we assume the detection decision is made as soon as possible after reception). We aggregate these results by counting the errors generated by *detection events*, not in terms of *sent messages* or *participants*. Which aggregation method is chosen is highly relevant for the interpretation of the results: in this work we focus on detection events to obtain a picture of the overall quality of the results. Aggregating by *message* provides information about how well a specific message sent by the attacker is detected, but presenting the results in terms of detected messages would mean that the amount of receivers is completely disregarded. Similarly, aggregation by *participant* ignores how much contact this vehicle has with the other vehicles. Since the amount of messages between vehicles is also indicative of a potential impact of an attack, aggregation by detection events is the best approach for an overall evaluation of detector performance. However, we point out that these metrics can also be implemented with our dataset, since we provide message and sender labels for every message.

3.1 Evaluating Detection Quality

The first metric we use to decide the quality of the detector is based on the well-established confusion matrix (which basically corresponds to an overview of true/false positives (TP/FP) and true/false negatives (TN/FN)). There are many options to choose from here; for example, *accuracy*, defined as the number of correct classifications ($TP+TN$) over all classifications ($TP+FP+TN+FN$), appears intuitive but suffers from the accuracy paradox for imbalanced sets. It is thus considered good practice [4,15] to always provide a quantification with two values, showing the trade-off between increased false positives to reduce false negatives and increased false negatives to reduce false positives. One such formulation is the use of *precision* and *recall*: precision quantifies the relevance of detection events ($TP/(TP + FP)$), while recall quantifies what rate of positives is actually detected $(TP/(TP+FN))$. An optimal detector thus has a precision and a recall of 1; how significant a deviation from this value is acceptable depends strongly on the application.

The state of the art [20] typically reports false positive $(FP/(FP + TN))$ and true positive $(TP/(FN + TP))$ rates, which provides a different and significantly skewed picture in certain situations, as discussed in machine learning literature [4,15]. Specifically, precision and recall are more informative in situations where a binary classification task (e.g., packet maliciousness decisions) is performed on an imbalanced dataset. As our dataset contains attackers in different degrees, and the amount of decisions made for attacker-transmitted messages $(TP + FN)$ compared to the amount of decisions made for benign messages $(FP + TN)$ is significantly different, we should thus prefer precision recall curves. As pointed out by other authors [4], a detector that is better in the PR graph is guaranteed to be better in the ROC graph; the interpretation process is generally similar (i.e., which curve is closer to the optimal point).

PR graphs provide us with an overall estimation of detector performance, but they have an important disadvantage: they are generally not as easy to interpret as a graph with FPR/TPR (referred to as an ROC curve). This greatly impacts the use of PR graphs in the literature: not only are they somewhat harder to understand fully, PR graphs often "look much worse", as demonstrated by Davis and Goadrich [4, Fig. 1]. This figure shows that the ROC curve can look close to optimal (the *area under curve* (AUC) is large), while the PR curve for the same data looks much worse (the AUC is small). This is partially related to the fact that interpolation between points on a PR curve is non-trivial; for details, refer to [4]. In addition to this issue, PR-graphs do not provide information about where potential flaws of individual mechanisms are, or whether a combination of multiple detectors can out-perform the individual mechanisms (as we argue in previous work [5]).

3.2   Evaluating Detector Limitations

To study the limitations of detectors without arbitrarily guessing which factors may influence such detectors, we design a new metric to find indications of such influences. The idea of our metric is quite simple: examine whether the distribution of erroneous classification rates (i.e., false positives and false negatives) is uniform over the receiving vehicles. If this metric says the distribution is uniform, the detector performance is not dependent on factors that are varied in the simulation, such as which vehicle executes it, or the relative position between the receiving and sending vehicle. On the other hand, if this distribution is extremely skewed, the conclusion is that the detector performance depends a lot on the context of the vehicle. We expect this is the case for many misbehavior detection schemes (and indeed most of the literature just assumes this is true), but it is also valuable information to know where the discrepancies occur. This enables further investigation into the detector's strengths and weaknesses, and finding a skewed distribution would suggest that combining the results of different mechanisms is the way forward. Note that this is *not a qualitative metric*: uniformly good or poor error dispersion does not imply that a metric is significantly better or worse, it only suggests whether there is room for improvement.

Given this intuition, we investigated and found a metric for statistical dispersion that is commonly used in sociology and economics to measure income inequality: the Gini coefficient or Gini index [3], originally defined in 1987 by Dixon et al. The idea can be visualized by sorting people by income in ascending order and then plotting the cumulative fraction of this list against the cumulative income of that group. More formally, the Gini index G of a population with mean size μ and value x_i assigned to individual i is defined as:

$$G = \frac{\sum_{i=1}^n \sum_{j=1}^n |x_i - x_j|}{2n^2 \mu} \tag{1}$$

The Gini index itself is not novel, nor is the application to quantify errors (see e.g. [6]), but our application of it is slightly different: we propose that it can be used effectively to determine the statistical dispersion in the error rates across vehicles. The reasoning is that computing the overall performance as discussed in the previous section hides localized effects associated with individual vehicles. Thus, if a mechanism has some regions where it performs really well (e.g., a highway), while it performs very poorly in other regions (e.g., urban settings with lots of traffic lights), these effects will be averaged out in the overall performance. If the overall performance is reasonable, one can use the dispersion in the error rates to determine whether this happens both for false positives and for false negatives (the latter being dependent on the attack): the higher the Gini index of these rates, the more differences exist between vehicles. However, if performance is poor overall, the Gini index can still be close to zero (or conversely, be close to 1); the arrays $(0.1, 0.1, 0.1, 0.1)$ and $(0.9, 0.9, 0.9, 0.9)$ have the same Gini index of zero. There are at least two main ways to use the result of this metric: (1) investigate the vehicles on either side of the skew and see whether the detector can be improved by changing its' functionality or (2) investigate whether fusion can be used to exploit low amounts of errors produced by different detectors in different scenarios.

4   Evaluation of Plausibility Detectors

This section shows an application of our dataset and metrics to analyze several data-centric plausibility detectors, which are detectors that verify a received message against data from local sources only. The decisions made by these detectors are practically instant (i.e., they do not depend on other data sources), and it does not generate additional attack vectors that can be used for *bad mouthing* and similar attacks, as is a risk in trust schemes and consistency mechanisms [20]. As plausibility mechanisms are often used as a basis for trust establishment [10,13,16,18], we focus on these. We implement detectors in our detection framework Maat[3], which is a detection and fusion framework based on

---

[3] https://github.com/vs-uulm/Maat.

subjective logic that we are currently developing. In this work, we compare four: the *acceptance range threshold* (ART), the *sudden appearance warning* (SAW), the *simple speed check* (SSC), and the *distance moved verifier* (DMV). Of these, the acceptance range threshold is the most well-studied, originally introduced by Leinmüller et al. [10] and later used by others, including Stübing et al. [18] and in our earlier work [19]. It basically uses the expected reception range as a measure for the plausibility of the position included in incoming single-hop beacon messages, which are the most important source of information for VANET applications. The sudden appearance warning was also introduced by Schmidt et al. [16], and is based on the assumption that vehicles will not suddenly appear, but rather always approach from a distance; if a message originates close by with an unknown sender, it is considered malicious. The simple speed check and distance moved verifier were implemented as part of our work on a detection framework, and both examine whether a new beacon confirms information claimed in an older beacon. The simple speed check decides maliciousness based on how the claimed speed relates to the speed implied by the position and time differences between the current and the previous beacon, and the claimed speed in the current beacon. If the deviation exceeds a threshold, this detector classifies the message as malicious (similar to, but much simpler than, a Kalman filter [18]). Finally, the distance moved verifier checks whether the vehicle moved a minimum distance (similar to the way the MDM proposed by Schmidt et al. [16]), and if this distance is too small, the message is considered malicious.

This selection of mechanisms is made for several reasons: (1) all of these mechanisms are exceedingly simple, (2) these mechanisms are designed to detect false positions in some sense, but as our analysis will show, different mechanisms detect different attacks, (3) the mechanisms rely on different data elements in the packet. Especially the simplicity is important for this discussion, since this allows us to not only compare the mechanism performance dependent on their respective thresholds, but also showcase how our metrics and dataset enable a useful and detailed analysis of mechanism behavior. We also focus on position verification as a specific application, in order to focus on a specific set of attacks, as discussed previously. Finally, these are the mechanisms for which the source code is available, unlike other mechanisms we have found in the literature – re-implementing mechanisms can be challenging, as often the implementation details are missing due to space limitations, and the code is not publicly available.

Table 3. Detector parameters, chosen based on earlier work.

Detector	Parameter	Values
ART	Est. reception range (m)	$100, 200, 300, 400, 450, 500, 550, 600, 700, 800$
SAW	Max. appearance distance (m)	$25, 100, 200$
SSC	Max. speed deviation (m/s)	$2.5, 5, 7.5, 10, 15, 20, 25$
DMV	Min. distance (m)	$1, 5, 10, 15, 20, 25$

4.1   Results: Detection Performance

Here we show the analysis results of our misbehavior detection framework, Maat, executing the detectors described above with different parameters, as listed in Table 3. Maat, which is currently in development within our institute, uses a graph representation to represent the data received by a vehicle, and is able to execute multiple detectors with multiple thresholds in parallel. In this paper, we focus on the outcomes of individual detection mechanisms: for a real-world deployment of Maat, this evaluation process is the first step. These results can be used to configure initial thresholds for each detector. For brevity, we focus on high and low density scenarios with high amounts of attackers (30%), as these provide the most notable output; we publish the entire set of figures and the underlying data as additional material[4]. The 10% and 20% attacker cases show comparable result for each set of graphs in Fig. 4; similarly, the medium density is comparable to the high density (as the application behavior is quite similar, as illustrated by Fig. 3).

As our dataset contains five simulation runs per behavior/attacker parameter set, each point in the graphs represents the mean of five runs, aggregated over vehicles as described previously. The error bars in these graphs show the sample standard deviation associated with this mean. The colors show the different detectors, also listed in the legend on the bottom; for black-and-white readers, we point out that the extremes of the threshold values (indicated with arrows at the extreme ends of each plot) are unique. Finally, note that the lines in these graphs are for illustrative purposes only – as previously discussed, interpolation between these points is a non-linear task [4].

4.2   Discussion: Detection Performance

In Fig. 4, the different attackers are listed from top to bottom as specified in Table 2. Overall, as one might expect, the type of attack is an important distinguishing factor in the effectiveness of the detection process (i.e., easily detected attacks generally have higher recall). One can observe immediately that the results for the different detectors vary greatly per attack, regardless of density. However, some detectors' performance is dependent on the density of the traffic (DMV is notable here). It can also be seen that the SAW has very poor performance for all attacks except for 16 – this corresponds to expectations from the detector design. We now focus on a brief discussion of each individual attacker.

For the first attacker, which falsifies position, the results show that in low density settings, all detectors except SSC very accurately detect the attack. A similar trend can be observed in the high density scenario; however, note that the ART performs slightly worse at very high thresholds (greater than 500); this conforms with results from an earlier study [19] (with different data and a different implementation). With regards to the SSC, which verifies whether the claimed speed in the current beacon corresponds to the distance moved

---

[4] https://github.com/vs-uulm/securecomm2018-misbehavior-evaluation.

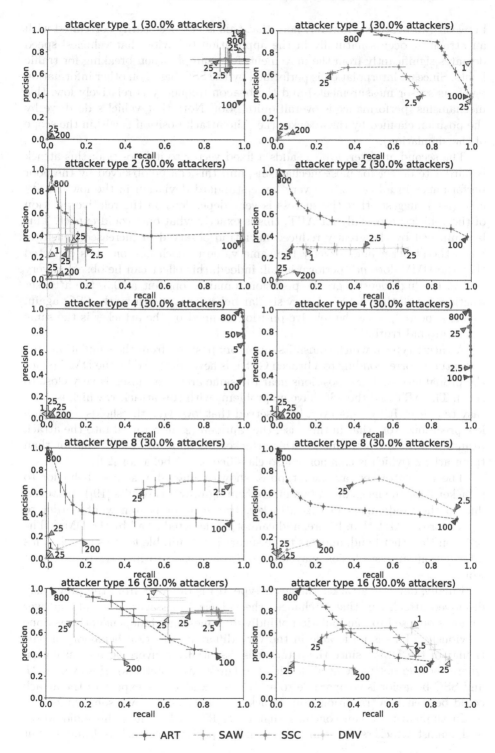

Fig. 4. Precision-recall graphs for low densities (left) and high densities (right).

between two beacons. However, note that this is not necessarily correlated with an attack: it occurs naturally in the application behavior that vehicles' speed deviates significantly from the movement, for example when breaking for traffic lights. Since no interpolation is performed by the SSC based on other information (such as sensor measurements) and the beacon frequency is relatively low, this mechanisms' performance is overall quite poor. Note that vehicles do drive by the position claimed by the attacker (i.e., the attack position is within the scope of the simulation).

The second attacker, type 2, adds a fixed vector to its' position; this attack is harder to detect for most mechanisms, and this can be observed by the poor performance in all cases. The very large standard deviation in the low density case (left) suggests that the success is very dependent on the relative position of the vehicles; especially for ART, this is exactly what one would expect. This is confirmed by the greatly reduced deviation observed in increased densities. Since the attacker adds exactly the same value to each beacon, it is expected that the DMV does not perform at all: indeed, this effect can be observed very well in the high density graph (precision remains constant at 0.3, the attacker fraction, for all thresholds). A very similar behavior is shown by the SSC; again, this is expected, since the relative position claimed by the attacker is the same as the ground truth.

Attacker type 4, which transmits a random position from the simulation area (essentially corresponding to a broken GPS), is never detected by the DMV (since the probability that two positions near the same area are chosen is very close to zero). The ART and the SSC have no problems with this attacker, which is quite easy to detect. It can, however, be observed that low ART thresholds result in a low precision. Note that in this case, the randomness introduced into the attack results in a poorer performance; this attacker fits more to faulty behavior than to an attack (which is commonly also classified as misbehavior [20]).

The next attacker, attacker type 8, shows remarkably similar behavior to attacker 2 for the mechanism (again, confirming previous results [19]). However, due to the randomness in this attacker, the attacker is somewhat harder to detect for the ART than before, and cannot be detected at all by the DMV. The SSC, on the other hand, appears to be surprisingly suitable for this attack. This information suggests fusion may be a suitable option to investigate in future work.

Finally, our last attacker (attacker type 16) is different from the previously discussed attacks, in that it changes the vehicles' messages in a pattern over time (as opposed to manipulation of individual messages independently, as done previously). This is noticeable in the very different detection behavior, in particular of the DMV, since the attacker is essentially converging to a situation where they do not move at all (which the DMV easily detects). However, ART and SSC behavior is comparable to attackers 8 and 1 – as expected: the attack could be seen as a transition from attacker 8 to attacker 1 over some time.

In summary, we can conclude that the ART with a high threshold works well against attackers that transmit erroneous positions (attackers 1 and 4), but has significant difficulties with those that are designed to confuse applications (attackers 2, 8 and 16). Against these malicious cases, the SSC works surprisingly well with lower thresholds, but it is subject to very poor performance against attacker 2. The DMV mechanism works best in dense traffic against attacker 16, and it also does well against attacker 1, but overall its' performance is very poor: this mechanism is clearly only suitable to identify very specific attacks. We also note that the SAW does not outperform any mechanism in any scenario; a future study that includes ghost vehicles (similar to for example, [11]) could show some benefit, but the extremely low precision will require some effort to make this scheme deployable. Finally, note that ART and SSC appear to outperform each other depending on the scenario (and the configured threshold): these are mechanisms we will focus on for our examination of the dispersion.

4.3   Results: Dispersion of Errors

Now that we have reviewed the detection performance in terms of precision-recall (PR), we examine our new metric based on the Gini index to study how to improve detection performance. Preliminary analysis has shown that the Gini index is not meaningful for small sample sizes as in our low density results, since the population is too small to make meaningful statements (because the sample standard deviation is very large for these results). The data and graphs are available for future analysis, but we caution against drawing conclusions from these for this reason. We therefore focus on a discussion of the high density scenario, which contains enough vehicles to allow for a meaningful analysis of the distribution of error rates. The results are shown in Fig. 5; as before, each point is the mean of five runs, and the sample standard deviation is indicated. Recall that in our setup, a Gini index closer zero means that the distribution of false positive/negative rates over the vehicles is closer to being equal, without making statements about the actual value.

4.4   Discussion: Dispersion of Errors

In this assessment, the Gini index for false positives rates is the same for every attacker: we first discuss the false negative dispersion per attacker. This dispersion gives us information about how different the detection performance is depending on the relative position of the attacker and the benign receiver.

For the ART, we observe that the dispersion of false negatives with regards to attacker 1 is very high: this can be explained by the fact that vehicles near the claimed constant false position will not be able to detect it with this mechanism. A similar effect can be observed for attacker 4, while for the other attacks, the dispersion only increases when the threshold is very low. This reflects the increasing recall discussed in the previous section, but remember that the precision also decreases significantly here. The SSC has a very low dispersion of errors for attacker 2, but unfortunately this is also the attacker against which its' precision is very low. Against attacker 8, the SSC outperforms the ART; the dispersion of errors suggests that this could be a localized effect, meaning that

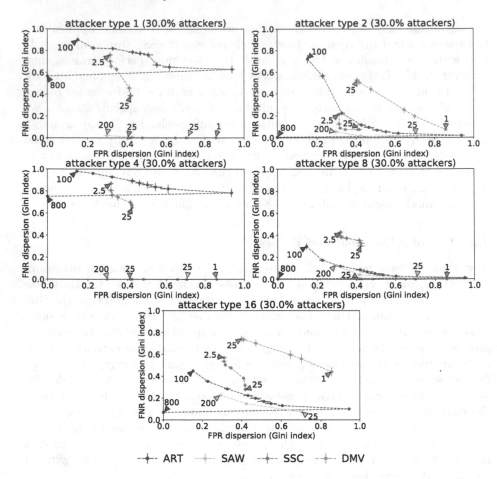

Fig. 5. Gini indices of FPR and FNR for different attackers

a combination of these mechanisms is likely to be feasible. For the mechanisms that perform very poorly against certain attackers (SAW and DMV), the Gini index shows that their poor performance is not easily fixed: the error dispersion is very close to zero in most cases. The exception is the DMV with regards to attackers 2 and 16: some performance improvement may be achievable by making changes to this detector. Finally, note that for attacker 1, the recall of the DMV is very high, while the Gini index for the false negative rate is very close to zero.

One can observe that the dispersion of false positives for the ART show that for higher thresholds, the amount of false positives is significantly skewed over the population; this reflects the intuition that receiving a message from up to 700 meters away is unlikely but not impossible; however, for a threshold of 800, the dispersion is zero. For the SSC, we observe that the threshold is much less relevant to the observed dispersion; this suggests that the mechanism would need to be changed more fundamentally to flatten the dispersion. A notable case is the DMV: this mechanism has a very high Gini index, and thus is an excellent candidate for fusion with other sources. In this particular setup, where detector assess the reliability of each message from the same source in isolation from other sources, an attack cannot lead to more false positives. Another class of attacks, where an attacker aims to convince a benign vehicle of a false perception of the traffic scenario (e.g., claiming a traffic jam where there is none, by convincing the target that the average speed is much lower than it actually is), this is not necessarily the case. Future work could use our metric to assess the real impact of this type of attack, as well as the use of this attack for *data-driven bad mouthing attacks*: causing a benign vehicle to incorrectly classify another benign vehicle as malicious by convincing it of a false aggregate.

5 Conclusion

In this paper, we have introduced a new dataset for misbehavior detection in vehicular networks, called *VeReMi*. The purpose of this extensible, publicly available dataset is to provide a basis on which researchers can compare detection results in a wide set of traffic behaviors and attacker implementations. We have additionally shown the application of this dataset to two existing, well-studied detection mechanisms (the acceptance range threshold and the sudden appearance warning), as well as two simple new detectors (simple speed check and distance moved verifier). We have also provided a detailed discussion on why precision-recall is the preferred method of comparison, as well as a new metric that enables the user to determine which detectors can potentially be improved. Using a combination of these metrics allows developers to have a more holistic view of a detector's assessment, which is information that can also be used in many fusion frameworks. In our continuing work, we will use these metrics and this dataset as a basis to assess other commonly employed mechanisms, such as fusion between mechanisms and trust establishment. This dataset will enable other researchers to compete with our detectors.

For future work, we see several directions beyond these detection performance improvements; one of these is to assess the feasibility of machine learning techniques for misbehavior detection. The dataset can be used to either learn the attacker behavior (enabling high-quality detection of specific attacker patterns) or the benign behavior (enabling the detection of deviations from this behavior). We expect that this direction is a feasible way to generate detector designs for specific scenarios that will also occur in the real world. However, we caution against using this data (or even our simulation code) as the sole foundation for the evaluation of such machine-learned models. Different real-world conditions (something as simple as a different speed limit on all roads) can impact the performance of such a learned model in a way that is not detectable without generating independent simulation results, or through the use of real-world data.

Future work should more closely investigate the available metrics from a security perspective. Although PR graphs are considered advantageous over most other options, they clearly do not give a complete picture of detector performance. The challenge in detection of malicious activity is that the difference between modeled behavior and observed behavior for both the attackers and the benign actors is fundamentally unknowable in advance of an attack. For example, benign actors will likely transmit messages with significant GPS errors in areas where urban valleys exist, and attackers may develop new methods or tune their parameters to avoid detection. Thus, although we feel that a dataset can function as a solid baseline for the behavior of different detection mechanisms, it is important to remark that such a dataset will always have the inherent limitation that the overall attacker prevalence is not generalizable. This is what makes misbehavior and anomaly detection distinct from a simple classification task (such as medical diagnostics), for which the prevalence can be estimated – dedicated metrics for misbehavior detection is likely the way forward.

Acknowledgement. The authors thank Florian Diemer and Leo Hnatek for the contribution of several detector implementations in Maat, and Henning Kopp for discussions regarding the Gini index. Experiments for this work were performed on the computational resource bwUniCluster funded by the Ministry of Science, Research and the Arts Baden-Württemberg and the Universities of the State of Baden-Württemberg, Germany, within the framework program bwHPC. This work was supported in part by the Baden-Württemberg Stiftung gGmbH Stuttgart as part of the project IKT-05 AutoDetect of its IT security research programme.

References

1. Cárdenas, A.A., Baras, J.S., Seamon, K.: A framework for the evaluation of intrusion detection systems. In IEEE Symposium on Security and Privacy, p. 15–pp. IEEE (2006)
2. Codeca, L., Frank, R., Faye, S., Engel, T.: Luxembourg SUMO traffic (LuST) scenario: traffic demand evaluation. IEEE Intell. Transp. Syst. Mag. **9**(2), 52–63 (2017)
3. Damgaard, C.: Gini coefficient. From MathWord - A Wolfram Web Resource, Created by Eric W. Weisstein. http://mathworld.wolfram.com/GiniCoefficient.html. Accessed 9 Feb 2018
4. Davis, J., Goadrich, M.: The relationship between precision-recall and ROC curves. In: Proceedings of the 23rd International Conference on Machine Learning, ICML 2006, pp. 233–240. ACM, New York (2006)
5. Dietzel, S., van der Heijden, R.W., Decke, H., Kargl, F.: A flexible, subjective logic-based framework for misbehavior detection in V2V networks. Proceeding of IEEE International Symposium on a World of Wireless, Mobile and Multimedia Networks 2014, pp. 1–6 (2014)
6. Eberz, S., Rasmussen, K.B., Lenders, V., Martinovic, I.: Evaluating behavioral biometrics for continuous authentication: challenges and metrics. In: Proceedings of the 2017 ACM on Asia Conference on Computer and Communications Security, ASIA CCS 2017, pp. 386–399. ACM, New York (2017)

7. Jimenez, I., Sevilla, M., Watkins, N., Maltzahn, C., Lofstead, J., Mohror, K., Arpaci-Dusseau, A., Arpaci-Dussea, R.: The popper convention: making reproducible systems evaluation practical. In: 2017 IEEE International Parallel and Distributed Processing Symposium Workshops (IPDPSW), pp. 1561–1570, May 2017

8. Joerer, S., Sommer, C., Dressler, F.: Toward reproducibility and comparability of IVC simulation studies: a literature survey. IEEE Commun. Mag. **50**(10), 82–88 (2012)

9. Kumar, V., Petit, J., Whyte, W.: Binary hash tree based certificate access management for connected vehicles. In: Proceedings of the 10th ACM Conference on Security and Privacy in Wireless and Mobile Networks, WiSec 2017, pp. 145–155. ACM, New York (2017)

10. Leinmüller, T., Schoch, E., Kargl, F., Maihöfer, C.: Decentralized position verification in geographic ad hoc routing. Security Commun. Netw. **3**, 289–302 (2008)

11. Lo, N.-W., Tsai, H.-C.: Illusion attack on VANET applications-a message plausibility problem. In: 2007 IEEE Globecom Workshops, pp. 1–8. IEEE (2007)

12. Mitchell, R., Chen, I.-R.: A survey of intrusion detection techniques for cyber-physical systems. ACM Comput. Surv. **46**(4), 55:1–55:29 (2014)

13. Raya, M., Papadimitratos, P., Gligor, V.D., Hubaux, J.P.: On data-centric trust establishment in ephemeral ad hoc networks. In: IEEE INFOCOM 2008 - The 27th Conference on Computer Communications, April 2008

14. Saini, M., Alelaiwi, A., Saddik, A.E.: How close are we to realizing a pragmatic VANET solution? a meta-survey. ACM Comput. Surv. **48**(2), 29:1–29:40 (2015)

15. Saito, T., Rehmsmeier, M.: The precision-recall plot is more informative than the ROC plot when evaluating binary classifiers on imbalanced datasets. PLoS ONE **10**(3), 1–21 (2015)

16. Schmidt, R.K., Leinmueller, T., Schoch, E., Held, A., Schaefer, G.: Vehicle behavior analysis to enhance security in VANETs. In: Proceedings of the 4th IEEE Vehicle-to-Vehicle Communications Workshop (V2VCOM2008) (2008)

17. Sommer, C., German, R., Dressler, F.: Bidirectionally coupled network and road traffic simulation for improved IVC analysis. IEEE Trans. Mob. Comput. **10**(1), 3–15 (2011)

18. Stübing, H., Firl, J., Huss, S.A.: A two-stage verification process for Car-to-X mobility data based on path prediction and probabilistic maneuver recognition. In: 2011 IEEE Vehicular Networking Conference (VNC), pp. 17–24. IEEE (2011)

19. van der Heijden, R.W., Al-Momani, A., Kargl, F., Abu-Sharkh, O.M.F.: Enhanced position verification for VANETs using subjective logic. In: 2016 IEEE 84th Vehicular Technology Conference (VTC-Fall), pp. 1–7, September 2016

20. van der Heijden, R.W., Dietzel, S., Leinmüller, T., Kargl, T.: Survey on misbehavior detection in cooperative intelligent transportation systems (2016). Arxiv Pre-Print http://arxiv.org/abs/1610.06810. Accessed 9 Feb 2018

21. van der Heijden, R.W., Kargl, F.: Evaluating misbehavior detection for vehicular networks. In: 5th GI/ITG KuVS FG Inter-vehicle Communication, p. 5 (2017)

22. van der Heijden, R.W., Lukaseder, T., Kargl, F.: Analyzing attacks on cooperative adaptive cruise control (CACC). In: 2017 IEEE Vehicular Networking Conference (VNC), pp. 45–52, November 2017

Birds of a Feather Flock Together: Fuzzy Extractor and Gait-Based Robust Group Secret Key Generation for Smart Wearables

Chitra Javali[1]($\boxtimes$) and Girish Revadigar[2]

[1] National Cybersecurity R&D Lab (NCL), National University of Singapore (NUS), Singapore, Singapore
chitraj@comp.nus.edu.sg
[2] Information Systems Technology and Design (ISTD), Singapore University of Technology and Design (SUTD), Singapore, Singapore
girish_shivalingappa@sutd.edu.sg

Abstract. The recent surge in the usage of smart wearables for health monitoring highlights securing the communication among a group of personal devices using group secret keys (GSK). Simultaneous GSK generation on multiple wearables is very challenging as finding a common feature among the devices that has good entropy is difficult. In this paper, we present two novel GSK protocols – FEAT-GSK and FEST-GSK, employing the unique gait characteristics of a person and fuzzy extractors. FEST-GSK eliminates the reconciliation and privacy amplification stages as it employs error correcting code and strong extractor. We implement our protocols on android devices and conduct various experiments. Our results demonstrate that the gait features extracted on user's devices show highest correlation (Pearson-correlation-coefficient >0.9), and guarantees matching group key generation e.g., 256-bit key in less than 4 s, whereas, the adversaries show as low as 20% key agreement with respect to the user.

Keywords: Group secret key generation · Fuzzy extractor
Secure sketch · Gait analysis · Accelerometer sensor

1 Introduction

The tremendous technological advancements in smart wearables and related domains have resulted in their increased usage in our day-to-day life. The built-in sensors and applications can perform impressive loads of tasks, like tracking our footsteps, monitoring health and other activities [4]. These smart wearables communicate with each other and transmit the sensitive health information usually through a wireless medium e.g., Bluetooth Low Energy (BLE) [1]. The wireless medium employed poses many serious security concerns like passive eavesdropping and data tampering/modification, etc. A recent demonstration of sniffing

© ICST Institute for Computer Sciences, Social Informatics and Telecommunications Engineering 2018
R. Beyah et al. (Eds.): SecureComm 2018, LNICST 254, pp. 338–357, 2018.
https://doi.org/10.1007/978-3-030-01701-9_19

attack [9] shows that the information like password, location, and attributes related to our health data can be leaked, which could lead to major security breach. For instance, a user's smart-phone uses Bluetooth to communicate with other wearables and also connects to the cloud-based services via internet to enable remote health monitoring, then, compromising a single wearable device can lead the attacker to gain access to a chain of devices and abundant useful information. Hence, robust and secure communication is essential among the wearable devices when they are communicating either in (i) peer-to-peer manner, or (ii) when a single device intends to communicate with all the body-worn devices of a subject [5]. Pair-wise encryption using the symmetric keys established between two devices, and the group secret keys (GSK) shared among a set of devices can achieve the confidentiality of the sensitive data.

Secure group communication is essential in many body area network-based applications [2,30], e.g., a base station may be required to securely update the software of all the devices simultaneously, or to transmit a broadcast message. The common methods employed for distributing the group keys are – manually loading the key to all the devices, or, manually loading a key to one of the devices, e.g., base station, which later distributes the key to other devices using the pre-distributed symmetric keys of individual devices. For security applications, the secret keys must not be utilized for a longer time as they can be compromised, and hence, the keys must be renewed periodically [5,30]. Every time a group key is renewed or regenerated, the above mentioned manual methods require human intervention to store a new key, and $\mathcal{N}$-number of communications are required for a base-station, $\mathcal{N}$ being the number of devices in a group. Hence, these methods are inefficient and cumbersome for a user. Ideally, the group secret key generation process must be automatic and unobtrusive, requiring very little or no human intervention.

Recent works have primarily focused on secret key generation between two wearable devices by employing biometrics like ECG [34], physical layer characteristics like received signal strength [19,20,28,29,31], link quality indicator (LQI) [22], and accelerometer sensor data on smart devices [36]. The most challenging part of secure group key generation is to identify and extract a common feature or characteristic among multiple devices. In addition, the features must possess enough randomness to ensure that the generated secret keys will have high entropy. A recent work [30] proposes a secure group key distribution scheme for smart wearable devices employing information-theoretically secure fuzzy vault technique. However, less attention has been paid to simultaneous group secret key generation for multiple smart wearables in the literature.

To address the above challenges and to meet the security requirements, in this paper, we propose two novel protocols to achieve simultaneous group secret key generation by a group of smart wearable devices using the unique gait characteristics of a person, i.e., walking style, extracted from the accelerometer sensor data recorded from the devices, and two cryptographic primitives: fuzzy extractors and secure sketch. A fuzzy extractor extracts nearly uniform randomness from its input and is error tolerant. It reproduces the randomness provided the input does not differ drastically with the original value. A secure sketch can recover its original input given another input value that is close to the original one. Hence, our fuzzy extractor, secure sketch and gait-based schemes can produce matching group secret keys on all the smart wearables of a subject. Following are our specific contributions:

1. We propose two novel group secret key generation schemes for smart wearables, (i) a Fuzzy Extractor And gaiT-based GSK (FEAT-GSK) protocol, and (ii) a Fuzzy Extractor, Secure sketch and gaiT-based GSK (FEST-GSK) protocol. Our FEST-GSK scheme employs hamming code and strong extractor SHA-256, and thus, eliminates the reconciliation and privacy amplification stages involved in traditional key generation schemes.
2. We implement our protocols on multiple off-the-shelf smart wearable devices and demonstrate experimentally that the proposed solutions are suitable for practical applications.
3. We conduct numerous experiments in various environments with multiple subjects, and the results reveal that, FEAT-GSK and FEST-GSK schemes achieve matching group secret key generation on all smart wearables of a user. The two protocols generate 256-bit secret keys with highest entropy i.e., >0.95 bits in just 3.72 and 1.81 s, respectively.
4. Our security analysis shows that, the correlation between the gait characteristics extracted on passive and active adversaries with respect to the same on legitimate devices of a user, will be minimal and hence the adversary cannot reproduce the same group secret key as the legitimate devices.

To the best of our knowledge, our work is the first to propose simultaneous group secret key generation schemes for multiple smart wearables using information theoretically secure fuzzy extractors and unique gait features of a user.

The rest of this paper is organized as follows: The preliminaries are presented in Sect. 2. Section 3 provides the details of our system and threat model. Section 4 presents the protocol designs. The evaluation of our protocol and security analyses are discussed in Sects. 5 and 6, respectively. Section 7 presents the literature review, and Sect. 8 concludes the paper.

2   Preliminaries

In this section, we present the preliminaries employed in our proposed protocol.

2.1   Secure Sketch and Fuzzy Extractor

Assume $\mathcal{M}$ be a metric space with a distance function dis, and threshold t.

Secure Sketch: A secure sketch $(\mathcal{M}, t)$ is a pair of randomized procedures, secure sketch SS and recovery Rec, with the following properties [14]:

– The secure sketch SS procedure takes an input $w \in \mathcal{M}$ and returns an output string $s \in \{0, 1\}^*$.

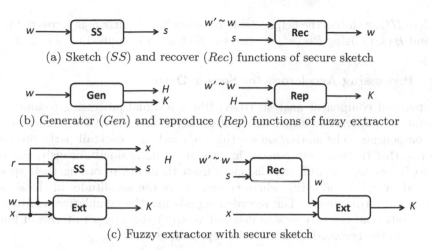

(a) Sketch (*SS*) and recover (*Rec*) functions of secure sketch

(b) Generator (*Gen*) and reproduce (*Rep*) functions of fuzzy extractor

(c) Fuzzy extractor with secure sketch

Fig. 1. Secure sketch and fuzzy extractor.

- The recovery procedure *Rec* takes input $w' \in \mathcal{M}$ and the bit string $s \in \{0, 1\}^*$ to produce w, i.e., $Rec(w', SS(w)) = w$, if $dis(w, w') \leq t$. This defines the correctness property of secure sketch. If $dis(w, w') > t$, then secure sketch algorithm does not ensure to produce the output w.

A secure sketch reproduces the precise input as shown in Fig. 1a and is secure, which implies that w is secure and no information is revealed about w, though s is made public.

Fuzzy Extractor: We employ fuzzy extractor [14] in our protocols as it is error tolerant and information theoretically secure [13]. It consists of two procedures, generator *Gen* and reproduce *Rep*, as shown in Fig. 1b.

- The *Gen* procedure takes an input $w \in \mathcal{M}$, and produces an output $K \in \{0,1\}^l$ that is uniformly random and a helper string H.
- If the input is changed to w' such that the distance between w and w' i.e., $dis(w, w') \leq t$, then K can be reproduced with the help of H by another procedure *Rep*.

The helper data H does not reveal any information about K, even if it is made public.

Fuzzy Extractor from Secure Sketch: Secure sketch can be also employed to construct fuzzy extractor [14]. Assume (*SS, Rec*) is a secure sketch and let *Ext* be a strong extractor, then the fuzzy extractor can be defined as follows:

- $Gen(w, r, x)$: set $H = (SS(r; w), x)$, $K = Ext(w; x)$ and output K.
- $Rep(w', H) : Rec(w', s) = w$, and output $K = Ext(w; x)$.

Figure 1c shows the constructs. In the first block, *SS* is applied to w and random string r to obtain s, and K is calculated by applying *Ext* to w and random string

x. Here $H(s, x)$ forms the helper data. To reproduce K, first w is recovered from w' and $H(s, x)$ using $Rec(w', s)$, then the $Ext(w, x)$ is applied to obtain K.

2.2   Processing Accelerometer Sensor Data

Independent component analysis (ICA) [18] is a signal processing technique to separate a multivariate signal into non-Gaussian and statistically independent subcomponents. The motivation for this approach is a cocktail party problem. Assume that there are two persons in a room speaking simultaneously, and two microphones kept at different distances from them are recording their speech denoted by $r_1(\tau)$ and $r_2(\tau)$, where r_1 and r_2 are the amplitudes of the signals and τ is the time index. The recorded signals are the cumulative addition of the signals from the two persons denoted as $s_1(\tau)$ and $s_2(\tau)$. In terms of linear equations, the recorded signals can be represented as:

$$r_1(\tau) = s_1 d_{11} + s_2 d_{12}; \quad r_2(\tau) = s_1 d_{21} + s_2 d_{22} \tag{1}$$

where d_{11}, d_{12}, d_{21} and d_{22} are the parameters related to the distances between the persons and microphones. Using the recorded signals, it is possible to separate the individual subcomponents i.e., s_1 and s_2 effectively by using ICA.

3   System and Threat Model

Figure 2a shows our system model. We consider four smart wearables viz., a smart-phone on the waist, which we denote as Hub, and three other devices – a smart-watch, a smart-glass and another smart-phone placed on the chest. Each smart device is associated with a unique device identifier id. The devices communicate with each other through Bluetooth. For the threat model, we consider two types of adversaries – passive and active. Both the adversaries wear similar type of devices as the legitimate user. The active adversary follows the walking style of the subject so that he/she can extract similar gait characteristics, and try to generate the secret key. The passive adversary walks as per his/her own style and does not try to mimic the legitimate subject, and captures the sensor data to generate secret key similar to user. The adversary can eavesdrop and try to analyse the content of the message, and can also modify the packets exchanged between the legitimate devices. We assume that all the on-body devices of user are legitimate, and we do not consider jamming attack by the adversary.

4   Protocol Design

In this section, we present our two protocol designs, FEAT-GSK and FEST-GSK. We first describe the procedure to extract gait features from the accelerometer data that is common to both the protocols, and subsequently present the protocols in detail.

4.1 Gait Feature Extraction

Accelerometer sensors are ubiquitous and can be found on every smart wearable. We extract the unique gait feature from accelerometer sensor data as follows:

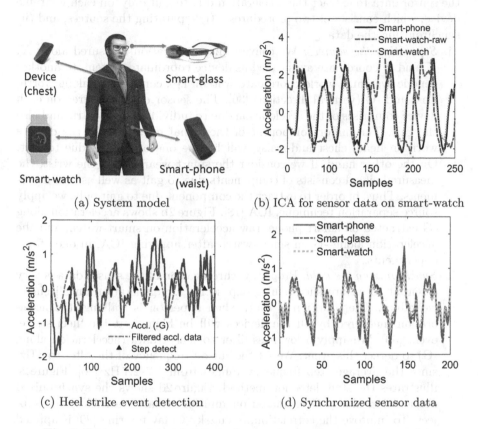

(a) System model

(b) ICA for sensor data on smart-watch

(c) Heel strike event detection

(d) Synchronized sensor data

Fig. 2. System model and stages of processing accelerometer sensor data.

1. *Initiating the process:* The Hub initiates the process of secret key generation. The Hub broadcasts a message $init = \{id_{Hub}||n_{Hub}||f_s||d_s||S\_CAPT\}$ to all the smart wearables while the subject is walking at a normal speed. Here, the identifier of the Hub $id_{Hub} = 1$, n_{Hub} is the nonce, and S_CAPT is the message identifier. The *init* also includes details like sampling frequency f_s and duration to capture the data d_s. All body-worn devices including Hub start recording the accelerometer sensor data for specified time duration upon receiving this message.
2. *Processing the sensor data:* The accelerometer sensor measures acceleration along three axes X, Y, and Z relative to the sensor's placement/orientation. Since the orientation of sensor on each device varies, and the placement of each

on-body device is different, the resulting acceleration measured on body-worn devices while the subject is walking, will be highly random and uncorrelated. Thus, the raw acceleration measured along different axes X, Y, and Z on each smart wearable does not provide any useful information. Hence, we process the sensor data to extract the acceleration due to gait only, on each wearable device, which consists of two procedures – (i) separating the sources, and (ii) synchronizing the data.

i. *Separating the sources:* We convert the acceleration measured along X, Y, and Z coordinate axes called as device coordinate system, to another generic system, a world coordinate system, i.e., components along North, East and -G (vertical direction) [36]. The sensor data measured on each device comprises of the acceleration due to individual body-parts and also the gait. The major component of the signal measured for the devices worn on head, chest and waist, will be the one originated due to gait. On the other hand, if we consider the smart wearable on the wrist, the measured signal consists of components due to gait as well as arm movements. Thus, in order to extract the component due to gait only, we apply source separation technique, ICA [18]. Figure 2b shows acceleration along -G extracted on smart-phone, raw acceleration on smart-watch, and the acceleration along -G on smart-watch after applying ICA, in one of our experiments.

ii. *Synchronizing the data:* Proper synchronization of the sensor data is very essential to ensure successful group secret key generation on all smart wearables. The intuition is that, when a person is walking, the acceleration measured by all the devices will be highest at the 'heel strike' event [30]. We apply a low pass filter to sensor data (acceleration along -G) to detect this event. We set the cut-off frequency of the filter to 3 Hz, since the average step frequency ranges from 1.7–2.7 Hz [36]. Figure 2c illustrates the step detection method. Figure 2d shows the synchronized acceleration along -G extracted on multiple smart wearables of a subject. To improve the correlation, Savitzsky-Golay filtering [29] is applied to acceleration along -G extracted on all the devices, which removes the noise components. Once synchronization and filtering are completed, all the smart wearables are ready for group secret key generation, using either our FEAT-GSK or FEST-GSK scheme explained in Sects. 4.2 and 4.3 respectively.

4.2   FEAT-GSK Protocol

In this section, we present Fuzzy Extractor And gaiT-based group secret key (FEAT-GSK) protocol. Algorithm 1 (Sect. 4.2) explains the procedure followed by Hub and other legitimate devices simultaneously, according to the sequence of execution. The symbols $\Leftarrow$ and $\Rightarrow$ in the algorithm denote over-the-air message transmission between the Hub and other smart wearables. The unique identifiers assigned for the devices are $id = 1, 2, 3$ and 4 for Hub, smart-glass, smart-phone (chest), and smart-watch, respectively. The Hub performs *Gen* operation on

Algorithm 1. FEAT-GSK

Entity: Hub
Input: $id_{Hub} = 1$; D; q; n_{Hub}
Output: Group secret key K
begin

  Gen:
  Key $K_1 \leftarrow$ Quantize D using q;
  $I_1 \leftarrow$ List of valid indexes;

  Recon_Hub:
  if $(SI(I_1, I_{id}) < 0.7)$ **then**
    Reject I_{id}; **(Attack detected)**
    $msg\_reqi \leftarrow \{I_{id}||id_{Hub}||n_{Hub}||REQ\_I\}$;
    Send msg_reqi to Device Id $= id \Rightarrow$ **goto** *Recon_Dev*;
    goto *Recon_Hub:*;
  else
    Accept I_{id}; **(No Attack)**
  end if
  Set $I = \{I_i\}_{i=1}^4 \leftarrow$ Construct set I;
  Set $I_{com} = \{I_{com_\delta}\}_{\delta=1}^\Delta$, where
  $\Delta = $ Num. common indexes in I_i, and
  $(I_{com_\delta} \in \bigcap_{I_i \in I} I_i) \Leftrightarrow (\forall I_i \in I, I_{com_\delta} \in I_i)$;
  $K \leftarrow$ Final key from (K_1, I_{com});
  Output secret key K;
  $bdl\_key \leftarrow \{I_{com}||id_{Hub}||n_{Hub}\}$;
  Send_list_Hub:
  $msg\_key \leftarrow \{bdl\_key, MAC(K, bdl\_key)\}$;
  Broadcast msg_key to all devices $\Rightarrow$

  goto *Send_list_Hub*;

end

Entity: Other smart wearables
Input: id; D'_{id}; $H = q$; n_{Hub}
Output: Group secret key K
begin

  Rep:
  Key $K_{id} \leftarrow$ Quantize D'_{id} using H;
  $I_{id} \leftarrow$ List of valid indexes;
  Recon_Dev:
  $msg\_recon \leftarrow \{id||I_{id}||n_{Hub}\}$;
  $\Leftarrow$ Send msg_recon to Hub

  Verify_key_Dev:
  $K'_{id} \leftarrow$ Final key from (K_{id}, I_{com});
  if $(MAC(K'_{id}, b) \neq MAC(K, b))$ **then**
    Reject I_{com}; **(Attack detected)**
    $msg\_reqi \leftarrow \{id||n_{Hub}||I_{com}||REQ\_I\}$;
    $\Leftarrow$ Send msg_reqi to Hub;
    goto *Verify_key_Dev*;
  else
    Accept I_{com}; **(No Attack)**
    Output key $K'_{id} = K$;
    $bdl\_match \leftarrow$
      $\{id||n_{Hub}||KEY\_MATCH\}$;
    $msg\_match \leftarrow$
      $\{bdl\_match, MAC(K'_{id}, bdl\_match)\}$;
    $\Leftarrow$ Send msg_match to Hub;
  end if

the extracted acceleration along -G (D), i.e., D is quantized using parameters $q = \{\mathcal{W}, n, \alpha\}$, to generate an initial key K_1 of length $l' > l$, where $\mathcal{W}$, n, α are the window size, number of bits per sample, and the guard band size respectively, and l is the length of the final group secret key. The parameters q are the public helper data H. The other wearable devices perform *Rep* operation on their acceleration along -G ($D'_{id} \sim D$) and generate an initial key $K_{id} \approx K_1$ using the public helper data H. The quantization method employed can be either single bit ($n = 1$) or multi-bit quantizer [30]. Also, all the devices generate a list of sample indexes I_{id} that are not discarded during quantization. At this stage, the keys $K_{id} \approx K_1$, however, as the sensor data is captured on each device separately, this may produce some bit disagreements. This is because the indexes discarded by different devices may be slightly different during quantization. To correct the bit mismatches, all the devices including Hub perform reconciliation. All the devices send their list I_{id} to Hub, along with their id and nonce n_{Hub}. The Hub verifies the authenticity of the message using device id, and calculates the similarity index (SI) [30] between its own list I_1 and I_{id} for integrity check. If SI > 0.7, meaning at least 70% of the indexes in I_{id} overlap with I_1, the I_{id} is considered as legitimate/non-modified (no attack) and accepted. If the SI < 0.7, the I_{id} is rejected suspecting an active attack/modification by an adversary. If the lists received from all the devices are authentic, then Hub constructs a list of common indexes I_{com} using all the lists I_1–I_4, and generates a final key K of length l, using only the bits corresponding to initial l indexes of I_{com} in K_1. The hub broadcasts $\{bdl\_key, MAC(K, bdl\_key)\}$ to all the devices, where $bdl\_key = \{id_{Hub}||I_{com}||n_{Hub}\}$, and $MAC(\cdot)$ is the message authentication code. Upon receiving this message, all the devices generate K'_{id} of length l from their respective K_{id} using I_{com}, and verify if the $MAC(K'_{id}, b)$ matches with the received $MAC(K, b)$. After the devices confirm the authenticity and integrity of the data, a confirmation message with identifier KEY_MATCH is sent to the Hub as shown in the algorithm. Once the Hub receives confirmation from all the legitimate devices, it broadcasts a message $msg\_res = \{bdl\_res, MAC(K, bdl\_res)\}$ to all the devices, where $bdl\_res = \{id_{Hub}||n_{Hub}||G\_KEY\_SUCCESS\}$, and $G\_KEY\_SUCCESS$ is a message identifier.

4.3   FEST-GSK Protocol

In this section, we present Fuzzy Extractor, Secure sketch and gaiT-based group secret key (FEST-GSK) protocol.

***Gen* Construct of Hub:** We design our protocol using distance metric-based fuzzy extractors [14] and hamming code for error correction. Figures 3a and b show our constructs *Gen* and *Rep*, used by Hub and other devices respectively, for group secret key generation. In the *Gen* construct, the acceleration due to gait (along -G) extracted on the Hub (D) is quantized in Q^n block using multi-bit quantization [30] with parameters $q = \{\mathcal{W}, n, \alpha\}$, to produce W and I. We employ Hamming (7, 4)-code for error correction, and hence, we set $n = 4$. In quantization, a guard band is introduced between successive quantization levels to reduce the bit-discrepancies that may occur during quantization [30]. The set $I = \{I_0, I_1, \ldots, I_{N-1}\}$ consists of the indexes of the samples that are not discarded during quantization. N is the total number of samples that are not discarded. We use Gray coding for generating the bits, with the code equivalent to decimal 0 at the lowest level and the code corresponding to 15 at the

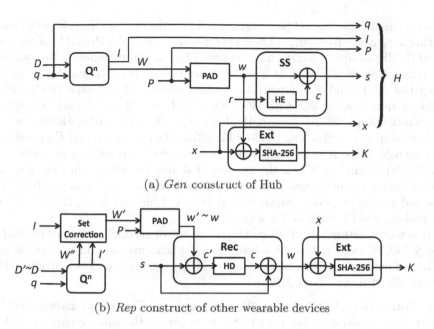

(a) *Gen* construct of Hub

(b) *Rep* construct of other wearable devices

Fig. 3. *Gen* and *Rep* constructs of FEST-GSK protocol using hamming code for error correction and SHA-256 strong extractor.

highest quantization level. The set $W = \{W_0, W_1, \ldots, W_{N-1}\}$ consists of the 4-bit strings W_i generated, corresponding to the indexes in I. The quantization parameters q and I form a part of helper data H. We append a 3-bit string P_i from a set of random bit strings P, to each W_i inside the block PAD to produce 7-bit strings for each W_i, i.e., $w = \{w_0, w_1, \ldots, w_{N-1}\}$ where $w_i = W_i \| P_i$. Inside the secure sketch block SS, the hamming encoder block HE encodes a series of 4-bit words r_i taken from a set of random bit strings $r = \{r_1, r_2, \ldots, r_{N-1}\}$ to produce a set of coded words $c = \{c_0, c_1, \ldots, c_{N-1}\}$ given by $c_i = C(r_i)$. The set c is combined with w to obtain $s = \{s_0, s_1, \ldots, s_{N-1}\}$ where $s_i = c_i \oplus w_i$. Finally, a 256-bit secret key $K = \mathcal{H}(x \oplus w)$ is generated in the extractor block Ext, using a strong-extractor $\mathcal{H}(\cdot) = $ SHA-256, with 128-bit w (series of w_i concatenated) as an input and a random bit string x of 128-bit length as a key, as shown in the Fig. 3a. The sets P, s and x form the remaining part of helper data H. The Hub constructs a bundle $bdl\_help = \{n_{Hub} \| id_{Hub} \| H\}$, and broadcasts a message $msg\_help = \{bdl\_help, MAC(K, bdl\_help)\}$ to all other smart wearables.

Generating the random bit strings P, r and x: Prior studies have shown that for security applications, a Random Number Generator (RNG) that depends on external events is preferred compared to Pseudo-RNGs [30,35]. Thus, we employ accelerometer sensor as a hardware RNG in our protocol. We generate the random strings P, r and x from the X, Y and Z components of accelerometer sensor data captured while the subject wearing/holding the device (Hub) is performing routine activities. To ensure highest entropy, we follow the Root Mean Square-based (RMS) sample selection method presented in [30] to generate the random bit strings. Specifically, we first generate three strings R_X, R_Y and R_Z by quantizing the X, Y, and Z components of accelerometer data, respectively, using multi-bit quantization [30] with $\mathcal{W} = 50$, $n = 4$, $\alpha = 0$, and binary coding for the quantization levels (0 - lowest, 15 - highest). After this, we interleave the bits of above strings to get a long random bit string R_{XYZ}. The string R_{XYZ} shows high entropy since it is derived from three different acceleration streams [30]. Finally, depending on N, i.e., the number of sensor recordings that are not discarded during quantization, R_{XYZ} is divided into non-overlapping sub strings P, r and x of appropriate length, e.g., if $W = 128$-bit and $n = 4$, then length of $P = 96$-bits, $r = 128$-bits, and $x = 128$-bits.

It is worth noting that, the accelerometer sensor reading consumes negligible energy [30,36] even on resource constrained platforms used in medical applications. Thus, our method of random bit string generation does not affect the battery life of smart-phone (Hub).

Rep Construct of Other Legitimate Devices: The other smart wearables employ *Rep* function of fuzzy extractor to generate the same group secret key as Hub, as shown in Fig. 3b. In *Rep* construct, we use general notations for sets, results etc., and omit the subscript *id* for easier understanding, though multiple devices execute this procedure separately and may have different parameter values e.g., the notation W'' is equivalent to W''_{id}. The first block in *Rep* function is Q^n, where the acceleration due to gait (along -G), i.e., D' is quantized using multi-bit quantization [30] with parameters $q = \{n, \alpha\}$ extracted from helper data H. Similar to Hub, Gray coding is used for the quantization levels, and the set of 4-bit strings $W'' = \{W''_0, W''_1, \ldots, W''_{N'-1}\}$ and a set of non-discarded indexes $I' = \{I'_0, I'_1, \ldots, I'_{N'-1}\}$ are generated. N' is the number of samples that are not discarded during quantization by the smart device.

The Hub and other smart wearables capture the sensor data individually, hence, there may be slight differences in the values recorded, and may result in bit errors during quantization. Figure 4a illustrates the quantization error due to difference in sample values. Thus, sample set correction is performed in *Rep* function to remove the errors. The block Set Correction takes inputs W'' and I' from Q^n, and I from helper data H, and outputs a corrected sample set W' that contains same indexes used by Hub. During correction, if an ith sample (discarded) is added to I', a 4-bit string W'_i is added to set W' and is assigned the same code word as $W'_{(i-1)}$.

After set correction, the next step is padding the bits. Inside the block PAD, each W'_i in W' is concatenated with a 3-bit string P_i to produce set $w' = \{w'_0, w'_1, \ldots, w'_N\}$, where $w'_i = W'_i \| P_i$. Once w' is obtained, inside the block Rec, set $c' = \{c'_0, c'_1, \ldots, c'_N\}$ is computed using s from helper data H as $c'_i = w'_i \oplus s_i$. After this step, each c'_i is decoded inside HD block to get set $c = \{c_0, c_1, \ldots, c_N\}$. The corrected set w is obtained using c and s as $w_i = c_i \oplus s_i$. Figure 4b shows the bit correction method using hamming code. Finally, Ext computes the key

$K' = \mathcal{H}(x \oplus w)$, where $\mathcal{H}(\cdot) = \text{SHA-256}$ is a strong extractor, and w, x are the parameters obtained from helper data H. After final key generation, all the devices including Hub verify the key agreement using MAC values, by following a procedure similar to FEAT-GSK protocol in Sect. 4.2.

The improved protocol FEST-GSK eliminates the two expensive steps of traditional key generation; (i) reconciliation, and (ii) privacy amplification, as our constructs employ error correcting codes and strong extractors. Hence, our scheme is suitable for IoT applications.

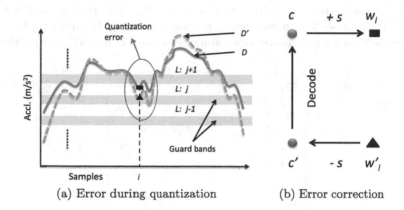

(a) Error during quantization   (b) Error correction

Fig. 4. Illustration of error correction.

5   Evaluation and Results

In this section, we describe our protocol implementations, evaluation and results. We have implemented the two protocols FEAT-GSK and FEST-GSK as applications that can run on Android-based smart-phone [6], smart-watch [7], and smart-glass [8]. For extracting the acceleration due to gait on smart-watch, we have employed FastICA [3] library. All the experiments were repeated for different environments, like small room, large office area, corridor, and cafeteria.

The experiments were conducted with 14 volunteers having equal number of male and female participants[1]. We categorized the experiments into two sets – one to evaluate our group secret key generation protocol on all the legitimate devices of the subject, and another, for security analysis. In both the sets, each experiment was conducted for 8–10 min with sampling frequency of sensor data set to 100 Hz, and repeated for 5 rounds. We collected the datasets while each subject was performing the assigned task in each experiment.

In the first set of experiments, each subject walked normally, following his/her usual style, and the datasets were captured. The average walking speed of each subject in these experiments was $\approx$1 m/s. For the security evaluation, we partitioned 14 subjects into 7 pairs. We again sub-divided the experiment into two

---

[1] The ethical approval has been obtained from the corresponding organization.

phases. In the first phase, one person in each group was selected as a legitimate user, and the other as an adversary. The legitimate user was asked to walk normally and the adversary was asked to follow/imitate the user's walking style at the same time. In the second phase, same tests were repeated by swapping the roles of legitimate user and adversary in each pair.

5.1   Evaluation of FEAT-GSK Protocol

For the protocol evaluation, we employ window-based one-bit quantization [30], and fix the parameters $\mathcal{W} = 50$, $n = 1$, and $\alpha = 0.5$. The Hub generates a key K_1 and all the other legitimate devices generate keys K_{id}, by applying Gen and Rep functions to their own acceleration along -G i.e., D and D'_{id}, respectively.

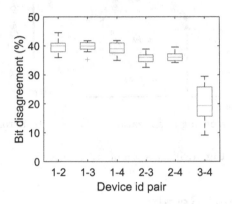

Fig. 5. Pair-wise bit disagreement for the initial keys generated by legitimate devices using FEAT-GSK protocol (before reconciliation).

To analyse the performance, we consider the dataset captured from each subject in the first set of experiments. We calculate the percentage bit-disagreement between the initial keys generated by all four legitimate devices of subject prior to reconciliation. We obtain a total of 6 pair-wise comparisons for the four devices, viz., 1-2, 1-3, 1-4, 2-3, 2-4, and 3-4, where the numbers denote device id. As seen in Fig. 5, the pair-wise bit disagreement for the initial keys generated by the legitimate devices was 19–40%. Our results show that the bit rate for generating initial keys was 69–82 bps. After employing reconciliation, the final keys generated by all legitimate devices were observed to match each other, confirming successful group key generation. To evaluate the randomness of the generated final group secret keys, we calculate the Shannon entropy. Our results show that the average entropy of the keys was 0.97–0.99 bits (1 is the maximum value for the entropy of binary strings), which shows that the keys generated by our protocol can be used for practical applications. The keys generated also pass the NIST [27] entropy test.

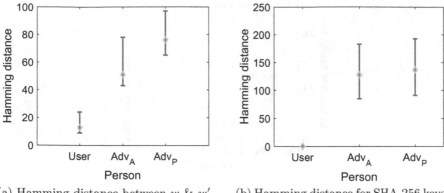

(a) Hamming distance between w & w' (b) Hamming distance for SHA-256 keys

Fig. 6. Hamming distances between w and w' and SHA-256 keys generated by legitimate devices, and passive/active adversaries (w.r.t. legitimate devices) using FEST-GSK protocol.

5.2 Evaluation of FEST-GSK Protocol

In the improved protocol FEST-GSK, since our constructs for fuzzy extractors are based on hamming code, for each key generation session, we calculate the hamming distance between the sets w and w' generated by Hub and other smart wearables respectively, to observe the error pattern among the devices. For quantization, we set $\mathcal{W} = 50$, $n = 4$, and $\alpha = 0.25$. The columns of resulting hamming distance matrix denote the pair-wise hamming distance between w and w' of the four smart wearables. Figure 6a shows the hamming distance calculated for w and w' of legitimate devices (User) for different datasets captured in our experiments. It can be observed that, the hamming distance varies between $\approx$8–23, that lies well within the maximum number of errors that can be corrected by the hamming code [14] in our setting.

Each legitimate smart wearable (of a subject) should generate matching secret key K' similar to Hub (K), in order to use K as a common group secret key. To analyse the number of bits that match in the keys generated by Hub and other smart wearables, we quantify this in terms of hamming distance between the keys K and K'. Figure 6b shows the pair-wise hamming distance calculated between K and K' for different datasets of all legitimate devices as 0. This is due to error correction codes used in our constructs, that eliminate any bit errors between w and w', and hence, the final secret key generated by the legitimate devices using strong extractor and random bit-string x will be the same. Our experimental results show that the bit rate for generating w/w' is $\approx$71 bps. Thus, our improved scheme FEST-GSK takes $\approx$1.81 s to generate a 128-bit w/w' which in-turn generates a strong final key of 256-bits. Figure 7 shows that the entropy of keys generated by legitimate devices is $>$0.975 bits, indicating very high randomness. Also, the generated group keys pass the NIST [27] entropy test which shows that the proposed scheme generates keys with high randomness.

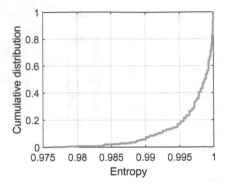

Fig. 7. The group secret keys of legitimate devices show entropy >0.975 bits.

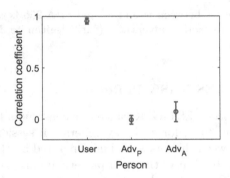

Fig. 8. Pearson correlation coefficient of acceleration on user and adversaries.

6   Security Analysis

In this section, we present the security analysis of our protocols. We basically consider two types of adversaries – passive and active adversaries as described in Sect. 3. In the following sub-sections, we evaluate the correlation of gait characteristics extracted on the smart wearables of user and passive/active adversaries, and measure the bit agreement of the keys and hamming distance for the w and w' generated by different entities.

6.1   Correlation of Gait Characteristics

An important point to ensure successful group secret key generation only by the legitimate smart wearables of a subject is that the processed sensor data on all the devices must be highly correlated [30,36]. To quantify the amount of correlation among the extracted gait characteristics, i.e., acceleration along -G on smart wearable of a user and that of an adversary, we calculate the Pearson Correlation Coefficient ($\mathcal{P}$) [29] for (i) Hub of user with other smart wearables of same user, and (ii) all legitimate devices of subject with all smart wearables

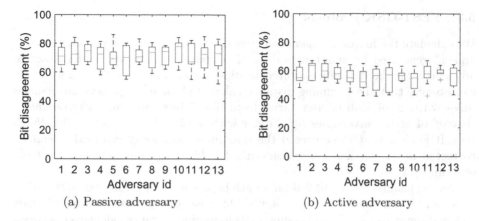

(a) Passive adversary   (b) Active adversary

Fig. 9. Bit disagreement between the final keys generated by adversaries and legitimate devices.

of (a) passive adversary $\mathsf{Adv_P}$, and (b) active adversary $\mathsf{Adv_A}$. The coefficient $\mathcal{P}$ measured for two sets provides a value in the range -1 to 1, with 1 indicating perfect or highest correlation, 0 no correlation, and -1 anti correlation. Figure 8 shows the mean (μ) and standard deviation (σ) of $\mathcal{P}$ calculated for the above three cases, from different datasets captured. It can be observed that, $\mathcal{P}$ for legitimate devices is very high i.e., >0.9 ($\mu = 0.9545$, $\sigma = 0.0287$), whereas, $\mathcal{P}$ for passive adversary is ≈ 0 ($\mu = -0.0080$, $\sigma = 0.0423$), showing no-correlation, since the passive adversary's sensor data will be totally different from that of the legitimate user. The coefficient $\mathcal{P}$ for active adversary is in the positive range, slightly more than 0 ($\mu = 0.0700$, $\sigma = 0.0963$), which shows that the sensor data on active adversary has a small amount of correlation, however, not as high as the legitimate devices of subject. Our observation on the correlation of user and adversary's gait characteristics adheres to the prior report [30]. The researchers have analysed that gait is a very complex and unique characteristic, and hence impersonating another user is extremely difficult [15,24,26,30]. This shows that, only the legitimate devices of a user can extract gait features with very high correlation, that can be used as a common source for secret key generation.

6.2 FEAT-GSK Protocol

In order to check the similarity between the bits generated by legitimate devices and an adversary during key generation, we evaluated the datasets captured during the second set of experiments. Figure 9 shows the bit disagreement between the final 128-bit group secret keys generated by the legitimate devices and passive/active adversaries. We observe that the passive adversaries have bit agreement of only 20–30% with respect to the legitimate devices, whereas, the active adversary's bit agreement is 32–45%. For enhanced security, we suggest generating 256-bit final group secret key and then truncating it to 128-bit by using XOR operation between the first and last 128-bits.

6.3 FEST-GSK Protocol

We calculate the hamming distance between the sets w (128-bit) of Hub of user, and w' generated by smart wearables of (i) passive adversary, and (ii) active adversary, for the datasets captured in different experiments. From Fig. 6a we can observe that the hamming distance calculated for w' of passive adversaries Adv_P w.r.t. w of Hub of user varies from 65–97 bits. Similarly, Fig. 6a shows that w' of active adversaries Adv_A differ with w of legitimate devices by 45–85 bits. It is clear that these exceed the maximum number of errors that can be corrected in our setting, i.e., considering 128-bit w/w', and 4-bits per sample encoding [14].

As the final secret key of 256-bit length is produced by strong extractor using w/w' and a random bit string x, any slight mismatch between w and w' leads to key disagreements. Figure 6b shows the hamming distance calculated between the group secret keys generated by Hub of user and smart wearables of (i) passive adversaries Adv_P, and (ii) active adversaries Adv_A, respectively. It is evident from the above figures that, since the adversaries fail to correct all the errors in w', both the passive and active adversaries cannot reproduce the same group secret key as the legitimate smart wearables of a user despite knowing the helper data H. To avoid brute force attack or guessing the bits of w, we recommend using larger bit strings e.g., 256-bits for w and w'.

7 Related Work

In this section, we explain the state-of-the-art for key generation using accelerometer data and gait, and fuzzy extractor and secure sketches-based applications. The accelerometer sensor present on devices has been exploited by many researchers for authentication/pairing [17,25], key sharing [16,30] and key generation [10,36]. The basic concept of utilizing the accelerometer sensor data for proximity detection of two devices was presented in [17] The authors in [25] have extended the above approach for pairing two mobile devices by observing the correlation pattern when shaken together in a same movement. The pairing devices can be distinguished from other devices that have concurrent movement. These schemes are suitable in a scenario when the two devices can be held in hand, however in the context of wearables, multiple devices are worn on different body parts and it is infeasible to shake them together. The researchers in [16] use heuristic trees to generate key for sensor devices. A threshold value is used to determine the error in key bits. However, an adversary can easily predict the generated key by brute-force attack. The researchers in [36] have proposed pair-wise secret key generation scheme for wearable devices using the acceleration data and gait characteristics of a person. The authors in [30] have presented a group secret key generation and distribution protocol for wearable devices, where, the group key is generated by a single device – hub, when the subject wearing/holding devices is performing routine activities. This key is shared securely with all other body-worn devices by using the gait features of the person by employing fuzzy-vault technique [21] when he/she is walking. In contrast, in our work a group secret key is generated by all the wearable devices simultaneously.

Fuzzy extractors and secure sketches for biometrics-based authentication were initially presented by Dodis et al. [14], and later employed by many researchers for other biometrics security applications, like, face [37] and multimodal systems [33]. The basic concept of these works is that, the user's biometric data is used as a key to authenticate a person in order to access his/her records or data stored in a server. Initially, the biometric data is converted to a uniform string in a noise-tolerant way, and a public helper data is also produced. Whenever the records are to be accessed, the user provides his/her biometrics to the server. If this input is close enough to the original data, the uniform string can be recovered with the help of helper data and the person can be considered as legitimate. Here, the user's biometric acts as the key and is not stored. Boyen et al. [11] have used fuzzy extractors for remote authentication of a client to a server, and the work in [12] extends it for mutual authentication when a secure channel is not available. Sutcu et al. [32] have presented practical challenges in the construction of secure sketch and also proposed secure sketch for face biometrics. The authors in [23] have proposed a secure sketch scheme for asymmetric representations of biometric data.

Our work is different from all the prior work. To the best of our knowledge, we are the first to propose secure group secret key generation for multiple smart wearable devices simultaneously using fuzzy extractors and unique gait features extracted from accelerometer sensor data.

8   Conclusion and Future Work

In this paper, we have presented two novel group secret key generation schemes for smart wearable devices – FEAT-GSK and FEST-GSK, exploiting the unique gait characteristics of a user extracted from accelerometer sensor data and the cryptographic primitives – fuzzy extractor and secure sketch. The FEST-GSK scheme employs error correcting code and strong extractor, and hence, does not require explicit reconciliation and privacy amplification stages of traditional key generation protocols. We have implemented our solutions on android-based smart-wearables and demonstrated experimentally that our FEAT-GSK and FEST-GSK protocols are robust, and can generate 256-bit group secret keys of entropy >0.95 bits in just 3.72 and 1.81 s, respectively, and hence are suitable for practical applications. The security properties of our protocols ensure that only the legitimate devices generate matching group secret keys, whereas the passive and active adversaries cannot reproduce the same keys.

In our future work, we would like to consider multiple smart wearables placed below the waist of a user, e.g., on the knees, legs, ankles, in the pockets, etc., for the evaluation of our protocols. Extracting acceleration due to gait on wearable devices placed on the lower body parts is challenging and needs different approach [30,36]. Also, in our future work we would like to consider other attacks like gait analysis using computer vision techniques.

References

1. Bluetooth Low Energy Specification. https://www.bluetooth.com. Accessed 21 Feb 2018
2. Continua Health Alliance. http://www.continuaalliance.org. Accessed 21 Feb 2018
3. FastICA Java Library. http://sourceforge.net/projects/fastica/. Accessed 21 Feb 2018
4. Fitness Ttrackers. http://www.wareable.com. Accessed 21 Feb 2018
5. IEEE 802.15 WPAN Task Group 6 (TG6) Body Area Networks. http://www.ieee802.org/15/pub/TG6.html. Accessed 21 Feb 2018
6. Moto E2 Phone. https://www.motorola.com. Accessed 21 Feb 2018
7. Samsung Smart Watch. https://www.samsung.com. Accessed 21 Feb 2018
8. Smart Glasses. https://www.vuzix.com/Products/M100-Smart-Glasses. Accessed 21 Feb 2018
9. Wearable Tech: A Developer's Security Nightmare. https://developers.redhat.com. Accessed 21 Feb 2018
10. Bichler, D., Stromberg, G., Huemer, M., Löw, M.: Key generation based on acceleration data of shaking processes. In: Krumm, J., Abowd, G.D., Seneviratne, A., Strang, T. (eds.) UbiComp 2007. LNCS, vol. 4717, pp. 304–317. Springer, Heidelberg (2007). https://doi.org/10.1007/978-3-540-74853-3_18
11. Boyen, X.: Reusable cryptographic fuzzy extractors. In: CCS (2004)
12. Boyen, X., Dodis, Y., Katz, J., Ostrovsky, R., Smith, A.: Secure remote authentication using biometric data. In: Cramer, R. (ed.) EUROCRYPT 2005. LNCS, vol. 3494, pp. 147–163. Springer, Heidelberg (2005). https://doi.org/10.1007/11426639_9
13. Cover, T.M., Thomas, J.A.: Elements of Information Theory. Wiley, New York (1991)
14. Dodis, Y., Ostrovsky, R., Reyzin, L., Smith, A.: Fuzzy extractors: how to generate strong keys from biometrics and other noisy data. SIAM J. Comput. 38(1), 97–139 (2008)
15. Gafurov, D., Snekkenes, E., Buvarp, T.E.: Robustness of biometric gait authentication against impersonation attack. In: OTM Confederated International Workshops (2006)
16. Groza, B., Mayrhofer, R.: SAPHE: simple accelerometer based wireless pairing with heuristic trees. In: MoMM (2012)
17. Holmquist, L.E., Mattern, F., Schiele, B., Alahuhta, P., Beigl, M., Gellersen, H.-W.: Smart-its friends: a technique for users to easily establish connections between smart artefacts. In: Abowd, G.D., Brumitt, B., Shafer, S. (eds.) UbiComp 2001. LNCS, vol. 2201, pp. 116–122. Springer, Heidelberg (2001). https://doi.org/10.1007/3-540-45427-6_10
18. Hyvärinen, A.: Fast and robust fixed-point algorithms for independent component analysis. IEEE TNN 10(3), 626–634 (1999)
19. Javali, C., Revadigar, G., Ding, M., Jha, S.: Secret key generation by virtual link estimation. In: BodyNets (2015)
20. Javali, C., Revadigar, G., Libman, L., Jha, S.: SeAK: secure authentication and key generation protocol based on dual antennas for wireless body area networks. In: Saxena, N., Sadeghi, A.-R. (eds.) RFIDSec 2014. LNCS, vol. 8651, pp. 74–89. Springer, Cham (2014). https://doi.org/10.1007/978-3-319-13066-8_5
21. Javali, C., Revadigar, G., Rasmussen, K.B., Hu, W., Jha, S.: I am alice, i was in wonderland: secure location proof generation and verification protocol. In: IEEE LCN (2016)

22. Kuruwatti, N., Nayana, N.Y., Sarole, N., Revadigar, G., Javali, C.: LQI-key: symmetric key generation scheme for internet-of-things (IoT) devices using wireless channel link quality. In: ICAECC (2018)
23. Li, Q., Guo, M., Chang, E.C.: Fuzzy extractors for asymmetric biometric representations. In: CVPRW (2008)
24. Liu, L.-F., Jia, W., Zhu, Y.-H.: Survey of gait recognition. In: Huang, D.-S., Jo, K.-H., Lee, H.-H., Kang, H.-J., Bevilacqua, V. (eds.) ICIC 2009. LNCS (LNAI), vol. 5755, pp. 652–659. Springer, Heidelberg (2009). https://doi.org/10.1007/978-3-642-04020-7_70
25. Mayrhofer, R., Gellersen, H.: Shake well before use: intuitive and secure pairing of mobile devices. IEEE TMC 8(6), 792–806 (2009)
26. Mjaaland, B., Bours, P., Gligoroski, D.: Gait mimicking - attack resistance testing of gait authentication systems. In: NISK (2009)
27. NIST: A Statistical Test Suite for Random and Pseudorandom Number Generators for Cryptographic Applications (2010)
28. Revadigar, G., Javali, C., Asghar, H.J., Rasmussen, K.B., Jha, S.: Mobility independent secret key generation for wearable health-care devices. In: BodyNets (2015)
29. Revadigar, G., Javali, C., Hu, W., Jha, S.: DLINK: dual link based radio frequency fingerprinting for wearable devices. In: IEEE LCN (2015)
30. Revadigar, G., Javali, C., Xu, W., Vasilakos, A.V., Hu, W., Jha, S.: Accelerometer and fuzzy vault-based secure group key generation and sharing protocol for smart wearables. IEEE TIFS 12(10), 2467–2482 (2017)
31. Shi, L., Yuan, J., Yu, S., Li, M.: ASK-BAN: authenticated secret key extraction utilizing channel characteristics for body area networks. In: WiSec (2013)
32. Sutcu, Y., Li, Q., Memon, N.: Protecting biometric templates with sketch: theory and practice. IEEE TIFS 2(3), 503–512 (2007)
33. Sutcu, Y., Li, Q., Memon, N.: Secure biometric templates from fingerprint-face features. In: IEEE CVPR, pp. 1–6 (2007)
34. Venkatasubramanian, K.K., Banerjee, A., Gupta, S.K.S.: PSKA: usable and secure key agreement scheme for body area networks. IEEE TITB 14(1), 60–68 (2010)
35. Voris, J., Saxena, N., Halevi, T.: Accelerometers and randomness: perfect together. In: WiSec (2011)
36. Xu, W., Javali, C., Revadigar, G., Luo, C., Bergmann, N., Hu, W.: Gait-key: a gait-based shared secret key generation protocol for wearable devices. ACM TOSN 13(1), 6:1–6:27 (2017)
37. Zhou, X.: Template protection and its implementation in 3D face recognition systems. SPIE 6539, 65390L (2007)

Unchained Identities: Putting a Price on Sybil Nodes in Mobile Ad Hoc Networks

Arne Bochem$^{(\boxtimes)}$, Benjamin Leiding, and Dieter Hogrefe

Institute of Computer Science, University of Goettingen, Goettingen, Germany
{arne.bochem,benjamin.leiding,hogrefe}@cs.uni-goettingen.de

Abstract. As mobile ad hoc networks (MANETs) and similar decentralized, self-organizing networks grow in number and popularity, they become worthwhile targets for attackers. Sybil attacks are a widespread issue for such networks and can be leveraged to increase the impact of other attacks, allowing attackers to threaten the integrity of the whole network. Authentication or identity management systems that prevent users from setting up arbitrary numbers of nodes are often missing in MANETs. As a result, attackers are able to introduce nodes with a multitude of identities into the network, thereby controlling a substantial fraction of the system and undermining its functionality and security. Additionally, MANETs are often partitioned and lack Internet access. As a result, implementing conventional measures based on central authorities is difficult. This paper fills the gap by introducing a decentralized blockchain-based identity system called *Unchained*. *Unchained* binds identities of nodes to addresses on a blockchain and economically disincentivizes the production of spurious identities by raising the costs of placing large numbers of Sybil identities in a network. Care is taken to ensure that circumventing *Unchained* results in costs similar or higher than following the protocol. We describe an offline verification scheme, detail the functionalities of the concept, discuss upper- and lower-bounds of security guarantees and evaluate *Unchained* based on case-studies.

Keywords: MANET · Security · Sybil attack · Blockchain
Identity · Authentication

1 Introduction

Stimulated by the persistent growth and expansion of the Internet of Things (IoT) [21,25], as well as progressing digitalization of our daily life, e.g., [15,29], wireless ad hoc networks such as mobile ad hoc networks (MANETs) or vehicular ad hoc networks (VANETs) become more common and popular. MANETs and their sub-types are often heavily partitioned, with transient connections occurring between nodes due to their mobility, resulting in a constantly changing network topology. Furthermore, communication in MANETs is usually organized in a decentralized manner without a connection to any central authority

© ICST Institute for Computer Sciences, Social Informatics and Telecommunications Engineering 2018
R. Beyah et al. (Eds.): SecureComm 2018, LNICST 254, pp. 358–374, 2018.
https://doi.org/10.1007/978-3-030-01701-9_20

or the Internet [19, 28]. As a result, these networks are worthwhile and easy targets for attackers. This raises the issue of providing proper security and privacy protection mechanisms in order defend them against attacks. Without such, the distributed nature of MANETs and their lack of a central authentication authority leaves them easy targets for Sybil attacks. This type of attack is a common issue in large-scale peer-to-peer (P2P) systems, where hostile or faulty computing elements threaten the security of the whole network. Single faulty entities may be able to present multiple identities, thereby controlling a substantial fraction of the system, consequently undermining its functionality and security [12].

Several techniques focus on preventing Sybil nodes from joining a network at all [11, 16]. Other approaches attempt to detect them when they are already part of the network [3, 30]. One of the key enablers of Sybil attacks is the absence of a mechanism that prevents attackers from setting up arbitrary numbers of (virtual) nodes. In MANETs, there usually is no central authority that controls or administers the network. Since detecting Sybil nodes after joining a network is a cumbersome and inaccurate task, we propose the *Unchained* protocol which introduces economic disincentives of introducing Sybil nodes to a network by leveraging blockchain technology and combining it with an offline verification approach.

Unchained uses blockchain technology to bind ad hoc network node identities to blockchain-based wallet addresses, i.e. public/private key pairs, and requires a certain deposit to be made on the blockchain in order to join the network. Circumventing the protocol and introducing a Sybil node means investing even more financial assets than it would cost to create an *Unchained* identity the regular way. Due to its offline verification approach, *Unchained* operates in environments without internet access and without direct access to the underlying blockchain, thereby "unchaining" its security mechanism. This allows its use in MANETs with no or merely intermittent Internet connectivity.

The remainder of this paper is structured as follows: Sect. 2 introduces related works and supplementary literature. Section 3 focuses on the operational details of the *Unchained* approach. Afterwards, Sect. 4 details security properties of the protocol and explains how to customize the protocol for various use cases, while Sect. 5 elaborates on different options to handle difficulty changes in the underlying cryptocurrency. Section 6 provides a discussion and evaluation based on case studies. Finally, Sect. 7 concludes this work and provides an outlook on future work.

2 Supplementary Literature and Related Works

This section provides background information and describes related works regarding previous approaches to solve the issue of Sybil attacks. Section 2.1 provides general information on the concepts of blockchain technology, terms and frameworks. Section 2.2 focuses on related works.

2.1   Blockchain Technology

A blockchain consists of a (theoretically) unlimited number of blocks which are chained together in a chronological order. Each block consists of transactions that successfully passed a validation procedure. As illustrated in Fig. 1, the collected valid transactions result in a new block that is added to the existing blockchain. The blockchain concept, also called distributed ledger system, is most notably known for providing the foundation of the peer-to-peer (P2P) cryptocurrency and payment system Bitcoin (₿) [22].

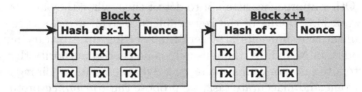

Fig. 1. Blockchain structure, adapted from [22].

A key enabler of blockchains is the so called mining process, allowing to achieve a global consensus on which transactions to include in the next block in a decentralized way. Currently, the most common blockchain consensus algorithm is based on proof-of-work, which is used by Bitcoin, Ethereum [32], and others. When collecting transactions to form a new block, participants have to solve a computationally hard puzzle that is referred to as proof-of-work. A proof of work is a piece of data that is difficult to produce but easy to verify and satisfies certain requirements. Bitcoin's proof-of-work is based on searching for a nonce (value) that when hashed together with a block header, begins with a number of zero bits. "The average work required is exponential in the number of zero bits required and can be verified by executing a single hash" [22]. The varying number of zero bits is used to adjust the difficulty of finding a valid block. Hardware speed ups and growing user participation in building blocks result in more computing power being available for the mining process. In order to publish new blocks in, on average, a given time intervals, the difficulty of the proof-of-work is adjusted depending on the available computing power. In the case of Bitcoin, the target time per block is ten minutes. In the case that new blocks are generated too fast, the difficulty increases, if new blocks are generated too slowly, it is decreases.

As soon as a block with a valid nonce is found, the block is published and attached to the chain. All participants verify the submitted proof-of-work for correctness, the included transactions for validity and accept it as the new latest block. Since each block depends on its predecessor, changing the content of a block requires an infeasible recalculation of all successor blocks. The first user to find a new block also receives a block reward. In the case of Bitcoin, this reward is, as of December 2017, 12.5 ₿ plus additional transaction fees. These block rewards have both the purpose of disseminating the currency among users, as well as incentivizing miners to spend energy on securing the blockchain. If multiple blocks are found at the same chain height, mining may proceed on either block and the longer chain is considered valid.

2.2 Related Works

Several other projects focus on Sybil attack prevention and Sybil attack detection in different network environments, therefore we only highlight some further publications. SybilGuard [35] is one of the well-known protocols that aims to limit the corruptive influence of Sybil attacks in peer-to-peer networks. The SybilLimit protocol is an advanced version of SybilGuard and aims to defend online social networks from Sybil nodes [34]. SybilGuard as well as SybilLimit rely on human-established trust relationships, hence they cannot be applied to mobile ad hoc networks.

[3,30] focus on Sybil attack detection in MANETs, whereas [33] targets the detection and localization of Sybil nodes in VANETs. In contrast to these approaches, Unchained focuses on preventing sybil nodes from joining a network instead of detecting them when they are already part of the network.

Furthermore, [11,23] try to prevent and detect Sybil attacks in sensor networks, whereas Unchained focuses on mobile ad hoc networks in general.

Blockchains matured and grew in popularity, resulting in various blockchain architectures, e.g., Ethereum [32], Qtum [10], or IOTA [27], as well blockchain-based applications and use cases, e.g., as a platform for IoT applications [9,26], applications in the automotive sector [18], in the finance sector [8,24] or as a part of security and authentication protocols [17,20,26].

3 Unchained Identities in MANETs

When setting up a new network, e.g., a MANET, each node is equipped with an identity that uniquely identifies the specific device within the network. When deployed, communicating devices have to validate each others identities for security and privacy reasons before exchanging information. The following section describes the general process of creating new identities when flashing the firmware to a device as well as validating identities. Both of these processes are based on blockchain technology and do not require any trusted third parties apart from a decentralized cryptocurrency's P2P network. For illustration purposes, we use the Bitcoin network in the following sections. However, *Unchained* can be implemented on all proof-of-work based Blockchains.

3.1 Creating a New Identity

The process of creating a new unchained identity is illustrated in Fig. 2 and assumes that a key pair, i.e. public and private key, presenting a Bitcoin wallet address already exists and that it holds a certain amount of Bitcoin. The amount contained within this address needs to be sufficient to make the deposit necessary in the first step of the identity creation process. First, the coins in the Bitcoin wallet are transferred to a pre-defined deposit address (step 2) and the resulting transaction is mined into a block by the Bitcoin network as part of Block$_X$ (step 3). In the subsequent step 4, an *Identity proof* is created based on the information from the minded block. The proof contains the block header (block number, block hash, difficulty target of the block), the deposit transaction, hashes for the merkle tree allowing to prove that the transaction is part of the block, the index number of the deposit address in the block as well as the public key.

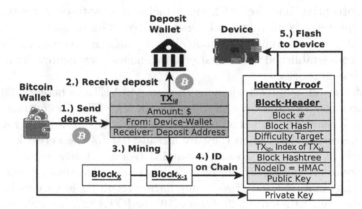

Fig. 2. Creating a new identity.

Furthermore, a unique *NodeID* is calculated based on the Hash Message Authentication Code (HMAC) as illustrated in Eq. 1–3. First, the block's proof-of-work hash is used as a key for the HMAC calculation in combination with the index number of the deposit transaction in the block. The purpose of this approach is to prevent attackers from attempting to create node IDs matching arbitrary attacker defined criteria. Since the ID depends on the deposit transaction, but also on the block's proof-of-work hash, guessing the node ID is equivalent to predicting the correct hash of the next block of the Bitcoin blockchain and therefore not feasible.

$$k_{\mathrm{HMAC}} := \mathrm{Block}_{\mathrm{PoWHash}} \tag{1}$$

$$\mathrm{TXindex} := \text{index of deposit TX in Block} \tag{2}$$

$$\mathrm{nodeID} := \mathrm{HMAC}(k_{\mathrm{HMAC}}, \mathrm{TXindex}) \tag{3}$$

Finally, the constructed *identity proof* and the node's private key are flashed onto the node, which is afterwards deployed in the network.

3.2   Identity Validation

Communication between nodes of a network is an essential functionality of ad hoc network. Before transmitting application data, nodes verify each others' identity in a bidirectional manner in order to secure and protect sensible network data.

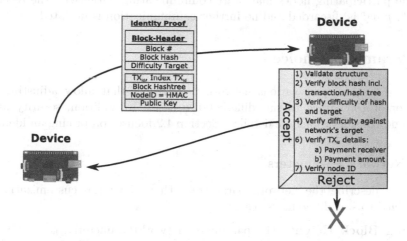

Fig. 3. Overview of the validation process.

The validation of node identities is performed upon first contact of each two nodes, such as a two-way handshake or the broadcasting of identity information to let nodes learn about their neighbors. In the following, we describe how participating nodes verify an identity upon receipt of its *identity proof*. A graphical overview of this procedure is given in Fig. 3. In the case of a two-way handshake, the procedure is simply repeated on each side after receiving the *identity proof*. Another potential scenario is a number of nodes broadcasting their *identity proofs* and verifying received *identity proofs*, allowing them to connect to surrounding peers when necessary.

First, the structure of the *identity proof* is validated. A valid *identity proof* contains a block header, a deposit transaction, the hashes of a merkle tree proving that the transaction is part of the specific block, a node ID and the public key of the node, which was also used to sign the deposit transaction. At this point, it is also verified that the block's height is above networkParameter$_{height}$ Afterwards, the block corresponding to the block header is verified based on the hashes from the merkle tree that is used to verify the transaction's presence in the block. Next, the node checks that the difficulty of the block hash matches the difficulty target in the block header and that the difficulty target is at least networkParameter$_{minDifficulty}$ for the given block height.

Once these properties are confirmed, the deposit transactions is verified. It contains a payment greater or equal to networkParameter$_{amount}$, which is sent to the mandatory receiver address networkParameter$_{receiver}$. The transaction has to be correctly signed with exactly one key pair that is also used for any future cryptographically secure (encryption, signatures, key exchange) communications with other nodes and the public key that is included in the *identity proof*. Finally, it is verified that the node ID matches the formula given in Eq. 3.

If all steps described above are successful, the validation process finishes and the participating nodes may start communicating. Otherwise the received *identity proof* is discarded and no further communication is initiated.

4   Parameter Choice

In Sect. 4.1 we discuss various network parameters that allow adjusting the behavior of *Unchained* to suit different use cases. In addition, security properties and considerations are detailed. Section 4.2 focuses on pricing an identity.

4.1   Network Parameters

First, we describe the network parameters that allow the customization of *Unchained* to suit different use cases.

Starting Block Height. The parameter $networkParameter_{height}$ defines the minimum block height that is accepted for *identity proofs*. The block height is defined by the number of blocks preceding a block on the blockchain. The genesis block's block height is zero [4]. The block height corresponds to the block height at the start of the network's lifetime. By rejecting *identity proofs* at lower block heights, there is no need to consider allowing blocks with significantly lower difficulties.

Deposit Address. $networkParameter_{receiver}$ is the deposit address to which a transaction, used when creating an *identity proof*, sends a certain amount of Bitcoin. The main property of this address is that funds sent there should not be recoverable by an attacker that is trying to create a large number of identities. Hence, using transaction fees instead of a deposit is not a viable option since an attacker may mine a valid block on their own and directly recover all funds. Currently, *Unchained* provides three different options that define what happens to the deposit.

The first option is proof-of-burn [7], where an invalid receiving address with no (known) existing private key is used. As a result, the sent deposit cannot be recovered. This method is secure, but not elegant since it destroys a certain amount of Bitcoin and the Bitcoin supply is strictly limited by the underlying Bitcoin protocol.

The second option is that the software of the network secured with *Unchained* is developed by a certain entity, or the network is maintained or controlled by a certain entity. The entity may choose to use an address under its control as the receiving address. This way, the developers or maintainers of the network could raise funds for further development by receiving Bitcoin through the creation of identities used by users of the network. As the developers have an interest in keeping the network secure, this approach is a viable choice that prevents attackers from recovering funds.

A third approach is to use the donation address of a charity. Unless the charity itself has an interest in attacking the network or is otherwise compromised, an attacker is unlikely to be able to recover the funds. If desired by a network operator, they may choose to allow multiple deposit addresses to be used. Hence, users may choose between different charities when making a donation to create an *Unchained* identity.

Deposit Amount. The networkParameter$_{amount}$ parameter determines the minimum deposit size required to set up a new identity. The amount is chosen in such a way that it is affordable for those who would like to participate in the network, while still being high enough to disincentivize the creation of large numbers of Sybil nodes. For larger networks, the deposit size may be lower since the network may tolerate higher numbers of spurious identities before an attacker gains a tangible benefit from their use. Section 4.2 details further considerations, limits and implications that depend on the deposit size.

A potential alternative is to use a small value for networkParameter$_{amount}$ and introducing a bigger networkParameter$_{lockedAmount}$ value. The first amounts gets sent to networkParameter$_{receiver}$, while the second amount is sent back to the identity's owner, but locked up using the `CheckLockTimeVerify` output [31] of a transaction or another type of smart contract. The locktime is equal to the lifetime of the identity. This way users may recover their funds after leaving the network, while ensuring that the creation of high numbers of concurrent identities still lock up significant amounts of capital.

Minimum Difficulty. This parameter defines the minimum amount of work that is required to generate a new block that may be used to build an *identity proof*. While Sect. 5 details more sophisticated approaches to control the allowable difficulty of blocks for *identity proofs*, the most basic way is to set a simple minimum difficulty parameter networkParameter$_{minDifficulty}$ that matches the underlying blockchain's difficulty at the time of setting up the network using *Unchained*. Alternatively, a value slightly below this value may be chosen to allow for drops in network difficulty.

If the parameter is hardcoded, it should be selected sufficiently low. If Bitcoin's target difficulty drops below the hardcoded value, it becomes impossible to create further identities. To avoid this issue, implementations should set networkParameter$_{minDifficulty}$ dynamically as described in Sect. 5.

Updates. Changes in the valuation of Bitcoin, difficulty or simply the general operating environment of the secured network may change over time. Therefore, it may become necessary to update the parameters described above to ensure that the network is operating as desired.

Assuming an entity that is maintaining and developing the network, it is possible to periodically distributed signed bundles of updated network parameters, including the block height at which this bundle should take effect. After the bundle is published, users who generate fresh identities should attach the update to their *identity proof* before flashing it onto their node. Similar considerations are also described in Sect. 5 with a special focus on difficulty updates.

4.2 Pricing an Identity

An attacker trying to create a large number of identities aims to minimize costs. One option is to mine a block conforming to the networkParameter$_{minDifficulty}$ parameter, filling it solely with deposit transactions, but never publishing it to the Bitcoin network. Since *Unchained* does not verify the full blockchain, these transactions do not even require valid inputs. However, mining a block with valid difficulty and not publishing it incurs a high opportunity cost, as well as energy cost. Hence, instead of paying for the identities, the attacker pays for the hashing power used to create the block. While the energy costs may vary, depending on location, the opportunity cost is easy to quantify and equal to the block reward plus additional transaction fees.

Given the current block size (1 MB), minimum transaction size (224 B) and block reward (12.5 ฿ plus fees) of Bitcoin, this also leads to an upper limit on the price for one identity, as given in Eq. 4, with the current maximum amount given in Eq. 5 [1,2,7].

$$\text{amount}_{\max} = \text{block reward} \cdot \frac{\min \text{ TX size}}{\max \text{ block size}} \tag{4}$$

$$= 12.5\text{฿} \cdot \frac{224\,\text{B}}{1\,\text{MB}} = 2.8\,\text{m฿} \tag{5}$$

Given the current price of Bitcoin as of 2017-10-29 at approximately \$10399 [5,6], the resulting maximum price per identity is roughly equivalent to \$29. Going above this limit makes it cheaper for an attacker to generate a fake block than simply paying for the identities, as long as fees and energy costs are disregarded. Most networks will likely set a lower value than 2.8 m฿ for networkParameter$_{amount}$, in order to make identities more affordable for users and anticipate volatility with regards to Bitcoin valuation.

5   Handling Difficulty Adjustments

Our system has to adapt to changes in the target difficulty of the underlying cryptocurrency. In the case of Bitcoin, the difficulty is adjusted every 2016 blocks. This is equivalent to roughly two weeks. These adjustments are made to keep the time interval between each block at, in the case of Bitcoin, on average 10 min. To handle these adjustments, we propose multiple approaches with different trade-offs.

Each node keeps a list of accepted target difficulties for each 2016 block interval. If the accepted target difficulty of an interval is adjusted upwards due to new information, identities confirmed using blocks with lower difficulty are retroactively invalidated. When the accepted target difficulty is lowered, it may be prudent to retroactively accept discarded peers into the network. However, since invalid identities are unlikely to be stored, the second case is unlikely to be implemented. The different approaches of handling difficulty changes concern the way this list of accepted target difficulties is updated.

5.1 Maximum Seen Difficulty

The first approach is both simple to implement as well as fully decentralized. The list of accepted target difficulties is initialized to zero or a known history at the point the node is initialized. Whenever an *identity proof* is received by a node, it looks up the target difficulty for that block in the list of difficulties. If both difficulty values match, the identity is accepted. In case the difficulty of the received *identity proof* is lower, the identity is discarded. Alternatively, when the difficulty of the received identity is higher, it is accepted and the target difficulty in the list is updated. If the list of accepted target difficulties was initialized with a known history however, these known-good values should not be overwritten even if an identity with a higher difficulty is encountered.

This solution allows the eventual detection and invalidation of forged identities that were validated using blocks of insufficiently high difficulty, as long as a connection to an honest node from the same two week period is made at some point. No infrastructure in addition to the previously described system is necessary.

As a caveat, this method is vulnerable to a denial of service attack. Assuming an attacker is able to mine a block targeting a difficulty that is higher than the difficulty of the underlying cryptocurrency and uses the block in an *identity proof*, the targeted nodes will update their lists of target difficulties accordingly, invalidating all regular identities that were generated during the timeframe corresponding to the malicious block. However, mining a block targeting a higher difficulty is even more expensive than mining a regular block. This issue can be mitigated by combining this approach with one of the two following methods. At the same time, this method can be used as a fallback solution for both of them.

5.2 Bundled Updates

Assuming network is run by a single operator, the operator may publish signed messages containing the target difficulty for each 2016 block range. The message is appended to each *identity proof*, setting the target difficulty in the list to the provided value. A drawback of this solution is that, in case the operator ceases to exist, no further difficulty updates can be broadcasted, leaving new nodes unable to join the network. However, when combining this approach with the mechanism from Sect. 5.1, only nodes worried about denial of service attacks need to attach update messages to their *identity proofs*. Nevertheless, joining the network without one of these messages also remains as an alternative. Nonetheless, when the operator ceases operations, the mitigation for the denial of service attack vector also ceases to be functional.

5.3   Majority Vote

Rather than relying on a single operator as in Sect. 5.2, nodes may choose to accept signed difficulty updates from multiple providers. One or more of these messages may then be attached to an *identity proof*. The values of each update provider are stored in the list of target difficulties. In the event that for any interval mismatching difficulty update messages are detected, the majority value is considered the true difficulty target. Whenever there is no majority, the highest value is treated as the true difficulty target. In the case of a majority, nodes might mistrust future update messages provided by providers belonging to the minority.

This approach has multiple benefits over the previous approach. There is no single point of failure that prevents the network from growing. Additionally, supposing an attacker is able to trick a difficulty update provider to forge an update, the result is not necessarily a successful attack, as the attacker is still missing a majority that accepts the update, Hence, the attacker has to compromise at least 50% of the update providers to perform a denial of service attack.

Moreover, this approach is compatible with the solution from Sect. 5.1, allowing nodes to join the network even without access to any signed difficulty update messages.

6   Evaluation

The following section focuses on evaluating the *Unchained* protocol and the provided security guarantees. Since *Unchained's* security guarantees mainly depend on the difficulty level as well as the token price of the underlying proof-of-work blockchain, we analyze how changing difficulty levels and token prices would have affected the Sybil attack prevention mechanism of a fictional MANET deployed in December 2016. Sections 6.1 and 6.2 perform analysis based on the assumption that the Bitcoin blockchain is used, and Sect. 6.3 uses the same scenario based on the Ethereum blockchain. We choose these two chains for several reasons: First, they are the most popular and most utilized proof-of-work blockchains that currently exist. Second, the different changes in difficulty and price cover important corner cases such as increasing and decreasing difficulties over time with sudden drops and raises. We assume a scenario of a MANET that was initially deployed in December 2016 with nodes continually joining and leaving the network and operated until the time of writing this work in November 2017.

6.1   Bitcoin Difficulty Analysis

The difficulty level of the Bitcoin blockchain is adjusted every 2016 blocks, which is equivalent to 14 days given a blocktime of ten minutes per block. As illustrated in Fig. 4a, the difficulty level is steadily rising with two minor exception in August and November 2017. At the same time, as shown in Fig. 4a, the Bitcoin price itself also increased almost steadily by a factor of ten within the last twelve months.

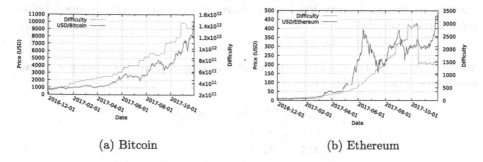

(a) Bitcoin   (b) Ethereum

Fig. 4. Average daily price in USD and block difficulty level between Dec. 2016 and Nov. 2017 (Source: [5,6,14]).

As already discussed in Sect. 4 the lower bound of security guarantees provided by *Unchained* is always the lowest level of difficulty and the lowest price per block that occurred during the existence of the network. Given the initial deployment of our hypothetical MANET in December 2016, all nodes joining at later stages have higher security guarantees than the initial nodes due to an increased block difficulty and price. As discussed in Sect. 4.2, the price is only a theoretical measurement for security guarantees, since it is up to the network operator to decide the minimum price of a node's identity. However, increasing token prices and therefore also increasing block prices, may also result in more expensive identities thereby raising the bar for a Sybil attacks.

Assuming a MANET setup at the beginning of November 2017, days before the decreasing Bitcoin price in (see Fig. 4a), reflects the exact opposite where it becomes less expensive to introduce new identities to the system for a short period of time. However, as discussed previously, it is up to the network operator to decided whether to pick the maximum possible identity-per-block-price or a lower price. For practical reasons it is likely that most operators pick a lower price and therefore minor price declines do not affect the security guarantees of our example MANET a lot. Moreover, it is also up to the network operator to define a minimum identity-price that is higher than the identity-per-block-price since it is still unlikely that a malicious entity has the computational power to mine a block with a matching difficulty level, given the vast hashing power of Bitcoin's mining pools.

6.2 Bitcoin Price Analysis

Using the historic price data gathered for Fig. 4a, going back until July 17th 2010, it is possible to calculate for each date, on which a network using *Unchained* could have been started, the highest drop in price and thus security level experienced by the network. While future developments cannot reliably predicted, this provides an intuition on the historic worst case performance of *Unchained*. In Table 1, the proportion of starting dates that would have lead to a drop on any subsequent day of at least a given percentage is given. Only for 0.1% of possible starting dates the security level would have at any later point dropped below 10% of the given date.

Table 1. Affected starting dates after which the Bitcoin price drops below a certain percentage of the given day's price.

Drop to	Affected started dates
<10%	0.1%
<20%	2.8%
<30%	8.5%
<40%	13.5%
<50%	18.0%
<60%	22.8%
<70%	27.2%
<80%	36.2%
<90%	49.5%
<100%	77.5%

Historically, high drops in security level only occur very rarely. Smaller drops occur more frequently, with almost 50% of possible starting days experiencing drops of at least 10% at some point in the future. While most networks will be able to tolerate smaller drops in security level, raising Bitcoin prices can also be an issue, as they can make identities too expensive for regular users. Considering this, for networks intended to exist over long time frames, provisions for an update mechanism for networkParameter$_{amount}$ should be made. In case mass adoption occurs, the volatility level of cryptocurrencies and fiat currency is expected to converge. Hence, Unchained's level of security will stabilize as well.

6.3   Ethereum Difficulty Analysis

Unchained is blockchain agnostic as long as the underlying chain architecture uses a proof-of-work consensus algorithm. Therefore, we also analyze how the changing difficulty levels and token prices of the Ethereum blockchain and how this would have affected the Sybil attack prevention mechanism of our fictional MANET deployed in December 2016.

Similar to the Bitcoin price, the Ethereum price also increased heavily, starting around $8 in December 2016 to more than $450 at the end of November

2017, even though the Ethereum price suffered some decreases in July 2017. Ethereum's block difficulty, illustrated in Fig. 4b, also increased over the last twelve month. However, a sudden drop occurred on October 16 due to a difficulty adjusting hard-fork of the Ethereum network [13]. Nevertheless, even the reduced difficulty level is far higher than the initial level in December 2016.

As a result, the security guarantee evaluation results are similar to the Bitcoin evaluation of Sect. 6.1. MANET nodes setup in December 2016 with the initial difficulty are cheaper and easier to create in terms of identity price and block difficulty. All nodes created afterwards provided higher security guarantees. When focusing on the timeframe briefly before and after the difficulty adjustment, identities created before the adjustment are less difficult than identities created afterwards. The same applies for the price of identities both before and after the price drop of Ether in July 2016 as illustrated in Fig. 4b.

In both the case of the Bitcoin as well as the Ethereum blockchain, price and difficulty increased heavily within the last 12 month. As a result, the lower bound of provided security is defined by the earliest nodes that joined the test MANET when created, since their *identity proofs* depends on the lowest block difficulty and identity price. All following node identities provide security guarantees above this lower bound. Furthermore, given the case that the difficulty levels will likely not increase indefinitely and remain somehow static (with minor fluctuations) at some point in the future, *Unchained's* lower and upper bounds will also converge and be less volatile.

7   Conclusion and Future Work

Detecting Sybil node attacks is major issue of large-scale P2P networks where malicious nodes threaten the security of the overall system. After joining a network, detecting such nodes is a cumbersome and inaccurate task. In this work we introduce a protocol for a decentralized blockchain-based identity system with offline verification that raises the difficulty of introducing high numbers of Sybil nodes to a network by providing economic disincentives.

Unchained uses blockchain technology to bind ad hoc network node identities to blockchain-based wallet addresses, i.e., public/private key pairs. In order to join the network, a proof-of-identity is created for each device. The proof is derived from a deposit transaction made from the wallet address to a deposit address and flashed to the node afterwards. Nodes validate each others' identities using the uniquely generated *identity proofs*.

Circumventing the protocol and introducing a Sybil node is equivalent to investing more financial assets than it would cost to create a malicious block on the blockchain. In addition, *identity proofs* are designed in such a way that no Internet access or direct connection to the underlying blockchain is required after the initial setup of the ad hoc network, thereby raising the bar to introduce Sybil nodes to even highly partitioned networks.

We detail the network parameters and update mechanism of *Unchained* and discuss upper- and lower-bounds of security guarantees. Finally, an evaluation based on a hypothetical MANET deployed leveraging the Bitcoin and Ethereum blockchain is used to analyze the protocol's security properties depending on the block difficulty and token prices between December 2016 and November 2017.

For future work, we plan to generalize the protocol and not only focus on MANETs or other ad hoc networks and instead integrate *Unchained* into IoT environments. Furthermore, we intend to explore the feasibility of adapting existing Sybil attack prevention or detection algorithms to consider the node's *identity proof* block difficulty and block price as attributes for their trust scoring systems.

We also aim to implement and deploy the *Unchained* protocol on the Bitcoin as well as Ethereum blockchain and evaluate real-world use-cases.

References

1. Mining - Bitcoin Wiki. https://en.bitcoin.it/w/index.php?title=Mining& oldid=64115#Reward. Accessed 11 Dec 2017
2. Transaction - Bitcoin Wiki. https://en.bitcoin.it/w/index.php?title=Transaction& oldid=63712. Accessed 11 Dec 2017
3. Abbas, S., Merabti, M., Llewellyn-Jones, D., Kifayat, K.: Lightweight sybil attack detection in MANETs. IEEE Syst. J. **7**(2), 236–248 (2013)
4. Bitcoin Project: Bitcoin Developer Guide (2017). https://bitcoin.org/en/developer-guide#proof-of-work. Accessed 18 Dec 2017
5. Bitcoincharts: Bitcoincharts API, Price data (MtGox, BTC-e, BitStamp, Coinbase). https://api.bitcoincharts.com/v1/csv/. Accessed 29 Nov 2017
6. Blockchain.info: Bitcoin Blockchain, Difficulty. https://api.blockchain.info/charts/difficulty?format=csv. Accessed 29 Nov 2017
7. Bonneau, J., Miller, A., Clark, J., Narayanan, A., Kroll, J.A., Felten, E.W.: SoK: research perspectives and challenges for bitcoin and cryptocurrencies. In: 2015 IEEE Symposium on Security and Privacy, pp. 104–121, May 2015
8. Bussmann, O.: The future of finance: fintech, tech disruption, and orchestrating innovation. In: Francioni, R., Schwartz, R.A. (eds.) Equity Markets in Transition: The Value Chain, Price Discovery, Regulation, and Beyond, pp. 473–486. Springer, Cham (2017). https://doi.org/10.1007/978-3-319-45848-9_19
9. Christidis, K., Devetsikiotis, M.: Blockchains and smart contracts for the internet of things. IEEE Access **4**, 2292–2303 (2016)
10. Dai, P., Mahi, N., Earls, J., Norta, A.: Smart-contract value-transfer protocols on a distributed mobile application platform (2017). https://qtum.org/uploads/files/a2772efe4dc8ed1100319c6480195fb1.pdf. Accessed 22 Nov 2017
11. Dhamodharan, U.S.R.K., Vayanaperumal, R.: Detecting and preventing sybil attacks in wireless sensor networks using message authentication and passing method. Sci. World J. **2015** (2015)
12. Douceur, J.R.: The sybil attack. In: Druschel, P., Kaashoek, F., Rowstron, A. (eds.) IPTPS 2002. LNCS, vol. 2429, pp. 251–260. Springer, Heidelberg (2002). https://doi.org/10.1007/3-540-45748-8_24
13. Ethereum Team: Byzantium HF Announcement (2017). https://blog.ethereum.org/2017/10/12/byzantium-hf-announcement/. Accessed 30 Nov 2017
14. Etherscan: Ethereum Charts and Statistics (2017). https://etherscan.io/charts. Accessed 30 Nov 2017

15. Horst, H.A., Miller, D.: Digital Anthropology. A&C Black, London (2013)
16. John, R., Cherian, J.P., Kizhakkethottam, J.J.: A survey of techniques to prevent sybil attacks. In: 2015 International Conference on Soft-Computing and Networks Security (ICSNS), pp. 1–6. IEEE (2015)
17. Leiding, B., Cap, C.H., Mundt, T., Rashidibajgan, S.: Authcoin: validation and authentication in decentralized networks. In: The 10th Mediterranean Conference on Information Systems - MCIS 2016, Cyprus, CY, September 2016
18. Leiding, B., Memarmoshrefi, P., Hogrefe, D.: Self-managed and blockchain-based vehicular ad-hoc networks. In: Proceedings of the 2016 ACM International Joint Conference on Pervasive and Ubiquitous Computing: Adjunct, pp. 137–140. ACM (2016)
19. Macker, J.: Mobile ad-hoc networking (MANET): routing protocol performance issues and evaluation considerations, RFC 2501 (1999)
20. McCorry, P., Shahandashti, S.F., Clarke, D., Hao, F.: Authenticated key exchange over bitcoin. In: Chen, L., Matsuo, S. (eds.) SSR 2015. LNCS, vol. 9497, pp. 3–20. Springer, Cham (2015). https://doi.org/10.1007/978-3-319-27152-1_1
21. van der Meulen, R.: Gartner says 8.4 billion connected "things" will be in use in 2017, up 31 percent from 2016 (2017). https://www.gartner.com/newsroom/id/3598917. Accessed 01 Nov 2017
22. Nakamoto, S.: Bitcoin: a peer-to-peer electronic cash system (2008). https://bitcoin.org/bitcoin.pdf. Accessed 26 Jan 2017
23. Newsome, J., Shi, E., Song, D., Perrig, A.: The sybil attack in sensor networks: analysis & defenses. In: Proceedings of the 3rd International Symposium on Information Processing in Sensor Networks, pp. 259–268. ACM (2004)
24. Nguyen, Q.K.: Blockchain - a financial technology for future sustainable development. In: International Conference on Green Technology and Sustainable Development (GTSD), pp. 51–54. IEEE (2016)
25. Nordrum, A.: Popular internet of things forecast of 50 billion devices by 2020 is outdated (2016). https://spectrum.ieee.org/tech-talk/telecom/internet/popular-internet-of-things-forecast-of-50-billion-devices-by-2020-is-outdated. Accessed 01 Nov 2017
26. Ouaddah, A., Elkalam, A.A., Ouahman, A.A.: Towards a novel privacy-preserving access control model based on blockchain technology in IoT. In: Rocha, Á., Serrhini, M., Felgueiras, C. (eds.) Europe and MENA Cooperation Advances in Information and Communication Technologies. AISC, vol. 520, pp. 523–533. Springer, Cham (2017). https://doi.org/10.1007/978-3-319-46568-5_53
27. Popov, S.: The Tangle - Version 1.3 (2017). https://iota.org/IOTA_Whitepaper.pdf. Accessed 22 Nov 2017
28. Raza, N., Aftab, M.U., Akbar, M.Q., Ashraf, O., Irfan, M.: Mobile ad-hoc networks applications and its challenges (2016)
29. Su, K., Li, J., Fu, H.: Smart city and the applications. In: 2011 International Conference on Electronics, Communications and Control (ICECC), pp. 1028–1031. IEEE (2011)
30. Tangpong, A., Kesidis, G., Hsu, H.Y., Hurson, A.: Robust sybil detection for MANETs. In: 2009 Proceedings of 18th International Conference on Computer Communications and Networks, ICCCN 2009, pp. 1–6. IEEE (2009)
31. Todd, P.: BIP 65 - OP_CHECKLOCKTIMEVERIFY (2014). https://github.com/bitcoin/bips/blob/6295c1a095a1fa33f38d334227fa4222d8e0a523/bip-0009.mediawiki. Accessed 11 Dec 2017
32. Wood, G.: Ethereum: a secure decentralized generalised transaction ledger (2014). http://gavwood.com/paper.pdf. Accessed 22 Nov 2017

33. Xiao, B., Yu, B., Gao, C.: Detection and localization of sybil nodes in VANETs. In: Proceedings of the 2006 Workshop on Dependability Issues in Wireless Ad Hoc Networks And Sensor Networks, pp. 1–8. ACM (2006)
34. Yu, H., Gibbons, P.B., Kaminsky, M., Xiao, F.: SybilLimit: a near-optimal social network defense against sybil attacks. In: 2008 IEEE Symposium on Security and Privacy, SP 2008, pp. 3–17. IEEE (2008)
35. Yu, H., Kaminsky, M., Gibbons, P.B., Flaxman, A.: SybilGuard: defending against sybil attacks via social networks. In: ACM SIGCOMM Computer Communication Review, vol. 36, pp. 267–278. ACM (2006)

Software Security

Understanding the Hidden Cost of Software Vulnerabilities: Measurements and Predictions

Afsah Anwar[1]([✉]), Aminollah Khormali[1], DaeHun Nyang[2], and Aziz Mohaisen[1]

[1] University of Central Florida, Orlando, FL 32816, USA
{afsahanwar,aminkhormali}@knights.ucf.edu, mohaisen@ucf.edu
[2] Inha University, Incheon, Republic of Korea
nyang@inha.ac.kr

Abstract. Vulnerabilities have a detrimental effect on end-users and enterprises, both direct and indirect; including loss of private data, intellectual property, the competitive edge, performance, etc. Despite the growing software industry and a push towards a digital economy, enterprises are increasingly considering security as an added cost, which makes it necessary for those enterprises to see a tangible incentive in adopting security. Furthermore, despite data breach laws that are in place, prior studies have suggested that only 4% of reported data breach incidents have resulted in litigation in federal courts, showing the limited legal ramifications of security breaches and vulnerabilities.

In this paper, we study the hidden cost of software vulnerabilities reported in the National Vulnerability Database (NVD) through stock price analysis. Towards this goal, we perform a high-fidelity data augmentation to ensure data reliability and to estimate vulnerability disclosure dates as a baseline for estimating the implication of software vulnerabilities. We further build a model for stock price prediction using the NARX Neural Network model to estimate the effect of vulnerability disclosure on the stock price. Compared to prior work, which relies on linear regression models, our approach is shown to provide better accuracy. Our analysis also shows that the effect of vulnerabilities on vendors varies, and greatly depends on the specific software industry. Whereas some industries are shown statistically to be affected negatively by the release of software vulnerabilities, even when those vulnerabilities are not broadly covered by the media, some others were not affected at all.

Keywords: Vulnerability economics · Prediction
National vulnerability database

1 Introduction

An ideal software should be defect-free, reliable and resilient. However, vulnerabilities are defects in software products, which expose the product and users

© ICST Institute for Computer Sciences, Social Informatics and Telecommunications Engineering 2018
R. Beyah et al. (Eds.): SecureComm 2018, LNICST 254, pp. 377–395, 2018.
https://doi.org/10.1007/978-3-030-01701-9_21

to risk alike, for e.g., Distributed Denial of Service attacks [1,2] or typosquatting attacks [3]. When such defects happen, users prefer vendors who take such defects as a priority, fix them, report them to their users, and keep the community as a whole immune to adversaries. Failure to do so would put vulnerable vendors at risk, whereby users seek different vendors, causing great losses.

In practice, vulnerabilities have multiple costs associated with them. For example, a vulnerability leads to loss of trust by users, tarnished brand reputation, and ultimately results in the loss of customer-base. To deal with vulnerabilities, vendors also incur additional costs in the form of developer-hours spent fixing them and redeploying fixes. As such, vulnerabilities could be a direct cause of losing a competitive edge in the global market to vendors less prone to them. For example, a study by the National Institute of Standards and Technology (NIST) estimated that the US economy looses about $60 Billion USD every year for patches development and redistribution, systems re-deployment, as well as direct productivity loss due to vulnerabilities [4].

To make matters worse, the number of security incidents and vulnerabilities have been growing exponentially, leading to a similar growth in resources required for fixing them. In 2012, for example, Knight Capital, a financial services company, lost $400 Million USD because of a bug in their code; the company bought shares at the *ask price* and sold them at the *bid price* [5]. Losses from WannaCry (2017), a ransomware attack in over 150 countries affecting more than 100,000 groups, is estimated to be $4 Billion USD [6]. Virus attacks, such as Love Bug (2000), SirCam (2001), Nimda (2001), and CodeRed (2001), have had an impact of $8.75 Billion, $1.25 Billion, $1.5 Billion and $2.75 Billion USD, respectively [7]. With deployment of software in critical infrastructure, vulnerabilities could have overwhelming impact. For example defects like the loss of radio contact between the air traffic controller and the pilots due to unexpected shutdown of voice communication system and crash of the backup system within a minute of it turning on, could cost lives [8].

The cost of vulnerabilities is a variable that does not depend only on the type of the vulnerability, but also the industry, potential users, and the severity of the vulnerability as seen by those users. For example, users of security or financial software are more likely to lose faith in their product, compared to general e-commerce applications. A more severe vulnerability is also more likely to impact a vendor than a minor software glitch. For example, a vulnerability that can be used to repeatedly launch a Denial of Service (DoS) attack could be viewed more severely by users than, say, an access control misconfiguration (e.g., 1-time access-token exposure).

For publicly-traded drug and auto vendors, Jarrell and Peltzman [9] demonstrated that recalling products has a detrimental impact on shareholder value. Conversely, though, researches have shown that software vendors may, on the one hand, not suffer any significant losses due to vulnerabilities [10], or, on the other hand, grow in profit and offerings despite the parallel growth in software vulnerabilities. However, there are also underlying costs associated with each software vulnerability, as mentioned above, and those costs are maybe invisible [10]. For example, Romanosky *et al.* [11] studied software-related data breaches in the United States, and found that 4% of them resulted in litigation in federal courts, out of which 50% (2% of the original studied cases) won by the plaintiffs.

Contributions. In this paper, we quantitatively analyze the loss faced by software vendors due to software vulnerabilities, through the lenses of stock price and valuation. To this end, this work has the following contributions. (i) An evaluation of vulnerabilities, disclosed in the year 2016, from the National Vulnerability Database (NVD) and their impact on their vendors. (ii) An accurate method for predicting stock price of the next day using NARX Neural Network. (iii) Industry-impact correlation analysis, demonstrating that some industries are more prone to stock loss due to vulnerabilities than others. (iv) Vulnerability type analysis, indicating that different types have different powers of affecting the stock price of a vendor.

Our work stands out in the following aspects, compared to the prior work (more in Sect. 2). First, unlike the prior work, which is event-based (tracks vulnerabilities that are only reported in the press), we use a comprehensive dataset of disclosed vulnerabilities in the National Vulnerability Database (NVD). Per Spanos and Angelis [12], 81.1% of the prior work they surveyed were limited to security breaches, while we focus on all software vulnerabilities. Furthermore, per the same source, 32.4% of the prior work used Lexis/Nexis (database of popular newspapers in the United States) as their source, 24.3% used the Data Loss Archive and Database (data for privacy breach), 13.5% used CNET (technology website), and 13.5% used Factiva (global news database). In this study, we uniquely focus on using NVD. (ii) We design a model to accurately predict stock for the next day to precisely measure the effect of a vulnerability. Our approach outperforms state-of-the-art approach using linear regression (e.g., while our mean-squared error (MSE) using ANN is below 0.6, using linear regression results in MSE of 6.24). (iii) Unlike the prior work, we did not exclude any vendors, as we considered publicly-traded vendors on NYSE, NASDAQ, Frankfurt, Other OTC, Taiwan, and LSE. Spanos and Angelis [12] in their survey found that 83.8% of the surveyed work used vendors that traded in a US stock market, 13.5% used vendors from different countries and only 2.9% (1 out of 34 works) used firms traded in TYO (the leading stock exchange in Japan) [12].

Organization. The rest of the paper is organized as follows: In Sect. 2, we revisit the literature. In Sect. 3, we present our approach to the problem. In Sect. 4, we present our prediction model. In Sect. 5, we evaluate the results. In Sect. 6 we further comment on the statistical significance of our results, followed by discussion, limitations and future work in Sect. 7. We conclude the paper in Sect. 8.

2   Related Work

Our work is an amalgam of different fields, where we connect the vulnerabilities to economic affect on vendor. Perceptions often relate vulnerabilities to effect on the end user. Little has been said and done from the vendor's perspective.

Effect on Vendor's Stock. Hovav and D'Archy [10], and Telang *et al.* [13] analyzed, in event-based studies, vulnerabilities and their impact on vendors. While Hovav and D'Archy have shown that market shows no signs of significant negative reaction due to vulnerabilities, Telang *et al.* show that a vendor on average loses 0.6% of its stock value due to vulnerabilities. Goel *et al.* [14] pointed out that security breaches have an adverse impact of about 1% on the market value of a vendor. Campbell *et al.* [15] observed a significant negative market reaction to information security breaches involving unauthorized access to confidential data, but no significant reaction to non-confidential breaches. Cavusoglu *et al.* [16] show that the announcement of Internet security breaches has a negative impact on the market value of vendors.

Bose *et al.* [17] show that each phishing alert leads to a loss of market capitalization that is at least US$ 411 million for a firm.

Vulnerability Analysis. Li and Paxson [18] outlined a method to approximate public disclosure date by scrapping reference links in NVD, which we use in this study. Nguyen and Massaci [19] pointed out that the vulnerable versions data in NVD is unreliable. Christey and Martin [20] outlined caveats with the NVD data, also suggesting its unreliability. Romanosky *et al.* [21] found that data breach disclosure laws, on average, reduce identity theft caused by data breaches by 6.1%. Similarly, Gordon *et al.* [22] found a significant downward shift in impact post the September 11 attacks.

Financial Impact of Defects. Jarrell and Peltzman [9] analyzed the impact of recall in the drug and auto industries on vendors' stock value loss. Towards calculating the effect of a vulnerability, it is crucial to predict a hypothetical stock valuation in the absence of a vulnerability. Kar [23] suggested the use of Artificial Neural Network (ANN) as a reliable method for predicting stock value. Farhang *et al.* [24], suggest that higher security investments in Android devices do not impose higher product prices on customers.

3   Methodology

Using the information available on the National Vulnerability Database (NVD), the goal of this study is to track the public disclosure date of vulnerabilities and capture their impact on vendors stock market valuation. As in the prior work [9], we consider the fluctuation in the stock price as a measure of the reported vulnerabilities' impact. To this end, we calculate the impact on the following days, with respect to the predicted value of the stock on the day of vulnerability disclosure. However, we limit ourselves up to the third day of the public disclosure of the vulnerability to reduce the likelihood of interference with factors that might affect the market value. The rest of this section explains in details the steps taken to achieve the above goal.

3.1   Data and Data Augmentation

Our main sources of data are NVD [25] and Yahoo Finance [26]. Figure 1 summarizes, at a high-level, the flow of data creation, from the source of data to the

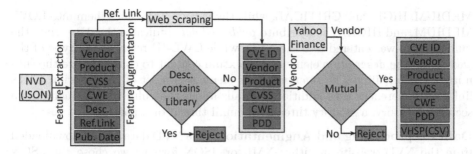

Fig. 1. Dataset creation flow. *Desc.* stands for the description of vulnerability, *Ref. Link* is the link referring to details corresponding to the vulnerability, *Pub. Date* is the Published Date, *CVSS* is Common Vulnerability Scoring System metrics, *CWE* is the Common Weakness Enumeration identifier, *PDD* is the Public Disclosure Date, approximated as the minimum of the dates gathered from the links corresponding to a vulnerability, and *VHSP* is the Vendor Historical Stock Price downloaded of mutual vendors from Yahoo Finance.

final dataset. In a nutshell, we extract information from JSON files downloaded from the National Vulnerability Database (NVD), scrape through the reference links for each vulnerability provided by NVD to approximate the disclosure date of the vulnerability, then check for indicative words, such as "lib" or "library" in the description of the vulnerability. If such words do not exist in the description, which means that those vulnerabilities are more likely associated with the vendor and not due to a third party, we consider the vulnerability for further analysis. We check for the vendor's historical stock prices using the Yahoo Finance. If the vendor exists in Yahoo Finance, we consider the vendor for our analysis, otherwise the vendor is rejected.

National Vulnerability Database (NVD) is a vulnerability database maintained by the National Institute of Standards and Technology (NIST) and contains all vulnerabilities reported to MITRE [27]. Analysts at NVD analyze the reported vulnerabilities, then insert them into the database after adding other necessary information, including (most importantly) a Common Vulnerabilities and Exposures Identifier (CVE-ID). In the following we elaborate on the other data elements in NVD associated with each vulnerability.

The NVD includes the following information (elements) for each reported vulnerability: the CVE-ID, vendor, product, Common Vulnerability Scoring System (CVSS) label, published date, Common Weakness Enumeration Identifier (CWE-ID) [28], description, and reference links. The CVSS label is provided using both version 2 and version 3 [29,30], which are widely used standard scoring techniques. The *vendor* element is the name of the vendor of the software that has the vulnerability, the *product* element is the name of the product which contains the vulnerability, and the *CVSS* is the severity of the vulnerability. CVSS version 3, released in the later half of 2015, labels vulnerabilities as LOW,

MEDIUM, HIGH, and CRITICAL, while the version 2 classifies them into LOW, MEDIUM, and HIGH. The attribute *published date* indicates the date when the vulnerability was entered into the NVD, while CWE-ID refers to the type of the weakness. The *description* element is a textual content to contextualize the submitted vulnerability. The *reference links* element is a set of the external URLs linking to references with additional details about the vulnerability, including a security advisory, a security thread, an email thread or a patch.

Data Preprocessing and Augmentation. The NVD data can be downloaded from the NVD website in either XML or JSON format; we chose the JSON format. The data is distributed in multiple JSON files with a file per year. We use the vulnerabilities reported in the year 2016, and limit our analysis to the severe ones. Since not all vulnerabilities have their CVSS version 3 assigned to them, we consider vulnerabilities with CVSS version 3 label as CRITICAL or version 2 label as "HIGH" to be severe. In our analysis we are interested in understanding the impact of core vulnerabilities in the software itself, rather than inherited vulnerabilities due to the use of third-party libraries. To this end, we filtered vulnerabilities due to third-party libraries by discarding those with the word "library" in their description. Given that a vulnerability may affect multiple vendors and products, we limit ourselves to the main source of the vulnerability by counting a vulnerability only under one vendor. For that, we checked the vendor name and the description in the vulnerability record, and found that the main vendor always appears in the description. Where multiple vendors appear in the description, we exclude those vulnerabilities from our analysis, since the vulnerability could be due to a third-party library common among products of those vendors. As a result, our dataset was reduced from 8,709 to 2,849 vulnerabilities.

Since the *published date* attribute captured in NVD is the date when the vulnerability was entered into the database and not the date when the vulnerability was actually found, the most important step in our analysis was to find the date when the vulnerability was disclosed to the public. We use the links present in the NVD to scrape through the web and label dates corresponding to each of the links, in an approach taken also by Li and Paxson [18]. We observed that some of the domains have stringent security measures preventing the automating scraping, while some did not have a date. For all such 1262 out of 8365 links, we manually visited the links and updated the corresponding URLs. For all URLs, we calculated the minimum of the dates corresponding to a vulnerability (when multiple dates are obtained from multiple URLs) and consider it as the public disclosure date. It should be noted that we ignore the links linking to patches, as the date of patching may or may not be same as the disclosure date, and market could only respond to public disclosure date.

In our dataset, we also found redundant vendor names, e.g., schneider-electric vs. schneider_electric, trendmicro vs. trend-micro, and palo_alto_networks vs. paloaltonetworks. We consolidate the various vendors under a consistent name, through manual inspection. For all the vendors in the above dataset we further augment them by incorporating stock price over time from Yahoo Finance, as highlighted in the following.

Yahoo Finance. For all the vulnerabilities in our dataset we gathered historical stock price information from Yahoo Finance. The historical data can be downloaded from Yahoo Finance as a Comma Separated Values (CSV) file. The file contains seven information attributes, namely, the date, open, low, high, close, adjusted Close, and volume. The *date* attribute corresponds to the date on which the stock's listed performance is captured. The *open* and *close* attributes are the stock value of the vendor on the given day at the opening and closing of the market, respectively. The *low* and *high* are the lowest and highest value of the vendor's stock achieved on the given day. The *adjusted close* attribute reflects the dividends and splits since that day. During an event of stock split, the adjusted closing price changes for every day in the history of the stock. For example, if stock for vendor X closed at $100 USD per share on December 5th, a 2:1 stock split is announced on December 6th, and the stock opened at $50 USD and closed at $60 USD, that represents a decline of $40 in the actual closing price. However, the adjusted close for December 5th would change to $50 USD, making the gain $10 at the end of December 6th. The *volume* attribute is the number of shares traded on the given day.

Price Prediction. We use the open, low, high, close, adjusted close, and volume of all preceding days as input to predict the close for a day, as explained in more details in Sect. 4. We use the predicted price as a baseline to estimate the cost of vulnerabilities upon their disclosure. Upon examining the vendors in our dataset, we found 60 of them available through Yahoo Finance. Out of the 60 vendors, only 41 of vendors had vulnerabilities in our selected dataset. Out of those 41 vendors, 5 vendors had missing data attributes (e.g., blackberry had several "null"-valued attributes).

Press. As a baseline for comparison with our results based on the approach used in the literature, we sample vulnerabilities reported in the media. We search for "software vulnerabilities in 2017" in *Forbes*, and *ZDNet*, and capture four vulnerabilities for comparison.

3.2 Assessing Vulnerability's Impact

To assess the impact of vulnerabilities, we separate our dataset by vendor. To find the effect of a vulnerability for the date on which the vulnerability was published, we look for the stock value on that particular date. It is worth noting that the stock markets do not open on weekends and holidays, making stocks unavailable on those days. For all dates with disclosed vulnerabilities whereby the stock data is unavailable, we approximate the open, low, high, close, adjusted close, and volume attributes in a linear relation with the last operating day and the next operating day. For example, suppose the value on the last operating day, d_0, is x, the market was closed on days d_1, d_2, and d_3, and the value on next operating day, d_4, is y. We first calculate the number of days between d_0 and d_4, denoted by d (here, 3). We then approximate the values on days d_i for $i \in \{1, 2, 3\}$ as $d_i = x + \frac{i \times (y-x)}{d}$.

Finding the effect of a vulnerability is done by comparing the predicted stock price assuming the vulnerabilities did not exist with the actual price which takes the existence of the vulnerability into account. Therefore, we first predict a stock price for the no-vulnerability case and calculate the impact of the vulnerability's Abnormal Return on day i (AR_i for $i \in \{1, 2, 3\}$), where $AR_i = R_i - \bar{R}$, such that Ri is the actual stock price on day i, and $\bar{R}$ is the expected stock without vulnerability (predicted). We then calculate the % of Abnormal Return on day i (PAR_i), where $i \in 1, 2, 3$, as $PAR_i = \frac{AR_i \times 100}{R_i}$.

Finally, we calculate the Overall (%) Abnormal Return on day i (OAR_i), where $i \in \{1, 2, 3\}$. For vendor $\{V_1, \ldots, V_m\}$ with vulnerability $\{v_1, \ldots, v_n\}$, the PAR values for a vulnerability v_j are denoted by PAR_i^j for $i \in \{1, 2, 3\}$. We calculate $OAR_i^k = \sum_{j=1}^{n} PAR_i^j$ on day i for a vendor V_k.

4   Prediction

The data of all vendors consists of the aforementioned features: date, open, close, high, low, volume and fractional change in the price from previous time step. All of these features, except date, are considered to predict the close value in the future. In order to increase the performance of the machine learning algorithm, data preprocessing is required. The general method for feature standardization is to consider the mean and standard deviation of each feature. In other words, feature standardization projects the raw data into a new space where each feature in the data has a mean and a standard deviation of zero and unit, respectively. This is, the mapping transforms the feature vector x into $z = \frac{x - \bar{x}}{\sigma}$, where $\bar{x}$ and σ, are the mean and standard deviation of the original feature vector x, respectively. These features are then fed into the nonlinear autoregressive neural network with exogenous factors (NARX) to predict the stock value of vendors.

4.1   NARX Neural Network

The NARX neural network, generally applied for prediction of the behavior of discrete-time nonlinear dynamical systems, is one of the most efficient tools of forecasting [31]. Unique characteristics of NARX provide accurate forecasts of the stock values by exploiting an architecture of recurrent neural network with limited feedback from the output neuron. In comparison with other architectures, which consider feedback from both hidden and output neurons, NARX is more efficient and yields better results [32]. Based on the NARX neural network model, the next value of the output at time t, $y(t)$, can be regressed on previous values of the output and exogenous input, represented using the following model:

$$y(t) = f[u(t-1), \ldots, u(t-d_u); y(t-1), \ldots, y(t-D_y)],$$

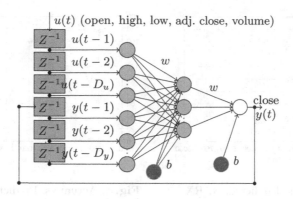

Fig. 2. General structure of the NARX neural network

Table 1. NARX parameter settings.

Parameter	Value
Number of input neurons	Five
Number of output neurons	One
Transfer functions	Tansig (hidden layer)
	Purelin (output layer)
Training, validation, testing	70%, 15%, and 15%
Evaluation function	Mean squared error
Learning Algorithm	Levenberg-Marquardt

where $u(t)$ and $y(t)$ are the input and output of the network at time t. d_u and d_y, are the lags of exogenous inputs and output of the system, and the function f is multi-layer feed forward network. The general architecture of the NARX neural network is shown in Fig. 2.

For each vendor, we divide the dataset into training, validation and test subsets (with 70%, 15%, and 15%, respectively). We use the training data to train a predictive model. The Mean Squared Error (MSE) is used to evaluate the performance of the corresponding models. The MSE is defined as:

$$\text{MSE} = \frac{1}{n} \sum_{i=1}^{n} (y_{t_i} - y_{p_i})^2,$$

where n is the number of samples. y_t and y_p are representing the actual value of the stock price and corresponding predicted value, respectively. A feed forward neural network with one hidden layer has been used as predictor function of the NARX. Levenberg-Marquardt (LM) back-propagation learning algorithm [33] has been employed to train the weights of the neural network. The specifications of the proposed NARX neural network are presented in Table 1.

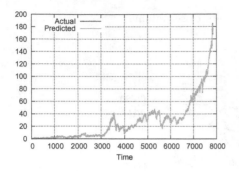

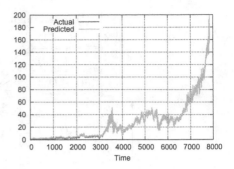

Fig. 3. Actual vs. Predicted: NARX.   **Fig. 4.** Actual vs. Predicted: ARIMA.

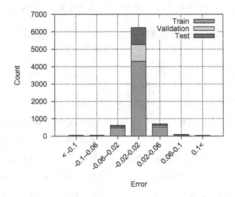

Fig. 5. Error histogram of Adobe stock.

Baseline for Comparison. In addition to the NARX neural network model, we also predicted the stock price of vendors using the Autoregressive Integrated Moving Average (ARIMA) model [34], one of the most popular time series prediction models, for comparison. To establish such a comparison with prior work using linear regression, we conducted the prediction for the stock price of one vendor, namely, Adobe. The AR portion of ARIMA signifies the variable to be predicted is regressed on its past values. Also, the MA portion in the ARIMA model indicates that the error in the regression model is a linear combination of error values in the past. The ARIMA model with external regressors, x, and for one-step ahead prediction can be represented by

$$y_p(t) - \phi_1 y_t(t-1) = \mu - \theta_1 e(t-1) + \beta(x(t) - \phi_1 x(t-1)),$$

where y_p and y_t are the predicted and actual prices of the stock, respectively. μ, θ, and ϕ are a constant, the MA coefficient, and the AR coefficient values.

The results are shown only for Adobe and for the rest of the vendors only the MSE is shown in Table 2. Figure 3 depicts the actual and predicted stock price. The low value of the error strongly suggests that the NARX model can forecast the stock values with high accuracy. In addition, The error histogram is

Table 2. Results for each vendor. Vul. stands for vulnerability count and OAR_1, OAR_2, and OAR_3 stand for the average effect at day 1, 2, and 3 (%), respectively. [2] Vendor names are abbreviated as follows: PAN=Palo Alto Networks, RWA=Rockwell Automation, TM=Trend Micro. ▲ indicates that the vulnerabilities had no overall impact on vendor's stock value while ▼ indicates that the stock of the vendor were impacted, overall.

Vendor	MSE	Vul	$OAR_1^{(1)}$	$OAR_2^{(1)}$	$OAR_3^{(1)}$	Vendor	MSE	Vul	$OAR_1^{(1)}$	$OAR_2^{(1)}$	$OAR_3^{(1)}$
Adobe	5.9E-4	494	▼0.65	▼0.37	▼0.50	Oracle	1.0E-3	130	▼0.48	▼0.81	▼1.51
Advantech	9.5E-4	9	▲0.61	▲0.89	▲0.96	Osram	7.8E-3	1	▲1.17	▼6.42	▼7.95
Apache	9.9E-4	37	▲0.60	▲0.98	▲1.17	PAN[2]	4.3E-3	2	▼1.09	▼1.13	▼8.54
Apple	2.8E-4	154	▲0.41	▲0.75	▲1.03	Redhat	1.6E-3	13	▲0.74	▲0.59	▲0.61
Atlassian	9.7E-3	4	▼3.85	▼3.86	▼3.12	RWA[2]	8.9E-4	5	▲1.47	▼0.87	▲0.06
Cisco	2.3E-3	111	▲0.10	▲0.33	▲0.42	Samsung	7.6E-3	10	▼0.08	▼0.08	▲2.95
Citrix	2.4E-3	9	▲0.14	▲0.01	▲0.57	Sap	2.3E-3	17	▲0.82	▲0.69	▲1.28
Facebook	1.1E-3	6	▲0.13	▼0.33	▲0.45	Schneider	3.1E-3	7	▼1.56	▼1.87	▼1.79
Fortinet	4.5E-3	7	▲0.37	▲0.19	▲0.92	Siemens	3.7E-3	14	▲0.51	▲0.83	▲0.32
GE	5.8E-4	3	▲0.12	▼0.58	▼0.39	Sophos	3.8E-3	3	▲1.72	▲1.87	▲0.89
Google	7.6E-4	410	▼0.08	▼0.21	▼0.08	Splunk	1.2E-2	1	▲0.88	▲3.17	▲1.11
Honeywell	4.3E-4	1	▼0.09	▲0.87	▲2.35	Symantec	1.3E-3	13	▲0.24	▲0.52	▲0.77
HP	7.6E-3	36	▲0.21	▲0.37	▲0.64	Teradata	3.6E-3	3	▼2.18	▼2.86	▼2.75
IBM	4.4E-3	51	▲0.22	▲0.32	▲0.26	TM[2]	9.3E-3	16	▼0.56	▼0.74	▲0.98
Juniper	6.3E-3	13	▼0.19	▼0.80	▼1.10	Vmware	6.1E-3	11	▲0.45	▲0.32	▲0.74
Lenovo	7.4E-3	9	▼0.75	▼1.12	▼0.55	Zyxel	5.2E-3	2	▲0.18	▼1.18	▲0.18
Microsoft	8.6E-3	279	▲0.45	▲0.39	▲0.56	Equifax	4.9E-4	1	▲1.52	▼14.02	▼24.19
Netapp	6.5E-3	4	▲1.08	▲0.76	▼1.19	Dow Jones	3.5E-4	1	▼0.08	▼0.34	▼0.03
Netgear	4.3E-3	14	▲1.18	▲1.61	▲0.10	Alteryx	4.8E-2	1	▼0.61	▼2.18	▼7.70
Nvidia	1.0E-3	38	▲0.56	▲1.46	▲4.39	Viacom	2.3E-3	1	▼1.60	▲0.60	▼0.62

provided in Fig. 5, and shows that the majority of the instances are forecasted precisely. In Fig. 4, although visual representation suggests a weakness of fit with ARIMA in prediction the stock values, the difference in the value of MSE for these to models, 6.42 for ARIMA and 0.59 for NARX, quantitatively justifies the goodness of the proposed method over methods used in the literature.

5 Results

We experimented with a large number of vulnerabilities, meaning that multiple vulnerabilities could correspond to a single date. Therefore, the effect we see could be due to one or more vulnerabilities. For every vulnerability disclosure date and vendor, we calculate % Abnormal Return on days 0, 1, and 2 (AR_1, AR_2, and AR_3 respectively as described above). The results are presented in Table 2. The table contains the normalized MSE, count of the vulnerabilities, and Abnormal Return on days 1, 2, and 3 for every vendor (as described above). We observe that vulnerabilities had an adverse impact on the stock price of 17 out of the 36 vendors.

Table 4 represents a breakdown of vendors by industry and their likelihood of their stock being impacted by vulnerabilities. For the classification of industries, the software industry contains vendors such as Adobe, Apache, Atlassian, Google, VMware, Sap, Oracle, Redhat, and Alteryx. The device industry includes Advantech and Apple. The networking industry includes Cisco, Citrix, Netgear, and Zyxel. The security industry includes Fortinet, Juniper, Paloalto Networks, Symantec, and Trendmicro. The consumer product industry includes Rockwell Automation, Osram, Splunk, Schneider, Teradata, Facebook, Netapp, and Viacom. The electronics & hardware industry includes Lenovo, and Nvidia. Finally, the finance industry includes Equifax and Dow Jones. To assign a likelihood of an industry's stock price being impacted by vulnerabilities, we use Highly-Likely when the number of vendors with stock price affected negatively by the vulnerabilities in the given industry is larger than those not affected, Less-Likely otherwise; we use Equally-Likely when the number of vendors affected equals the number of vendors not affected.

We look at vulnerabilities from 10 vendors to find the reason for the nearly no-effect of vulnerabilities in some industries. We see that in every dataset there are a few dates which have no significant positive effect (from vendors perspective) on the market leading the results to be negative. By referring to the description of the vulnerabilities, we observe that:

1. Vulnerabilities affecting vendors' stock negatively are of critical severity (vulnerabilities with CVSS version 3 label of CRITICAL) while the rest were less severe (vulnerabilities with CVSS labels of HIGH or MEDIUM).
2. Vulnerabilities affecting vendors' stock price negatively have a combination of version 3 label of HIGH or CRITICAL, and a description containing phrases such as "denial of service", "allows remote attacker to read/execute", "allows context-dependent attackers to conduct XML External Entity XXE attacks via a crafted PDF", and "allows context-dependent attackers to have unspecified impact via an invalid character". Additionally, vulnerabilities description such as "allows authenticated remote attacker to read/execute", "remote attackers to cause a denial of service", and "allows remote attackers to write to files of arbitrary types via unspecified vectors" have little (on days 0, 1, and 2) to no effect on the stock price. Therefore, we can conclude that vulnerabilities involving unauthorized accesses have a higher cost, seen in their detrimental effect on the stock price.
3. Vulnerabilities with phrases such as "local users with access to" and "denial of service" in the description have no impact on the stock. Therefore, DoS attacks lacking confidentiality factor lead to no impact on stock value.

For the vulnerabilities gathered from the press, we followed the same steps. We found that these vulnerabilities have an adverse effect on vendor stock price in almost every case.

6 Statistical Significance

To understand the statistical significance of our results, we use the confidence interval of the observations as a guideline. Particularly, we measure the statistical confidence of overall effect of vulnerabilities corresponding to a vendor on days 1, 2, and 3, respectively. Table 3 shows the confidence intervals (lower and upper limit) on days 1, 2, and 3, measured with 95% confidence.

95% Confidence Interval. 95% Confidence Interval (CI) is a range that contains the true mean of a population with 95% certainty. For a smaller population, the CI is almost similar to the range of the data, while only a tiny sample of data lies within the confidence interval for a large population. In our study, we have noticed that our data populations are diverse, where some vendors have a small number of samples, and others have larger number of samples. For example, Figs. 6, 7 and 8 show the distribution of observations of effect for multiple example vendors and several vulnerabilities associated with each vendor. The shown histogram captures counts of the effect of vulnerabilities; the x-axis includes brackets of the effect (measured by OAR) and the y-axsis captures the count for the given effect. The diversity of the effect is well-captured by the count distribution; high severity impact is seen in a vendor where the counts are focused in the negative side of the interval, whereas lower (or no) impact is seen where the count focus is in the positive side. The confidence interval with 95% confidence for a given population (distribution) can be calculated as,

$$CI = \left(\bar{x} - 1.96\frac{\sigma}{\sqrt{n}}, \bar{x} + 1.96\frac{\sigma}{\sqrt{n}} \right),$$

where $\bar{x}$ is the mean of the population, σ is the standard deviation, and n is the number of samples in the population.

Putting it into perspective, while OAR_i, where $i \in \{1, 2, 3\}$, captures the overall effect of vulnerabilities corresponding to a vendor, the Confidence Interval (CI_i, where $i \in \{1, 2, 3\}$) gives the confidence for the effect to lie within its upper and lower bound. In Table 3, and by considering the data associated with Adobe, for example, we can say with 95% confidence that the confidence interval for the population, CI_i, contains the true mean, OAR_i. We also observe that:

1. Our OAR_i in Table 2 are within their respective confidence intervals, which means that our results reported earlier are statistically significant.
2. The true mean values for Adobe, Palo Alto Networks, Schneider Electric, and Teradata, on the day a vulnerability is disclosed, are bounded in negative intervals. Thus, the probability for a vulnerability having an effect on the day a vulnerability is disclosed on the vendor's stock price is highly likely.
3. The true mean for Oracle, Palo Alto Networks, Schneider Electric, and Zyxel on days after the day a vulnerability is disclosed are bounded in negative intervals. Thus, the probability for a vulnerability having a negative impact on days succeeding the day a vulnerability is disclosed on the vendor's stock price is highly likely.
4. The true mean for every vendor on the three days is bounded from below by negative value. Although the confidence intervals do not say anything about the percentage of population that would fall in the negative side of the interval, the lower bound indicate a likelihood that the population would

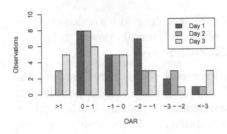

Fig. 6. Histogram of the effect of vulnerabilities on stock value: Adobe

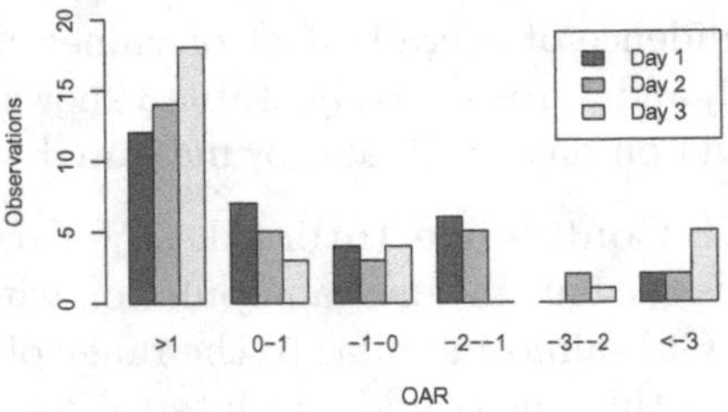

Fig. 7. Histogram of the effect of vulnerabilities on stock value: Apache

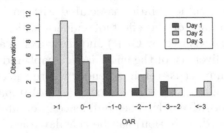

Fig. 8. Histogram of the effect of vulnerabilities on stock value: Apple

have samples with negative effect on the vendor's stock. Thus, given the various vulnerabilities on a specific vendor, it is likely that some of those vulnerabilities would have a negative effect on the vendor's stock value, even though the overall effect (measured by the mean) would be nullified. This, as well, is well captured in our analysis.

7   Discussion and Comparison

There has been several works dedicated to understanding the hidden cost of software vulnerabilities in the literature, which we discuss in the following across multiple aspects by comparison.

7.1   Comparison of Findings with Prior Work

The prior work has made various conclusions concerning the effect of the software vulnerabilities, and whether they are associated with a certain feature of those vulnerabilities, including correlation with types, publicity, etc. In the following, we compare our work and findings with the prior work across multiple factors, including vulnerability type, publicity, data source, methodology, and sector.

Confidentiality vs. Non-confidentiality Vulnerabilities (Confirmation). Campbell *et al.* [15] observed a negative market reaction for information security

Table 3. Statistical confidence for each vendor. OAR_1, OAR_2, and OAR_3 stand for the average effect at day 1, 2, and 3 (percent), respectively. CI_i is the confidence interval for day$_i$, where i $\epsilon\{1,2,3\}$. [(2)] Vendor names are abbreviated; PAN = Palo Alto Networks, RWA = Rockwell Automation, TM = Trend Micro.

Vendor	CI_1		CI_2		CI_3		Vendor	CI_1		CI_2		CI_3	
	Low	High	Low	High	Low	High		Low	High	Low	High	Low	High
Adobe	−1.10	−0.20	−0.96	0.22	−1.23	0.23	Oracle	−1.08	0.12	−1.19	−0.43	−2.10	−0.92
Advantec	−0.96	2.18	−2.20	3.98	−3.02	4.94	PAN[(2)]	−1.80	−0.37	−2.10	−0.15	−24.23	7.15
Apache	−0.17	1.45	−0.40	2.36	−0.64	2.98	Redhat	−0.19	1.68	−0.33	1.51	−0.64	1.86
Apple	−0.25	1.07	−0.11	1.62	−0.17	2.24	RWA[(2)]	−0.19	3.13	−2.18	2.00	−1.67	1.79
Atlassian	−2.05	0.53	−3.41	1.62	−2.77	2.50	Samsung	−0.21	0.06	−0.21	0.06	−3.07	8.96
Cisco	−0.22	0.41	−0.20	0.85	−0.17	1.02	Sap	−0.31	1.94	−0.57	1.94	−0.10	2.66
Citrix	−0.46	0.75	−0.93	0.94	−0.69	1.83	Schneider	−2.95	−0.17	−3.36	−0.37	−4.17	0.58
Facebook	−0.38	0.63	−0.74	0.08	−2.37	3.27	Siemens	−0.19	1.22	−0.60	2.26	−1.10	1.73
Fortinet	−1.04	2.98	−0.76	2.66	−1.48	3.07	Sophos	−0.19	3.64	0.77	2.96	−1.03	2.80
GE	−1.05	1.30	−1.54	0.37	−2.28	1.50	Symantec	−0.20	0.69	−0.05	1.09	−0.09	1.63
Google	−0.41	0.25	−0.76	0.34	−0.75	0.60	Teradata	−2.50	−1.86	−4.63	−1.10	−8.29	2.79
HP	−0.38	0.79	−0.35	1.09	−0.34	1.63	TM[(2)]	−1.71	0.60	−1.90	0.42	−0.41	2.37
IBM	−0.04	0.48	−0.11	0.74	−0.17	0.69	Vmware	−0.51	1.41	−0.79	1.42	−0.86	2.34
Juniper	−1.66	1.29	−2.38	0.79	−3.57	1.37	Zyxel	−0.52	0.88	−1.42	−0.95	−2.27	2.64
Lenovo	−1.55	0.05	−2.67	0.42	−2.69	1.59	Nvidia	−0.49	1.60	−0.57	3.49	1.10	7.67
Microsoft	−0.03	0.92	−0.31	1.08	−0.20	1.33	Netgear	−0.16	2.52	0.21	3.00	−2.28	2.48
Netapp	−0.44	2.59	−0.27	1.80	−4.13	1.74							

breaches involving unauthorized access to confidential data, and reported no significant reaction to non-confidentiality related breaches. Through our analysis, we had a similar conclusion. Particularly, we found that vulnerabilities affecting vendor's stock negatively have descriptions containing phrases indicating confidentiality breaches, such as "denial of service", "allows remote attacker to read/execute", "allows context-dependent attackers to conduct XML External Entity XXE attacks via a crafted PDF", and "allows context-dependent attackers to have unspecified impact via an invalid character".

How Publicity Affects Price (Contradiction). There has been several works in the literature on attempting to understand how the coverage by media and other forms of publicity for viruses and data breaches affect the stock value of a given vendor associated with such vulnerabilities. For example, Hovav and D'Arcy [10] demonstrated that virus-related announcements do not impact stock price of vendors. Our results partly contradict their claims, as we show that vulnerabilities impact the stock value a vendor, sometimes significantly (negatively), regardless to whether such vulnerabilities are announced or not.

Data Source and Effect (Broadening Scopes). Goel et al. [14] and Telang and Wattal [13] estimated the impact of vulnerabilities on the stock value of a given vendor by calculating a Cumulative Abnormal Rate (CAR) and using a linear regression model. Their results are based on security incidents: while both gather data from the press, Telang and Wattal [13] also use a few incidents from Computer Emergency Response Team (CERT) reports. On the other hand, we

Table 4. Per industry stock impact likelihood analysis.

Industry	Likeliness
Software	Highly likely
Consumer products	Highly likely
Finance	Highly likely
Security	Equally likely
Electronics & hardware	Equally likely
Conglomerate	Less likely
Device	Less likely
Networking	Less likely

consider a wide range of vulnerabilities regardless of being reported by the press. Our results show various trends and indicate the dynamic and wide spectrum of effect of vulnerabilities on the stock price of vendors.

Methodology (Addressing Caveats of Prior Work). The prior work shows the impact of vulnerabilities using CAR, which aggregates AR's on different days. However, we refrain from using CAR because of the following. First, CAR does not effectively capture the impact of a vulnerability, due to information loss by aggregation. For example, CAR would indicate no-effect if the magnitude (upward) of one or more days analyzed negate the magnitude (downward) of other days. Second, we consider a vulnerability as having had an impact if the stock shows a downward trend on d_1, d_2, or d_3, irrespective of the magnitude. Third, our results, through a rigorous analysis are statistically significant. To demonstrate the caveats of CAR and show the benefits of our approach in capturing a better state of the effect of vulnerabilities on the stock price, we consider both Samsung and Equifax in Table 2. On the one hand, the impact of vulnerability on Equifax on days 2 and 3 was significant (-14.02 and -24.09 vs. $+1.52$ on day 1), where CAR would capture the effect. On the other hand, such an effect would not be captured by CAR with Samsung (-0.08 and -0.08 on days 1 and 2 vs. $+2.95$ on day 3). Our approach, however, considers the effect of the vulnerability the stock price over the different days separately (and does not lose information due to aggregation).

Sector-Based Analysis. A general hypothesis is that the cost of security and vulnerabilities on vendors is sector-dependent. One of the main shortcomings of the prior work, however, is that it overlooks analyzing the cost based on sectors of the software industry. By classifying vendors based a clear industry sector, our results show the likelihood of effect to be high in software and consumer product industry, while the likelihood is less in the device, networking or conglomerate industries. Table 4 further highlights the industries with highest losses, by tracking losses by individual vendors. Although Table 2 shows that a vulnerability may or may not have an effect on its vendor's stock price, Table 3 shows that individual vulnerabilities may affect the stocks' value.

Shortcomings. In this study we found a significant effect of vulnerabilities on a given day and limited ourselves to the second day after the release of the vulnerability in order to minimize the impact of other factors. However, other factors may affect the stock value than the vulnerability, making the results unreliable, and highlight the correlational-nature of our study (as opposed to causational). Eliminating the effect of those factors, once known, is an open question. Furthermore, apart from the effect on stock, a vendor may sustain other hidden and long-term losses, such as consumers churn (switching to other products or vendors), loss of reputation, and internal losses (such as man-hour for developing remedies), which we do not consider in our evaluation, and open various directions for future work.

7.2   Breaches and Disclosure

Our analysis of the vulnerabilities show that while vulnerabilities may or may not have an impact on the stock price, a vulnerability reported by the press is highly likely to impact the stock price. The diverse results for the vulnerabilities collected from NVD are explained by the diverse severity of the vulnerabilities, whereas (1) the press may report on highly critical vulnerabilities that are more likely to result in loss, or (2) the reported vulnerabilities in the press may create a negative perception of the vendor leading to loss in their stock value. This, as a result, led many vendors to not disclose vulnerabilities in order to cope with bad publicity. For example, Microsoft did not disclose an attack on its bug tracking system in 2013 [35], demonstrating the such a behavior in vendors when dealing with vulnerabilities [36]. Recent reports also indicate a similar behavior by Yahoo when their online accounts were compromised, or by Uber when their employees and users personal information were leaked. More broadly, a recent survey of 343 security professionals worldwide indicated that the management of 20% of the respondents considered cyber-security issues a low priority, alluding to the possibility of not disclosing vulnerabilities even when they affect their systems [37].

8   Conclusion and Future Work

We perform an empirical analysis on vulnerabilities from NVD and look at their effect on vendor's stock price. Our results show that the effect is industry-specific, and depends on the severity of the reported vulnerabilities. We also compare the results with the vulnerabilities found in popular press: while both vulnerabilities affect the vendor's stock, vulnerabilities reported in the media have a much more adverse effect. En route, we also design a model to predict the stock price with high accuracy. Our work is limited in a sense that we do not consider other external factors affecting the stock or internal factors affecting long term users behavior and deriving vulnerabilities cost. Exploring those factors along with regional differences in effect will be our future work.

Acknowledgement. This work is supported in part by NSF grant CNS-1809000 and NRF grant NRF-2016K1A1A2912757. Part of this work has been presented as a poster at ACM AsiaCCS 2018 [38].

References

1. Wang, A., Mohaisen, A., Chang, W., Chen, S.: Delving into internet DDoS attacks by botnets: characterization and analysis. In: Proceedings of the 45th International Conference on Dependable Systems and Networks (DSN), Rio de Janeiro, Brazil, pp. 379–390 (2015)
2. Wang, A., Mohaisen, A., Chang, W., Chen, S.: Measuring and analyzing trends in recent distributed denial of service attacks. In: Proceedings of the 17th International Workshop on Information Security Applications (WISA), pp. 15–28 (2016)
3. Spaulding, J., Nyang, D., Mohaisen, A.: Understanding the effectiveness of typosquatting techniques. In: Proceedings of the 5th ACM/IEEE Workshop on Hot Topics in Web Systems and Technologies, p. 9 (2017)
4. Tassey, G.: The economic impacts of inadequate infrastructure for software testing. National Institute of Standards and Technology, RTI Project, vol. 7007, no. 011 (2002)
5. Strasburg, J., Bunge, J.: Loss swamps trading firm, knight capital searches for partner as tab for computer glitch hits $440 million. Wall Street Journal (2012). http://search.proquest.com/docview/1033163975
6. Berr, J.: "WannaCry" ransomware attack losses could reach $4 billion", May 2017. http://cbsn.ws/2yYjif2
7. The cost impact of major virus attacks since 1995. http://www.computereco nomics.com/article.cfm?id=936
8. Geppert, L.: Lost radio contact leaves pilots on their own. IEEE Spectr. **41**(11), 16–17 (2004)
9. Jarrell, G., Peltzman, S.: The impact of product recalls on the wealth of sellers. J. Polit. Econ. **93**(3), 512–536 (1985)
10. Hovav, A., D'arcy, J.: Capital market reaction to defective it products: the case of computer viruses. Comput. Secur. **24**(5), 409–424 (2005)
11. Romanosky, S., Hoffman, D., Acquisti, A.: Empirical analysis of data breach litigation. J. Empir. Leg. Stud. **11**(1), 74–104 (2014)
12. Spanos, G., Angelis, L.: The impact of information security events to the stock market: a systematic literature review. Comput. Secur. **58**, 216–229 (2016)
13. Telang, R., Wattal, S.: An empirical analysis of the impact of software vulnerability announcements on firm stock price. IEEE Trans. Softw. Eng. **33**(8), 544–557 (2007)
14. Goel, S., Shawky, H.A.: Estimating the market impact of security breach announcements on firm values. Inf. Manag. **46**(7), 404–410 (2009)
15. Campbell, K., Gordon, L.A., Loeb, M.P., Zhou, L.: The economic cost of publicly announced information security breaches: empirical evidence from the stock market. J. Comput. Secur. **11**(3), 431–448 (2003)
16. Cavusoglu, H., Mishra, B., Raghunathan, S.: The effect of internet security breach announcements on market value: capital market reactions for breached firms and internet security developers. Int. J. Electron. Commer. **9**(1), 70–104 (2004)
17. Bose, I., Leung, A.C.M.: Do phishing alerts impact global corporations? A firm value analysis. Decis. Support. Syst. **64**, 67–78 (2014)

18. Li, F., Paxson, V.: A large-scale empirical study of security patches. In: Proceedings of the 24th ACM Conference on Computer and Communications Security (CCS), Dallas, TX, October–Novvember 2017, pp. 2201–2215 (2017)
19. Nguyen, V.H., Massacci, F.: The (un)reliability of NVD vulnerable versions data: an empirical experiment on Google chrome vulnerabilities. In: Proceedings of the 8th ACM Symposium on Information, Computer and Communications Security (ASIACCS), Sydney, Australia, pp. 493–498, March 2013
20. Christey, S., Martin, B.: Buying into the bias: why vulnerability statistics suck. BlackHat, Las Vegas, Technical report, vol. 1 (2013)
21. Romanosky, S., Telang, R., Acquisti, A.: Do data breach disclosure laws reduce identity theft? J. Policy Anal. Manag. **30**(2), 256–286 (2011)
22. Gordon, L.A., Loeb, M.P., Zhou, L.: The impact of information security breaches: has there been a downward shift in costs? J. Comput. Secur. **19**(1), 33–56 (2011)
23. Kar, A.: Stock prediction using artificial neural networks. Department of Computer Science and Engineering, IIT Kanpur (1990)
24. Farhang, S., Laszka, A., Grossklags, J.: An economic study of the effect of android platform fragmentation on security updates, arXiv preprint arXiv:1712.08222 (2017)
25. National Vulnerability Database (NVD). https://nvd.nist.gov/
26. Symbol lookup from Yahoo! finance. https://finance.yahoo.com/lookup/
27. CVE - common vulnerabilities and exposures (CVE). https://cve.mitre.org/
28. Common weakness enumeration. https://cwe.mitre.org/
29. Common vulnerability scoring system SIG. https://www.first.org/cvss/
30. CVSS version 3. https://www.first.org/cvss/cvss-v30-user_guide_v1.1.pdf
31. Elman, J.L.: Finding structure in time. Cogn. Sci. **14**(2), 179–211 (1990)
32. Horne, B.G., Giles, C.L.: An experimental comparison of recurrent neural networks. In: Proceedings of the Advances in Neural Information Processing Systems 7, [NIPS Conference], pp. 697–704 (1994)
33. Moré, J.J.: The levenberg-marquardt algorithm: implementation and theory. In: Watson, G.A. (ed.) Numerical Analysis. LNM, vol. 630, pp. 105–116. Springer, Heidelberg (1978). https://doi.org/10.1007/BFb0067700
34. Box, G.E., Pierce, D.A.: Distribution of residual autocorrelations in autoregressive-integrated moving average time series models. J. Am. Stat. Assoc. **65**(332), 1509–1526 (1970)
35. Menn, J.: Exclusive: Microsoft responded quietly after detecting secret database hack in 2013, October 2017. http://reut.rs/2ysNpw2
36. A social science approach to information security. http://bit.ly/2l7IefL
37. Violino, B.: Data breaches rising because of lack of cybersecurity acumen, December 2017. http://bit.ly/2CbIQKR
38. Anwar, A., Khormali, A. Mohaisen, A.: POSTER: understanding the hidden cost of software vulnerabilities: measurements and predictions. In: Proceedings of the 13th ACM Symposium on Information, Computer and Communications Security (ASIACCS), Incheon, Korea, June 2018

Privacy-Enhanced Fraud Detection
with Bloom Filters

Daniel Arp[1](✉), Erwin Quiring[1], Tammo Krueger[2], Stanimir Dragiev[2],
and Konrad Rieck[1]

[1] Technische Universität Braunschweig, Braunschweig, Germany
d.arp@tu-braunschweig.de
[2] Zalando Payments GmbH, Berlin, Germany

Abstract. The online shopping sector is continuously growing, generating a turnover of billions of dollars each year. Unfortunately, this growth in popularity is not limited to regular customers: Organized crime targeting online shops has considerably evolved in the past years, causing significant financial losses to the merchants. As criminals often use similar strategies among different merchants, sharing information about fraud patterns could help mitigate the success of these malicious activities. In practice, however, the sharing of data is difficult, since shops are often competitors or have to follow strict privacy laws. In this paper, we propose a novel method for fraud detection that allows merchants to exchange information on recent fraud incidents without exposing customer data. To this end, our method pseudonymizes orders on the client-side before sending them to a central service for analysis. Although the service cannot access individual features of these orders, it is able to infer fraudulent patterns using machine learning techniques. We examine the capabilities of this approach and measure its impact on the overall detection performance on a dataset of more than 1.5 million orders from a large European online fashion retailer.

1 Introduction

The electronic commerce sector (e-commerce) is rapidly growing world-wide, offering a large variety of products which are delivered directly to the customers' home. In order to stay competitive with traditional shops, online retailers try to send out products as soon as possible after being purchased, thus leaving only little time to check for fraudulent activity. Following this strategy, the online merchant *Amazon* alone generated a sales revenue of about 177.87 billion dollars in 2017 [34]. However, the great success of these shops and their high incomes also attract cybercriminals that cause significant financial losses to the merchants.

The creativity of the cybercriminals is virtually unlimited and ranges from individual fraudsters refusing to pay for products to highly organized cybercriminals. So called *reshipping scams* are, for instance, a common fraud scheme which causes an estimated financial loss of 1.8 billion US dollars each year [14]. In these scams, the fraudsters use stolen payment data and let the shop send the products to middlemen who relabel the goods and forward them to the criminals. In consequence, it becomes rather impossible for law enforcement to catch these cybercriminals due to the lack of any actual information about their identity.

As a reaction to the growing threat caused by cybercriminals, merchants have started to rely on fraud detection systems which automatically scan incoming orders for fraudulent patterns. According to a report published by Lexis-Nexis [19], these systems often combine multiple fraud detection techniques, such as identity and address verification or device fingerprinting. Despite these efforts to automate the detection process, manual reviews are often additionally necessary to verify that an order is indeed malicious. Still, there remains a large number of undetected fraud incidents. As fraudsters tend to use similar fraud patterns among various merchants, an exchange of current fraud incidents between online retailers could effectively reduce the number of successful fraud attempts. In practice, however, this exchange of information is difficult because competitive merchants are often unwilling to share their data and also privacy laws pose a big hurdle for sharing customer data among different parties.

In this paper, we propose a novel approach that allows merchants to exchange information on recent fraud incidents without exposing customer data to other retailers. In particular, each merchant pseudonymizes incoming orders on the client side before uploading them to a central analysis service. This service in turn applies machine learning techniques to the pseudonymized data accumulated from all participating online retailers. In this way, the analysis service does not have access to orders in plaintext and each merchant cannot see data from the others. The resulting detection method, however, is capable of uncovering patterns in the pseudonymized data that may indicate global fraud and would have been missed otherwise.

Our pseudonymization method is based on Bloom filters as proposed by Schnell et al. [29]. We extend this data representation to improve the privacy of customers and empirically evaluate the probability of de-pseudonymization attacks. Based on these results, we calibrate the parameters of our pseudonymization method such that a machine learning algorithm can find actual fraud patterns while still providing a good protection of the underlying data.

We apply our method to a large data set consisting of more than 1.5 million actual orders collected by a large European online retailer and evaluate several learning methods on the pseudonymized data. We compare our results against a baseline that the merchant obtains without the use of pseudonymization. Although the detection performance decreases due to the information loss introduced by the pseudonymization, significant fraud patterns still remain in the data which can help to inform merchants about potential fraudulent activity.

In summary, we make the following contributions:

1. We present an approach that allows the sharing of data between different merchants without directly exposing sensitive information about their customers.
2. We determine the strength of the proposed pseudonymization method while assuming a realistic attack scenario.

3. We evaluate the detection performance of our approach on a large dataset containing 1,840,582 actual orders and demonstrate its ability to extract useful fraud patterns from the data despite the loss of information introduced by the pseudonymization.
4. To foster future research in this area, we make our method publicly available to the community[1].

The remainder of this paper is structured as follows. Section 2 provides some background information about the fraud ecosystem and common fraud patterns. In Sect. 3 we define a threat model which allows us to design a system for privacy-enhanced detection of online fraud. The resulting system is evaluated in Sect. 4. We discuss the challenges and limitations that we have faced throughout our research in Sect. 5 and discuss related work in Sect. 6. Section 7 concludes this paper.

2   Background

Online retailers are nowadays facing a large variety of different types of fraud. Due to convenience for the customers, it is not possible to simply enforce a strict verification process before delivering the purchase. Instead, the merchant needs to carefully weigh up the chance of losing a legitimate customer against the chance of being scammed by a cybercriminal. This decision is far from being trivial since fraudsters are continuously improving their patterns in order to remain undetected. In the following, we briefly discuss three prevalent fraud patterns of different complexity.

The so-called *chargeback fraud* [19,38] represents a simple, yet common kind of fraud. A scammer purchases several products that are paid by credit card. After receiving the purchased goods, the fraudster requests a chargeback from her bank, thus getting the spent money refunded. This type of fraud understandably works just once at each merchant. Consequently, professional fraud often additionally involves identity theft where stolen credit card data or other personal information of other people are used to commit fraud repeatedly. Similar fraud activities also emerge in the context of bank transfers. For example, SEPA transfers can be canceled within a few days as part of a chargeback fraud.

Another type of fraud involves the payment by invoice, a popular payment method in some European countries. Normally, a customer purchases products that are delivered together with the invoice. This allows for *invoice fraud* which is similar to chargeback fraud in the sense that the payment is postponed to a later time. However, compared to chargeback fraud, it poses the additional risk to the retailer that no financial information about the customer is available—not even the minimal guarantee of a valid solvent bank account. This further lowers the threshold for committing fraud: while for chargeback fraud at least a (possibly stolen) credit card number is required, for the invoice the retailer has no interaction with the fraudster whatsoever. The fraudster obtains the products, but is never paying the invoice.

---

[1] http://www.github.com/darp/abbo-tools.

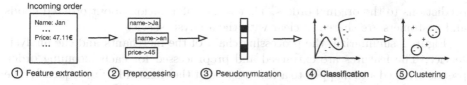

Fig. 1. Overview of the different steps of a privacy-enhanced fraud detection. A merchant (1) extracts features from an incoming order that are subsequently (2) preprocessed and (3) pseudonymized. Next, the analysis service applies (3) classification and (4) clustering methods to uncover fraudulent activities.

A more involved group of fraudulent activities combining various scamming patterns is known as *re-shipping scams* [14], commonly applied by professional cybercriminals. The fraudsters purchase goods from merchants by using stolen credit card data or benefit from deferred payment solutions like invoice. They hire middlemen commonly referred to as *drop points* via job announcements in newspapers or online portals. These drop points accept the packages and forward them to the fraudsters. The fraudsters' identity remains unknown while the possibly unwitting middleman might be approached by law enforcement. These middlemen are often used by multiple fraudsters to scam different merchants and are active for less than a month.

The exchange of fraudulent orders among multiple vendors and the application of a global classifier could effectively hinder fraudulent orders involving common drop points, stolen identities or credit card numbers. Overall, these fraud patterns highlight the need and benefit of a shared fraud detection that is discussed in the remainder of this manuscript.

3 Methodology

In this section we develop the overall setting of a shared analysis service among several merchants. We then derive a threat model and discuss the resulting privacy risks. Based on this step, we finally design a pseudonymization method to protect the customers' privacy during fraud detection.

3.1 The Analysis Service

Each participating merchant pseudonymizes its incoming orders before uploading them to the analysis service. A classification model trained on the pseudonymized data returns a prediction score which describes the potential risk of a submitted order. In contrast to a classifier solely trained on the data from a single retailer, the proposed classifier has access to the orders from all participating merchants. In this way, it is capable to identify global fraud incidents that could be missed by a single vendor. As consequence of this design, the analysis service does not have access to data in plaintext and only the merchants can link reported fraud predictions to the original orders. That is, no information about ordered goods and customers are shared in clear with the analysis service.

Figure 1 summarizes the processing chain of the merchants and the analysis service. The features are extracted and preprocessed for each incoming order, pseudonymized and mapped to a vector space at the client side. Subsequently, the analysis service performs classification and clustering to identify fraud incidents. We discuss these steps in more detail in the following.

3.2   Features for Fraud Detection

To identify online fraud effectively, the classification model needs access to a set of discriminating features. The participation of a diverse range of online retailers also requires the definition of a meaningful subset of features that every retailer can contribute to. Thus, we focus on a minimal set of features which on the one hand are naturally available due to the purchase process and on the other hand enable the classification model to discriminate fraudsters from normal orders:

Address Data. Every online fraud needs to be delivered to a certain physical address before the fraudster is able to resell the stolen goods and generate profit. The drop points are often reused since it is difficult to organize a multitude of delivery places without the help of a sophisticated organizational structure which is often not available. By collecting address data from multiple merchants it becomes easier to identify suspicious behavior for one particular address.

Cart Items. The ultimate goal of the fraudster is to get goods for free which she can easily resell. In most cases she will therefore focus on specific brands and types of goods which have a good market value. This highly resaleable combination of goods in correlation with fraud will emerge naturally in the data pool of the analysis service and thus can be exploited by the classifier. We describe the ordered goods as a list of unique article identifiers and their respective prices.

Iterations. Fraudsters try to optimize their shopping cart by repeatedly adding or removing items until they can fool the checkout system and get the delivery. This is the single point where they can receive feedback from the fraud detection system and try to uncover the black box by exploiting common assumptions, for instance that a lower basket size increases the chance to get through.

Solvency Score. Online retailers usually include a solvency score in their assessment of a customer. This score describes more or less accurately the probability that a customer will default. In the context of fraud detection, this feature helps to discriminate benign orders from fraud orders: If a customer has a good solvency score she is most of the time an actual person with a positive shopping history and is thus less likely to commit fraud.

This minimal set of features allows the analysis service to build classification models that balance out the amount of used features with the benefit of the pooling effect.

3.3   Threat Model

Sharing this kind of data between several parties obviously raises serious privacy and competition concerns. An order contains sensitive information about a customer such as her name, address and purchased products. To derive a secure pseudonymization method, we therefore need to define a threat model that describes the involved parties and their capabilities.

Merchants. The analysis service is used by multiple, possibly competitive merchants. A fraudulent merchant might thus try to abuse the analysis service to access confidential information from other merchants, such as the amount and type of commonly sold goods, the addresses of active customers and so on.

   Hence, we design the analysis service such that the participating online retailers do not need to trust each other. In particular, each merchant has only access to its own uploaded data, that is, no retailer ever needs to have explicit access to the pseudonymized data of other participating merchants. Instead, the information of fraud incidents from other retailers is implicitly contained in the classification model trained by the analysis service.

Analysis Service. A fraudulent operator of the analysis service has access to the data of all merchants, thus posing a serious risk to the confidentiality of the data. We assume that the operator is not one of the participating retailers but knows the names and addresses of some customers in the dataset. Using this information, she tries to deduce the goods that a particular customer has bought from one or several merchants.

   In consequence, we have to ensure that the analysis service never has access to the plain data but only to pseudonymized orders. Still, the possibility is given that the operator of the analysis service attempts to break the pseudonymization using her background knowledge about certain customers. Thus, we need to strengthen our pseudonymization technique accordingly.

3.4   Pseudonymization

After discussing the utilized features and defining the threat model, we can finally develop a suitable pseudonymization technique. This technique has to fulfill certain requirements in our scenario. Most importantly, it should not be possible to easily reconstruct the information stored within the pseudonymized orders. At the same time, it should allow a machine learning algorithm to still extract fraudulent patterns from the data. Moreover, the approach should be capable of handling different data types as the discussion of the features in the previous subsection highlights.

Preprocessing the Data. Our proposed pseudonymization technique is based on Bloom filters [1], which we describe afterwards. The conversion of an incoming order into this data structure requires a preprocessing that can be divided into two distinct steps.

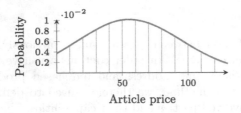

Fig. 2. Instead of using the exact value of the numerical features, their values are discretized by binning them.

First, non-string values are converted into a string representation. For numerical features like the article price, this is done by simply binning their values. In particular, the size of these bins is selected regarding to the value distribution of the considered feature. Figure 2 depicts an example of this procedure for the *article price*. The selection of the bin size affects both the detection performance and the pseudonymization strength. By selecting a large bin size, more articles get assigned to the same price. This makes it harder for an attacker to derive whether the filter contains a particular article solely based on its price value.

In the second step, all strings are decomposed into smaller substrings before being inserted into the Bloom filter. Overall, different types of decompositions exist which can be applied.

- *Word Decomposition.* The order is split at the whitespaces and the resulting elements are inserted into the Bloom filter. While the decomposition of orders through this method is rather simple, it is not possible to match strings whose spelling only slightly differ.
- *N-Gram Decomposition.* In contrast to the word decomposition, the extraction of *n-grams* allows us to compensate for spelling mistakes and thus to decide whether two Bloom filters contain similar strings [8].
- *Entity Decomposition.* This decomposition is similar to the word decomposition, but additionally stores the information to which part of the order a particular word belongs. This, for instance, allows determining whether the shipping and billing address of an order differ—a pattern indicative for fraudulent activity.
- *Colored N-Grams Decomposition.* Similar to the decomposition in entities, colored n-grams store to which part of an order the extracted n-gram belongs. Figure 1 shows an example for a colored 2-gram decomposition.

Bloom Filters. After the preprocessing of an order, the resulting strings are finally put into a Bloom filter. For each order, we initialize a separate Bloom filter. This probabilistic data structure enables storing large sets of elements within a limited amount of memory while simultaneously allowing an efficient comparison between different filters. At the same time, it does not allow an attacker to recover the information stored inside the data structure without

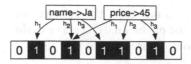

Fig. 3. Two elements are inserted into the Bloom filter using three hash functions (with a collision at the 4th bit).

background knowledge. Initially proposed for spell checking, Bloom Filters have already been successfully applied in several privacy-sensitive fields including the linkage of health records [11,21,26,29].

Figure 3 depicts the basic concept behind Bloom filters schematically. The filter is a bit array of fixed length m where all bits are initialized as 0 s. To insert an element x into the filter, a predefined number of k independent hash functions $h_i(x)$ are applied on the element. Each hash function maps the element to a particular position in the filter where the corresponding bit is set to 1. Similarly, it is possible to check whether the filter contains a particular element by applying these hash functions to the element and checking whether the corresponding bits are set to 1. If one of the bits is not set, the element has definitely not been inserted into the filter. In contrast, a positive match may be a false positive if the bits are set to 1 by other inserted elements.

These so-called collisions are usually an unwanted property of Bloom filters. However, collisions are desirable in our case since they already thwart an attacker from certainly reconstructing information stored within the filter. Nonetheless, this mechanism on its own is not sufficient to protect sensitive data as our evaluation in Sect. 4 underlines.

Hardening the Bloom Filter. We examine several extensions of Bloom filters to strengthen their security properties.

- *Noise Insertion.* Adding noise to the Bloom filter can help to protect the data stored inside of it [11,21] but can also partially destroy important information. We examine the effects of this approach for our application scenario by randomly setting bits in the filter.
- *Merging Filters.* Instead of just setting random bits, it is also possible to sample fake items from their respective distributions and add them to the Bloom filter. While this approach is more complex, it also further lowers the probability of successful frequency analysis attacks [16]. We implement a similar approach by merging multiple filters into a single one before sending it to the analysis service. Thus, an attacker has no possibility to assign a specific feature, e.g. an article, to a particular customer.
- *Keyed Hash Functions.* If an attacker has knowledge of the underlying distributions of the dataset and exact parameters used to pseudonymize the data, she can perform a dictionary attack and reconstruct the information stored inside the filters. This kind of attack can be effectively thwarted by keyed

hash functions [28,29]. In our case, the retailers share a secret key which is unknown to the operator of the analysis service, thus significantly improving the protection of the data stored inside the filters.

With these extensions at hand, it should be possible to clearly lower the probability of a de-pseudonymization. However, these techniques can simultaneously affect the detection performance of the classifier. We examine and discuss the effects of these techniques in Sect. 4.2.

3.5   Learning-Based Fraud Detection

In the last step, we apply machine learning techniques for automatically detecting fraudulent patterns in the pseudonymized data. The usage of machine learning relieves a fraud analysis from manually constructing detection rules. In particular, we consider *classification* and *clustering* techniques. In the classification step, a learning model distinguishes between fraud and non-fraud cases. Afterwards, fraudulent patterns are extracted from the data by applying clustering techniques. This allows a fraud analyst to interpret these patterns and to take further actions if necessary.

Classification. The application of machine learning requires an appropriate vector representation of each Bloom filter. To this end, we associate each bit of the Bloom filter with a dimension in an m-dimensional vector space, where each dimension is either 0 or 1 and m corresponds to the length of the Bloom filter:

$$x \in \mathbb{R}^m = (b_1, b_2, \ldots, b_m), \quad b_i = \{0, 1\} \,. \tag{1}$$

This yields very sparse high-dimensional data on which machine learning techniques can be applied. We examine the performance of *Linear Support Vector Machines* [10] and *Gradient Boosted Trees* [7] on this representation.

Clustering. In the next step, we try to find fraudulent patterns within the pseudonymized data by applying clustering methods such as k-means [9]. The identified clusters are ranked according to their ratio between fraud and benign samples. That is, clusters that contain many fraud incidents and preferably no benign samples are ranked at the top.

We can then extract (pseudonymized) fraudulent patterns from the highest ranked clusters. Figure 4 schematically visualizes an example for this process. Each Bloom filter of a fraud case is represented as a row in the left image. Red pixels represent set bits, black pixels unset bits. In addition, white horizontal lines separate the different clusters from each other. This representation easily uncovers fraudulent patterns as a unique combination of red vertical stripes in the image. In practice, the analysis service can extract these patterns and send them to each online retailer. Since they have complete knowledge of the underlying pseudonymization technique, they are able to map back the fraud pattern to plaintext. Figure 4 shows an example on the right where an uncovered combination of n-grams indicates fraudulent activity.

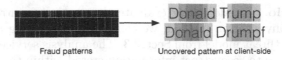

Fraud patterns   Uncovered pattern at client-side

Fig. 4. Schematic visualization of the process to uncover fraud patterns on the client-side.

4   Evaluation

A successful operation of the central analysis service rests on two key requirements: First, we need to hinder a de-pseudonymization as good as possible. Second, we should be able to apply machine learning techniques to detect fraudulent orders. To evaluate whether we can balance these opposing requirements, we conduct the following experiments:

1. *Calibrating the data protection.* We examine the strength of our implemented pseudonymization method under the given threat model. Based on the results, we preselect a range of parameters that ensure a good data protection.
2. *Calibrating the detection performance.* We pseudonymize a sample of the data using the selected parameter ranges and train a classifier for each combination. We pick the parameter combination that yields the best detection results.
3. *Classification.* We pseudonymize the complete dataset of orders and evaluate the detection performance on this data. Subsequently, we compare the results with the detection performance achieved on the unprotected data.
4. *Clustering.* Finally, we cluster the pseudonymized data and extract common patterns of professional fraud from it. We then discuss how these patterns can help merchants to identify fraud more quickly.

4.1   Evaluation Dataset

Our dataset consists of 1,840,582 orders including 14,179 fraud incidents from 2016 provided by Zalando, a large European online fashion retailer. The data was carefully cleaned to ensure a high data quality. To discriminate between benign and fraudulent orders, we consider the actual payment. We flag each order as fraudulent that is not payed after three months. We have conducted our experiments in close consultation with Zalando. In each step, we have carefully followed German data privacy laws.

4.2   Calibrating the Data Protection

We first examine the pseudonymization method described in Sect. 3.4 to preselect a range of promising Bloom filter parameters that provide high pseudonymization strength.

Attack Scenario. To adequately evaluate the protection introduced by the proposed pseudonymization method, we consider the following attack scenario according to the threat model from Sect. 3.3. The analysis service represents the adversary and tries to reconstruct information stored within the Bloom filters.

Without background knowledge, such an attack is not possible. The adversary needs to know the parameters that have been used to create the Bloom filters, such as the type of hash functions. In addition, the service needs a list of possible addresses or articles. Without this information, a Bloom filter simply appears to the adversary as random bit sequence. Therefore, we grant the service full knowledge of the underlying method and assume that it has collected a list of customer addresses and possible articles, for example, by crawling the web. Its objective is now to gain knowledge about the shopping behavior of the customers in the dataset. In particular, the service wants to derive which goods a particular customer has bought.

With the necessary background knowledge the attacker can create own Bloom filters with the names and addresses of targeted customers and compare them with the pseudonymized orders. To this end, the adversary uses the *Jaccard similarity* [33] which is defined between two Bloom filters B_1 and B_2 as

$$J(B_1, B_2) = \frac{|B_1 \cap B_2|}{|B_1 \cup B_2|} = \frac{|B_1 \wedge B_2|}{|B_1 \vee B_2|}. \tag{2}$$

$B_1 \wedge B_2$ represents the bitwise intersection, $B_1 \vee B_2$ the respective union between the two vectors. The attacker can now match two Bloom filters if their similarity score is greater than a particular threshold. After having identified a particular customer in one of the pseudonymized orders, the adversary can run a dictionary attack in order to determine which goods have been purchased by this customer.

Results. For measuring the influence of different pseudonymization parameters, we sample an artificial dataset consisting of 1,000 distinct orders. Using this data, we evaluate the impact of several Bloom filter parameters on the pseudonymization strength. The obtained results are averaged over 5 repetitions.

Decompositions. The results for different decompositions types are presented in Fig. 5a. The plot depicts the fraction of correctly re-identified customers for different decomposition types depending on the Bloom filter length. For all examined decompositions, the attacker is able to re-identify the majority of customers even when a small Bloom filter size of 500 Bits is selected. Further reducing the size of the filters increases the collision probability and in turn also lowers the de-pseudonymization probability. However, the high number of collisions destroys valuable patterns for the detection of fraud at the same time.

Overall, we find that the collision probability does not provide proper protection of the sensitive data and we require further protection mechanisms. Moreover, the selected decomposition type has only little impact on the de-pseudonymization probability. Hence, we select two decomposition types that should allow deriving the best detection performance, i.e., *n-grams and colored*

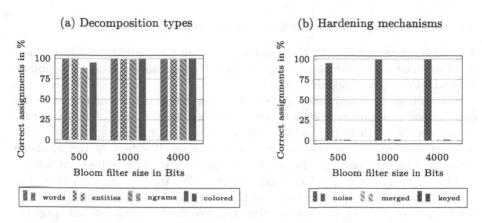

Fig. 5. (a) and (b) depict the impact of different decomposition types and hardening mechanisms on the pseudonymization strength.

n-grams. While both allow handling spelling mistakes, colored n-grams also allow distinguishing between different parts of an order.

Hardening Mechanisms. Since the collision probability does not provide sufficient protection, we have to rely on the hardening extensions described in Sect. 3.4. The results of their evaluation are depicted in Fig. 5b. In this experiment, we add 10% of noise to the Bloom filters and measure the impact on the de-pseudonymization performance. Surprisingly, the addition of noise has almost no effect on the success of the attacker. The reason for this is that the attacker has knowledge about the name and address of a customer in our attack scenario. If both are re-identified in a particular Bloom filter, the probability is very high that the pseudonymized order indeed belongs to that customer—despite the presence of noise.

In contrast to adding noise, the two other hardening mechanisms succeed in protecting the customer data. If we merge k orders during the pseudonymization with $k = 3$, the attacker is unable to re-identify the order of a particular customer. However, if the merged order is identified as fraud, the merchant needs to check which one of the k orders actually contains fraud patterns. The hardening mechanism of keyed hash functions also successfully thwarts de-pseudonymization without the drawback of the merge method. In this case, the mechanism requires that the key remains unknown to the attacker.

In summary, the adversary in our attack scenario can be effectively thwarted when merging multiple orders or by using keyed hash functions. These two mechanisms provide a good protection independent from the size of the Bloom filters. In the following, we thus examine the effects of both hardening mechanisms on the detection performance using Bloom filter sizes between 1000 and 10,000 Bits.

4.3   Calibrating the Detection Performance

The parameters selected in the previous step ensure a good data protection. It thus remains to calibrate our approach such that also a good detection of fraudulent activity is possible—if at all.

Overall, we have 384 different parameter combinations to evaluate after the preselection of parameters, such as the size of the Bloom filter, the regularisation parameter of the learning method and the lengths of the n-grams. In order to cope with this large number, we use only a small subset of the available training data and perform the model selection on it. This subset consists of 11,145 samples including 5,591 fraud incidents. We train a linear SVM on the data and measure its performance using the area under the ROC curve (AUC) [2]. We bound the AUC at 1% false positives to favor models with low false-positive rates. Having large false positive rates could otherwise lead to the rejection of legitimate customers, thus causing even greater financial loss to the merchants.

Based on the results of these experiments, we select a Bloom filter size of 4000 bits and a colored 2-gram decomposition. Moreover, we choose a bin size of 10 and 1 for the article price and the solvency score, respectively.

4.4   Classification

We finally examine the change in detection performance on the full dataset. We pseudonymize the dataset using the previously determined parameter values. We then split the dataset into two distinct sets and compare the detection performance obtained on the pseudonymized data with the original performance. The results are presented in Fig. 6a. The baseline provided by Zalando is depicted in black whereas the results obtained on the pseudonymized data are shown as colored lines.

Note, that all classifiers have been trained on the same set of features in order to ensure comparability. Using keyed hash functions as hardening mechanism, we achieve a detection performance of about 75% compared to the results obtained by Zalando at 1% false positives. As can be seen from Fig. 6a, this ratio remains nearly constant, even for significantly lower false positive rates such as 0.1%. We credit the difference in detection performance compared to Zalando to the information loss induced by the pseudonymization. While Zalando, for instance, trains the learning algorithm based on the exact numerical values, we lose information due to the binning of numerical features as described in Sect. 3.4. Nonetheless, we can uncover a large fraction of the fraud cases without access to the original orders, demonstrating that a central analysis service is technically feasible.

We also evaluate the detection performance after merging the filters. In particular, we randomly pick three Bloom filters and merge them into one. If at least one of the merged filters has been labeled as fraud, the resulting Bloom filter is also considered to be malicious. We notice a significant drop in the detection rate, thus achieving only about 30% of the original detection rate. We deduce

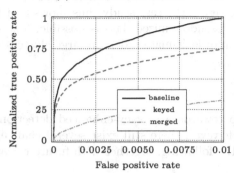

(a) Classification results

(b) Clustering results

Rank #	Fraud #	Benign	Ratio
1	17	0	100.0%
2	31	0	100.0%
3	15	1	93.8%
4	357	41	89.7%
5	151	26	85.3%

Fig. 6. Classification results on 1,840,582 orders with a Bloom filter size of 4000 and two different hardening mechanisms. Each ROC curve shows the normalized true positive rate by using the performance of the baseline classifier as reference. Moreover, the table in (b) presents the purity of the top-ranked clusters obtained on a dataset of 11,145 orders.

that merging the Bloom filters changes the underlying distributions drastically and thus has a large impact on the detection rate.

In summary, we achieve a detection performance of about 75% compared to the unprotected data while at the same time clearly enhancing the protection of the underlying data. In the following, we evaluate whether it is possible to extract fraudulent patterns from the data using clustering despite the information loss introduced by the pseudonymization.

4.5   Clustering

We apply a k-means clustering to the dataset of 11,145 samples which has also been used to perform the parameter selection as discussed in Sect. 4.3. In particular, we test different values for k and pick the one which yields the best results, that is, a clustering where the top ranked clusters have the highest purity. Figure 6b shows the top ranked clusters obtained when selecting $k = 100$.

We investigate these best-ranked clusters to determine whether they contain schemes of organized cybercrime. By de-pseudonymizing the data at the merchant, we find that the orders in the first three clusters are mainly grouped together due to specific articles or addresses they share. However, after consultation with Zalando, they can not be considered professional fraud and rather correspond to simple chargeback scams.

By contrast, cluster 4 and 5 exhibit typical patterns of professional scam. In particular, the forth cluster mainly contains orders of expensive clothes which are delivered to drop points in Berlin. Moreover, these orders show a high iteration count, indicating that the fraudsters tried to optimize their shopping cart. Similar patterns can also be found in the cluster 5 where the fraudsters ordered rather high-priced accessories like watches or bags and let them send to drop points in Cologne. It is worth noting that both clusters contain 41 and 26 presumably legitimate orders, respectively. Overall, the case study thus shows that the extraction of fraud patterns from the pseudonymized data is possible, however, it requires tuning to lower the fraction of legitimate orders in large clusters.

5   Limitations

Our approach represents a first step towards a privacy-enhanced detection of fraudulent activity in e-commerce. However, there still exist several challenges and limitations which we discuss in the following, together with future research directions.

Malicious Collaborations. In our threat model we do not consider the collaboration between a malicious merchant and a malicious analysis service. In this scenario, the key for the pseudonymization could be leaked to the analysis service, thus enabling its operator to run dictionary attacks on the Bloom filters. Fortunately, the collaboration of multiple merchants or a malicious analysis service alone do not pose a risk. It therefore remains future research to find extensions that also protect the customer data in scenarios where a malicious merchant and service collaborate.

Consistent Data Labeling. A consistent procedure for labeling the input data fed to the machine learning algorithm is essential to achieve a good classification performance. While this seems to be an obvious requirement, it is far from trivial in practice. This is because various online retailers often have their own definition of fraud and thus varying labeling procedures. In order to apply our approach in practice, it would be necessary that the participating online retailers agree on a common labeling scheme.

Data Access. We only have access to the data of a single merchant to conduct our experiments. In order to demonstrate that our approach is indeed capable of identifying global fraud patterns, we thus require further data from other merchants. Still, the obtained results indicate that the identification of fraud is possible on pseudonymized data using our method and thus can help us acquire a larger group of participating merchants.

Frequency Analysis Attacks. Several researchers have shown that Bloom filters are prone to frequency analysis attacks [15–17]. Although these attacks pose a real threat in practice, they require the adversary to have exact background knowledge about the underlying distributions from which the features are drawn. While this is a realistic assumption for publicly available information such as names or addresses, it requires insider knowledge for other features like the solvency score.

By adding noise to the filters, the risk of a successful attack can be further reduced and should thus be negligible in our case. Nonetheless, measuring the actual risk needs further research since it highly depends on the particular application scenario and the knowledge available to the adversary.

6 Related Work

In the following, we discuss related work which contains research of mainly three different disciplines. First, we discuss research that provides insights into the underground ecosystem related to reshipping scams. Second, we describe papers that deal with fraud and malware detection. Finally, we review related literature which focusses on privacy-preserving technologies.

Underground Ecosystem. The first in-depth study on reshipping scams is presented by Hao et al. [14] who have analyzed the log files from seven reshipping scam operations that took place between 2010 and 2015. Their paper provides a detailed overview of the inner workings of this underground economy and estimates the overall financial loss caused by reshipping scams to be around 1.8 billion US dollars per year. In addition, they have been able to identify several possible ways how these criminal activities can be disrupted. However, the suggested countermeasures need to be enforced by the shipping service companies, thus requiring the online retailers to rely on these companies. In contrast, we focus on defenses that can be directly applied by the merchants themselves.

Other research groups have examined fraudulent activity closely related to reshipping scams. In particular, reshipping scams mostly imply identity theft [3,30,35] and mule recruitment [12,22]. A survey on hijacking of online accounts for identity theft has been conducted by Shay et al. [30]. The authors have interrogated 294 people about their experience with account hijacking. Surprisingly, about 30.3% of the participants report that they have experienced compromise attempts on their email or social network accounts at least once. A similar study has been conducted by Bursztein et al. [3] but focusses on manual account hijacking. While identity theft allows fraudsters to distribute malware or spam using the stolen identities [18], it also poses a crucial part in reshipping scams. Consequently, some countermeasures initially proposed for spam or malware might also help to impede fraud in e-commerce.

Fraud Detection in e-Commerce. A large strain of research examines techniques to efficiently detect credit card fraud [5,23]. Chan et al. [6] present a survey of different techniques for detecting credit card fraud. Likewise, other researchers have studied approaches to detect related fraud variants. In particular, Pandit et al. [25] propose a fraud detection system based on a *Markov Random Field* to discover fraud in online auctions. Their approach has been evaluated on a data set containing more than 60,000 actual users from eBay. Another method by Maranzato et al. [20] targets frauds against reputation systems in e-markets. An orthogonal strategy to defend against online fraud is the application of fingerprinting techniques like browser fingerprinting and device fingerprinting [4], which unfortunately raises serious privacy concerns [24]. The most similar method to ours has been proposed by Preuveneers et al. [27]. The authors present a system which provides fraud detection as a service to the merchants. However, their approach does not consider data protection. Moreover, they use individual detection rules for each merchant instead of a global classifier trained on the data of several online retailers.

Privacy-Preserving Technologies. When processing personal data, it is particularly important to ensure that the data is protected from unauthorized access. Techniques to achieve a high protection level for sensitive patient data have been widely studied in the field of medical databases [16,29,37]. In particular, Schnell et al. [29] present an approach for privacy-preserving record linkage based on Bloom filters. Personal identifiers are stored in Bloom filters which can then be used to re-identify the database entry of a person within different databases without revealing its identity. Several researchers have demonstrated attacks on Bloom filters [15–17] using frequency analysis techniques. However, these attacks require the attacker to have background knowledge on the underlying distributions. While this is a realistic assumptions for publicly available information such as names or addresses, it requires insider knowledge for other features like the solvency score.

In addition, various researchers have recently demonstrated several successful information leakage attacks against machine learning models [13,32,36]. As a result of these attacks, the adversary is able to deduce some potentially sensitive information from the data that has been used to train the classifiers. In order to fend off some of these attacks, Shokri and Shmatikov [31] propose a system to jointly learn a neural network without exposing too much information of the local datasets. However, since random weights from locally trained neural networks are exchanged between the different parties, the exact privacy implications of this approach are still unclear. A similar defense technique has been presented by Wu et al. [39] to privately evaluate random forests and decision trees, but is limited to two parties and thus not applicable in our scenario.

7   Conclusion

This paper takes a first step towards an earlier detection of fraudulent orders committed against online retailers. As scammers often use similar strategies among several merchants, an exchange of information about recent fraud schemes between merchants could effectively impede the success of these scams. However, merchants are often unwilling to share this data with competitors and, moreover, have to follow strict privacy laws.

As a remedy, we propose an analysis service that allows multiple merchants to upload incoming orders that are pseudonymized in advance. In this way, the analysis service is able to extract global fraud patterns from the shared but pseudonymized data. This enables the service to inform the merchants about recent fraud schemes in a privacy-friendly way.

We implement a pseudonymization technique based on Bloom filters and evaluate its impact on the overall detection performance. To this end, we use a large dataset of actual orders collected by a large European online fashion retailer. In the pseudonymized setting we are able to spot 75% of the fraud cases detected by the privacy-unaware analysis at the same false positive rate. An additional clustering step further demonstrates that we are able to identify common patterns of professional fraud.

Although our approach does not provide perfect results, we demonstrate that balancing privacy and performance in fraud detection is technically feasible and direct access to sensitive information is not strictly necessary. Our approach is generic and can be extended using different pseudonymization techniques and learning methods. As a consequence, we are optimistic that future work can further narrow the gap between unprotected and privacy-enhanced fraud detection.

Acknowledgments. The authors would like to thank Alwin Maier and Paul Schmidt for their assistance during the research project. Moreover, the authors gratefully acknowledge funding from the German Federal Ministry of Education and Research (BMBF) under the project ABBO (FKZ: 13N13634).

References

1. Bloom, B.H.: Space/time trade-offs in hash coding with allowable errors. Commun. ACM **13**(7), 422–426 (1970)
2. Bradley, A.: The use of the area under the ROC curve in the evaluation of machine learning algorithms. Pattern Recogn. **30**(7), 1145–1159 (1997)
3. Bursztein, E., et al.: Handcrafted fraud and extortion: manual account hijacking in the wild. In: Proceedings of Conference on Internet Measurement Conference (IMC) (2014)
4. Bursztein, E., Malyshev, A., Pietraszek, T., Thomas, K.: Picasso: lightweight device class fingerprinting for web clients. In: Proceedings of ACM Workshop on Security and Privacy in Smartphones and Mobile Devices (SPSM) (2016)
5. Caldeira, E., Brandao, G., Pereira, A.C.M.: Fraud analysis and prevention in e-commerce transactions. In: Proceedings of Latin American Web Congress (LA-WEB) (2014)
6. Chan, P.K., Fan, W., Prodromidis, A.L., Stolfo, S.J.: Distributed data mining in credit card fraud detection. IEEE Intell. Syst. **14**(6), 67–74 (1999)
7. Chen, T., Guestrin, C.: XGBoost: a scalable tree boosting system. In: Proceedings of ACM SIGKDD Conference on Knowledge Discovery and Data Mining (2016)
8. Damashek, M.: Gauging similarity with n-grams: language-independent categorization of text. Science **267**(5199), 843–848 (1995)
9. Duda, R., Hart, P.E., Stork, D.G.: Pattern Classification, 2nd edn. Wiley, Hoboken (2001)
10. Fan, R.E., Chang, K.W., Hsieh, C.J., Wang, X.R., Lin, C.J.: LIBLINEAR: a library for large linear classification. J. Mach. Learn. Res. (JMLR) **9**, 1871–1874 (2008)
11. Fanti, G., Pihur, V., Erlingsson, Ú.: Building a RAPPOR with the unknown: privacy-preserving learning of associations and data dictionaries. In: Proceedings of Privacy Enhancing Technologies Symposium (PETS) (2016)
12. Florencio, D., Herley, C.: Phishing and money mules. In: Proceedings of IEEE International Workshop on Information Forensics and Security (WIFS) (2010)
13. Fredrikson, M., Lantz, E., Jha, S., Lin, S., Page, D., Ristenpart, T.: Privacy in pharmacogenetics: an end-to-end case study of personalized warfarin dosing. In: Proceedings of USENIX Security Symposium (2014)
14. Hao, S., et al.: Drops for stuff: an analysis of reshipping mule scams. In: Proceedings of ACM Conference on Computer and Communications Security (CCS) (2015)

15. Kroll, M., Steinmetzer, S.: Automated cryptanalysis of bloom filter encryptions of health records. In: Proceedings of the International Conference on Health Informatics (HEALTHINF) (2015)
16. Kroll, M., Steinmetzer, S., Niedermeyer, F., Schnell, R.: Cryptanalysis of basic bloom filters used for privacy preserving record linkage. J. Priv. Confidentiality 6(2), 59–79 (2014)
17. Kuzu, M., Kantarcioglu, M., Durham, E., Malin, B.: A constraint satisfaction cryptanalysis of bloom filters in private record linkage. In: Proceedings of Privacy Enhancing Technologies Symposium (PETS) (2011)
18. Levchenko, K., et al.: Click trajectories: end-to-end analysis of the spam value chain. In: Proceedings of IEEE Symposium on Security and Privacy (2011)
19. LexisNexis: True cost of fraud study (2016)
20. Maranzato, R., Pereira, A., do Lago, A.P., Neubert, M.: Fraud detection in reputation systems in e-markets using logistic regression. In: Proceedings of ACM Symposium on Applied Computing (SAC) (2010)
21. Mor, N., Riva, O., Nath, S., Kubiatowicz, J.: Bloom cookies: web search personalization without user tracking. In: Proceedings of Network and Distributed System Security Symposium (NDSS) (2015)
22. Motoyama, M., McCoy, D., Levchenko, K., Savage, S., Voelker, G.M.: Dirty jobs: the role of freelance labor in web service abuse. In: Proceedings of USENIX Security Symposium (2011)
23. Ngai, E.W.T., Hu, Y., Wong, Y.H., Chen, Y., Sun, X.: The application of data mining techniques in financial fraud detection: a classification framework and an academic review of literature. Decis. Support Syst. 50(3), 559–569 (2011)
24. Nikiforakis, N., Kapravelos, A., Joosen, W., Kruegel, C., Piessens, F., Vigna, G.: Cookieless monster: exploring the ecosystem of web-based device fingerprinting. In: Proceedings of IEEE Symposium on Security and Privacy (2013)
25. Pandit, S., Chau, D.H., Wang, S., Faloutsos, C.: NetProbe: a fast and scalable system for fraud detection in online auction networks. In: Proceedings of the International World Wide Web Conference (WWW) (2007)
26. Perl, H., Yassene, M., Brenner, M., Smith, M.: Fast confidential search for biomedical data using bloom filters and homomorphic cryptography. In: International Conference on eScience (2012)
27. Preuveneers, D., Goosens, B., Joosen, W.: Enhanced fraud detection as a service supporting merchant-specific runtime customization. In: Proceedings of ACM Symposium on Applied Computing (SAC) (2017)
28. Schneier, B.: Applied Cryptography. Wiley, Hoboken (1996)
29. Schnell, R., Bachteler, T., Reiher, J.: Privacy-preserving record linkage using bloom filters. BMC Med. Inform. Decis. Mak. 9, 41 (2009)
30. Shay, R., Ion, I., Reeder, R.W., Consolvo, S.: "My religious aunt asked why I was trying to sell her viagra": experiences with account hijacking. In: Proceedings of ACM Conference on Human Factors in Computing Systems (CHI) (2014)
31. Shokri, R., Shmatikov, V.: Privacy-preserving deep learning. In: Proceedings of ACM Conference on Computer and Communications Security (CCS) (2015)
32. Shokri, R., Stronati, M., Song, C., Shmatikov, V.: Membership inference attacks against machine learning models. In: Proceedings of IEEE Symposium on Security and Privacy (2017)
33. Sokal, R., Sneath, P.: Principles of Numerical Taxonomy. W.H. Freeman and Company, New York (1963)

34. Statista: Net sales revenue of Amazon from 2004 to 2017 (2018). https://www.statista.com/statistics/266282/annual-net-revenue-of-amazoncom/.   Accessed April 2018
35. Thomas, K., Iatskiv, D., Bursztein, E., Pietraszek, T., Grier, C., McCoy, D.: Dialing back abuse on phone verified accounts. In: Proceedings of ACM Conference on Computer and Communications Security (CCS) (2014)
36. Tramèr, F., Zhang, F., Juels, A., Reiter, M.K., Ristenpart, T.: Stealing machine learning models via prediction APIS. In: Proceedings of USENIX Security Symposium (2017)
37. Vatsalan, D., Christen, P., Verykios, V.S.: A taxonomy of privacy-preserving record linkage techniques. Inf. Syst. **38**(6), 946–969 (2013)
38. Worldpay: Fragmentation of fraud (2014)
39. Wu, D.J., Feng, T., Naehrig, M., Lauter, K.E.: Privately evaluating decision trees and random forests. In: Proceedings of Privacy Enhancing Technologies Symposium (PETS) (2016)

FriSM: Malicious Exploit Kit Detection via Feature-Based String-Similarity Matching

Sungjin Kim and Brent ByungHoon Kang[✉]

Graduate School of Information Security, School of Computing,
Korea Institute of Science Technology (KAIST), Daejeon, Republic of Korea
{r3dzon3,brentkang}@kaist.ac.kr

Abstract. Since an exploit kit (EK) was first developed, an increasing number of attempts has been made to infect users' PCs by transmitting malware via EKs. To tackle such malware distribution, we propose herein an enhanced *similarity-matching* technique that determines whether the test sets are similar to the pattern sets in which the structural properties of EKs are defined. A key characteristic of our *similarity-matching* technique is that, unlike typical pattern-matching, it can detect isomorphic variants derived from EKs. In an experiment involving 36,950 datasets, our *similarity-matching* technique provides a TP rate of 99.9% and an FP rate of 0.001% with a performance of 0.003 s/page.

Keywords: Exploit kits · Pattern matching · Similarity matching

1 Introduction

Many PCs are infected by malware during web surfing. Infections can also be caused by clicking on malicious links in email. Recent malware, called `Princess` ransomware, has been propagated across various countries via behaviors without users' knowledge. Such malware distribution is closely associated with webpages that contain exploit kits (EKs) such as RIG and Magnitude. Adversaries have long attempted to use EKs to target users. To tackle them, previous studies [1–5] used machine learning (ML)-, pattern-, and behavior-based approaches.

The ML-based model [1–3] checks the space in the hyperplanes built by benign/malicious training sets and determines the space to which a test sample is close. This classification is sometimes weak for cases involving benign samples encoded with packers, such as Dean Edwards [6] or benign JavaScript codes that contain `eval()` and `escape()` functions, which are commonly used as malicious attributes. This model also encounters difficulties in detecting browser-plugin-based attacks loaded immediately from the start page. Such attacks accompany a redirect seen as a legitimate URL (e.g., a fake Flash executable).

The pattern-based analysis [4] offers rapid detection with patterns. However, this approach can be applied only to content that contains pattern forms that can

© ICST Institute for Computer Sciences, Social Informatics and Telecommunications Engineering 2018
R. Beyah et al. (Eds.): SecureComm 2018, LNICST 254, pp. 416–432, 2018.
https://doi.org/10.1007/978-3-030-01701-9_23

be clearly classified. In this case, the number of patterns (or signatures) increases along with the increase in EK variants. The performance of such a model depends on the number of patterns and rule policies, which include simple matching or counting of the repeats of some patterns.

```
<embed id="frqbtvwm" src="/rich/bGNudXBOdg.swf" play="true" height="404" width="717" plugins
page="http://www.macromedia.com/go/getflashplayer" align="middle" loop="false" type="applica
tion/x-shockwave-flash" allowScriptAccess="sameDomain" quality="high" name="frqbtvwm"/>

<embed id="ahzhnlubpu" allowScriptAccess="sameDomain" align="middle" src="/1978/12/04/deal/m
any-draught-east-balance.html.swf" type="application/x-shockwave-flash" quality="high" loop=
"false" width="164" play="true" name="ahzhnlubpu" pluginspage="http://www.macromedia.com/go/
getflashplayer" height="496"/>
```

Fig. 1. Same Neutrino EKs, but different code sequences.

Dynamic analysis [5] provides a high detection rate, but this model encounters difficulties in detecting malicious traces that are not activated (i.e., malicious behaviors are exposed only when an attack is active). There is a myriad of web servers to prepare a resurgence for disseminating malware. These web servers and malicious links are hidden. In this circumstance, we propose similarity-matching-based malicious webpage detection to detect EKs by harnessing previous advantages. The main contributions of this study are as follows:

- We propose a new string-similarity-matching model. We introduce new string-similarity-related features for EK classification.
- The number of patterns is comparable to the size of typical pattern-matching or training sets in machine learning.
- This model provides a detection rate of 99.9% and can determine the maliciousness of a webpage every 0.0033 s. The performance is comparable to that of ML-based models.

The remainder of this paper is organized as follows: Sect. 2 presents related work; Sect. 3 provides an overview of the proposed model; Sect. 4 explains the details of our implementation; Sect. 5 describes our experimental results; and Sect. 6 discusses the limitations and conclusions.

2   Related Work

This section introduces previous models and their difference with our model.

2.1   Similarity Matching Models

We introduce four string metrics based on the nature of measurement. The *Levenshtein distance* [7] computes the minimum number of edits needed to transform one string into another. It measures the distance difference between two string sequences. This is expressed by the minimum number of single/multiple-character edits (insertions, deletions, or substitutions) required to change one character into the other. For example, the *Levenshtein distance* between "hack" and "acks" requires 2 (delete "h"; insert "s"). It is highly dependent on whether the elements of the compared sets are sequentially similar. Hence, this algorithm is disadvantageous when a string order is mingled nonsequentially even though the two strings are composed of the same words, as shown in Fig. 1. The time complexity for the worst case is $O(m \times n)$, where m and n are the lengths of the two strings.

SequenceMatcher uses the *Ratcliff/Obershelp* algorithm [8]. This is obtained by applying $\frac{2 \times M}{T}$, where T is the total number of elements in both strings, and M is the number of matches. For instance, when comparing the two strings "abc" and "a", it returns 0.5 by considering T = 4 and M = 1 (i.e., $2 \times 1/4 = 0.5$). *SequenceMatcher* provides solutions in a quadratic time for the worst case. It is advantageous only when a similarity exists in pairs of the same code sequences. Our experiment indicates that *SequenceMatcher* is not good at detecting EKs, except in cases where the code sequence is the same.

The *Sørensen-Dice index* [9] is known as the F1 score. When taken as a string-similarity measure, the coefficient can be calculated for two strings, x and y, using bigrams. For instance, in calculating the similarity between "virus" and "pacus", we find the set of bigrams in each word. Each set has four elements, and the intersection of two sets has one element: *us*. The statistic is calculated as s = $(2 \times 1)/(4 + 4) = 0.25$.

The *Jaccard index* [10,11] is defined as the size of the intersection divided by the size of the union of two sets. The *Jaccard distance*, which measures the dissimilarity between two sets of text, is obtained by subtracting the *Jaccard coefficient* from 1 by applying $J(A, B) = \frac{|A \cap B|}{|A \cup B|}$, and $d_J(A, B) = 1 - J(A, B)$.

Similarity-related studies [12–14] have attempted an index of malicious link trees built during exploitation. In particular, two studies [11,12] compared two trees using a variant of the *Jaccard* approach. These models need to correctly render tree structures, but attackers can hinder the operation by obfuscating the flows, which might decrease the detection rate because of discretized trees. Studies in this domain (e.g., Hamming distance-based [13] and *Ratcliff* algorithm-based [14]) mostly focus on the similarity in the generated tree structure and call sequences in malicious webpages. Kizzle [15] focused on the automatic antivirus signature extraction of EKs based on an algorithm generating regular-expression-based signatures. It used 50 machines for initial clustering. Jobs take approximately 90 min on average. Thus, this model is resource-heavy. Kizzle obtained datasets from 2014 on four major EKs, such as Nuclear, Sweet Orange, Angler, and RIG. However, our dataset consisted of 12 different EKs from 2014 to 2017. The coding structures of the EKs differ from each other and have numerous variants. We developed a formula for measuring the degree of similarity based on features.

2.2 Limitations

We calculated similarity measures using *SequenceMatcher*, *Levenshtein distance*, *Sorensen*, and *Jaccard index* to understand the problem of the current string metrics to be used for EK detection. Table 1 lists the test result, in which *Levenshtein* exhibited a high matching rate. The results for *Sorensen* and *Jaccard* overlapped.

Table 1. Angler FP results obtained by the string-matching algorithm.

	#	SequenceMatcher	Levenshtein	Jaccard
Type I	114	115	5	23
Type II	5	225	0	221
Type III	51	88	0	2
Type IV	29	146	0	88
Type V	27	203	1	116

We performed an experiment, in which we assessed the number of false positives (FPs) that occurred when each string metric classified all EK samples of the same type. Five types existed among 226 samples of Angler. These types had entirely different code structures from each other and denoted as types I, II, III, IV, and V. They contained 114, 5, 51, 29, and 27 samples, respectively. For instance, Angler Type I contained 114 variants. Their code sequences or used codes are similar to each other, as shown in Fig. 1. We compared the FPs with 226 Angler samples to determine how exactly the string metrics classify I−V types. We selected one sample from each type to establish a pattern and compared the 226 samples.

Levenshtein produced five FPs while matching 114 samples, as listed in Table 1. *Levenshtein* classified five other samples from types II to V when exactly classifying 114 samples of Type I. The minimum measure value for *Levenshtein* was 0.236 while it evaluated the 114 samples. It showed FPs of 4.386, 0, 0, 0, and 3.703% for Angler types I, II, III, IV, and V, respectively. The respective minimum values were measured as 0.236, 0.249, 0.27, 0.289, and 0.2435.

We performed the same experiment for Fiesta, Gondad, Nebula, and Magnitude. Similar tendencies were observed for these EKs. In this test, *Levenshtein* provided minimum similarity values of 0.2125−0.192 for three Fiesta types, 1−0.2805 for four Gondad types, 1−0.567 for five Magnitude types, and 0.5205 for a Nebula type. As seen in this experiment, *Levenshtein* provided low FPs for the EK classification.

However, using *Levenshtein* for malicious webpage detection has two limitations. First, the string metrics require the original source codes of both samples being compared. The file sizes of these sources range from hundreds of bytes to hundreds of kilobytes. That is, these metrics require a considerable amount of space. Second, a variety of similarity scores, which are uncontrolled, exists. Hence, we cannot establish a baseline for judging the maliciousness of a webpage.

In resolving these drawbacks, we need to reduce the size to a level suitable for practical use and configure a fixed baseline. In brief, we formulate them as $\{g(A_1 - B), \cdots, g(A_{10} - B)\} \leq threshold$ when we compare 1 test sample (B) with 10 patterns (A) for EK detection. This condition is satisfied when the difference between A_n and B meets the threshold, and the model then infers that B is malicious.

3 Design

Similarity matching provides a better performance in a scenario with slight changes. However, current similarity metrics cannot easily detect variants of an EK. Hence, we propose an alternative model that can classify EKs with the equality in the code sequence and the structural format. We introduce similarity-related features before designing a model to distinguish exploit codes.

3.1 Features

Table 2 categorizes the features into three classes: probabilistic, size-based, and distance-based features. The probabilistic features specify the frequencies of letters. Size-based features describe the characteristics relevant to the size. Distance-based features denote the difference in the distribution of alphanumeric and nonalphanumeric characters. The details of our features are as follows:

Table 2. Features used in the similarity measures.

Feature class	#	Feature name	Description	cited
Probabilistic	1	WordNum	Number of words	New
	2	MaxWordSize	Size of word with maximum length	New
	3	MaxRepeatWordSize	Size of word with maximum repeats	New
	4	MaxRepeatWordNum	Number of word with maximum repeats	New
	5	FunctionName	Existence of critical JavaScript functions	[16]
Size-based	6	StringSize	String size without space	New
	7	LongestLine	Length of a longest line	[16]
	8	FileSize	File size of webpage	[17]
	9	LineNum	Number of lines	[17, 18]
Distance-based	10	SimilarCharDistribution	Code string similarity	New
	11	RatioNonalphanumeric	Ratio of nonalphanumeric characters	New
	12	SubstringOverlap	Measure repeats of a specific string	New
	13	RatioAlphanumeric	Ratio of alphanumeric characters	New

WordNum. The word number is the count of different words. We find key-value pairs in a string. In the (key, value) tuple, the key represents the word size whereas the value represents the word count of the same size. This provides information related to how EKs are constructed using different word sizes. From this property, we compare the distribution ratio of words between the EKs and benign pages. The total number of different words in Angler is 18.2 on an average. The counts of benign webpages were extensively distributed between 1 and 928. By contrast, most EKs were centralized between 1 and 165, as plotted in Fig. 2.

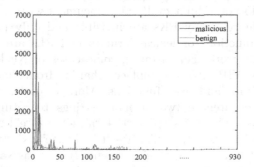

Fig. 2. Distribution of word lengths used in EKs and benign webpages. The x-axis represents the length of words, and the y-axis represents the number of samples in our dataset.

MaxWordSize. We consider the maximum word size because many EKs contain a long string word resulting from obfuscation. For example, 48.7% of the Angler samples in our dataset include a word with more than 1000 characters. Among the remaining samples, 50.4% have words with an average length of 15.75 characters. In other words, the Angler contains a word with a long size or multiple short words with a very high probability. Magnitude, Nuclear, RIG, and Sundown EKs showed a trend similar to that of Angler. The maximum word size of Fiesta, Sweet Orange, and Blackhole is generally over 3000, 90000, and 100000 characters, respectively. However, most Neutrino EKs were less than 120 characters. Thus, word sizes in EKs show distinct properties that can be divided into several ranges.

MaxRepeatWordSize or MaxRepeatWordNum. The codes of most EKs are obfuscated. The obfuscation pattern often shows the recurrence of same strings with fixed sizes. Therefore, we extract a word with the most repeats. This property fully expresses the characterization of EKs using iteration. We parse codes and produce key-value pairs with maximum repeats. For instance, from this code, "AdgSf344_42 AdgSf344_42 AdgSf344_42 AdgSf344_42 AdgSf344_42 AdgSf344_42   AdgSf344_42   AdgSf344_42tAdgSf344_42rAdgSf344_42yAdgSf3 44_42 AdgSf344_42AdgSf344_42", we yield a {11, 7} tuple, which refers to the word size of maximum repeats and its counts. In addition, three different word sizes exist. The size of maximum word contains 47 characters.

FunctionName. Attackers reuse CVE codes and add new CVE codes [17]. They rarely remove old ones to increase exploit probabilities. Furthermore, new vulnerabilities related to Java, Flash, IE, and browser-plugins are limited, thereby increasing code reusability. Thus, the differences in code are relatively small. This tendency is strongly exposed in EKs of the same type, where code sharing is high. During the information collection stage, EKs gather user agent/application environments such as browser (e.g., MSIE) version, cookies, and swf information. EKs then run an unpacking code to de-obfuscate their attack payloads by calling eval() and document.writeln(). However, recent EKs do not exhibit eval() and document.write() in codes because of obfuscation.[1] Hence, many EKs are invisible and only partially readable. These JavaScript functions or lexical formats in URLs are widely used, but may not extensively work. For instance, some cases of Nuclear, Fiesta, Nebula, RIG, and CK VIP EKs use replace, charAt, fromCharCode, unescape, split, getElementById, and exec functions. More recently, attackers use the + operator and concatenate two or more strings to return a single function name, such as ["r" + "e" + "p" + "l" + "a" + "c" + "e"], "sc" + "r" + "ipt," eval("unes" + "cape"), ['s' + 'p' + 'l' + 'i' + 't'], ["", "e", "x", "e", "c", ""], 'inde' + 'xOf', "createE" + "lement," "getEle" + "mentsBy" + "TagName," 'cha' + 'rAt,' and "VBs" + "cri" + "pt." This format is often changed to other combinations. Thus, an EK can be detected by checking for the presence of these keywords before and after removing operator and quotation marks. We return the result as 0 or 1. In such cases, YARA [19] is not enough (delete and sum).

Some types of Angler use navigator. User agent, Trident, MSIE [0–7], eval, Math, var, and substr. Other Angler EKs include string formats with $<span$ $class = $ "text" $id =$, $<p\ class =$ "text" $id =$, or $<p\ ui =$ ". This form can be used as a signature for Angler detection. Some types of Magnitude use eval, execute, unescape, and CreateObject functions. In addition, EKs often use *try-catch* statements; however, the keyword is also used in benign JavaScripts.

StringSize. Many EKs are composed of webpages of a certain size. This feature is counted by multiplying key-value pairs. The result is approximately similar with the longest line, except spaces. Neutrino and Redkit EKs generally have a short string size (between 26 and 370 characters); however, most EKs have string sizes that range from several thousands up to nearly 400,000 characters. Specifically, Sweet Orange has large strings. Thus, the distribution ratio is distinguished from benign pages.

LongestLine, FileSize, and LineNum. Our main considerations are performance. In considering this parameter, we only take a specific body of the entire

---

[1] To avoid detection, attackers use split(), escape(), eval(), XOR/8-bit ASCII/BASE64 or their own encoding, and JavaScript compression tools. The outputs of these methods yield obfuscated strings with %, +, \x, or $ as the first character. In recent years, EKs often hide JavaScript functions.

code, namely the longest line. From a piece of code, we extract all attribute values of features, except FunctionName, FileSize and LineNum in Table 2. In reality, we only read 4500 bytes from the longest line even if the length of the longest line is more than 4500 bytes because this size of code is enough to extract features and detect EKs.[2] The detection rate in the experiment is slightly different, with the longest line having a length of 3500−5500 bytes. Consequently, the detection rate is dependent on the features rather than the length. The surface for detection is reduced, but the performance increases. On this feature, while some might say that adversaries can generate a large number of short lines of codes to avoid the longest line feature, multiple code lines can also be used in a high-impact feature.

A file size is distributed to 137−933,612 bytes in our malicious dataset, which influences the attributes of features. In line numbers, some EKs only contain a longest line. Some of the Magnitude, Rig, Sundown, Terror, and Blackhole EKs are composed of a line number of 1. By contrast, some EKs are distributed between 1 and 1000 line numbers. Remarkably, many EKs, except Neutrino, exhibit a property that the file size and longest line have similar sizes. For instance, the longest line is 264,338 bytes if a file size is 267,827 bytes. Neutrino EKs mostly contain less than 400 characters in the longest line.

SimilarCharDistribution. EK variants show two types of tendencies: differences in the code sequence and differences in the letters used. EK variants differ in word sequence despite having the same code, as shown in Fig. 1. Most variants make different EKs using different characters. With regard to the characters, we transform each character to a one-to-one corresponding number. More specifically, we change special characters to negative numbers and alphanumeric characters to positive numbers. This bijection is expressed as $f\colon S \to N$, where S is a set of characters, and N is a set of integers. After this correspondence, we sum all numbers in a set of N and divide by the size of N. For instance, "abc" is changed by considering "a" as 1, "b" as 2, and "c" as 3.

We formulate $\sum_1^n S_n$. S is applied to this principal: $x := y$. x is a character, and y is a number mapped to x. We then sum all the numbers to discover the existence of the same character distribution and detect scrambled codes, such as "abc def" and "def abc". This mangled code is common in the Angler. The detection of strings with different code sequence relies on this feature. Subsequently, we determine the reciprocal of the sum as a float in the range [-1, 1]. The sum is close to -1 if a webpage contains many nonalphanumeric characters, such as arithmetic operators. By contrast, the sum is close to 1 if a webpage is composed of alphanumeric ASCII or Unicode characters, such as 0−9, A−Z, and a−z. This property is useful when the two string samples being compared are structurally similar in terms of the character distribution.

---

[2] See https://drive.google.com/open?id=1tfBCB1tcfxg3GNo7yZwYUCqhABjbbN-P.

RatioNonalphanumeric. The exploit codes contain nonalphanumeric characters because they are often obfuscated to nonalphanumeric forms. Hence, the
relative magnitude of nonalphanumeric characters in an entire string is highly
exposed. We express nonalphanumeric characters as negative numbers between
-1 and 0. The more nonalphanumeric characters there are, the lower the negative
number becomes. Thus, we reflect the magnitude of nonalphanumeric character
distribution. For instance, an underscore and a hyphen each have a different
value. In this approach, the score of nonalphanumeric characters increases by
multiplying distance n according to a character sequence, $d: n \to [0, 4500]$, where
d is distance. In fact, when the nonalphanumeric letters are '!@#', the !, @, and
are 10, 20, 30, respectively. The magnitude of the mapped nonalphanumeric
is $10 * 1 + 20 * 2 + 30 * 3$.

SubstringOverlap. Many EKs contain properties that repeat a specific word.
They also have high overlaps of words, such as "ALal3ALal3ALal3 ALal3
ALal3ALal3 ALal3ALal3ALal3" and "0011 * 0011 * 0011 * 0011 * 0011 * 0011 *
0011 *". A specific substring overlap that shows a high frequency is recognized
as having a high level of similarity between a pair of strings. We reconstruct an
original string to a new form, which consists of 1, 1 and 0, to measure repeats
of specific words. To do this, we first classify words from a string. Alphanumeric
characters are then transformed to 1 (alphabetic characters) and 0 (Arabic numbers), while nonalphanumeric characters are transformed to 1 for each character
in the words. After changing characters to numbers, we check for the existence
of the same string. This feature extends the detection rate by searching the overlap of words. For instance, 'ALal3' and '0011*' are transformed to '11110' and
'00001.' This approach generally provides extensive coverage and is more effective than exact matching trials because of the countless variants. In calculating
the frequency of overlapping words, we divide the number of intersections by the
number of words in original strings, where m is the number of words matched,
and n is the overall size of the words.

$$f_1 = \frac{m}{n+1} \tag{1}$$

RatioAlphanumeric. If two strings show code similarity even though they
use different characters, the model should present that they are significantly
similar. In measuring this similarity, we sum the positive and negative values
separately in order until the end of the string. We apply Eq. (2), where n and m
denote cardinality. According to the frequencies, the scores differ. The count of
alphanumeric characters is more critical in practice than the nonalphanumeric
characters because the alphanumeric ratio is more common in EKs (Table 4).

$$f_2 = \left(\frac{1}{\sum_{i=1}^{n} x_i} - \frac{1}{|\sum_{j=1}^{m} y_j|} \right) \times (n+m) \tag{2}$$

Such a feature-based string matching method can effectively overcome string
sequence problems and the computational issues of naive string matching over

long strings. We compute the feature values of two strings S_1 and S_2, measure the similarity degree between them, and recognize their similarity.

3.2 Proposed Model

As shown in Fig. 3, we first cluster the EKs to the same EK groups to design the model. We then select a representative EK from the group. Subsequently, we extract 13 attribute values from representatives, which compose of nine integers and four floating-point numbers between -1 and 1. The values significantly reduce the file size through two steps because EKs can be denoted as float type instead of a large string. We use 118 pattern instances with 13 attribute values. We also extract the same attribute values from test webpages. Subsequently, this model classifies EKs by comparing the scores of each attribute's values in the same array.

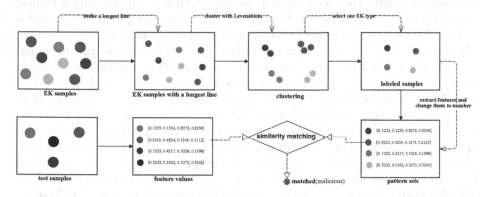

Fig. 3. Modeling procedure of our similarity matching.

Pattern Collection and Feature Extraction. We build a set of features to be used for patterns. Every EK contains multiple EK versions, and each version has innumerable variants. In this model, we select one sample representing each version. For instance, Angler in our dataset has seven different EK versions. The representatives of EKs are a subset of all Angler EKs. We used the *Levenshtein distance* to select the EKs. We only use the selected EKs for building patterns. We do not need benign patterns because our matching method determines the closest one among EKs, unlike an ML-based approach. In building the set, this model gathers the attribute values of features after reading 4500 bytes of selected EK samples, which comprises a small portion of the overall code. These values are designed to inspect whether repeating words exist or check whether code sequences coincide. We also map each character of exploit codes to each different number. The numbers are counted and summed. Their outputs are transformed to floats scoring of [-1, 1] range to express the feature level with original exploit codes. This transformation considerably reduces the size of a pattern set.

Afterwards, this model estimates the existence of similarity by sequentially comparing each feature value of two strings $s1$ and $s2$, where $s1$ is the 13 attribute values obtained from a test sample, and $s2$ is the 13 attribute values from the pattern instances. The proposed model executes 13 feature comparisons per given test sample one at a time until a match is achieved or until it reaches the end of the pattern set. The test case is considered malicious when a match is found. In other words, the test case satisfies the scope of the threshold, which is a similarity ratio for acceptance. The total number of comparisons is N(f × P), where P is the number of patterns, and f is the number of features that takes 13 attribute values. The worst-case time complexity is $O(N)$, where N is the number of compared patterns. We terminate further execution after achieving a match to avoid this worst case.

String Matching. Our measure quantifies the similarity, which is mainly based on a character-based statistical comparison. We elicit the repeated exposure of the same elements. The model then measures whether an input string is similar to our patterns. To overcome the problem of previous string metrics (described in Sect. 2), we build a decision boundary (θ), called a threshold, to determine whether a webpage is malicious or benign. We use θ 0.05 as the threshold. Accordingly, the feature attribute values should satisfy the following condition to be malicious: $|pattern\ attribute\ values - test\ attribute\ values| \leq threshold$. The equation is represented as $|P_n - f_n| \leq C$, where $A = \{P_1, \cdots, P_n\}$, and $B = \{f_1, \cdots, f_{13}\}$. A is a set of patterns, and B is a set of attribute values extracted from the test sample. P_n and f_n are finite sets. In this formula, C is the threshold and f_n is a partial of the attribute values. $C = P_n \times$ decision boundary (θ) between 1 and 0.01, which is the range of the similarity that we define. When the similarity comparison result $|P_n - f_n|$ is located in the scope of our threshold, this model decides that the matching of the two strings is similar. In other words, one of A is structurally identical to B.

4   Implementation

This section explains the implemented feature extraction and matching modules.

The feature extraction module starts to load a headless WebKit browser with URLs. Our model then gathers links occurring in webpage rendering and collects webpage sources with the links. Next, the model collects features from the sources.[3] The extraction module aims to gather webpage sources, and is a component for extracting attribute values. The feature extraction stage is based on the longest line of the input data.

The similarity-matching module is a component used to decide whether a webpage is malicious. We consider two more procedures in this stage: probabilistic/size- and distance-based matching. The probabilistic/size-based matching distinguishes suspicious webpages among test webpages to be compared. The proposed model executes nine feature comparisons using features

---

[3] The feature extraction uses the JavaScript, HTML, and VBScript codes. We use the original code before it is interpreted by JavaScript engines, such as jscript.dll or V8.

1−9 in Table 3. For the first filtering, the model changes the extracted attribute values to generalized formats. For instance, attribute values "6 56 11 1 149 154 154 1" are changed to "1 2 2 1 3 3 3 1".[4] In reality, this model compares normalized formats of test samples with those of 118 rules predefined. The filtered outputs are suspect and highly likely to be EKs. Distance-based matching uses only the outputs that pass through this step. A final decision is accomplished by distance matching.

Six matching steps are employed in the distance-matching step: (1) This work reads each attribute value of the patterns and test string. (2) This model measures the difference of each attribute value from the pattern sets A and test sets B at the same location. (3) The result of difference is compared with the threshold. (4) The model determines whether it satisfies the range of the threshold. (5) The matching for the features should be true for all. If not true, the algorithm moves to the next pattern. (6) The comparison is performed in a similar manner until the end of the patterns. We introduce the pseudocode in Algorithm 1 to illustrate these steps.

Algorithm 1: Matching algorithm

Input   : Floats x and y, which are a pattern file and a test file
Output: True (malicious) or False (benign)
procedure SIMILARITY_MATCH(A, B)
  $A = |A|$
  $B = |B|$
  $\theta = 0.05$
  $C = A \times \theta$
  if $|A−B| \leq C$ **then** return $True$;
  else return $False$;
end procedure

procedure BEGIN(x, y)
  TestAttributeValue $\leftarrow y$
  $n \leftarrow 0$
  while *not at end of pattern or unmatched* **do**
    PatternAttributeValue $\leftarrow$ read a line from x
    for $n <$ *number of attributes* **do**
      $n += 1$
      $test_n \leftarrow$ TestAttributeValue $[n]$
      $pattern_n \leftarrow$ PatternAttributeValue $[n]$
      $M_n \leftarrow$ SIMILARITY_MATCH($pattern_n$, $test_n$)
    if *all* $M_n == True$ **then** break;
    else move to next pattern;
end procedure

The collection modules for the test samples are mainly programmed using *phantomJs* [20] with 148 lines of code, whereas the feature extraction and matching modules were implemented using Python 2.7 with 389 lines of code.

---

[4] See https://drive.google.com/open?id=1UVg-gbfIv7NTabq90UkVKt3CeleBEBY9. Patterns for classification (left) and clustered patterns for matching (right).

5   Evaluation

5.1   Dataset and Experimental Setup

We collected publicly available datasets (from Jan. 2013 to Apr. 2017) from http://www.malware-traffic-analysis.net/ [21] and a third-party antivirus company to demonstrate our approach. Out of the 36,950 webpages, 15,620 were used as benign webpages and gathered from the Alexa Top 5000 sites [22]. A total of 21,330 were used as malicious webpages. All these samples were labeled by VirusTotal [23] and commercial sandbox inspection. EKs include Angler (230), Gondad (2,174), Neutrino (129), Nuclear (84), Sundown (23), Sweet Orange (1,508), RIG (471), Blackhole (402), Redkit (599), CK VIP(1,183), Caihong (1,005), Fiesta (10), and Unknown (13,512). The entire dataset was processed using Weka 3.8. We applied both 10- and 5-fold cross-validations.

We ran the experiments inside VirtualBox on Windows 7 with an Intel Core™ i7-7700HQ CPU, 2.80 GHz with 8 GB memory.

Table 3. Detection rate as weighted average (a 10-fold cross-validation was applied.)

Classifier	TP Rate	FP Rate	Precision	Recall	F1 score	ROC area
RandomForest	0.999	0.001	0.999	0.999	0.999	1.000
J48	0.997	0.003	0.997	0.997	0.997	0.998
SVM	0.926	0.054	0.937	0.926	0.926	0.936
Logistic	0.882	0.140	0.885	0.882	0.881	0.945
BayesNet	0.979	0.016	0.980	0.979	0.979	0.999

5.2   Detection Rate and Performance

We verified the validation of features that can be used in string similarity using ML approaches. *RandomForest* (RF) had a TP rate of 99.9% and an FP rate of 0.01%. In the model, bagging was applied using 100 iterations and the base learner. This classifier exhibited a high detection rate and a high performance (approximately 0.00186 s/page), as listed in Table 3. The experiment applying a 5-fold cross validation method showed the difference of 0.004 at most in SVM, but most classifiers showed same/similar results. *RandomForest* misclassified 38 false negatives (FNs) and 11 FPs. The FNs occurred in Angler, Neutrino, and Sundown EKs. The most common cause of misclassified FPs was the similar obfuscation by packers. The errors in the FNs were revealed in the malicious pages of short codes with simple link tags.

In addition, we evaluated the relevance for each attribute using the class *Info-GainAttributeEval*, which provides a method for scoring the features in Weka. A higher information gain ratio indicates a better discriminative power for classification. In this experiment, the size of the longest line had a high gain ratio, as listed in Table 4. We recognized that the size-based feature was one of the most distinguishable properties. In string matching, we assumed that the use of features with a higher *info gain* helped achieve a higher detection rate.

Table 4. Features ranked by the information gain ratio for 36,950 datasets.

Rank	Info gain	Feature	Rank	Info gain	Feature
1	0.796	LongestLine	8	0.554	WordNum
2	0.780	StringSize	9	0.513	SimilarCharDistribution
3	0.757	MaxWordSize	10	0.458	MaxRepeatWordSize
4	0.739	RatioAlphanumeric	11	0.337	MaxRepeatWordNum
5	0.726	FileSize	12	0.043	RatioNonalphanumeric
6	0.668	LineNum	13	0.001	FunctionName
7	0.587	SubStringOverlap			

Table 5. Detection rate comparison.

	# sample	ClamAV		F-Prot		BitDefender		Sophos		RF		FriSM	
		FN	FP	FN	FP	FN	FP	FN	FP	FN	FP	FN	FP
Malicious	21330	21105		19869		14944		1562		38		1	
Benign	15620		0		0		0		1		11		11

The accuracy of each test was measured based on the area under the receiver operating characteristic (ROC) curve. An area of 1 represents success, whereas an area of 0.5 represents failure in general. In our experiment, the ROC area was close to 1 (area under curve (AUC) = 0.9902), indicating that a classifier successfully classified almost all the positive and negative cases.

We compared our model with four antivirus products, all of which were operated in a Linux environment. In this evaluation, our model showed 1 FNs and 11 FPs[5] at θ 0.05 as presented in Table 5. The 11 FPs largely originated from two cases: short benign pages with a redirect (with a file size of less than 10 Kb) and obfuscated webpages. Unreadable benign webpages using obfuscator tools (base64, Dean Edwards' JavaScript packers or compressors) were very similar to EKs. Another cause of FP was a short html tag with a redirect.[6]

The results showed that the TP rate was 99.99%, and the FP rate was 0.001%. The TP and FP rates were similar to those of typical ML-based models. Nonetheless, the proposed model was more advantageous than ML- or pattern-based models in terms of the number of patterns and training datasets. If 118 patterns are used, these models may demonstrate a low detection rate. The

---

[5] See https://drive.google.com/open?id=143nOUCKBMgB8t7g8PEJvh8yryBLYhAK-.

[6] We offer brief sample outputs for both TNs and FP cases at this website: https://drive.google.com/open?id=1QDl1Kpyq85arwHCuvU7qiJGVoWOhUuhP.

proposed model can detect similar strings even though the exact rules are not defined in pattern lists. This also results in a rapid performance. For detecting an obfuscated webpage that does not have any traces or even function names and parameters, similarity matching provides a high detection rate. As regards the testing time, RF and FriSM demonstrated 0.0026 s and 0.0033 s per page, respectively. In this regard, antivirus products were 0.0165 s on average.

5.3   Error Analysis

FriSM searched seemingly similar malicious webpages. Thus, FriSM showed high FPs. Three methods can be used to reduce the error ratio and remediate FN problems: (1) applying new features, (2) increasing threshold, and (3) upgrading patterns. In particular, in this model, finding the optimal threshold is very important for the best classification. We prove this by performing an experiment to determine the appropriate decision threshold that will minimize the overall classification error. The threshold uses theta to classify a webpage as either benign or malicious. FNs can be reduced by increasing θ; however, consequently, FPs also increase. This model only accepts cases that closely resemble each other (i.e., almost same), where two strings are considered similar if theta is quite low, but less similar if theta is high. At present, our theta is low, and our model detects cases wherein the similarity of two strings is high.

We can increase the threshold by increasing θ (e.g., $0.05 \rightarrow 0.051$) to increase the detection rate. In this situation, the misclassified FNs were reduced from 1 to 0; however, the misclassified FPs also increased from 11 to 13. The threshold used to control the similarity simultaneously affected the FN and FP rates. We evaluated the accuracy for θ (between 0.049–0.051). In this range, TP on θ 0.049, 0.05, and 0.051 was 11, 1, and 0, respectively. FP was 9, 11, and 13. Thus, the accuracy was the highest at θ 0.05 and 99.97%. Our θ 0.05 did not ensure that the similarity rate was more than 99.95%. Instead, θ provided a baseline to determine the similarity of character distribution of the x and y strings. Hence, in terms of the detection rate, we needed to moderate the optimized threshold. We can add more patterns to increase the detection rate; however, this decreased the performance because of the increase in the number of patterns being considered.

Lastly, we evaluated 129 additional EK samples (111 were prior EK types, and 18 were new) collected between Apr. 11, 2017 and Feb. 12, 2018 from [21] to understand the detection methods between FriSM and RF. A total of 111 EKs consisted of KaiXin, RIG, Magnitude, and Terror. The 18 Magnitude and Terror EKs were not defined as patterns in our model. In this experiment, our model exhibited a high detection rate of 96.9% (100% in prior EKs, 78% in new EKs); however, RF showed low detection rates of 83.7%. New EKs showing a structural similarity with our EK patterns were detected even though they had not been specifically defined as patterns.

6 Discussion and Conclusions

This model may not be applicable if the structure of EKs drastically changes or patterns do not exist. Hence, in future work, we need to develop a new method to avoid FPs and TNs. In addition, the threshold in our model requires the range of the similarity comparison to be narrowed to reduce FNs. This increases the number of patterns and can be a nontrivial task even though the rule sets are small compared to the ones of previous models. Nonetheless, this approach is still useful for rapidly detecting EKs unless EKs show a distinct increase. The proposed method, which depends on feature, attribute values, and threshold for a high detection rate, had a TP rate of 99%.

Acknowledgements. This research was supported by the Ministry of Science, ICT and Future Planning, Korea, under the Human Resource Development Project for Brain Scouting Program (IITP-2017-0-01889) supervised by the IITP.

References

1. Stringhini, G., Kruegel, C., Vigna, G.: Shady paths: leveraging surfing crowds to detect malicious web pages. In: Proceedings of the 2013 ACM SIGSAC Conference on Computer and Communications Security, pp. 133–144. ACM (2013)
2. Eshete, B., Venkatakrishnan, V.N.: Webwinnow: leveraging exploit kit workflows to detect malicious URLs. In: Proceedings of the 4th ACM Conference on Data and Application Security and Privacy, pp. 305–312. ACM (2014)
3. Šrndić, N., Laskov, P.: Hidost: a static machine-learning-based detector of malicious files. EURASIP J. Inf. Secur. 22 (2016)
4. Thug. https://www.honeynet.org/taxonomy/term/218. Accessed 6 Nov 2017
5. Kim, S., Kim, S., Kim, D.: LoGos internet-explorer-based malicious webpage detection. ETRI J. **39**, 406–416 (2017). https://doi.org/10.4218/etrij.17.0116.0810
6. Edwards, D.: http://dean.edwards.name/packer/. Accessed 12 Oct 2017
7. Levenshtein distance. https://en.wikipedia.org/wiki/Levenshtein_distance. Accessed 12 Oct 2017
8. Ratcliff, J.W., Metzener, D.E.: Pattern-matching-the gestalt approach. Dr Dobbs J. **13**(7), 46 (1988)
9. Dice similarity coefficient. https://en.wikipedia.org/wiki/sorensen-Dice_coefficient. Accessed 12 Oct 2017
10. Jaccard, P.: Distribution de la flore alpine dans le bassin des Dranses et dans quelques régions voisines. Bulletin de la Société Vaudoise des Sciences Naturelles pp. 241–272 (1901)
11. Taylor, T., et al.: Detecting malicious exploit kits using tree-based similarity searches. In: Proceedings of the Sixth ACM Conference on Data and Application Security and Privacy, pp. 255–266. ACM (2016)
12. Perdisci, R., Lee, W., Feamster, N.: Behavioral clustering of HTTP-based malware and signature generation using malicious network traces. In: NSDI, vol. 10, p. 14 (2010)
13. Cui, Q., Jourdan, G.V., Bochmann, G.V., Couturier, R., Onut, I.V.: Tracking phishing attacks over time. In: Proceedings of the 26th International Conference on World Wide Web International World Wide Web Conferences Steering Committee, pp. 667–676 (2017)

14. Kapravelos, A., Shoshitaishvili, Y., Cova, M., Kruegel, C., Vigna, G.: Revolver: an automated approach to the detection of evasive web-based malware. In: USENIX Security Symposium, pp. 637–652 (2013)
15. Stock, B., Livshits, B., Zorn, B.: Kizzle: a signature compiler for detecting exploit kits. In: 46th Annual IEEE/IFIP International Conference Dependable Systems and Networks (DSN), IEEE (2016)
16. Canali, D., Cova, M., Vigna, G., Kruegel, C.: Prophiler: a fast filter for the large-scale detection of malicious web pages. In: Proceedings of the 20th International Conference on World Wide Web, pp. 197–206. ACM (2011)
17. Eshete, B., Villafiorita, A., Weldemariam, K.: BINSPECT: holistic analysis and detection of malicious web pages. In: Keromytis, A.D., Di Pietro, R. (eds.) SecureComm 2012. LNICST, vol. 106, pp. 149–166. Springer, Heidelberg (2013). https://doi.org/10.1007/978-3-642-36883-7_10
18. Choi, H., Zhu, B.B., Lee, H.: Detecting malicious web links and identifying their attack types. WebApps 11, 11 (2011)
19. YARA. https://virustotal.github.io/yara/. Accessed 25 Nov 2017
20. PhantomJS. http://phantomjs.org/. Accessed 25 Nov 2017
21. Malware-Traffic-Analysis.Net.   http://www.malware-traffic-analysis.net/. Accessed 20 Feb 2018
22. Alexa. http://www.alexa.com/topsites. Accessed 18 Nov 2017
23. VirusTotal. https://www.virustotal.com/. Accessed 18 Nov 2017

A Machine Learning Framework for Studying Domain Generation Algorithm (DGA)-Based Malware

Tommy Chin[1]($\boxtimes$), Kaiqi Xiong[2], Chengbin Hu[2], and Yi Li[2]

[1] Department of Computing Security, Rochester Institute of Technology,
Rochester, USA
`tommy.chin@ieee.org`
[2] Florida Center for Cybersecurity, University of South Florida, Tampa, USA
`xiongk@usf.edu,{chengbin,yli13}@mail.usf.edu`

Abstract. Malware or threat actors use a Command and Control (C2) environment to proliferate and manage an attack. In a sophisticated attack, a threat actor often employs a Domain Generation Algorithm (DGA) to cycle the network location in which malware communicates with C2. Network security controls such as blacklisting, implementing a DNS sinkhole, or inserting a firewall rule is a vital asset to an organization's security posture. However, all of them are typically ineffective against a DGA. In this paper, we propose a machine learning framework for identifying and clustering domain names to circumvent threats from a DGA. We collect a real-time threat intelligent feed over a six month period where all domains have threats on the public Internet at the time of collection. We then apply the proposed machine learning framework to study DGA-based malware. The proposed framework contains a two-level model, which consists of classification and clustering is used to first detect DGA domains and then identify the DGA of those domains. Our extensive experimental results demonstrate the accuracy of the proposed framework. To be precise, we achieve accuracies of 95.14% for the first-level classification and 92.45% for the second-level clustering, respectively.

Keywords: Malware · Domain Generation Algorithm
Machine learning · Security · Networking

1 Introduction

A computer network and its assets are frequently under a variety of attacks including malware attacks, where threat actors attempt to infiltrate layers of protection and defensive solutions [1–3]. Anti-malware software, for the longest time, is a critical asset for an organization as it provides a level of security on computer systems to deter and remove malicious threats. However, many anti-malware solutions typically utilize static string matching approaches, hashing

© ICST Institute for Computer Sciences, Social Informatics and Telecommunications Engineering 2018
R. Beyah et al. (Eds.): SecureComm 2018, LNICST 254, pp. 433–448, 2018.
https://doi.org/10.1007/978-3-030-01701-9_24

schemes, or network communication whitelisting [4]. Sophisticate threat actors and authors/developers to new malware strands purposely integrate evasive techniques and covert communication channels to bypass most detection techniques, which presents a grand challenge in securing an enterprise.

One component to some variations of malware strands is a method to communicate with a centralized server to service a Command and Control (C2) using either a static or dynamic method [5]. In the static method, the malware has been pre-written with a value such as an IP address or a domain name that becomes permanently fixed throughout the lifespan of the malware and that once a security operator identifies such an illicit network, a simple firewall rule will relieve the threat. In the dynamic method, the creator of the malware implements a technique to communicate back to a variety of servers, based on a sequencing approach known as Domain Generation Algorithm (DGA) [6]. The dynamics of a DGA commonly utilizes a seeded function. That is, given an input such as a timestamp, a deterministic output would follow as pre-defined by the DGA. The challenge behind deterring a DGA approach is that an administrator would have to identify the malware, the DGA, and the seed value to filter out past malicious networks and future servers in the sequence.

Network security measures such as Access Control List (ACL), firewalls, and Domain Name System (DNS) sinkholes have been the prominent best practice to reduce the proliferation of unauthorized access and the spread of malware strands. A DGA, however, increases the difficulty to control malicious communication as a sophisticated threat actor implements the ability to change the server or location periodically the malware communicates back (callback) to the C2 in an automated fashion. Overall, utilizing a DGA would primarily establish a game of cat and mouse for both security operators mitigating the threat while the centralized server for the C2 would frequently change location.

This study evaluates known malicious domains that exclusively belong to DGAs and we attempt to apply machine learning approaches including multiple feature extractions, classification, and clustering techniques. Computer systems frequently query domain names using DNS due to vastly broad running applications and services [7]. Security appliances that monitor and evaluate each DNS query needs to determine whether a particular domain has some level of maliciousness and specifically, whether or not a specific query originates from a DGA. If so, which one. Moreover, this study utilizes a real-time threat intelligence feed that has been collected over a six-month period on a daily basis while leveraging high-performance nodes [8,9] from the Global Environment for Network Innovation (GENI) [10] to conduct extensive data processing. We further propose a machine learning framework to classify and detect DGA malware and experimentally evaluate the proposed framework through a comparison of various machine learning approaches. Specifically, our machine learning framework consists of the following three main components: (1) Blacklist with a pattern filter that first filters the incoming DNS queries and stores them in the blacklist. (2) Feature extractor that extracts features from those domains that are not in the blacklist. The domains will be sent to the next component. (3) Two-level classification and clustering. To identify DGA domains, we start with the first-level classification to classify DGA domains and normal domains. We then apply the second-level clustering to group domains sequenced by the DGA. The overall goal is to determine the technique the DGA employs so that our proposed framework can prevent future communication to the C2. Our evaluation results show that we can achieve the accuracy of 95.14% for the first-level classification and the accuracy 92.45% for the second-level clustering, respectively.

The rest of the paper is organized as follows. Section 2 defines the research problem while Sect. 3 demonstrates existing related work. Section 4 presents data collection and the proposed machine learning framework and Sect. 5 dicusses the experimental and evaluation of the framework. Lastly, Sect. 6 concludes our studies and presents future work.

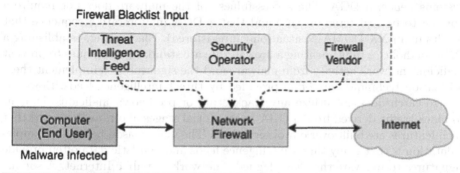

DGA Sequence	Firewall Blacklist	Internet Domain	Filtered
swgqwmnpxuorh.com	swgqwmnpxuorh.com	swgqwmnpxuorh.com	Yes
ghluburrkboax.net	ghluburrkboax.net	ghluburrkboax.net	Yes
veivkqvvamlgx.biz	veivkqvvamlgx.biz	veivkqvvamlgx.biz	Yes
wykwohntbxrlh.org		wykwohntbxrlh.org	No
kjpbsprvnertx.co.uk			
ahmsbkdcffkst.info		ahmsbkdcffkst.info	No

Fig. 1. Threat models: multiple conditions for a DGA to function in a network environment where filtering results in a firewall that prevents the communication and an empty cell in Internet domain that results in an NX domain error. Note, the domains listed in the figure belong to existing live threats.

2   Problem Statement

Firewall blacklisting constantly expands as the multiple sources of inputs expand filtering rules. However, sequences in a DGA may not be known to these inputs promptly. Moreover, for the malware to communicate correctly to an appropriate domain, a threat actor must register each respective domain name in the sequence to maintain the C2 or risk the loss of a node in the distribution. Figure 1 demonstrates an example scenario for such a case.

Our research problem is to accurately identify and cluster domains that originate from known DGA-based techniques where we target to obtain a security apparatus that autonomously mitigates network communication to unknown threats in a sequence.

2.1   Assumptions and Threat Models

Threat actors need a method to control and maintain the malware in a C2 environment while operating in an unnoticeable manner from network security systems hence, a DGA. The successfulness of the malware does not require a domain to be registered or valid and that a DGA may iterate a sequence that results in an NX DOMAIN situation (unregistered). Blacklisting, establishing a DNS sinkhole, or implementing a firewall rule are standard techniques to prevent malicious network activity from malware and the signatures to implement these mitigation techniques are often provided by threat intelligence feeds. However, this research does not utilize any blacklisting or pre-known malicious domains to block traffic derived from a DGA in the initial stages of our analysis and that such features are built over our observations. The main reason behind our implementation is that many threat intelligence feeds and heuristic data often provide signatures to malware that has plagued a network or public Internet. A sophisticated threat actor would implement or utilize a 0-day style malware (malicious code that has never been seen or known to the public) and therefore, blacklisting would be inappropriate for our analysis. Our proposed machine learning framework aims to solve the problem of detecting DGA sequences using machine learning techniques derived from observations in a network.

3   Related Work

Current Internet and end-user systems are frequently plagued with the hazards of malware. The landscape of the modern Internet grows as mobile devices, Internet of Things (IoT), and network connected vehicles expand where a threat actor may attack the increasing number of potential targets a daily basis [11,12]. Many of such systems are susceptible to malware attacks due to mismanagement issues, poor patching behaviors, and dangerous 0-day attacks [13].

Because DGA-generated domain names contain significant features that can be used to differentiate DGA domain names from normal ones [14]. Therefore, many studies aim to target blocking those DGA domain names as an defense approach [15,16]. The DGA that generates the domain fluxing botnet needs to be known so that we can take countermeasures. Several studies have looked at understanding and reverse engineering the inner workings of botnets [17,18]. Thomas et al. [19] proposed an automatic method to extract DGA from current malware. Their study focused on domain fluxing malware and relied on the binary extraction for DGA. Their approach is only effective for certain types of malware [20]. Besides blocking and extracting DGAs from normal domains, deeper study has been explored based on the features of DGA domain names.

Since the DGA domains names are usually randomly generated, the lengths of DGA domains are very long, which is a good feature that can be used for detecting DGA domains. However, shorter DGA domain names are more difficult to detect. This is because most normal domains are tend to be short. Ahluwalia et al. [21] proposed a detection model that can dynamically detect DGA domains. They apply information theoretic features based on the notion of domain length threshold. Their approach can dynamically detect the DGA domains with any length. Many other works have been done on DGA detection based on the DGA domain features.

Ma et al. [22] proposed a lightweight approach to detect DGA domains based on URLs using both lexical and host-based features. They consider lexical features of the URL such as length, number of dots, and special characters in the URL path. Antonakakis et al. [23] propose a novel detection system, called Pleiades. They extract a number of statistical features related to the NXDomain strings, including distribution of n-grams. Wang et al. [24] proposed using word segmentation to derive tokens from domain names to detect malicious domains. The proposed feature space includes the number of characters, digits, and hyphens. Similar to Ma et al. [22], McGrath et al. [25] also take a close look at phishing URLs and found that the phishing URLs and DGA domains have different characteristic when compared with normal domains and URLs. Therefore, they proposed a model for detecting DGA domains based on domain length comparison and character frequencies of English language alphabets. The similar approach based on DGA features can be find in [15,26].

In order to classify DGA domain names, Schiavoni et al. [5] proposed a feasible approach for characterizing and clustering DGA-generated domains according to both linguistic and DNS features. In the study, they proposed that DGA domains have groups of very significant characters from normal domains. By grouping the domains according to their features, the authors applied a machine learning classifier could distinguish them from all the domains easily. Several machine-learning techniques have been studied to classify malicious codes. They include neural networks, support vector machines (SVM) and boosted classifiers [27]. There are also several studies aiming to predict DGA domain names from historical DGA domains [28]. Woodbridge et al. [29] used DNS queries to find the pattern of different families of DGAs. Their approach does not need a feature extraction step but requires a long short-term memory (LSTM) network, which needs time to accumulate data. Similar to Woodbridge et al. [29], Xu et al. [30] checked DNS similarity and pattern to predict future DGA domains. Their approach is effective for some DGAs. Recently, researches have proposed deep learning techniques for detecting DGAs learn features automatically, which require no effort from human for feature analysis [31,32].

4 Design

Establishing a viable source for this research requires two components: (1) domains derived from a DGA; (2) machine learning that (2a) would encompass multiple feature extraction techniques and (2b) would entail clustering the domains. Multiple online sources from simple Google searching provide example codes for a DGA construction. However, a majority of these techniques are trivial and fundamental at best. Online threat intelligence feeds give a more realistic approach to examine current and live threats that roam the public Internet. This section describes the approach for data collection and proposed a machine learning framework for DGA malware analysis.

4.1 Threat Intelligence Feed and Ongoing Threat Data

DGAs are plentiful through multiple online examples that are found from Google searching and Github repositories. However, sophisticated threat actors purposely create tailored DGA to evaluate current detection systems. Using real-time active malicious domains derived from DGAs on the public Internet measures the accuracy of the proposed approach. Specifically, threat intelligence feeds collected from Bambenek Consulting [33] over a period of six months were obtained through daily manual querying demonstrated trends of ongoing threats. The structure of the data is presented in a CSV format of domain names, originating malware, and DGA membership with the daily file size of approximate 110 MB. Figure 2 demonstrates an example feed from the collected data.

```
sjthgkvsnpkfq.net,Domain used by Cryptolocker - Flashback DGA for 16 Jan 2018,2018-01-16
tfysaplgjhsnp.biz,Domain used by Cryptolocker - Flashback DGA for 16 Jan 2018,2018-01-16
ubvjhbndmsjoj.ru,Domain used by Cryptolocker - Flashback DGA for 16 Jan 2018,2018-01-16
vwbubgdqikrwr.org,Domain used by Cryptolocker - Flashback DGA for 16 Jan 2018,2018-01-16
wlxnxfvwqsnyu.co.uk,Domain used by Cryptolocker - Flashback DGA for 16 Jan 2018,2018-01-16
```

Fig. 2. Example sample dataset from Bambenek consulting gives domain names, malware origins, DGA schema, and date collected.

4.2 The Machine Learning Framework

We propose a machine learning framework that consists of three important steps, as shown in Fig. 3. We first have the input DNS queries with the payload, then it will be passing into our process step, which consists of 4 important components: (1) We first use a domain-request packet filter to get domain names and store them in the blacklist. If the input is a known domain, we will skip (2)–(4), and directly go to the output, otherwise, we will proceed to next component. (2) Then, a feature extractor is used to extract domain features. (3) Next, we apply the first-level classification to distinguish DGA domains and non-DGA domains and second-level clustering to group similar DGA domains. (4) Finally, we detect the DGA domains. After the domain name goes through the process step, we will append this domain to the blacklist.

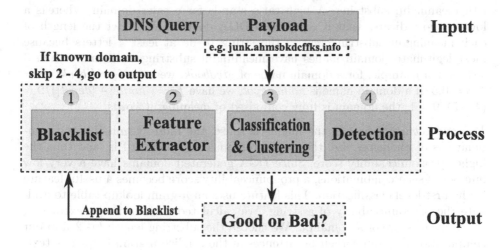

Fig. 3. Machine learning framework.

The rest of this section discusses these important steps in details.

Blacklist. To perform the classification and clustering in our following steps, we only need the information of domain names. Since the collected raw data contains some trivial information that is useless in our experiment, we apply a domain-request packet filter to remove that trivial information to obtain only domain names. This is done by using the Gruber Regex Pattern Filter [34]. All the network traffics undergo this filtering process. The filtered domain names are stored in the blacklist [35] and then sent to the feature extractor in next step.

Feature Extractor. The second step is to extract features from the domain names obtained from the first step. We consider each domain name as a string. To efficiently classify domains, we use two types of features: linguistic features and DNS features. We start with the discussions of linguistic features and then the DNS features.

There are six linguistic features: Length, Meaningful Word Ratio, Pronounce-ability Score, Percentage of Numerical Characters, Percentage of the Length of the Longest Meaningful String (LMS), and Levenshtein Edit Distance. The detailed description and calculation of each linguistic feature are given as follow:

Length: This feature is simply the length of a domain name, denoted by $|d|$.

Meaningful Word Ratio: This feature measures the ratio of meaningful words in a string (domain name). It can be calculated as follow:

$$f_1 = \sum_{i=1}^{n} \frac{|w_i|}{|d|} \qquad (1)$$

where w_i is the i-th meaningful substring of this string, $|w_i|$ is the length of i-th meaningful substring. A high ratio stands for a safer domain, whereas a lower ratio indicates that it could be a DGA domain. We strict the length of each meaningful substring $|w_i|$ in the string to be at least 4 letters because most legitimate domain names have meaningful substrings with more than 3 letters. For example, for a domain name of $yivdbook$, we have $f_1 = (|book|)/8 = 4/8 = 0.5$. If a domain name is $homedepot$, we have $f_1 = (|home| + |depot|)/9 = (4 + 5)/9 = 1$, the domain is fully composed of meaningful words.

Pronounceability Score: In the linguistic sense, the more permissible the combinations of phonemes are, the more pronounceable the word is, and thus the higher pronounceability score. Since DGA generated domains have a very low number of such combinations, a pronounceability score becomes a useful feature in the first-level classification. This feature uses an n-gram lookup table to evaluate the pronounceability of a string. We calculated the feature by extracting the n-grams score of a domain d. We choose the substring length $l \in 2, 3$ in our computation and count their occurrences in the English n-gram frequency text. For a domain d, the n-grams score is calculated as follow:

$$f_2 = \frac{\sum n - gram(d)}{|d| - n + 1} \qquad (2)$$

where n is the length of the matching word in the n-gram list.

Percentage of Numerical Characters: This feature measures the percentage of numerical characters in a string. It can be simply calculated by $f_3 = |n|/|d|$, where $|n|$ is the number of numerical characters.

Percentage of the Length of LMS: This feature is to measure the length of the longest meaningful string in a domain name. The calculation can be written as $f_4 = |l|/|d|$, where $|l|$ is the length of longest meaningful string.

Levenshtein Edit Distance: This feature measures the minimum number of single-character edits between a current domain and its previous domain. For example, given two strings "kitten" and "sitting", the Levenshtein Edit Distance between them is 3, because the characters that need to be edited are k to s, e to i and adding a g at the end.

Aside from linguistic features, we also look into DNS features where 27 DNS features in Table 1 are used in this research. We utilize DNS features because a DGA domain usually contains less information, whereas a legitimate domain does. For example, DGA domains tend to have short time and their creation dates are typically within one year.

Table 1. DGA classification features

Features	Description	(+/−)
Expiration date	If longer than 1 year	+
Creation date	If longer than 1 year	+
DNS record	If DNS record is documented	+
Distinct IP addresses	#. IP addresses related to this domain	+
Number of distinct countries	#. countries related this domain	+
IP shared by domains	#. domains are shared by the IP	−
Reverse DNS query results	If DN in top 3 reverse query results	+
Sub-domain	If domain is related to other sub-ones	+
Average TTL	DNS data time cached by DNS servers	+
SD of TTL	Distribution SD of TTL	−
% usage of the TTL ranges	Distribution range of TTL	+
# of distinct TTL values	Different value of TTL on server	−
# of TTL change	How frequently TTL changes	+
Client delete permission	If client has delete permission	−
Client update permission	If client has update permission	−
Client transfer permission	If client has transfer permission	−
Server delete permission	If server has delete permission	−
Server update permission	If client has update permission	−
Server transfer permission	If client has transfer permission	−
Registrar	The domain name registrar	+
Whois Guard	If use Whois guard to protect privacy	−
IP address same subnet	If IP address is in the same subnet	−
Business name	If domain has a corporation name	+
Geography location	If domain provides address	+
Phone number	If domain provides a phone number	+
Local hosting	If use local host machine	+
Popularity	If on the top 10000 domain list	+

Note: DN - Domain name. TTL - Time-To-Live. SD - Standard deviation. All the features used in our model. (+/−): "+" stands for positively related to normal domain, whereas "−" stands for negatively.

Two-Level Model: Classification and Clustering. To understand DGA domains, we propose a two-level machine learning model consisting of the first-level classification and the second-level clustering. In the former, we use a classification model called J48 classifier to classify input domains into DGA domain (bad domain) and non-DGA domain (good domain). Then, the classified DGA domains will be sent to the second-level clustering, where we use the DBSCAN-based clustering [5] to divide the DGA domains into several groups, as shown in Fig. 4.

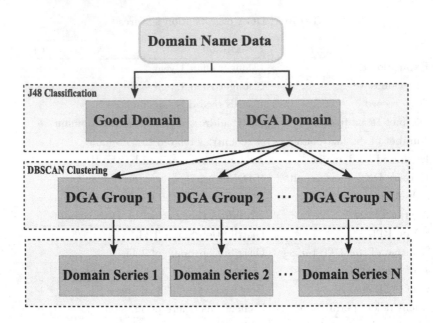

Fig. 4. Two-level model of classification and clustering

First-Level Classification: A perfect classification algorithm for classifying DGA domains and non-DGA domains requires the maximal difference between them. By using the features obtained above, we test different machine learning classifiers including Decision Tree-J48, Artificial Neural Network (ANN), Support Vector Machine (SVM), Logistic Regression and Naive Bayes to find the best classifier. Among those classifiers, we notice that J48 is the best to classify DGA domains (its detailed discussion is given in Sect. 5), so J48 is chosen as a classifier in our first-level classification.

Second-Level Clustering: Only the classified DGA domains are used for the second-level clustering. Our clustering model is based on the DBSCAN algorithm, where we use domain features to compute the distance of their domain names and to group these domains according to their domain feature difference. Let d_i and d_j be domain names, where $i \neq j$. We first set $i = 0$ representing the first domain and then calculate the overall distance between d_i and all other domains. Since we have two types of features: linguistic feature and DNS feature, the overall distance is a combination of linguistic distance and DNS similarity. The linguistic distance is computed based on the six linguistic features followed by the following equation:

$$D_l(d_i, d_j) = \sqrt{\sum_{k=1}^{6} dis_k(d_i, d_j)}, \tag{3}$$

where $dis_k(d_i, d_j)$ is the distance of each linguistic features between two domains d_i and d_j. To get the DNS similarity, we first construct a weight matrix $\mathbf{M} \in \mathbb{R}^{K \times L}$, where K and L are the number of DNS features and linguistic features of all the DGA domains $\mathbb{D}$ classified from the first-level classification, respectively. The relationship between K and L is represented by a bipartite graph that is represented in $\mathbf{M}$, where each component $\mathbf{M}_{k,l}$ holds the weight of an edge (l, k). For each DNS record, weight $\mathbf{M}_{k,l}$ is computed by:

$$\mathbf{M}_{k,l} = \frac{1}{|\mathbb{D}(k)|}, \text{ for any } l = 1, ..., L, \tag{4}$$

where $|\mathbb{D}(k)|$ is the cardinality of the subset of domains that are pointed to the DNS record. We then use a matrix $\mathbf{S} \in \mathbb{R}^{L \times L}$ to store DNS similarity information, where for each component, $\mathbf{S}_{d_i, d_j}$ is the similarity value of domains d_i and d_j. Our intuition is that when two domains point to the same DNS record k, they should have high similarity. Therefore, we could calculate the similarity matrix based on the weight matrix $\mathbf{M}$. Let $\mathbf{N}$ be $\mathbf{M}$ normalized by columns. We have:

$$\mathbf{N} \equiv \mathbf{M} \text{ when } \left(\sum_{k=1}^{K} M_{k,l} = 1, \forall l = 1, \cdots, L \right). \tag{5}$$

Final similarity matrix is calculated by:

$$\mathbf{S} = \mathbf{N}^T \odot \mathbf{N} \in \mathbb{R}^{L \times L}. \tag{6}$$

The overall distance is a combination of linguistic distance and DNS similarity, which is calculated by:

$$D(d_i, d_j) = S_{d_i, d_j} + log(\frac{1}{D_l(d_i, d_j)}) \tag{7}$$

After we have the overall distance, we can get all points density-reachable from d_i based on the threshold distance, ϵ. If $D(d_i, d_j) > \epsilon$, we add those points d_j to a cluster C. The minimal cluster points, $MinPts$, is used to determine a core point. Let d_i be a core point. If the number of point in $C > MinPts$, then a cluster is formed. If d_i is a border point, implying that no points are density-reachable from d_i, then our DBSCAN model visits the next domain. The above steps will be repeated until all of the domains have been processed.

5   Evaluation

5.1   Global Environment for Network Innovation

GENI is an NSF funded heterogenous testbed solution. Leveraging high-performance nodes aided in the ability to process large volumes of real-time data feeds in a timely manner. The nodes selected for the evaluation consisted of systems running: Intel(R) Xeon(R) CPU E5-2450 @ 2.10 GHz, 16 GB of hard drive space, and 1GB of memory where the size could be manipulated, based on reservation.

Experimental Setup. To evaluate our model thoroughly, we use five datasets of DGA domain data: CryptoLocker, Tovar, Dyre, Nymaim, and Locky from the latest DGA-feed [36–38]. We collected the DGA domain names over a period of six months in 2017. 160,000 domain names were tested in our model. To provide a list of normal control group domain names, we choose the top 1 million most popular Internet domains listed in domain punch [39]. We mix the control domain names and DGA domains names with a 1:1 ratio for the first-level classification. In the second-level clustering, we use classified DGA domain names from the first-level classification to cluster different groups of DGA domains.

5.2   Our Execution and Results

Experimental Results. To find the best model for the first-level classification, we test five different machine learning models, J48, ANN, SVM, Logistic Regression, and Naive Bayes. Figures 5(A) and (B) show the performance of different algorithms on the classification of the DGA domains. We find that J48 has the highest average accuracy, 95.14%, compared to other machine learning algorithms. Figure 5(B) also shows that J48 is the fastest one with an average of 0.0144 ms to classify the domain names. To see the accuracy of J48 associated with scalability, we test five groups of samples for each DGA generated domain with a total number of 1000, 5000, 15000, 20000, 50000 domain names. We find that J48 performs the best for CryptoLocker domain names.

Figure 6(A) shows how the second-level clustering algorithm performs on different DGAs. When we use both linguistic distance and DNS similarity as the overall distance, its average accuracy is 87.64%, whereas if we only use DNS similarity as the overall distance, the average accuracy is 89.02%. This is because most of DGAs have very similar string composition and length. These features can not help the clustering algorithm to identify similar DGA domains from each other. Furthermore, we test the accuracy of clustering when more groups are mixed together.

As Fig. 6(B) shows, we test all the two group combinations for all the five DGAs. When we mix Cryptolocker with other DGAs, the average accuracy for clustering is 81.43% for all the features. However, when we use only DNS features as the DBSCAN distance, its accuracy increases to 92.45%, which means that most Cryptolocker domains are clustered into one group. Similarly, when testing other groups, we find that the accuracies of clustering are 91.05%, 92.22%, 92.89%, and 92.57% for ovar, Dyre, Nymaim, and Locky, respectively. The result demonstrates that the clustering model is efficient to group the same DGA domains into one group.

5.3   Discussions

As seen in our experimental evaluation, the proposed machine learning framework has demonstrated the efficient way to predict a future DGA domain name. We have evaluated the proposed machine learning framework with most latest DGA domain names from DGA-feed to cluster and predict DGA domains

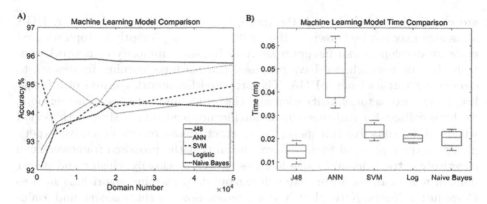

Fig. 5. (A) Accuracy of different machine learning algorithms (B) Classification time of different machine learning algorithms.

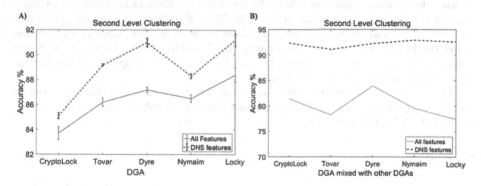

Fig. 6. (A) Clustering accuracy for each DGA. (B) Clustering accuracy for each two DGAs group.

from these real-world data. Our evaluation has shown that with 33 features we proposed in our model, the J48 classification algorithm performed the most effective and efficient in comparison to ANN, SVM, Logistic, and Naive Byes due to the minimal classification time, 0.0144 ms, and the highest accuracy, 95.14%. We have also tested the clustering accuracy. Our result has shown that the DBSCAN clustering model has the accuracy of 92.45%. We have noticed that the best accuracy we get from clustering is the one where only DNS query features are used. The experimental results have proved that a cluster of DGA domains usually points to several specific server IPs. DNS information of these domains are very similar and therefore clustering them with only DNS features is very accurate.

6   Conclusions and Future Work

The dichotomy of DGA in malware presents a grant challenge in securing an organization. Firewall blacklisting is constantly expanded since filtering rules are constantly added through the multiple sources of inputs. However, DGA sequences may not be known by the multiple sources promptly as sophisticated malware developers can integrate DGA to bypass a majority of network controls. In this research, we have proposed the machine learning framework to circumvent threats from a DGA. The proposed framework consists of a blacklist, feature extractor, classification and clustering, and detection. Furthermore, we have collected a real-time threat intelligence feed over a six month period where all domains live threats on the Internet. Based on our extensive experiments on the real-world feed, we have shown that the proposed framework can effectively extract domain name features as well as classify, cluster and detect domain names. In the future, we will explore deep learning algorithms such as Convolution Neural Network (CNN) via tensor-flow for this research and evaluate them on a real-world testbed such as GENI [40–42].

Acknowledgments. We acknowledge National Science Foundation (NSF) to partially sponsor the research work under grants #1633978, #1620871, #1636622, #1651280, and #1620862, and BBN/GPO project #1936 through an NSF/CNS grant. We also thank the Florida Center for Cybersecurity (FC2) located at the University of South Florida (USF) to support the research through its funding that is open to all institutions in the State University System of Florida.

The views and conclusions contained herein are those of the authors and should not be interpreted as necessarily representing the official policies, either expressed or implied of NSF, FC2, and USF.

References

1. Rieck, K., Holz, T., Willems, C., Düssel, P., Laskov, P.: Learning and classification of malware behavior. In: Zamboni, D. (ed.) DIMVA 2008. LNCS, vol. 5137, pp. 108–125. Springer, Heidelberg (2008). https://doi.org/10.1007/978-3-540-70542-0_6

2. Chin, T., Xiong, K., Rahouti, M.: SDN-based kernel modular countermeasure for intrusion detection. In: Lin, X., Ghorbani, A., Ren, K., Zhu, S., Zhang, A. (eds.) SecureComm 2017. LNICST, vol. 238, pp. 270–290. Springer, Cham (2018). https://doi.org/10.1007/978-3-319-78813-5_14

3. Ghosh, U., et al.: An SDN based framework for guaranteeing security and performance in information-centric cloud networks. In: Proceedings of the 11th IEEE International Conference on Cloud Computing (IEEE Cloud) (2017)

4. Khancome, C., Boonjing, V., Chanvarasuth, P.: A two-hashing table multiple string pattern matching algorithm. In: Tenth International Conference on Information Technology: New Generations (ITNG), pp. 696–701. IEEE (2013)

5. Schiavoni, S., Maggi, F., Cavallaro, L., Zanero, S.: Phoenix: DGA-based botnet tracking and intelligence. In: Dietrich, S. (ed.) DIMVA 2014. LNCS, vol. 8550, pp. 192–211. Springer, Cham (2014). https://doi.org/10.1007/978-3-319-08509-8_11

6. Sood, A.K., Zeadally, S.: A taxonomy of domain-generation algorithms. IEEE Secur. Priv. **14**(4), 46–53 (2016)

7. Xiong, K.: Multiple priority customer service guarantees in cluster computing. In: Proceedings of the IEEE International Symposium on Parallel & Distributed Processing (IPDPS), pp. 1–12. IEEE (2009)

8. Xiong, K.: Resource optimization and security for cloud services. Wiley, Hoboken (2014)
9. Xiong, K.: Resource optimization and security for distributed computing (2008). https://repository.lib.ncsu.edu/handle/1840.16/3581
10. Mark, B., et al.: GENI: a federated testbed for innovative network experiments. Comput. Netw. **61**, 5–23 (2014)
11. Xiong, K., Chen, X.: Ensuring cloud service guarantees via service level agreement (SLA)-based resource allocation. In: Proceedings of the IEEE 35th International Conference on Distributed Computing Systems Workshops, ICDCS Workshops, pp. 35–41. IEEE (2015)
12. Chin, T., Xiong, K.: Dynamic generation containment systems (DGCS): A moving target defense approach. In: Proceedings of the 3rd International Workshop on Emerging Ideas and Trends in Engineering of Cyber-Physical Systems (EITEC), vol. 00, pp. 11–16, April 2016
13. Sornalakshmi, K.: Detection of DoS attack and zero day threat with SIEM. In: International Conference on Intelligent Computing and Control Systems (ICICCS), pp. 1–7. IEEE (2017)
14. Yadav, S., Reddy, A.L.N.: Winning with DNS failures: strategies for faster botnet detection. In: Rajarajan, M., Piper, F., Wang, H., Kesidis, G. (eds.) SecureComm 2011. LNICST, vol. 96, pp. 446–459. Springer, Heidelberg (2012). https://doi.org/10.1007/978-3-642-31909-9_26
15. Yadav, S., Reddy, A.K.K., Reddy, A.N., Ranjan, S.: Detecting algorithmically generated domain-flux attacks with DNS traffic analysis. IEEE/ACM Trans. Netw. **20**(5), 1663–1677 (2012)
16. Guo, F., Ferrie, P., Chiueh, T.: A study of the packer problem and its solutions. In: Lippmann, R., Kirda, E., Trachtenberg, A. (eds.) RAID 2008. LNCS, vol. 5230, pp. 98–115. Springer, Heidelberg (2008). https://doi.org/10.1007/978-3-540-87403-4_6
17. Holz, T., Steiner, M., Dahl, F., Biersack, E., Freiling, F.C., et al.: Measurements and mitigation of peer-to-peer-based botnets: a case study on storm worm. LEET **8**(1), 1–9 (2008)
18. Zhang, L., Yu, S., Wu, D., Watters, P.: A survey on latest botnet attack and defense. In: IEEE 10th International Conference on Trust, Security and Privacy in Computing and Communications (TrustCom), pp. 53–60. IEEE (2011)
19. Barabosch, T., Wichmann, A., Leder, F., Gerhards-Padilla, E.: Automatic extraction of domain name generation algorithms from current malware. In: Proceedings of NATO Symposium IST-111 on Information Assurance and Cyber Defense, Koblenz, Germany (2012)
20. Gardiner, J., Nagaraja, S.: On the security of machine learning in malware c&c detection: a survey. ACM Comput. Surv. (CSUR) **49**(3), 59 (2016)
21. Ahluwalia, A., Traore, I., Ganame, K., Agarwal, N.: Detecting broad length algorithmically generated domains. In: Traore, I., Woungang, I., Awad, A. (eds.) ISDDC 2017. LNCS, vol. 10618, pp. 19–34. Springer, Cham (2017). https://doi.org/10.1007/978-3-319-69155-8_2
22. Ma, J., Saul, L.K., Savage, S., Voelker, G.M.: Beyond blacklists: learning to detect malicious web sites from suspicious URLs. In: Proceedings of the 15th ACM SIGKDD International Conference on Knowledge Discovery and Data Mining, pp. 1245–1254. ACM (2009)
23. Antonakakis, M., et al.: From throw-away traffic to bots: detecting the rise of DGA-based malware. In: USENIX security symposium, vol. 12 (2012)
24. Wang, W., Shirley, K.: Breaking bad: detecting malicious domains using word segmentation. arXiv preprint arXiv:1506.04111 (2015)

25. McGrath, D.K., Gupta, M.: Behind phishing: an examination of phisher modi operandi. LEET **8**, 4 (2008)
26. Mowbray, M., Hagen, J.: Finding domain-generation algorithms by looking at length distribution. In: IEEE International Symposium on Software Reliability Engineering Workshops (ISSREW), pp. 395–400. IEEE (2014)
27. Shabtai, A., et al.: Detection of malicious code by applying machine learning classifiers on static features: a state-of-the-art survey. Information Security Technical Report (2009)
28. Sharifnya, R., Abadi, M.: A novel reputation system to detect DGA-based botnets. In: 3th International eConference on Computer and Knowledge Engineering (ICCKE), pp. 417–423. IEEE (2013)
29. Woodbridge, J., Anderson, H.S., Ahuja, A., Grant, D.: Predicting domain generation algorithms with long short-term memory networks. arXiv preprint arXiv:1611.00791 (2016)
30. Xu, W., Sanders, K., Zhang, Y.: We know it before you do: predicting malicious domains. In: Virus Bulletin Conference (2014)
31. Yu, B., Gray, D.L., Pan, J., De Cock, M., Nascimento, A.C.: Inline DGA detection with deep networks. In: IEEE International Conference on Data Mining Workshops (ICDMW), pp. 683–692. IEEE (2017)
32. Saxe, J., Berlin, K.: eXpose: A character-level convolutional neural network with embeddings for detecting malicious URLs, file paths and registry keys. arXiv preprint arXiv:1702.08568 (2017)
33. Bambenek: OSINT feeds from bambenek consulting. Bambenek Consulting
34. Yang, L., Karim, R., Ganapathy, V., Smith, R.: Fast, memory-efficient regular expression matching with NFA-OBDDs. Comput. Netw. **55**(15), 3376–3393 (2011)
35. Kührer, M., Rossow, C., Holz, T.: Paint it black: evaluating the effectiveness of malware blacklists. In: Stavrou, A., Bos, H., Portokalidis, G. (eds.) RAID 2014. LNCS, vol. 8688, pp. 1–21. Springer, Cham (2014). https://doi.org/10.1007/978-3-319-11379-1_1
36. JBT Organization: Domain feed of known DGA domains (2017)
37. Jarvis, K.: Cryptolocker ransomware. Viitattu **20**, 2014 (2013)
38. Chaignon, P.: A collection of known domain generation algorithms (2014)
39. Technologies: Top million websites & TLDs (2016)
40. Chin, T., Mountrouidou, X., Li, X., Xiong, K.: An SDN-supported collaborative approach for DDoS flooding detection and containment. In: 2015 IEEE Military Communications Conference, MILCOM 2015, pp. 659–664. IEEE (2015)
41. Lenkala, S.R., Shetty, S., Xiong, K.: Security risk assessment of cloud carrier. In: 2013 13th IEEE/ACM International Symposium on Cluster, Cloud and Grid Computing (CCGrid), pp. 442–449. IEEE (2013)
42. Xiong, K., Perros, H.: SLA-based service composition in enterprise computing. In: 16th International Workshop on Quality of Service, IWQoS 2008, pp. 30–39. IEEE (2008)

Cloud Security

Se-Lambda: Securing Privacy-Sensitive Serverless Applications Using SGX Enclave

Weizhong Qiang[✉], Zezhao Dong, and Hai Jin

Services Computing Technology and System Lab, Cluster and Grid Computing Lab,
Big Data Technology and System Lab, School of Computer Science and Technology,
Huazhong University of Science and Technology, Wuhan 430074, China
wzqiang@hust.edu.cn

Abstract. Serverless computing is an emerging trend in the cloud, which represents a new paradigm for deploying applications and services. In the serverless computing framework, cloud users can deploy arbitrary code and process data on the service runtime. However, as neither cloud users nor cloud providers are trustworthy, serverless computing platform suffers from trust issues caused by both sides. In this paper, we propose a new serverless computing framework called Se-Lambda, which protects the API gateway by using SGX enclave and the service runtime by leveraging a two-way sandbox that combines SGX enclave and WebAssembly sandboxed environment. In the proposed service runtime, users' untrusted code is confined by WebAssembly sandboxed environment, while SGX enclave prevents malicious cloud providers from stealing users' privacy-sensitive data. In addition, we implement a privilege monitoring mechanism in SGX enclave to manage the access control of function modules from users. We implement the prototype of Se-Lambda based on the open source project OpenLambda. The experimental results show that the Se-Lambda imposes a low performance penalty, while buying a significantly increased level of security.

Keywords: Serverless computing · Cloud security
Runtime security · Intel SGX · WebAssembly

1 Introduction

With the rapid development of cloud computing, serverless computing has become a new paradigm for deploying applications and services [7]. Serverless computing is based on event-driven programming, in which application logic is implemented as functions and events that trigger them, and then the cloud provider executes functions following an event stream. When a serverless application is deployed, the price is dependent on the actual amount of computing resources consumed by each request, thus cutting the costs of cloud users. In addition, application scaling is automatically handled by the cloud platform

© ICST Institute for Computer Sciences, Social Informatics and Telecommunications Engineering 2018
R. Beyah et al. (Eds.): SecureComm 2018, LNICST 254, pp. 451–470, 2018.
https://doi.org/10.1007/978-3-030-01701-9_25

itself, rather than by users or tenants that create application or virtual machine instances. By taking the advantages of serverless computing, we can leverage it to build web, *Internet of Things* (IoT), and mobile applications.

In the serverless computing framework, an application invokes different APIs to realize a functionality as its logic is split into different functions. During an API call, API gateway is responsible for obtaining an API token, resolving the URL and invoking the corresponding service runtime. Therefore, API gateway is the core component of serverless computing, which always suffers from a variety of malicious attacks. Once a module of API gateway is compromised, it will affect other modules. In addition, the service runtime of serverless computing platform also faces severe security challenges.

On the one hand, unlike *Infrastructure-as-a-Service* (IaaS) model which has strong isolation guarantee due to good isolation between virtual machine instances, the serverless architecture, which is mostly based on containers for executing functions, only achieves weak isolation guarantee. The reason is that containers depend on the isolation provided by the host OS kernel, and the kernel often leverages software mechanisms for isolation and needs to protect a larger interface [2]. In addition, users of the serverless computing framework can deploy arbitrary function module which may contain malicious code to be executed on the service runtime. Therefore, a malicious cloud user can compromise the platform's host runtime, even the underlying system, by exploiting vulnerabilities of the container or OS kernel. On the other hand, the serverless computing framework shares the same issue as other cloud computing models, with which is that malicious or curious cloud providers may steal cloud users' privacy-sensitive data, such as encryption keys, since they control the whole software stack of the service runtime.

It is a challenge to allow trustworthy execution of programs in hostile environments, such as a public cloud, without trusting the cloud provider. Previous approaches either use homomorphic encryption or leverage *Trusted Execution Environment* (TEE). As we know, because of the expensive computing cost, it is not practical to use homomorphic encryption for securing data in clouds. Intel *Software Guard Extensions* (SGX), as a hardware-based TEE that provides an isolated environment called enclave to secure the execution of a program, can protect the running enclave against malicious software, including the operating system, hypervisor, and even low-level firmware.

In particular, SGX enclaves have been applied to existing data-processing services, such as MapReduce framework [22], log server [15], and coordination services [5]. Unfortunately, these researches need to customize specialized enclaves for protecting the confidentiality and integrity of users' data. In additional, Haven [3] and Graphene-SGX [31] leverage library OS to execute unmodified legacy applications in clouds, which suffers from a large amount of *Trusted Computing Base* (TCB) and a high performance overhead. In order to minimize the TCB of applications, researchers put part of an application into the enclave, such as SCONE [2] and Panoply [27]. All these architectures protect the confidentiality of users' data, assuming that any application running inside an SGX enclave are trusted.

However, cloud applications themselves may contain malicious code, and thus are untrusted, which is the case particularly for serverless computing architecture. To address the issue of untrusted applications, Minibox [18] combines hypervisor-based isolation technique [19] and native client sandbox [35] to protect applications in *Platform-as-a-Service* model, which is limited to x86 native code, and with a TCB that is too large to be directly applied in the serverless architecture. In addition, Ryoan [13] uses a distributed sandbox to protect data-processing service, which focuses on preventing untrusted code from leaking users' data. Ryoan has an increased TCB and brings much performance overhead, which is not suitable for the service runtime of serverless computing platform, such as *Node.js* runtime.

In this paper, we propose Se-Lambda, a serverless computing framework that can secure the processing of users' data without trusting the whole software stack of the cloud provider. In Se-Lambda, both API gateway and service runtime are protected. For API gateway, Se-Lambda leverages the SGX enclave to protect the core modules of API gateway, which avoids the negative influence of malicious attacks. In addition, Se-Lambda uses SGX's remote attestation to provide a function validation module in the API gateway, which verifies the integrity of a function module before it is executed.

For service runtime, Se-Lambda leverages a two-way sandbox, which places WebAssembly sandboxed environment into the SGX enclave, to provide shield execution for users' function modules. The WebAssembly sandboxed environment is the state-of-art sandbox that supports both web embedding and non-web embedding environment, which isolates users' function modules to prevent malicious code from compromising the host runtime, even the cloud platform. In addition, the SGX enclave prevents cloud provider from leaking users' data by taking the advantages of SGX's strong isolation. Moreover, the two-way sandbox leverages the dynamic function execution technique to reduce the overhead of unnecessary enclave creation and destruction.

Based on the design, neither function modules nor cloud providers are supposed to be trustworthy. The integration of the two-way sandbox into service runtime will impose a little performance overhead, while introducing an increased level of security.

The main contributions of this paper are as follows:

- We propose a detailed design of Se-Lambda, including the securing of API gateway and service runtime. In API gateway, Se-Lambda utilizes the SGX enclave to protect the core modules of API gateway and leverages SGX's remote attestation to verify the integrity of function module.
- We provide a two-way sandbox for the service runtime, which prevents untrusted users' function module from compromising the host runtime, even the cloud platform. In addition, it protects users' privacy-sensitive data from the malicious cloud provider.
- We implement a prototype of Se-Lambda and evaluate it. It introduces a significantly increased level of security while imposing a little performance overhead.

In the next section, we describe the background and threat model. Then, we introduce system design in Sect. 3. Then, we describe implementation details in Sect. 4, followed by evaluation results in Sect. 5. Finally, we discuss related work in Sect. 6 and draw conclusions in Sect. 7.

2   Background

2.1   Software Guard Extensions

Intel *Software Guard Extensions* (SGX) is an extension of the Intel architecture, which is used to enhance software security. With SGX, developers can place the trusted portion of the software in the enclave to protect select code and data from disclosure or modification, as neither privileged nor unprivileged software can access enclaves that are protected areas of execution in memory. In the context of SGX, enclaves are isolated execution units, with encrypted code and data. The data is placed in the *Enclave Page Cache* (EPC), the memory in the EPC is encrypted by the *Memory Encryption Engine* (MEE) to prevent known memory attacks. The contents of the memory in the EPC will be decrypted only when it enters the CPU package and will be encrypted when it leaves the CPU package. Therefore, the TCB of an enclave contains only itself and the underlying CPU.

SGX provides a CPU-based remote attestation mechanism that enables third parties to verify the integrity of the code running in an enclave, and a data sharing mechanism between enclaves over a secure channel established by the remote attestation mechanism. An enclave can only execute unprivileged instructions in user space. When an application in the enclave needs a system call to get the underlying system service, the enclave needs to be switched out to execute this system call.

2.2   WebAssembly

WebAssembly (WASM) [33] is an experimental, low-level programming language that is usually applied to the web, which defines a small, portable and load-time-efficient format suitable for compilation to the web. Up to now, web browsers such as Chrome, Microsoft Edge, Safari, and Firefox, have begun to support the initial version of WebAssembly.

WebAssembly leverages *Software Fault Isolation* (SFI) to build the sandboxed environment, which is isolated from the host runtime. The sandboxed environment is applied to prevent buggy or malicious modules from leaking users' data. Each WebAssembly module is subject to the security policies of its embedding. For example, modules running in a web browser follows the same origin policy as the browser, while modules in a non-browser environment follows the same POSIX security policy as the system. A WebAssembly module must declare all accessible methods and their related types at the time of loading, including the dynamic link functions it used. Therefore, we can leverage *Control-Flow*

Integrity (CFI) implicitly to check whether an application is hijacked during program execution.

The way of function call in WebAssembly is different from C/C++ function call in the following aspects: (1) A function call must specify target index corresponding to effective entries in function index or table index space. (2) Indirect function calls need to specify the type signature of the target function at the calling, then the type signature must be exactly matched before the function is called. Through the above mechanism, WebAssembly can effectively avoid control-flow hijacking attacks.

2.3   Threat Model

We assume that cloud users and cloud providers do not trust each others, but trust their own codes and platforms. At the cloud platform level, we assume a powerful adversary who controls the entire software environment of the cloud platform, including the operating system, hypervisor, and even low-level firmware. In addition, the adversary may physically get access to the service's server to perform hardware attacks, such as cold boot attack. At the cloud user level, we assume that the adversary can deploy arbitrary code on the service runtime of serverless architecture, especially malicious code. The adversary may break the container's isolation by exploiting the vulnerabilities of softwares, which may compromise the host runtime, even the cloud platform.

We assume that the following components are trusted: (1) the Intel SGX instruction set extension; (2) the Intel SGX kernel driver, and the `aesmd` which approves the enclave creation by verifying attributes in the enclave signature; (3) the WebAssembly sandboxed environment. Other than these components above, there is no need to trust any other part in Se-Lambda.

We do not consider denial of service that an attacker may terminate the execution of the enclave or crash the enclave. Additionally, side channel attacks, such as page faults and cache timing, are beyond the scope of our model due to the infeasibility of exploiting these channels in practice.

3   System Design

The purpose of designing Se-Lambda is to provide a secured serverless computing environment where cloud users and cloud providers do not trust each others. The serverless computing framework needs to protect cloud users' data from being leaked as well as the host runtime of cloud providers from being compromised.

3.1   Architecture

Due to the architectures of various serverless platforms are a little different, we refer to the architecture of Amazon's AWS Lambda, which includes an API gateway and a service runtime. Figure 1 shows a detailed overview of the Se-Lambda architecture.

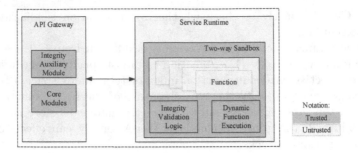

Fig. 1. Architecture of Se-Lambda

Se-Lambda prevents the untrusted software on API gateway from compromising core modules by leveraging hardware to isolate them. In addition, Se-Lambda offers an integrity validation to verify the integrity of cloud users' function modules. The integrity validation contains an auxiliary module in API gateway and the validation logic in two-way sandbox (see Sect. 3.2).

Se-Lambda prevents the service runtime from leaking cloud users' data and malicious code from compromising the host runtime of cloud providers by introducing a two-way sandbox, which provides a two-way protection between cloud users' function modules and the cloud provider. When deploying a serverless application on the protected service runtime, both cloud users and cloud providers do not need to worry about trust issues (see Sect. 3.3).

Se-Lambda offers a dynamic function execution mechanism to improve the performance of the two-way sandbox by optimizing the life cycle of the two-way sandbox to reduce the times of creating and destroying it (see Sect. 3.4).

3.2 API Gateway

We use SGX enclave to isolate the core module of API gateway and provide an integrity auxiliary module in API gateway.

Core Modules Isolation. API gateway is the key component of Se-Lambda, which contains various core modules, such as authentication and authorization. Figure 2 shows the workflow for API gateway handling user requests, which briefly includes the following steps. First, API gateway handles a user request by parsing the request information and performing security checks to prevent malicious attacks. Then, when the request is verified, API gateway calls the user authentication and access control modules in service mediation. Finally, after the authentication succeeds, API gateway invokes the corresponding service runtime to execute function modules and outputs the result to the user.

Se-Lambda does not trust other software on the API gateway, including the operating system and hypervisor. Placing all modules of API gateway into SGX enclave will cause a large TCB. Instead, we only place the privacy-sensitive core

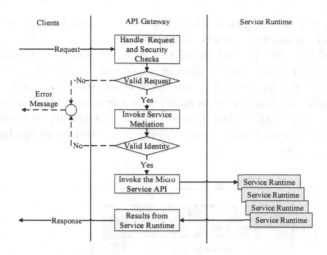

Fig. 2. Workflow of serverless computing gateway

modules into SGX enclave to isolate them from being compromised. As we only protect part of API gateway, we can offer a fine-grained isolation as well as a small TCB.

Function Validation. Se-Lambda ensures that function modules running on the service runtime are what the cloud users expect through integrity validation for those modules. However, previous software based integrity validation can be bypassed or compromised by attackers, which may drop a validation request or tamper with the validation code itself. Se-Lambda leverages SGX's remote attestation to provide an integrity validation for function modules by taking the advantage of hardware attestation.

In detail, after the protected service runtime creates the two-way sandbox, the sandbox attests to API gateway that it is trusted and establishes an authenticated communication channel by launching a remote attestation. When API gateway invokes the protected service runtime to execute a function module, it sends function module's hash value, which is from user's request, to the two-way sandbox by the above authenticated channel. Then, before the function module is executed, the two-way sandbox leverages hash checking to verify the integrity of this function module.

3.3   Two-Way Sandbox

The service runtime is the engine that executes users' function modules in the serverless computing framework. However, neither cloud users nor cloud providers are trustworthy, since malicious users' code may compromise the host runtime and malicious cloud providers may steal users' data. Some solutions provide trusted environment to address these issues, which are not suitable for the serverless programming model. In this section, we provide a protected service runtime, which includes a two-way sandbox.

Figure 3 shows the architecture of the two-way sandbox, which includes a gray part of trusted and a white part of untrusted. The trusted part contains CPU, SGX driver, and a two-way sandbox is an SGX enclave that includes a WebAssembly sandboxed environment. The two-way protection provided by the sandbox is that SGX enclave protects the confidentiality of users' data and WebAssembly sandboxed environment protects the security of the host runtime of the cloud provider.

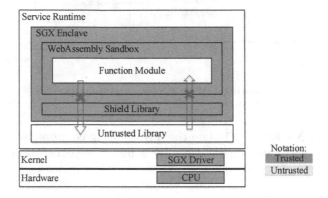

Fig. 3. Architecture of two-way sandbox

However, the code inside SGX enclave cannot execute privileged instructions and needs to switch to the outside world to execute them, which may faces malicious attacks, such as Iago attacks [8] in which a malicious kernel could manipulate system call return values and then induce a protected process to act against its interests. In addition, although WebAssembly sandboxed environment prevents software vulnerabilities from compromising host runtime, it does not prevent the execution from exceeding the permissions.

One of the safety functions of the two-way sandbox is to manage the interface between the function module and the outside world. Thus, the two-way sandbox includes a privilege monitoring module within SGX enclave to manage the access control for a function module, which recodes system calls of the function module and filters them according to permission set. In order to prevent Iago attacks, we share the same approach as previous works [3,27] by letting the privilege monitoring module perform checks on the return values of system calls.

In addition, the two-way sandbox achieves the dynamic function execution technique, which is discussed in Sect. 3.4, by dynamically allocating memory during the execution of function modules. For example, when executing a function module, the two-way sandbox loads it into dynamically allocated memory. After the function module is executed, the dynamically allocated memory is freed to the OS, which greatly reduces the memory footprint.

3.4 Optimization of Two-Way Sandbox Life Cycle

According to the limitations of serverless architecture, the execution time of each function is ephemeral, which means that the enclave that provides the sandbox will also be short-lived. However, the time overhead of creating and destructing an enclave is high [13]. As shown in Fig. 4(a), the life cycle of the two-way sandbox contains creation, initialization, integrity attestation, function's execution, result return, and destruction. The two-way sandbox starts with creating and initializing SGX enclave. Then, API gateway validates the integrity of the function module. After the function module is executed, the two-way sandbox outputs the result and then is destructed.

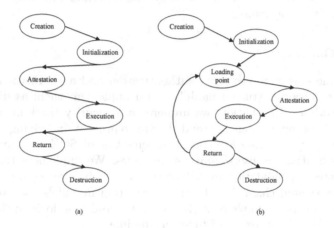

Fig. 4. The life cycle of the two-way sandbox

Se-Lambda avoids the duplicated creation and destruction of the two-way sandbox as well as reduces the memory footprint of the sandbox by introducing the dynamic function execution technique, which adds a loading-point after the initialization of SGX enclave. As shown in Fig. 4(b), after the two-way sandbox creates and initializes the SGX enclave, it reaches a loading-point and then waits for loading function module. When the API gateway schedules the sandbox based service runtime to execute a function module, the function module is dynamically loaded into the two-way sandbox. After the function module is executed, the two-way sandbox will clear it through the dynamic function execution mechanism. At the same time, the two-way sandbox will be restored to the state of waiting for dynamically loading function module.

4 Implementation

Se-Lambda's prototype system is based on the open source serverless computing framework *OpenLambda*. We choose *Node.js* (version 8.7) as the service runtime, which is built on the Google V8 JavaScript engine. We use the WebAssembly sandboxed environment in the V8 engine to protect the host runtime from being compromised by malicious code. In addition, we migrate the V8 engine into SGX enclave to prevent users' data from being leaked by malicious or buggy underlying systems.

In the API gateway of *OpenLambda*, we implement an isolated environment to protect some trusted modules, as well as an auxiliary module to assist the integrity validation of users' function modules. Because the SGX enclave can only execute unprivileged code, we provide a secure underlying system service for users' function modules to offer functionalities such as dynamic memory allocation and privilege monitoring. Based on the features of interpreted language, we optimize the life cycle of the two-way sandbox and introduce a dynamic function execution mechanism.

4.1 API Gateway

We treat some core modules (e.g., authentication and authorization modules) in the API gateway as trusted modules, and implement them as dynamically extensible modules. In addition, we implement a security check mechanism on the interface between SGX enclave and the OS to prevent underlying OS attacks.

We leverage the remote attestation mechanism of SGX to implement the integrity verification for users' function modules. We implement the auxiliary module of integrity validation in API gateway, which is responsible for establishing authenticated channel and sending function module's hash to the two-way sandbox. Then, we implement the integrity validation logic in the two-way sandbox to verify the integrity of function module.

4.2 Dynamic Memory Allocation

The dynamic memory allocation is needed by the two-way sandbox in Se-Lambda. SGX2 adds instructions such as *EACCEPT*, *EMODT*, and *EMODPR* to support dynamic memory allocation in the enclave, which can dynamically increase enclave memory or swap out rarely used enclave pages. After the CPU that supports SGX2 obtains a memory page from the system kernel, it calls the *EACCEPT* instruction to accept this page. In addition, after using *EMODT* and *EMODPR* instruction to modify the permission of an existing EPC page, the CPU needs to call *EACCEPT* instruction to accept this.

However, there is no hardware that supports SGX2 available at present. Instead, in the implementation, we use a pre-allocated memory mechanism in SGX1. When creating an enclave in the service runtime, we allocate a large amount of memory that meets the requirements of the two-way sandbox during the execution of a function module. In addition, we implement a simple user-space memory management module to manage pre-allocated memory, which gets a fixed length of memory when an enclave is created. After the SGX enclave is destroyed, the pre-allocated memory will be freed.

4.3   Shield Module

We implement a shield library in SGX enclave to avoid constraints of SGX enclave and WebAssembly sandboxed environment, which includes privilege monitoring and I/O control. In the two-way sandbox, although code in WebAssembly sandboxed environment cannot exploit vulnerabilities to compromise the host runtime, they can perform the operations that are beyond the normal permissions. We leverage system call filtering and permission checking to implement the privilege monitoring module, which is responsible for monitoring code behavior in WebAssembly sandboxed environment. When a function module triggers a system call in WebAssembly sandboxed environment, the privilege monitoring module records the system call parameters. Then, it checks permissions of the function module and filters it according to the permissions defined in the creation process of this function module. In addition to privilege monitoring, the shield library is also responsible for managing the interaction between the SGX enclave and untrusted OS.

4.4   Dynamic Function Execution

To realize dynamic function execution, we implement a loading-point after the two-way sandbox is created and initialized. Once the execution of a function module ends, the two-way sandbox restores to the loading-point for the next function module. As it is very complicated to restore a program to the previous state, we leverage the features of interpreted language, which launches a virtual machine to execute code. Fortunately, the WebAssembly is a stack-based interpreted language, which is interpreted by the virtual machine in the JavaScript engine. When porting the WebAssembly sandboxed environment into SGX enclave, we change source code to allocate the used resources dynamically during the execution of the WebAssembly virtual machine.

For example, when the service runtime executes a function module, it loads this function module into the newly allocated memory of SGX enclave. Then, the two-way sandbox starts the instance of WebAssembly virtual machine to interpret this function module. Once the execution of this function module ends, the WebAssembly virtual machine outputs the result and automatically shuts down itself. Because resources used by the WebAssembly virtual machine is dynamically allocated, we implement a mechanism to free all the resources after the virtual machine is shut down. As a result, the two-way sandbox reverts to loading-point and continues to wait for the execution of the next function module.

5   Evaluation

Se-Lambda is designed to provide a lightweight and secure serverless framework for cloud users. The evaluation of Se-Lambda includes three parts. First, we evaluate the security guarantee of Se-Lambda. Then, we compare the performance of API gateway with SGX enclave against native variants. Finally, we conduct an empirical experiment on Se-Lambda's service runtime to evaluate the performance impact of the two-way sandbox. We choose Google brotli [6] and OpenCV [20] as the evaluation benchmarks. In addition, we quantify the memory footprint and time overhead of the two-way sandbox.

All benchmarks are conducted on a Dell Precision Tower 3620 workstation with Intel Xeon E3-1225 v5 3.3 GHz processor (with Skylake microarchitecture, 4 cores, and SGX version 1) and 8 GB RAM. We install Intel's SGX Linux Driver and SDK 2.0 on the Ubuntu 16.04.3 LTS with Linux kernel version 4.10. All the performance measurements are averaged on 100 runs.

5.1 Security Evaluation

Since Se-Lambda provides security mechanism for both service runtime and API gateway, we evaluate the confidentiality and integrity of these components. In the evaluation, we simulate some attack events against the two-way sandbox inside service runtime and API gateway, to verify the security guarantee. In addition, we compare the security guarantee of the two-way sandbox and Ryoan [13].

As shown in Table 1, Se-Lambda can defend against all the listed attacks. Firstly, Se-Lambda can ensure the integrity of SGX enclave and users' code. Since the two-way sandbox and isolated function modules of API gateway are attested via SGX's remote attestation, they can prevent attackers from being tampered with. Se-Lambda validates the integrity of users' code through function validation. Thus Se-Lambda can detect tampered users' code and refuse its execution.

Then, in terms of confidentiality, Se-Lambda can protect users' sensitive data. Since both the two-way sandbox and API gateway process sensitive data inside SGX enclave, attackers cannot steal sensitive data. Finally, Se-Lambda can prevent untrusted code from compromising host runtime. The two-way sandbox can execute untrusted code, which is due to the protection of WebAssembly sandbox. In order to verify privilege monitoring, we invoke the two-way sandbox to run an application with different system calls. The results show that only system calls in the permission set can succeed.

We also compare the two-way sandbox with Ryoan in terms of security guarantee. Table 2 shows the comparison results. The results show that both the two-way sandbox and Ryoan can confine untrusted code and prevent sensitive data leakage because of the two-way protection. However, the two-way sandbox can perform privilege monitoring to avoid system call abuse, while Ryoan does not support.

5.2 API Gateway Performance

The API gateway is the key component of serverless computing framework, which handles requests from users and dispatches service runtime to execute function modules. In our evaluation, we use ApacheBench [1] to post the request and fetch the response. We gradually increase the concurrency of ApacheBench to test the throughput and per-request latency of API gateway. Meanwhile, we evaluate the

Table 1. The security guarantee of Se-Lambda

Component	Attack event	Security threat	Defense ability
Two-way sandbox	Executing untrusted code on sandbox	Confidentiality	Yes
	Stealing the sensitive data of users	Confidentiality	Yes
	Executing arbitrary system calls	Confidentiality	Yes
	Tampering with users' code	Integrity	Yes
	Tampering with the integrity validation	Integrity	Yes
API gateway	Stealing isolated modules' sensitive data	Confidentiality	Yes
	Tampering with the isolated module	Integrity	Yes

Table 2. Comparison of two-way sandbox and Ryoan

Security guarantee	Two-way sandbox	Ryoan
Confining untrusted code	Yes	Yes
Preventing sensitive data leakage	Yes	Yes
Privilege monitoring	Yes	No

CPU utilization of API gateway, with SGX enabled and disabled, respectively. The baseline is to run API gateway without SGX, which is also called *Gateway*, while API gateway with SGX is called *Gateway-SGX*.

Figure 5 shows the throughput and per-request latency of *Gateway* and *Gateway-SGX*. *Gateway-SGX* achieves approximately 11,600 requests per second, while the latency increases dramatically when the throughput is more than this value. *Gateway* achieves 16,000 requests per second. We observe that *Gateway* performs better than *Gateway-SGX*, since the bulk of the *Gateway-SGX*'s latency is cost to create and destroy an enclave.

As shown in Fig. 6, the CPU utilization grows with throughput. As *Gateway-SGX* needs extra CPU cycles to maintain SGX enclave environment, the CPU utilization of *Gateway-SGX* is slightly higher than *Gateway*. The CPU utilization peak of *Gateway* and *Gateway-SGX* is about 125%, since the API gateway is a multi-thread program with different threads running on multiple CPU cores. This demonstrates that the overhead imposed by SGX is acceptable.

5.3 Service Runtime Workloads

One of the most popular deployment models of serverless computing is to build web services on cloud platform. We choose two libraries that are frequently used to construct web services, including *Brotli* (version 1.0.1) for compressing and decompressing web data [6], and *OpenCV* (version 3.3) for image processing [20],

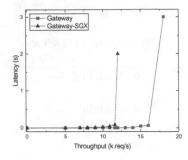

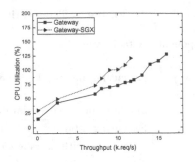

Fig. 5. Throughput versus latency for API gateway

Fig. 6. CPU utilization for API gateway

to conduct the experiments. All these workloads are implemented in C/C++. In order to make them run in the WebAssembly sandboxed environment, we compile these C/C++ source code into WebAssembly by a precompiled toolchain, including *emscripten* [9] and *binaryen* [4]. In the experiments, we evaluate the execution time and the memory cost of these libraries.

Execution Time Overhead. Brotli is a data format specification, which compresses data streams with a combination of generic-purpose lossless compression algorithm. We choose the datasets of squash compression benchmark [28], which ranges from 10 KB to 100 MB, to test the total time of compressing and decompressing a file. As shown in Fig. 7(a), the execution time overhead increases with the size of the tested file. We find that the most time of a small workload is spent in creating enclave while the overhead of enclave creation is less significant for a large workload. For example, a large workload like compressing *enwik8* (100 MB) running in the two-way sandbox is 1.8x slower than the native variant.

OpenCV is an open source computer vision library, which can be deployed on the cloud as an image processing service. In this experiment, we compile *OpenCV* into *Node.js* module with the WebAssembly format, which can be loaded into the two-way sandbox. We evaluate the time overhead of *OpenCV*, with or without the two-way sandbox, by performing image processing on pictures, ranging from 11 KB to 3.5 MB. As shown in Fig. 7(b), when processing a large image (3.5 MB), the overhead of *OpenCV* with the two-way sandbox is 35% higher compared to the native variant, since image processing involves heavy computation. When processing a large image, most of the overhead is spent in loading file into the enclave and privilege monitoring.

Optimization Evaluation. In this experiment, we evaluate the effect of optimizing the life cycle of two-way sandbox. We continuously invoke the two-way sandbox at 100 times, with optimization enabled or disabled, to execute *Brotli* application, which compressing and decompressing a file, ranging from 10 KB to 10 MB.

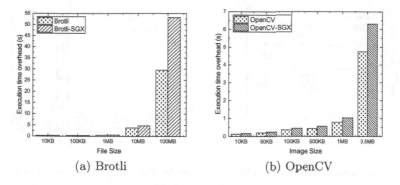

(a) Brotli

(b) OpenCV

Fig. 7. Execution time for *Brotli*, *OpenCV*

As shown in Fig. 8, the execution time of two-way sandbox is reduced with optimization enabled. The effect of optimization is getting better as the file size grows, because the overhead of creating and initializing an SGX enclave increases with the file size and the optimization avoids it.

Memory Overhead. In this experiment, we choose five different stages during the life cycle of the two-way sandbox, including creation, loading-point, attestation, execution, and return, to evaluate the memory footprint of the two-way sandbox. As shown in Fig. 9, each workload has five peaks, which represent the memory footprint at different states, such as before creation (*Static Stage*), before loading function (*Loading Stage*), after attestation (*Attested Stage*), after functions' execution (*Executed Stage*), and after outputting results (*Returned Stage*).

We find that the memory footprint of the two-way sandbox gradually increases after enclave creation. As discussed in Sect. 3.4, instead of destroying the two-way sandbox, we optimize the life cycle of the two-way sandbox by making the sandbox still exist after it outputs the result of the function module. The highest memory overhead during the life cycle of the two-way sandbox is spent at functions' execution, which is reasonable because the memory is dynamically allocated at the execution of function modules. As the maximum file of *Brotli*'s dataset is *enwik8* (100 MB), the memory overhead of it at functions' execution is much higher than the others.

6 Related Work

In this section, firstly, we discuss solutions against untrusted platform and software protection for untrusted code. Then we discuss containers and sandboxes using SGX enclave, the security of SGX enclave and homomorphic encryption.

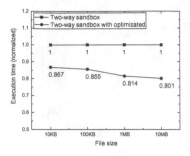

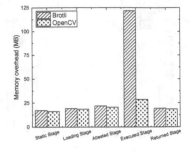

Fig. 8. Optimizing the life cycle of two-way sandbox

Fig. 9. The memory overhead of two-way sandbox

Solutions Against Untrusted Platform. Software solutions leverage a trusted hypervisor to prevent untrusted OS from compromising trusted applications, such as InkTag [12] and Sego [16], which have a large TCB. Hardware solutions use a trusted hardware to protect a trusted application from untrusted OS, such as SGX.

VC3 [22] provides an SGX-based execution environment for MapReduce jobs to prevent malicious underlying systems from disclosing privacy-sensitive data. Secure-Zookeeper [5] protects privacy-sensitive modules of zookeeper coordination services across multiple SGX enclaves and provides secure communications between enclaves. SGX-Log [15] leverages a secure log system based on SGX enclave to protect the confidentiality and integrity of system logs. Opaque [36] leverages SGX enclave to construct new distributed oblivious relational operators for distributed data analytics platform, which hides access patterns. In addition, some researchers also used SGX enclave to protect network applications, such as S-NFV [24], content-based routing [21]. However, all of these systems need specialized SGX enclaves to protect cloud applications.

Haven [3] is the first to use library OS to provide a SGX enclave environment for applications, which could execute any Windows application without modifying the application. Graphene-SGX [31] provides a trusted execution environment that based on Graphene library OS for Linux applications and supports multiple processes. In order to improve the performance of library OS, SGX-kernel [30] provides user-level asynchronous cross-enclave communication and preemptible multi-threading in SGX enclave. Compared to Graphene-SGX, Panoply [27] reduces the application TCB by two orders of magnitude and supports event management in SGX enclave. All these systems protect the confidentiality of users' data, assuming that any application running inside SGX enclave are trusted.

Software Protection for Untrusted Code. In order to prevent malicious code from compromising the underlying host runtime, some researchers propose solutions which are based on software fault isolation techniques. NaCl [35] leverages SFI to isolate untrusted native code, which can run native code in the web browser to improve the security and performance of native code. TxBox [14] is a sandbox that executes untrusted applications in system transactions and allows parallel security checks. MiniBox [18] leverages a two-way sandbox to prevent x86 native code and the OS from each other, which uses Native Client and TrustVisor [19] to build two-way sandbox. Unlike the two-way sandbox of Se-Lambda, it has a large TCB to run function module directly inside these systems.

Containers and Sandboxes Using SGX Enclave. SCONE [2] provides a protection mechanism for containers, which uses SGX enclave inside the Docker container to protect container processes from outside attacks. To reduce enclave transition cost when issuing system calls inside an enclave, SCONE implements asynchronous system calls. However, SCONE does not consider malicious code inside the SGX enclave.

Ryoan [13] provides a distributed two-way sandbox for request-oriented data processing services, which inspires us. Ryoan places an *Native Client* [35] instance into SGX enclave, and implements a series of security policies and optimizations. However, Ryoan's implementation has a large TCB, and *Native Client* can only execute x86 native code. The two-way sandbox of Se-Lambda can execute code with arbitrary language that can be compiled into WebAssembly, such as JavaScript, C, C++, and Rust.

Security of SGX Enclave. Recent work [34] points out that a malicious OS can use in-enclave thread synchronization vulnerability to compromise users' code. Since SGX enclave shares system resources with non-enclave, such as page table, cache, and branch predictor, these sharing mechanisms may introduce many side channels. Side channel attacks [17,26,32] leverage page table or branch predictor to leak information. Some mitigation measures, such as SGX-Shield [23] and T-SGX [25], can be integrated into Se-Lambda.

Homomorphic Encryption. Homomorphic encryption allows untrusted code to perform computations directly on encrypted data without revealing users' data, which shares similar threat model with Se-Lambda. However, fully homomorphic encryption [10,11] can perform arbitrary computations on the encrypted data, which suffers from significant performance overhead. Partial homomorphic encryption applies only to confined scenarios, such as MapReduce jobs [29] running on the encrypted data. In comparison, Se-Lambda provides similar protections for users' data, while imposing much less performance overhead.

7   Conclusion and Future Work

In this paper, we propose Se-Lambda, which improves the integrity and confidentiality of serverless computing services. Cloud users can use Se-Lambda to process privacy-sensitive data on the service platform, which they do not control;

at the same time, the service platform does not have to worry about malicious user code breaking the host runtime. Thus, Se-Lambda is beneficial to both cloud users and service platforms.

Our prototype system is based on the open source project *OpenLambda*, which is an experimental project. With the development of serverless computing, we will add new features to Se-Lambda. In order to improve the security of API gateway, we consider placing most of the API gateway modules into SGX enclave. In addition, we will implement a complete programming framework and toolchain for developers.

Since WebAssembly is an experimental underlying language, it is still under continuous and iterative development. Our prototype system leverages the *Minimum Viable Product* (MVP) version of WebAssembly. When WebAssembly implements features such as garbage collection, tail call, bulk memory operations, we will integrate them into the two-way sandbox. Additionally, we will provide protection for WebAssembly to avoid sandbox bypassing attacks.

Acknowledgment. This work is supported by National Basic Research Program of China (973 Program) under grant No. 2014CB340600, National Natural Science Foundation of China under grant No. 61772221, and the Shenzhen Fundamental Research Program under grant No. JCYJ20170413114215614.

References

1. ApacheBench (2018). https://httpd.apache.org/docs/2.4/programs/ab.html
2. Arnautov, S., et al.: SCONE: secure Linux containers with Intel SGX. In: Proceedings of the 12th USENIX Symposium on Operating Systems Design and Implementation, pp. 689–703. USENIX Association (2016)
3. Baumann, A., Peinado, M., Hunt, G.: Shielding applications from an untrusted cloud with haven. In: Proceedings of the 11th USENIX Conference on Operating Systems Design and Implementation, pp. 267–283. USENIX Association (2014)
4. Binaryen (2018). https://github.com/WebAssembly/binaryen
5. Brenner, S., et al.: SecureKeeper: confidential ZooKeeper using Intel SGX. In: Proceedings of the 17th International Middleware Conference, pp. 1–13. ACM (2016)
6. Brotli (2018). https://github.com/google/brotli/
7. Buyya, R., et al.: A manifesto for future generation cloud computing: research directions for the next decade. CoRR abs/1711.09123 (2017)
8. Checkoway, S., Shacham, H.: Iago attacks: why the system call API is a bad untrusted RPC interface. In: Proceedings of the Eighteenth International Conference on Architectural Support for Programming Languages and Operating Systems, pp. 253–264. ACM (2013)
9. Emscripten (2018). https://github.com/kripken/emscripten
10. Gentry, C.: A fully homomorphic encryption scheme. Ph.D. thesis, Stanford University (2009)
11. Gentry, C., Halevi, S., Smart, N.P.: Homomorphic evaluation of the AES circuit. In: Safavi-Naini, R., Canetti, R. (eds.) CRYPTO 2012. LNCS, vol. 7417, pp. 850–867. Springer, Heidelberg (2012). https://doi.org/10.1007/978-3-642-32009-5_49

12. Hofmann, O.S., Kim, S., Dunn, A.M., Lee, M.Z., Witchel, E.: Inktag: secure applications on an untrusted operating system. In: Proceedings of the Eighteenth International Conference on Architectural Support for Programming Languages and Operating Systems, pp. 265–278. ACM (2013)
13. Hunt, T., Zhu, Z., Xu, Y., Peter, S., Witchel, E.: Ryoan: a distributed sandbox for untrusted computation on secret data. In: Proceedings of the 12th USENIX Conference on Operating Systems Design and Implementation, pp. 533–549. USENIX Association (2016)
14. Jana, S., Porter, D.E., Shmatikov, V.: TxBox: building secure, efficient sandboxes with system transactions. In: Proceedings of the 2011 IEEE Symposium on Security and Privacy, pp. 329–344. IEEE (2011)
15. Karande, V., Bauman, E., Lin, Z., Khan, L.: SGX-log: securing system logs with SGX. In: Proceedings of the 2017 ACM on Asia Conference on Computer and Communications Security, pp. 19–30. ACM (2017)
16. Kwon, Y., Dunn, A.M., Lee, M.Z., Hofmann, O.S., Xu, Y., Witchel, E.: Sego: pervasive trusted metadata for efficiently verified untrusted system services. In: Proceedings of the Twenty-First International Conference on Architectural Support for Programming Languages and Operating Systems, pp. 277–290. ACM (2016)
17. Lee, S., Shih, M.W., Gera, P., Kim, T., Kim, H., Peinado, M.: Inferring fine-grained control flow inside SGX enclaves with branch shadowing. In: Proceedings of the 26th USENIX Security Symposium, pp. 557–574. USENIX Association (2017)
18. Li, Y., McCune, J., Newsome, J., Perrig, A., Baker, B., Drewry, W.: MiniBox: a two-way sandbox for x86 native code. In: Proceedings of the 2014 USENIX Annual Technical Conference, pp. 409–420. USENIX Association (2014)
19. McCune, J.M., et al.: TrustVisor: efficient TCB reduction and attestation. In: Proceedings of the 2010 IEEE Symposium on Security and Privacy, pp. 143–158. IEEE (2010)
20. OpenCV (2018). https://opencv.org/
21. Pires, R., Pasin, M., Felber, P., Fetzer, C.: Secure content-based routing using Intel software guard extensions. In: Proceedings of the 17th International Middleware Conference, pp. 1–10. ACM (2016)
22. Schuster, F., et al.: VC3: trustworthy data analytics in the cloud using SGX. In: Proceedings of the 2015 IEEE Symposium on Security and Privacy, pp. 38–54. IEEE (2015)
23. Seo, J., et al.: SGX-shield: enabling address space layout randomization for SGX programs. In: Proceedings of the 2017 Annual Network and Distributed System Security Symposium (2017)
24. Shih, M.W., Kumar, M., Kim, T., Gavrilovska, A.: S-NFV: securing NFV states by using SGX. In: Proceedings of the 2016 ACM International Workshop on Security in Software Defined Networks and Network Function Virtualization, pp. 45–48. ACM (2016)
25. Shih, M.W., Lee, S., Kim, T., Peinado, M.: T-SGX: eradicating controlled-channel attacks against enclave programs. In: Proceedings of the 2017 Annual Network and Distributed System Security Symposium (2017)
26. Shinde, S., Chua, Z.L., Narayanan, V., Saxena, P.: Preventing page faults from telling your secrets. In: Proceedings of the 11th ACM on Asia Conference on Computer and Communications Security, pp. 317–328. ACM (2016)
27. Shinde, S., Le Tien, D., Tople, S., Saxena, P.: Panoply: low-TCB Linux applications with SGX enclaves. In: Proceedings of the 2017 Annual Network and Distributed System Security Symposium (2017)

28. Squash-benchmark (2018). http://quixdb.github.io/squash-benchmark/
29. Tetali, S.D., Lesani, M., Majumdar, R., Millstein, T.: MrCrypt: static analysis for secure cloud computations. In: Proceedings of the 2013 ACM SIGPLAN International Conference on Object Oriented Programming Systems Languages, and Applications, pp. 271–286. ACM (2013)
30. Tian, H., Zhang, Y., Xing, C., Yan, S.: SGXKernel: a library operating system optimized for Intel SGX. In: Proceedings of the Computing Frontiers Conference, pp. 35–44. ACM (2017)
31. Tsai, C.C., Porter, D.E., Vij, M.: Graphene-SGX: a practical library OS for unmodified applications on SGX. In: Proceedings of the 2017 USENIX Annual Technical Conference, pp. 645–658. USENIX Association (2017)
32. Van Bulck, J., Weichbrodt, N., Kapitza, R., Piessens, F., Strackx, R.: Telling your secrets without page faults: stealthy page table-based attacks on enclaved execution. In: Proceedings of the 26th USENIX Security Symposium, pp. 1041–1056. USENIX Association (2017)
33. WebAssembly (2018). http://webassembly.org/
34. Weichbrodt, N., Kurmus, A., Pietzuch, P., Kapitza, R.: AsyncShock: exploiting synchronisation bugs in Intel SGX enclaves. In: Askoxylakis, I., Ioannidis, S., Katsikas, S., Meadows, C. (eds.) ESORICS 2016. LNCS, vol. 9878, pp. 440–457. Springer, Cham (2016). https://doi.org/10.1007/978-3-319-45744-4_22
35. Yee, B., et al.: Native client: a sandbox for portable, untrusted x86 native code. In: Proceedings of the 2009 IEEE Symposium on Security and Privacy, pp. 79–93. IEEE (2009)
36. Zheng, W., Dave, A., Beekman, J.G., Popa, R.A., Gonzalez, J.E., Stoica, I.: Opaque: an oblivious and encrypted distributed analytics platform. In: Proceedings of the 14th USENIX Conference on Networked Systems Design and Implementation, pp. 283–298. USENIX Association (2017)

CAVAS: Neutralizing Application and Container Security Vulnerabilities in the Cloud Native Era

Kennedy A. Torkura[✉], Muhammad I. H. Sukmana,
Feng Cheng, and Christoph Meinel

Hasso-Plattner-Institute for Digital Engineering, University of Potsdam,
Potsdam, Germany
{kennedy.torkura,muhammad.sukmana,feng.cheng,christoph.meinel}@hpi.de

Abstract. The security challenges of container technologies such as Docker and Kubernetes are key issues in software development and other industries. This has increased interest on application container counter-measures e.g. detection and mitigation of the high number of vulnerabilities affecting container images, in particular images retained at DockerHub. However, investigations on application-layer vulnerabilities in Microservice Architectures (MSA) such as Cloud Native Environments (CNE) is lacking. In this paper, we investigate both image and application layer vulnerabilities and apply *vulnerability correlation* to understand the dependence relationships between vulnerabilities found in these layers. The outcome of this analysis offers interesting insights applicable to risk management and security hardening of microservices e.g. deployment of *vulnerability correlation-based* security policies that are useful for vulnerability detection, risk prioritization and resource allocation. Our prototype implementation extends our previous security system: Cloud Aware Vulnerability Assessment System (CAVAS), which employs the *Security Gateway* concept for security policy enforcement. The Security Gateway leverages the *client side discovery and registry* cloud pattern for discovering microservices and the notion of *dynamic document stores* for exploring and testing *RESTful microservices*. Our experimental evaluation shows that the security gateway's *vulnerability detection rate* out-performs that of traditional testing approaches with 31.4%. Also, we discover that about 26.2% of severity metrics for vulnerabilities detected by image security scanners is in-correct. Hence, correcting this information is a prerequisite step to vulnerability correlation. Our proposal can therefore be employed for efficient continuous security and risk assessments in CNE.

Keywords: Cloud-security · Vulnerability assessment
Vulnerability correlation · Cloud native environments
Application container security

© ICST Institute for Computer Sciences, Social Informatics and Telecommunications Engineering 2018
R. Beyah et al. (Eds.): SecureComm 2018, LNICST 254, pp. 471–490, 2018.
https://doi.org/10.1007/978-3-030-01701-9_26

1   Introduction

Container technologies like Docker and Kubernetes are enabling rapid application development and deployment. These technologies enhance productivity when combined with cloud infrastructure and *DevOps* [1] and are key components of Microservice Architectures (MSA) and Cloud Native Environment (CNE). However, container-based infrastructure is challenged by several security concerns, requiring novel security paradigms as effective counter-measures. An emerging security concept is the *shift-left* approach which proposes continuous security by wiring security tests early and throughout the Continuous Integration (CI) and Continuous Development (CD) pipeline [2]. These set of activities that implement these practices are generally referred to as *SecDevOps* (also called *RuggedOps, DevSecOps, SecOps*) [3]. However there are no set guidelines for *SecDevOps* and most research efforts focus on image-level vulnerabilities ignoring application-level vulnerabilities especially those affecting REST-based MSA. Most MSA adopt REST [4] for inter-service communication [5], however automated security testing of REST is challenging[1]. Traditional security assessment techniques fail to explore REST applications, yet the exploration phase is a prerequisite for vulnerability detection through identification of *entry/exit points*. This exploration difficulty emerges since REST applications are not implemented with well defined interfaces as web applications. Also, holistic vulnerability analysis of CNEs e.g. cloud-based microservices requires proper scrutiny of vulnerabilities at all levels [6].

Contribution. This work proposes a cloud native, continuous security methodology that employs security policies for detecting vulnerabilities in Docker container images and microservice applications. Our approach employs the *shift left* concept, achieved via our previously introduced concept- *Security Gateway* [7], a core component of Cloud Aware Vulnerability Assessment System (CAVAS). The *security gateway* serves as a security control for enforcing security policies. The notion of the *security gateway* here refers to security assessments, which is different from how the term is used in other contexts e.g. application firewalls [8] and network routers [9]. We support the *security gateway* with two innovative concepts: *dynamic document store* and *security health endpoints*. The dynamic document store overcomes the aforementioned challenge of detecting vulnerabilities in REST microservices by leveraging OpenAPI[2](formerly Swagger) documents for vulnerability detection. Similarly, the security health endpoint provides security observability by easily presenting security information for deployed microservices. The *client side discovery and registry* cloud pattern is leveraged for microservices discovery. Furthermore, we validate the accuracy of the vulnerability information contained in image vulnerability scan results. Figure 1 illustrates our analysis of inaccuracies in vulnerability information returned by container image vulnerability scanners. We develop a technique for rectifying these anomalies and thereafter correlate the vulnerabilities detected at both

---

[1] https://www.owasp.org/index.php/REST_Assessment_Cheat_Sheet.
[2] https://github.com/OAI/OpenAPI-Specification.

image and application levels, within and across containers of the same application. The knowledge gained via *vulnerability correlation* [10] provides effective risk management techniques, e.g. we employ this insights for adding *correlation-based rules* in security policies. These rules prioritize detection of correlated vulnerabilities given the greater security risks posed by correlated vulnerabilities. To the best of our knowledge, this work is the first that applies the principle of vulnerability information validation and correlation in the context of MSAs and CNEs.

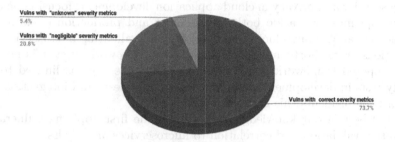

Fig. 1. Incorrect vulnerability security metrics in 12 analyzed microservices

The rest of this paper is structured as follows, the next section presents related works, followed by a background of application container image vulnerabilities, challenges to security assessments in CNEs and problem definition. In Sect. 3, the design and system model of CAVAS is described based on specified requirements. The implementation details of CAVAS is presented in Sect. 5. In Sect. 6, we evaluate our work and Sect. 7 concludes the paper.

2 Related Work

Gummaraju et al.'s [11] security analysis of DockerHub revealed that over 30% and 40% of official and community of Docker images respectively, have severe vulnerabilities. In [12], the authors conducted a vulnerability oriented security analysis of the Docker ecosystem and highlighted several security implications for deploying Docker-based applications. Bila et al. [13] presented a continuous security architecture for cloud-based container clusters that leverages OpenWhisk[3] serverless architecture for instant vulnerability alert notification. Harbor [14] is an open-source, enterprise grade registry similar to CAVAS, however it does not integrate with software supply chains and cloud container orchestration. Tak et al. [15] demonstrated the existence of *drift* in containers i.e. a situation where declared containers differ from deployed containers owing to un-tracked changes. The authors recommended continuous security testing for containers since *one-time* static analysis tests do not detect *image drifts*. Some of these

---

[3] https://openwhisk.apache.org/.

recommendations are considered in this work. Zhnag et al. [16] used Harbormaster for policy enforcement in Docker environments, but the policies are for access control while our policies are for vulnerability detection. Antunes et al. [17] investigated on vulnerability testing tools for web services including an analysis of current approaches, tools and architectures. Their investigation tackles traditional monolithic web services and is therefore not fitted for CNEs.

In [18] the challenges of deploying microservices to cloud platforms were highlighted including the security issues, however the authors offered no practical solutions to the raised issues. Thanh et al. [19] proposed approaches for integrating security and privacy in cloud application development, focusing on development pipelines, we tackle both development and production environments. Savchenko et al. [20] introduced a methodology for validating microservice cloud applications. Two shortcomings are identified in this work, first it is not clear if the proposed framework is evaluated, secondly, the work is limited to non-security tests in development environments e.g. unit tests and integration tests, our work complements this gap.

To the best of our knowledge, this work is the first applying vulnerability information validation and correlation to microservices and CNEs.

3   Background and Problem

3.1   Application Container Vulnerabilties

The NIST Application Container Guide [6] outlines major risks to the core components of container technologies. We outline subsets of these risks most relevant to this paper.

Insecure Container Runtime Configurations. Container runtimes provide options for customization which can expose the security of the system if improperly configured. For example, a container executed with *root* permissions naturally has access to the OS devices, kernel and other containers. This privilege might be abused by compromised containers.

Image Vulnerabilities. Images are essentially static, archive files composed of several package definitions. Images might be free of vulnerabilities at *creation time* but become vulnerable after some time if vulnerabilities are discovered in one or more of its components. Containers derived from images are not automatically updated like traditional software packages, thus, a common risk in is existence of vulnerable containers whose parent image versions are outdated i.e. *stale images*. These *stale images* pose serious security risks upon execution.

Image Configuration-Based Vulnerabilities. Similar to normal software, images are prone to configuration-based vulnerabilities which might either be intentional or un-intentional. For example, an image might include an SSH daemon, running with default credentials. Attackers might exploit this vulnerability to successfully attack containerized environments.

Images from Untrusted Sources. This is one of the most high-risk image vulnerabilities. Due to publicly available images on DockerHub and other public image registries, images are easily *pulled* and executed without due validation.

Application Vulnerabilities. Applications are commonly built into images essentially providing those applications access to the host containers internals upon execution. Vulnerable applications use containers for conducting *side-channel attacks* [21].

3.2   Security Assessments in Cloud-Native Environments

Several security issues are introduced when applications are deployed to CNEs [5]. Security assessments are imperatives for timely detection and mitigation of vulnerabilities associated with these security issues. However, CNEs present several challenges for security assessments, We highlight some of these security challenges next.

Microservices Discovery. Microservices are subject to constantly changing environmental parameters such as ip addresses, port numbers and service endpoints. This dynamism presents an overhead for security e.g. security assessments which are traditionally configured for static network resources, hosts and applications. Essentially, security tools are challenged with discovering microservice endpoints e.g. after scaling operations. This discoverability challenge is similar to that of virtualized environments, but occurs at the application layer hence virtualization-based approaches do not suffice.

Security Testing of REST Services. REST is a favoured architectural style for microservices [5]. REST exposes resources using endpoints easily accessible for a wide range of applications e.g. mobile and IoT devices. However, unlike web applications, automated security assessments for RESTful applications is difficult [17]. Security scanners detect vulnerabilities in web applications by iteratively fetching and crawling through web-page links to discover entry/exit points. This is possible since web applications have well defined interfaces. Then random requests are sent and responses are analyzed for security vulnerabilities. Conversely, REST services do not have such well defined interfaces, and while responses from web applications are predictable, REST services dynamically generate responses.

Technological Diversity. Microservices are built with different business capabilities by different development teams, which may use different technologies i.e. different programming languages and frameworks [20]. The motivation for this approach is to use the best tools for specific problems. While this aids productivity, it complicates security. For example, the Spring PetClinic application[4] consists of four microservices, three developed in Java and one developed in JavaScript (*UI-Service*). Effective vulnerability detection therefore requires employment of different testing configurations for each microservice e.g. different policies. This is due to the uniqueness of vulnerabilities per technology. Furthermore, developers integrate several open source components, which could be laden with vulnerabilities [22].

3.3 Problem Definition

Challenges to Continuous Security Assessments and Vulnerability Management. Continuous security assessments are useful for identifying vulnerabilities in applications and networks. Identification of vulnerabilities and timely patching reduces attack surfaces thereby thwarting cyber-attacks. Security assessments for traditional applications/environments involve statically deployed applications/systems, but CNEs are ephemeral. Microservices are dynamically launched and de-registered, owing to scaling requirements and complexities in distributed systems. Hence, a *discoverability* challenge emerges for security assessment i.e. the capacity to constantly locate deployed microservices. Furthermore, the diversity of technologies in microservices increases possibilities for security vulnerabilities. The desire for fast-paced development cycles in microservice-based architectures (to meet *time-to-market*) further complicates these challenges by overlooking comprehensive security tests in CD pipelines. Consequently, vulnerable microservices could be launched to production environments. Novel security assessments techniques specifically adapted and integrated to CNEs are therefore required to tackle these security challenges.

Limitations of Prior Research. Current research tackling security of CNEs focus on other of security aspects e.g. authentication and authorization, security monitoring and anomaly detection. These are critical challenges affecting CNEs, but vulnerability detection and security assessments are not yet in focus. Effective security evaluation microservices aids timely detection of compromised microservices and reduces attack surfaces. Moreover, security evaluations are key regulatory and compliance requirements especially for cloud applications [23]. For example, the Centre for Internet Security recommends implementation of continuous vulnerability assessments to identify and mitigate vulnerabilities.[5] To the best of our knowledge, there are no research efforts focused in this direction. Traditional security assessment methods do not handle the challenge of effectively conducting security assessments in CNE. We aim at helping security teams implement robust vulnerability management and mediation systems that are native to the cloud i.e. suited for CNE. Similarly, several research works have analyzed the severity of security vulnerabilities infecting container images

---

[4] https://github.com/spring-petclinic/spring-petclinic-microservices.

[5] https://www.cisecurity.org/controls/continuous-vulnerability-assessment-and-remediation/.

yet there are no works that demonstrate practical remediation approaches e.g. automated integration of container and application vulnerability analysis for cloud based CI and productive environments. Our approach is consistent with the current *SecDevOps* move which emphasizes integration of security into the development and operations teams and operations.

4   Design and System Model

Ensuring continuous security in CNEs requires innovative approaches which can be identified by outlining security requirements. These requirements are discussed in this section, followed by a description of how we fulfill them.

4.1   Requirements for Security Assessments in Cloud Native Environments

We identified five requirements necessary for continuous security assessments in microservices-based and CNEs. First, the security assessment solution should automatically discover deployed microservice instances. This requirement has several security benefits e.g. inserting security controls. Next is support for security policies, given their usefulness for security automation and control. Fine grained security policies provide for security efficiency. Accordingly, the solution should support and enforce a wide range of security policies. Third, the solution must be *tamper-proof* i.e. isolated from possible attacks. It should not be discoverable by only the core services e.g. *service registry and discovery* and *API Gateway*. We apply the concept of *security VMs* [24] to achieve this, VMs are replaced with containers. Security containers are isolated from application containers using cloud networks *security groups*. Fourth, the solution must effectively resolve the technologies used in developing microservices. Microservices within an application may be developed using diverse technologies, employing generic security testing policies might not be as effective as policies that specifically tackle the development technology. For example, a Java application should be tested with a *Java-biased* policy. Hence the solution should automatically identify technologies. We satisfy this requirement by implementing the *dynamic document stores*, details are at Sect. 4.4. The last requirement is the need to validate the vulnerability information returned by images vulnerability scanners. We realized several anomalies in the security metrics assigned to detected vulnerabilities, details are at Sect. 4.6.

4.2   Security Automation with the Security Gateway

The notion of a *Security Gateway* adopts the concept of Security Enforcement Points (SEP), which are commonly used to enforce security policies at run-time. For example in [25], Almorsy et al. leveraged SEP to enforce security policies by intercepting and validating requests sent against critical components. The

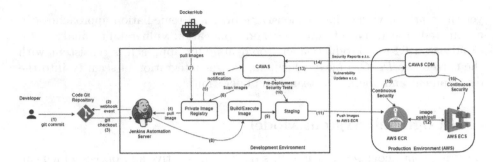

Fig. 2. CAVAS workflow: *SecDevOps* in the continuous development/integration environment and continuous security in production environment (AWS ECS)

security gateway, differs from the microservices *gateway pattern*[6] operationally. The security gateway enforces defined security requirements in the CI pipeline as well as production environments. Conversely, API-Gateways are concerned with efficient routing of incoming and outgoing traffic, the security gateway serves as a SEP for the policies described in Sect. 6.2. Our definition also differs from the use of the term *security gateways* in the context of application firewalls [8] and network routers [9]. By leveraging *client-side service discovery and registry*, the security gateway automatically overcomes two challenges: discoverabilty and inventory of microservices. Client side discovery is an approach that forces incoming microservices to first contact the *discovery server* in order to gain situational awareness of other microservices[7]. Similarly, the embedded *registry* component maintains *living* record of deployed microservices. The CAVAS workflow (illustrated in Fig. 2) describes automated steps within the development environment (*steps 1–11*) and the cloud-based production environment (*steps 12–16*). The Security Gateway is positioned in the staging phase i.e. *steps 9–11*.

4.3   Support for Security Policies

Security policies are best practices for automating security [26] through the definition of risk levels and appropriate actions to be taken when thresholds are breached. The Security Gateway acts as a SEP for enforcing the following policies:

– Container Image Security Policies - Automated vulnerability analysis of container images is enforced through container security policies. These policies define the permissible security risk levels with rules as advised in the NIST Application Container Guide [6]. Container-based microservices are vulnerable to several security issues e.g. over 30% of official images in Docker hub were infected with severe vulnerabilities [11]. Policies also enforce scheduled security assessments in production environments.

---

[6] http://microservices.io/patterns/apigateway.html.
[7] http://microservices.io/patterns/client-side-discovery.html.

- Microservice-Specific Security Policies - Ideally, every microservice would have a specific policy used for continuous security assessment. These policies are defined based on the implementation details of each microservice. This approach aims at improving efficiency of security testing by targeting specific microservice implementation technologies. For example, a microservice developed in Ruby programming language. A security policy specifying vulnerabilities announced at the Ruby security advisories[8] or OWASP Ruby Cheatsheet[9] would be used for testing the service. Standard application security rating systems e.g. WASC and CWE are defined in these policies.
- Baseline Security Policies - Detailed security scanning for vulnerabilities requires time, 30–60 min for an average web application and 6–12 h for medium-scale web applications. Given the speedy turnout rate for microservices, lengthy tests are no long feasible. Therefore, to strike the balance between speed and security, we propose *baseline security policies* for conducting *Pre-deployment security tests*. These tests are time-based i.e. 2–3 min and produce either **PASS** or **FAIL** results.

4.4   Using OpenAPI Documents for Microservice Security Testing

The challenges of using security scanners for conducting security tests against REST*ful* resources were previously highlighted in Sect. 3. An approach for overcoming this challenge consists in leveraging web service description documents [17]. Web service description documents are machine readable documents containing information e.g. operations of web services. Vulnerability scanners can ingest these documents and extract information requisite for security testing. Given that there are no standardized conventions for documenting REST resources, we use OpenAPI (formerly called Swagger) for our use case. OpenAPI uses JSON and YAML for formatting documents. We propose microservices contain OpenAPI documents, this can be achieved through two approaches: on-demand generation and file-based. We support both approaches, documents are retained in *policy stores* in accordance with *externalized configuration* cloud native design pattern[10]. Furthermore, OpenAPI documents aid discovery of first and second order vulnerabilities in REST APIs [27]. Security policies earlier described in Sect. 4.3 can be also retained in the dynamic document stores. The store can be protected with token-based authentication e.g. JSON Web Token (JWT) or other automated authentication methods.

4.5   Security Observability

Health Endpoint Monitoring Pattern provides resiliency by enforcing periodic heartbeats against microservices [28]. This checks aid timely failure identification[11]. This technique can also be applied for maintaining security states of

---

[8] https://www.ruby-lang.org/en/security/.

[9] https://www.owasp.org/index.php/Ruby_on_Rails_Cheatsheet.

[10] http://microservices.io/patterns/.

[11] http://microservices.io/.

Listing 1.1. Example Image Scan Result with "Negligible" Severity Metric

```
{
  "fix" :  "None",
  "package":  "dpkg −1.17.27",
  "severity":  "Negligible",
  "url" :  "https:// security −tracker . debian . org / tracker /CVE−2017−8283",
  "vuln" :  "CVE−2017−8283"
}
```

microservices. Given that the distributed nature of microservices further complicates security monitoring, approaches for easily verifying security statuses of microservices is imperative. Thus, we proposed the concept of *Security Health Endpoints* in [7]. Scan reports are made easily accessible for other security tools via predefined URLs e.g. *http://localhost:8090/security-health* whereas the health checks are accessed at *http://localhost:8090/health*. The information can be directly extracted for security tasks e.g. automated configuration of AWS Security group rules and integration of vulnerability information into SIEMs [29].

4.6   Vulnerability Information Correlation and Validation

The accuracy of vulnerability information is critical for proper risk assessment hence the need to validate information retrieved from vulnerability information sources and vulnerability scanners results. For example, in probabilistic threat models where CVSS scores are used for calculating probabilities, hence the need for comprehensive and accurate security metrics. Several sources offer vulnerability information e.g. software vendors, security software vendors and independent researchers. Relying on single sources is not sufficient since sources could either provide incomplete or wrong information. Listing 1.1 is an example result where CVE-2017-8283 is assigned CVE severity *"Negligible"* whereas the NVD entry has a CVSSv2 score of 7.5 (**HIGH**)[12]. Therefore, correlating vulnerabilities from several sources improves accuracy and creates better understanding of security risks and vulnerabilities [30]. This feature is integrated in CAVAS by using HPI-VDB[13], a publicly available vulnerability database that correlates vulnerability information from numerous sources. Currently the database contains about 96410 vulnerabilities, originating from over 225420 different applications and over 17430 software vendors. Details of our methodology is provided in Sect. 5.5.

5   Implementation

This section provides implementation details of our prototype implementation: CAVAS. These implementations extend the features of CAVAS introduced in

---

[12] https://nvd.nist.gov/vuln/detail/CVE-2017-8283.
[13] https://hpi-vdb.de/vulndb.

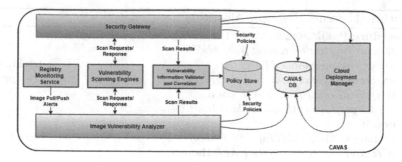

Fig. 3. CAVAS architecture

our earlier works [7,31,32]. CAVAS is implemented using cloud native design patterns. Figure 3 illustrates the microservices-based architecture of CAVAS, described in the following subsections:

5.1   Security Gateway

The Security Gateway concept leverages cloud design patterns for security testing by adapting the behaviour of the *service discovery and registry* server to suit security testing. This approach enables integration of SEPs for security policies enforcement. The Security Gateway consists of a customized Eureka server deployed in the staging environment with a config server, these are core components of CNEs. In [7], we described our adaptation of the Netflix Eureka server to serve as the Security Gateway. The *dynamic document stores* supports automated security testing for REST applications using OpenAPI documents. These OpenAPI documents are retained in the Config Server, with other configuration files as specified in the microservice *externalized configuration* tenet. The Security Gateway performs *Pre-deployment Security Tests* using a Algorithm 1, and can be easily adapted to enforce enterprise security policies e.g. *PASS* mandatory for deployments. Listing 1.2 is a baseline security policy for detecting *SQL Injection, XSS and CSRF* vulnerabilities.

5.2   Image Vulnerability Analyzer

The Image Vulnerability Analyzer (IVA) interacts with Anchore and Docker Security Bench for appropriate vulnerability analysis. It depends on the Registry Monitoring Service for alerts on when to conduct test and the image or container to be tested. We implemented this component in Java using Spotify Docker Java client library[14].

---

[14] https://github.com/spotify/docker-client.

Algorithm 1. SecurityGateway Algorithm

1: **procedure** PREDEPLOYMENTSECTEST($MuTInfo, SecPolicy$)
2:     *Receive registration request from MuT*
3:     *assign instanceStatus STARTING*   ▷ testing mode
4:     *appSecTests (MuTInfo, SecPolicy)*   ▷ app tests
5:     **if** *appSecTests.equals FAIL* **then**
6:         *denydeploymentRequest (MuTInfo)*
7:     **end if**
8:     *complianceTests (MuTInfo, SecPolicy)*   ▷ config tests
9:     **if** *complianceTests.equals FAIL* **then**
10:        *denyDeploymentRequest (MuTInfo)*
11:        **if** *currentTimeStamp − latestTimeStamp > 24hours* **then**
12:            *imageSecTest (MuTInfo, SecPolicy)*   ▷ conditional image tests
13:            **if** *imageSecTest.equals FAIL* **then**
14:                *denyDeploymentRequest (MuTInfo)*
15:            **end if**
16:            **if** *imageLastSecTest.equals FAIL* **then**   ▷ most current image tests
17:                *denyDeploymentRequest (MuTInfo)*
18:            **end if**
19:        **end if**
20:    **end if**
21:    *assign instanceStatus UP*   ▷ deploy to prod
22: **end procedure**

5.3   Registry Monitoring Service

The Representational State Transfer (RMS) serves as a notification endpoint for receiving webhook event notifications from the our private registry. Our development environment has a private image registry based on Docker Registry 2.0. This approach affords control over image entry and exit by using the Docker Registry API[15]. All events in the registry such as *pull* and *push* commands as illustrated in *steps 4–7* of Fig. 2, are sent to the endpoint as event notifications. On receipt of notifications, the RMS sends scanning requests to the IVA. Images not available in the local registry are pulled from DockerHub, in this case IVA scans these in-coming images for security vulnerabilities, a PASS is required for entry.

5.4   Vulnerability Scanning Engines

We use Anchore and OWASP ZAP as scanning engines for vulnerability detection. Anchore is an open-source tool for conducting static vulnerability analysis of application containers[16]. Anchore retrieves vulnerability information from several sources and has an API for 3rd party integration. For application vulnerability analysis, we leverage OWASP ZAP[17], a popular open-source dynamic

---

[15] https://docs.docker.com/registry/spec/api/.
[16] https://github.com/anchore/anchore-engine.
[17] https://www.owasp.org/index.php/OWASP_Zed_Attack_Proxy_Project.

vulnerability scanner. OWASP ZAP's API enables automation and integration with CAVAS, it also supports OpenAPI documents ingestion. The community edition of Docker Bench Security[18] is integrated into CAVAS for detecting security mis-configurations. Docker Bench security implements the Centre for Internet Security (CIS) benchmark[19] which specifies best practices for establishing secure configuration baselines for Docker environments.

5.5 Correcting Vulnerability Information

In order to correlate vulnerabilities, several steps are required. This approach was prompted when we discovered *negligible* and *unknown* returned as vulnerability severity metrics. Since these security metrics are not defined in the Common Platform Enumeration[20] vulnerability structure, we carefully inspected the results and discovered several anomalies. Thus, a technique for validating and correcting these anomalies was devised. Essentially, vulnerabilities with either *unknown* or *negligible* severity metrics were filtered and crosschecked against the HPI-VDB using API calls. Anomalies are thereafter replaced with the correct metrics: CVSSv2 scores e.g. *10.0, 3.5*, CVE severity e.g. *HIGH, LOW* or CVE status e.g. *AWAITING ANALYSIS, DEFERRED*[21]. The next step was *vulnerability correlation*, done by identifying commonalities in image and application vulnerabilities. We used Common Weakness Enumeration (CWE) since it is commonly used for classifying application vulnerabilities as well as an additional classification for software packages, hence some vulnerabilities are assigned both CVEs and CWEs. Our technique queries our internal vulnerability database i.e. persisted results of application and image scans, for matching CWEs/CVEs within microservices that consists an application. The knowledge gained can be used in several security scenarios e.g. policy formulation, risk assessment and vulnerability prioritization.

5.6 Cloud Deployment Manager

To satisfy the need for continuous security *in-production environments*, the Cloud Deployment Manager (CDM) manages microservices deployed in the production AWS environment. The CDM can be deployed either in development or production environments as illustrated in Fig. 2. CDM integrates with several AWS services e.g. Elastic Container Service (ECS), Elastic Container Registry (ECR) and Elastic Computing Cloud (EC2). CDM conducts in production security testing e.g. *fuzzing* by spawning identical instances of microservices scheduled for security tests, for tests in the staging environment. This safeguards deployed microservices from unforeseen behavior consequent of tests e.g. fuzzing tests. This is possible since containers are *immutable* hence testing microservices

---

[18] https://github.com/docker/docker-bench-security.
[19] https://www.cisecurity.org/benchmark/docker/.
[20] https://nvd.nist.gov/products/cpe.
[21] https://nvd.nist.gov/vuln.

Listing 1.2. Example Baseline Security Policy

```
{
"policy_name":"version2tests",
"policy_type" : "Baseline Security Policy",
"attack_strength" : "medium",
"max_permissible_risk" : "low",
"scope" : {
    "depth_limit" : 5
},
"checks" : ["sql_injection","xss","csrf"],
"plugins" : {"discovery checks":"mild",
"cross_site_scripting":"medium",
"cross_site_request_forgery":"medium",
"sql_injection":"medium"}
}
```

with the same source image is sufficient to identify vulnerabilities without testing the production microservice. The CDM also conducts continuous inspection of the processes running in deployed microservices to identify malicious activities (*steps 15 and 16*). As earlier discussed in Sect. 4.5, we propose the inclusion of security health endpoints in CNEs. To afford this feature, we implement *security health endpoint resources* in each microservice. These resources are capable of retrieving the current security assessment results, e.g. on receipt of a GET request, the most recent security testing report is returned in json format.

Table 1. Summary of test environment

Environment variable	Value
Local host operating system	Ubuntu 14.04 Trusty Tahr
Local host RAM/HDD	32 GB/500 GB
Automations server/Git	Jenkins/Github
Cloud container orchestration	AWS ECS, AWS EC2

6   Evaluation

We evaluated *CAVAS* through practical experiments in a private CI/CD pipeline, the details are illustrated in Table 1. Three types of experiments were conducted, first the *vulnerability detection rate* [33] for CAVAS is determined and evaluated. Next, we show the efficiency of our proposed technique for vulnerability information validation and correlation. Lastly, the effectiveness of our security policies is evaluated.

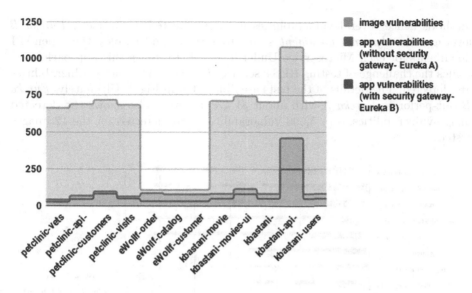

Fig. 4. CAVAS vulnerability detection rate

6.1   Vulnerability Detection Rate

Three container-based microservice applications were used for this experiment: Spring PetClinic (See footnote 4), Movie recommendation Service[22] and an eShop Application from Eberhard Wolff's book [34], also available on GitHub[23]. We will thereafter refer to these applications as *PetClinic,kbastani* and *eWollf* respectively. The applications were cloned from their GitHub repositories and support for OpenAPI documents generation was added. The applications were selected based on popularity as reference microservice architectures, evidenced through their high GitHub ratings. Each application consists of several microservice instances, e.g. PetClinic consists of: *petclinic-vets, petclininc-api-gateway, petclininc-customers* and *petclininc-visits*. The core microservices components e.g. *service registry and discovery* are not tested. To measure the image vulnerabilities, the corresponding images for each microservice is built and analyzed for security vulnerabilities using the integrated Anchore scanning engine. The results are thereafter collected and persisted in CAVAS reports database. To measure the application vulnerabilities, the images are executed i.e. *containerized* and tested using dynamic security testing techniques. This step is necessary for detecting the vulnerabilities existing in the application code. In this testing phase, two Eureka servers are deployed: with traditional OWASP ZAP vulnerability scanner and with the Security Gateway, we refer to them as *Eureka A* and *Eureka B* respectively. The *baseline security policy* is used for testing. *Eureka A* conducts the test using conventional web application testing

---

[22] https://github.com/kbastani/spring-cloud-microservice-example.
[23] https://github.com/ewolff/microservice.

methods hence several vulnerabilities are not detected. Conversely, *Eureka B* leverages the *dynamic document stores* to retrieve and employ the OpenAPI documents for each Microservice Under Test (MuT). Since this approach overcomes the challenge of testing REST services (see Sect. 3.2), more vulnerabilities are detected. The details of the tests are illustrated in Fig. 4. Ultimately, *Eureka B* out-performs *Eureka A* with about 31.4%. Figure 5, also shows the detected image vulnerabilities, over 5,600 vulnerabilities were detected for the 12 images tested.

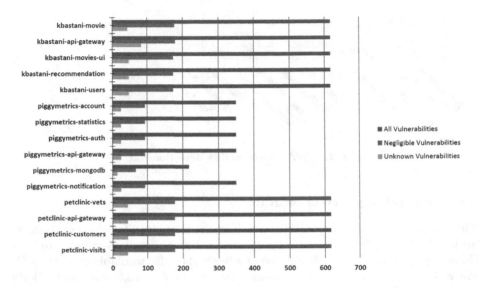

Fig. 5. Anomalies in images vulnerability severity metrics

Vulnerability Information Validation and Correlation. To verify the efficiency of our vulnerability correlation and validation approach, we conducted two tests. In the first test, we investigated the correctness of vulnerability information returned from the image vulnerability tests. To conduct a broader test, a fourth application, PiggyMetrics[24] (thereafter called *piggymetrics*) was added. We discovered that about 20.8% of detected vulnerabilities were marked *negligible*, while about 5.4% were marked as *unknown*. This error-rate is unhealthy for risk assessment hence CAVAS has a component for automatically detecting and correcting vulnerability information. Additionally, we wanted to investigate the correlation between container images and application vulnerabilities. According to [30], vulnerability correlation provides deeper visibility into vulnerability analysis and provides more effective risk management approaches. As seen in Figs. 4 and 5, the image vulnerabilities detected per application are almost identical. This is the first level of correlation, the second level is to detect the correlation between the vulnerabilities detected in the application as well as the image. To

---

[24] https://github.com/sqshq/PiggyMetrics.

do this, a common factor is used as the base, for our experiments, we used the CWE which is used for both packages and web application vulnerability classification. Other types of classifications are not feasible e.g. few web applications have CVEs. Due to space limitations, details of the results are not shown, however Table 2, briefly shows the CVEs, corresponding CVSS, severity metrics and CWE id for the vulnerabilities correlated in the *kbastani* application. All the vulnerabilities correlate with CWE-200: *An information exposure is the intentional or unintentional disclosure of information to an actor that is not explicitly authorized to have access to that information*[25]. The correlation results can be applied to different scenarios, e.g. the vulnerabilities in Table 2 could be prioritized for patching because the possibility of successful attacks using these vulnerabilities could be higher since they exist at both application and image layer. Hence more efforts could be implemented towards rectifying correlated vulnerabilities.

Table 2. Vulnerabilities correlated in the kbastani application

kbastani application			
CVE Id	CVSS score	Severity	CWE Id
CVE-2017-9526	4.3	Medium	CWE-200
CVE-2017-1000100	4.3	Medium	CWE-200
CVE-2017-7407	2.1	low	CWE-200
CVE-2015-5276	5.0	Medium	CWE-200
CVE-2018-1000007	5.0	Medium	CWE-200

6.2   Security Policy Enforcement

To demonstrate the efficiency of the security gateway in enforcing security policies, we commit code to the *petclinic-customers* code repository and generally follow *steps 1–10* of the CAVAS workflow (Fig. 2). At the *staging area*, the *baseline security policy* is implemented against the MuT as a process of the *pre-deployment test*. Since the MuT does not satisfy the rules expressed in the policy, it fails the test and cannot be pushed to production. We also evaluate a policy based on the knowledge gained from the vulnerability correlation effort. *kbastani-movies-ui* is the MuT and a rule is added to the *baseline security policy* to check for correlated vulnerabilities i.e. *CWE-200* and *CVE-2018-1000007*. Again, following *steps 1–10* of CAVAS workflow, the MuT fails the test and the deployment request is canceled.

7   Conclusion and Future Work

This paper presents an innovative *shift-left* and *continuous security* approach suited for detecting application and container image vulnerabilities in development and production environments. Our prototype implementation extends our

---

[25] https://cwe.mitre.org/data/definitions/200.html.

previous work: Cloud Aware Vulnerability Assessment System (CAVAS), which employs the *Security Gateway* concept for security policy enforcement by acting like a SEP. The *Security Gateway* employs *dynamic document stores* and takes advantage of *client side discovery and registry* cloud pattern for identifying and testing microservices for security vulnerabilities. Ultimately, our evaluations show that the security gateway's vulnerability detection rate is better than that of traditional testing techniques by 31.4%. Additionally, we propose techniques for validating vulnerability information returned from image vulnerability scans given that over 26.2% of this information is incorrect. After correcting these anomalies, we employ *vulnerability correlation* for identifying dependence relationships between image and application vulnerabilities. The result of this analysis is interesting and prospective since microservices of an application are composed of virtually identical packages, thus very similar vulnerabilities. This vulnerability commonality can be exploited by attackers e.g. a successful attack against one microservice might expose other microservices to the same attack vector. To counter this type of attack, we propose *vulnerability correlation derived policies* that identify and prevent deployment of vulnerable containers. In the future, we intend to conduct more complex experiments for vulnerability correlation to measure its efficiency for risk assessment. Therefore, supporting schemes like *vulnerability correlation matrix* for CNEs might be relevant.

References

1. Fitzgerald, B., Stol, K.-J.: Continuous software engineering: a roadmap and agenda. J. Syst. Softw. **123**, 176–189 (2017)
2. Bird, J.: DevOpsSec Securing Software through Continuous Delivery. O' Relliy Media Inc., Sebastopol (2016)
3. Rahman, A.A.U., Williams, L.: Software security in devops: synthesizing practitioners' perceptions and practices. In: Proceedings of the International Workshop on Continuous Software Evolution and Delivery (2016)
4. Fielding, R.T., Taylor, R.N.: Architectural styles and the design of network-based software architectures, Ph.D. thesis (2000)
5. Dragoni, N., et al.: Microservices: yesterday, today, and tomorrow. In: Mazzara, M., Meyer, B. (eds.) Present and Ulterior Software Engineering, pp. 195–216. Springer, Cham (2017). https://doi.org/10.1007/978-3-319-67425-4_12
6. Souppaya, M., Morello, J. Scarfone, K.: Application container security guide (2017). https://doi.org/10.6028/NIST.SP.800-190
7. Torkura, K.A., Sukmana, M.I., Meinel, C.: Integrating continuous security assessments in microservices and cloud native applications. In: Proceedings of the 10th International Conference on Utility and Cloud Computing (2017)
8. Scott, D., Sharp, R.: Abstracting application-level web security. In: Proceedings of the 11th International Conference on World Wide Web, pp. 396–407. ACM (2002)
9. Oppliger, R.: Security at the internet layer. Computer **31**(9), 43–47 (1998)
10. Chen, P.-Y., Kataria, G., Krishnan, R.: Correlated failures, diversification, and information security risk management. MIS Q. **35**, 397–422 (2011)
11. Gummaraju, J., Desikan, T., Turner, Y.: Over 30% of official images in docker hub contain high priority security vulnerabilities. Technical report, BanyanOps (2015)

12. Combe, T., Martin, A., Di Pietro, R.: Containers: vulnerability analysis. Technical report, Nokia Bell Labs
13. Bila, N., Dettori, P., Kanso, A., Watanabe, Y., Youssef, A.: Leveraging the serverless architecture for securing linux containers. In: 2017 IEEE 37th International Conference on Distributed Computing Systems Workshops (ICDCSW) (2017)
14. VMWare. Harbor. http://vmware.github.io/harbor/
15. Tak, B., Isci, C., Duri, S., Bila, N., Nadgowda, S., Doran, J.: Understanding security implications of using containers in the cloud. In: USENIX Annual Technical Conference (USENIX ATC 2017) (2017)
16. Zhang, M., Marino, D., Efstathopoulos, P.: Harbormaster: policy enforcement for containers. In: 2015 IEEE 7th International Conference on Cloud Computing Technology and Science (CloudCom) (2015)
17. Antunes, N., Vieira, M.: Designing vulnerability testing tools for web services: approach, components, and tools. Int. J. Inf. Secur. **16**, 1–23 (2016)
18. Esposito, C., Castiglione, A., Choo, K.-K.R.: Challenges in delivering software in the cloud as microservices. IEEE Cloud Comput. **3**(5), 10–14 (2016)
19. Thanh, T.Q., Covaci, S., Magedanz, T., Gouvas, P., Zafeiropoulos, A.: Embedding security and privacy into the development and operation of cloud applications and services. In: 2016 17th International Telecommunications Network Strategy and Planning Symposium (Networks). IEEE (2016)
20. Savchenko, D.I., Radchenko, G.I., Taipale, O.: Microservices validation: mjolnirr platform case study. In: 2015 38th International Convention on Information and Communication Technology, Electronics and Microelectronics (MIPRO) (2015)
21. Schwarz, M., Weiser, S., Gruss, D., Maurice, C., Mangard, S.: Malware guard extension: using SGX to conceal cache attacks. In: Polychronakis, M., Meier, M. (eds.) DIMVA 2017. LNCS, vol. 10327, pp. 3–24. Springer, Cham (2017). https://doi.org/10.1007/978-3-319-60876-1_1
22. Wichers, D.: Owasp top-10 2013. OWASP Foundation, February 2013
23. Alliance, C.S.: Domain 4: complaince and audit management (2011). https://cloudsecurityalliance.org/wp-content/uploads/2011/09/Domain-4.doc
24. Sun, Y., Nanda, S., Jaeger, T.: Security-as-a-service for microservices-based cloud applications. In: 2015 IEEE 7th International Conference on Cloud Computing Technology and Science (CloudCom) (2015)
25. Almorsy, M., Grundy, J., Ibrahim, A.S.: Adaptable, model-driven security engineering for SaaS cloud-based applications. Autom. Softw. Eng. **21**(2), 187–224 (2014)
26. Subashini, S., Kavitha, V.: A survey on security issues in service delivery models of cloud computing. J. Netw. Comput. Appl. **34**(1), 1–11 (2011)
27. Davis, S.: Using the open API specification to find first and second order vulnerabilities in restful APIS (2016). https://2016.appsec.eu/wp-content/uploads/2016/07/AppSecEU2016-Scott-Davis-Scanning-with-Swagger.pdf
28. Homer, A., Sharp, J., Brader, L., Narumoto, M., Swanson, T.: Cloud Design Patterns. Microsoft Press (2014)
29. Roschke, S., Cheng, F., Schuppenies, R., Meinel, C.: Towards unifying vulnerability information for attack graph construction. In: Samarati, P., Yung, M., Martinelli, F., Ardagna, C.A. (eds.) ISC 2009. LNCS, vol. 5735, pp. 218–233. Springer, Heidelberg (2009). https://doi.org/10.1007/978-3-642-04474-8_18
30. Wang, L., Ma, R., Gao, H.R., Wang, X.J., Hu, C.Z.: Analysis of vulnerability correlation based on data fitting. In: Xu, M., Qin, Z., Yan, F., Fu, S. (eds.) CTCIS 2017. CCIS, vol. 704, pp. 165–180. Springer, Singapore (2017). https://doi.org/10.1007/978-981-10-7080-8_13

31. Torkura, K.A., Meinel, C.: Towards cloud-aware vulnerability assessments. In: 2015 11th International Conference on Signal-Image Technology & Internet-Based Systems (SITIS) (2015)
32. Torkura, K.A., Sukmana, M.I. Cheng, F., Meinel, C.: Leveraging cloud native design patterns for security-as-a-service applications. In: 2017 IEEE International Conference on Smart Cloud (SmartCloud) (2017)
33. Bau, J. Bursztein, E., Gupta, D. Mitchell, J.: State of the art: automated black-box web application vulnerability testing. In: IEEE Symposium on Security and Privacy (SP), pp. 332–345. IEEE (2010)
34. Wolff, E.: Microservices: Flexible Software Architecture. Addison-Wesley Professional, Boston (2016)

Shuffler: Mitigate Cross-VM Side-Channel Attacks via Hypervisor Scheduling

Li Liu[1]([✉]), An Wang[1], WanYu Zang[2], Meng Yu[3], Menbai Xiao[1], and Songqing Chen[1]

[1] George Mason University, Fairfax, USA
lliu8@masonlive.gmu.edu
[2] TAMU at San Antonio, San Antonio, USA
[3] University of Texas at San Antonio, San Antonio, USA

Abstract. Cloud computing relies on resources sharing to achieve high resource utilization and economy of scale. Meanwhile, contention on shared resources opens doors for co-located virtual machines (VMs) to have negative impacts on each other, and even introduces vulnerabilities such as information leakage. For example, via CPU cache-based side-channel attacks, an attacker VM can extract crypto keys from a victim VM.

To cost-effectively secure the cloud against those threats without sacrificing resource sharing, in this paper, we first investigate the factors that can impact the success of such attacks. Our investigation reveals that the root cause of such attacks is the constant sharing patterns of hardware resources between VMs. Based on our findings, we quantify the negative impacts a VM can have on another VM on the same machine using the *vulnerable probability*, and propose lightweight and generic scheduler-based defense mechanisms called *Shuffler schedulers*, which can effectively limit the vulnerable probability of all VMs. The key is that distributing CPU time to vCPUs with equal probability would reduce the overall vulnerable probability of the system. Our analyses and experimental results show that the Shuffler schedulers can effectively reduce information leakage to mitigate cross-VM side-channel attacks, with little performance penalty while preserving high resource utilization.

1 Introduction

Cloud has become as an extremely successful paradigm for conveniently storing, accessing, processing and sharing information. One of the building blocks of the cloud computing economy is its resource sharing empowered by virtualization techniques. Virtualization provides a logical abstraction for multiple VMs to share the same hardware resources, where VM isolation and resource sharing are regulated by the hypervisor.

© ICST Institute for Computer Sciences, Social Informatics and Telecommunications Engineering 2018
R. Beyah et al. (Eds.): SecureComm 2018, LNICST 254, pp. 491–511, 2018.
https://doi.org/10.1007/978-3-030-01701-9_27

However, such sharing among VMs may cause potential vulnerabilities. For example, sophisticated attacks could exploit the underlying shared resources to extract sensitive information from neighboring VMs, resulting in security and privacy breaches. Studies showed that co-location can be achieved by normal cloud users with little cost [28,32,39] in the public clouds. As a result, side-channel attacks are demonstrated be to a real threat to cloud tenants [15,28].

Cache-based side-channel attacks, among others, represent the primary and most threatening concerns of cloud security in previous studies [7]. Many solutions are proposed. One category of solutions [10,27] is to harden the targeted operations being attacked, so that the victim is no longer vulnerable to attacks in the insecure cloud environment. However, the hardened programs may still be vulnerable to other side-channel attacks [41]. Compared to hardening vulnerable programs individually, a more general solution is to secure the cloud environment. For example, dedicated host service provided by the cloud provider [2] physically isolates a user's VMs from all other VMs, thus preventing those VMs being attacked. An alternative is to dedicate a portion of CPU caches to each VM [17,19]. Both solutions close the cache side channel at the cost of resource sharing, which is not favorable for the cloud paradigm. There are solutions employing the moving target defense philosophy by frequently migrating VMs [25] to other hosts. However, Liu et al. [20] reported to complete the attacks in minutes. To defend against such attacks, live migration will introduce unaffordable overhead.

Therefore, to mitigate this continuous threat, it is imperative to have a solution that can (1) effectively mitigate cache-based side-channel attacks without sacrificing resource sharing, and (2) incur as little overhead as possible without significant performance or monetary cost. These objectives become even more challenging to achieve, given that one cannot tell in advance which VM(s) is (are) the attacker(s) in a cloud environment. That is, we should assume that any VM could be an attacker.

In this paper, we set to find such a solution. For this purpose, an important question to ask is "what makes the victim vulnerable to side-channel attacks?" We reveal that it is the runtime sharing patterns that enable the attacker to spy the victim via the shared resources. Furthermore, we quantify the time such patterns last by the vulnerable probability. By reproducing the Prime+Probe attack [15,20], we confirm that the attack results are limited by the vulnerable probability. Therefore, the attacks could be mitigated by reducing the vulnerable probability.

Motivated by our previous work [21], we find that distributing CPU time to candidate vCPUs with equal probability would effectively reduce the overall vulnerable probability. Thus, we propose our shuffling scheduling scheme based on a random virtual CPU (vCPU) selection mechanism. The *Local Shuffler (LS)* scheduler and the *Global Shuffler (GS)* scheduler are designed and implemented. Our experimental results show that the Shuffler schedulers can significantly reduce the vulnerable probability without sacrificing performance. In addition, when repeating the side-channel attack on a 4096 bits RSA key, the

Shuffler schedulers reduce the (key bits) recovery rate from 100% to below 72%. Note that this is for the worst-case scenario which favors the attacker as much as possible. Furthermore, we show that this recovery rate reduction can effectively mitigate such attacks.

Compared to other solutions, our scheme has several advantages: (1) it preserves high resource utilization, (2) it is lightweight in terms of overhead, (3) the implementation requires only minor revisions to the current hypervisor scheduler, thus making it easy to deploy, and (4) it is effective not only to cache-based side-channel attacks, but also to attacks exploiting other shared resources in runtime, such as DRAM [26] and processor interconnect [16].

The remainder of the paper is organized as following: Sect. 2 introduces related background information. Section 3 describes our motivation examples along with the identification of the vulnerable probability. Section 4 discusses detailed design and implementation of our defense mechanism. Section 5 demonstrates the evaluation results of the Shuffler schedulers. Some closely related issues are further discussed in Sect. 6. Related work is summarized in Sect. 7. Finally, Sect. 8 concludes our work.

2   Background

2.1   Cross-VM Side-Channel Attacks

In cross-VM side-channel attacks, the attacker VM resides in the same physical host as the victim VM, and spies the victim VM's memory accesses by frequently interleaving with the victim VMs on the shared resources. In such a spying process, the victim VM's memory accesses are only exposed to the attacker during runtime.

As exposed by Zhang et al. [43], an attacker could spy the victim's memory accesses by frequently preempting the victim. However, this is no longer possible in recent version of Xen [31]. Cross-core shared resources such as CPU last level cache (LLC) [15,20,40], processor interconnect [16], DRAM [26], etc., can still be utilized to launch cross-VM side-channel attacks in the cloud. In such attacks, the victim's memory accesses are only exposed to the attacker when the attacker VM and the victim VM run concurrently on different cores. In Sect. 3.1, we will introduce the vulnerable probability to quantify such a vulnerability of a victim during this process, and demonstrate that this value limits the side-channel leakage.

2.2   Hypervisor Scheduling Mechanisms

As each memory access usually takes tens of nanoseconds, fine grained view of how the attacker VM and the victim VM run in time is needed to analyze the spying process of cache-based side-channel attacks. To understand the vCPU scheduling trace made by the hypervisor scheduler, we take the hypervisor schedulers of Xen as an example.

Virtualization enables multiple (guest) VMs to run on the same host. The hypervisor mediates the requests for shared CPU resources by multiple VMs through built-in schedulers. To facilitate the scheduling of CPU, the concept of vCPU is introduced, which refers to the virtual processor of a VM. Each VM can have one or more vCPUs. Upon this, the hypervisor schedules physical CPUs (cores) for vCPUs using different schemes. Additionally, Xen provides a flexible scheduler interface, via which customized scheduling algorithms can be implemented.

For recent versions of the Xen hypervisor, there are four different schedulers, namely the Credit scheduler, the Credit2 scheduler, the Real-Time Deferrable Server scheduler (RTDS), and the ARINC653 scheduler. By default, the Credit scheduler [1] is utilized. It is a general-purpose scheduler that aims to provide proportional fair share of CPU resources to different VMs. We built our prototype based on this scheduler.

3   Motivation

As introduced in Sect. 2.1, in cross-VM side-channel attacks, the victim is vulnerable to attacks when the victim and the attacker run concurrently on different cores. Such a runtime pattern enables the attacker to effectively spy the victim via shared resources. To precisely capture this vulnerability, we define a new measurement metric called the *vulnerable probability*, which is the normalized time during which the victim runs concurrently with the attacker using the victim's accumulative running time as a measure of scale.

To verify the impact of the vulnerable probability on the attack results, we reproduce cross-VM side-channel attacks and demonstrate through experiments our key observations along with their insights. These insights further motivate us to study how the victim can avoid being attacked, and to design our solution in the next section.

3.1   Vulnerable Probabilities in Attacks

Prime+Probe via LLC has been thoroughly studied [7] and demonstrated in the public cloud [15,28]. This attack is used in our discussion, but our discussion is effective to other attacks such as Flush+Reload [40] as well.

We use HP ProLiant DL380 G6 equipped with two Xeon E5540 CPUs. All 4 cores in each CPU package share the same LLC. Xen hypervisor version 4.6.0 with the Credit scheduler is used to manage VMs running on the host. The victim VM repeats signing a file with 4096 bits RSA key using GnuPG-1.4.13. The attacker VM spies the square-and-multiply implementation of modular exponentiation used by GnuPG-1.4.13 via shared LLC as described in [15,20]. We also run additional background VMs (2–10) during the attacks. To reduce the noise introduced by Dom0, we pin Dom0 to one CPU package and all DomUs (guest VMs, including the attacker and the victim) to the other CPU package. Each DomU is configured to have one vCPU.

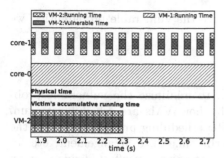
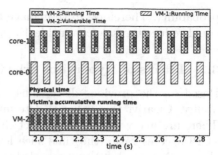

(a) An attack case in which the attacker collects 99.5% key bits. 100% of the victim's crypto execution is under the attacker's spy.

(b) An attack case in which the attacker collects 48.5% key bits. 49% of the victim's crypto execution is under the attacker's spy.

Fig. 1. Vulnerable probabilities in the two attacks

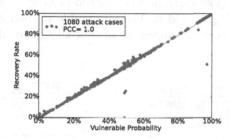

Fig. 2. Recovery rates versus vulnerable probabilities in 1080 attacks

In each attack, the attacker can collect a portion of the secret key bits as a partial key. We define this rate as the *(key bits) recovery rate*, which is used to quantify the attack results. To verify the impact of the vulnerable probabilities on the attack results, we repeat attack $30, 60, 90, \ldots 240$ times when running 5-12 VMs, including the attacker VM and the victim VM, respectively.

Figure 1 demonstrates how the attacker (VM-1) and the victim (VM-2) were scheduled to run in two independent attacks. In the first attack (Fig. 1a), 100% of the victim's crypto execution on core-1 is spied by the attacker running on core-0, while in the other attack (Fig. 1b), only 49% of the victim's crypto execution is exposed to the attacker. Meanwhile, the attacker collects 99.5% and 48.5% key bits separately in these two attacks. The vulnerable probabilities (100% and 49%) and the recovery rates (99.5% and 48.5%) are closely correlated.

Intuitively, the vulnerable probabilities determine the attack results. To verify this hypothesis, we compare the vulnerable probabilities and the recovery rates of all 1080 attacks, as shown in Fig. 2. We calculate the Pearson correlation coefficient (PCC) that quantifies dependencies and correlations. The PCC value is 1.0, suggesting that the attack result is largely determined by the vulnerable probability. Therefore, if we manage to reduce the vulnerable probabilities, we could reduce the side-channel leakage.

3.2 Effects of Hypervisor Scheduler

Based on the previous discussions, we aim to minimize the vulnerable probability. Clearly, this value is determined by how VMs are scheduled to run. There are many factors that affect the vCPU scheduling process, including the vCPUs/cores ratio, the time slice length, the time slice arrangement, etc. In the previous work [21], we revealed that slice arrangement affected side-channel leakage more significantly than other factors. Below we demonstrate the effects of the slice arrangement to the vulnerable probability.

The scheduling trace t_1 in Fig. 3a shows the original slice arrangement in an attack collected in Sect. 3.1, while t_2 in Fig. 3b shows another slice arrangement in the same attack. Compared to t_1, t_2 assigns the vCPUs more evenly to all the available cores. Correspondingly, how the victim (VM-2) is spied by the attacker (VM-1) is shown in Fig. 3c and d. The vulnerable probability is reduced from 100% to 68%. Thus, proper arrangement of time slices can effectively reduce the vulnerable probability.

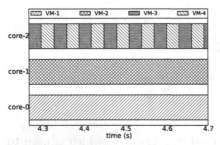

(a) Scheduling trace t_1, original slice arrangement.

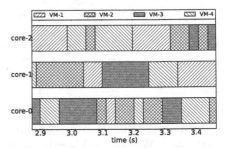

(b) Scheduling trace t_2, another slice arrangement.

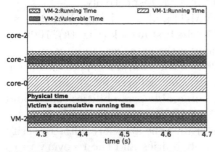

(c) VM-2's vulnerable probability is 100%, when spied by VM-1 in t_1.

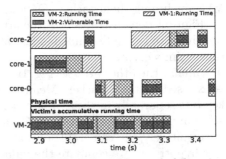

(d) VM-2's vulnerable probability is 68%, when spied by VM-1 in t_2.

Fig. 3. Vulnerable probability of the same attack with different slice arrangements. In both scheduling traces, the victim (VM-2) completes the same crypto operation.

Motivated by this result, we move on to design and implement a scheduler-based mechanism that can significantly reduce the vulnerable probability.

4 Our Solution

As shown in the last section, the slice arrangement largely determines the vulnerable probability. In this section, we will revisit the design of the hypervisor scheduler, particularly focusing on the slice arrangement in the vCPU scheduling process. From the scheduler's perspective, we begin by scoping the attacker's goals and capabilities.

4.1 Threat Model

We assume that in each attack, the goal of an attacker is to extract as much information as possible. Under this condition, we consider a threat model meeting the common requirements in published the attacks [15,20,40], with the following characteristics:

- Co-location: the attacker VM runs in the same physical host with the victim VM.
- Unknown attacker: from the perspective of the hypervisor scheduler, attacker is unknown in advance, meaning that any VM could be the attacker.
- Single attacker: we assume the state-of-the-art setting in which each attacker vCPU spies the victim individually. We discuss colluding attacks involving multiple vCPUs in Sect. 6.1. Below we use *attacker*, *attacker vCPU* and *attacker VM* interchangeably.
- CPU overcommitment: we assume that there are more vCPUs than cores in the host. We discuss this assumption in Sect. 6.2.
- Effective spy during runtime: we assume that the attacker can effectively spy the victim's memory access via shared resources during runtime, and that the third party VMs introduce minimum noise to the side channels.
- Persistent attacks: we assume the attacker can repeat the same attack for a reasonable large number of times. For example, Liu et al. [20] repeated the same attack for more than 20,000 times to recover the secret key.

4.2 Problem Statement

We aim to reduce the vulnerable probability by scheduling. In a given attack with scheduling trace t, the victim (vCPU or VM) v and the attacker a, the vulnerable probability is represented as $P(t, v, a)$, which is defined by the time of the victim runs concurrently with the attacker on the scale of the victim's accumulative running time. For example, in Fig. 3, $P(t_1, VM_2, VM_1) = 100\%$ and $P(t_2, VM_2, VM_1) = 68\%$.

Since it is not possible to pinpoint the specific attacker, the goal for the hypervisor is to mitigate the overall vulnerability of the system, which is bound by the most vulnerable vCPU pairs quantified as:

$$P(t) = \max_{\forall v,a}\{P(t,v,a)\} \tag{1}$$

Therefore, an effective defense mechanism can be mathematically captured by the solution to $\min_t P(t)$. To this end, we conduct a mathematical analysis on the problem and propose a scheduler-based scheme to achieve the optimization accordingly.

4.3   Problem Analysis and Solution

In the discussion below, we assume that there are m available cores and n ($n > m$) active vCPUs in a host. For a given scheduling trace t and victim vCPU v, there are $m - 1$ vCPUs run concurrently whenever v runs. Thus, its vulnerable probabilities against to all potential attackers are subject to:

$$\sum_{\forall a} P(t,v,a) = m - 1$$

Then the largest vulnerable probability an attacker can obtain can be calculated by Eq. 2. Here we assume the worst-case that any of the $n - 1$ vCPUs may be the attacker.

$$\max_{\forall a}\{P(t,v,a)\} \geq \frac{\sum_{\forall a} P(t,v,a)}{n-1} = \frac{m-1}{n-1} \tag{2}$$

The intuitive interpretation of Eq. 2 suggests that the balanced allocation of the CPU time would guarantee the minimal vulnerable probability for a specific victim vCPU. Take the scheduling traces t_1 and t_2 in Fig. 3 as an example.

$$\text{subject to} \quad \sum_{\forall a} P(t_1, VM_2, a) = \sum_{\forall a} P(t_2, VM_2, a) = 2$$

$$\max_{\forall a} P(t_1, VM_2, a) = \max_{\forall a \in \{VM_1, VM_3, VM_4\}} P(t_1, VM_2, a)$$

$$= \max\{1, 0.52, 0.48\} = 1$$

$$\max_{\forall a} P(t_2, VM_2, a) = \max_{\forall a \in \{VM_1, VM_3, VM_4\}} P(t_2, VM_2, a)$$

$$= \max\{0.68, 0.60, 0.72\} = 0.72$$

From the results, we can infer that the victim in t_2 has a smaller worst-case vulnerable probability. This advantage stems from a more balanced distribution of CPU time. Combining Eqs. 1 and 2 we can obtain that:

$$P(t) = \max_{\forall a,v}\{P(t,v,a)\} = \max_{\forall v}\{\max_{\forall a}\{P(t,v,a)\}\} \geq \frac{m-1}{n-1}$$

Thus,

$$\min_t P(t) \geq \frac{m-1}{n-1} \tag{3}$$

Based on the above discussions, distributing CPU time to vCPUs with equal probability would reduce the overall vulnerable probability of the system. Thus, we propose to select all candidate vCPUs with equal probability when making scheduling decisions. Later we will demonstrate that such a scheme effectively reduces the overall vulnerable probability to the near optimal value through experiments.

4.4   Implementation of the Shuffler Schedulers

To demonstrate the effectiveness of our solution, we use Xen's Credit scheduler as an example, and the scheme could be applied to other schedulers as well. Revisiting the example shown in Fig. 3, we can observe that the vulnerable probability could reach as high as 100% due to the constant runtime patterns of vCPUs, which originate from two scheduling schemes.

- The tendency of vCPUs to be scheduled to the same core. In the credit scheduler, each core maintains a local run queue (runq) of the active vCPUs. Each time the scheduling routine is triggered, the vCPU currently running on this core is returned to its runq, and the next vCPU to run is selected from this runq.
- VCPU's scheduling in round-robin order. Each runq is managed in a round-robin fashion in the runq. The returned vCPU is appended to the end of the runq of the same priority and the next vCPU to run is selected from the head of the runq.

Intuitively, we can design a deterministic scheduler, which records the vulnerable probability of all vCPU pairs, and each time greedily selects a vCPU that minimizes $P(t)$ in Sect. 4.3. However, the scheduling decision of a deterministic scheduler is predictable. Zhang *et al.* [43] abused the open source Xen hypervisor to trick the Credit scheduler to behave in the attacker's favor. Gullasch *et al.* [11] utilized similar feature in the Linux process scheduler to launch attacks as well.

Thus, we propose to integrate the uniform and random selections in the design of the Xen's Credit scheduler. Following this scheme, we implement the *Local Shuffler (LS)* scheduler. We minimize the modifications to make the implementation lightweight. Specifically, we have the following changes:

1. Runq selection: during the scheduling, a runq is uniformly and randomly selected from all available runqs.
2. VCPU selection: within the selected runq, the next vCPU to run is uniformly and randomly selected from all candidate vCPUs with the highest priority, and the current running vCPU is returned to the same runq.

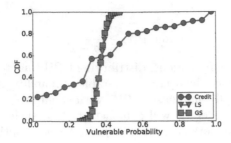

Fig. 4. Vulnerable probabilities distributions

In the LS scheduler, a runq is still maintained for each core. In addition, we further propose and implement the *Global Shuffler (GS)* scheduler, where only one global runq is maintained for all cores. In the GC scheduler, the scheduling scheme is modified as following:

1. Runq selection: during the scheduling, all candidate vCPUs are kept in a globally shared runq.
2. VCPU selection: the same with that of the LS scheduler within the selected runq.

We limit the above changes to relevant functions in the source code of the Credit scheduler (*sched_credit.c*). In the following section, we will evaluate and compare the schedulers LS and GS with Credit from multiple perspectives.

5   Performance Evaluation

In this section, we evaluate the effectiveness of our proposed schedulers from different perspectives. We use the same hardware and configurations as used in Sect. 3.1. The hypervisor utilized for our evaluations is the Xen hypervisor version 4.6.0.

5.1   Vulnerable Probability

To evaluate the vulnerable probabilities when different schedulers are used, we repeated the experiment 30 times when running 9 VMs and collected 2160 (30 · $\binom{9}{2}$)) potential attacker and victim pairs for each scheduler. Figure 4 shows the cumulative distribution function (CDF) of the vulnerable probabilities for all possible attacks.

In this figure, the x-axis represents the vulnerable probabilities while the y-axis shows the CDF values. The distributions of the vulnerable probabilities for each scheduler are distinguished by different markers. "Credit", "LS" and "GS" represents the default Credit scheduler, the Local Shuffler scheduler and the Global Shuffler scheduler separately. Furthermore, the maximum vulnerable probability illustrates the worst-case scenario when the potential attackers could obtain the most information from the victim.

In this figure, we can clearly observe that Credit leads to the most widely distributed values, with the worst-case value being 100%. This suggests that an attacker could obtain an almost complete data set of the victim's memory accesses in persistent attacks. In contrast, LS and GS can limit this worst-case value to 49%. Since the attacker can repeatedly launch the same attack in our threat model, the worst-case value indicates the effectiveness of the attacks. We use it in the following evaluations. Another observation is that the vulnerable probabilities of LS and GS is more evenly distributed within a smaller range of 25%–49% than that of Credit.

There are many factors that may affect the scheduling trace in attacks, including the running time, the vCPUs/cores ratio, the workloads, and the time slice length. Next, we compare the worst-case vulnerable probabilities using different schedulers under various settings (among 2160 possible attacks if not otherwise specified).

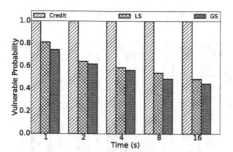
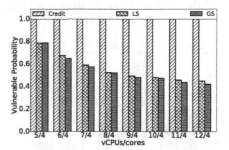

Fig. 5. The worst-case vulnerable probabilities with different running time

Fig. 6. The worst-case vulnerable probabilities with different vCPUs/cores

Table 1. Sysbench workloads

Workloads	Description	Parameters
CPU intensive	Verify prime numbers by doing standard division of the number starting from 1	--test=cpu --max-time=10
Memory intensive	Allocate a memory buffer and then write from it randomly	--test=memory --max-time=10
I/O intensive	Randomly read/write previously created files	--test=fileio --max-time=10 --file-test-mode=rndrw

We first varied the running time from 1 second to 16 seconds and the results are shown in Fig. 5. In this figure, the x-axis represents the running time and the y-axis represents the worst-case vulnerable probabilities. Furthermore, each group of data represents the results of the three schedulers.

We can observe from the figure that for Credit, the worst-case vulnerable probabilities can always reach 100% despite the variation of the running time. While for other schedulers, the worst-case vulnerable probabilities can be effectively reduced by 20%–50%. In addition, the worst-case vulnerable probability continuously decrease as the running time increases for our proposed schedulers. This suggests that the effectiveness of our schemes is more remarkable for long-term executions due to the more even distribution of time slices to vCPUs.

We further evaluate the worst-case vulnerable probabilities with different vCPUs/cores ratios as shown in Fig. 6. By increasing the number of VMs, we changed the number of vCPUs from 5 to 12 running on 4 cores as represented on the x-axis in the figure. From this figure, we can see that our solution can also achieve 20%–50% reductions. Furthermore, we also observe that the result approximates the optimal value calculated by Eq. 3.

For different workloads, using sysbench [18], we generated CPU intensive workloads, memory intensive workloads and I/O intensive workloads to evaluate different schedulers. The configuration is shown in Table 1. The results are displayed in Fig. 7. With the Shuffler schedulers, the worst-case vulnerable probabilities can be reduced to below 60%.

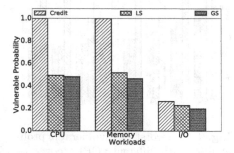

Fig. 7. The worst-case vulnerable probabilities with different workloads

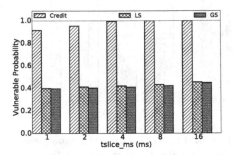

Fig. 8. The worst-case vulnerable probabilities with different time slice lengths

Finally, we changed the time slice length configured with parameter *tslice_ms* (default 30) in Xen, from 1 ms to 16 ms for all schedulers. The result is shown in Fig. 8. Our schedulers can effectively reduce the worst-case vulnerability by more than 50%.

To sum up, for the worst-case vulnerable probability in various settings:

1. It can reach almost 100% in most settings when the default Credit scheduler is used.
2. Our proposed Shuffler schedulers can reduce it to below 80%.
3. The GS scheduler is slightly more effective than the LS scheduler, suggesting a global queue implementation is preferable for evenly distributing CPU time.

5.2 Recovery Rate

In this section, we reproduce the same Prime+Probe attack used in Sect. 3.1, and evaluate how the Shuffler schedulers reduce the (key bits) recovery rate compared to the Credit scheduler.

Figure 9 shows the CDF of the recovery rates for repeated attacks. From the figure, we can clearly observe that Credit leads to the most widely distributed values, with the worst-case recovery rate being 99%. In contrast, LS and GS limit the worst-case recovery rate to 66% and 78%, respectively. The worst-case recovery rate indicates the effectiveness of persistent attacks. We use it in the following evaluations.

We further evaluate the worst-case recovery rates with different vCPUs/cores ratios as shown in Fig. 10. We also changed the number of vCPUs from 5 to 12 running on 4 cores as represented on the x-axis in the figure, and present the highest recovery rates on the y-axis. The number of attacks repeated for different vCPUs number is $30, 60, 90, ..., 240$, respectively.

From the figure, we can see that our solution can limit the recovery rates to below 85%. In our experiment, all background VMs run CPU intensive workloads that introduce little noise to the attacks. In the cloud environment, the existence of error bits will further reduce the worst-case recovery rates.

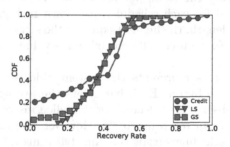

Fig. 9. Recovery rates distributions

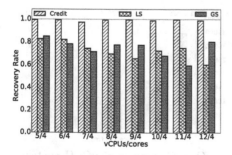

Fig. 10. The worst-case recovery rates with different vCPUs/cores

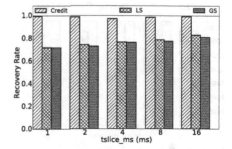

Fig. 11. The worst-case recovery rates with different time slice lengths

Furthermore, the worst-case recovery rates can be further reduced to the near optimized value shown in Eq. 3. This can be confirmed by repeating the same attack while setting smaller tslice_ms value, as shown in Fig. 11. We configured vCPUs/cores to 5/4, and changed the tslice_ms from 1 ms to 16 ms for all schedulers. The worst-case recovery rates are reduced to below 72% for the Shuffler schedulers, from 99% for the Credit scheduler, when tslice_ms is set to 1 ms. The worst-case recovery rate of 72% makes reconstructing the full key infeasible, as we will discuss in Sect. 6.3.

5.3   Scheduling Overhead

Besides security, we also evaluate the performance overhead of the Shuffler schedulers. The overhead incurred by the schedulers mainly comes from the CPU time consumed for scheduling operations and performance penalty due to extra context switches. We will evaluate them separately.

For the CPU time consumption, we measure the system-wide performance when executing CPU intensive workloads in all VMs. The performance of each VM is reported by sysbench [18]. During a given period, the more CPU time consumed by the scheduling operations, the less number of events can be executed in the VMs. For the performance penalty, we count the total number of vCPU context switches during the same period. We use these two metrics together to profile the overhead for each scheduler, as shown in Fig. 12. Intuitively, the smaller the time slice length, the higher frequency the scheduler is triggered, thus the higher overhead. So we used different tslice_ms values in this experiment as shown in the x-axis.

In Fig. 12a, the y-axis represents the system-wide performance during 10 seconds. The higher the better. Each bar shows the average value among 150 repetitions. We can observe that decreasing the tslice_ms values always imposes extra overhead, which can reach up to 2%. However, the extra overhead introduced by the Shuffler schedulers using the same tslice_ms values is less than 0.5% compared to the Credit scheduler.

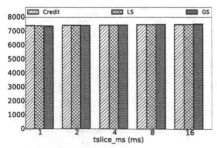

(a) Overall number of events executed in all VMs

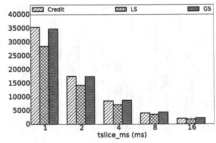

(b) Overall number of vCPU context switches

Fig. 12. Overhead of different schedulers

In Fig. 12b, the y-axis represents the total number of vCPU context switches during the same period. The lower the better. As expected, the number of vCPU context switches decreased by half as we doubled the tslice_ms value. Furthermore, we also find that GS caused similar number of vCPU context switches compared to Credit, while LS reduced this number by 13%–20%. It is because the current running vCPU has higher probability to continue running when the LS scheduler is used.

To sum up, the Shuffler schedulers introduce negligible overhead compared to the Credit scheduler, since they neither consumed more CPU time in scheduling operations, nor generated more vCPU context switches.

6 Discussion

6.1 Colluding Attacks

In our threat model, we assumed the state-of-the-art attacking scenarios in which a single attacker vCPU was used [15,20,40]. We argue that colluding attacker vCPUs could hardly gain more advantages over single attacker vCPU, based on two observations: (1) To avoid the mutual pollution of the monitored cache sets, no overlapping executions of the attacker vCPUs are desired, since they spy the shared resources by "writing". This requires the cooperation of the hypervisor, which is not possible without compromising the hypervisor. (2) To stitch the collected information together, the attacker vCPUs need to synchronize at overly high frequency, which is not readily available. Thus, the capability of colluding attacks is limited by our proposed solution as well.

6.2 CPU Overcommitment

In our thread model, we assumed CPU is overcommitted in the physical hosts. CPU overcommitment is commonly used to consolidate the VMs to save power consumption and to improve resource utilization [6,8,22]. For example, the default vCPUs/cores ratio is 16 in OpenStack [4]. Though for public clouds, the vCPUs/cores ratio is not disclosed by the cloud providers, there are some clues to overcommitment. For example, for the latest general purpose T2 instances in Amazon EC2, the vCPUs/cores ratio may be 5 (12 credits/hour), 10 or 20, etc. [3].

If CPU is not overcommitted, the idle cores can be used to inject noise to the side channels to mitigate attacks. Zhang et al. [42] had discussions in this direction. Such a mechanism can be a good complement to our solution.

6.3 Key Reconstruction

The evaluation shows that when our proposed Shuffler schedulers were used, the attacker could only collect less than 72% key bits in a single attack. As a result, the side-channel attacks fail since it is infeasible to guess the missing 28% key bits.

One may wonder if advanced crypto key analysis techniques enable the attacker to reconstruct the full key string from such partial keys. For example, when there was bits corruption in the partial keys, Heninger and Shacham [12] managed to reconstruct the full key string by utilizing the redundant information in the key string. However, such key reconstruction methods cannot directly apply to our case, since the partial keys have missing bits at random, and key bits positions are incorrect.

Alternatively, the attacker could accumulate collected information across multiple partial keys to reconstruct the complete key. Similar problem was discussed in the context of deletion channel [13,23,24]. In this model, a transmitter sends a bit and the receiver either receives the bit (with probability $1 - P$) or does not receive anything without being notified (with probability P). Similarly, we state the key reconstruction problem when the Shuffler schedulers are used:

For a victim's key bits sequence $X = x_1 x_2 ... x_l$ of length l. In each attack, the attacker can collect a subsequence, $Y_1, Y_2, ..., Y_n$, where each Y_i is obtained independently by deleting each of X's element with probability P. Under these conditions, what is the number of subsequences (n) needed to reconstruct X with high probability?

We model the attacker's data collection in this way, since the hypervisor scheduling is transparent to the attacker, and the Shuffler schedulers promised vulnerable probabilities to be smaller than 72%. Then bits deletion is inevitable with $P \geq 28\%$.

The state-of-the-art result of this problem to the best of our knowledge is [13]:

$$\begin{cases} n = O(l \cdot poly(logl)), & P \leq (1/\sqrt{l}) \\ n = exp(\sqrt{l} \cdot poly(logl)), & \text{any } P \end{cases}$$

Considering $P = 28\%$ and $l = 4096$, only the second result applies to our key reconstruction problem. In this case, the number of repeated attacks required to reconstruct the full key increases exponentially with $\sqrt{l} = \sqrt{4096} = 64$, making the attacking time unaffordable when our proposed Shuffler schedulers are used.

To sum up, our scheduling-based scheme effectively mitigates cross-VM side-channel attacks.

7   Related Work

Side-channel attacks have attracted a lot of attention during the past and many schemes have been proposed to mitigate such attacks. For many attacks, visible timing difference for different hardware events is required. Askarov et al. [5] provided a timing mitigator to bound the information leaked through the timing channel. To eliminate the timing channel, Stefan et al. [30] proposed an instruction-based scheduling, Vattikonda et al. [34] suggested to remove the fine grained timer in Xen. However, obfuscating timing information negatively affects benign cloud tenants as well, and the attacker may obtain precise timing information using other methods [29]. Zhang et al. [42] introduced bystander VMs running configurable workloads to inject noise to covert channels, which could be a good complement to our solution.

Crypto operations are often the target of side-channel attacks. Gueron [10] proposed a new modular exponentiation implementation to secure RSA against side-channel attacks. Raccoon [27] was also proposed to harden programs against side-channel attacks by obfuscating the program at the source code level. However, the modified programs may still be vulnerable to new side-channel attacks [41].

Compared to harden individual program, a more general solution is to secure the cloud environment against side-channel attacks. Dedicated host service provided by the cloud providers [2] can be used to physically isolate VMs from all other VMs, thus preventing them being attacked. However, dedicated hosts come at the cost of higher price for the cloud user and lower resource utilization for the cloud provider. Alternatively, certain degree of VM isolation could be achieved by carefully placing and frequently migrating VMs in its life-cycle [25,32,39]. Based on prior studies [25,35] and confirmed by our measurements, it took about 1.47 seconds to live migrate an instance with 2048 MB RAM and 7 GB hard drive via 1Gbps network. Furthermore, the latency of such migrations could be translated into monetary cost of the providers ranging from $1 to $100.

Once the attacker and the victim run their cloud tenants in the same host, different shared resources may be exploited to launch side-channel attacks. Various prior efforts focused on mitigating known attacks via different shared resources, such as networks-on-chip [37], memory controller [36], memory pages [44], CPU caches [9,17,19,38], etc. Specifically, to mitigate cache side-channel attacks, Godfrey and Zulkernine [9] proposed to flush caches during context switches, Wang and Lee [38] suggested a new cache design, Liu et al. [19] proposed to partition the LLC for each cloud tenant using Intel's Cache Allocation Technology, Kim et al. [17] designed a memory page coloring scheme to prevent usage patterns of sensitive data being leaked. These defenses are often effective to a specific group of attacks. However, they usually introduced significant overhead, reduced resource utilization, and even required far-reaching changes to the hardware.

A finer-grained isolation via scheduling is more economically desirable for both the cloud user and the cloud provider. Hu [14] discussed the impact of scheduling policy on hardware timing covert-channel and proposed a lattice scheduler for process scheduling. In virtualized environment, the impact of various scheduling factors, including load balancing, weight, cap, time slice and (context-switch) rate limiting, on covert-channel attacks were studied [33]. Varadarajan et al. [31] found that the attacker needed to measure the cache state frequently in side-channel attacks, and that the efficacy of such attacks can be dramatically reduced by enabling the minimum runtime guarantee feature in Xen. They both targeted side-channel attacks via core-shared resources such as L1 cache. In comparison, our previous work [21] studied how different factors affected the more advanced side-channel attacks via cross-core shared resources such as LLC. In this work, we revealed that the root cause of the side-channel leakage is the runtime resources sharing patterns between cloud tenants. We had an in-depth discussion of it, defined the vulnerable probability to quantify it, and proposed a scheduling-based mechanism to reduce it. In addition, the extra overhead is less than 0.5% in our evaluation.

8   Conclusion

The multi-tenancy in the cloud infrastructure enables side-channel attacks to be launched by co-locating VMs. In this paper, we revisit the cache-based side-channel attacks where the attackers exploit the shared hardware resources such as CPU cache. Unfortunately, existing solutions either fail to provide sufficient protections at economic costs or limit their scope to specific attacks. In this paper, we propose a lightweight and generic solution to eliminate a wide range of cross-VM and possibly unknown attacks. Our thorough analyses have demonstrated that the efficacy of such attacks could be dramatically reduced by distributing CPU resource as evenly as possible to all candidate vCPUs. Accordingly, we have designed and implemented the Shuffler schedulers by incorporating this strategy and randomization into Xen's Credit scheduler. The evaluation results show that the Shuffler schedulers significantly reduce the vulnerable probabilities of all VMs, thus mitigating attacks without sacrificing the original resource sharing or performance.

Acknowledgment. We appreciate constructive comments from anonymous referees. This work is partially supported by an ARO grant W911NF-15-1-0262, a NIST grant 70NANB16H166. and NSF grants CNS-1422355, CNS-1524462, and CNS-1634441.

References

1. Credit Scheduler (2017). http://wiki.xen.org/wiki/Credit_Scheduler. Accessed 19 Feb 2018
2. Amazon EC2 Dedicated Hosts (2018). https://aws.amazon.com/ec2/dedicated-hosts/. Accessed 19 Feb 2018
3. Amazon EC2 Instance Types (2018). https://aws.amazon.com/ec2/instance-types/. Accessed 19 Feb 2018
4. Overcommitting CPU and RAM (2018). https://docs.openstack.org/arch-design/design-compute/design-compute-overcommit.html. Accessed 19 Feb 2018
5. Askarov, A., Zhang, D., Myers, A.C.: Predictive black-box mitigation of timing channels. In: Proceedings of the 17th ACM Conference on Computer and Communications Security, pp. 297–307. ACM (2010)
6. Cortez, E., Bonde, A., Muzio, A., Russinovich, M., Fontoura, M., Bianchini, R.: Resource central: understanding and predicting workloads for improved resource management in large cloud platforms. In: Proceedings of the 26th Symposium on Operating Systems Principles, pp. 153–167. ACM (2017)
7. Ge, Q., Yarom, Y., Cock, D., Heiser, G.: A survey of microarchitectural timing attacks and countermeasures on contemporary hardware. J. Cryptogr. Eng. **8**, 1–27 (2016)

8. Ghosh, R., Naik, V.K.: Biting off safely more than you can chew: predictive analytics for resource over-commit in IaaS cloud. In: 2012 IEEE 5th International Conference on Cloud Computing (CLOUD), pp. 25–32. IEEE (2012)

9. Godfrey, M., Zulkernine, M.: A server-side solution to cache-based side-channel attacks in the cloud. In: 2013 IEEE Sixth International Conference on Cloud Computing (CLOUD), pp. 163–170. IEEE (2013)

10. Gueron, S.: Efficient software implementations of modular exponentiation. J. Cryptogr. Eng. **2**(1), 31–43 (2012)

11. Gullasch, D., Bangerter, E., Krenn, S.: Cache games - bringing access-based cache attacks on AES to practice. In: Proceedings of the 2011 IEEE Symposium on Security and Privacy, SP 2011, pp. 490–505. IEEE Computer Society, Washington, DC (2011)

12. Heninger, N., Shacham, H.: Reconstructing RSA private keys from random key bits. In: Halevi, S. (ed.) CRYPTO 2009. LNCS, vol. 5677, pp. 1–17. Springer, Heidelberg (2009). https://doi.org/10.1007/978-3-642-03356-8_1

13. Holenstein, T., Mitzenmacher, M., Panigrahy, R., Wieder, U.: Trace reconstruction with constant deletion probability and related results. In: Proceedings of the Nineteenth Annual ACM-SIAM Symposium on Discrete Algorithms, pp. 389–398. Society for Industrial and Applied Mathematics (2008)

14. Hu, W.M.: Lattice scheduling and covert channels. In: Proceedings of 1992 IEEE Computer Society Symposium on Research in Security and Privacy, pp. 52–61. IEEE (1992)

15. Inci, M.S., Gulmezoglu, B., Irazoqui, G., Eisenbarth, T., Sunar, B.: Seriously, get off my cloud! cross-VM RSA key recovery in a public cloud. Technical report, IACR Cryptology ePrint Archive (2015)

16. Irazoqui, G., Eisenbarth, T., Sunar, B.: Cross processor cache attacks. In: Proceedings of the 11th ACM on Asia Conference on Computer and Communications Security, pp. 353–364. ACM (2016)

17. Kim, T., Peinado, M., Mainar-Ruiz, G.: STEALTHMEM: system-level protection against cache-based side channel attacks in the cloud. In: Proceedings of the 21st USENIX Conference on Security Symposium, Security 2012, p. 11. USENIX Association, Berkeley (2012)

18. Kopytov, A.: Sysbench: a system performance benchmark (2004). http://sysbench.sourceforge.net

19. Liu, F., et al.: Catalyst: defeating last-level cache side channel attacks in cloud computing. In: 2016 IEEE International Symposium on High Performance Computer Architecture (HPCA), pp. 406–418. IEEE (2016)

20. Liu, F., Yarom, Y., Ge, Q., Heiser, G., Lee, R.B.: Last-level cache side-channel attacks are practical. In: IEEE Symposium on Security and Privacy, San Jose, CA, US (2015)

21. Liu, L., Wang, A., Zang, W., Yu, M., Chen, S.: Empirical evaluation of the hypervisor scheduling on side channel attacks. In: 2018 IEEE International Conference on Communications (ICC). IEEE (2018)

22. Lowe, S.D.: Best practices for oversubscription of CPU, memory and storage in vSphere virtual environments. Technical Whitepaper, Dell (2013)

23. McGregor, A., Price, E., Vorotnikova, S.: Trace reconstruction revisited. In: Schulz, A.S., Wagner, D. (eds.) ESA 2014. LNCS, vol. 8737, pp. 689–700. Springer, Heidelberg (2014). https://doi.org/10.1007/978-3-662-44777-2_57

24. Mitzenmacher, M., et al.: A survey of results for deletion channels and related synchronization channels. Probab. Surv. **6**, 1–33 (2009)

25. Moon, S.J., Sekar, V., Reiter, M.K.: Nomad: mitigating arbitrary cloud side channels via provider-assisted migration. In: Proceedings of the 22nd ACM SIGSAC Conference on Computer and Communications Security, pp. 1595–1606. ACM (2015)

26. Pessl, P., Gruss, D., Maurice, C., Schwarz, M., Mangard, S.: Drama: exploiting dram addressing for cross-CPU attacks. In: 25th USENIX Security Symposium (USENIX Security 16), Austin, TX, 2016, pp. 565–581. USENIX Association (2016)

27. Rane, A., Lin, C., Tiwari, M.: Raccoon: closing digital side-channels through obfuscated execution. In: USENIX Security, pp. 431–446 (2015)

28. Ristenpart, T., Tromer, E., Shacham, H., Savage, S.: Hey, you, get off of my cloud: exploring information leakage in third-party compute clouds. In: Proceedings of the 16th ACM Conference on Computer and Communications Security, pp. 199–212. ACM (2009)

29. Schwarz, M., Weiser, S., Gruss, D., Maurice, C., Mangard, S.: Malware guard extension: using SGX to conceal cache attacks. In: Polychronakis, M., Meier, M. (eds.) DIMVA 2017. LNCS, vol. 10327, pp. 3–24. Springer, Cham (2017). https://doi.org/10.1007/978-3-319-60876-1_1

30. Stefan, D., et al.: Eliminating cache-based timing attacks with instruction-based scheduling. In: Crampton, J., Jajodia, S., Mayes, K. (eds.) ESORICS 2013. LNCS, vol. 8134, pp. 718–735. Springer, Heidelberg (2013). https://doi.org/10.1007/978-3-642-40203-6_40

31. Varadarajan, V., Ristenpart, T., Swift, M.: Scheduler-based defenses against cross-VM side-channels. In: 23rd USENIX Security Symposium (USENIX Security 14), pp. 687–702. USENIX Association, San Diego (2014)

32. Varadarajan, V., Zhang, Y., Ristenpart, T., Swift, M.M.: A placement vulnerability study in multi-tenant public clouds. In: USENIX Security, pp. 913–928 (2015)

33. Vateva-Gurova, T., Suri, N., Mendelson, A.: The impact of hypervisor scheduling on compromising virtualized environments. In: 2015 IEEE International Conference on Computer and Information Technology; Ubiquitous Computing and Communications; Dependable, Autonomic and Secure Computing; Pervasive Intelligence and Computing (CIT/IUCC/DASC/PICOM), pp. 1910–1917. IEEE (2015)

34. Vattikonda, B.C., Das, S., Shacham, H.: Eliminating fine grained timers in Xen. In: Proceedings of the 3rd ACM Workshop on Cloud Computing Security Workshop, CCSW 2011, pp. 41–46. ACM, New York (2011)

35. Wang, H., Li, F., Chen, S.: Towards cost-effective moving target defense against DDoS and covert channel attacks. In: Proceedings of the 2016 ACM Workshop on Moving Target Defense, pp. 15–25. ACM (2016)

36. Wang, Y., Ferraiuolo, A., Suh, G.E.: Timing channel protection for a shared memory controller. In: 2014 IEEE 20th International Symposium on High Performance Computer Architecture (HPCA), pp. 225–236. IEEE (2014)

37. Wang, Y., Suh, G.E.: Efficient timing channel protection for on-chip networks. In: 2012 Sixth IEEE/ACM International Symposium on Networks on Chip (NoCS), pp. 142–151. IEEE (2012)

38. Wang, Z., Lee, R.B.: New cache designs for thwarting software cache-based side channel attacks. In: Proceedings of the 34th Annual International Symposium on Computer Architecture, ISCA 2007, pp. 494–505. ACM, New York (2007)

39. Xu, Z., Wang, H., Wu, Z.: A measurement study on co-residence threat inside the cloud. In: 24th USENIX Security Symposium (USENIX Security 2015), pp. 929–944. USENIX Association, Washington, D.C., August 2015

40. Yarom, Y., Falkner, K.: FLUSH+RELOAD: a high resolution, low noise, L3 cache side-channel attack. In: 23rd USENIX Security Symposium (USENIX Security 2014), pp. 719–732. USENIX Association, San Diego (2014)
41. Yarom, Y., Genkin, D., Heninger, N.: Cachebleed: a timing attack on openssl constant-time rsa. J. Cryptogr. Eng. **7**(2), 99–112 (2017)
42. Zhang, R., Su, X., Wang, J., Wang, C., Liu, W., Lau, R.W.: On mitigating the risk of cross-vm covert channels in a public cloud. IEEE Trans. Parallel Distrib. Syst. **26**(8), 2327–2339 (2015)
43. Zhang, Y., Juels, A., Reiter, M.K., Ristenpart, T.: Cross-VM side channels and their use to extract private keys. In: Proceedings of the 2012 ACM Conference on Computer and Communications Security, CCS 2012, pp. 305–316. ACM, New York (2012)
44. Zhou, Z., Reiter, M.K., Zhang, Y.: A software approach to defeating side channels in last-level caches. In: Proceedings of the 2016 ACM SIGSAC Conference on Computer and Communications Security, pp. 871–882. ACM (2016)

Building Your Private Cloud Storage on Public Cloud Service Using Embedded GPUs

Wangzhao Cheng[1,2,3], Fangyu Zheng[1,2(✉)], Wuqiong Pan[1,2], Jingqiang Lin[1,2], Huorong Li[1,2,3], and Bingyu Li[1,2,3]

[1] Data Assurance and Communication Security Research Center, Beijing, China
[2] State Key Laboratory of Information Security, Institute of Information Engineering, CAS, Beijing, China
{chengwangzhao,zhengfangyu,panwuqiong,linjingqiang,lihuorong, libingyu}@iie.ac.cn
[3] School of Cyber Security, University of Chinese Academy of Sciences, Beijing, China

Abstract. When the public cloud provides infrastructure as a service (IaaS), the customer can outsource its data to the public cloud and release itself from the burden of storing data locally. At this point, the customer can not guarantee the security of the data in the public cloud. Encrypting data before using cloud storage is a viable solution, but frequent data encryption operations cause the original limited local computing resources to be even more stretched. In this paper, we used Jetson TX1 to build a client-side data encryption device that proxies the customer's data encryption and decryption operations. Firstly, a GPU-based SM4 implementation is carefully scheduled in the integrated GPU on Jetson TX1, including instruction-level optimization and variable improvement for data arrangement. Secondly, using zero-copy access on the device, we reduce the impact of explicit data transfer operations on overall performance. Finally, our SM4 kernel is capable of encrypting data at 30.30 Gbps on Jetson TX1, it is 26.6 times faster than the CPU-based implementation on the same platform. Furthermore, data processing throughput of the device reaches 30.19Gbps, a single Jetson TX1 owns sufficiently redundant computational power for the customer in 10 Gigabit fiber network environment.

Keywords: Symmetric cryptographic algorithm · Jetson TX1 CUDA · SM4 implementation · Virtual private cloud storage

W. Cheng—This work was partially supported by National 973 Program of China under Award No. 2014CB340603, National Natural Science Foundation of China under Award No. 61772518 and National Key R&D Program of China under Award No. 2017YFB0802103.

1   Introduction

With the advent of networking technology, companies and individuals are dealing with more and more online affairs, and it has led to a dramatic rise in networking, data storage and computing needs. Simple addition of local computing infrastructure often results in a sharp increase in costs and unnecessary waste of resources, and it prompts these organizations to seek affordable solutions from public cloud technologies. Using Microsoft's Azure storage service and Amazons S3 as examples, compared with building and maintaining a private storage infrastructure, customers can simply move their data to public clouds, and then public clouds provide scalable and dynamic storage at a relatively inexpensive price. For most customers, public cloud solutions have obvious advantages in cost control, management and maintenance.

Using public cloud service has significant benefits, it brings new security and privacy risks at the same time. For storage services based on public clouds, all infrastructures are owned and totally controlled by the cloud service provider. Customers make use of the storage infrastructure through the provider, and they have no administrative rights for the infrastructure that is not located locally. There is no way for the customer to ensure that cloud service providers are legally authorized (In private cloud, the infrastructure is located in customer's region of control, but the cost of building and maintaining a private cloud platform remains substantial, and public cloud is still the main choice). Security protocols like SSL, TLS, IPSec, can be applied to guarantee the confidentiality and integrity of data during transmission over the Internet. However, in these protocols, both the cloud service provider and the client can obtain the secret key. It means that user's privacy data could be maliciously acquired by the cloud service provider, even these security protocols were well applied. On the other hand, these large cloud service providers are also the target of various malicious attacks, secret keys in the cloud service provider also has the risk of being stolen. Public cloud security incidents, like Apple's iCloud leaking user's private photos [17] and Dropbox leaking user's passwords [7], seriously affected the prospect of public cloud.

Kamara and Lauter think that concerning data's confidentiality and integrity is the biggest obstacle for the adoption of cloud storage and cloud computing [10]. In their work, they proposed an idea of using mature symmetric cryptographic techniques to provide virtual private storage service on public cloud infrastructure, which helps users to get credible cloud storage services on untrusted public cloud. Their work offered no concrete implementation, and under practical situations, frequently encrypting data on the client side brings intense consumption on the limited local computing resources. It runs counter to our original intention of using public cloud to save local resources.

In this paper, we solve these problems above by using Jetson TX1 to build a data encryption and decryption proxy device that locates in client's intranet and controlled by the customer. The device encrypts the data sent to the public cloud and decrypts the returned ciphertext, so customers do not need to change the original network architecture, nor do they need to add data encryption and decryption operations on the client side, they can convert the unreliable, uncontrollable cloud storage services provided by public clouds into virtual private cloud services, which is reliable and controllable.

In fact, Jetson TX1 and other embedded GPUs are wildly applied in many research fields, like deep neural networks [24] and computer-vision [23], however, they are seldom involved in research of cryptography. Motivated by this situation, we introduce Jetson TX1 to build virtual private cloud storage on public cloud infrastructure. Our work focuses on the following aspects.

1. Speeding up the SM4 kernel on Jetson TX1. First, we implemented a PTX-version round function on Jetson TX1 for SM4 algorithm. Then we reasonably allocated Jetson TX1's storage resources, and found the most suitable choice through comparison. Finally, our GPU-based SM4 implementation reached 30.30Gbps at its peak rate, which is 26.6 times faster than the CPU-based one on the same platform.
2. Designing secret key's architecture. First, setting secret key and generating round keys were completed before the data processing stage, it saved unnecessary cost of round key generation. On the other hand, the device had no IP address while working, so secret key was safer in it, as it was harder to be attacked remotely.
3. Reducing the performance degradation caused by data transfer. The CPU and the GPU on Jetson TX1 shared an unified DRAM memory, and compared with the multi-stream technology commonly used on desktop GPUs, we found that zero-copy memory is more efficiency on Jetson TX1 with no negative effects, and this can also be applied to other symmetric cryptographic algorithms, not only to our SM4 implementation.

The rest of our paper is organized as follow: Sect. 2 reviews the related works on GPUs, especially on embedded GPUs. Section 3 presents the overview of Jetson TX1, CUDA, and SM4 symmetric algorithm. Section 4 describes in detail about how to enhance SM4 on Jetson TX1, and the strategy to build our data processor for cryptographic cloud storage. Section 5 evaluates the performance of proposed implementation. Section 6 concludes the paper.

2   Related Works

The SM4 algorithm was declassified in 2006 and standardized in 2012 as Chinese standard symmetric cipher. Researchers have done a lot of works on its security problems and attacking methods [13]. At the same time, there are relatively few studies on high performance SM4 implementation, and in practical applications, the performance bottleneck severely limits the usability of SM4 algorithm.

As the dedicated graphics processor, GPUs are originally developed to accelerate the manipulation for computer graphics, and its main content of the research is concentrated in this field. However, researchers have been trying to expand GPU's general-purpose computing power [1] in the field of cryptographic algorithms. Before CUDA even exists, using libraries specifically developed for

3D image processing, like Direct3D and OpenGL, AES has been run and accelerated successfully on GPUs [3]. Moss et al. [18] and Fleissner et al. [5] used GPUs to implement the modular exponentiation. In 2007, NVIDIA corporation introduced the CUDA (Compute Unified Device Architecture) API [12], which made it simplified for developers to involve the GPU hardware when designing parallelization within applications [16]. Since then, more cryptographic algorithms were scheduled in GPUs for better performance, including both symmetric algorithms (like AES [15] and DES [14]) and asymmetric algorithms (like ECC [31] and RSA [30]). Compared with other implementations, GPUs can greatly improve the algorithm's implementing rate, and reduce the delay, Gilger et al. used GPUs to accelerate all these symmetric algorithms in OpenSSL cryptographic library [8]. GPUs were also used as a general-purpose accelerator to improve whole system's computing capability [2].

Compared with desktop GPUs, which has been broadly studied and addressed in cryptography, fewer studies are contributing to mobile and embedded GPUs. In fact, embedded GPUs have huge advantages in achieving the higher performance and better power efficiency, which is purposed in practical applications, and also valuable to the customer in public cloud environment. Declared as *"the ideal platform for compute-intensive embedded projects"* by Nvidia [20], Jetson TX1 has been widely used in the field of computer vision [23], deep neural networks [24], and even for the classical molecular dynamics algorithms [19]. Due to the hardware and software constraints and dependencies, naively porting optimizations for desktop GPUs to embedded GPUs might not work. Furthermore, embedded devices have limited storage capacity available, realization of high-performance symmetric algorithms on low-power embedded GPUs platform is still challenging due to its massive computational and storage requirements.

3   Background

3.1   NVIDIA Jetson TX1 and CUDA

The embedded platform we used in the paper is Nvidia's Jetson TX1, which is a single-board computer containing low power consumption ARM CPUs and an integrated GPU. Its architecture is shown in Fig. 1. Jetson TX1 is based on the 64-bit Tegra X1 SoC [19], the integrated GPU owns 1 copy engine for data transfer, and 2 streaming multiprocessors (SM) for data processing. Each SM contains 128 single precision CUDA cores and 512 bytes texture alignment, and they shared 256 KB L2 cache. When using this GPU to complete transactions, 32 threads within one SM grouped as a warp and ran in a clock concurrently. All GPU threads followed the Single Instruction Multiple Threads (SIMT) architecture. In order to improve resource utilization, the warp may be preempted when it is stalled, and the runtime context switches to another one, so SMs are always hold occupied. Multiple warps of threads assigned to one SM are called block. A block can contain up to 1024 GPU threads, and each block could access 48 KB fast shared memory and 32 KB registers.

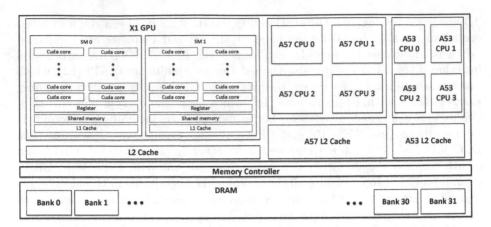

Fig. 1. NVIDIA Jetson TX1's architecture

Apart from the integrated GPU, Jetson TX1 contains 4 high performance Cortex-A57 cores (1.9 GHz), and 4 lower performance Cortex-A53 cores (1.3 GHz) [29], Cortex-A53 cores are only available to software in low-power modes. Each Cortex-A57 core has 48 KB L1 instruction cache and 32 KB L1 data cache, and these four cores shared 2 MB L2 cache together. Cortex-A53 cores owns 32 KB L1 instruction cache and 32 KB L1 data cache, and shared 512 KB L2 cache.

3.2 SM4 Symmetric Algorithm

As a 32 round unbalanced Feistel cipher, both the processing block and the key of SM4 are 128-bit. It is Chinese standard symmetric cipher for data confidentiality [13] and its security strength is same to that of AES-128.

4 Implementation Architecture

As mentioned above, when the public cloud provides IaaS [27], the customer was able to build a virtual private cloud based on public cloud infrastructure and obtain encrypted cloud storage [10,25]. However, it required to complete data encryption locally, which would result in a shortage of local computing resources. To solve this problem, we schedule a fast SM4 kernel on the integrated GPU, and designed sane usage strategy that suits the public cloud application environment. We used Jetson TX1 to build a data encryption and decryption proxy device located in the customer's network, and this section describes the detail.

4.1 Scheduling SM4 on Jetson TX1

To accelerate SM4 algorithm on integrated GPUs, naively porting a software implementation is unable to meet the requirement. On the other hand, optimizations for desktop GPUs cannot be directly used on mobile platforms due to hardware and software constraints and dependencies. Therefore, we need to redesign complete optimization solutions for SM4 algorithm on Jetson TX1.

As mentioned above, the algorithm needs 32 times of round function to complete a data block encryption, and we tried to speed up this part using the *parallel thread execution* (PTX) instruction set [22]. PTX is a pseudo-assembly language used in Nvidia's CUDA programming environment [28]. When compiling the CUDA source code, which is written in a C-like language or other forms, the *nvcc* compiler translates it into PTX instructions, then the graphics driver turns these translated PTX instructions into binary codes that can run on the CUDA core. Using the PTX instruction set, we are able to accurately control the usage of GPU's resources, thereby improving the overall program's operational efficiency.

The main commands of the round operation in SM4 encryption are bitwise exclusive OR, left circular shift operation and non-linear transformation. Among them, bitwise exclusive OR and left circular shift operation were accomplished by PTX instructions. For bitwise exclusive OR, *xor.b32* was the option. For left circular shift operation, we first left-shifted the input with *shl.b32*, then use *shr.b32* to right-shifted the input by corresponding bits, and finally used *or.b32* to generate the result. For non-linear permutations, using arithmetic calculations is very computationally expensive and complex. Querying the pre-allocated and assigned memory space [8] is a common practice to achieve non-linear permutation. And in our work, we built a 256 bytes size S-Box. To implement the non-linear permutations for a 32-bit block, it needed to query the S-Box for 4 times. Algorithm 1 shows the detailed implementation of the round function.

In order to evaluate whether our optimization is effective, we compared the overall throughput of the algorithm before and after optimization. In the test, the program owned one block with 512 GPU threads in it, and every thread encoded 1024 bytes data. Finally, the overall throughput of the optimized kernel was 2.864 Gbps, and the unoptimized result was 2.128 Gbps, Our optimization method improved the utilization of hardware resources and the overall performance under the same test environment. In the following process, we would still do similar comparisons to confirm the effectiveness of our optimizations.

To enhance the performance of the SM4 kernel, reasonable memory arrangement was also needed. CUDA-enabled GPUs provide a variety of storage resources, including global memory, constant memory, shared memory, and 32-bit register. It is essential to choose proper arrangement for data used in the algorithm, including *S-Box* (as mentioned above, it was used to achieve non-linear transformation) and *plaintext/ciphertext*.

For the S-Box, constant memory, shared memory, and 32-bit register are all options to speed up its accessing rate. Among them, register is the fastest. However, on-chip register is scarce, overuse would decline the number of concurrent threads running on each SM and result in overall performance degradation. In order to reduce the usage of register, we made 32 GPU threads within a warp to co-store a set of 256 bytes S-Box, the specific implementation is as follows: In the warp, a 256 bytes S-Box was equally assigned to 32 GPU threads, and what

Algorithm 1. The Round Function

Input:

   $X_i, X_{i+1}, X_{i+2}, X_{i+3}, rk_i$:

   $X_i, X_{i+1}, X_{i+2}, X_{i+3}, rk_i \in Z_2^{32}$ and $i = 0, 1, ..., 31$;

Output:

   X_{i+4}: $X_{i+4} \in Z_2^{32}$ and $i = 0, 1, ..., 31$;

1: unsigned int t;

2: asm volatile

3: ("{\t\n"

4:      "$xor.b32$ %0, %1, %2 ; \t\n"

5:      "$xor.b32$ %0, %0, %3 ; \t\n"

6:      "$xor.b32$ %0, %0, %4 ; \t\n"

7:      "}"

8:      :" + r"(t): "r"(X_{i+1}), "r"(X_{i+2}),

                "r"(X_{i+3}), "r"(rk_i)

9:);

10: unsigned char *$pchar$ = (unsigned char *)&t;

11: **for** $i = 0$ to 3 **do**

12:    $pchar[i] = device\_sbox[pchar[i]]$;

13: **end for**

14: asm volatile

15: ("{\t\n"

16:      ".$reg.b32$ a ; \t\n"

17:      ".$reg.b32$ b ; \t\n"

18:      "$xor.b32$ %0, %0, %1 ; \t\n"

19:      "$shl.b32$ a, %1, 2 ; \t\n"

20:      "$shr.b32$ a, %1, 30 ; \t\n"

21:      "$or.b32$ a, a, b ; \t\n"

22:      "$xor.b32$ %0, %0, a ; \t\n"

23:      "$shl.b32$ a, %1, 10 ; \t\n"

24:      "$shr.b32$ a, %1, 22 ; \t\n"

25:      "$or.b32$ a, a, b ; \t\n"

26:      "$xor.b32$ %0, %0, a ; \t\n"

27:      "$shl.b32$ a, %1, 18 ; \t\n"

28:      "$shr.b32$ a, %1, 14 ; \t\n"

29:      "$or.b32$ a, a, b ; \t\n"

30:      "$xor.b32$ %0, %0, a ; \t\n"

31:      "$shl.b32$ a, %1, 24 ; \t\n"

32:      "$shr.b32$ a, %1, 8 ; \t\n"

33:      "$or.b32$ a, a, b ; \t\n"

34:      "$xor.b32$ %0, %0, a ; \t\n"

35:      "}"

36:      : " + r"(X_i) : "r"(t)

37:);

38: return $X_{i+4} = X_i$;

a thread got depends on its thread ID. When to perform non-linear transformation, the thread used the instruction *shuffle* twice to share its own two register to all threads and get the data it needed. In this way, every thread only used 2 registers, instead of 64. In addition to this scheme, constant memory and shared memory can also be used to store S-Box. We tested these three optimization solutions separately, and when the S-Box was stored in constant memory, the implementation was the fastest. Due to multiple usage of instruction *shuffle*, this implementation of using registers had a sharp decline in performance, however, it is resistant to key recovery timing attack [9].

For the plaintext/ciphertext, they were both stored in global memory. Compared with other memory space, the bandwidth of global memory was lower, and non-optimal global memory access had a higher impact on the performance. We took advantage of coalesced access to reduce the generated transactions when accessing the global memory. First, when accessing data in the global memory, each GPU thread accessed a 128-bit block at one time (This is exactly the size of input block for SM4 algorithm). Further, we split the concatenated plaintext into several 128-bit blocks and rearranged their location, and ensuring when GPU threads were ordered to access plaintext/ciphertext in the global memory, the warp was accessing a continuous memory space, not multiple discrete data fragments. Then we evaluated the effect of our optimization. Before optimization, the kernel's throughput is 4.44 Gbps, and after optimization, it increased to 6.048 Gbps. Coalesced access improved the accessing speed of the plaintext/ciphertext in the global memory, thereby enhanced the overall performance of the implementation.

It is worth mentioning, that these optimization methods for SM4's S-Box and plaintext/ciphertext on Jetson TX1, could also be applied to other symmetric cryptographic algorithms as well. Take AES for an example, it can also achieve non-linear transformation by accessing pre-allocated space, and its plaintext/ciphertext would also be stored in the global memory due to its size.

Finally, we adjusted the integrated GPU's concurrency strategy. Compared with desktop GPU, SMs in Jetson TX1 own less register. In GTX1080 [26], there is 64 K 32-bit register on each SM, and in Jetson TX1, the number dropped to 32k. When we did the algorithmic acceleration on the GTX1080, we set 1024 threads per block, however, on Jetson TX1, we cut it down by half to 512, and used 4 block to make the most of Jetson TX1's 2 SMs.

Fig. 2. How Jetson TX1 works in public cloud

4.2 Key's Architecture

Secret key is an integral part of data encryption. In SM4 algorithm, the secret key needed to be expanded into round keys, and then used for each round of data processing. To release the GPU from repeated round keys extension, the program expanded round keys just after the device administrator set the secret key at the beginning of the system startup. When GPU threads processed data, the program first loaded these round keys into shared memory, and then did following steps. Compared with the global memory, shared memory is on chip, so its accessing rate is much higher, and on the other hand, register is too small to store round keys.

To protect user's data on the public cloud, we added one Jetson TX1 to the original network topology, and how it works was shown in Fig. 2. Our device was working at the MAC layer, and it was transparent to both the customer and the service provider. Both its two physical network interfaces, one was connected to the customer and another was connected to the Internet, had no IP address. It increased the difficulty of remote access by attackers, and it was a safer environment for the secret key. On the basis of the original service, when the customer uploaded data to the public cloud, plaintext data first needed to pass through Jetson TX1. After Jetson TX1 encrypted these data packets, it forwarded them to the public cloud. So data stored in the public cloud was ciphertext. When the customer downloaded data from the public cloud, ciphertext data first was decrypted by Jetson TX1 and then forwarded to the customer. In this way, we provide virtual private storage service on public cloud, and the whole process is transparent to both the customer and the service provider.

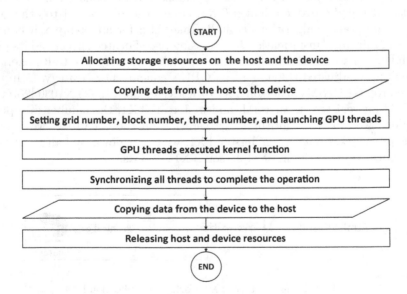

Fig. 3. The flow of a normal CUDA-based program

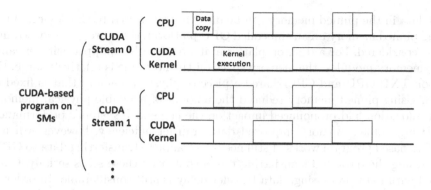

Fig. 4. How a multi-stream CUDA-based program works

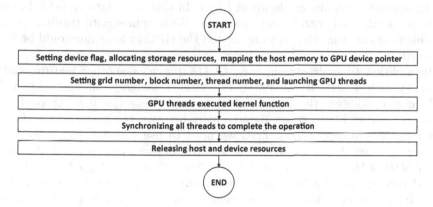

Fig. 5. The flow of a zero-copy access CUDA-based program

4.3   Using Jetson TX1 as the Cryptographic Engine

After optimizing SM4 kernel on Jetson TX1, we used the kernel to complete the data encryption operation. Figure 3 shows the flow of how a normal CUDA-based program works. For a CUDA-based realized layer, the input data first must be transferred from the host (CPU) memory to the device (GPU) memory, then CUDA cores follow the kernel function to process data, finally copy the output back to the host memory. For SM4 algorithm, the amount of its input and output data is huge, data transfer is inevitable and affects the overall performance of the system.

By default, memory allocated on the host memory are pageable. To transfer the data from the pageable host memory to the device memory, the CUDA driver first needs to allocate and copy the data to a pinned memory (page-lock memory), and then transfers the data from the pinned memory to the device memory. These extra pinned memory allocation and data transfer from pageable host memory to pinned host memory can be avoided. CUDA provides special APIs, like *"cudaHostAlloc()"*, to allocate pinned memory in the host memory, and data in the pinned memory can be directly transferred to the device. When using pinned memory on an embedded GPU platform, there are some constraints to be considered. For a desktop platform, it was usually equipped with expandable memory modules, the memory space on the host side is relatively large. On Jetson TX1, GPU and CPU shared a piece of physical memory that is fixed at 4GB. Using pinned memory reduced the amount of available physical memory, over-allocation had pronounced impact on the embedded system's performance.

Using pinned memory improved data transfer efficiency, however, when a CUDA-based program works, it still needs to complete transferring data to GPU, processing the data and transferring the output back these steps serially. Compared with data processing, data transfer delay is still considerable. In order to improve the overall performance on this basis, we scheduled and pipelined the kernel function and data transfer between the host memory and the device memory in multiple streams, as shown in Fig. 4. In this way, data transfer latency could be overlapped with kernel execution. With appropriate turning, it was possible to ensure that the copy engine and the GPU at least one could be fully occupied.

In addition to multi-stream way, CUDA provides another feature, called zero-copy access [21]. By mapping the pinned memory on host side to a GPU device pointer, the kernel function can access the data through the device pointer without explicit data transfer between the host and the device. When using zero-copy access, first, we need to use the statement "*cudaSet-DeviceFlags(cudaDeviceMapHost)*" to set the device flag, and call the function"*cudaHostAlloc*" with a special flag "*cudaHostAllocMapped*" to allocate pinned memory on the host side. Then using the function "*cudaHostGetDevicePointer*" to map the allocated memory space to device pointers. When these operations are completed, the kernel can directly fetch data from the host through the device pointers. So the flow of a zero-copy access CUDA-based program was simplified and optimized as shown in Fig. 5.

Compared with Fig. 3, the new program had no data transfer operation between the host and the device, and those extra configurations and function call operations for zero-copy access could be set up in the system initialization phase. In this way, data transfer posed little overhead on the whole performance, and the program used the single default stream to achieve the best performance.

Comparing these two optimization strategies, the program using zero-copy access do not need explicit data transfer. However, due to the black-box nature of CUDA, when programmers used the function "*cudaMemcpy*" to complete the data transfer, its efficiency can not be precisely controlled. Similarly, there is a potential compromise in data accessing rate when using zero-copy memory. Zero-copy access is completed under CUDA's assistant, both its working mechanism and operating efficiency are not clear to us. In [4], programmers thought that zero-copy access was not the best choice when there is not much computation to perform. So we tried both these two strategies on Jetson TX1 and compared their results to find out which is better.

5   Performance Assessment

Based on our GPU-based SM4 implementation, we have achieved ECB, CBC and CTR these mainstream data encryption modes. And in this section, we evaluated the performance of our SM4 kernel on Jetson TX1, and compared it with the common CPU-based implementation. In the meantime, we analyzed the impact of these two optimization strategies on data transfer, data access, and kernel execution efficiency (multi-stream and zero-copy access, used to reduce performance degradation from data transfer, as mentioned above). And chose the appropriate one for our device. Detailed information about Jetson TX1's hardware was provided in Sect. 3, and the OS runs on the platform was Ubuntu 16.04, the compiler we used is GCC 5.4.0 and CUDA toolkit 8.0.

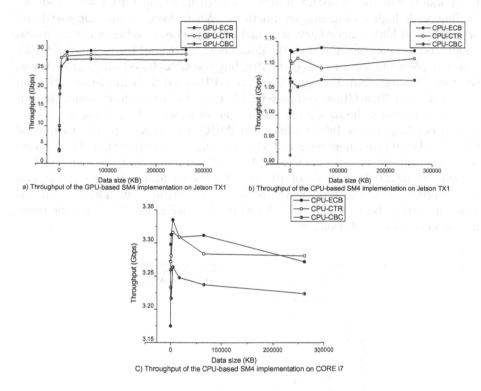

a) Throughput of the GPU-based SM4 implementation on Jetson TX1

b) Throughput of the CPU-based SM4 implementation on Jetson TX1

C) Throughput of the CPU-based SM4 implementation on CORE i7

Fig. 6. Throughput of GPU-based SM4 implementation and CPU-based SM4 implementation

5.1   Kernel Speed

The performance text was run on Jetson TX1. To evaluate our GPU-based SM4 implementation, we used our kernel to encrypt data of different sizes and counted the throughput. In our implementation, the S-Box was stored in the constant memory, plaintext/ciphertext was stored in the global memory, round keys were generated by the CPU in the initial stage and then stored in the shared memory. Each block had 512 threads, and a total of four blocks were called to maximize the computing power of the integrated GPU on Jetson TX1. For the CPU-based SM4 implementation, we tested its performance both on Jetson TX1's quad core CPU and on a laptop with a Intel CORE i7-6820HQ CPU and 16 GB memory. To make the most of CPU's capability, multiple threads was called, and all these data, including S-Box, round keys and plaintext/ciphertext were stored in the host memory, and round keys were also pre-generated before the data encryption operation starts. When measuring the consumption time, we only considered the data encoding time, without considering the data transfer delay.

We tested the performance of both GPU-based SM4 implementation and CPU-based SM4 implementation when they encrypted data in ECB, CBC and CTR mode, and the final test results is shown in Fig. 6. GPUs were good at dealing with high concurrent transactions. When data volume increased, its advantages of high concurrency were highlighted. The experimental results also supported this conclusion. When the data grew, the overall throughput of GPU-based implementation increased rapidly, but the CPU-based one's growth was limited. The maximum throughput of our GPU-based SM4 implementation on Jetson TX1 is 30.30 Gbps, compared with the CPU-based implementation on the same platform, the maximum throughput of which is 1.14 Gbps, it is about 26.6 times higher. On Intel CORE i7-6820HQ, the maximum throughput of the CPU-based implementation is 3.34 Gbps, and compared with it, GPU-based implementation still has obvious advantages. Considering that the bandwidth of current 10 Gigabit fiber is about 10 Gbps, for the customer, the computational power provided by the SM4 kernel is sufficiently redundant. The CPU-based implementation, both on Jetson TX1 and Intel CORE i7-6820HQ, has the problem of insufficient performance.

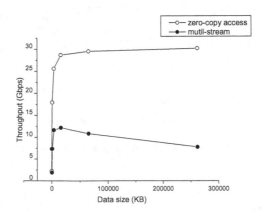

Fig. 7. Throughput of CUDA-based program using multi-stream and zero-copy memory on Jetson TX1

5.2 Multi-stream Vs. Zero-Copy Access

Using GPUs to complete the symmetric cryptographic operation, the impact of data transfer between the host memory and the device memory can not be ignored. On the desktop GPU, it is a common practice to use multi-stream method to overlap data transfer with data process operation. However, even after optimization, data transfer is still the performance bottleneck in practical applications. On embedded GPUs like the TX1, the CPU and the GPU shared a unified DRAM memory, and CUDA provides other efficient mechanism to omit explicit data transfer operation, which is called zero-copy access. The working mechanism is not clear, and its optimization effect also needs to be judged, so we compared the performance of programs using these two strategies, to find out which is better. In the experiment, two CUDA-based programs using different strategies encrypted varied sizes of data on Jetson TX1, and we tested the throughput. For the program that uses multi-stream, memory allocation, data initialization and round key generation were completed in the initialization phase, We measured only the time consumed by the necessary operations for data encryption, including data transfer and data processing. For the program that uses zero-copy access, data was not explicitly copied from the CPU to the GPU and vice versa, so we measured GPU's computing time. Similarly, device flag setting, memory allocation, mapping device pointer to the host memory were also done with other operations in the system initialization phase.

The kernel optimization strategies for both program were the same, for zero-copy access program, its default stream owns 4 blocks, but for the multi-stream one, it has 8 streams and each stream owns only one block to achieve the best performance. The test result of these programs is shown in Fig. 7. The maximum throughput of the zero-copy access program is 30.19 Gbps, compared with that of the multi-stream program, which is 12.16 Gbps, it is 2.48 times higher. It should be noted that, compared to the multi-stream, zero-copy access program significantly reduces the precious memory consumption on the DRAM, as the DRAM on Jetson TX1 is fixed and non-expandable. At least, there is no need to allocate memory space for the device in the DRAM. For GPU-based SM4 implementation on Jetson TX1, zero-copy access was a more suitable optimization strategy. On the other hand, we found that when using zero-copy memory, the throughput of the program is almost the same to the kernel when only considering the data encryption on the GPU (as shown in Fig. 6(a), the maximum throughput of the kernel is 30.30 Gbps). It proved that using zero-copy memory had no negative impact on the data accessing nor on the kernel execution, and it released GPU's computing capability from the bottleneck of data transfer on Jetson TX1. Zero-copy access can also be applied to enhance the performance of other symmetric cryptographic algorithms on the Jetson TX1.

6 Conclusion

In this paper, we have presented how to use embedded GPUs to build virtual private cloud environment on public cloud infrastructure to provide secure and inexpensive encrypted cloud storage service. On the integrated GPU in Jetson TX1, the maximum throughput of our GPU-based SM4 kernel reaches 30.30 Gbps, it is 26.6 times faster than the CPU-based implementation on the same platform. We have omitted explicit data transfer operation from our program with no negative impacts on the kernel's performance, and the data encryption and decryption proxy device can provide 30.19 Gbps data processing capabilities, it means that one single Jetson TX1 is sufficient for the customer in 10 Gigabit fiber network environment. And we also found, for symmetric cryptographic algorithms or other GPU applications with heavy data transfer burden on Jetson TX1, data transfer was no longer the performance bottleneck.

In the future, we would continue to improve the performance of our GPU-based SM4 implementation on Jetson TX1. On the other hand, our existing work was vulnerable to timing-attack [6], malicious public cloud service providers and users hidden in customer's intranet (for example, a malicious programs buried in the customer's intranet) can collaborate to recover the secret key [9]. Using register to store S-Box that mentioned in our article might be a solution, but it drew down the performance. Timing-attack resistant bitsliced implementation [11] is another possible solution, and this would be our following work.

References

1. General Purpose Computation Using Graphics Hardware. http://gpgpu.org/. Accessed 10 Dec 2014
2. Cheng, W., Zheng, F., Pan, W., Lin, J., Li, H., Li, B.: High-performance symmetric cryptography server with GPU acceleration. In: Qing, S., Mitchell, C., Chen, L., Liu, D. (eds.) ICICS 2017. LNCS, vol. 10631, pp. 529–540. Springer, Cham (2018). https://doi.org/10.1007/978-3-319-89500-0_46
3. Cook, D.L., Ioannidis, J., Keromytis, A.D., Luck, J.: CryptoGraphics: secret key cryptography using graphics cards. In: Menezes, A. (ed.) CT-RSA 2005. LNCS, vol. 3376, pp. 334–350. Springer, Heidelberg (2005). https://doi.org/10.1007/978-3-540-30574-3_23
4. CygnusX1. Default Pinned Memory Vs Zero-Copy Memory. https://stackoverflow.com/questions/5209214/default-pinned-memory-vs-zero-copy-memory (2017). Accessed 10 Dec 2014
5. Fleissner, S.: GPU-accelerated montgomery exponentiation. In: Shi, Y., van Albada, G.D., Dongarra, J., Sloot, P.M.A. (eds.) ICCS 2007. LNCS, vol. 4487, pp. 213–220. Springer, Heidelberg (2007). https://doi.org/10.1007/978-3-540-72584-8_28
6. Fomin, D.B.: A timing attack on CUDA implementations of an AES-type block cipher. Mat. Vopr. Kriptogr. **7**(2), 121–130 (2016)
7. Gibbs, S.: Dropbox hack leads to leaking of 68m user passwords on the internet. https://www.theguardian.com/technology/2016/aug/31/dropbox-hack-passwords-68m-data-breach (2016). Accessed 8 Dec 2014
8. Gilger, J., Barnickel, J., Meyer, U.: GPU-acceleration of block ciphers in the OpenSSL cryptographic library. In: Gollmann, D., Freiling, F.C. (eds.) ISC 2012. LNCS, vol. 7483, pp. 338–353. Springer, Heidelberg (2012). https://doi.org/10.1007/978-3-642-33383-5_21

9. Jiang, Z.H., Fei, Y., Kaeli, D.: A complete key recovery timing attack on a GPU. In: 2016 IEEE International Symposium on High Performance Computer Architecture (HPCA), pp. 394–405. IEEE (2016)

10. Kamara, S., Lauter, K.: Cryptographic cloud storage. In: Sion, R., Curtmola, R., Dietrich, S., Kiayias, A., Miret, J.M., Sako, K., Sebé, F. (eds.) FC 2010. LNCS, vol. 6054, pp. 136–149. Springer, Heidelberg (2010). https://doi.org/10.1007/978-3-642-14992-4_13

11. Käsper, E., Schwabe, P.: Faster and timing-attack resistant AES-GCM. In: Clavier, C., Gaj, K. (eds.) CHES 2009. LNCS, vol. 5747, pp. 1–17. Springer, Heidelberg (2009). https://doi.org/10.1007/978-3-642-04138-9_1

12. Kirk, D.B., Wen-Mei, W.H.: Programming Massively Parallel Processors: A Hands-on Approach. Morgan kaufmann, Burlington (2016)

13. Liu, F., Ji, W., Hu, L., Ding, J., Lv, S., Pyshkin, A., Weinmann, R.-P.: Analysis of the SMS4 block cipher. In: Pieprzyk, J., Ghodosi, H., Dawson, E. (eds.) ACISP 2007. LNCS, vol. 4586, pp. 158–170. Springer, Heidelberg (2007). https://doi.org/10.1007/978-3-540-73458-1_13

14. Luken, B.P., Ouyang, M., Desoky, A.H.: AES and DES encryption with GPU. In: ISCA PDCCS, pp. 67–70 (2009)

15. Manavski, S.A.: CUDA compatible GPU as an efficient hardware accelerator for AES cryptography. In: 2007 IEEE International Conference on Signal Processing and Communications. ICSPC 2007, pp. 65–68. IEEE (2007)

16. Mei, C., Jiang, H., Jenness, J.: CUDA-based AES parallelization with fine-tuned GPU memory utilization. In: 2010 IEEE International Symposium on Parallel & Distributed Processing, Workshops and Phd Forum (IPDPSW), pp. 1–7. IEEE (2010)

17. Molina, B.: iCloud not breached in celebrity photo leak. https://www.usatoday.com/story/tech/personal/2014/09/02/apple-icloud-leak/14979323/ (2014). Accessed 10 Dec 2014

18. Moss, A., Page, D., Smart, N.P.: Toward acceleration of RSA using 3D graphics hardware. In: Galbraith, S.D. (ed.) Cryptography and Coding 2007. LNCS, vol. 4887, pp. 364–383. Springer, Heidelberg (2007). https://doi.org/10.1007/978-3-540-77272-9_22

19. Nikolskiy, V.P., Stegailov, V.V., Vecher, V.S.: Efficiency of the Tegra k1 and x1 systems-on-chip for classical molecular dynamics. In: 2016 International Conference on High Performance Computing & Simulation (HPCS), pp. 682–689. IEEE (2016)

20. NVIDIA: Embedded Systems. https://www.nvidia.com/en-us/autonomous-machines/embedded-systems/. Accessed 8 Dec 2014

21. NVIDIA: CUDA Toolkit Documentation v9.1.85. http://docs.nvidia.com/cuda/ (2017). Accessed 10 Dec 2014

22. NVIDIA: Parallel Thread Execution ISA Version 6.1. http://docs.nvidia.com/cuda/parallel-thread-execution/ (2017). Accessed 10 Dec 2014

23. Otterness, N., et al.: An evaluation of the nvidia tx1 for supporting real-time computer-vision workloads. In: 2017 IEEE Real-Time and Embedded Technology and Applications Symposium (RTAS), pp. 353–364. IEEE (2017)

24. Rizvi, S.T.H., Cabodi, G., Francini, G.: Optimized deep neural networks for real-time object classification on embedded GPUS. Appl. Sci. **7**(8), 826 (2017)

25. Wikipedia: Cloud computing. https://en.wikipedia.org/wiki/Cloud_computing (2017). Accessed 10 Dec 2014

26. Wikipedia. GeForce 10 series. https://en.wikipedia.org/wiki/GeForce_10_series (2017). Accessed 10 Dec 2014

27. Wikipedia: Infrastructure as a service. https://en.wikipedia.org/wiki/Infrastructure_as_a_service (2017). Accessed 10 Dec 2014
28. Wikipedia: Parallel Thread Execution. https://en.wikipedia.org/wiki/Parallel_Thread_Execution (2017). Accessed 10 Dec 2014
29. Wikipedia: Tegra. https://en.wikipedia.org/wiki/Tegra#Jetson_TX1 (2017). Accessed 10 Dec 2014
30. Zheng, F., Pan, W., Lin, J., Jing, J., Zhao, Y.: Exploiting the floating-point computing power of GPUs for RSA. In: Chow, S.S.M., Camenisch, J., Hui, L.C.K., Yiu, S.M. (eds.) ISC 2014. LNCS, vol. 8783, pp. 198–215. Springer, Cham (2014). https://doi.org/10.1007/978-3-319-13257-0_12
31. Zheng, F., Pan, W., Lin, J., Jing, J., Zhao, Y.: Exploiting the potential of GPUs for modular multiplication in ECC. In: Rhee, K.-H., Yi, J.H. (eds.) WISA 2014. LNCS, vol. 8909, pp. 295–306. Springer, Cham (2015). https://doi.org/10.1007/978-3-319-15087-1_23

Secure and Efficient Outsourcing of Large-Scale Overdetermined Systems of Linear Equations

Shiran Pan[1,2,3], Wen-Tao Zhu[2(✉)], Qiongxiao Wang[1,2], and Bing Chang[4]

[1] State Key Laboratory of Information Security,
Institute of Information Engineering, Chinese Academy of Sciences,
Beijing, China
{panshiran,wangqiongxiao}@iie.ac.cn
[2] Data Assurance and Communication Security Research Center,
Chinese Academy of Sciences, Beijing, China
wtzhu@ieee.org
[3] School of Cyber Security, University of Chinese Academy of Sciences,
Beijing, China
[4] School of Information Systems, Singapore Management University,
Singapore, Singapore
bingchang@smu.edu.sg

Abstract. We address overdetermined systems of linear equations, where the number of unknowns is smaller than the number of equations so that only approximate solutions exist instead of exact solutions. Such systems are prevalent in many areas of science and engineering, and finding the optimal solutions is mathematically known as the linear least squares (LLS) problem. Real-world overdetermined systems are often large-scale and computationally expensive to solve. Consequently, we are interested in connecting the LLS problem with cloud computing, where a resource-constrained client outsources the problem to a powerful but untrusted cloud. Among several security considerations is that the input of and solution to the LLS problem usually contain the client's private information, which necessitates privacy-preserving outsourcing. In this paper, we present a construction called Sells, which employs a mathematical method called QR decomposition to solve the above problem, in a masked yet verifiable manner. One advantage of adopting QR decomposition is that in certain circumstances, solving a batch of LLS problems only requires fully executing Sells once, where certain intermediate result can be reused and the overall efficiency is greatly improved. Theoretical analysis shows that our proposal is verifiable, recoverable, and privacy-preserving. Experiments demonstrate that a client can benefit from the scheme not only reduced computation cost but also accelerated problem solving.

Keywords: Linear equations · Overdetermined system
Linear least squares · Cloud computing · Verifiable outsourcing
Privacy preserving

© ICST Institute for Computer Sciences, Social Informatics and Telecommunications Engineering 2018
R. Beyah et al. (Eds.): SecureComm 2018, LNICST 254, pp. 529–548, 2018.
https://doi.org/10.1007/978-3-030-01701-9_29

1   Introduction

We consider, over the set of real numbers, a system of m simultaneous but independently obtained linear equations involving n unknowns $x_1, \ldots, x_n$:

$$a_{i,1}x_1 + a_{i,2}x_2 + \cdots + a_{i,n}x_n = b_i, \ i = 1, \ldots, m.$$

1.1   Overdetermined System of Linear Equations

The above system of linear equations can be equivalently represented in the matrix form of $Ax = b$, where $A = (a_{i,j}) \in \mathbb{R}^{m \times n}$ is the coefficient matrix, $b = (b_i) \in \mathbb{R}^{m \times 1}$ is the column vector of constant terms, and $x = (x_j) \in \mathbb{R}^{n \times 1}$ is the column vector of unknowns. Basically, when $m < n$, the system has an infinite number of solutions, and is said to be underdetermined. When $m = n$, under certain condition (A is invertible) the system has an exact solution $x = A^{-1}b$. This is the familiar "textbook" case. When $m > n$, the system is said to be *overdetermined*, and usually has no exact solution. This is, however, the dominant case in practice. For example, to evaluate n unknown variables in the physical world, each instance of measurement (where measurement errors are inevitable) corresponds to an independent equation; the number of measurements, m, can be sufficiently large, and the resultant overdetermined system helps lower certain deviation including measurement errors.

Concerning the above linear system $Ax = b$ we are interested in the "$m > n$" case, because a large number of real-world problems from various application fields (e.g., weather forecasts [1], wireless localization [2], and harmonics estimation in power systems [3]; more examples will be given and discussed in Sect. 4) can be reduced to solving overdetermined systems, for which approximate solutions are pursued instead of exact ones (which in fact usually do not exist). The method of linear least squares (LLS) can be used to find an *optimal* approximate solution to $Ax = b$ w.r.t. $\min_x \|b - Ax\|^2$, where $\| \cdot \|$ is the Euclidean norm (we will be more specific in Sect. 2). Finding such an optimal solution is known as the LLS problem, which is mathematically equivalent to solving the overdetermined system. Typically, the QR decomposition (a.k.a. QR factorization) [4] of the coefficient matrix is employed in favor of numerical accuracy.

1.2   Solving Large-Scale Overdetermined Systems with the Cloud

Many scientific calculation scenarios involve *large-scale* overdetermined linear systems (i.e., $m > n \gg 1$) [5], solving which often incurs prohibitive computation costs. For example, a modern laptop computer may spend as long as 2.5 min to solve an overdetermined system with ($m = 12,000, n = 6,000$), while solving an even larger one may become completely infeasible as this may cause the computer to run out of memory. A straightforward solution is to employ more powerful hardware, e.g., a workstation/desktop computer with more powerful CPU and sufficiently large memory. However, this will bring extra expenditures on hardware, and thus is uneconomical and impractical for wide use. Specifically, when a large number of independent users are involved, such hardware expenditure is inevitable for each of them and the total costs are considerably expensive. Therefore, a more cost-saving and more practical solution is preferable. Consequently, in this paper we consider the cloud computing paradigm in which a resource-constrained user, referred to as a tenant or a client, turns to a powerful cloud for assistance. That is, the majority of the workload is shifted to the cloud, which aids the client to solve large-scale overdetermined systems (equivalently, the LLS problems). By such outsourcing, the client can be freed from hardware/software constraints and enjoy the cloud's nearly unlimited computing resources in a pay-per-use manner.

An attending issue with cloud computing is that the cloud might be untrustworthy, which arouses several assurance concerns [6]. First, for commercial incentives, the cloud may be so "lazy" that it provides inaccurate or even invalid computation results, hoping not to be detected by the client. Second, the data processed and generated during the computation in the cloud often contains sensitive information about the client (proprietary scientific measurements, private financial or medical records, etc.), which may be exploited by the cloud for various purposes [7–9]. Therefore, it is of significant importance for the client to be able to verify the computation results and also to deploy appropriate mechanisms to protect sensitive data.

To address the above concerns, it is necessary for the client to transform a "local" problem like LLS into a masked yet verifiable cloud computing task. The "auxiliary" operations by the client such as transformation and verification have to be efficient (at least they should be lightweight as compared to the original problem itself, herein LLS); otherwise, the "auxiliary" operations simply negate the benefits of using cloud computing. Interestingly, as to be demonstrated in this paper, certain auxiliary operation itself can be aided by the (untrustworthy) cloud, which renders the "masked yet verifiable problem solving" a sophisticated and subtle interaction between the client and the cloud. Overall, we find secure outsourcing of LLS not only technically challenging but also intriguing.

1.3   Motivation and Technical Contributions

In the literature, observable work has been done on secure outsourcing of large-scale linear systems ([7, 9, 10], just to name a few). Nevertheless, we make the observation that previous studies focus on the familiar "textbook" case (where exact solutions exist); little has been done to address the overdetermined system (where only approximate solutions exist), or equivalently, the LLS problem. So far, how to connect cloud computing to linear least squares seems to be an unexplored question. In this paper, we make an effort to "securely" solve the LLS problem with the aid of the cloud. The technical contributions of this paper are summarized as follows:

- For the first time, we define the problem of secure outsourcing of LLS, to which the problem of solving overdetermined system of linear equations is mathematically equivalent. Accordingly, we propose a framework for privacy-preserving outsourcing, formulate the basic components, and identify the design goals.

- We present a concrete solution known as Sells (which stands for secure and efficient LLS outsourcing). Thorough theoretical analysis shows that our proposal fulfills all the design goals and simultaneously maintains efficiency. To the best of our knowledge, Sells is the first secure outsourcing scheme eligible for solving large-scale LLS problems.
- We implement and evaluate Sells concerning LLS problems of different scales (i.e., with various combinations of parameters m and n satisfying $m > n \gg 1$). Extensive experimental results obtained from our prototype demonstrate that Sells can benefit a client with reduced computation cost as well as accelerated problem solving.

This paper is organized as follows. Mathematical preliminaries are briefed in Sect. 2. The problem statement regarding solving overdetermined system with the aid of the cloud is in Sect. 3. Section 4 presents our proposal known as Sells. Theoretical analysis is conducted in Sect. 5, while efficiency performance is evaluated in Sect. 6. We discuss related work in Sect. 7. Concluding remarks are in Sect. 8.

2   Preliminaries

2.1   Matrix-Matrix Multiplication and Matrix-Vector Multiplication

For dense matrices $X \in \mathbb{R}^{l \times m}$ and $Y \in \mathbb{R}^{m \times n}$, their product is $XY \in \mathbb{R}^{l \times n}$. The computation complexity of such dense-matrix-dense-matrix multiplication is $\mathcal{O}(lmn)$. When each row of X has only 1 non-zero element, X is actually a sparse matrix and the computation complexity of the sparse-matrix-dense-matrix multiplication XY is $\mathcal{O}(ln)$. Similarly, when each column of Y has only 1 non-zero element, Y is a sparse matrix and the computation complexity of the dense-matrix-sparse-matrix multiplication XY is $\mathcal{O}(ln)$.

When $n = 1$, $Y \in \mathbb{R}^{m \times n}$ is reduced to a column vector $y \in \mathbb{R}^{m \times 1}$. The product of matrix X and vector y is also a column vector $Xy \in \mathbb{R}^{l \times 1}$. The computation complexity of such matrix-vector multiplication is $\mathcal{O}(lm)$.

2.2   Linear Least Squares (LLS)

Essentially, the LLS problem is to solve an overdetermined system of linear equations $Ax = b$, where $A \in \mathbb{R}^{m \times n}$, $b \in \mathbb{R}^{m \times 1}$, and m (the number of equations) $> n$ (the number of unknowns). As the system usually has no exact solution, we are interested in the optimal approximate solution $\tilde{x} \in \mathbb{R}^{n \times 1}$, which fits the system best. For any $x \in \mathbb{R}^{n \times 1}$, define $r = b - Ax \in \mathbb{R}^{m \times 1}$ as the residual vector. Then, the best approximation (i.e., the LLS solution) $\tilde{x}$ is attained by minimizing (the square of) r's Euclidean norm [11]:

$$\tilde{x} = \arg\min_{x} \|b - Ax\|^2 = \arg\min_{x} \|r\|^2 = \arg\min_{x} (r^T r). \tag{1}$$

2.3   Solving LLS with QR Decomposition

In linear algebra, the QR decomposition of a matrix $A \in \mathbb{R}^{m \times n}$ $(m \geq n)$ is to factor it as $A = QR$, where $Q \in \mathbb{R}^{m \times m}$ is an orthogonal matrix (i.e., $QQ^{\mathrm{T}} = I$, which is the identity matrix) and $R \in \mathbb{R}^{m \times n}$ is an upper triangular matrix. QR decomposition is one of the standard approaches to solving the LLS problem [4], which is presented as the minimization problem shown in Eq. (1).

For an overdetermined linear system $Ax = b \in \mathbb{R}^{m \times 1}$, we conduct the QR decomposition of the coefficient matrix $A \in \mathbb{R}^{m \times n}$ as

$$A = QR = \begin{bmatrix} Q_1 \in \mathbb{R}^{m \times n}, Q_2 \subset \mathbb{R}^{m \times (m-n)} \end{bmatrix} \begin{bmatrix} R_1 \in \mathbb{R}^{n \times n} \\ 0_{(m-n) \times n} \end{bmatrix},$$

where R_1 is upper triangular and $0_{(m-n) \times n}$ is a zero matrix. For any $x \in \mathbb{R}^{n \times 1}$, left-multiplying the residual vector $r = b - Ax$ with Q^{T}, we have

$$Q^{\mathrm{T}}r = Q^{\mathrm{T}}(b - Ax) = \begin{bmatrix} Q_1^{\mathrm{T}} \\ Q_2^{\mathrm{T}} \end{bmatrix} b - Q^{\mathrm{T}}Q \begin{bmatrix} R_1 \\ 0 \end{bmatrix} x = \begin{bmatrix} Q_1^{\mathrm{T}}b - R_1x \\ Q_2^{\mathrm{T}}b \end{bmatrix} = \begin{bmatrix} u \\ v \end{bmatrix}.$$

Since $QQ^{\mathrm{T}} = I$, $\|r\|^2 = r^{\mathrm{T}}r = (r^{\mathrm{T}}Q)(Q^{\mathrm{T}}r) = u^{\mathrm{T}}u + v^{\mathrm{T}}v$. Because $v = Q_2^{\mathrm{T}}b$ is independent of x, $\min \|r\|^2$ is attained only when u is a zero vector. That is, the LLS solution $\tilde{x}$ is found by solving $R_1x = Q_1^{\mathrm{T}}b$.

According to [12, Sect. 3.3.2], the QR decomposition of a matrix is not unique, and the computation cost of the decomposition is $\mathcal{O}(mn^2)$.

2.4   Random Permutation Function and Invertible Sparse Matrix

A random permutation of a set $S = \{s_1, \cdots, s_n\}$ is defined as a bijection from S to itself, denoted as $\pi : S \to S$. In Cauchy's two-rows notation [13], the elements of S are in the first row and the corresponding image elements are in the second row. The random permutation function can be expressed as:

$$\pi = \begin{pmatrix} s_1 \ s_2 \ \cdots \ s_n \\ t_1 \ t_2 \ \cdots \ t_n \end{pmatrix},$$

where $\pi(s_i) = t_i$, $i = 1, \cdots, n$. When $t_i = \pi(s_i) = s_i$, the permutation function is called identical permutation. The inverse function of π is denoted as π^{-1}, i.e., $\pi^{-1}(t_i) = s_i$. Algorithm 1 demonstrates the random permutation generation.

Based on random permutation function, an invertible sparse matrix $P \in \mathbb{R}^{m \times m}$ can be generated with the following Algorithm 2. In addition, P's inverse matrix $P^{-1} = (P^{-1}(i, j)) \in \mathbb{R}^{m \times m}$ is also a sparse matrix and can be quickly computed as

$$P^{-1}(i, j) = \omega_j^{-1} \delta_{\pi^{-1}(i), j}, \ 1 \leq i, j \leq m, \tag{2}$$

where $P^{-1}(i, j)$ is the element on the i-th row and j-th column of P^{-1}.

Algorithm 1. Generation of random permutation

Input: $S = \{s_1, \cdots, s_n\}$
Output: random permutation π of S
 1: set π to be the identical permutation of S.
 2: **for** $i = n : 2$ **do**
 3:     select a random integer j where $1 \leq j \leq i$;
 4:     swap $\pi(s_i)$ and $\pi(s_j)$.
 5: **end for**

Algorithm 2. Generation of random invertible sparse matrix

Input: security parameter λ, matrix dimension m
Output: random invertible sparse matrix $\boldsymbol{P} \in \mathbb{R}^{m \times m}$
 1: taking as input the security parameter λ, randomly, uniformly, and independently
    select m non-zero real numbers from $\mathbb{R}$: $\{\omega_1, \cdots, \omega_m\} \subset \mathbb{R}$.
 2: invoke Alg. 1 to yield a random permutation π of the integer set $\{1, 2, \cdots, m\}$.
 3: generate a sparse matrix $\boldsymbol{P} = (\boldsymbol{P}(i,j)) \in \mathbb{R}^{m \times m}$ as $\boldsymbol{P}(i,j) = \omega_i \delta_{\pi(i),j}, 1 \leq i, j \leq m$,
    where $\delta_{x,y}$ denotes the Kronecker delta function that returns 1 if $x = y$ or 0
    otherwise.

---

3   Problem Statement

3.1   System Model

Denote an LLS problem as $\mathcal{P}(\boldsymbol{A}, \boldsymbol{b})$, which takes as input $\boldsymbol{A} \in \mathbb{R}^{m \times n}$ and $\boldsymbol{b} \in \mathbb{R}^{m \times 1}$ $(m > n \gg 1)$. The solution to $\mathcal{P}$ is $\tilde{\boldsymbol{x}} \in \mathbb{R}^{n \times 1}$ sat. $\tilde{\boldsymbol{x}} = \arg\min_{\boldsymbol{x}} \|\boldsymbol{b} - \boldsymbol{A}\boldsymbol{x}\|^2$. To securely solve $\mathcal{P}(\boldsymbol{A}, \boldsymbol{b})$ with the aid of the cloud, the client needs to transform the problem $\mathcal{P}$ into a masked yet verifiable cloud computing task $\mathcal{P}'$. To this end, we consider the framework shown in Fig. 1, where the solid lines indicate certain data flows while the dashed line indicates the workflow.

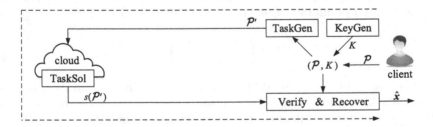

Fig. 1. Framework of LLS outsourcing involving two players, the client and the cloud. The client first generates a secret key K and uses it to convert the original LLS problem $\mathcal{P}$ to an outsourced computing task $\mathcal{P}'$. Then, it receives and verifies the solution to $\mathcal{P}'$ by the cloud, based on which it recovers $\hat{\boldsymbol{x}}$, which is expected to be the solution to $\mathcal{P}$ (i.e., to equal $\tilde{\boldsymbol{x}}$).

In this cloud computing paradigm, an LLS outsourcing scheme comprises 5 algorithms (**KeyGen, TaskGen, TaskSol, Verify, Recover**), where only

TaskSol is conducted by the cloud while others are initiated by the client. First, the client calls **KeyGen** to generate its secret key K. Then, it invokes **TaskGen** to transform a given problem $\mathcal{P}$ into a masked task $\mathcal{P}'$, which is outsourced to the cloud. Upon receiving $\mathcal{P}'$, the cloud executes **TaskSol** to return the client the solution to $\mathcal{P}'$. This intermediate result is subsequently verified by the client with **Verify**. If the result passes the verification, the client then invokes **Recover** to derive $\hat{x}$, which is expected to be the solution to the original problem $\mathcal{P}$. To prevent the cloud from acquiring sensitive information associated with $\mathcal{P}$, the secret key K is employed by the client for masking the problem, verifying the received result, and recovering the real solution.

A subtle issue may arise in the above framework. Since the client is assumed to be resource-constrained, even transforming $\mathcal{P}$ into $\mathcal{P}'$ may be too heavyweight. Actually, in our case study, the computation complexity of problem transformation happens to be on par with solving $\mathcal{P}$ itself. Thus, the client has to turn to the cloud for generating the masked task, which means the **TaskGen** module is interactive. At this stage the client does not care about the correctness of such "cloud-aided problem transformation"; all examinations are left to the **Verify** module. It may be feasible for one to design a non-interactive **TaskGen**, i.e., an algorithm that only involves the client's local processing instead of certain assistance from the cloud. We leave investigation on such feasibility as part of our future work.

3.2 Threat Model

Following [7,8,14,15], we adopt a "fully malicious" threat model where the cloud is a deceptive and/or curious adversary. Specifically, the cloud may return an invalid computation result while hoping not to be detected by the client, and/or try to infer, based on all the information it receives (referred to as the cloud's knowledge), the input of the LLS problem $\mathcal{P}$ or the solution to it.

3.3 Components: Formalized Description

1. **KeyGen**$(\lambda) \mapsto K$: Given the security parameter λ, the client executes this probabilistic key generation algorithm to yield its secret key K.
2. **TaskGen**$(\mathcal{P}, K) \mapsto \mathcal{P}'$: The client executes this probabilistic task generation algorithm to transform with K the original problem $\mathcal{P}$ into a masked computing task $\mathcal{P}'$, which is outsourced to the cloud.
3. **TaskSol**$(\mathcal{P}') \mapsto s(\mathcal{P}')$: The cloud invokes this probabilistic task solving algorithm to compute an intermediate result $s(\mathcal{P}')$, which is supposed to be a solution to the masked task $\mathcal{P}'$.
4. **Verify**$(\mathcal{P}, K, s(\mathcal{P}')) \mapsto$ `true`/`false`: The client invokes this probabilisitc verification algorithm to check with the secret key K whether $s(\mathcal{P}')$ is a valid solution to $\mathcal{P}'$ (i.e., the result of **TaskGen**$(K, \mathcal{P})$). If so, the client outputs `true`; otherwise, it outputs `false` and terminates.
5. **Recover**$(\mathcal{P}, K, s(\mathcal{P}')) \mapsto \hat{x}$: The client executes this deterministic recovery algorithm to restore $\hat{x}$ from $s(\mathcal{P}')$ with K. The final $\hat{x}$ is expected to be the solution $\tilde{x}$ to the original problem $\mathcal{P}$.

3.4   Design Goals

We identify three design goals for LLS outsourcing schemes.

Definition 1 (Verifiability). *An LLS outsourcing scheme is said to be verifiable if for any $s(\mathcal{P}')$ that is returned by the cloud but not a valid solution to $\mathcal{P}'$, there exists a function $nelg(\cdot)$ negligible in the security parameter λ satisfying $\Pr(\mathbf{Verify}(\mathcal{P}, K, s(\mathcal{P}')) \mapsto \mathtt{true}) \leq nelg(\lambda)$.*

Definition 2 (Recoverability). *An LLS outsourcing scheme is said to be recoverable if for any $s(\mathcal{P}')$ that is returned by an honest cloud following the designed algorithms, then $\mathbf{Recover}(\mathcal{P}, K, s(\mathcal{P}')) = \tilde{x}$.*

Definition 3 (Privacy preserving). *An LLS outsourcing scheme is said to be privacy-preserving if the cloud cannot infer any of the coefficient matrix $\boldsymbol{A}$, the constant vector $\boldsymbol{b}$, and the LLS solution $\tilde{x}$ based on its knowledge.*

4   Proposed Scheme: Sells

Following the QR decomposition method introduced in Sect. 2.3, we construct an LLS outsourcing scheme known as Sells to solve an overdetermined linear system $\boldsymbol{Ax} = \boldsymbol{b}$. The basic idea is as follows. The client converts the coefficient matrix $\boldsymbol{A}$ to a masked form $\boldsymbol{A}'$, and transforms the LLS problem into an outsourced task, which is the QR decomposition of $\boldsymbol{A}'$. Based on the decomposition result by the cloud, the client then "locally" derives the solution to the original LLS problem.

A very remarkable feature of our design is that the constant vector $\boldsymbol{b}$ is always kept by the client and thus completely blind to the cloud. Besides obvious security benefit, this also accelerates solving different overdetermined linear systems $\boldsymbol{Ax}^{(i)} = \boldsymbol{b}^{(i)}$ with the same $\boldsymbol{A}$ but different $\boldsymbol{b}^{(i)}$'s: the client only needs to turn to the cloud once for the QR decomposition and then it can reuse the intermediate result to locally deduce any instance of $\boldsymbol{x}^{(i)}$. Indeed, many scientific calculation tasks (e.g., acoustic signal processing [21], image restoration [22], and electromagnetic scattering characterizing [23]) can be reduced to solving such linear systems, for which Sells is particularly beneficial.

Next, one by one we elaborate on the components of Sells, some of which are relatively simple but others are a bit complex.

4.1   KeyGen(λ) $\mapsto K = (\boldsymbol{M}, \boldsymbol{N})$

Given the security parameter λ, the client invokes **KeyGen** to generate as its secret key a random orthogonal matrix $\boldsymbol{M} \in \mathbb{R}^{m \times m}$ (e.g., following [12, Sect. 3.4]) and a random invertible upper triangular matrix $\boldsymbol{N} \in \mathbb{R}^{n \times n}$.

4.2 TaskGen$(A, K) \mapsto A'$

To protect the privacy of the coefficient matrix $A \in \mathbb{R}^{m \times n}$, the client intends to mask it via left and right multiplications with M and N, respectively. However, following Sect. 2.1, the computation complexity of locally calculating MA is $\mathcal{O}(m^2 n)$, that of $(MA)N$ is $\mathcal{O}(mn^2)$, and thus that of $A' = MAN$ is $\mathcal{O}(m^2 n)$ in total (considering $m > n$), which is at least as large as that of the QR decomposition of A ($\mathcal{O}(mn^2)$, cf. Sect. 2.3). Hence, the client needs the cloud's assistance for such masking.

For efficiently computing MAN, we adopt and modify the secure outsourcing protocol for matrix multiplication proposed in [16], which utilizes sparse matrices of specific structure (cf. Sect. 2.4) for privacy protection. This technique has been employed as a building block for securely outsourcing various scientific calculations such as matrix inversion [17], matrix determinant [24], and quadratic programs [25]. Our **TaskGen** is illustrated in Table 1, which involves only one-round client-cloud interaction. In **TaskGen**, as P_k and P_k^{-1} ($k \in [1,4]$) are all sparse matrices (cf. Algorithm 2), the client only needs to perform several relatively lightweight dense-matrix-sparse-matrix and sparse-matrix-dense-matrix multiplications to compute X, Y, Z, and A'. Therefore, the client's total computation complexity for computing MAN is reduced from $\mathcal{O}(m^2 n)$ to only $\mathcal{O}(m^2)$. Lemma 1 tells the correctness of our protocol.

Table 1. A one-round interactive **TaskGen**, via which the client can efficiently compute $A' = MAN$ with the aid of the cloud. The total computation complexity of the client's operations is only $\mathcal{O}(m^2)$.

client	cloud
1. independently and repeatedly invoke Alg. 2 to generate 4 random sparse matrices $P_1, P_2 \in \mathbb{R}^{m \times m}$, $P_3, P_4 \in \mathbb{R}^{n \times n}$, where $P_k(i,j) = \omega_{k,i} \delta_{\pi_k(i),j}$, $k \in [1,4]$. 2. $X = P_1 M P_2^{-1}, Y = P_2 A P_3^{-1}, Z = P_3 N P_4^{-1}$.	
	3. X, Y, Z $\longrightarrow$
	4. $S = XYZ$.
	5. S $\longleftarrow$
6. $A' = P_1^{-1} S P_4$.	

Lemma 1. *If the cloud honestly executes* **TaskGen**, *then* $A' = MAN$.

Proof. If the cloud follows the protocol, then

$$S = XYZ = (P_1 M P_2^{-1})(P_2 A P_3^{-1})(P_3 N P_4^{-1}) = P_1 MAN P_4^{-1}.$$

$$\therefore \ A' = P_1^{-1} S P_4 = P_1^{-1}(P_1 MAN P_4^{-1}) P_4 = MAN.$$

$\square$

4.3   TaskSol(A') $\mapsto$ (Q', R')

Upon receiving $A' \in \mathbb{R}^{m \times n}$, the cloud conducts the QR decomposition for A' and returns the computation result ($Q' \in \mathbb{R}^{m \times m}, R' \in \mathbb{R}^{m \times n}$) to the client. For the decomposition, the cloud can choose from several feasible approaches.

4.4   Verify($A, K, (Q', R')$) $\mapsto$ true/false

To detect possible cheating behaviors by the cloud, the client should check the correctness of the "cloud-aided problem transformation" as well as the solution to the masked task received from the cloud. In Sells, it suffices to verify whether (Q', R') forms a QR decomposition of MAN. Specifically, the client needs to check whether Q' is orthogonal (i.e., $Q'Q'^{\mathrm{T}} = I$), whether R' is upper triangular, and whether $Q'R' = MAN$.

Since the computation costs for calculating $Q'Q'^{\mathrm{T}}$, $Q'R'$, and MAN are as high as $\mathcal{O}(m^3)$, $\mathcal{O}(m^2 n)$, and $\mathcal{O}(m^2 n)$, respectively, we do not really perform these matrix multiplications for a deterministic verification. Instead, following [17,18] we employ Freivalds' technique [19] to design a probabilistic but efficient verification procedure shown in Algorithm 3, which involves constant rounds of checks. The computation complexity of Algorithm 3 is only $\mathcal{O}(m^2)$ thanks to the matrix-vector multiplications. The client accepts (Q', R') if Algorithm 3 returns true, or terminates otherwise.

Algorithm 3. Verification of received solution to the masked task (**Verify**)

Input: coefficient matrix A, secret key $K = (M, N)$, and received (Q', R')
Output: true / false
1: **if** R' is not upper triangular **then**
2:     return false
3: **end if**
4: **for** $i = 1$ to l ($\ll m$) **do**
5:     select a random ($m \times 1$)-dimensional 0/1 vector α, compute $p = Q'(Q'^{\mathrm{T}}\alpha) - I\alpha$
6:     **if** $p \neq (0, 0, \cdots, 0)^{\mathrm{T}}$ **then**
7:         return false
8:     **end if**
9:     select a random ($n \times 1$)-dimensional 0/1 vector β, compute $q = Q'(R'\beta) - M(A(N\beta))$
10:     **if** $q \neq (0, 0, \cdots, 0)^{\mathrm{T}}$ **then**
11:         return false
12:     **end if**
13: **end for**
14: return true

We shall capture in the next section the effectiveness of the verification algorithm, which can balance between security and efficiency. For example, $l = 40$ seems enough for achieving almost perfect verifiability, yet such an l is still far smaller than a typical m or n (recall Sect. 1.2).

4.5   Recover$(b, K, (Q', R')) \mapsto \hat{x}$

Given the verified decomposition result (Q', R'), the client invokes Algorithm 4 to calculate $\hat{x}$ with b and K. A favorable feature of our Algorithm 4 is that (like **Verify**) it does not involve any matrix-matrix multiplication; particularly, in steps 2 and 4, only matrix-vector multiplications are employed for efficiency. In step 3, since R_1' is an upper triangular matrix, $R_1' y = b'$ can be efficiently solved with an iterative method called back substitution [12, Sect. 2.3], the computation complexity of which is $\mathcal{O}(n^2)$.

Algorithm 4. Solution recovery (**Recover**)

Input: constant vector b, secret key $K = (M, N)$, and verified (Q', R')
Output: column vector $\hat{x}$

1: parse Q' as $\left[Q_1' \in \mathbb{R}^{m \times n}, Q_2' \in \mathbb{R}^{m \times (m-n)} \right]$, parse R' as $\begin{bmatrix} R_1' \in \mathbb{R}^{n \times n} \\ 0_{(m-n) \times n} \end{bmatrix}$.

2: compute $b' = Q_1'^{\mathrm{T}}(Mb)$.
3: solve $R_1' y = b'$ to get y.
4: compute $\hat{x} = Ny$.

---

5   Analytic Evaluation

5.1   Security

Theorem 1. Sells *is a verifiable LLS outsourcing scheme.*

Proof. For Algorithm 3 to yield **true**, the R' returned by the cloud has to be upper triangular; otherwise, the client rejects $s(\mathcal{P}') = (Q', R')$ immediately. Now let us focus on the check on p in the **for** loop. Let $Prob_1$ be the probability that a non-orthogonal Q' passes one-round check, and $Prob_f$ be the probability that it passes all l rounds of checks. (We will also take q into consideration shortly.) Let $\alpha = (\alpha_1, \cdots, \alpha_m)^{\mathrm{T}}$, $D = Q'Q'^{\mathrm{T}} - I = (d_{i,j})$ ($d_{i,j}$ is the element on the i-th row and j-th column of D), $p = Q'Q'^{\mathrm{T}}\alpha - I\alpha = D\alpha = (p_1, \cdots, p_m)^{\mathrm{T}}$. For a non-orthogonal Q', $Q'Q'^{\mathrm{T}} \neq I \Rightarrow D \neq 0_{m \times m}$, so at least one element of D is nonzero. Assume w.l.o.g. that $d_{x,y} \neq 0$. Let $\gamma = \sum_{j=1, j \neq y}^{m} d_{x,j}\alpha_j$. Because the x-th element of p is $p_x = \gamma + d_{x,y}\alpha_y$ and $\Pr(\alpha_y = 0) = \Pr(\alpha_y = 1) = \frac{1}{2}$,

$$\therefore \begin{cases} \Pr(p_x = 0 | \gamma = 0) = \Pr(d_{x,y}\alpha_y = 0) = \Pr(\alpha_y = 0) = \frac{1}{2}, \\ \Pr(p_x = 0 | \gamma \neq 0) = \Pr(d_{x,y}\alpha_y = -\gamma | \alpha_y = 1)\Pr(\alpha_y = 1) \leq \Pr(\alpha_y = 1) = \frac{1}{2}, \end{cases}$$

$$\therefore \Pr(p_x = 0) = \Pr(p_x = 0 | \gamma = 0)\Pr(\gamma = 0) + \Pr(p_x = 0 | \gamma \neq 0)\Pr(\gamma \neq 0)$$
$$\leq \frac{1}{2}\Pr(\gamma = 0) + \frac{1}{2}\Pr(\gamma \neq 0) = \frac{1}{2}(\Pr(\gamma = 0) + \Pr(\gamma \neq 0)) = \frac{1}{2}.$$

$$\therefore Prob_1 = \Pr(\boldsymbol{p} = (0, \cdots, 0)^{\mathrm{T}} \mid \boldsymbol{Q}' \text{ is non-orthogonal})$$

$$\leq \Pr(p_x = 0 \mid \boldsymbol{Q}' \text{ is non-orthogonal}) \leq \frac{1}{2},$$

$$\therefore Prob_f = (Prob_1)^l \leq 2^{-l}.$$

Now let us focus on the check on q in the **for** loop, according to which the client checks whether $\boldsymbol{Q}'\boldsymbol{R}'$ equals $\boldsymbol{MAN}$. Similarly, any $(\boldsymbol{Q}', \boldsymbol{R}')$ that does not satisfy $\boldsymbol{Q}'\boldsymbol{R}' = \boldsymbol{MAN}$ can pass the verification with a probability no more than 2^{-l}. We omit the details for simplicity.

The client accepts $(\boldsymbol{Q}', \boldsymbol{R}')$ iff $\boldsymbol{R}'$ is upper triangular, $\boldsymbol{Q}'\boldsymbol{Q}'^{\mathrm{T}} = \boldsymbol{I}$, and $\boldsymbol{Q}'\boldsymbol{R}' = \boldsymbol{MAN}$. Therefore, for any $(\boldsymbol{Q}', \boldsymbol{R}')$ that does not form a QR decomposition of $\boldsymbol{MAN}$, $\Pr(\mathbf{Verify}(\boldsymbol{A}, K, (\boldsymbol{Q}', \boldsymbol{R}')) \mapsto \mathtt{true}) \leq 2^{-2l}$. □

Theorem 2. Sells *is recoverable for the LLS problem.*

Proof. Consider an orthogonal matrix $\boldsymbol{Q}' = [\boldsymbol{Q}'_1, \boldsymbol{Q}'_2] \in \mathbb{R}^{m \times m}$ and an upper triangular matrix $\boldsymbol{R}' = \begin{bmatrix} \boldsymbol{R}'_1 \\ \boldsymbol{0} \end{bmatrix} \in \mathbb{R}^{m \times n}$, which form a QR decomposition of $\boldsymbol{A}' = \boldsymbol{MAN}$. Let $\boldsymbol{Q} = \boldsymbol{M}^{-1}[\boldsymbol{Q}'_1, \boldsymbol{Q}'_2] = [\boldsymbol{Q}_1, \boldsymbol{Q}_2]$ and $\boldsymbol{R} = \begin{bmatrix} \boldsymbol{R}'_1 \\ \boldsymbol{0} \end{bmatrix} \boldsymbol{N}^{-1} = \begin{bmatrix} \boldsymbol{R}_1 \\ \boldsymbol{0} \end{bmatrix}$.

Since $\boldsymbol{M}$ (thus $\boldsymbol{M}^{-1}$) and $\boldsymbol{Q}'$ are orthogonal, $\boldsymbol{Q} = \boldsymbol{M}^{-1}\boldsymbol{Q}'$ is also orthogonal. On the other hand, as $\boldsymbol{N}$ (thus $\boldsymbol{N}^{-1}$) and $\boldsymbol{R}'_1$ are upper triangular, $\boldsymbol{R}_1 = \boldsymbol{R}'_1\boldsymbol{N}^{-1}$ is also upper triangular. Last, multiplying $\boldsymbol{Q}$ by $\boldsymbol{R}$, we have

$$\boldsymbol{QR} = (\boldsymbol{M}^{-1}\boldsymbol{Q}')(\boldsymbol{R}'\boldsymbol{N}^{-1}) = \boldsymbol{M}^{-1}\boldsymbol{A}'\boldsymbol{N}^{-1} = \boldsymbol{M}^{-1}(\boldsymbol{MAN})\boldsymbol{N}^{-1} = \boldsymbol{A}.$$

Thus, $\boldsymbol{Q}$ and $\boldsymbol{R}$ form a QR decomposition of the original coefficient matrix $\boldsymbol{A}$.

For the $\hat{\boldsymbol{x}}$ calculated in step 4 of Algorithm 4, noticing $(\boldsymbol{M}^{-1})^{\mathrm{T}} = \boldsymbol{M}$ we have

$$\boldsymbol{R}_1\hat{\boldsymbol{x}} = \boldsymbol{R}_1\boldsymbol{N}\boldsymbol{y} = \boldsymbol{R}_1\boldsymbol{N}(\boldsymbol{R}'^{-1}_1\boldsymbol{b}') = (\boldsymbol{R}'_1\boldsymbol{N}^{-1})\boldsymbol{N}\boldsymbol{R}'^{-1}_1(\boldsymbol{Q}'^{\mathrm{T}}_1\boldsymbol{Mb})$$
$$= (\boldsymbol{Q}'^{\mathrm{T}}_1\boldsymbol{M})\boldsymbol{b} = (\boldsymbol{M}^{-1}\boldsymbol{Q}'_1)^{\mathrm{T}}\boldsymbol{b} = \boldsymbol{Q}^{\mathrm{T}}_1\boldsymbol{b}.$$

According to Sect. 2.3, such an $\hat{\boldsymbol{x}}$ equals the LLS solution $\tilde{\boldsymbol{x}}$ to $\mathcal{P}(\boldsymbol{A}, \boldsymbol{b})$. This proves the recoverability of Sells. □

For proving the privacy preserving of Sells, we first present the following lemma.

Lemma 2. *In* **TaskGen**, *for* $\boldsymbol{X} = \boldsymbol{P}_1\boldsymbol{M}\boldsymbol{P}_2^{-1}$, *it holds that*

$$\boldsymbol{X}(i, j) = (\omega_{1,i}/\omega_{2,j})\boldsymbol{M}(\pi_1(i), \pi_2(j)),$$

where $\boldsymbol{X}(i, j)$ *and* $\boldsymbol{M}(i, j)$ *denote the elements on the* i-*th row and* j-*th column of* $\boldsymbol{X}$ *and* $\boldsymbol{M}$, *respectively.*

Proof. Following step 1 of **TaskGen**, $\boldsymbol{P}_1 = (\boldsymbol{P}_1(i, j))$ and $\boldsymbol{P}_2 = (\boldsymbol{P}_2(i, j))$ are generated by independently and repeatedly invoking Algorithm 2. That is, $\boldsymbol{P}_1(i, j) = \omega_{1,i}\delta_{\pi_1(i),j}$, $\boldsymbol{P}_2(i, j) = \omega_{2,i}\delta_{\pi_2(i),j}$, $1 \leq i, j \leq m$. Then, the element on the i-th row and j-th column of $P_1 M$ is computed as $\sum_{k=1}^{m} P_1(i,k) M(k,j)$. Since $\delta_{x,y}$ (i.e., the Kronecker delta function) returns 1 if $x = y$ or 0 otherwise,

$$\sum_{k=1}^{m} P_1(i,k) M(k,j) = \sum_{k=1}^{m} \omega_{1,i} \delta_{\pi_1(i),k} M(k,j) = \omega_{1,i} M(\pi_1(i),j).$$

Next, we consider the matrix multiplication $(P_1 M) P_2^{-1}$. According to Eq. (2), the element on the i-th row and j-th column of P_2^{-1} is $P_2^{-1}(i,j) = \omega_{2,j}^{-1} \delta_{\pi_2^{-1}(i),j}, 1 \leq i,j \leq m$. As $\delta_{\pi_2^{-1}(k),j} = 1$ iff $\pi_2^{-1}(k) = j$ (i.e., $k = \pi_2(j)$), the element on the i-th row and j-th column of $X = (P_1 M) P_2^{-1}$ is computed as

$$X(i,j) = \sum_{k=1}^{m} \left(\omega_{1,i} M(\pi_1(i),k) \right) P_2^{-1}(k,j) = \sum_{k=1}^{m} \left(\omega_{1,i} M(\pi_1(i),k) \right) \left(\omega_{2,j}^{-1} \delta_{\pi_2^{-1}(k),j} \right)$$
$$= \omega_{1,i} \omega_{2,j}^{-1} M(\pi_1(i), \pi_2(j)). \qquad \square$$

Similarly, for $Y = P_2 A P_3^{-1}$, $Z = P_3 N P_4^{-1}$, $Y(i,j) = (\omega_{2,i}/\omega_{3,j}) A(\pi_2(i), \pi_3(j))$ and $Z(i,j) = (\omega_{3,i}/\omega_{4,j}) N(\pi_3(i), \pi_4(j))$. We omit the proof for simplicity.

Theorem 3. Sells *is privacy-preserving in the fully malicious model.*

Proof. In Sells, as the column vector of constant terms b is always kept by the client, the privacy of b and $\tilde{x}$ (solved according to $R_1 x = Q_1^T b$, cf. Sect. 2.3) is naturally guaranteed. Following Definition 3, next we only need to prove the privacy of A.

In Sells, A is masked by left and right multiplications of randomly generated matrices M and N, respectively. Without knowing M and N, the adversary cannot recover A from $A' = MAN$. Next, we show that the adversary cannot derive any of M, A, and N though it knows (X, Y, Z).

First, we consider X, Y, and Z separately. According to **TaskGen**, M is masked with two random invertible sparse matrices P_1 and P_2 to generate $X = P_1 M P_2^{-1}$, where following Lemma 2 $X(i,j) = (\omega_{1,i}/\omega_{2,j}) M(\pi_1(i), \pi_2(j))$. Such mask can be regarded as a two-phase operation:

- Phase 1: The position of each element in M is randomly rearranged with two permutations to generate $\tilde{M}$, i.e., $\tilde{M}(i,j) = M(\pi_1(i), \pi_2(j))$.
- Phase 2: The value of each element in $\tilde{M}$ is further obfuscated by multiplying a factor to generate X, i.e., $X(i,j) = (\omega_{1,i}/\omega_{2,j}) \tilde{M}(i,j)$.

According to Algorithm 1, there are $m!$ possible cases of both random permutations π_1 and π_2. This implies that in Phase 1 there are $(m!)^2$ possible ways to rearrange the elements of M to yield $\tilde{M}$. In Phase 2, each element in $\tilde{M}$ is further masked by two non-zero numbers randomly, uniformly, and independently chosen from $\mathbb{R}$ (which is an infinite space, i.e., $|\mathbb{R}| = \infty$). Therefore, the expected time for the adversary without knowing (P_1, P_2) to recover M from X is $\mathcal{O}\left((m!)^2 \cdot |\mathbb{R}|^{2m}\right)$, which is obviously a non-polynomially bounded quantity.

In fact, even if the client simply sets each $\omega_{k,i}$ $(k = 1, 2)$ to a λ-bit random integer, the expected time to recover M from X is still $\mathcal{O}\big((m!)^2(2^\lambda)^{2m}\big)$, which is a non-polynomially bounded quantity in terms of m. Thus, the adversary cannot recover M by directly decrypting X. As A and N are masked in the similar way, the adversary also cannot recover A (from decrypting Y) nor N (from decrypting Z) in polynomial time (we omit the proof for simplicity).

Second, we consider the computation results by the adversary based on (X, Y, Z). The adversary can obtain $XY = P_1 M A P_3^{-1}$ and $YZ = P_2 A N P_4^{-1}$. Following the above analysis, without knowing P_k $(k \in [1, 4])$, the adversary cannot recover MA (from XY) nor AN (from YZ). Thus, although it additionally knows $A' = MAN$, it is unable to acquire any of M and N using (XY, YZ). Next we consider $S = XYZ = P_1 M A N P_4^{-1}$. According to Algorithm 2, there are $m!$ and $n!$ possible positions of non-zero elements in P_1 and P_4, respectively. Therefore, when the adversary attempts to solve (P_1, P_4) by constructing linear equations based on (A', S), the possibility of successfully recovering the exact (P_1, P_4) is only $\frac{1}{(m!n!)}$, which is a negligible quantity in terms of m and n (both are sufficiently large, recall Sect. 1.2).

To sum up, the adversary cannot recover any of M, A, and N based on its knowledge. Therefore, Sells is privacy-preserving in the fully malicious model. $\square$

5.2   Complexity

Now we investigate the computation complexity on the client side.

- In **TaskGen**, P_1, P_2, P_3, and P_4 are all sparse matrices and each of them has only one non-zero element in each row, so the client only needs to spend $\mathcal{O}(m^2)$, $\mathcal{O}(mn)$, and $\mathcal{O}(n^2)$ costs computing $P_1 M P_2^{-1}$, $P_2 A P_3^{-1}$, and $P_3 N P_4^{-1}$, respectively.
- In **Verify**, since $l \ll m$ is a constant, the client spends $\mathcal{O}(m^2)$ computation costs checking whether $Q'(Q'^{\mathrm{T}}\alpha) - I\alpha = 0$ and $Q'(R'\beta) - M\big(A(N\beta)\big) = 0$.
- In **Recover**, the client first spends $\mathcal{O}(m^2)$ cost computing $b' = Q_1'^{\mathrm{T}}(Mb)$; then, through back substitution, the client spends $\mathcal{O}(n^2)$ cost solving y from $R_1' y = b'$; finally, it takes the client $\mathcal{O}(n^2)$ cost to map y to $\hat{x}$.

To sum up, the overall computation complexity is $\mathcal{O}(m^2)$. When m and n are of the same order, this is lower than that of locally solving an LLS problem with the QR decomposition method, which is $\mathcal{O}(mn^2)$.

6   Experimental Evaluation

In this section, we evaluate Sells with large-scale overdetermined systems of linear equations of varying dimensions, each of which is in the form of $Ax = b$ with $A \in \mathbb{R}^{m \times n}$, $b \in \mathbb{R}^{m \times 1}$, $m > n \gg 1$. All algorithms are implemented with MATLAB. As input, we employ random A and b in all experiments: any element in A or b is randomly, uniformly, and independently sampled from the same interval $[-1024.0, 1024.0]$.

We implement the client on a laptop computer with an Intel i3-2330M processor running at 2.20 GHz and 4 GB memory, and emulate the cloud with a desktop workstation with an Intel i7-6700K processor running at 4.00 GHz and 8 GB memory. Although the laptop does not look so "resource-constrained" (particularly when compared to our "cloud"), it turns out that it is impossible to conduct many of our experiments on "clients" with memory less than 4 GB.

6.1   Efficiency of Sells

To evaluate the computation overhead for solving overdetermined systems under various scales, we adopt the processing time as the performance metric. Two scenarios are tested for comparison.

- In the first scenario, the client deploys Sells, and the processing time on both the client and the cloud sides is measured. However, we exclude the **KeyGen** algorithm (which is fairly lightweight, as specified in Sect. 4.1) and step 1 of the **TaskGen** algorithm (as specified in Table 1) for measurement because they can be conducted offline. Specifically, $K = (M, N)$ and P_k ($k \in [1, 4]$) are all independent of A or b; they can be generated by the client beforehand (as long as m and n are determined). For our interactive **TaskGen**, time costs on the client and the cloud sides are measured respectively. For **Verify**, the parameter l (the number of check rounds in Algorithm 3) is set to 40, which assures almost perfect verifiability following Theorem 1.
- In the second scenario, the client computer does not turn to the cloud. It directly adopts the QR decomposition method specified in Sect. 2.3 to solve the overdetermined systems "locally." It is worth noting that MATLAB has implemented certain optimization for QR decomposition, which actually biases the performance comparison in favor of this local approach.

Table 2 illustrates the client's processing time (averaged from repeated but independent experiments) in the two scenarios. In all experiments, the client's processing time in the second scenario (i.e., local computing) is significantly larger than the total time in the first scenario (i.e., privacy-preserving cloud computing). To make this clear, we adopt their ratio as the indicator for cost savings. Just for simplicity, the condition $m > n$ is instantiated with $m = 2n$. Then, we make the observation that this indicator increases as the scale of the overdetermined system increases, which means the larger the overdetermined system is the more performance gain is obtained.

Moreover, regarding the same settings, Table 3 compares the total processing time of Sells (on both the client and the cloud sides) and the time of employing local QR decomposition. For Sells, the computation cost on the (relatively more powerful) cloud is observably larger than that on the client. The explanation is straightforward: conforming to the philosophy of cloud computing, Sells indeed assigns expensive parts of the computation to the cloud, while the client only performs relatively lightweight operations. According to Table 3, the total elapsed time of Sells is far less than that of the local scenario, implying that Sells

Table 2. The client's processing time (in seconds) for solving overdetermined systems of different scales. It takes $t_{\mathsf{Sells.client}}$ in all when employing **Sells** (which is the sum of the online time costs of **TaskGen** on the client side, **Verify**, and **Recover**), or t_{direct} when adopting local QR decomposition, which in our case benefits from MATLAB's built-in acceleration.

m, n	t_{Sells}				t_{direct}	$\frac{t_{\mathsf{direct}}}{t_{\mathsf{Sells.client}}}$
	TaskGen	Verify	Recover	client (Σ)		
2000, 1000	0.18	0.08	0.03	0.29	1.09	3.76
4000, 2000	0.41	0.17	0.08	0.66	4.79	7.23
6000, 3000	0.97	0.43	0.19	1.59	20.21	12.71
8000, 4000	1.86	0.72	0.33	2.91	47.92	16.47
10000, 5000	3.46	1.13	0.66	5.25	96.38	18.35
12000, 6000	7.85	1.63	1.17	9.65	211.97	21.96

Table 3. Processing time (in seconds) for solving overdetermined systems of different scales, where $t_{\mathsf{Sells.client}}$ and $t_{\mathsf{Sells.cloud}}$ represent the costs of the client and the cloud in **Sells**, respectively. Note that $t_{\mathsf{Sells.cloud}}$ is spent on not only **TaskSol** but also part of **TaskGen**.

m, n	$t_{\mathsf{Sells.client}}$	$t_{\mathsf{Sells.cloud}}$	t_{Sells} (Σ)	t_{direct}
2000, 1000	0.29	0.26	0.55	1.09
4000, 2000	0.66	1.82	2.48	4.79
6000, 3000	1.59	5.98	7.57	20.21
8000, 4000	2.91	13.72	16.63	47.92
10000, 5000	5.25	25.16	30.41	94.38
12000, 6000	9.65	40.91	50.56	211.97

is a pragmatic proposal. This can be made more apparent if we implement the client on a more resource-constrained computer and/or emulate the cloud with a more powerful server. Overall, besides bringing significant cost savings to the client, **Sells** also shortens the actual time for the problem solving.

6.2 Performance Comparison

To the best of our knowledge, **Sells** is the first secure outsourcing scheme eligible for solving a large-scale overdetermined system, where only approximate solutions exist. Nevertheless, we are still interested in a performance comparison between **Sells** and "related" schemes from the state of the art that are dedicated to solving linear equations where exact solution exist (usually this means $m = n$), which include proposals from Salinas et al. [9] and Yu et al. [10]. Fortunately, the intended performance comparison is still applicable, as the two schemes do accommodate the $m > n$ case. In this case, the two schemes still try to find the exact solution to the linear equations, wishing that there are just enough *linearly dependent* equations such that the system can be exactly reduced to n independent equations. If so, the two schemes [9, 10] yield valid solutions that are exact and unique. However, in our experiments with completely random A and b, the wished "just enough" condition generally does not hold, and the two schemes [9, 10] only yield invalid solutions. In our comparison, because we focus on efficiency instead of effectiveness, we do not care whether the solutions returned by [9, 10] are valid or not. Note that though the "related" scheme in [7] also focuses on outsourcing large-scale linear systems of equations, it is specifically designed for the linear systems with square coefficient matrix (i.e., the $m = n$ case); therefore, we exclude this scheme for comparison.

Table 4. Processing time (in seconds) of the client by deploying Sells and other two schemes [9, 10] for solving large-scale overdetermined systems.

m, n	2000, 500	4000, 1000	6000, 1500	8000, 2000	10000, 2500	12000, 3000
Salinas et al.'s [9]	0.18	0.31	0.65	1.19	1.96	2.71
Yu et al.'s [10]	0.23	0.89	2.23	3.71	5.66	8.76
Sells	0.13	0.49	1.15	2.34	4.33	5.42
m, n	2000, 1000	4000, 2000	6000, 3000	8000, 4000	10000, 5000	12000, 6000
Salinas et al.'s [9]	0.47	1.77	3.96	7.01	10.93	16.89
Yu et al.'s [10]	0.27	1.05	2.34	4.35	6.86	10.01
Sells	0.29	0.66	1.59	2.91	5.25	9.65
m, n	2000, 1500	4000, 3000	6000, 4500	8000, 6000	10000, 7500	12000, 9000
Salinas et al.'s [9]	2.06	8.51	19.68	41.19	54.18	94.71
Yu et al.'s [10]	0.32	1.23	2.83	5.43	8.23	12.16
Sells	0.41	0.91	2.07	4.97	9.19	14.08

For a fair comparison, all three secure outsourcing schemes ([9], [10], and Sells) are implemented with MATLAB on the same laptop/workstation configuration specified in the previous subsection. Again we adopt the total processing time on the client side (as in Table 2) to measure the performance. In doing so, however, we fail to find any operations in [9] which correspond to **Verify**, and thus we conjecture that [9] actually sacrifices security for efficiency. In favor of Yu et al.'s scheme [10] we deliberately optimize it and exclude measuring certain operations that can be conducted offline. The results are shown in Table 4, where the condition $m > n$ is instantiated with cases of $(m : n) = (4 : \{1, 2, 3\})$. Generally, the experimental results demonstrate that Sells is comparable to the other two schemes in terms of efficiency. In many cases, Sells still outperforms both existent schemes.

7 Related Work

In the literature, extensive work has been done on secure outsourcing of large-scale systems of linear equations, but with a focus on the "textbook" case (where exact solution exists) instead of the overdetermined case. Wang et al. [14,15] employed homomorphic encryption to securely outsource large-scale linear systems based on the Jacobi method, where the client encrypts the coefficient matrix with certain homomorphic algorithm and sends it to the cloud, which then interacts with the client for iterative problem solving. Nevertheless, Wang et al.'s schemes [14,15] only work for certain kind of linear systems where the coefficient matrices are diagonally dominant. To break through this limit, Salinas et al. [9] developed a new scheme based on the conjugate gradient method [20], where the coefficient matrix only needs to be full-rank. Without using homomorphic encryption, Salinas et al.'s scheme [9] is more computationally efficient compared with [14,15]. However, all [9,14,15] are iterative and thus involve intensive communications between the client and the cloud, as pointed out in [7,10]. In addition, we note that although [9] considers a threat model where the cloud may be cheating, it seems that the outsourcing scheme presented there does not bother to verify any result returned by the cloud to detect possible misbehavior.

Recently, several non-iterative schemes [7,10] have been proposed. Chen et al. [7] employed sparse matrices to protect the coefficient matrix and designed an outsourcing scheme for linear systems, which requires only 1 round of communication between the client and the cloud. However, their scheme is specifically designed for the linear systems with square coefficient matrices (i.e., the $m = n$ case). As a following study, Yu et al. [10] utilized a series of obfuscation techniques to design another non-iterative scheme, which can accommodate the $m > n$ case and can better protect the data privacy (including the number and positions of zero elements in the coefficient matrix) at the cost of two rounds of interactions.

Although there have been many research efforts on secure outsourcing of linear systems, they are dedicated to exact solutions instead of approximate solutions; none of them (whether iterative or non-iterative) can be readily applied to tackle overdetermined systems where optimal solutions are pursued.

8 Conclusions

In this paper, we are interested in solving an overdetermined system of linear equations, which is mathematically equivalent to the linear least squares (LLS) problem and becomes a challenging task for a resource-constrained client when the scale of the problem increases. In practice, large-scale overdetermined systems abound in many fields of science and engineering. To confront such challenges, we propose to harness the cloud to solve overdetermined systems, in a privacy-preserving manner. To this end, first, we have formalized the problem of secure outsourcing of LLS. We have identified the system/threat model, formulated the scheme components, and established the design goals. We hope our formalization efforts can pave the way for rigorous treatment on the LLS outsourcing problem and consequently inspire more proposals.

Second, we have presented a secure and efficient LLS outsourcing scheme called Sells, which employs the QR decomposition technique. It is possible to solve overdetermined systems with other techniques (e.g., SVD decomposition [12, Sect. 3.3.3], as employed in [3]), but employing the QR decomposition one for LLS outsourcing reaps a few evident benefits. For example, in Sells the column vector of constant terms b is always kept by the client; its original form (or even any scrambled form) is completely inaccessible to the cloud. Therefore, the privacy of b (thus the solution to the LLS problem) is intrinsically guaranteed. For another example, Sells particularly lends itself to solving a series of overdetermined linear systems $Ax^{(i)} = b^{(i)}$ with the same coefficient matrix but different constant vectors. Interestingly, this is indeed a common case in many research fields [21–23]. In this case, the client turns to the cloud for the QR decomposition only once, and can then reuse the result. One can check our Algorithm 2 to make sure that the (Q', R') received (and verified) from the cloud can be reused for quickly deriving from any given $b^{(i)}$ a corresponding $x^{(i)}$.

Third, we have evaluated Sells with overdetermined systems under various scales. Extensive experiments have demonstrated that Sells is efficient and practical: it brings significant cost savings to the client and simultaneously shortens the entire time needed for the problem solving. Further experiments have shown that in terms of efficiency, Sells is comparable to existent solutions that are dedicated to solving linear systems with exact solutions only.

To the best of our knowledge, Sells is the first secure outsourcing scheme that is readily applicable to the LLS problem. For future work, we are interested in a non-interactive (hence more communication-efficient) **TaskGen** algorithm, which transforms, without any assistance from the cloud, the LLS problem into a masked task. We would also like to explore approaches other than the QR decomposition technique to securely outsource an overdetermined system of linear equations (e.g., SVD decomposition [12]).

Acknowledgment. The authors would like to thank the anonymous reviewers for their valuable comments. This work was supported by the National Basic Research Program of China (973 Program) under Grant 2014CB340603.

References

1. Baldwin, M.P., Stephenson, D., Thompson, D.W., Dunkerton, T.J., Charlton, A.J., O'Neill, A.: Stratospheric memory and skill of extended-range weather forecasts. Science **301**, 636–640 (2003)
2. So, H.C., Lin, L.: Linear least squares approach for accurate received signal strength based source localization. IEEE Trans. Signal Process. **59**, 4035–4040 (2011)
3. Lobos, T., Kozina, T., Koglin, H.J.: Power system harmonics estimation using linear least squares method and SVD. IEE Proc. Gener. Transm. Distrib. **148**, 567–572 (1999)
4. Bjorck, A.: Numerical Methods for Least Squares Problems. SIAM, Philadelphia (1996)
5. Edelman, A.: Large dense numerical linear algebra in 1993: the parallel computing influence. Int. J. High Perform. Comput. Appl. **7**, 113–128 (1993)
6. Ren, K., Wang, C., Wang, Q.: Security challenges for the public cloud. IEEE Internet Comput. **16**, 69–73 (2012)

7. Chen, X., Huang, X., Li, J., Ma, J., Lou, W., Wong, D.S.: New algorithms for secure outsourcing of large-scale systems of linear equations. IEEE Trans. Inf. Forensics Secur. **10**, 69–78 (2015)
8. Pan, S., Zheng, F., Zhu, W.-T., Wang, Q.: Harnessing the cloud for secure and efficient outsourcing of non-negative matrix factorization. In: the 6th IEEE Conference on Communications and Network Security (CNS 2018). IEEE (2018)
9. Salinas, S., Luo, C., Chen, X., Li, P.: Efficient secure outsourcing of large-scale linear systems of equations. In: 2015 IEEE Conference on Computer Communications (INFOCOM 2015), pp. 1035–1043. IEEE (2015)
10. Yu, Y., Luo, Y., Wang, D., Fu, S., Xu, M.: Efficient, secure and non-iterative outsourcing of large-scale systems of linear equations. In: 2016 IEEE International Conference on Communications (ICC 2016), p. 6. IEEE (2016)
11. Lawson, C.L., Hanson, R.J.: Solving Least Squares Problems. SIAM, Philadelphia (1974)
12. Demmel, J.W.: Applied Numerical Linear Algebra. SIAM, Philadelphia (1997)
13. Lyndon, R.C., Schupp, P.E.: Combinatorial Group Theory. CM, vol. 89. Springer, Heidelberg (2001). https://doi.org/10.1007/978-3-642-61896-3
14. Wang, C., Ren, K., Wang, J., Wang, Q.: Harnessing the cloud for securely outsourcing large-scale systems of linear equations. IEEE Trans. Parallel Distrib. Syst. **24**, 1172–1181 (2013)
15. Wang, C., Ren, K., Wang, K., Urs, K.M.R.: Harnessing the cloud for securely solving large-scale systems of linear equations. In: 31st IEEE International Conference on Distributed Computing Systems (ICDCS 2011), pp. 549–558. IEEE (2011)
16. Atallah, M.J., Pantazopoulos, K.N., Rice, J.R., Spafford, E.E.: Secure outsourcing of scientific computations. Adv. Comput. **54**, 215–272 (2002)
17. Lei, X., Liao, X., Huang, T., Li, H., Hu, C.: Outsourcing large matrix inversion computation to a public cloud. IEEE Trans. Cloud Comput. **1**, 78–87 (2013)
18. Zhou, L., Li, C.: Outsourcing eigen-decomposition and singular value decomposition of large matrix to a public cloud. IEEE ACCESS **4**, 869–879 (2016)
19. Motwani, R., Raghavan, P.: Randomized Algorithms. Cambridge University Press, Cambridge (1995)
20. Hestenes, M.R., Stiefel, E.: Methods of conjugate gradients for solving linear systems. J. Res. Natl. Bur. Stand. **49**, 409–436 (1952)
21. Plemmons, R.J.: FFT-based RLS in signal processing. In: 1993 IEEE International Conference on Acoustics, Speech, and Signal Processing (ICASSP 1993), pp. 571–574 (1993)
22. Solomon, C., Breckon, T.: Fundamentals of Digital Image Processing: A Practical Approach with Examples in MATLAB. Wiley-Blackwell, Hoboken (2011)
23. Smith, C.F., Peterson, A.F., Mittra, R.: A conjugate gradient algorithm for the treatment of multiple incident electromagnetic fields. IEEE Trans. Antennas Propag. **37**, 1490–1493 (1989)
24. Lei, X., Liao, X., Huang, T., Li, H.: Cloud computing service: the case of large matrix determinant computation. IEEE Trans. Serv. Comput. **8**, 688–700 (2015)
25. Salinas, S., Luo, C., Liao, W., Li, P.: Efficient secure outsourcing of large-scale quadratic programs. In: 11th ACM on Asia Conference on Computer and Communications Security (ASIA CCS 2016), pp. 281–292. ACM (2016)

Privacy-Preserving Multiparty Learning for Logistic Regression

Wei Du[1]([✉]), Ang Li[2], and Qinghua Li[2]

[1] Department of Electrical and Computer Engineering, Michigan State University,
East Lansing, USA
duwei1@msu.edu
[2] Department of Computer Science and Computer Engineering,
University of Arkansas, Fayetteville, USA
{angli,qinghual}@uark.edu

Abstract. In recent years, machine learning techniques are widely used in numerous applications, such as weather forecast, financial data analysis, spam filtering, and medical prediction. In the meantime, massive data generated from multiple sources further improve the performance of machine learning tools. However, data sharing from multiple sources brings privacy issues for those sources since sensitive information may be leaked in this process. In this paper, we propose a framework enabling multiple parties to collaboratively and accurately train a learning model over distributed datasets while guaranteeing the privacy of data sources. Specifically, we consider logistic regression model for data training and propose two approaches for perturbing the objective function to preserve ϵ-differential privacy. The proposed solutions are tested on real datasets, including Bank Marketing and Credit Card Default prediction. Experimental results demonstrate that the proposed multiparty learning framework is highly efficient and accurate.

1 Introduction

The past few decades have witnessed an increasing role that machine learning techniques play in both academic and industry communities. These techniques can be widely used to extract useful information from datasets in various fields [14]. At the same time, the advent of the big data era provides a better platform for its further development. For example, some advertisement companies collect massive data from social media, such as search history from Google and individuals' interactions from Facebook, and analyze the data to lock in targeted customers and improve accuracy of posting advertisements. Machine learning algorithms also have applications in the medical area. Taking cancer scan for instance, some types of cancers are really difficult for even experienced doctors to accurately determine cancer staging, but it has been reported that intelligent computers can help do this with higher accuracy. The combination of

---

W. Du—This work was done when Wei Du was at the University of Arkansas.

© ICST Institute for Computer Sciences, Social Informatics and Telecommunications Engineering 2018
R. Beyah et al. (Eds.): SecureComm 2018, LNICST 254, pp. 549–568, 2018.
https://doi.org/10.1007/978-3-030-01701-9_30

data analytics and efforts by doctors can give better medical treatment plans. Machine learning also exerts its effect in the field of finance. Financial companies accumulate a large amount of data records of their customers including purchase history, credit level, and loans and mortgage repayment activities. Then these companies could develop automatic, intelligent fraud detection systems to actively learn the behaviors of customers and distinguish potential threats and bankrupt cases, which can significantly reduce asset loss and bad debts.

A typical machine learning paradigm is to make targeted predictions based on a single dataset [26]. However, the data resources are increasingly distributed and stored by different owners. For example, medical data can be distributed in several hospitals and healthcare institutes; personal credit history, asset status, and accounting information can be distributed across multiple financial companies. Combining data from multiple sources for learning can usually derive better prediction performance. As a result, the traditional paradigm of learning from a single dataset is experiencing transitions towards collaborative learning, i.e., data from multiple parties are used to collaboratively train a learning model. A conventional collaborative learning approach is to have a central party, i.e., a virtual server and let multiple data owners directly upload their data to the server for training [5, 20–22].

Although collaborative learning achieves better performance than singe dataset based learning, concerns on privacy are arising. It is possible that during the process, the private information of each party, e.g. health data records, can be disclosed, which will cause privacy leakage. Furthermore, the privacy leakage issue will cause mistrust between participating parties, preventing them from sharing their data to the central server. Therefore, it becomes increasingly important to design a protocol to train a learning model from the datasets from multiple parties, while at the same time preserving their privacy.

Some work has been done for privacy-preserving machine learning in the past few years, and those protection techniques can be mainly divided into three groups. The first group perturbs the original data with randomized algorithms [13, 17, 24]. Although the perturbation techniques can protect confidential information, perturbed data may differ from the original data to a large extent, and thus decrease the accuracy of the resulted training model. Secondly, anonymization is also a popular method to protect users' sensitive information [12]. For example, we can remove the name and identification number from individual history records. Then the accuracy of the training model will not be affected and the privacy of data owners can also be preserved. However, such anonymization techniques are vulnerable to attacks involving auxiliary information. Thirdly, some cryptographic techniques have also been reported in previous studies [4, 10]. In [10], Graepel et al. reported a homomorphic encryption scheme to retain both the privacy of training and testing examples. However, homomorphic encryption techniques will incur intensive computations, making it impractical for large-scale applications.

Recently, differential privacy [7] as an arising notation has attracted much attention in the field of privacy. Theoretically, it could offer formal privacy guarantees no matter what auxiliary information the attackers have. There has been a lot of work on the realization of machine learning models under differential privacy. A typical approach is first generating noise via Laplace mechanism or exponential mechanism and then building a noisy model for their dataset using these generated noises [7]. Some other approaches modify the objective function of the training model [8]. These mechanisms can perturb the objective function by adding noise, and output predictions of the perturbed noisy model. However, most of them are focusing on the single-party setting, and have not applied to multiparty learning.

In this paper, we propose a framework for privacy-preserving multiparty learning among multiple data owners. The proposed framework achieves differential privacy, providing theoretical guarantees for each party's privacy. The framework focuses on the application of logistic regression for model building, but can be easily applied or extended to other machine learning models. In this framework, each data owner first trains its model locally, and each of them will obtain an output objective function for their local model. We design two approaches of noise generation in this process to meet differential privacy. Then these data owners will upload their learned local parameters to a central server for sharing. The central server will average the uploaded local parameters and send the averaged parameters back to those data owners. Local data owners will then incorporate the averaged parameters to retrain their local model. The above process will be repeated iteratively until the parameters converge. The proposed framework is based on the weighted parameter averaging mechanism since the number of data records for different data owners might be different. Experimental results show that the proposed framework is computationally efficient. The main contributions of this paper are summarized as follows:

- We propose a differentially private framework for multiple parties to collaboratively build learning models using logistic regression, which provides theoretical privacy guarantees for those parties.
- Two efficient mechanisms are designed for generating noise during local learning to achieve differential privacy for multiparty learning.
- We propose a weighted parameter sharing mechanism for multiple data owners with different sizes of data records.
- We run extensive experiments to evaluate the performance of the proposed framework using real datasets, and the results show high efficiency and accuracy of the proposed solution.

The rest of the paper is organized as follows. Section 2 introduces preliminary background knowledge. Section 3 elaborates the two different approaches for realizing differentially private learning in a multiparty setting. In addition, theoretical privacy analysis for the proposed mechanism is also provided. Section 4 presents evaluation results. Section 5 discusses related work and their difference from our work, and Sect. 6 concludes the paper.

2   Preliminaries

2.1   Differential Privacy

Differential privacy is an important concept in the area of privacy. It formally guarantees that no matter what change has been made to any particular element in a database an attacker cannot tell the difference in the output of a randomized algorithm [13].

Definition 1. A randomized algorithm $\mathcal{M}$ that takes the elements in $\mathcal{D}$ and outputs a function $\mathcal{M}(\mathcal{D})$ achieves ϵ-differential privacy if

$$\frac{P(\mathcal{M}(\mathcal{D}) \in S)}{P(\mathcal{M}(\mathcal{D}') \in S)} \leq e^{\epsilon} \tag{1}$$

where S is the output range of $\mathcal{M}(\mathcal{D})$. $\mathcal{D}$ and $\mathcal{D}'$ are a pair of neighborhood databases differing in a single item. ϵ is a privacy budget that controls the strength of the privacy of the algorithm $\mathcal{M}$ for any pair of neighborhood databases. For smaller ϵ, the output $\mathcal{M}(\mathcal{D})$ is almost the same for any pair $\mathcal{D}$ and $\mathcal{D}'$, making it hard for the adversarial party to identify the difference between these two neighborhood databases. To make it more clear, we have:

$$e^{-\epsilon} \leq \frac{P(\mathcal{M}(\mathcal{D}) \in S)}{P(\mathcal{M}(\mathcal{D}') \in S)} \leq e^{\epsilon} \tag{2}$$

The derivation of Eq. (2) is based on the interchangeability of the *Definition* 1. For smaller ϵ, we have the approximation formula:

$$e^{\epsilon} = 1 - \epsilon \tag{3}$$

The combination of Eqs. (2) and (3) will give:

$$1 - \epsilon \leq \frac{P(\mathcal{M}(\mathcal{D}) \in S)}{P(\mathcal{M}(\mathcal{D}') \in S)} \leq 1 + \epsilon \tag{4}$$

Since $0 < P(\mathcal{M}(\mathcal{D}) \in S), P(\mathcal{M}(\mathcal{D}') \in S) < 1$, the expansion of Eq. (4) can be rewritten as:

$$|P(\mathcal{M}(\mathcal{D}) \in S) - P(\mathcal{M}(\mathcal{D}') \in S)| < \epsilon \tag{5}$$

It can be clearly seen from Eq. (5), if ϵ is a negligible variable, any malicious party inquiring $\mathcal{M}(\mathcal{D})$ cannot distinguish $\mathcal{D}$ and $\mathcal{D}'$. Then strong privacy of the data owner will be achieved.

Several methods have been used to satisfy ϵ-differential privacy and Laplace mechanism is a commonly used one [7]. In particular, the Laplace mechanism adds a random noise to the output of an algorithm, where the random noise is drawn from Laplace distribution depending on the global sensitivity of the algorithm [8].

Definition 2. Given a real-valued vector mapping function: $\mathcal{D} \rightarrow \mathcal{M}(\mathcal{D})$, the sensitivity of $\mathcal{M}(\mathcal{D})$ is denoted as:

$$\Delta S_{\mathcal{M}} = \max \|\mathcal{M}(\mathcal{D}) - \mathcal{M}(\mathcal{D}')\|_1 \tag{6}$$

where $\mathcal{D}$ and $\mathcal{D}'$ are any pair of neighborhood databases, and $\|\mathcal{M}(\mathcal{D}) - \mathcal{M}(\mathcal{D}')\|_1$ is the l_1 distance between $\mathcal{M}(\mathcal{D})$ and $\mathcal{M}(\mathcal{D}')$. The sensitivity $\Delta S_{\mathcal{M}}$ describes the maximum variation of the output $\mathcal{M}(\mathcal{D})$ under single-item changes.

Definition 3. The Laplace distribution centered at μ, and scaled with b has the following probability density function:

$$Lap(x|\mu, b) = \frac{1}{2b} exp(-\frac{|x - \mu|}{b}) \tag{7}$$

Then to compute the noisy output on database $\mathcal{D}$, we will have:

$$\mathcal{M}'(\mathcal{D}) = \mathcal{M}(\mathcal{D}) + Lap(x|0, \frac{\Delta S_{\mathcal{M}}}{\epsilon}) \tag{8}$$

where $Lap(x|0, \frac{\Delta S_{\mathcal{M}}}{\epsilon})$ indicates that the Laplace distribution follows zero mean and $\frac{\Delta S_{\mathcal{M}}}{\epsilon}$ scale. The noise generation mechanism in Eq. (8) can provide ϵ-differential privacy for any randomized algorithm $\mathcal{M}$.

2.2 Linear Regression and Logistic Regression

Consider a basic machine learning task for binary classification, where a database $\mathcal{D}$ is given. Suppose $\mathcal{D}$ consists of N samples $X_1, X_2, X_3, \cdots, X_n$. Each sample X_i is denoted as $(x_{i1}, x_{i2}, x_{i3}, \cdots, x_{im}, y_i)$, where $x_{i1}, x_{i2}, x_{i3}, \cdots, x_{im}$ are the m attributes of sample X_i, and $y_i \in \{0, 1\}$ is the corresponding binary label. For example, when we record cancer history of patients, we need to write down some basic information, such as age, weight, height, and so on. In addition, we also need some high-level information, including blood pressure, heart rate, and medical related indexes. All these information corresponds to the m attributes of a data record. The label $y_i \in \{0, 1\}$ indicates existence of a disease. A patient will be labeled as 1 if diagnosed with a particular cancer, and otherwise will be labeled as 0.

From the perspective of machine learning scientists, it is assumed that there exists a hidden relationship between the m attributes $x_{i1}, x_{i2}, x_{i3}, \cdots, x_{im}$ and the recorded label $y_i \in \{0, 1\}$. The objective of a machine learning algorithm is to learn this particular relationship which empowers us to predict the label of a data record as accurate as possible given the corresponding attributes logged. Suppose the prediction function f taking the input of ith element $(\mathbf{x}_i : x_{i1}, x_{i2}, x_{i3}, \cdots, x_{im})$, and outputting the predicted label $\hat{y}_i$ is expressed as the following:

$$\hat{y}_i = f(\mathbf{x}_i) \tag{9}$$

The above function f is usually formulated as an optimization problem that one would like to maximize the prediction accuracy. The number of errors made by the prediction function f over the entire dataset is shown as:

$$\sum_{n=1}^{N} \Pi_{\hat{y}_i \neq y_i} \tag{10}$$

where Π is a loss function that evaluates the difference between the predicted label and the real label. Our goal is to minimize the number of prediction errors, and the optimization problem is stated as [15]:

$$\mathbf{w}^* = \arg \min_{\mathbf{w}} \sum_{n=1}^{N} \Pi_{\hat{f}(\mathbf{x}_i) \neq y_i} \tag{11}$$

where $\mathbf{w}$ is the parameter of the function f, and $\mathbf{w}^*$ is the optimal result of Eq. (11).

The types of objective function and loss evaluation could vary. In this paper, we focus on the application of logistic regression, which is a commonly used classification technique. In the following part, we will first introduce linear regression and then extend to logistic regression.

Linear regression is the basic regression model, and the prediction function f is assumed to be linearly dependent on the m attributes. The predicted label $\hat{y}_i$ can be stated as:

$$\hat{y}_i = \mathbf{w}^T \mathbf{x}_i + \alpha \tag{12}$$

where $(\mathbf{x}_i : x_{i1}, x_{i2}, x_{i3}, \cdots, x_{im})$ are the m attributes of the ith data record, $(\mathbf{w} : w_{i1}, w_{i2}, w_{i3}, \cdots, w_{im})$ are the corresponding parameters related to m attributes, and α is the bias factor of the linear function that helps increase the prediction accuracy.

To measure the error between predicted label and real label, the Euclid distance of a particular data record $\mathbf{x}_i$ is expressed as:

$$d = (\mathbf{w}^T \mathbf{x}_i + \alpha - y_i)^2 \tag{13}$$

From Eq. (13), we can easily reach the sum of errors over the entire database:

$$(\mathbf{w}^*, \alpha^*) = \arg \min_{(\mathbf{w}, \alpha)} \sum_{i=1}^{m} (\mathbf{w}^T \mathbf{x}_i + \alpha - y_i)^2 \tag{14}$$

Equation (14) is an optimization problem with respect to the parameters $(\mathbf{w}, \alpha)$. In general, the goal of linear regression is to construct a linear function to learn the real label according to attributes of the data sample.

In real world applications, sometimes people are more interested in the probability prediction for particular tasks. Taking the bankrupt prediction as an example, finance companies would like to learn the bankrupt probability of their customers based on payment history and salary level. Logistic regression is developed to learn the probability for some tasks, and is widely used in various areas to predict the occurrence of particular events, such as incidence of a disease, repurchase probability of a product, and failure rates of facilities. In fact, logistic regression is an extended version of linear regression, but the difference is that we have to map the linear function to a probability prediction. The most commonly used mapping function is sigmoid function written as:

$$y = \frac{1}{1 + e^{-x}} \tag{15}$$

Substituting Eq. (12) into Eq. (15), we have:

$$y_i = \frac{1}{1 + e^{-(\mathbf{w}^T \mathbf{x}_i + \alpha)}} \tag{16}$$

Also, Eq. (16) can be rewritten as:

$$ln \frac{y_i}{1 - y_i} = \mathbf{w}^T \mathbf{x}_i + \alpha \tag{17}$$

If we treat y_i as the probability of positive case and $1 - y_i$ as the probability of negative case, and then $\dfrac{y_i}{1 - y_i}$ represents the relative possibility of data sample $\mathbf{x}_i$ to be a positive case. It can be seen in Eq. (16) that logistic regression is to use linear regression results to predict the logarithm probability for occurrence of the real label.

If we treat y_i as the poster probability estimation $p(y_i = 1|\mathbf{x}_i)$, then we can rewrite Eq. (17) as:

$$ln \frac{p(y_i = 1|\mathbf{x}_i)}{p(y_i = 0|\mathbf{x}_i)} = \mathbf{w}^T \mathbf{x}_i + \alpha \tag{18}$$

It can be derived from Eq. (18) that:

$$p(y_i = 1|\mathbf{x}_i) = \frac{e^{\mathbf{w}^T \mathbf{x}_i + \alpha}}{1 + e^{\mathbf{w}^T \mathbf{x}_i + \alpha}} \tag{19}$$

$$p(y_i = 0|\mathbf{x}_i) = \frac{1}{1 + e^{\mathbf{w}^T \mathbf{x}_i + \alpha}} \tag{20}$$

As a consequence, we can use the maximum likelihood method to estimate $\mathbf{w}$ and α over the entire dataset [15]:

$$l(\mathbf{w}, \alpha) = \sum_{i=1}^{N} \ln p(y_i|\mathbf{x}_i; \mathbf{w}, \alpha) \tag{21}$$

Let $p_1(\mathbf{x}; \mathbf{w}, \alpha) = p(y = 1|\mathbf{x}; \mathbf{w}, \alpha)$, $p_0(\mathbf{x}; \mathbf{w}, \alpha) = p(y = 0|\mathbf{x}; \mathbf{w}, \alpha) = 1 - p_1(\mathbf{x}; \mathbf{w}, \alpha)$. Then the likelihood term in Eq. (21) can be rewritten as:

$$p(y_i|\mathbf{x}_i; \mathbf{w}, \alpha) = y_i p_1(\mathbf{x}_i; \mathbf{w}, \alpha) + (1 - y_i) p_0(\mathbf{x}_i; \mathbf{w}, \alpha) \tag{22}$$

Substituting Eq. (22) in to Eq. (21), and according to Eqs. (19), (20), the maximization of Eq. (22) is equivalent to minimizing the following problem:

$$l(\mathbf{w}, \alpha) = \sum_{i=1}^{m} (-y_i(\mathbf{w}^T \mathbf{x}_i + \alpha) + \ln(1 + e^{\mathbf{w}^T \mathbf{x}_i + \alpha})) \tag{23}$$

The above optimization problem is a differentiable convex function, and can be easily solved by the gradient decent method, or the Newton method.

2.3   System Architecture and Threat Model

The system architecture of the collaborative multiparty learning is illustrated in Fig. 1. It is assumed that N parities are included in this system, and each party has its own local dataset for training. All of the parties agree to train the same model, and logistic regression is applied. The central sever is to maintain the parameters of all these participating parties, including storing, updating, offloading, downloading, and so forth. As we discussed before, each participant constructs a local logistic regression model based on its own dataset. In the initialization step, every participant will obtain a set of parameters $(\mathbf{w}_i, \alpha_i)$, where $i \in [1, N]$. After obtaining the first round parameters, all these participants will upload their parameters to the central server for sharing. Now the central sever can act as a restoring and exchanging system that allows each participant to download the parameters of others. The advantage is that each participant can use other datasets in learning without knowing the original data of other parties. In addition, each party will not interfere with each other during the training process since the only interaction is the parameter exchanging. It should be noted that weighted parameter sharing is used such that the central server averages the parameters in proportional to the size of each party's data.

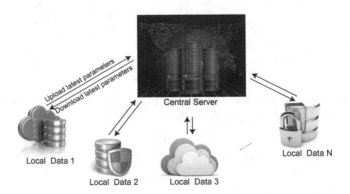

Fig. 1. System framework for multiparty learning.

However, the above multiparty learning system also induces privacy challenges. Since every participant maintains its own dataset which may contain sensitive information, directly uploading the parameters to the central sever might cause release of private information. As a result, the parameters of each participant should be protected before being sent to the central sever for sharing. In this paper, we will employ two methods to protect the parameters that will ensure differential privacy. The experimental results in Sect. 4 will show that both methods can achieve good performance.

3 Privacy-Preserving Logistic Regression

3.1 Output Function Perturbation Approach (OFPA)

As mentioned in the previous section, the parameters $(\mathbf{w}, \alpha)$ may contain sensitive information which cannot be uploaded to the central server directly. Every run of the logistic regression model by the local participant will produce a new set of parameters $(\mathbf{w}, \alpha)$. As we will discuss in Algorithm 1, it is very challenging to directly apply the Laplace mechanism due to the difficulty of calculating the global sensitivity of the objective function. As a result, we choose to develop ways to perturb the objective function and then we can easily apply the Laplace mechanism to preserve differential privacy. Let us first start with a simple approach which directly adds Laplace noise to the parameters $(\mathbf{w}, \alpha)$ [13], as described in *Algorithm 1*.

Algorithm 1. Laplace noise addition to parameters

Input:
    Input a local database $\mathcal{D}$;
Output:
    Encrypted parameter $(\mathbf{w}, \alpha)$;
1: Construct a local logistic regression model $\mathcal{M}$ over the database $\mathcal{D}$;
2: Compute the optimal parameter $(\mathbf{w}^*, \alpha^*)$ for $\mathcal{M}$;
3: Compute $\Delta S_{\mathcal{M}}$ from Eq. (6);
4: Generate a random noise vector $\mathbf{v}$ with elements from the Laplace distribution
$$Lap(x|0, \frac{\Delta S_{\mathcal{M}}}{\epsilon}) = \frac{\epsilon}{2\Delta S_{\mathcal{M}}} exp(-\frac{|x|\epsilon}{\Delta S_{\mathcal{M}}});$$
5: Compute $(\mathbf{w}, \alpha) = (\mathbf{w}^*, \alpha^*) + \mathbf{v}$;
6: **return** $(\mathbf{w}, \alpha)$;

Theorem 1. The output $(\mathbf{w}, \alpha) = (\mathbf{w}^*, \alpha^*) + \mathbf{v}$ from *Algorithm* 1 satisfies ϵ-differential privacy.

Proof: The proof is omitted due to space limit.

From Theorem 1, we know that *Algorithm* 1 provides a way to realize ϵ-differential privacy with respect to parameters $(\mathbf{w}, \alpha)$ of each local participant. However, the disadvantage of *Algorithm* 1 is the complexity of computing global sensitivity $\Delta S_{\mathcal{M}}$, which may not be preferable for model training.

Next we will develop a more brief and stable method to realize ϵ-differential privacy for the parameters $(\mathbf{w}, \alpha)$. Instead of adding noise to the parameters directly, we decide to generate a noise vector $\mathbf{v}$ via the Laplace mechanism, and adding this generated noisy vector into objective function which will give:

$$l'(\mathbf{w}, \alpha) = l(\mathbf{w}, \alpha) + \mathbf{v}^T \mathbf{w}$$
$$= \sum_{i=1}^{m} (-y_i(\mathbf{w}^T \mathbf{x}_i + \alpha) + ln(1 + e^{\mathbf{w}^T \mathbf{x}_i + \alpha})) + \mathbf{v}^T \mathbf{w} \tag{24}$$

It can be proved that the output of Eq. (24) meets ϵ-differential privacy as stated in Theorem 2. The detailed computational procedures for collaborative learning of OFPA is shown in *Algorithm 2*.

The 3rd line of *Algorithm 2* points out the stop criteria for collaborative learning. If the variation at the central server is below the preset threshold, we assume the result is optimal and the parameters obtained are global optimal for all participants. In the 7th line, it can be seen that for every participant's objective function, we will add a Laplace noise vector to protect the privacy. The 8th line is the core part of collaborative learning that every participant will download the weighted averaging parameters for the next-round training. The main function of the central server is stated in line 12; i.e., it will calculate the weighted average of the uploaded parameters from all participants. From the whole process, participants can enjoy the benefits of multiple data sources without worrying about information leakage.

Theorem 2. The output of $l'(\mathbf{w}, \alpha) = l(\mathbf{w}, \alpha) + \mathbf{v}_{ik}^T \mathbf{w}$ for each participant in *Algorithm 2* satisfies ϵ-differential privacy.

Proof: To prove the ϵ-differential privacy for any pair of neighbor databases $\mathcal{D}$ and $\mathcal{D}'$, we need to show that *Definition 1* holds for any randomized algorithms.

Without loss of generality, suppose the last element of $\mathcal{D}$ and $\mathcal{D}'$ is different, such that $\mathcal{D}$ is composed of $(\mathbf{x}_1, y_1), (\mathbf{x}_2, y_2), \cdots, (\mathbf{x}_{n-1}, y_{n-1}), (\mathbf{x}_n, y_n)$, and $\mathcal{D}'$ is composed of $(\mathbf{x}_1, y_1), (\mathbf{x}_2, y_2), \cdots, (\mathbf{x}_{n-1}, y_{n-1}), (\mathbf{x}_n', y_n')$. In addition, we also assume that $\| \mathbf{x}_i \| \leq 1$, which can be normalized to 1 if not. We know that the minimization of Eq. (24) will lead to the zero derivative. In addition, let $(\mathbf{w}, \alpha)$ and $(\mathbf{w}', \alpha')$ be what are obtained for $\mathcal{D}$ and $\mathcal{D}'$ after every round of training.

To prove ϵ-differential privacy between $\mathcal{D}$ and $\mathcal{D}'$, we only need to show ϵ-differential privacy of the output from $l'(\mathbf{w}, \alpha)$. The zero derivative of Eq. (24) for the last element of $\mathcal{D}$ and $\mathcal{D}'$ will give:

$$\mathbf{v} - y_n \mathbf{x}_n - \frac{\mathbf{x}_n}{1 + exp(\mathbf{w}_n^T \mathbf{x}_n + \alpha)}$$
$$= \mathbf{v}' - y_n \mathbf{x}_n' - \frac{\mathbf{x}_n'}{1 + exp(\mathbf{w}_n^{T'} \mathbf{x}_n' + \alpha')} \tag{25}$$

Since $\| \mathbf{x}_n \|_1 \leq 1$, $\| \mathbf{x}_n' \|_1 \leq 1$, $exp(\mathbf{w}_n^T \mathbf{x}_n + \alpha) > 0$, and $exp(\mathbf{w}_n^{T'} \mathbf{x}_n' + \alpha') > 0$. Thus for any pair of $\mathbf{v}$ and $\mathbf{v}'$, we will get $\| \mathbf{v} - \mathbf{v}' \|_1 \leq 4$ from Eq. (25). Then for any $(\mathbf{w}, \alpha)$ we have the following:

$$\frac{P((\mathbf{w}, \alpha)|(\mathbf{x}_1, y_1), (\mathbf{x}_2, y_2), (\mathbf{x}_3, y_3), \cdots, (\mathbf{x}_n, y_n))}{P((\mathbf{w}, \alpha)|(\mathbf{x}_1, y_1), (\mathbf{x}_2, y_2), (\mathbf{x}_3, y_3), \cdots, (\mathbf{x}'_n, y'_n))}$$

$$= \frac{\Pi_{i=1}^m e^{\frac{-4}{\epsilon} v_i}}{\Pi_{i=1}^m e^{\frac{-4}{\epsilon} v'_i}} \tag{26}$$

$$= e^{\frac{-4}{\epsilon} \|\mathbf{v}\|_1 - \|\mathbf{v}'\|_1} \leq e^{\epsilon}$$

Algorithm 2. Privacy-Preserving Collaborative Logistic Regression of OFPA

Input:
    Input N databases $\mathcal{D}_1, \mathcal{D}_2, \mathcal{D}_3, \cdots, \mathcal{D}_N$;
Output:
    Output global optimal parameter $(\mathbf{w}, \alpha)$;
1: Initialize $k = 0$;
2: Initialize $(\mathbf{w}_k, \alpha_k) = \mathbf{0}$;
3: **while** $|\Delta(\mathbf{w}_k, \alpha_k)| > \eta$
4:     **for** i = 1 : N
5:         Local data owner i constructs its own logistic regression model $l(\mathbf{w}, \alpha)$ from Eq. (23);
6:         Generate a random vector $\mathbf{v}_{ik}$ with elements from Laplace distribution $Lap(x|0, 4/\epsilon)$;
7:         Compute perturbed objective function $l'(\mathbf{w}, \alpha) = l(\mathbf{w}, \alpha) + \mathbf{v}_{ik}^T \mathbf{w}$;
8:         Download weighted parameters from central server, and update $(\mathbf{w}_{ik}, \alpha_{ik}) = (\mathbf{w}_k, \alpha_k)$;
9:         Compute $(\mathbf{w}_{ik}^*, \alpha_{ik}^*) = \arg\min l'(\mathbf{w}, \alpha)$;
10:        Upload $(\mathbf{w}_{ik}^*, \alpha_{ik}^*)$ to the central server;
11:     **end for**;
12:     Central server computes weighted averaging parameter $(\mathbf{w}_k, \alpha_k)$;
13:     $k = k + 1$;
14: **return** $(\mathbf{w}, \alpha) = (\mathbf{w}_k, \alpha_k)$;

3.2 Output Function Approximation Approach (OFAA)

For OFPA, we add a noise vector into the objective function according to Laplace mechanism. However, one can see that the generated noise is from a constant scale Laplace distribution, and we cannot adjust the noise level. As a result, a preferable mechanism should be able to adjust the noise level according to particular forms of the objective function. In the following, we will develop an approach by injecting noise to coefficients of the objective function's approximation form.

Before delving into details of the function approximation approach, we first discuss the structure of the objective function of logistic regression. It can be verified that $l(\mathbf{w}, \alpha)$ in Eq. (23) is a continuous and differentiable function. According to Stone-Weierstrass Theorem [23], we can approximate $l(\mathbf{w}, \alpha)$ with a polynomial function with respect to $(\mathbf{w}, \alpha)$. Parameter $(\mathbf{w}, \alpha)$ is a $m + 1$ dimensional vector variable $(w_1, w_2, w_3, \cdots, w_m, \alpha)$. Let Φ_j be the set of products of $(w_1, w_2, w_3, \cdots, w_m, \alpha)$ at the jth degree expressed as:

$$\Phi_j = \{w_1^{d_1} \cdot w_2^{d_2} \cdot w_3^{d_3} \cdots w_m^{d_m} \cdot \alpha^{d_{m+1}} | \sum_{i=1}^{m+1} d_i = j\} \qquad (27)$$

where $d_1, d_2, d_3, \cdots, d_{m+1} \in \mathcal{N}$, and let $\phi(\mathbf{w}) = w_1^{d_1} \cdot w_2^{d_2} \cdot w_3^{d_3} \cdots w_m^{d_m} \cdot \alpha^{d_{m+1}}$. Then we can get the approximation expression of $l(\mathbf{w}, \alpha)$ according to Stone-Weierstrass Theorem as follows:

$$l(\mathbf{w}, \alpha) = \sum_{j=0}^{J} \sum_{\phi \in \Phi_j} \sum_{s_i \in \mathcal{D}} \lambda_{\phi s_i} \phi(\mathbf{w}) \qquad (28)$$

where s_i is the ith element in database $\mathcal{D}$, and $\lambda_{\phi s_i}$ is the coefficient of polynomial for data record s_i. It can be seen from Eq. (28) that the objective function $l(\mathbf{w}, \alpha)$ can be approximated with a formula consisting of polynomial function only. As a result, it occurs to us that we can add noise to the coefficients of each degree in the polynomial form. The following *Algorithm* 3 will give detailed steps about adding noise to the coefficients of the polynomial expression.

From *Algorithm* 3, we can see that the central server plays the same role of the previous algorithm, but the difference lies in the noise generation mechanism. The determination of the noise level is from the 7th and 8th steps of *Algorithm* 3. For the jth degree of the approximate polynomial expression, we choose the maximum coefficient $\| \lambda_{\Phi_j} \|_{max}$, and set $\Delta S = 2(J + 1) \| \lambda_{\Phi_j} \|_{max}$ as the scale for Laplace distribution. Then in the 10th step, we will obtain a new perturbed approximate objective function $\hat{l}(\mathbf{w}, \alpha)$. The parameter $(\mathbf{w}, \alpha)$ from $\hat{l}(\mathbf{w}, \alpha)$ satisfies ϵ-differential privacy, and the proofs will be given in Theorem 3.

Theorem 3. In *Algorithm* 3, the perturbed approximate objective function $\hat{l}(\mathbf{w}, \alpha)$ satisfies ϵ-differential privacy for Laplace distribution with scale ΔS.

Proof: Firstly, without loss of generality, we suppose $\mathcal{D}$ and $\mathcal{D}'$ differ with the last data record, and let s_n and s'_n be the corresponding last data records. We have that:

$$\frac{P((\mathbf{w}, \alpha)|(s_1, s_2, s_3, \cdots, s_n)}{P((\mathbf{w}, \alpha)|(s_1, s_2, s_3, \cdots, s_n')}$$

$$= \frac{\Pi_{j=0}^{J} \Pi_{\phi \in \Phi_j} \Pi_{s_i \in \mathcal{D}} \, e^{\left(\frac{\epsilon \| \lambda'_{\phi s_i} - \lambda_{\phi s_i} \|_1}{\Delta S}\right)}}{\Pi_{j=0}^{J} \Pi_{\phi \in \Phi_j} \Pi_{s_i \in \mathcal{D}'} \, e^{\left(\frac{\epsilon \| \lambda'_{\phi s_i} - \lambda_{\phi s_i} \|_1}{\Delta S}\right)}}$$

$$\leq \Pi_{j=0}^{J} \Pi_{\phi \in \Phi_j} \, e^{\left(\frac{\epsilon(\| \sum_{s_i \in \mathcal{D}} \lambda'_{\phi s_i} - \sum_{s_i \in \mathcal{D}'} \lambda'_{\phi s_i} \|_1)}{\Delta S}\right)} \quad (29)$$

$$= \Pi_{j=0}^{J} \Pi_{\phi \in \Phi_j} \, e^{\left(\frac{\epsilon(\| \lambda'_{\phi s_n} - \lambda'_{\phi s_n'} \|_1)}{\Delta S}\right)}$$

$$= \Pi_{j=0}^{J} \, e^{\left(\frac{\epsilon(\| \lambda'_{\Phi_j s_n} - \lambda'_{\Phi_j s_n'} \|_1)}{\Delta S}\right)}$$

$$\leq \Pi_{j=0}^{J} \, e^{\left(\frac{\epsilon(2\max(\| \lambda'_{\Phi_j} \|_1, \| \lambda'_{\Phi_j} \|_1))}{\Delta S}\right)}$$

$$= e^{\sum_{j=0}^{J} \epsilon/(J+1)} = e^{\epsilon}$$

The first inequity is derived from the triangle formula $\| a \|_1 - \| b \|_1 \leq \| a \pm b \|_1$, where a and b are real numbers. The second inequality is derived as follows:

$$\| \lambda'_{\Phi_j s_n} - \lambda'_{\Phi_j s_n'} \|_1 \leq \| \lambda'_{\Phi_j s_n} \| + \| \lambda'_{\Phi_j s_n'} \|_1$$
$$\leq 2\max(\| \lambda'_{\Phi_j} \|_1, \| \lambda'_{\Phi_j} \|_1)$$

Then Eq. (29) holds, and the proof is complete.

It can be seen that the noise addition mechanism of *Algorithm* 3 guarantees ϵ-differential privacy. As a result, releasing the parameter of $\hat{l}(\mathbf{w}, \alpha)$ will not cause information leakage. In addition, the noise addition mechanism in *Algorithm* 3 is designed for objective function with polynomial expression, but $l(\mathbf{w}, \alpha)$ is not of polynomial form yet. We have stated that $l(\mathbf{w}, \alpha)$ can be approximated with a polynomial form by the Stone-Weierstrass Theorem and next we will find a way to derive the approximation polynomial form of $l(\mathbf{w}, \alpha)$.

It is well known that Taylor expansion is commonly used in approximating a continuous and differentiable function with arbitrary precision. In this paper, we decide to use Taylor expansion to derive the approximation polynomial expression for our objective function $l(\mathbf{w}, \alpha)$. For convenience, we can rewrite $l(\mathbf{w}, \alpha)$ as the following:

$$l(\mathbf{w}, \alpha) = \sum_{i=1}^{m} [l_1(\theta_1) - l_2(\theta_2)] \quad (30)$$

where $l_1(t) = \ln(1 + \exp(t))$, $l_2(t) = t$, $\theta_1 = \mathbf{w}^T \mathbf{x}_i + \alpha$, and $\theta_2 = y_i(\mathbf{w}^T \mathbf{x}_i + \alpha)$. In addition, the Taylor expansion of a differentiable and continuous function $f(x)$ at point a is expressed as:

Algorithm 3. Privacy-Preserving Collaborative Logistic Regression of OFAA

Input:
    Input N databases $\mathcal{D}_1, \mathcal{D}_2, \mathcal{D}_3, \cdots, \mathcal{D}_N$;
Output:
    Output global optimal parameter $(\mathbf{w}, \alpha)$;
1: Initialize $k = 0$;
2: Initialize $(\mathbf{w}_k, \alpha_k) = \mathbf{0}$;
3: **while** $| \Delta(\mathbf{w}_k, \alpha_k) | > \eta$
4:     **for** i $= 1 : N$
5:         Let $l(\mathbf{w}, \alpha)_i = \sum_{j=0}^{J} \sum_{\phi \in \Phi_j} \sum_{s_k \in \mathcal{D}_i} \lambda_{\phi s_k} \phi(\mathbf{w}, \alpha)$;
6:         **for** j $= 0 : J$
7:             Let $\Delta S = 2(J + 1) \parallel \lambda_{\Phi_j} \parallel_{max}$;
8:             Let $\lambda'_{\Phi_j} = \lambda_{\Phi_j} + Lap(x | 0, \dfrac{\Delta S}{\epsilon})$;
9:         **end for;**
10:        Let $\hat{l}(\mathbf{w}, \alpha)_i = \sum_{j=0}^{J} \sum_{\phi \in \Phi_j} \sum_{s_k \in \mathcal{D}_i} \lambda_{\phi' s_k} \phi(\mathbf{w}, \alpha)$;
11:        Download weighted parameters from central server,
           and update $(\mathbf{w}_{ik}, \alpha_{ik}) = (\mathbf{w}_k, \alpha_k)$;
12:        Compute $(\mathbf{w}_{ik}^*, \alpha_{ik}^*) = \arg \min \hat{l}(\mathbf{w}, \alpha)_i$;
13:        Upload $(\mathbf{w}_{ik}^*, \alpha_{ik}^*)$ to central server;
14:    **end for;**
15:    Central server computes weighted averaging param-
       eter $(\mathbf{w}_k, \alpha_k)$;
16:    $k = k + 1$;
17: **return** $(\mathbf{w}, \alpha) = (\mathbf{w}_k, \alpha_k)$;

$$\sum_{n=0}^{\infty} \frac{f^{(n)}(a)}{n!} (x - a)^n \tag{31}$$

where $f^{(n)}(a)$ is the nth derivative of function f evaluated at point a. If we apply Taylor expansion to $l(\mathbf{w}, \alpha)$, we will have the following:

$$l(\mathbf{w}, \alpha) = \sum_{i=1}^{m} \sum_{n=0}^{\infty} [\frac{l_1^{(n)}(\theta_1')}{n!} (\theta_1 - \theta_1')^n - \frac{l_2^{(n)}(\theta_2')}{n!} (\theta_2 - \theta_2')^n] \tag{32}$$

where $l_1^{(n)}(\theta_1')$ is the nth derivative of function θ_1 evaluated at point θ_1', and $l_2^{(n)}(\theta_2')$ is the nth derivative of function θ_2 evaluated at point θ_2'. Note that $l_2^{(n)} = 0$ for $n > 1$. As a result, we can simplify Eq. (32) by setting $\theta_1' = \theta_2' = 0$, and we will have the following:

$$l(\mathbf{w}, \alpha) = \sum_{i=1}^{m} \sum_{n=0}^{\infty} \frac{l_1^{(n)}(0)}{n!} (\mathbf{w}^T \mathbf{x}_i + \alpha)^n - \sum_{i=1}^{m} (y_i \mathbf{w}^T \mathbf{x}_i + \alpha) \tag{33}$$

Up to now, we have derived the polynomial expression of the objective function $l(\mathbf{w}, \alpha)$. However, we cannot apply Eq. (33) directly due to the infinite summation. We can remove higher order polynomial terms of the Taylor expansion and only keep terms with orders $n \leq 2$. Then the approximate polynomial form of Eq. (33) is expressed as:

$$l(\mathbf{w}, \alpha) = \sum_{i=1}^{m} \sum_{n=0}^{2} \frac{l_1^{(n)}(0)}{n!} (\mathbf{w}^T \mathbf{x}_i + \alpha)^n - \sum_{i=1}^{m} (y_i \mathbf{w}^T \mathbf{x}_i + \alpha) \qquad (34)$$

and calculation of the derivative shows that $l_1^{(0)}(0) = \ln 2$, $l_1^{(1)}(0) = 1/2$, and $l_2^{(0)}(0) = 1/4$. With these derivative results, we can calculate the scale in $Algorithm$ 3. As described in $Algorithm$ 3, for the polynomial expression with different order j, we will choose the according $\Delta S = 2(J+1) \parallel \lambda_{\Phi_j} \parallel_{max}$ as the scale of the Laplace distribution. Taking $j = 1$ as an example, ΔS is expressed as:

$$\Delta S = 2 \max(\frac{f_1^0(0)}{1!} \sum_{i=1}^{d} x_i + \alpha + y_i \sum_{i=1}^{d} x_i + \alpha) * 3$$
$$\leq \frac{9}{2} d \qquad (35)$$

where d is the number of attributes of data records. As a result, we can inject the noise into the coefficients of the first order polynomial term with Laplace distribution $Lap(x|0, \frac{9d}{2\epsilon})$ according to $Algorithm$ 3, and inject noise to the polynomial form of other orders with the same approach.

4 Experiments

In this section, we evaluate the performance of the two proposed approaches OFPA and OFAA, and compare them with regular logistic regression without privacy protection denoted as $LR\_NoPrivacy$ which is trained as a single party who holds the entire dataset. All experiments are conducted using Python 2.7 on a Macbook with a 2.2 GHz Intel Core i7 CPU and 16 GB RAM.

We choose two real datasets for experiments, $Bank$ $Marketing$ [19] used to predict whether the client will subscribe a term deposit and $Default$ of $Credit$ $Card$ $Clients$ [27] for predicting whether a credit owner will default or not. The $Bank$ $Marketing$ dataset contains 45211 records and 17 attributes, including bank client attributes (e.g., age), current campaign attributes (e.g., contact communication type), and social and economic context attributes (e.g., employment variation rate). For the $Default$ of $Credit$ $Card$ $Clients$ dataset, it contains 30000 records and 24 attributes, including credit card owner attributes (e.g., gender), history of past payment, amount of bill statement attributes, and amount of previous payment attributes. Since several attributes in both datasets are categorical variables, we encode such categorical values into integers for our model training using $LabelEncoder$ [1]. Without loss of generality, we assume three parties are included intending to collaboratively learn the logistic regression model, which hold 40%, 30% and 10% of each dataset separately, while the remained 20% of each dataset is treated as test set.

We conduct logistic regression on each dataset by varying three different parameters, namely the privacy budget ϵ, dataset cardinality, and dataset dimensionality. According to Eq. (19), if $p(y_i = 1|\mathbf{x}_i) = \dfrac{e^{\mathbf{w}^T\mathbf{x}_i+\alpha}}{1 + e^{\mathbf{w}^T\mathbf{x}_i+\alpha}} > 0.5$, we make prediction to be 1, and otherwise to be 0. The accuracy of logistic regression models is measured by *misclassification rate*, which is defined as the fraction of data records that are incorrectly classified. Additionally, in each experiment, the logistic regression model is trained 40 epochs 10 times, and the average results are reported.

4.1   Classification Accuracy vs. Privacy Budget

To explore how privacy budget ϵ affects the performance of the proposed algorithms, experiments are performed by varying ϵ from 0.1 to 3.2. Figure 2 shows the misclassification rate of each algorithm against the privacy budget ϵ. The accuracy of LR_NoPrivacy almost stays stable on both datasets. Both OFPA and OFAA produce less misclassifications with increasing ϵ, since a larger ϵ means that a smaller amount of noise is added to the objective function. Furthermore, it shows that the performance of OFPA is slightly better than OFAA, but both of them are robust against the varied ϵ and close to regular logistic regression.

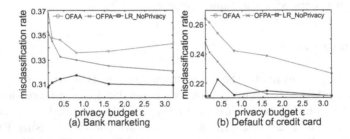

Fig. 2. Classification accuracy vs. privacy budget.

4.2   Classification Accuracy vs. Dataset Cardinality

To evaluate the classification accuracy against the variation of dataset cardinality, we generate random subsets of the two original datasets with sampling rate from 0.2 to 1, while keeping ϵ as 0.8. As shown in Fig. 3, the accuracy of LR_NoPrivacy slightly outperforms that of OFPA and OFAA, but the performance of OFPA and OFAA improves rapidly with the increase of dataset cardinality. More importantly, the misclassification rate of OFPA and OFAA is comparable with LR_NoPrivacy when we use the full dataset, indicating that our proposed algorithms can make accurate predictions while protecting data privacy.

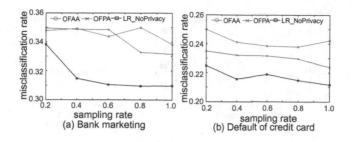

Fig. 3. Classification accuracy vs. dataset cardinality.

4.3 Classification Accuracy vs. Dataset Dimensionality

To demonstrate the effectiveness of the proposed algorithms against the change of dataset dimensionality, we vary the dimensions of *Bank Marketing* dataset from 5 to 17, and change the dimensionality of *Default of Credit Card Clients* from 8 to 24, while setting ϵ as 0.8. Figure 4 shows that although the performance of LR_NoPrivacy still performs slightly better than that of OFPA and OFAA, the accuracy of our proposed approaches improves with the increasing of dataset dimensionality.

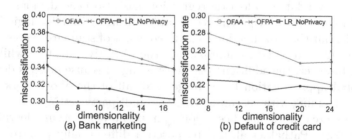

Fig. 4. Classification accuracy vs. dataset dimensionality.

4.4 Training Time vs. Privacy Budget

In order to evaluate how noise injection affects the training time, we train each logistic regression model with 40 epochs 10 times. The average training time is reported in Fig. 5. It shows that time cost of training LR_NoPrivacy is less than that of OFPA and OFAA, which is reasonable since the latter needs more time to stabilize the noisy model. Note that the training of logistic model using OFAA is slower than that of OFPA, since the injected noise in OFPA is constant, but we have to generate more noise to perform OFAA.

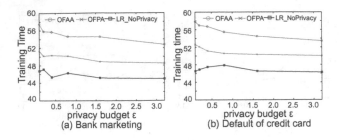

Fig. 5. Training time vs. privacy budget.

5   Related Work

Dwork et al. first proposed the notion of ϵ-differential privacy [7], and provided Laplace mechanism to achieve it. Later, differential privacy has been developed as a platform to deal with privacy analysis and extensive work employed it to address different types of tasks. For example, Friedman et al. [9] achieved ϵ-differential privacy decision tree to predict adult incomes. Bhaskar et al. [3] reported a differential privacy solution for frequent pattern mining. Other types of work preserving differential privacy have also been done, including support vector machines [16], recommendation system [18], and neural networks [2]. Differential privacy related to logistic regression has also been demonstrated. For instance, Chaudhuri et al. [6] enforced ϵ-differential privacy for logistic regression analysis, but the cost function considered is not of standard regression form. Zhang et al. [28] proposed to approximate the objective function while adding noise to it; however, the addition noise level is high because noise is determined by the global approximation form. In general, all of the above work focus on single party training without considering the multiparty setting.

Some research work has been done on privacy-preserving learning from multiparty data. Pathak et al. [21] proposed a differentially private algorithm based on parameter averaging through secure multiparty computation. Rajkumar et al. [22] designed a privacy-preserving multiparty learning scheme, which is enforced by private exchange of gradient information to minimize empirical risks incrementally. In addition, other works using different forms of noise scaling to achieve differential privacy over distributed data have also been reported [11,25]. Different from previous work, we propose a weighted sharing scheme which will help increase the accuracy of model. In addition, we propose to approximate the objection and then inject noise to each degree separately, providing a more efficient, more concise and faster method to complete data training. Furthermore, the schemes designed here feature easy extension to other machine learning tasks.

6   Conclusion

In this paper, we proposed two differentially private approaches for collaboratively training logistic regression classifiers among multiple parties. The proposed approaches enable users to enjoy well-trained logistic regression classifiers based on distributed datasets without disclosing their raw data to each other. Experimental results show that the effectiveness, robustness, and training cost of the proposed algorithms are close to that of regular logistic regression on the aggregate dataset without privacy protection. Although this work mainly focuses on logistic regression, the proposed schemes can also be extended to other classification problems in the context of collaborative learning.

References

1. sklearn.preprocessing.LabelEncoder. http://scikit-learn.org/stable/modules/generated/sklearn.preprocessing.LabelEncoder.html
2. Abadi, M., et al.: Deep learning with differential privacy. In: Proceedings of the 2016 ACM SIGSAC Conference on Computer and Communications Security, pp. 308–318. ACM (2016)
3. Bhaskar, R., Laxman, S., Smith, A., Thakurta, A.: Discovering frequent patterns in sensitive data. In: Proceedings of the 16th ACM SIGKDD International Conference on Knowledge Discovery and Data Mining, pp. 503–512. ACM (2010)
4. Bos, J.W., Lauter, K., Naehrig, M.: Private predictive analysis on encrypted medical data. J. Biomed. Inform. **50**, 234–243 (2014)
5. Bouwen, R., Taillieu, T.: Multi-party collaboration as social learning for interdependence: developing relational knowing for sustainable natural resource management. J. Community Appl. Soc. Psychol. **14**(3), 137–153 (2004)
6. Chaudhuri, K., Monteleoni, C.: Privacy-preserving logistic regression. In: Advances in Neural Information Processing Systems, pp. 289–296 (2009)
7. Dwork, C.: Differential privacy: a survey of results. In: Agrawal, M., Du, D., Duan, Z., Li, A. (eds.) TAMC 2008. LNCS, vol. 4978, pp. 1–19. Springer, Heidelberg (2008). https://doi.org/10.1007/978-3-540-79228-4_1
8. Dwork, C., Roth, A., et al.: The algorithmic foundations of differential privacy. Found. Trends® Theor. Comput. Sci. **9**(3–4), 211–407 (2014)
9. Friedman, A., Schuster, A.: Data mining with differential privacy. In: Proceedings of the 16th ACM SIGKDD International Conference on Knowledge Discovery and Data Mining, pp. 493–502. ACM (2010)
10. Graepel, T., Lauter, K., Naehrig, M.: ML confidential: machine learning on encrypted data. In: Kwon, T., Lee, M.-K., Kwon, D. (eds.) ICISC 2012. LNCS, vol. 7839, pp. 1–21. Springer, Heidelberg (2013). https://doi.org/10.1007/978-3-642-37682-5_1
11. Heikkilä, M., Okimoto, Y., Kaski, S., Shimizu, K., Honkela, A.: Differentially private Bayesian learning on distributed data. arXiv preprint arXiv:1703.01106 (2017)
12. Inan, A., Kantarcioglu, M., Bertino, E.: Using anonymized data for classification. In: 2009 IEEE 25th International Conference on Data Engineering, ICDE 2009, pp. 429–440. IEEE (2009)
13. Kabir, S.M., Youssef, A.M., Elhakeem, A.K.: On data distortion for privacy preserving data mining. In: 2007 Canadian Conference on Electrical and Computer Engineering, CCECE 2007, pp. 308–311. IEEE (2007)
14. Kotsiantis, S.B., Zaharakis, I., Pintelas, P.: Supervised machine learning: a review of classification techniques (2007)
15. Kutner, M.H., Nachtsheim, C., Neter, J.: Applied Linear Regression Models. McGraw-Hill/Irwin, New York (2004)

16. Li, H., Xiong, L., Ohno-Machado, L., Jiang, X.: Privacy preserving RBF kernel support vector machine. BioMed Res. Int. **2014**, 1–10 (2014)
17. Liu, K., Kargupta, H., Ryan, J.: Random projection-based multiplicative data perturbation for privacy preserving distributed data mining. IEEE Trans. Knowl. Data Eng. **18**(1), 92–106 (2006)
18. McSherry, F., Mironov, I.: Differentially private recommender systems: building privacy into the net. In: Proceedings of the 15th ACM SIGKDD International Conference on Knowledge Discovery and Data Mining, pp. 627–636. ACM (2009)
19. Moro, S., Cortez, P., Rita, P.: A data-driven approach to predict the success of bank telemarketing. Decis. Support Syst. **62**, 22–31 (2014)
20. Ohrimenko, O., et al.: Oblivious multi-party machine learning on trusted processors. In: USENIX Security Symposium, pp. 619–636 (2016)
21. Pathak, M., Rane, S., Raj, B.: Multiparty differential privacy via aggregation of locally trained classifiers. In: Advances in Neural Information Processing Systems, pp. 1876–1884 (2010)
22. Rajkumar, A., Agarwal, S.: A differentially private stochastic gradient descent algorithm for multiparty classification. In: Artificial Intelligence and Statistics, pp. 933–941 (2012)
23. Rudin, W., et al.: Principles of Mathematical Analysis, vol. 3. McGraw-hill, New York (1964)
24. Shobana, S., Nagajothi, P.: Deriving private information from randomized dataset using data reorganization techniques. Data Min. Knowl. Eng. **4**(4), 191–194 (2012)
25. Shokri, R., Shmatikov, V.: Privacy-preserving deep learning. In: Proceedings of the 22nd ACM SIGSAC Conference on Computer and Communications Security, pp. 1310–1321. ACM (2015)
26. Witten, I.H., Frank, E., Hall, M.A., Pal, C.J.: Data Mining: Practical Machine Learning Tools and Techniques. Morgan Kaufmann, Cambridge (2016)
27. Yeh, I.C., Lien, C.H.: The comparisons of data mining techniques for the predictive accuracy of probability of default of credit card clients. Expert Syst. Appl. **36**(2), 2473–2480 (2009)
28. Zhang, J., Zhang, Z., Xiao, X., Yang, Y., Winslett, M.: Functional mechanism: regression analysis under differential privacy. Proc. VLDB Endow. **5**(11), 1364–1375 (2012)

Privacy-Preserving Outsourcing of Large-Scale Nonlinear Programming to the Cloud

Ang Li[1]([✉]), Wei Du[2]([✉]), and Qinghua Li[1]

[1] Department of Computer Science and Computer Engineering,
University of Arkansas, Fayetteville, USA
{angli,qinghual}@uark.edu
[2] Department of Electrical and Computer Engineering, Michigan State University,
East Lansing, USA
duwei1@msu.edu

Abstract. The increasing massive data generated by various sources has given birth to big data analytics. Solving large-scale nonlinear programming problems (NLPs) is one important big data analytics task that has applications in many domains such as transport and logistics. However, NLPs are usually too computationally expensive for resource-constrained users. Fortunately, cloud computing provides an alternative and economical service for resource-constrained users to outsource their computation tasks to the cloud. However, one major concern with outsourcing NLPs is the leakage of user's private information contained in NLP formulations and results. Although much work has been done on privacy-preserving outsourcing of computation tasks, little attention has been paid to NLPs. In this paper, we for the first time investigate secure outsourcing of general large-scale NLPs with nonlinear constraints. A secure and efficient transformation scheme at the user side is proposed to protect user's private information; at the cloud side, generalized reduced gradient method is applied to effectively solve the transformed large-scale NLPs. The proposed protocol is implemented on a cloud computing testbed. Experimental evaluations demonstrate that significant time can be saved for users and the proposed mechanism has the potential for practical use.

1 Introduction

Cloud computing has gained an increasing popularity in both academia and industry communities, and been widely used due to its huge computing power, on-demand scalability and low usage cost [15]. It offers many services to users, such as data storage, data management and computing resources via the Internet. Besides personal uses such as data storage service represented by Dropbox, cloud computing also has enterprise applications such as big data analytics and

---

Ang Li and Wei Du equally contributed to this work. This work was done when Wei Du was at the University of Arkansas.

© ICST Institute for Computer Sciences, Social Informatics and Telecommunications Engineering 2018
R. Beyah et al. (Eds.): SecureComm 2018, LNICST 254, pp. 569–587, 2018.
https://doi.org/10.1007/978-3-030-01701-9_31

business intelligence. One fundamental feature of cloud computing is computation outsourcing, allowing users to perform computations at the resource-rich cloud side and no longer be limited by limited local resources.

Despite the tremendous benefits, outsourcing computation to the cloud also introduces security and privacy concerns. The first concern is data privacy including both input data privacy and output data privacy [14,16,20]. The outsourcing paradigm deprives users' direct control over the systems where their data is hosted and computed. The data input to the cloud may contain sensitive information such as medical records and financial asset status. The leakage of these data will breach users' privacy. To protect data against unauthorized leakage, data has to be encrypted before outsourcing. Another concern is the verifiability of results returned from the cloud. Usually users cannot oversee all details of the computations in the cloud. There do exist some motives for the cloud service provider to behave dishonestly and deliver incorrect results to users. One motive is that since intensive computing resources are usually needed to perform outsoursed computation tasks, the cloud service provider might not do all the needed computations to save computing resources. If the cloud server is under outside attacks during the computing process or suffering from internal software failures, the correctness of returned results will also be at risk. Consequently, the verifiability of results returned from cloud should be provided. A third concern is that the computation at the cloud should be efficient; otherwise there is no need for users to outsource computations to the cloud. The time needed by the client to offload the computation to the cloud should be much less than the time needed by the client to solve the computation task by itself [5,6,16,21].

In this paper, we investigate privacy-preserving outsourcing of large-scale NLPs with nonlinear constraints. NLP is a general optimization problem [2,3]. For instance, finding the optimal investment portfolio is a typical NLP optimization problem subjecting to nonlinear constraints, where an investor wants to maximize expected return and minimize risk simultaneously for investment. In the deep learning area, researchers are always making efforts to find the optimal solution for loss function, which can also be formulated as an NLP with nonlinear constraints [18]. NLPs with nonlinear constraints are also common in various industry domains, such as the minimum cost of transport and logistics, optimal design, emission-constrained minimum fuel, and so forth [2,3]. It is very challenging for resource-limited users to solve large-scale NLPs with nonlinear constraints, since it requires intensive computation resources.

In this work, we propose a privacy-preserving and efficient mechanism to offload large-scale NLPs with nonlinear constraints to the cloud. To the best of our knowledge, privacy-preserving outsourcing of NLPs with nonlinear constraints has never been studied before and this paper is the first. We first formulate the private NLP with nonlinear constraints as a set of matrices and vectors. Then the user generates random vectors and matrices and performs mathematical transformation to protect the original NLP formulation. It is proved that the transformed NLP with nonlinear constraints is computationally indistinguishable from the original one, which means that the cloud cannot infer any useful information about the original NLP from the transformed NLP. At the cloud side, the generalized reduced gradient method is employed to solve the encrypted NLP, which is experimentally demonstrated to be efficient and practical. Finally, the user can verify the correctness of the returned solution to NLP.

The contributions of this paper can be summarized as follows:

- For the first time, we propose an efficient and practical privacy-preserving mechanism for outsourcing large-scale NLPs with nonlinear constraints to the cloud.
- For the proposed solution, we mathematically prove that the input privacy and output privacy of users can be protected. The solution also provides verifiability of cloud-returned results.
- The proposed mechanism is implemented, and its performance is evaluated through experiments. The results show high efficiency and practicality of the proposed mechanism.

The rest of the paper is organized as follows. Section 2 reviews related work. Section 3 introduces system model and security definitions. Section 4 presents how to use transformation schemes to protect the original NLP and formal proofs are given. Section 5 applies the generalized reduced gradient method to solve the outsourced NLP with nonlinear constraints. Section 6 shows evaluation results. Section 7 concludes this paper.

2   Related Work

Much work has been done on privacy-preserving outsourcing of computation-intensive tasks to the cloud. Some work focused on outsourcing arbitrary computation functions [1,8,11], mainly using fully homomorphic encryption (FHE) schemes such as [10]. Although theoretical guarantees of privacy can be achieved with FHE, current FHE schemes have very high computation cost, making them impractical for large-scale computations such as large-scale NLPs addressed in this paper. Other work designed secure outsourcing protocols for specific problems, such as linear programming [19], system of equations [20], distributed linear programming [17], quadratic programming [21], and linear regression [4]. Outsourcing basic mathematical computations has also been studied, such as matrix determinant computation [13], matrix inversion [14], and modular exponentiations [7]. However, previous work mostly focused on linear systems and some other particular problems. Outsourcing NLPs has received little attention

Very recently, we also studied securely outsourcing NLPs in our previous work [9], but that work only considers NLPs with *linear* equality constraints. Different from it, this paper addresses NLPs with *nonlinear* inequality and equality constraints which are more complicated and general.

3   Problem Formulation

3.1   NLPs Formulation

The general form of NLP is expressed as follows [2,3]:

$$
\begin{aligned}
\mathbf{P}_1 : \text{Minimize} \quad & f(\mathbf{x}) \\
\text{subject to} \quad & g_i(\mathbf{x}) = 0, \qquad i = 1, \cdots, m \\
& h_j(\mathbf{x}) \leq b_j, \qquad j = 1, \cdots, l \\
& a_k \leq x_k \leq u_k,\ k = 1, \cdots n
\end{aligned}
\tag{1}
$$

where $\mathbf{x} = (x_1, x_2, \cdots, x_n)$ is an n dimensional vector of variables, $f(\mathbf{x})$ is a non-linear objective function, $g_i(\mathbf{x}) = 0$ are m equality constraints, and $h_j(\mathbf{x}) \leq b_j$ are l inequality constraints. In this paper, the NLP is considered as feasible indicating that there exists at least one point $\mathbf{x}^*$ satisfying all of the inequality and equality constraints. Also, it should be noted that the inequality and equality constraints are both of nonlinear form in this paper. NLPs appear many practical applications, such as machine learning, finance budget allocation, and some decision-making problems. Taking the typical support vector machine (SVM) classification as an example. It is known that SVM consists of linear and nonlinear form according to the selection of classification functions. A large portion of the classification tasks require using the nonlinear form of hyperplanes due to the complexity of data. As a result, the training of the SVM classifier is transformed to solve the nonlinear function subjecting to nonlinear constraints, where nonlinear function is the loss function of SVM model, and nonlinear constraints are nonlinear forms of hyperplanes.

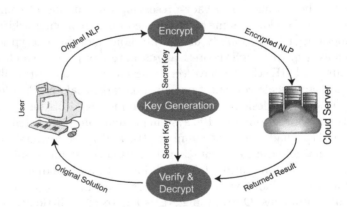

Fig. 1. System model for outsourcing large-scale NLPs with nonlinear constraints.

3.2 System Model

The outsourcing model has two parties, the user and the cloud server, as illustrated in Fig. 1. The user has an NLP problem to solve. However, the user cannot solve this large-scale problem due to his limited computation power. Thus, he outsources the NLP problem to the cloud server. In order to protect the original NLP problem Φ from being known to the cloud, the user generates a private key K to encrypt the problem Φ, and sends the encrypted NLP problem $\Phi(K)$ to the cloud server. The cloud server solves $\Phi(K)$ using the generalized reduced gradient method, and returns the solution back to the user. During the computing process, the cloud server is supposed to learn nothing or very little information about the original NLP problem. When the user receives the solution for $\Phi(K)$ from the server, the user verifies its correctness. If it is incorrect, the user will reject it; if it is correct, the user will accept it and decrypt it with the private key K to get the solution for the original NLP problem Φ.

3.3 Security Model and Goal

The security concerns and threats are mainly from the untrusted cloud server. A malicious cloud server may try to learn about the original NLP problem. It may also not follow the correct computing process of the problem and derive a wrong solution. As a result, the security goal is two-fold: hiding the original NLP problem from the cloud in order to protect the user's privacy, and providing a verification mechanism for the user to check the correctness of returned result so that the cloud server cannot cheat.

3.4 Security Requirements

This section gives a formal security definition for the outsourcing protocol. Let us first look at the scope of private information within this context. In the original NLP problem $\mathbf{P}_1$, the coefficient matrices of the equality and inequality constraints contain sensitive information. The positions of elements in the coefficient matrices may also contain private information, e.g. the node distribution graph of an optimal digital circuit layout path. In addition, the solution $\mathbf{x}^*$ of the original NLP problem $\mathbf{P}_1$ should also be protected.

The concept of computational indistinguishability is used in this paper to design a secure outsourcing protocol.

Definition 1: A randomized algorithm $\mathcal{A}$ satisfies computational indistinguishability if and only if for any two databases D and D', for every probabilistic polynomial-time adversary machine M, there exists a negligible function $neg(\cdot)$ such that [12]:

$$|Pr[M^{\mathcal{A}}(D)] - Pr[M^{\mathcal{A}}(D')]| \leq neg(\cdot) \qquad (2)$$

where the notation $M^{\mathcal{A}}(D)$ (similarly for $M^{\mathcal{A}}(D')$) means that adversary machines have access to the database and try to extract private information from the data. Definition 1 measures the information leakage level of the encryption scheme that encrypts the original NLP problem. If computational indistinguishability is achieved, the cloud server cannot learn anything significant about the original NLP problem.

4   NLP Transformation

4.1   Input Privacy Protection

In order to protect the coefficient matrices and vectors of the constraints as shown in the general form of NLP P_1, they are encrypted by the user's privacy key K.

Protecting Equality Constraints. Suppose the coefficient matrix and the vector of the equality constraints in P_1 are denoted as $G \in \mathbb{R}^{m \times n}$ and $b \in \mathbb{R}^{m \times 1}$, respectively. G and b can be efficiently hidden by employing matrix multiplications. In particular, the user can protect the equality constraint matrix and vectors as follows:

$$\hat{G} = PQG$$
$$\hat{b} = PQb \tag{3}$$

where $P \in \mathbb{R}^{m \times m}$ is a diagonal matrix, with the elements defined as follows:

$$P_{i,j} = \begin{cases} r_i & i = j \\ 0 & i \neq j \end{cases} \tag{4}$$

Here the value of r_i comes from the uniform distribution defined as:

$$r_i = \begin{cases} r & -N < r < N \\ 0 & \text{otherwise} \end{cases} \tag{5}$$

$Q \in \mathbb{R}^{m \times m}$ in Eq. (3) is a positive constant diagonal matrix, which is expressed as:

$$Q_{i,j} = \begin{cases} C & i = j \\ 0 & i \neq j \end{cases} \tag{6}$$

It can be seen from Eq. (3) that the matrices G and b are masked by the multiplying a random diagonal matrix P and a constant diagonal matrix Q. It should be noted that the rank of matrix G stays the same due to the full rank of P and Q. From the encryption form, one cannot extract any useful information without releasing P and Q. We will give detailed mathematical analysis of the above transformation in the next section.

Inequality Constraints Protection. The coefficient matrix of the inequality constraints is denoted as $\mathbf{H} \in \mathbb{R}^{l \times n}$. A similar approach can be used to encrypt $\mathbf{H}$ as follows:

$$\hat{\mathbf{H}} = \mathbf{TSH} \tag{7}$$

where $\mathbf{T} \in \mathbb{R}^{l \times l}$ is a diagonal matrix with elements generated following the uniform distribution defined in Eq. (5) and $\mathbf{S} \in \mathbb{R}^{l \times l}$ is set to be a diagonal constant matrix.

4.2 Output Privacy Protection

The above matrix multiplication mechanism is able to protect the input privacy, but the output privacy has not been addressed yet. The user sends the NLP to the cloud server, and will receive a solution $\mathbf{x}^*$ back from the cloud. The result $\mathbf{x}^*$ might contain sensitive information, e.g., the asset allocation strategy in a financial company. In fact, the output privacy can be easily protected by vector addition. We can just replace the original variable vector $\mathbf{x}$ with the following:

$$\mathbf{z} = \mathbf{x} + \mathbf{r} \tag{8}$$

where the elements of vector $\mathbf{r}$ are also taken from the uniform distribution defined in Eq. (5). After completing the protection of the input and output privacy, we can rewrite the original problem $\mathbf{P}_1$ as the following:

$$
\begin{aligned}
\mathbf{P}_2 : \text{Minimize} \quad & f(\mathbf{z}) \\
\text{subject to} \quad & \hat{g}_i(\mathbf{z}) = 0, \qquad i = 1, \cdots, m \\
& \hat{h}_j(\mathbf{z}) \leq \hat{b}_j, \qquad j = 1, \cdots, l \\
& \hat{a}_k \leq z_k \leq \hat{u}_k, \, k = 1, \cdots n
\end{aligned} \tag{9}
$$

where $\hat{\mathbf{G}} = \mathbf{PQG}$, $\hat{\mathbf{b}} = \mathbf{PQb}$, $\hat{\mathbf{H}} = \mathbf{TSH}$, $\mathbf{z} = \mathbf{x} + \mathbf{r}$, $\hat{a}_k = a_k + r_k$, and $\hat{u}_k = u_k + r_k$.

4.3 Structure Privacy Protection

The above matrix transformations can protect the element values within the input and output matrix; however, the structure of the input and output matrix (i.e., positions of non-zero elements) still needs to be protected, which might also contain sensitive information. For example, the circuit layout is of vital importance in the area of electronics design, and one of the common methods is to construct matrices according to the node distribution. Thus, it is easy to recover the original circuit layout if we know the circuit matrices. As a result, the position of the elements in a matrix sometimes will contain sensitive and valuable information which needs to be hidden. Next we will introduce a matrix permutation mechanism to protect the position information of the original matrix.

Algorithm 1. Key generation.

Input:
   Input size n;
Output:
   Random uniformly distributed vector $\mathbf{r}$;
   Random uniformly distributed matrix $\mathbf{S}$;
   Constant matrix $\mathbf{M}$;
   Random permutation matrix $\mathbf{W}$;
1: Generate a uniformly distributed random vector $\mathbf{r}$ according to Eq. (5);
2: Generate uniformly distributed diagonal matrices $\mathbf{S}$ according to Eq. (5);
3: Generate constant diagonal matrix $\mathbf{M}$ according to Eq. (6);
4: Set $S = \{1, 2, 3, \cdots, n\}$;
5:     **for** $j = 1$ to n
6:         select i randomly from $i \in (1, j)$;
7:         swap $S(i)$ and $S(j)$;
8:     **end for**
9:     **for** $i = 1$ to n
10:         **for** $j = 1$ to n
11:             φ outputs the ith element from S with $\varphi(i)$;
12:             σ outputs value with $\sigma_{\varphi(i),j}$;
13:             set $W(i,j) = \sigma_{\varphi(i),j}$;
14:         **end for**
15:     **end for**
16: **return** $\mathbf{r}$, $\mathbf{S}$, $\mathbf{M}$, $\mathbf{W}$;

The permutation of a matrix starts from permuting a set S. Consider a two line notation representing an original set S and its permutation set S' denoted as [2]:

$$\left\{ \begin{matrix} s_1, s_2, s_3 \cdots, s_n \\ s'_1, s'_2, s'_3 \cdots, s'_n \end{matrix} \right\} \tag{10}$$

Here the upper line is the elements of the original set S and the bottom line is the elements from the permutation set S'. Note that S and S' have the same elements but with different orders. Here we define $s'_i = \theta(s_i)$ to represent the function mapping from Eq. (10), indicating that for an upper line element s_i as the input, the output will be the corresponding element s'_i in the bottom line. Then the permutation matrix can be obtained as follows:

$$M(i,j) = \sigma_{\theta(i),j} \quad 1 \leq i, j \leq n \tag{11}$$

where $\sigma_{i,j}$ is the Kronecker delta function, which is commonly used in engineering field and defined as [5]:

$$\sigma_{i,j} = \begin{cases} 0 & i \neq j \\ 1 & i = j \end{cases} \tag{12}$$

and $\theta(i)$ is defined as above, outputting the ith element of the permutation set. Then we can protect the position information of matrix $\hat{\mathbf{G}}$ and $\hat{\mathbf{H}}$ with the following expression:

$$\mathbf{G}' = \mathbf{X}\hat{\mathbf{G}}\mathbf{Y}$$
$$\mathbf{H}' = \mathbf{X}\hat{\mathbf{H}}\mathbf{Y} \tag{13}$$

where $\mathbf{X}$ and $\mathbf{Y}$ are random permutation matrices generated from Eq. (11). It can be seen that matrices $\mathbf{X}$ and $\mathbf{Y}$ are used to randomly permute the positions of rows and columns of the matrix, respectively. Since the permutation matrices are randomly generated, they will permute the original matrix to random-order rows and columns. As a result, the cloud server will not be able to learn any structure information from the reordered matrices.

Up to now, we have finished transforming the original NLP, and the problem $\mathbf{P}_3$ can be rewritten as:

$$\mathbf{P}_3 : \text{Minimize} \quad f(\mathbf{z})$$
$$\text{subject to} \quad g_i'(\mathbf{z}) = 0, \quad i = 1, \cdots, m \tag{14}$$
$$h_j'(\mathbf{z}) \leq b_j', \quad j = 1, \cdots, l$$
$$\hat{a}_k \leq z_k \leq \hat{u}_k, \ k = 1, \cdots n$$

where $\mathbf{G}' = \mathbf{X}\hat{\mathbf{G}}\mathbf{Y}$, $\mathbf{H}' = \mathbf{X}\hat{\mathbf{H}}\mathbf{Y}$, and $\mathbf{b}' = \mathbf{X}\hat{\mathbf{b}}$.

Both key generation and matrix transformation are performed by the user locally, and the procedures are summarized in Algorithms 1 and 2, respectively.

Algorithm 2. Transformation mechanism.

Input:
  Objective function $f(\mathbf{x})$;
  Equality coefficient matrix $\mathbf{G}$ and inequality coefficient vector $\mathbf{b}$;
  Inequality coefficient matrix $\mathbf{H}$;
Output:
  Encrypted objective function $f(\mathbf{z})$;
  Encrypted matrix $\mathbf{G}'$ and vector $\mathbf{b}'$;
  Encrypted matrix $\mathbf{H}'$;
1: Generate a random vector $\mathbf{r}$ from *Algorithm 1* to obtain $\mathbf{z} = \mathbf{x} + \mathbf{r}$, $f(\mathbf{z}) = f(\mathbf{x} + \mathbf{r})$;
2: Generate two random diagonal matrices $\mathbf{P}$ and $\mathbf{T}$ from *Algorithm 1*;
3: Generate two constant diagonal matrices $\mathbf{Q}$ and $\mathbf{S}$ from *Algorithm 1*;
4: Calculate $\hat{\mathbf{G}} = \mathbf{PQG}$ and $\hat{\mathbf{b}} = \mathbf{PQb}$;
5: Calculate $\hat{\mathbf{H}} = \mathbf{TSH}$;
6: Generate matrices $\mathbf{X}$ and $\mathbf{Y}$ from line 4 to 15 in *Algorithm 1* , corresponding to matrix $\mathbf{W}$;
7: Calculate $\mathbf{G}' = \mathbf{X}\hat{\mathbf{G}}\mathbf{Y}$ and $\mathbf{b}' = \mathbf{X}\hat{\mathbf{b}}$;
8: Calculate $\mathbf{H}' = \mathbf{X}\hat{\mathbf{H}}\mathbf{Y}$;
9: **return** $f(\mathbf{z}), \mathbf{G}', \mathbf{b}', \mathbf{H}'$;

4.4   Privacy Analysis

In order to show why the aforementioned transformation schemes can protect input privacy and output privacy, next we will derive a theorem proving that the input matrix and the output vector are computationally indistinguishable from a randomly generated matrix and vector, respectively.

Theorem 1. Let the elements of $\mathbf{R} \in \mathbb{R}^{m \times n}$ and $\mathbf{r} \in \mathbb{R}^{n \times 1}$ be generated from the uniform distribution defined in Eq. (5). Then the matrices $\hat{\mathbf{G}} = \mathbf{PQG}$ and $\hat{\mathbf{H}} = \mathbf{TSH}$ are computationally indistinguishable from a random matrix $\mathbf{R}$, and vector $\mathbf{z} = \mathbf{x} + \mathbf{r}$ is computationally indistinguishable from a random vector $\mathbf{r}$.

Proof: Firstly, to prove the computational indistinguishability between matrices $\hat{\mathbf{G}}$ and $\mathbf{R}$, we need to show for any probabilistic polynomial-time adversary machines M having access to database $M^{\mathcal{A}}$, it can only tell the difference between $\hat{G}_{i,j}$ and $R_{i,j}$ with negligible success probability, where $\hat{G}_{i,j}$ is the element in the ith row and jth column of $\hat{\mathbf{G}}$ and $R_{i,j}$ is the element in the ith row and jth column of $\mathbf{R}$. Suppose the adversary machine M sending inquiry to database D, it will output $Pr[M^{\mathcal{A}}(D)]$, which is the probability of the element coming from a specific database D. It is obvious that if M determines the element coming from a specific database D with full confidence, it will output 1. Suppose the element $\hat{G}_{i,j}$ is chosen from $\hat{\mathbf{G}}$ by adversary machine M, the success probability to identify it from $\hat{\mathbf{G}}$ is expressed as the following:

$$
\begin{aligned}
Pr[M^{\mathcal{A}}(\hat{G}_{i,j})] &= \frac{1}{2}Pr[-N < \hat{G}_{i,j} < N] \\
&\quad + Pr[\hat{G}_{i,j} \le -N] + Pr[\hat{G}_{i,j} \ge N] \\
&= \frac{1}{2}[1 - Pr[\hat{G}_{i,j} \le -N]] - Pr[\hat{G}_{i,j} \ge N]] \\
&\quad + Pr[\hat{G}_{i,j} \le -N] + Pr[\hat{G}_{i,j} \ge N]
\end{aligned}
\tag{15}
$$

Here is brief explanation of the above expression, if the inquiry $\hat{G}_{i,j}$ by M is within the range $(-N, N)$, the probability of it coming from $\hat{\mathbf{G}}$ is $1/2$ since it is possible for both $\mathbf{R}$ and $\hat{\mathbf{G}}$ owing elements falling in the range $(-N, N)$. However, if the inquiry $\hat{G}_{i,j}$ by M is out of the range $(-N, N)$, it must be from matrix $\hat{G}_{i,j}$ that the probability is 1. To calculate Eq. (15), we first have that

$$
\begin{aligned}
Pr[\hat{G}_{i,j} \ge N] &= Pr[Q_{i,i}P_{i,i}G_{i,j} \ge N] \\
&= Pr[P_{i,i}G_{i,j} \ge \frac{N}{C}] \\
&= \alpha Pr[P_{i,i} \ge \frac{N}{CG_{i,j}}] + (1-\alpha)Pr[P_{i,i} \le \frac{N}{CG_{i,j}}] \\
&\le \alpha Pr[P_{i,i} \ge \frac{N}{CL}] + (1-\alpha)Pr[P_{i,i} \le \frac{-N}{CL}] \\
&= 1 - \frac{1}{CL}
\end{aligned}
\tag{16}
$$

where $P_{i,i}$ and $Q_{i,i}$ is the element in ith row and ith column of matrix $\mathbf{P}$ and $\mathbf{Q}$, respectively; L is the maximum value of elements in $\hat{\mathbf{G}}$, C is the constant in $\mathbf{Q}$ defined in Eq. (6), α is the probability for the element $G_{i,j}$ to be positive and $1 - \alpha$ is the probability for the element $G_{i,j}$ to be negative.

In addition, we can similarly obtain :

$$Pr[\hat{G}_{i,j} \leq -N] = 1 - \frac{1}{CL} \tag{17}$$

Thus, the success probability for adversary machine M determining $\hat{G}_{i,j}$ chosen from matrix $\hat{\mathbf{G}}$ in Eq. (15) will be:

$$Pr[M^{\mathcal{A}}(\hat{G}_{i,j})] \leq \frac{3}{2} - \frac{1}{CL} \tag{18}$$

The success probability for $R_{i,j}$ to be identified by the distinguisher M is expressed as follows :

$$Pr[M^{\mathcal{A}}(\hat{R}_{i,j})] = \frac{1}{2} \tag{19}$$

The comparison of Eqs. (18) and (19) will lead to

$$|Pr[M^{\mathcal{A}}(\hat{G}_{i,j})] - Pr[M^{\mathcal{A}}(\hat{R}_{i,j})]| \leq \frac{CL - 1}{CL} \tag{20}$$

By comparing Eqs. (20) and (2), we can define

$$neg(C) = \frac{CL - 1}{CL} \tag{21}$$

Since we can choose any positive constant C, we can choose a value of C that makes CL be close to 1, which will make Eq. (21) be a negligible value. As such, the encrypted matrix $\hat{\mathbf{G}}$ and random generated $\mathbf{R}$ meet the property of computational indistinguishability. Similarly, we can also prove the computational indistinguishability between $\hat{\mathbf{H}}$, $\mathbf{R}$, and $\mathbf{z}$, $\mathbf{r}$, respectively. The proof is complete.

It can be concluded from **Theorem** 1 that even if the adversary machines have full access to the data, it still cannot learn any useful information. As a result, sending the encrypted data via the transformation mechanism to the cloud will not release any private information, proving the security of the proposed protocol.

5   Secure Outsourcing Algorithm for Encrypted NLPs

In this section, we will design an efficient outsourcing algorithm to solve the encrypted large-scale NLPs. To solve large-scale NLPs, the generalized reduced gradient (GRG) method [2,9] is employed to get the optimal solution of $\mathbf{P}_3$. The strategy of GRG is based on an iterative way to repeatedly generate feasible improving directions optimizing NLPs.

5.1   Gradient Decent Method for Unconstrained NLPs

Before delving into details of the GRG to solve large-scale NLPs subjecting to a system of constraints, we first introduce how to find the optimal solution of an unconstrained objective function. A popular and widely used algorithm for solving unconstrained problem is gradient decent method. Suppose $f(\mathbf{z})$ is convex and differentiable within the neighborhood of $\mathbf{z}_0$. The decent method is to produce a sequence of $\mathbf{z}_k$ $(k = 0, 1, 2, ...)$ which can continuously decrease the objective function, expressed as:

$$\mathbf{z}_{k+1} = \mathbf{z}_k + \lambda \mathbf{d} \tag{22}$$

where $\mathbf{d}$ is called search direction, $k = 0, 1, 2, ...$ is iteration number, and λ is termed as step length.

The decent method means that for every iteration of the algorithm, we must have

$$f(\mathbf{z}_{k+1}) < f(\mathbf{z}_k) \tag{23}$$

except when $\mathbf{z}_k$ is already an optimal solution of the objective function.

The convexity of the objective function indicates that the search direction $\mathbf{d}$ must satisfy the following expression:

$$\nabla f(\mathbf{z}_k)\mathbf{d} < 0 \tag{24}$$

It can be seen from Eq.(24) that search direction $\mathbf{d}$ must form an acute angle with the negative gradient, thus as such it is called as a decent direction. As a result, an obvious choice for $\mathbf{d}$ is along the negative gradient direction $-\nabla f(\mathbf{z}_k)$. Once the selection of the search direction is completed, next step is to determine step size as the following:

$$\lambda = \arg \min_{s \geq 0} f(\mathbf{z} + s\mathbf{d}) \tag{25}$$

An exact line search method can be used to solve the one variable optimization task, just as Eq. (25). However, the above gradient decent method cannot be applied to $\mathbf{P}_3$ due to the existence of constraints. The reason is that if we directly move $\mathbf{z}_k$ along the negative gradient direction $\mathbf{z}_{k+1} = \mathbf{z}_k - \lambda \nabla f(\mathbf{z}_k)$, the feasibility of the constraints may be destroyed. As a result, it occurs to us that we have to figure out a way to generate a series of feasible directions gradually approaching the optimal solution of the constrained large-scale NLPs, which will be shown as next section.

5.2   Generalized Reduced Gradient Method for Constrained NLPs

GRG method is robust and efficient in solving large-scale nonlinear problems practically. The constraints in $\mathbf{P}_3$ includes both equality and inequality equations. In fact, we can make all of the inequality constraints $\hat{h}_j(\mathbf{z}) \leq \hat{b}_j, j =$

$1, \cdots, l$ to equality constraints by introducing a bunch of slack variables as follows:

$$\hat{h}_j(\mathbf{z}) + s_j - \hat{b}_j = 0, \quad j = 1, \cdots, l$$
$$s_j \geq 0, \qquad\qquad j = 1, \cdots, l \tag{26}$$

Thus we can rewrite $\mathbf{P}_3$ in the following general form:

$$\mathbf{P}_4 : \text{Minimize} \quad f(\mathbf{z}, \mathbf{s})$$
$$\text{subject to} \quad \hat{e}_i(\mathbf{z}, \mathbf{s}) = 0, \quad i = 1, \cdots, m, \cdots, m + l$$
$$\hat{a}_k \leq z_k \leq \hat{u}_k, \; k = 1, \cdots n \tag{27}$$
$$0 \leq s_p < \infty, \quad p = 1, \cdots l$$

where $\hat{e}_i(\mathbf{z}, \mathbf{s}) = 0$ is the combination of equality and inequality constraints in $\mathbf{P}_3$. For simplicity of notation, we can use $\mathbf{y} = (\mathbf{z}, \mathbf{s})$ to represent the variable vector, and $\mathbf{v} \leq \mathbf{y} \leq \mathbf{w}$ to denote the range of the variables. It should be noted that for some slack variables, the corresponding components of $\mathbf{w}$ can be set as infinite.

As described before, the constraints are of nonlinear forms. To make the logic more clear and algorithm more understandable, we will first describe how to solve the linear constraints and then extend to the nonlinear forms of the constraints. Suppose the equality constraints in $\mathbf{P}_4$ are in the linear form that $\mathbf{E}\mathbf{y} = \mathbf{c}, \mathbf{y} \geq \mathbf{0}$, where $\mathbf{E} \in \mathbb{R}^{(m+l) \times n}$ and $\mathbf{c} \in \mathbb{R}^{(m+l) \times 1}$. In addition, an non-degeneracy assumption is made here that every $m + l$ columns of the matrix $\mathbf{E}$ are linearly independent and every basic solution to the constraints has at least $m + l$ strictly positive values. This assumption can be easily satisfied since we can apply elementary transformation of matrix which will reduce the matrix be composed of independent columns or rows. With this assumption, every feasible point to the constraints will have at most $n - m - l$ variables with values setting to zero. For any feasible point $\mathbf{y}$, it can be partitioned into two groups that $\mathbf{y} = (\mathbf{y}_B, \mathbf{y}_N)$, where $\mathbf{y}_B$ has the dimension $m + l$ termed as basic variables, and $\mathbf{y}_N$ with dimension $n - m - l$ is called as non-basic variable. Accordingly, matrix $\mathbf{E}$ can be decomposed as $\mathbf{E} = [\mathbf{E}_B, \mathbf{E}_N]$, where $\mathbf{E}_B$ and $\mathbf{E}_N$ are the columns corresponding to $\mathbf{y}_B$ and $\mathbf{y}_N$, respectively.

From the algebra we know that for each stage, the optimization of this problem is only dependent on the non-basic variables $\mathbf{y}_N$, since basic variable vector $\mathbf{y}_B$ can be uniquely determined from $\mathbf{y}_N$. A simple modification of the gradient decent method will provide a feasible improving direction $\mathbf{d}$ to optimize the objective function. A feasible improving direction $\mathbf{d}$ at the point $\mathbf{y}$ must follow:

$$\mathbf{E}\mathbf{d} = \mathbf{0}, \qquad\qquad (a)$$
$$\nabla f(\mathbf{y})^T \mathbf{d} < 0, \qquad\quad (b) \tag{28}$$

where $\nabla f(\mathbf{y})^T$ is the gradient vector of objective function $f(\mathbf{y})$ at point $\mathbf{y}$. Equation (28a) means that if a feasible point $\mathbf{y}$ moves along the direction $\mathbf{d}$, the feasibility of the constraints will not be damaged. Equation (28b) indicates that moving along $\mathbf{d}$ will make the objective function $f(\mathbf{y})$ approach the optimal point. The *reduced gradient* method as the following will find such moving direction $\mathbf{d}$ that satisfies Eq.(28).

The gradient vector corresponding to $\mathbf{y}_N$ (also called as *reduced gradient*) can be found by the following expression:

$$\mathbf{r}^T = \nabla_N f(\mathbf{y})^T - \nabla_B f(\mathbf{y})^T \mathbf{E}_B^{-1} \mathbf{E}_N \tag{29}$$

where $\nabla_N f(\mathbf{y})^T$ is the gradient vector of $\nabla f(\mathbf{y})^T$ that corresponds to $\mathbf{y}_N$ and $\nabla_B f(\mathbf{y})^T$ is the gradient vector corresponding to $\mathbf{y}_B$. From above reduced gradient, we can construct the feasible moving direction $\mathbf{d}_N$ that will move $\mathbf{y}_N + \lambda \mathbf{d}_N$ in the feasible working space, where $\mathbf{d}_N$ can be determined as the following:

$$d_{Ni} = \begin{cases} -r_i & r_i \leq 0 \\ -y_{Ni} r_i & r_i > 0 \end{cases} \tag{30}$$

where d_{Ni} is the ith element of $\mathbf{d}_N$, r_i is the ith element of $\mathbf{r}^T$, and y_{Ni} is the ith element of $\mathbf{y}_N$. Equation (30) provides the rules for finding improving feasible direction for non-basic variables $\mathbf{y}_N$. Once the improving feasible direction for $\mathbf{y}_N$ is determined, we can get the corresponding moving direction $\mathbf{d}_B$ for $\mathbf{y}_B$ by expanding Eq. (28a):

$$\mathbf{E}_N \mathbf{d}_N + \mathbf{E}_B \mathbf{d}_B = 0$$
$$\mathbf{d}_B = -\mathbf{E}_B^{-1} \mathbf{E}_N \mathbf{d}_N \tag{31}$$

Eq. (31) shows that $\mathbf{d}_B$ can be uniquely calculated from $\mathbf{d}_N$, and the moving direction is composed that $\mathbf{d} = [\mathbf{d}_B, \mathbf{d}_N]$. It can be proved that $\mathbf{d} = [\mathbf{d}_B, \mathbf{d}_N]$ satisfies Eqs. (28a) and (28b), indicating both feasibility and improvability will be achieved for $\mathbf{d}$.

The reduced gradient method dealing with the linear constraints can be generalized and extended to address the nonlinear constraints. Similar to linear constraints, we first partition the variables into basic and non-basic variable vector as $\mathbf{y} = (\mathbf{y}_B, \mathbf{y}_N)$, and the corresponding Jacobi matrix of $\hat{\mathbf{e}}(\mathbf{y})$ in $\mathbf{P}_4$ can also be grouped into:

$$\frac{\partial \hat{\mathbf{e}}}{\partial \mathbf{y}} = (\frac{\partial \hat{\mathbf{e}}}{\partial \mathbf{y}_B}, \frac{\partial \hat{\mathbf{e}}}{\partial \mathbf{y}_N}) \tag{32}$$

and a nondegeneracy assumption is made here that for any point $\mathbf{y}$, $\dfrac{\partial \hat{\mathbf{e}}}{\partial \mathbf{y}_B} \in \mathbb{R}^{(m+l) \times (m+l)}$ is nonsingular.

For the case of nonlinear constraints, the *reduced gradient* $\mathbf{r}^T$ with respect to $\mathbf{y}_N$ is expressed as:

$$\mathbf{r}^T = \nabla_N f(\mathbf{y})^T - \nabla_B f(\mathbf{y})^T (\frac{\partial \hat{\mathbf{e}}}{\partial \mathbf{y}_B})^{-1} \frac{\partial \hat{\mathbf{e}}}{\partial \mathbf{y}_N} \tag{33}$$

Now we specify the direction $\mathbf{d}_N$ as follows:

$$d_{Ni} = \begin{cases} 0 & y_{Ni} r_i > 0 \text{ and } y_{Ni} = v_i \\ 0 & y_{Ni} r_i < 0 \text{ and } y_{Ni} = w_i \\ -y_{Ni} r_i & \text{otherwise} \end{cases} \tag{34}$$

where v_i is the lower bound of the variable y_i and w_i is the upper bound of the variable y_i. However, the difference with the linear form is that $\mathbf{y}_N$ moves a straight line along $\mathbf{d}_N$, the nonlinear form of the constraints requires $\mathbf{y}_N$ move nonlinearly to continuously walk in the feasible space formed by the constraints. To address this, we can first move $\mathbf{y}_N$ along the direction defined by Eq. (34), then a correction procedure is employed making $\mathbf{y}_N$ return to working space to satisfy the feasibility of the constraints. Once a tentative move along $\mathbf{d}_N$ is made, the following iterative method can be used for the correction. Supposing $\mathbf{y}_k$ is the current feasible point, we first move the non-basic variable vector $\mathbf{y}_{N(k+1)} = \mathbf{y}_{Nk} + \lambda \mathbf{d}_{Nk}$, to return point $\mathbf{y} = (\mathbf{y}_{Bk}, \mathbf{y}_{N(k+1)})$ near $\mathbf{y}_k$ back to the constraint space, we can solve the following equation:

$$\hat{\mathbf{e}}(\mathbf{y}_{Bk}, \mathbf{y}_{N(k+1)}) = 0 \tag{35}$$

for $\mathbf{y}_{Bk}$ where $\mathbf{y}_{N(k+1)}$ is fixed. This is done by the following iterative procedure, which is described in Algorithm 3 from line 11 to 14:

$$\mathbf{y}_{Bk_{j+1}} = \mathbf{y}_{Bk_j} - \left(\frac{\partial \hat{\mathbf{e}}(\mathbf{y}_{Bk_j}, \mathbf{y}_{N(k+1)})}{\partial \mathbf{y}_{Bk}} \right)^{-1} \hat{\mathbf{e}}(\mathbf{y}_{Bk_j}, \mathbf{y}_{N(k+1)}) \tag{36}$$

where $\mathbf{y}_{Bk_j}$ is the basic variable vector of $\mathbf{y}_B$ in the jth iteration step according to Eq. (36). When this iterative process produces a feasible point $\mathbf{y}_{B(k+1)}$, we have to check if following conditions are satisfied:

$$f(\mathbf{y}_{B(k+1)}, \mathbf{y}_{N(k+1)}) < f(\mathbf{y}_{Bk}, \mathbf{y}_{Nk})$$
$$\mathbf{v} \le \mathbf{y}_{B(k+1)}, \mathbf{y}_{N(k+1)} \le \mathbf{w} \tag{37}$$

If Eq. (37) holds true, it indicates that the new point is feasible and improvable. Then we set $\mathbf{y}_{k+1} = (\mathbf{y}_{B(k+1)}, \mathbf{y}_{N(k+1)})$ as a new approaching point, otherwise we will decrease the step length λ when we first make the tentative move for $\mathbf{y}_{Nk}$ and repeat the above iterative process. The procedure of generalized reduced gradient method is summarized as Algorithm 3.

Regrading verification of the correctness of the returned result, the users can apply KKT conditions of $\mathbf{P}_3$ [8] to check if the return result is valid or not.

6   Performance Evaluation

In this section, we evaluate the performance of our proposed secure outsourcing protocol for large-scale NLPs with nonlinear constraints. For the experimental setup, the client side is implemented on a computer with Intel(R) Core(TM) i5-5200 U CPU processor running at 2.2 GHz, 8 GB memory. For the cloud side, the experiment is conducted on a computer with Intel(R) Core(TM) i7-4770 U CPU processor running at 3.40 GHz, 16 GB memory. We implement the proposed protocol including both the client and cloud side processed in Python 2.7. We also ignore the communication latency between users and the cloud for this experiment, since the computation dominates running time as demonstrated by our experiments.

Algorithm 3. Secure outsourcing scheme for large-scale NLPs

Input:
 Starting point $\mathbf{y}_0$ that $\hat{\mathbf{e}}(\mathbf{y}_0) = 0$;
Output:
 Optimal result $\mathbf{y}^*$ for $\mathbf{P}_4$;
1: Initialize $k = 0$;
2: Decompose $\mathbf{y}_0 = (\mathbf{y}_{B0}, \mathbf{y}_{N0})$;
3: Calculate Jacobi matrix of $\hat{\mathbf{e}}(\mathbf{y}_0)$ and decompose the Jacobi matrix $\dfrac{\partial \hat{\mathbf{e}}}{\partial \mathbf{y}} =$
 $(\dfrac{\partial \hat{\mathbf{e}}}{\partial \mathbf{y}_B}, \dfrac{\partial \hat{\mathbf{e}}}{\partial \mathbf{y}_N})$ corresponding to $(\mathbf{y}_{B0}, \mathbf{y}_{N0})$;
4: Compute $\mathbf{d}_{N0}$ from Eq. (34);
5: **while** $\| \mathbf{d}_{Nk} \|_1 > \epsilon$
6:   Choose $\lambda > 0$ and compute $\mathbf{y}_{N(k+1)} = \mathbf{y}_{Nk} + \lambda \mathbf{d}_{Nk}$;
7:   If not $\mathbf{v} \leq \mathbf{y}_{N(k+1)} \leq \mathbf{w}$:
     $\lambda = 1/2\lambda$;
8:    go to (6) and repeat;
9:   Initialize j $= 0$;
10:   Let $\mathbf{y}_{Bj} = \mathbf{y}_{Bk}$;
11:   **while** $\| \hat{\mathbf{e}}(\mathbf{y}_{Bj}, \mathbf{y}_{N(k+1)}) \|_1 > \epsilon$
12:    Let $E = (\dfrac{\partial \hat{\mathbf{e}}(\mathbf{y}_{Bj}, \mathbf{y}_{N(k+1)})}{\partial \mathbf{y}_{Bk}})^{-1}$;
13:    $\mathbf{y}_{B(j+1)} = \mathbf{y}_{Bj} - E\hat{\mathbf{e}}(\mathbf{y}_{Bj}, \mathbf{y}_{N(k+1)})$;
14:    $j = j + 1$;
15:   end **while**;
16:   If Eq. (37) holds true:
17:    $\mathbf{y}_{B(k+1)} = \mathbf{y}_{Bj}$;
18:    $\mathbf{y}_{k+1} = (\mathbf{y}_{B(k+1)}, \mathbf{y}_{N(k+1)})$;
19:   else:
20:    go to (6) and repeat;
21:   $k = k + 1$;
22:   Calculate $\mathbf{d}_{Nk}$ from Eq. (34);
23: end **while**;
24: Let $\mathbf{y}^* = (\mathbf{y}_{Bk}, \mathbf{y}_{Nk})$;
25: **return** $\mathbf{y}^*$;

We randomly generate a set of test cases that cover the small and large sized NLPs with nonlinear constraints, where the number of variables is increased from 1000 to 16000. The objective function here is randomly generated second-degree polynomial function, and nonlinear constraints are randomly generated with first-degree polynomial functions for equality constraints and second-degree polynomial functions for inequality constraints, respectively. All these test cases are carefully designed so that there are feasible under corresponding nonlinear constraints.

For the experiments, we first solve the original NLP in the client side, then solve the encrypted NLP in cloud side. Table 1 shows the experiment results, and each entry in this table represents the mean of 20 trials. As illustrated in this table, the size of original NLPs is reported in the first three columns. Besides, several parameters are adopted to evaluate the performance of proposed protocol. $T_{original}$ is defined as the time to solve original NLP by client side. The time to solve encrypted NLP is divided into time for the cloud server T_{cloud} and time for the client T_{client}. T_{cloud} is defined as the time that cloud used to operate the encrypted NLP by the cloud server. T_{client} is the time cost to encrypt and decrypt the original NLP by the client. Furthermore, we propose to assess the practical efficiency by two metrics calculated from $T_{original}$, T_{client} and T_{cloud}. The *speedup* is calculated as $\frac{T_{original}}{T_{client}}$, representing time savings for the client to outsource the NLP to the cloud using proposed protocol. The speedup is expected to be greater than 1, otherwise there is no necessity for the client to outsource NLP to the cloud server. The *cloud efficiency* is measured as $\frac{T_{original}}{T_{cloud}}$, indicating the time savings enabled by the cloud. It is expected that the encryption of the problem should not introduce great overhead for solving the large-scale NLP. Moreover, due to more powerful computation capabilities of cloud server, the cloud efficiency is expected be grater than 1.

It can be seen that from the Table 1 that the encryption can be finished in a very short time by the client. For instance, the time consumption of the encryption for the problem with 16000 variables is only 166.68 s. However, the time cost to find the optimal solution by the cloud server is much longer but reasonable, and increases rapidly with growing number of variables. As shown in the penultimate column of the table, the speedup of proposed protocol increases dramatically when the size of the problem gets larger. Hence, a substantial amount of time can be saved for the client by proposed protocol. For example, the speedup is 49.66 for the problem with 16000 variables, indicating 97.9% of time is saved for the client. The cloud efficiency is shown in the last column, and it can be seen that the cloud efficiency increases with the increasing size of the problem, indicating the powerful computation capabilities of cloud server. Consequently, the experiment results demonstrate our proposed secure outsourcing protocol is practical and efficient.

Table 1. Performance evaluation

Test cases				Original NLP	Encrypted NLP		Speedup	Cloud efficiency
#	# variables	# equality constraints	# inequality constraints	$T_{original}$(sec)	T_{cloud}(sec)	T_{client}(sec)	$\frac{T_{original}}{T_{client}}$	$\frac{T_{original}}{T_{cloud}}$
1	1000	300	300	3.17	2.28	0.09	35.22	1.39
2	2000	600	600	27.61	18.66	0.72	38.34	1.48
3	4000	1200	1200	182.05	112.38	4.48	40.62	1.62
4	8000	2400	2400	1236.42	695.79	36.50	34.33	1.77
5	12000	3600	3600	2777.04	1368.55	75.32	37.02	2.03
6	16000	4800	4800	8245.51	3720.11	166.68	49.66	2.21

7   Conclusion

In this paper, for the first time, we design an efficient and practical protocol for securely outsourcing large-scale NLPs with nonlinear constraints. The transformation technique is applied to protect the sensitive input/output information. In addition, we adopt the generalized reduced gradient method to solve the transformed NLP. A set of large-scale simulations are performed to evaluate the performance of proposed mechanism, and results demonstrate its high practicality and efficiency. It is expected that the proposed protocol can not only be deployed independently, but also serves as a building block to solve more sophisticated problems in the real world.

References

1. Barbosa, M., Farshim, P.: Delegatable homomorphic encryption with applications to secure outsourcing of computation. In: Dunkelman, O. (ed.) CT-RSA 2012. LNCS, vol. 7178, pp. 296–312. Springer, Heidelberg (2012). https://doi.org/10.1007/978-3-642-27954-6_19
2. Bazaraa, M.S., Sherali, H.D., Shetty, C.M.: Nonlinear Programming: Theory and Algorithms. Wiley, Hoboken (2013)
3. Bertsekas, D.P.: Nonlinear Programming. Athena scientific, Belmont (1999)
4. Chen, F., Xiang, T., Lei, X., Chen, J.: Highly efficient linear regression outsourcing to a cloud. IEEE Trans. Cloud Comput. 2(4), 499–508 (2014)
5. Chen, F., Xiang, T., Yang, Y.: Privacy-preserving and verifiable protocols for scientific computation outsourcing to the cloud. J. Parallel Distrib. Comput. 74(3), 2141–2151 (2014)
6. Chen, X., Huang, X., Li, J., Ma, J., Lou, W., Wong, D.S.: New algorithms for secure outsourcing of large-scale systems of linear equations. IEEE Trans. Inf. Forensics Secur. 10(1), 69–78 (2015)
7. Chen, X., Li, J., Ma, J., Tang, Q., Lou, W.: New algorithms for secure outsourcing of modular exponentiations. IEEE Trans. Parallel Distrib. Syst. 25(9), 2386–2396 (2014)
8. Chung, K.-M., Kalai, Y., Vadhan, S.: Improved Delegation of computation using fully homomorphic encryption. In: Rabin, T. (ed.) CRYPTO 2010. LNCS, vol. 6223, pp. 483–501. Springer, Heidelberg (2010). https://doi.org/10.1007/978-3-642-14623-7_26
9. Du, W., Li, Q.: Secure and efficient outsourcing of large-scale nonlinear programming. In: 2017 IEEE Conference on Communications and Network Security (CNS), IEEE (2017)
10. Gentry, C.: Fully homomorphic encryption using ideal lattices
11. Kalai, Y., Raz, R., Rothblum, R.: How to delegate computations: the power of no-signaling proofs
12. Katz, J., Lindell, Y.: Introduction to Modern Cryptography. CRC Press, Boca Raton (2014)
13. Lei, X., Liao, X., Huang, T., Li, H.: Cloud computing service: the case of large matrix determinant computation. IEEE Trans. Serv. Comput. 8(5), 688–700 (2015)
14. Lei, X., Liao, X., Huang, T., Li, H., Hu, C.: Outsourcing large matrix inversion computation to a public cloud. IEEE Trans. Cloud Comput. 1(1), 1–1 (2013)

15. Murugesan, S., Bojanova, I.: Encyclopedia of Cloud Computing. Wiley, Hoboken (2016)
16. Ren, K., Wang, C., Wang, Q.: Security challenges for the public cloud. IEEE Internet Comput. **16**(1), 69–73 (2012)
17. Shen, W., Yin, B., Cui, X., Cheng, Y.: A distributed secure outsourcing scheme for solving linear algebraic equations in ad hoc clouds. IEEE Trans. Cloud Comput. (2017)
18. Sutskever, I., Martens, J., Dahl, G., Hinton, G.: On the importance of initialization and momentum in deep learning. In: International Conference on Machine Learning, pp. 1139–1147 (2013)
19. Wang, C., Ke, R., Wang, J.: Secure and practical outsourcing of linear programming in cloud computing
20. Wang, C., Ren, K., Wang, J., Wang, Q.: Harnessing the cloud for securely outsourcing large-scale systems of linear equations. IEEE Trans. Parallel Distrib. Syst. **24**(6), 1172–1181 (2013)
21. Zhou, L., Li, C.: Outsourcing large-scale quadratic programming to a public cloud. IEEE Access **3**, 2581–2589 (2015)

A Verifiable and Dynamic Multi-keyword Ranked Search Scheme over Encrypted Cloud Data with Accuracy Improvement

Qi Zhang[1(✉)], Shaojing Fu[1,2,3], Nan Jia[1], and Ming Xu[1]

[1] College of Computer, National University of Defense Technology, Changsha, China
zqi6@outlook.com
[2] State Key Laboratory of Cryptology, Beijing, China
[3] Science and Technology on Information Assurance Laboratory, Beijing, China

Abstract. With the widely application of cloud computing, more and more data owners prefer to outsource their data on the remote cloud servers to reduce the overhead. Searchable encryption is proposed in an urgently need for searching on the encrypted data. In this paper, we present a tree-based privacy-preserving and efficient multi-keyword ranked search scheme supporting verification and dynamic update. Considering the effect of the keywords location on the weight in most documents, the traditional $TF \times IDF$ algorithm can be optimized with location information to get more accurate similarity score. To improve the efficiency, we combine the vector space model and binary tree to construct a tree-based index structure. And the index tree is encrypted by secure kNN computation. Finally, We analyze the security against two threat model, and implement the experiment on the real paper set to evaluate the performance.

Keywords: Keyword location · Searchable symmetric encryption
Tree-based index · Verification · Dynamic update

1 Introduction

In recent years, cloud computing has sprung up in various fields due to its unique advantages. More and more data owners choose to outsource their large amounts of local data to remote cloud servers to reduce their storage and computation overhead.

Despite those benefits, data stored on the cloud servers, especially the sensitive information, faces serious security risks and privacy challenges since cloud servers are honest-but-curious. A general way to reduce this leakage is encrypting the data before outsourcing. However, encryption will bring other difficulties. For example, if we want to search an exact document on the server, we have to download all the encrypted data and decrypt it locally which lead to large storage and computation cost. Therefore, searching on encrypted data becomes a valuable research issue.

© ICST Institute for Computer Sciences, Social Informatics and Telecommunications Engineering 2018
R. Beyah et al. (Eds.): SecureComm 2018, LNICST 254, pp. 588–604, 2018.
https://doi.org/10.1007/978-3-030-01701-9_32

Searchable encryption is proposed to settle these problems since it can guarantee the security and usability of data. These years, lots of works has been proposed on this field, such as single keyword search, multi-keyword search, ranked search. Furthermore, verification and dynamic update are added to fulfill the functionality.

In this paper, we present a tree-based secure and efficient multi-keyword ranked search scheme supporting verification and dynamic update. Our paper takes the keyword location into account. In plaintext area, the information retrieval mechanism is first returning all the results whose title contains the keywords and later returning the results whose body contains them. That is to say the keyword location will greatly influence the similarity of the documents with query request. However, in ciphertext, traditional TF value only consider the number of the keywords in a document. Introducing the location information in the TF value will counts. Moreover, the length of the paper also have impact on the similarity. We construct a tree-based index structure to improve the efficiency of search. Moreover, the verification and dynamic update function are also designed based on the tree-base index structure. We choose to implement the experiment on the data set of paper for its typical fixed format which composed of title, abstract, body, conclusion and preferences so that we can easily assign the different significance to the keyword in different part. Our Contribution can be summarized as follows:

(1) We present a tree-based secure and efficient multi-keyword ranked search scheme supporting verification and dynamic update.
(2) We introduce the keyword location and length of document to optimize the $TF \times IDF$ algorithm to improve the accuracy.
(3) We analyze the security against two threat model, and implement the experiment on the real paper set to evaluate the performance.

The rest of this paper is organized as follows. Section 2 gives the related word on searchable encryption. Section 3 gives a brief introduction of the scheme. Section 4 describes the scheme in detail. Section 5 presents the performance analysis. Finally, we conclude in Sect. 6.

2 Related Work

Song et al. [15] first proposed a solution for searching single keyword on encrypted data with sequential scan which was provably secure but in high cost. Boneh [1] first proposed public key searchable encryption scheme. Based on these scheme, a great deal of improvement had been produced.

Single Keyword Search. Goh [8] defined a secure index using a bloom filter and pseudo-random functions which will introduce false positive results. Chang and Mitzenmacher [4] developed two index schemes using dictionaries. Li et al. [14] developed a single keyword search scheme to support fuzzy search.

Multi-keyword Search. Lots of research [2,9,19] achieve the conjunctive multi-keyword search. Boneh et al. [2] proposed a public-key scheme and supported conjunctive and disconjunctive search like subset and range query. Wang et al. [19] designed a inverted index based public-key searchable encryption scheme. They used private set intersection to support conjunctive multi-keyword search. Wang et al. [21] utilized the bloom filter with LSH and construct two schemes using homomorphic encryption and pseudorandom padding to deal with high-dimensional feature-rich data.

Rank Search. Rank search is proposed to deal with the drawbacks of boolean search. Wang et al. [20] used inverted index and $TF \times IDF$ to construct a order-preserving symmetric encryption. However this scheme only support single keyword search. Cao et al. [3] first proposed a basic multi-keyword ranked search scheme (MRSE) using secure inner product computation which had low overhead on computation and communication. However, this scheme ignored the different importance of the keywords. Fu et al. [7] proposed a scheme supporting both fuzzy and rank search by processing stemming algorithm, LSH and bloom filter. Sun et al. [17] developed the scheme by MDB-tree index structure. Chen et al. [5] used k-means algorithm to construct the hierarchical cluster index tree. Xia et al. [22] designed a special KBB index tree to provide efficient multi-keyword ranked search which we refer to in this paper.

Dynamic Search. In practice, the data on the server could not be immutable. Therefore, update should be considered. Goh [8] realized the update based on the bloom filter. Kamara et al. [11] constructed a new dynamic encrypted index to give a dynamic SSE scheme. Later, they improved the scheme by KBB tree in [10]. Wang et al. [21] provide efficient index dynamic over homomorphic encryption and pseudorandom padding. Wan and Deng [18] applied update based on bilinear-map accumulation tree. Lai and Chow [12] developed a dynamic symmetric structured encryption scheme with random binary tree.

Verifiable Search. Wan and Deng [18] gave a solution to apply verification based on homomorphic MAC. Sun et al. [17] combined MDB-tree and Merkle hash tree to realize. And later proposed public and private verification scheme based on bilinear-map accumulation [16].

3   Problem Formulation

3.1   System Model and Threat Model

System Model. The system model involves three entities: data owner, cloud server and data user, as shown in Fig. 1.

Data Owner: The data owner owns the plaintext dataset F locally. First data owner encrypts the plaintext document collection F by symmetric encryption algorithm, and generates the secure index tree T to improve the search efficiency. Later, outsource the index tree to the cloud server along with the encrypted document collection C. And the secret keys for document encryption and secure kNN algorithm are sent to the data user via a secure channel. When data owner wants to update the data on the cloud, update request will be sends to cloud.

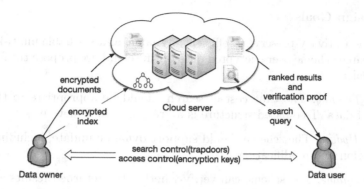

Fig. 1. The architecture of our scheme.

Cloud Server: The cloud server is responsible for the data storage. The encrypted document collection and encrypted index tree from data owner are stored on the cloud. After receiving the search trapdoor from the data user, cloud server traverses the secure index tree to search for the relevant documents and sends back the top-k most similar results to the data user. Meanwhile the cloud server also sends back information to the data user for verification. When receiving the update request from data owner, the cloud server uses the information from data owner to update the document collection and index tree.

Data User: The data user who has access to the data can upload a search request consisting of some of keywords in the keyword dictionary. The data user uses the secret key to generate a query trapdoor and sends it to the cloud. When receiving the results from cloud server, data user can decrypts the results with the symmetric key locally. The verification proof returned can be used to verify the correctness, completeness and freshness of the results.

Threat Model. We assume the data user is authorized and trusted so that we don't consider the leakage in the data user side. Nor do we consider the leakage of secret key on the channel of key distribution. But the cloud server is assumed to be honest-but-curious. In other words, the cloud server will follow the processes honestly but will be curious to the content of data, keywords and other additional information. We mainly consider two threat models.

Known Ciphertext Model. In this model, the cloud server only knows encrypted information, specifically, the encrypted document collection C, the encrypted tree-based index I and the encrypted trapdoor.

Known Background Model. In this model, the cloud server knows additional backgrounds, such as the document frequency and keyword frequency. These information will be used to conduct statistical attack to infer the keywords in the query request.

3.2 Design Goals

To achieve a privacy-preserving, efficient, dynamic and verifiable multi-keyword ranked search scheme over encrypted data on the cloud, we propose the following design goals:

Search Efficiency. The time cost of search should be appropriate to the large amount of data. Tree-based structure is a great way to achieve it.

Dynamic Update. The scheme should support dynamic update, including insertion, deletion and modification.

Result Verifiable. The scheme can verify whether the returned results are what the data user want or not. (1) Correctness. The results should satisfy the query request and all originated from data owner with unmodified version. (2) Completeness. The results should contain all the search results which match the query request. (3) Freshness. The results should be the freshest and unmodified.

Privacy. The scheme can prevent the data or any other information from being analyzed by cloud server. (1) Data privacy. The server cannot recover the plaintext documents by analyzing the ciphertext. Cryptography is always used to protect the data. (2) Index and query privacy. The index and query are represented by vectors which contain the information of keywords such as the TF value in the index and the IDF value in the trapdoor which should be protected. (3) Keyword privacy. The cloud server could not make out the specific keywords. (4) Trapdoor unlinkability. The trapdoor need to be indistinguishable for the same query.

3.3 Notations

See Table 1.

Table 1. The notations in our scheme.

F	The plaintext document collection stored in data owner side, which contains N documents, and denoted as $F = \{f_1, f_2, \ldots, f_N\}$
W	The dictionary of n keywords shared between data owner and data user, denoted as $W = \{w_1, w_2, \ldots, w_n\}$
C	The encrypted document collection stored in cloud server side, denoted as $C = \{c_1, c_2, \ldots, c_N\}$
T	The unencrypted index tree generated from the document collection C
I	The encrypted index tree generated from tree T
Q	The query vector submitted by data user contains m keywords in W, denoted as $Q = \{q_1, q_2, \ldots, q_m\}$
TD	The trapdoor generated from the query vector Q and will upload to cloud server
R	The top-k encrypted document search results returned from cloud server for decryption and verification
PR	The plaintext document results decrypted by R

3.4   Preliminaries

Vector Space Model with TF × IDF. Vector space model is one of the most widely used models for information retrieval whose basic idea is to represent the document and query as a vector. Each dimension of the vector corresponds to a keyword, and the value is the weight of the keyword, which can be calculated using the $TF \times IDF$ mechanism [23]. The term frequency, TF, the frequency of the word in the document which reveals the significance of the word. The inverse document frequency, IDF, is the number of documents which contain the word among the document collection. And the $TF \times IDF$ algorithm uses the product of TF and IDF to measure the correlation between the keywords and document:

$$
\begin{aligned}
S &= \sum_{w_i \in Q} TF_{f_i, w_i} \times IDF_{w_i} \\
&= \sum_{w_i \in Q} \frac{ln(1 + N_{f, w_i})}{\sqrt{\sum_{w_i \in W} (ln(1 + N_{f, w_i}))^2}} \times \frac{ln(1 + N/N_{w_i})}{\sqrt{\sum_{w_i \in W} (ln(1 + N/N_{w_i}))^2}}
\end{aligned} \tag{1}
$$

where N_{f_i, w_i} is the number of keyword w_i in document f_i. N is the total number of documents in collection, N_{w_i} is the number of documents that contain the keyword w_i.

This method is intuitive, also the processing speed is fast. However, it neglects many other characteristics. Fully considering the effect of the word location and the document length on the weight, we optimize the algorithm by introducing them into $TF \times IDF$. The optimized $TF \times IDF$ is denoted as:

$$
\begin{aligned}
S &= \sum_{w_i \in Q} TF'_{f_i, w_i} \times IDF_{w_i} \\
&= \sum_{w_i \in Q} \frac{\frac{n_{w_i}}{L_{f_i}} \times \sum_1^k (\gamma_{f_j} \times tf_{j, w_i})}{\sqrt{\sum_{w_i \in W} (\frac{n_{w_i}}{L_{f_i}} \times \sum_1^k (\gamma_{f_j} \times tf_{j, w_i}))^2}} \times IDF_{w_i}
\end{aligned} \tag{2}
$$

where the document can be divided into k parts, γ_{f_j} is the weighting coefficient of the jth part of the document, and the sum of the coefficient is 1, tf_{j, w_i} is the number of keyword w_i in the jth part, n_{w_i} is the number of the keyword w_i, L_{f_i} is the length of the whole document f_i.

Tree-Based Index Construction. As shown in Fig. 2, we construct the indexes to a binary tree based on the Xia's scheme [22]. This tree-based index structure can greatly improve the efficiency of search.

In this structure, each node u in the tree is defined as:

$$
u = (ID, P_l, P_r, D, h). \tag{3}
$$

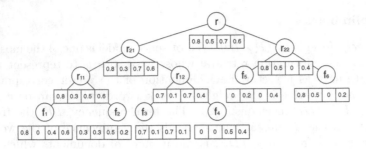

Fig. 2. Index tree.

where ID is the identity of the node, P_l and P_r is the pointers to the left and right child node, D is the index vector whose dimensions are the TF weight of keywords, and h is the hash value of node u for verification. Each leaf node is linked to a document. The building process is shown in Algorithm 1.

Algorithm 1. BuildTree(F)

Input: the plaintext documents F, the encrypted indexes I
Output: the index tree T
1: **for** each document f_i in F **do**
2:     Initial the leaf node. $u.ID = ID(f_i), u.P_l = null, u.P_r = null, u.D[i] = TF_{f_i, w_i}$ for $i \in [1, n]$
3: **end for**
4: **while** the root node is not generated **do**
5:     Generate the parent node for each two nodes u' and u''. $u.ID = ID(u), u.P_l = u', u.P_r = u'', u.D[i] = max\{u'.D[i], u''.D[i]\}$ for $i \in [1, n]$
6: **end while**
7: **return** the tree T

---

4   The Proposed Scheme

4.1   Detail Scheme

The detail scheme is as follows.

Algorithm 2. Search(u)

Input: index tree node u, trapdoor TD, threshold TH
Output: k documents R
1: compute the relevance score $S = u.D \cdot TD$
2: **if** the node u is not a leaf node **then**
3:     **if** $S > TH$ **then**
4:         $Search(u.P_l)$
5:         $Search(u.P_r)$
6:     **end if**
7: **else**

8:      **if** $S > TH$ **then**
9:          insert the node and the score into r
10:     **if** $length(R) > k$ **then**
11:         sort R and delete the result with minimum score
12:         $TH = min\{R\}$
13:     **end if**
14:    **end if**
15: **end if**
16: **return** R

- $\{SK, sk\} \leftarrow Initial(1^l)$. This algorithm generates the secret keys for encrypting the documents, indexes and query. The data owner generates the secret key sk for encrypting and decrypting the documents, and the secret key SK for encrypting indexes. SK is composed of three elements, one $(n + U + 1)$-bit vector as S, and two $(n + U + 1) \times (n + U + 1)$ invertible matrices as $\{M1, M2\}$, where U is a random number of dummy keywords to insert. Thus, $SK = \{S, M1, M2\}$.

- $C \leftarrow Enc(F, sk)$. The data owner uses a symmetric encryption algorithm such as AES to encrypt the plain document collection F.

- $I \leftarrow BuildIndex(F, SK)$. It is used to generate the encrypted index for each document. The data owner generates a n bit index vector for each document f_i in document collection F. Then, every vector is extended to $(n + U + 1)$-bit vector p_i. The $(n + j)^{th}$ bit where $j \in [1, U]$, is set to a random number $\epsilon^{(j)}$. And the $(n + U + 1)^{th}$ bit is set as 1. Then, call the algorithm $T \leftarrow BuildTree(F)$ to construct a index tree. Next, the index vector p_i on each node of the tree is split into two random vectors $\{p_i{}', p_i{}''\}$ by the secret vector S for splitting. Namely, if $S[j] = 0$, we set $p_i{}'[j] = p_i{}''[j] = p_i[j]$; if $S[j] = 1$, we set $p_i{}'[j]$ and $p_i{}''[j]$ as random numbers and $p_i{}'[j] + p_i{}''[j] = p_i[j]$. The index is encrypted as $I_i = \{M_1^T p_i{}', M_2^T p_i{}''\}$.

- $TD \leftarrow Trapdoor(Q, SK)$. The data user generates a n bit index vector for the search query Q, in which each dimensions are set to the IDF_{w_i} of the keywords w_i, and for other keywords, $Q[i] = 0$. Then, the query vector is extended to $(n + U + 1)$-bit vector q. Choose a random number v out of U, the v random positions in $[n, n + U]$ are set to 1, others are set to 0. And the $(n + U + 1)^{th}$ bit is set to a random number $t(t \in [0, 1])$. Scale the first $n + U$-bit, denoted as Q', by a random number r, then the query $q = (rQ', t)$. Next, the query vector q is split into two random vectors $\{q', q''\}$ by the secret vector S for splitting. Namely, if $S[j] = 1$, we set $q'[j] = q''[j] = q[j]$; if $S[j] = 0$, we set $q'[j]$ and $q''[j]$ as random numbers and $q'[j] + q''[j] = q[j]$. Then, the trapdoor is encrypted as $TD = \{M_1^{-1} q', M_2^{-1} q''\}$.

- $R \leftarrow Search(I, TD)$. This algorithm uses indexes and trapdoor to calculate the similarity to get the top-k research results, showed in Algorithm 2. After receiving the trapdoor TD from the data user, the cloud server calculates the relevance score between TD and the index vector stored in each node to get the top k relevant results. The relevance score is calculated as:

$$
\begin{aligned}
S &= I_i \cdot TD \\
&= (M_1^T p_i{}') \cdot (M_1^{-1} q{}') + (M_2^T p_i{}'') \cdot (M_2^{-1} q{}'') \\
&= p_i{}' \cdot q{}' + p_i{}'' \cdot q{}'' \\
&= p_i \cdot q
\end{aligned}
\tag{4}
$$

- $PR \leftarrow Dec(R, sk)$. The data user uses the secret key sk transmitted from the data owner by a secret channel to decrypt the secret results R and get the plaintext results PR.

4.2   Result Verification

Algorithm 3. hash tree construction

1: **for** each leaf node **do**
2:     $u.h = hash(u.ID \| \Phi(f_i))$ // $\Phi(f_i)$ means the content of the document.
3: **end for**
4: **for** each nonleaf node **do**
5:     $u.h = hash(u.ID \| h_{p_l} \| h_{p_r})$
6:     **if** the node is root node **then** // signature
7:         $\sigma_r = Sign(u.h \| ts)$ // ts is the timestamp
8:     **end if**
9: **end for**

Algorithm 4. minimum hash sub-tree

Input: returned results R, index tree T
Output: minimum hash sub-tree $mintree$
1: **for** each node u in R **do**
2:     insert u into $mintree$
3:     **while** u is not root node **do**
4:         insert u's father node and u's brother node into $mintree$
5:         $u = u.parent$
6:     **end while**
7: **end for**
8: **return** $mintree$

Algorithm 5. Verify

Input: minimum hash sub-tree $mintree$, returned results R
1: **if** the signature of root node is true **then** // freshness and authentic
2:     **if** verification of each node in $mintree$ is true **then**   // authentic
3:         recompute the hash value of nodes in R
4:         **if** the value after recomputing $=$ the value in $mintree$ **then**
5:             re-search the $mintree$ using the same trapdoor // correctness
6:             **if** the re-search result $= R$ **then** // correctness and completeness

```
 7:                return True
 8:            end if
 9:        end if
10:    end if
11: end if
```

We refer to the Merkle tree to design our verification scheme. The data owner construct the hash tree based on the index tree using Algorithm 3. For example, in Fig. 2, the hash value of leaf node f_1 is $hash(f_1.ID||\Phi(f_1))$, and the non-leaf node $r_{11}.h = hash(f_1.h||f_2.h)$ and the root node $r.h = hash(r_{21}.h||r_{22}.h)$. And generate the signature of the root node by signature algorithm like RSA signature algorithm. Then cloud server will return necessary proof for verification with the results. The proof includes the signature of the root node σ_r and the minimum hash sub-tree $mintree$ generated by Algorithm 4. In Fig. 2, if the returned result is f_2, the proof is $(\sigma_r, f_2, r_{11}, r_{21}, r, f_1, r_{12}, r_{22})$. After receiving the proof and results, data user verifies the results to be completeness, correctness and freshness by Algorithm 5.

4.3 Dynamic Update

Since the data stored at the cloud server may be deleted and modified, new documents may be added, the scheme should support dynamic update. There are two aspects should be take into consideration. One is the keywords dictionary. This can be settled by keeping some blank space in the document vector in advance. We have a premiss that the dictionary is relatively fixed and with small increments. Therefore, this process can satisfy most of the situations and the overhead is relatively low.

The other is the update of file collection which will influence both the encrypted index tree and the encrypted file collection. The data owner preserves a plaintext index tree locally, and generates sufficient information for updating in an encrypted way showed in Algorithm 6. Enlightened by the minimum hash sub-tree, we will neither need to re-construct whole encrypted index tree nor to proceed $BuildIndex$ on whole tree, which will reduce the efficiency since this algorithm contains many matrix operation.

Algorithm 6. Update proof

Input: the update file f_{upd}
```
 1: flag = {insert, delete, modify}
 2: encrypt the file f_upd to c_upd
 3: if flag = insert then
 4:     insert the c_upd into the leaf nodes
 5: end if
 6: if flag = delete then
 7:     search and set the node of c_upd to null
 8: end if
 9: if flag = modify then
```

10:      search and update the node of c_{upd}
11: **end if**
12: re-build a new index tree
13: construct minimum sub-tree t_{upd} for c_{upd} by Algorithm 4
14: **return** $\{t_{upd}, flag, c_{upd}\}$

After receiving the information for updating, the cloud server use the information u_{upd} to update the corresponding nodes in the index tree and document c_{upd} to update the file collection. This process is showed below.

Algorithm 7. Update

Input: updated file c_{upd}, sub-tree t_{upd}, update operation $flag$
1: **if** $flag = insert$ **then**
2:      insert the c_{upd} into the Collection C
3: **end if**
4: **if** $flag = delete$ **then**
5:      search and delete the document
6: **end if**
7: **if** $flag = modify$ **then**
8:      search and replace the document to c_{upd}
9: **end if**
10: replace corresponding nodes in T to t_{upd}

---

5   Performance Analysis

In order to estimate the performance, we implement the scheme on real data set using C# language on a Windows 7 server with Inter(R) Core(TM) i5-6500 3.20 GHz.

For ease of experiment, we choose the formatted paper set as our study object for they have typically fixed format such as title, abstract, body, conclusion and preferences. The data set contains 4529 papers with 2964 keywords. We refer to the parameter setting under the plaintext in other works and set the parameter as shown in Table 2. We analyze our scheme from precision, security and efficiency.

Table 2. The parameter in data labelling.

γ_0	0.45	Title
γ_1	0.35	Abstract
γ_2	0.1	Body
γ_3	0.07	Conclusion
γ_4	0.03	References

5.1 Precision

Precision is the fraction of real retrieved documents among all the returned document. Since the similarity score of a document will be greatly influenced and randomized, the process will produce false positive results and reduce the precision of the results. The precision is defined as: $Precision = k'/k$, where k' is the number of real documents and k is the number of returned top-k documents. The results are shown in Fig. 3.

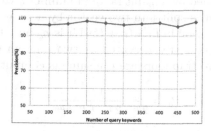

Fig. 3. The precision of search.

5.2 Security Analysis

Known Ciphertext Model. In this model, the cloud server can only obtain the encrypted document and encrypted index. The adversary distinguishes two documents mainly depending on the index generation $I \leftarrow BuildIndex(F, SK)$ and document encryption $C \leftarrow Enc(F, sk)$. The document vector is $(n + U + 1)$-bit. The first n-bit are the weight of the keywords. The U-bit are randomly chosen, and the last bit is set to 1.

For index generation, the documents are first split into two vectors and the number is set randomly if the number in S is "1". Assume the number of "1" in first n-bit and the last bit is μ_1 and each dimension of F is η_f, there are $(2^{\eta_f})^\mu \cdot (2^{\eta_f})^U$ possible values. Then the two vector are encrypted by two random $(n + U + 1) \times (n + U + 1)$-bit matrixes. Assume each elements in matrixes is η_M-bit, there are $(2^{\eta_M})^{(n+U+1)^2 \times 2}$ possible values for two matrixes. Thus the probability that indexes of two document are the same can be computed as follows:

$$P_d = \frac{1}{(2^{\eta_f})^{\mu_1} \cdot (2^{\eta_f})^U \cdot (2^{\eta_M})^{(n+U+1)^2 \times 2}}$$

$$= \frac{1}{2^{\mu_1 \eta_f + U \eta_f + 2\eta_M (n+U+1)^2}} \qquad (5)$$

The larger μ_1, U, η_f and η_M are, the more difficult to distinguish. If we choose $\eta_f = 1024$, $P_d < 1/2^{1024}$ can be negligible. As a result, the encrypted indexes are indistinguishable.

For document encryption, since we choose the symmetric encryption with semantic secure, the encrypted documents are secure against known ciphertext model.

Known Background Model. In this model, the adversary can obtain some statistical information to infer the keywords or any other information.

The trapdoor is a $n + U + 1$-bit vector. The first n-bit represents whether the keyword exists in the query or not. U-bit dimension is included v out of U bit "1" and the other bits are "0". The last bit is set to a η_t-bit random number t. First the vector is scaled by a η_r-bit random number r which have 2^{η_r} possible values. Then the vector is split into two vector by a $(n + U + 1)$-bit S with μ_0 "0". Assume each dimension in first $(n + U)$-bit is η_q bits, there are $(2^{\eta_q})^{\mu_0} \cdot 2^{\eta_t}$. Then the two query vector are encrypted by two random matrixes. As a result the probability that two trapdoors are the same is computed as follows:

$$P_q = \frac{1}{2^{\eta_r} \cdot 2^{\eta_t} \cdot (2^{\eta_q})^{\mu_0}} \tag{6}$$

It can be proved to be indistinguishable by setting large number of η_r, η_t, η_q and μ_0. For example, if $\eta_r = 1024$, $P_q < 1/2^{1024}$ and can be negligible.

Privacy

- *Data privacy.* Document collection is encrypted by a traditional symmetric encryption algorithm like AES which has been proved to be semantically secure.
- *Index and trapdoor privacy.* In our scheme, index I and trapdoor TD are encrypted by secure kNN algorithm. And the dummy keywords, the vector S for splitting and two matrixes M_1, M_2 for encrypting are all generated randomly which hide the plaintext in each dimension. As long as the secret key $SK = \{S, M1, M2\}$ is kept confidential, the cloud server can not identify the index or trapdoor by analyzing the ciphertext. It has been proved to be secure in the known ciphertext model [3].
- *Query unlinkability.* The random number r, t and v randomly chosen ϵ_i protect the search pattern and make the trapdoor indistinguishable even for the same search query. And thus, the similarity score will be different for each query and the cloud server cannot identify the relationship.
- *keyword privacy.* By introducing the random number ϵ_i in the index vector to randomize the similarity score, the keyword privacy can be well protected under known background model.

5.3   Efficiency Analysis

Index Construction. The index tree construction includes two process, building and encrypting by secure kNN algorithm. In building process, the tree is generated by all the documents in collection. The complexity of building is linear to the number of document $\mathcal{O}(N)$. Since encrypting process includes a split

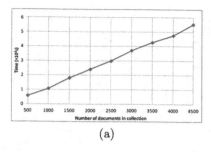
(a)

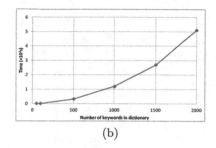
(b)

Fig. 4. The time cost of index tree construction. (a) For the different number of documents in collection with the fixed keyword dictionary $n = 1000$. (b) For the different number of keywords in dictionary with the fixed document collection $N = 1000$.

vector and two secret matrix, the complexity of encryption process depends on the number of keyword dictionary $\mathcal{O}(n^2)$. As a result, the time cost of index construction is mainly influenced by the number of document collection and keyword dictionary. The time cost are shown in Fig. 4. Since the process is one-time computation on the data owner, the time cost is acceptable.

Trapdoor Generation. The complexity of trapdoor generation depends on the split vector and secret matrix. Thus the complexity is related to the number of keyword dictionary $\mathcal{O}(n^2)$. And the number of keyword query has little influence of the time cost. The time cost is shown in Fig. 5.

Search. The search process can be briefly summarized as the product of each tree node and query vector. Thus the complexity of search mainly depends on the number of tree nodes and the number of keyword in dictionary. Actually, we don't need to compute the similarity score for every nodes. Based on the tree structure, we can compare the similarity score of nonleaf node with the threshold and eliminate the nodes which will apparently not be included in the final results. The time cost is shown in Fig. 6.

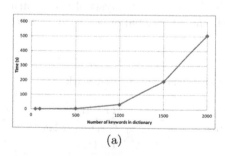
(a)

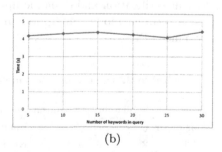
(b)

Fig. 5. The time cost of trapdoor generation. (a) For the different number of keywords in dictionary with the fixed keywords in query $m = 5$. (b) For the different number of keywords in query with the fixed keyword dictionary $n = 500$.

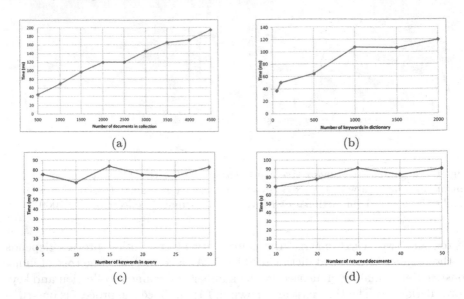

Fig. 6. The time cost of search. (a) For the different number of documents in collection with $n = 500, m = 5$ and $k = 20$. (b) For the different number of keywords in dictionary with $N = 1000, m = 5$ and $k = 20$. (c) For the different number of keywords in query with $N = 1000, n = 500$ and $k = 20$. (d) For the different number of return documents with $N = 1000, m = 5$ and $n = 500$.

6   Conclusion and Future Work

In this paper, we present a privacy-preserving, efficient ranked multi-keyword search scheme. We first focus on the formatted data set such as paper, project plan and so on. So that the keyword location and document length are introduced into the computation of TF value in our search scheme. A tree structure for index is designed to improve the efficiency of search. And we extend the functionality to implement verification and dynamic update. We give an analysis of the security against two threat model and apply our scheme on real paper set to analyze the performance (Table 3).

Table 3. The comparison among our scheme and related work.

Scheme	Verifiability	Dynamism	Construction	TF × IDF
Our paper	√	√	Binary tree	Location & length
[22]	×	√	KBB-tree	Tradition
[6]	×	×	MDB-tree & interest model	Tradition
[17]	√	×	MDB-tree	Tradition

This work still have further improvements. Inspired by Li et al. [13], the query can be extended to support operations with "AND", "OR", "NOT" by well designed parameters. And we can extend the scheme to support semantic-based sentence query. Furthermore, the nodes in the tree can be well designed such as clustering and partition to have a much better efficiency improvement.

Acknowledgments. This work is supported by the National Nature Science Foundation of China (NSFC) under grant 61379144 and 61572026, Open Foundation of State Key Laboratory of Cryptology (No: MMKFKT201617) and the Foundation of Science and Technology on Information Assurance Laboratory.

References

1. Boneh, D., Di Crescenzo, G., Ostrovsky, R., Persiano, G.: Public key encryption with keyword search. In: Cachin, C., Camenisch, J.L. (eds.) EUROCRYPT 2004. LNCS, vol. 3027, pp. 506–522. Springer, Heidelberg (2004). https://doi.org/10.1007/978-3-540-24676-3_30
2. Boneh, D., Waters, B.: Conjunctive, subset, and range queries on encrypted data. In: Vadhan, S.P. (ed.) TCC 2007. LNCS, vol. 4392, pp. 535–554. Springer, Heidelberg (2007). https://doi.org/10.1007/978-3-540-70936-7_29
3. Cao, N., Wang, C., Li, M., Ren, K., Lou, W.: Privacy-preserving multi-keyword ranked search over encrypted cloud data. IEEE Trans. Parallel Distrib. Syst. **25**(1), 222–233 (2013). https://doi.ieeecomputersociety.org/10.1109/TPDS.2013.45
4. Chang, Y.-C., Mitzenmacher, M.: Privacy preserving keyword searches on remote encrypted data. In: Ioannidis, J., Keromytis, A., Yung, M. (eds.) ACNS 2005. LNCS, vol. 3531, pp. 442–455. Springer, Heidelberg (2005). https://doi.org/10.1007/11496137_30
5. Chen, C., et al.: An efficient privacy-preserving ranked keyword search method. IEEE Trans. Parallel Distrib. Syst. **27**(4), 951–963 (2016)
6. Fu, Z., Ren, K., Shu, J., Sun, X., Huang, F.: Enabling personalized search over encrypted outsourced data with efficiency improvement. IEEE Trans. Parallel Distrib. Syst. **27**(9), 2546–2559 (2016)
7. Fu, Z., Wu, X., Guan, C., Sun, X., Ren, K.: Towards efficient multi-keyword fuzzy search over encrypted outsourced data with accuracy improvement. IEEE Trans. Inf. Forensics Secur. **11**(12), 2706–2716 (2017)
8. Goh, E.J.: Secure indexes. Cryptology ePrint Archive, Report 2003/216 (2003). https://eprint.iacr.org/2003/216
9. Golle, P., Staddon, J., Waters, B.: Secure conjunctive keyword search over encrypted data. In: Jakobsson, M., Yung, M., Zhou, J. (eds.) ACNS 2004. LNCS, vol. 3089, pp. 31–45. Springer, Heidelberg (2004). https://doi.org/10.1007/978-3-540-24852-1_3
10. Kamara, S., Papamanthou, C.: Parallel and dynamic searchable symmetric encryption. In: Sadeghi, A.-R. (ed.) FC 2013. LNCS, vol. 7859, pp. 258–274. Springer, Heidelberg (2013). https://doi.org/10.1007/978-3-642-39884-1_22
11. Kamara, S., Papamanthou, C., Roeder, T.: Dynamic searchable symmetric encryption. In: ACM Conference on Computer and Communications Security, pp. 965–976 (2012)

12. Lai, R.W.F., Chow, S.S.M.: Parallel and dynamic structured encryption. In: Deng, R., Weng, J., Ren, K., Yegneswaran, V. (eds.) SecureComm 2016. LNICST, vol. 198, pp. 219–238. Springer, Cham (2017). https://doi.org/10.1007/978-3-319-59608-2_12

13. Li, H., Yang, Y., Luan, T., Liang, X., Zhou, L., Shen, X.: Enabling fine-grained multi-keyword search supporting classified sub-dictionaries over encrypted cloud data. IEEE Trans. Dependable Secur. Comput. **13**(3), 312–325 (2016)

14. Li, J., Wang, Q., Wang, C., Cao, N., Ren, K., Lou, W.: Fuzzy keyword search over encrypted data in cloud computing. In: Conference on Information Communications, pp. 441–445 (2010)

15. Song, D., Wagner, D., Perrig, A.: Practical techniques for searches on encrypted data. In: Proceeding 2000 IEEE Symposium on Security and Privacy, SP 2000, pp. 44–55 (2000)

16. Sun, W., Liu, X., Lou, W., Hou, Y.T., Li, H.: Catch you if you lie to me: efficient verifiable conjunctive keyword search over large dynamic encrypted cloud data. In: 2015 IEEE Conference on Computer Communications (INFOCOM), pp. 2110–2118, April 2015

17. Sun, W., et al.: Verifiable privacy-preserving multi-keyword text search in the cloud supporting similarity-based ranking. IEEE Trans. Parallel Distrib. Syst. **25**(11), 3025–3035 (2014)

18. Wan, Z., Deng, R.H.: VPsearch: achieving verifiability for privacy-preserving multi-keyword search over encrypted cloud data. IEEE Trans. Dependable Secur. Comput. **PP**(99), 1 (2017)

19. Wang, B., Song, W., Lou, W., Hou, Y.T.: Inverted index based multi-keyword public-key searchable encryption with strong privacy guarantee. In: Computer Communications, pp. 2092–2100 (2015)

20. Wang, C., Cao, N., Li, J., Ren, K., Lou, W.: Secure ranked keyword search over encrypted cloud data. In: Proceedings of the 2010 IEEE 30th International Conference on Distributed Computing Systems, pp. 253–262 (2010). https://doi.org/10.1109/ICDCS.2010.34

21. Wang, Q., He, M., Du, M., Chow, S.S., Lai, R.W., Zou, Q.: Searchable encryption over feature-rich data. IEEE Trans. Dependable Secur. Comput., 1 (2016), http://doi.ieeecomputersociety.org/10.1109/TDSC.2016.2593444

22. Xia, Z., Wang, X., Sun, X., Wang, Q.: A secure and dynamic multi-keyword ranked search scheme over encrypted cloud data. IEEE Trans. Parallel Distrib. Syst. **27**(2), 340–352 (2016). http://doi.ieeecomputersociety.org/10.1109/TPDS.2015.2401003

23. Zobel, J., Moffat, A.: Exploring the similarity space. ACM SIGIR Forum **32**(1), 18–34 (1998)

Author Index

Printed in the United States
By Bookmasters